LIST - 68

Spanish Cultural Studies

Spanish
Cultural Studies

An Introduction

The Struggle for Modernity

Edited by Helen Graham
and Jo Labanyi

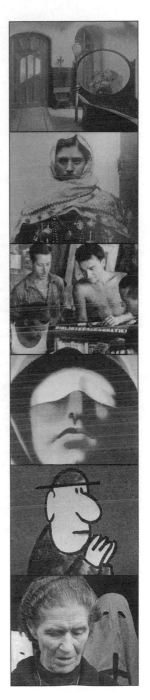

OXFORD UNIVERSITY PRESS

1995

Oxford University Press, Walton Street, Oxford OX2 6DP

Oxford New York

Athens Auckland Bangkok Bombay
Calcutta Cape Town Dar es Salaam Delhi
Florence Hong Kong Istanbul Karachi
Kuala Lumpur Madras Madrid Melbourne
Mexico City Nairobi Paris Singapore
Taipei Tokyo Toronto

and associated companies in
Berlin Ibadan

Oxford is a trade mark of Oxford University Press

Published in the United States
by Oxford University Press Inc., New York

British Library Cataloguing in Publication Data
Data available

Library of Congress Cataloging in Publication Data
Spanish Cultural Studies: an introduction: the struggle for modernity
edited by Helen Graham and Jo Labanyi.
Includes bibliographical references and index.
   1. Spain—Intellectual life—20th century.   2. Popular culture—
Spain—History—20th century.   3. Spain—Politics and government—
20th century.
I. Graham, Helen, 1959–   .   II. Labanyi, Jo.
DP233.5.S7   1995
306'.0946—dc20   95–15071

ISBN 0–19–815199–3 (Pbk.)
ISBN 0–19–815195–0

1 3 5 7 9 10 8 6 4 2

Typeset by Graphicraft
Printed in Great Britain
on acid-free paper by
Bookcraft Ltd.
Midsomer Norton, Bath

Editors' Preface

SPANISH cultural studies are in their infancy. Despite the excellent work being done in individual areas, there has to date been little attempt at interdisciplinary co-ordination. This is partly due to institutional compartmentalization, even stronger in Spanish universities than in the American or British systems where interdisciplinary programmes—particularly with the growth of gender studies— are expanding. The problem is compounded outside Spain by the fact that in other European countries Spanish is still regarded as a minority interest, and few history or media or anthropology departments—to take some key examples—have Spanish experts. In addition, teachers wanting to introduce Spanish material into interdisciplinary courses constantly come up against the lack of availability of texts (secondary as well as primary) in translation. This book is an attempt to overcome these handicaps. Given the rudimentary state of the art, it is conceived not as a collection of model case-studies (though some of the essays are that), but as a sourcebook providing an overview of trends and issues.

Because of the lack of existing interdisciplinary work in the Spanish field, we have commissioned a large number of short essays from a wide range of specialists working in Britain, Spain, France, and the USA. A high proportion of our contributors are leading experts whose names will be familiar to many readers, and we are delighted that they found this project sufficiently exciting to want to be part of it. We have also made a point of commissioning work from young researchers bringing new ideas and approaches into their respective areas of study. All the essays have been written specially for this volume, and represent the most recent research in their fields. Although the whole of the twentieth century is covered, proportionally more space is given to the contemporary period to make the book as up to date as possible. Our aim is not so much to show what Spanish cultural studies have achieved so far as to stimulate others to do further work that will establish Spanish cultural studies as a discipline, both by introducing new material into their courses and by undertaking research of their own.

We have given quotations in English to make the book accessible to students following courses in comparative or European studies (whether in literature, film, history, politics, or gender studies), who may not have a knowledge of Spanish.

We hope that this book will facilitate the inclusion of Spanish material in such courses. Throughout we have been concerned to situate Spain in a European context, for its historical development has been a response to the same dynamic processes of capitalist modernization which define the rest of the continent. Many of the essays included here explore the complex relations between the national and the international (including increasingly the United States) which simultaneously erode and define Spain's cultural specificity. Given the glaring lack—in English or Spanish—of any equivalent interdisciplinary survey of twentieth-century Spanish culture, and particularly of studies which view the latter not as a collection of individual works of art but as a complex network of processes and relations crossing the institutionalized boundary between 'high' and 'low' cultural forms, we also hope that this book will interest all those wanting to familiarize themselves with modern Spanish culture in its broadest sense. Indeed, one of the objectives of this volume is to show that an understanding of cultural formations is central to understanding the tensions and contradictions that are modern Spain.

To facilitate accessibility, footnotes have been kept to a minimum or omitted but the suggestions for further reading at the end of each essay indicate the sources used. We have limited these suggestions to items that are available in bookshops or university libraries, giving priority to works in English. Students of Spanish culture wanting to cross disciplinary boundaries have in the past been deterred by the practical difficulty of not knowing where to start when venturing into new territory: the suggestions for further reading in this volume should provide a toehold from which to explore.

For the benefit of readers with little or no previous knowledge of twentieth-century Spain, we have provided a chronology listing events of key cultural significance, and a glossary giving explanations of terms marked in the text with an asterisk. The book is divided into four parts corresponding to discrete historical periods, with the Franco era subdivided into two sections; within these divisions, essays are grouped in related clusters. An opening introductory essay by the editors provides an overview of cultural developments in modern Spain, situating them in a comparative socio-historical context and identifying key debates in cultural theory. In addition, editors' introductions to each section point readers to the issues and problems raised by the essays that follow. Readers wanting information on a particular cultural area or topic should use the index, as well as the list of contents, to locate the relevant sections, since many of the essays refer to a wide range of material and issues.

Of all the areas of modern Spanish cultural production, literature has been the most studied. The essays in this volume that deal with literature have avoided straightforward literary history and the analysis of individual works—both of these things have been done well elsewhere—in order to pinpoint and problematize cultural issues. Readers should thus not expect to find in this book a comprehensive survey of major writers. Above all, we have wanted to stress the complex relationship between élite and popular or mass cultural forms, so as to get beyond the restrictive, non-dynamic notion of culture as a collection of set texts. Our aim in so doing is not to discourage detailed textual analysis but to provide a context of cultural debate into which such analysis can be inserted.

Throughout the volume, we have paid special attention to the ways in which diverse forms of cultural production enmesh with changing life-styles to construct and deconstruct forms of national, regional, class, and gender identity. In particular, we have tried to high-light the contradictions and paradoxes inherent in all cultural systems—culture being the medium through which social antagonisms are negotiated. We have, in other words, wanted to stress that culture is a plural set of possibilities moving in different directions, with the result that there is always the potential for things to be otherwise. As this volume shows, the confrontation between those who have sought to impose a single, monolithic cultural model and those who have struggled to keep open a space for cultural debate and difference has been particularly acute in twentieth-century Spain. We have subtitled this book *The Struggle for Modernity* both to emphasize the role that culture has played in constructing—and resisting—modernity, and to stress the notion that culture is—as the civil war would show so dramatically—a form of struggle.

There are many omissions in this volume, partly for lack of space, partly because many areas of modern Spanish culture have not been adequately explored, if at all. We would signal the following as areas where work needs urgently to be done. In the broad cultural field of lived practices and values: popular cultures and nationalism (from 1898 onwards); integrist Catholicism and the construction of social values/political culture in twentieth-century Spain; popular religion; the social histories of Republican modernization and civil war; the social history of the 1940s—especially the popular cultural impact of Francoist repression, the black market, and autarky (including cultural 'autism' and the phenomenon of inner exile); popular cults, beliefs, and miracles, particularly in the 1940s; prostitution; the social history of the Sección Femenina;* race and the imperial idea in Francoism; the social history of the economic miracle (e.g. migration and continuity/change in popular and labour cultures); the impact on values and life-styles of the new consumerism of the 1960s and 1970s, and of 1980s enterprise culture; youth cultures, and urban subcultures in particular. In the field of cultural production and the culture industries: popular song; romance (e.g. the novels of Corín Tellado, much mentioned by commentators on the early Franco period but never adequately studied); comics,[1] particularly in the post-Franco period; teenage magazines and *fotonovelas*; TV soap operas; rock music; audience reception of the visual and performing arts (including TV, radio, recorded music, and video); the construction of, and changes in, the reading public; science fiction; counter-cultural magazines; pornography; advertising; museums and the heritage industry. Even the history of the Madrid *movida** has still to be written.[2]

We should like to thank the many contributors to this volume, whose insights have been enormously beneficial to our own work. Contributors' essays represent their own views, which are not necessarily those of the editors, nor do the editors' views always coincide; where divergences between essays occur, these have been allowed to stand in order to reflect differences of opinion and approach in the various fields. We hope that readers will feel stimulated by this variety, and that some of them will go on to write the essays missing in this collection. Translations of essays written originally in Spanish are by the editors, who would also like to thank John Maher for his assistance here, and Pauline Shaw for her help with picture research.

We dedicate this book to the memory of Montserrat Roig (1946–91), novelist, historian, journalist, and critic. In celebrating her creative talent, political clarity, and rich humanity, we take the measure of our loss.

Notes

1 Pioneering work has been done here by S. Vázquez Parga, *Los comics del franquismo* (Barcelona, 1980), and J. A. Ramírez, *La historieta cómica de postguerra* (Madrid, 1975) and *El 'comic' femenino en España, arte sub y anulación* (Madrid, 1975): all on the early Franco period.
2 J. L. Gallero, *Sólo se vive una vez: esplendor y ruina de la movida madrileña* (Madrid, 1991) gives an endearing oral account.

Acknowledgements

Responsibility for researching and selecting the visual material included in this book lies with the editors, who have made every effort to contact the copyright holders in each case. Where no acknowledgement is given, the material is owned by the editors. We should like to thank the following for providing photographs and/or giving permission to reproduce:

Archivo Histórico Nacional (Sección Guerra Civil), Salamanca (Plate 8)
Biblioteca Nacional, Madrid (Plates 4, 10, 11a, 11b, 13)
Bodleian Library, Oxford (Plate 18)
Centre d'Estudis d'Història Contemporània (Biblioteca Figueras), Barcelona (Plates 9, 12)
Centro de Arte Reina Sofía, Madrid (Plate 3)
D.A.C.S (Plate 24) D.A.C.S 1995
El Deseo, SA, Madrid (Plate 28)
Editorial Gustavo Gili, Barcelona (Plate 1)
Filmoteca Española, Madrid (Plates 15, 17, 20, 28, 29, 30)
Fonomusic, Madrid (Plate 23)
Foto Kollar, Paris (Plate 7)
Galería Balmes 21, Barcelona (Plate 2)
Cristina García Rodero (Plate 31)
IVAM Centre Julio González, Valencia (Plates 24, 25)
Basilio Martin Patino (Plates 15, 17)
Antón Reixa (Plate 26)
Jordi Sarra (Plate 27)
Sogetel, SA, Madrid (Plate 30)
Teide, SA, Madrid (Plate 29)

Our thanks also to Jon Wilson, of the Photographic Unit, Birkbeck College, for photographing much of the original material.

Contents

List of Illustrations

Notes on Contributors

Dawn Ades is Professor of Art History and Theory at the University of Essex. Her publications include *Dada and Surrealism Reviewed* (1978), *Salvador Dalí* (1982), *Photomontage* (1986), *Art in Latin America: The Modern Era 1820–1980* (1989), and 'Morphologies of Desire', in *Salvador Dalí: The Early Years* (1994).

Alicia Alted is a member of the Department of Contemporary History at the UNED, Madrid. She is the author of *Política del nuevo Estado sobre el patrimonio cultural y la educación durante la guerra civil española* (1984). She has published extensively on the cultural history and politics of the civil war, Francoism, anti-Franco opposition, and Republican exile, most recently *El archivo de la República española en el exilio, 1945–1977* (1993) and 'La oposición republicana, 1939–1977', in N. Townson (ed.), *El republicanismo en España (1830–1977)* (1994).

José Alvarez Junco holds the Príncipe de Asturias Chair in Spanish Culture and Civilization at Tufts University. He is the author of *La comuna en España* (1971), *La ideología política del anarquismo español* (1976), and *Populismo, caudillaje y discurso demagógico* (1987). His most recent book *El emperador del paralelo* (1990) is a study of populism and anticlericalism in turn-of-the-century Spain. His current research interests focus especially on nation-building processes in late nineteenth- and early twentieth-century Spain.

Sebastian Balfour is Senior Lecturer in Spanish and Latin American Studies at Goldsmiths' College, University of London. He is the author of *Dictatorship, Workers and the City: Labour in Greater Barcelona since 1939* (1989) and *Castro* (1990, revised edn. 1995) and was historical adviser for the BBC's 1992 Emmy award-winning documentary on the Cuban Missile Crisis. He has published numerous other articles on twentieth-century Spanish history and is currently writing a book on the end of the Spanish empire, the Disaster of 1898, and the crisis of the liberal state in Spain.

Borja de Riquer i Permanyer is Professor of Contemporary History at the Autónoma University, Barcelona. His major research interests are in Catalan history, nationalist movements, and the Franco period. His numerous publications include: *Lliga Regionalista: la burgesia catalana i el nacionalisme* (1977), 'El Franquisme i la transició democràtica, 1939–1988', in P. Vilar (ed.), *La història de Catalunya*, vol. vii (1989). He is currently writing a book on conservative Catalan nationalism during the civil war and the Franco period. He is also co-ordinating research work on the process of nation-building in nineteenth-century Spanish society.

Catherine Boyle is Lecturer in Spanish and Spanish American Studies at King's College, University of London, specializing in the performing arts. She has published on Spanish and Spanish American theatre, women's writing, and cultural studies, including *Chilean Theater 1973–1985: Marginality, Power and Selfhood* (1991), and 'Chilean Song since 1973: An Overview', in *Chile after 1973: Elements for the Analysis of Military Rule* (1985). She is co-editor of *Travesía: Journal of Latin American Cultural Studies*.

Enrique Bustamante is Professor of Audiovisual Communications and Head of the Department of Media Studies at the Universidad Complutense, Madrid. He is also editor of the magazine *Telos: Cuadernos de Comunicación, Tecnología y Sociedad*. His publications include *Los amos de la información en España* (1982) and *Las industrias culturales en España* (1986, co-editor).

Richard Cleminson is Lecturer in Spanish Studies at the University of Bradford. He is currently writing a Ph.D. thesis on the sexual politics of anarchism. His publications include: 'First Steps towards Mass Sex-Economic Therapy? Wilhelm Reich and the Spanish Revolution', in *Anarchist Studies*, 1 (1993); *Anarquismo y homosexualidad: antología de artículos de la 'Revista Blanca', 'Generación Consciente', 'Estudios' e 'Iniciales'* (Madrid, 1994); 'Anarchists for Health: Spanish Anarchism and Health Reform in the 1930s', in *Health Care Analysis*, 3 (Feb. and May 1995); 'Eugenics by Name or by Nature? The Spanish Anarchist Sex Reform of the 1930s', in *History of European Ideas* (1995).

Emma Dent Coad is a design and architectural journalist specializing in Spain. She has written for various British and American art journals, and contributed to cultural programmes for BBC television and radio. She is author of *Spanish Design and Architecture* (1990) and *Javier Mariscal: Designing the New Spain* (1992).

Christopher Cobb is Emeritus Professor in the Faculty of Human Sciences, Kingston University. He is the author of *La cultura y el pueblo: España 1930–39* (1981); *Los milicianos de la cultura* (1994); 'Teatro proletario: teatro de masas', in *Literatura popular y proletaria* (1986); 'The Educational and Cultural Policies of the Popular Front Government in Spain', in *The French and Spanish Popular Fronts: Comparative Perspectives* (1991), and numerous other articles on popular culture and education in Republican Spain.

Elías Díaz is Professor of the Philosophy of Law at the Autónoma University, Madrid. He was a founder member of the seminal cultural journal *Cuadernos para el Diálogo* in 1963 and he currently edits the philosophy and social science journal *Sistema*. His research and published work have been both in the history of social and political ideas in nineteenth- and twentieth-century Spain and in political, legal, and moral philosophy. Among his many books are included: *Estado de derecho y sociedad democrática* (1966), *La filosofía social del Krausismo español* (1973), *Pensamiento español en la era de Franco (1939–1975)* (1983), *La transición a la democracia: claves ideológicas 1976–1986* (1987), *Ética contra política: los intelectuales y el poder* (1990).

Sheelagh Ellwood is Principal Research Officer (Iberia) at the Foreign and Commonwealth Office. She is author of various articles on the extreme right in Spain, and of the books *Prietas las filas* (1983), *Spanish Fascism in the Franco Era* (1987), *The Spanish Civil War* (1990), and *Profiles in Power: Franco* (1993).

Antonio Elorza is Professor in the Department of Political Theory at the Complutense University, Madrid. His publications include *La ideología liberal en la ilustración española* (1970), *Socialismo utópico español* (1970), *Ideologías del nacionalismo vasco* (1978), *La razón y la sombra: una lectura política de Ortega y Gasset* (1984), and *La modernización política en España*

(1990). His current research interests focus on the historical development of nationalisms in Spain.

Peter Evans is Professor of Spanish and Film Studies at the University of Nottingham. He has published widely on Spanish and American cinema, and has co-authored *Challenges to Authority: Fiction and Film in Contemporary Spain* (1988), *Blue Skies and Silver Linings: Aspects of the Hollywood Musical* (1985), *Affairs to Remember: The Hollywood Comedy of the Sexes* (1989), and *Biblical Epics: Sacred Narrative in the Hollywood Cinema* (1993). His book on the films of Luis Buñuel will be published by OUP in 1995.

Josep-Anton Fernández is Lecturer in Catalan at Queen Mary and Westfield College, University of London. He is currently writing a Ph.D. thesis on modern Catalan fiction at King's College, University of Cambridge.

Sue Frenk is Lecturer in Spanish at the University of Durham. She has published various articles on Spanish American literature and cultural magazines, and is co-author of *Voices from the Rainforest* (1994). Her research interests are in gender and cultural studies.

Helen Graham is Lecturer in the Department of History at Royal Holloway, University of London. She is the author of *Socialism and War: The Spanish Socialist Party in Power and Crisis 1936–1939* (1991) and has edited (with Paul Preston) *The Popular Front in Europe* (1987) and (with Martin Alexander) *The French and Spanish Popular Fronts: Comparative Perspectives* (1989). She has published various articles on the Spanish left in the 1930s and is currently writing a book on the Second Spanish Republic during the civil war with the aid of a Leverhulme Research Fellowship. Her main research interests are in the social and cultural history of 1930s and 1940s Spain.

Anny Brooksbank Jones is Head of Spanish at Nottingham Trent University, where she lectures and researches in Hispanic cultural and area studies, and feminist theory. Recent and forthcoming publications include articles on the 1993 Spanish election campaign; Hispanic feminisms; and women, politics, and social change in contemporary Spain. She is currently writing a book on Spanish women and co-editing a collection of essays on Latin American women's writing.

Barry Jordan is Professor of Hispanic Studies and Head of Modern Languages and European Studies at De Montfort University, Leicester. He has published articles on post-war Spanish drama, fiction, and (more recently) film; recent books include *Writing and Politics in Franco's Spain* (1990) and *Carmen Laforet: 'Nada'* (1993). He is currently writing a book (with Rikki Morgan) on Spanish cinema.

Jo Labanyi is Reader in Modern Spanish and Spanish American Literature at Birkbeck College, University of London. She has published articles on nineteenth- and twentieth-century Spanish and Spanish American fiction; her books include *Myth and History in the Contemporary Spanish Novel* (1989), *Galdós* (1992), a translation of Galdós, *Nazarín* (1993), and (with Lou Charnon-Deutsch) *Culture and Gender in Nineteenth-Century Spain* (in press). She is currently writing a book on the politics of the family in the Spanish realist novel, and researching Spanish cinema of the 1940s with a British Academy/Leverhulme Trust Senior Research Fellowship.

Frances Lannon is Fellow and Tutor in Modern History at Lady Margaret Hall, University of Oxford. She is the author of *Privilege, Persecution and Prophecy: The Catholic Church in Spain 1875–1975* (1987) and various articles on the Church and Catholicism in twentieth-century Spain. She edited (with Paul Preston) *Elites and Power in Twentieth-Century Spain:*

Essays in Honour of Sir Raymond Carr (1990) and is currently researching a book on women, the Second Republic, and the Spanish civil war.

Jesús María Lasagabaster is Professor of Literature and Literary Criticism in the Departments of Basque and Spanish at the Universidad de Deusto, San Sebastián. His publications on Basque literature include *La novela de Ignacio Aldecoa* (1978) and *Antología de la narrativa vasca contemporánea* (1986; English translation *Contemporary Basque Fiction*, 1990).

John London is Alexander von Humboldt Research Fellow at the Institut für Theaterwissenschaft of the Freie Universität Berlin. His research interests are in modern Spanish theatre and public spectacle. His publications include *Claves de 'La verdad sospechosa'* (1990), *El teatre de la pàgina* (1993), (with David George) *Contemporary Catalan Theatre* (1995), and a translation of *The Unknown Lorca* (1994). His *Reception and Renewal in Modern Spanish Theatre: 1939–1963* is currently in press.

Clare Mar-Molinero is Lecturer in Spanish and Sociolinguistics at the University of Southampton. Her main research interests are in language policies and planning, with particular reference to those of contemporary Spain. Her publications include work on Catalan language planning and language education programmes and on Spain's language policies. She is currently contributing to a book on language and nationalism in the European context.

Enrique Montero wrote his doctoral thesis on Spanish republicanism, the birth of mass politics, and the coming of the Second Republic. He has continued to work on related themes, most recently publishing an essay on the republicanization of the professional associations and the collapse of the monarchy in N. Townson (ed.), *El republicanismo en España (1830–1977)* (1994).

Rosa Montero is a novelist and journalist. She has worked for *El País* since 1977 in numerous capacities including as foreign correspondent in Europe, the United States, and Latin America. Her novels include *Crónica del desamor* (1979), *La Función Delta* (1981), *Te trataré como a una reina* (1983), *Temblor* (1990), *Bella y oscura* (1993).

Chris Perriam is Lecturer in Spanish at the University of Durham, and has published on modern Spanish and Spanish American poetry, including *The Late Poetry of Pablo Neruda* (1989), and a book on Luis Antonio de Villena currently in press. His research interests include gay writing, the representation of masculinity, and film.

Paul Preston is Professor of International History at the London School of Economics. His books include: *The Coming of the Spanish Civil War* (1978, 2nd edn. 1994), *The Triumph of Democracy in Spain* (1986), *The Spanish Civil War 1936–1939* (1986), *The Politics of Revenge: Fascism and the Military in 20th Century Spain* (1990), and *Franco: A Biography* (1993). He is currently working on a history of the anti-Franco opposition and a biography of King Juan Carlos.

Mike Richards currently teaches in the Department of History at the University of Sheffield. He is completing a Ph.D. thesis on the political economy of Francoism.

Serge Salaün is Professor of Modern Spanish Literature at the Université de la Sorbonne Nouvelle (Paris III). He has published extensively on modern Spanish poetry and on various forms of popular culture, including the *zarzuela*, the *género chico*, cabaret, and working-class culture. His books include *La poesía de la guerra de España* (1985), *El cuplé* (1990), and (with Carlos Serrano) *1900 en España* (1991).

Antonio Sánchez is currently writing a Ph.D. thesis on contemporary Spanish culture and theories of postmodernism at Birkbeck College, University of London.

Arthur Terry is Emeritus Professor of Literature at the University of Essex. He has published many books and articles on Spanish, Catalan, and Latin American literature, including: *La poesia de Joan Maragall* (1963); *An Anthology of Spanish Poetry (1500–1700)*, 2 vols. (1965, 1968); *Catalan Literature* (1972); *Antonio Machado: 'Campos de Castilla'* (1973); *Selected Poems of Ausias March* (1976); *Sobre poesia catalana contemporania: Riba, Foix, Espriu* (1985); *Quatre poètes catalans: Ferrater, Brossa, Gimferrer, Xirau* (1991); *Seventeenth-Century Spanish Poetry: The Power of Artifice* (1993). In 1982 he was awarded the Creu de Sant Jordi by the Catalan government for his work as a critic of Catalan literature and his services to Catalan culture.

Mike Thompson is Lecturer in Spanish at the University of Durham, and has published articles on modern Spanish theatre, plus a translation of Buero Vallejo, *A Dreamer for the People* (1993).

Xelís de Toro Santos is Xunta de Galicia Lecturer in Galician at the University of Oxford and is currently writing an M.Phil. thesis at the University of Birmingham on 'Literature and Nation in the Magazine *Nós*'. He has published three novels in Galician: *Non hai misericordia* (1990), awarded the Cidade de Lugo Prize, (under the pseudonym Roque Morteiro) *Seis cordas e un corazón* (1989), awarded the Consorcio de Santiago Detective Fiction Prize, and *Terminal* (1994). He has written for Galician radio, television, and press, and is co-founder of an independent publishing company.

Augusto M. Torres is a critic, film director, and novelist. He has published books on the cinemas of eastern Europe (1972), Latin America (1973), North America (1973, 1992), France (1976), and Italy (1994); and monographs on Glauber Rocha (1970), Fassbinder (1983), and Cukor (1992). His books on Spanish cinema include *Cine español, años sesenta* (1973), *Conversaciones con Manuel Gutiérrez Aragón* (1985), and *Diccionario del cine español* (1994); he also edited the important collective volume *Cine español: 1896–1983* (1984). He has directed two feature films and nine shorts.

Enric Ucelay Da Cal teaches in the Department of Contemporary History at the Autónoma University, Barcelona. He is the author of *La Catalunya populista (imatge, cultura i política en l'etapa republicana 1931–39)* (1982) and studies of Estat Català (1979), and Francesc Macià (1984, 1988). He has published extensively on Catalan history in the contemporary period, with particular reference to the social and political history of nationalism in comparative perspective.

Julian White studied at the Royal Academy of Music and King's College, University of London. He currently teaches, as well as researching on twentieth-century Spanish music in general and Roberto Gerhard in particular. Two recent articles on Gerhard have appeared in *Tempo*: 'National Traditions in the Music of Roberto Gerhard', 184 (Mar. 1993); and 'Roberto Gerhard's Piano Music', 187 (Dec. 1993).

Introduction

HELEN GRAHAM

JO LABANYI

Never again will a single story be told as though it
were the only one.   (John Berger)

Culture and Modernity: The Case of Spain

HELEN GRAHAM AND JO LABANYI

The starting-point of any volume that claims to have as its aim
the establishment of Spanish cultural studies as a discipline must
be to ask why the discipline has been so slow to develop. We
should also like in this introductory essay to define what we
understand by culture, to raise what we see as the key issues
involved in the study of culture (and of Spanish culture in
particular), and to outline the ways in which the concept of
culture is bound up with that of modernity and with the related terms 'modernization' and 'modernism' (and its sequel
'post-modernism').

   We do not wish to discuss here the ways in which the teaching of Spanish culture at educational institutions in Spain and
abroad has inhibited the development of interdisciplinary approaches and the study of popular and mass cultural forms. It
is however instructive to consider the wider socio-historical
factors that have conditioned the growth of cultural studies
in other countries, in order to understand why a tradition of
cultural theory is lacking in Spain. What emerges is not that
similar issues do not obtain in Spain's case, nor that Spanish
intellectuals have been unconcerned with the critical analysis of
culture (the essay is after all a major genre in twentieth-century

Spain), but rather that the considerable attention given by Spanish thinkers to the role of culture has not been constructed as a body of cultural theory able to provide the intellectual underpinning for cultural studies as a discipline. The frequent élitism of these cultural theorists and their concern with national identities —or, all too often, with national identity in the singular—perhaps makes their work unattractive to cultural historians today. But both of these features are common— in various ways—to the founding fathers of cultural studies in other European countries: the discipline grew out of the nineteenth-century concern with the role of culture in nation formation, and out of subsequent worries—from the 1930s to the 1950s—about the growth of mass culture.

The nationalist stress of much Spanish cultural analysis paradoxically places it in a European context. As several essays in this volume point out, early twentieth-century Spanish intellectuals inherited a reformist tradition going back to the Enlightenment, and continued in the later nineteenth century by the Krausist* thinkers grouped around the Institución Libre de Enseñanza,* who constructed a version of post-Kantian ethics that stressed the individual's civic responsibility, and who saw the diffusion of culture as the key to the transformation—and modernization—of society. Parallels can be drawn here with the 'culture and civilization' tradition associated in Britain with Matthew Arnold, generally seen as the starting-point of British cultural theory. Although they would have deplored Arnold's explicit political conservatism, the Krausists shared his notion that 'civilizing' the masses through education was a way of deflecting the threat of social revolution: culture was something the masses did not have but ought to; social revolution was seen not as an alternative cultural model but as the destruction of culture. The Spanish Republican intellectuals of the 1930s who continued this reformist tradition (many of them educated at the Institución Libre de Enseñanza) have much in common with F. R. Leavis who, at the same time in Britain, was promoting the humanizing value of culture from a similarly paternalistic centrist/liberal perspective. Leavis was, however, worried by the threat to high culture (and to a national tradition) posed by what he saw as the dehumanization of (American) mass culture, a phenomenon still too recent in Spain to cause concern. Leavis's cultural analysis was continued, but given a different political slant, in the 1950s by Richard Hoggart (founder of the Birmingham Centre for Contemporary Cultural Studies), Raymond Williams, and E. P. Thompson, writing from within a marxist tradition, who were equally worried about the effects of the mass media but who saw this as a threat to the popular cultural traditions of working-class communities. This debate is in many ways anticipated in 1930s Spain, with the polarization of class allegiances produced by civil war, as Republican intellectuals found themselves torn between a Leavisite 'culture and civilization' position and the defence of popular culture (which, as in the work of Hoggart, Williams, and E. P. Thompson, is viewed as an expression of organic community hard to reconcile with modernity, at least in its present capitalist form). It is significant that those liberal intellectuals who eventually broke with the Republic were those who, like Ortega y Gasset, maintained an élitist view of culture; Ortega went further than most in praising modernist art precisely because it was dehumanized and therefore, in his view, of no interest to the masses. The lack of a cultural studies tradition in Spain should not be blamed on Ortega, but rather on those (not always Spaniards) who have turned his essay *The Dehumanization of Art* (1926) into the classic—if not sole—expression of Spanish cultural theory, ignoring the substantial humanist tradition against which he was reacting.

A simple explanation for the failure of this humanist critical tradition to develop into a body of cultural theory is that Nationalist victory in the civil war, restoring power to the traditional élite, ruled out any continued interest in popular culture or in the modern mass media. But this needs qualifying. If Francoism exercised particularly strict control over popular and mass forms of cultural expression, this was because Nationalist intellectuals were well aware of the importance of culture as a tool of national unification and political 'pacification' (the instilling of politically acceptable values into the populace thus takes the form of apparent depoliticiza-tion).[1] Indeed, as various essays in this book show, they paid particular attention to promoting popular and mass forms of entertainment: folklore, song, sport, and cinema. The Church, while reinforcing social hierarchy, also drew on a tradition of popular religious spectacle. What Francoism discouraged was not popular and mass culture, but the exercise of independent critical thought necessary to the development of any form of cultural analysis.

The parallels here—which serve to highlight the differences—are with Germany. Cultural studies first developed there in the 1930s with the work of the Frankfurt School—Walter Benjamin, Theodor Adorno, Max Horkheimer—which was informed by an acute awareness of the Nazi exploitation of mass culture as a political tool. Their (not always orthodox) marxist analysis consequently insists on material and political issues of the ownership and control of the means of cultural production, as well as on its reception; the public is viewed as a basically passive receiver of cultural messages, hence their worries about political abuse. Adorno and Horkheimer—writing in exile in the United States, where they would have a decisive influence on cultural theory—went on, in *The Dialectic of Enlighten-ment* (1947), to develop their experience of the Nazi 'aestheticization of politics' (Benjamin's term) into an analysis of the capitalist organization of leisure time through the 'culture industry', as they called it in a now classic phrase. Increasing Americanization through the mass media was now seen as the enemy of critical thinking. One of the reasons why the huge number of Spanish Republican intel-lectuals who went into exile did not produce a parallel body of cultural theory is no doubt because they mostly left Spain before the cultural effects of Nationalist victory were felt. It was left to the younger generation of opposition intelligentsia that emerged in Spain in the 1950s—consisting largely of writers, film-makers, and artists—to draw conclusions from their experience of cultural manipulation. While censorship prevented the free expression of their ideas, they were in fact—through officially tolerated magazines and intellectual encounters, and through their creative work—able to articulate a coherent body of cultural theory. Having grown up during and after the war, they had only a flimsy grasp of marxist theory, despite the fact that their ideas were largely channelled through the Communist Party. And being mostly children of well-to-do Nationalist families, they had little direct experience of class realities. The well-intentioned naïvety of their work led the majority to repudiate it in later life; consequently it was never incorporated into a historical tradition of Spanish cultural theory. Their cultural thinking was based largely on post-war Italian neo-realism, which in turn attempted to put into practice Gramsci's notion of the 'national-popular' as a progressive cultural form rooted in the national tradition and in popular life.[2] The Gramscian theoretical roots of Spanish social realism deserve critical attention, particularly since Gramsci's writings on culture have been the dominant force behind British cultural studies and, more recently, Latin American cultural theory.

Gramsci's main contribution to cultural theory has been his concept of hegemony: that is, the notion that power is not so much imposed from above by force (though violent methods may be used as well; Franco's Spain is a classic example) as the result of a negotiation process whereby the ruling classes secure the consent of the people by cultural means; in turn, the people resist by resorting to counter-hegemonic cultural tactics. This concept has been fertile not only because it sees culture as a site of power, but also because it insists on the two-way nature of the struggle. Mass culture thus acquires a more positive value than it had for Williams or Adorno, since the public are no longer seen as passive but as being able to control their response to the media, even though they have no control over the production and distribution systems. The emphasis is thus on audience reception as a process of contestation and resignification. With the rise of postmodernist theory in the Anglo-Saxon world and France in the late 1970s and 1980s, this developed into a stress on cultural difference and otherness, which in turn allowed important insights to be borrowed from anthropological theory. This was useful in pointing out that 'the public' is a complex network of heterogeneous groups, in which overlapping factors such as class, race, and gender have to be taken into account; the notion of contestatory 'subcultures' also became important. At the same time, the stress on the audience's agency—and particularly on irony and pleasure as liberatory forms of resignification—has tended to eclipse the issue of control of the production and distribution systems, forgetting that the audience is just that—an audience—and that the role of the mass media is, precisely, to construct the different individuals who make up the public as 'the masses'.

The postmodern stress on heterogeneity—allied with the Gramscian notion of hegemony—has been especially fertile in Latin American cultural theory, where issues of race and cultural imperialism are paramount, and where anthropological work has produced impressive results.[3] If contemporary Spain has not produced an equivalent body of theory, this is possibly because race is an issue still only reluctantly acknowledged, and because the cultural heterogeneity legitimized by regional autonomy has tended to lead to a converse stress on the construction of homogeneous local cultural identities. It is perhaps a measure of the success of Francoist political indoctrination that 'others' still tend to be seen as existing without rather than within. Spanish anthropology has tended to concentrate on the folk-loric (yet more studies of Andalusian village life): valuable work remains to be done in the area of ethnographic analysis of modern urban social practices, par-ticularly those of subcultural groups; an ethnographic approach to the social his-tory of the economic miracle would also be fruitful. Additionally, questions of cultural dependency are now urgently posed by the increasing globalization of the media (including a controlling stake in the private TV channel Telecinco by Berlusconi's company Fininvest). The postmodern nature of much Spanish cul-tural production since the early 1970s (poetry, fiction, film, design and architec-ture, photography, song)—in the sense that it is marked by heterogeneity, pastiche, the conversion of history into representation, and the mixing of high and low cultural forms—makes it fertile territory for cultural analysis at a time when postmodernist theory, which has put cultural issues at the centre of contemporary intellectual debate, has become the dominant framework in cultural studies.

In this volume we take 'culture' to mean both lived practices and artefacts or performances, understood as symbolic systems. The notion of 'performance' effectively ties the various categories together, inasmuch as they are all forms of signification produced for an audience. For this reason it has become common to talk of lived practices, as well as artefacts and performances, as 'texts' designed to be 'read'. One must, however, remember that lived practices have material effects on human beings that are more deadly than those of any art object; as someone once pointed out on hearing the Spanish civil war referred to as a text: 'my father died in that text.' Nevertheless, all cultural forms—whether lived practices or artefacts and performances—have an underlying narrative: culture can be defined as the stories people tell each other to explain what and where they are. This brings us to the second point we have wanted to stress: that culture is a site of power that is always negotiated and contested. The concept of mediation is im-portant here: not just in the sense of the mediation of contradiction—as in the classic marxist definition of the function of ideology—but particularly in the sense it has acquired in media theory of the ways in which (to use Jesús Martín-Barbero's formulation) the media alter the fields they enter.[4] In other words, the media are never neutral but are vehicles of particular historical processes, whose reception is contingent on the historically defined cultural characteristics of the various receiving publics. Questions of production and consumption thus cannot be di-vorced. And consumption is never a passive or homogeneous process: not only do different sectors of the public respond differently, but the same sector can respond in ways that are simultaneously conformist and contestatory; indeed the same response can be both at the same time. Nor can it be assumed that the institutions that control the production of meaning identify themselves monolithically with the state, or with the establishment (not necesarily the same thing). (Neither, of

course, should one assume that state power is always repressive rather than enabling, nor that the response of subaltern groups is always subversive of dominant
norms.) The history of twentieth-century Spanish culture is—as the civil war made
particularly apparent—the history of a struggle between different ways of interpreting the world, and different ways of interpreting Spanish society in particular:
a battle of meanings which shaped individual and collective identities, and affected
the material conditions of individual and collective existence. The third point that
we hope emerges from this volume is the need for historical contextualization. In
order fully to understand cultural processes and forms, one needs to know what
are the issues of legitimation at stake at any given conjuncture, why they should
have acquired urgency at that particular moment, and who are the antagonists—
or partners—in the struggle to impose certain meanings at the expense of others.

One of the main questions raised by cultural studies is that of how notions of
'high' and 'low' culture are constructed. As Bourdieu has noted, this discrimination is the prime way in which cultural practice determines what in any given
society is legitimate and what is not:

The most intolerable thing for those who regard themselves as the possessors of legitimate
culture is the sacrilegious reuniting of tastes which taste dictates shall be separated. [. . .]
At stake in every struggle over art there is also the imposition of an art of living, that is,
the transmutation of an arbitrary way of living into the legitimate way of life which casts
every other way of living into arbitrariness.[5]

'High' culture, in other words, is possessed by the 'cultured'; 'low' culture is what
is enjoyed by the 'uncultured', by those who do not 'have culture'. The implication is that 'high' culture possesses 'ethical' values lacking in 'low' culture. In
effect, three categories are involved here: 'high' culture, which we shall also refer
to in this volume as 'élite' culture, to make clear its discriminatory social function;
and 'popular' and 'mass' culture. The history of the last two terms sums up the
history of cultural theory, and is especially pertinent in the case of Spain. The term
'popular culture', as the expression of 'the people' or 'folk', is a Romantic coinage,
inescapably linked to the liberal project of nation-building which sought to incorporate the rural population into the modern state, in an attempt to make 'the
people' and the nation coincide. This creates a slippage whereby 'the people' can
be seen as those who resist incorporation or as those who embody the nation.
Popular culture—as pre-literate, oral folk culture—can thus be denigrated as 'uncultured' or turned into an emblem of the national tradition. The important point
is that 'the popular' is a construction of the modern state, which turned peasants
into 'the people'. The use of the term *pueblo* by the educators of the Institución
Libre de Enseñanza, and by the Republican intellectuals who were their products,
deserves analysis; as does its use in Nationalist rhetoric, more blatantly concerned
with incorporating resistant sectors of the population into the state (while at the
same time stigmatizing them by constructing them as 'other').

By the mid-nineteenth century (*c*.1830 in Britain, *c*.1870 in Spain), the term 'masses' emerges as a way of referring to the industrial proletariat or the urban lower classes: that is, those sectors of 'the people' who have left the land and been incorporated into the capitalist process of industrialization and urbanization. Again, the 'masses' are a product of modernity. Indeed, Raymond Williams notes that the English word 'culture' itself only acquired its modern meaning of 'cultural processes or products' (having originally referred to the cultivation of crops or animals, and from the sixteenth century, by extension, to the 'cultivation' of human beings) in the late eighteenth century, becoming common only in the mid-nineteenth century (that is, at the time Arnold wrote his famous *Culture and Anarchy*).[6] The modern usage of the term thus coincides with, and indeed is a product of, bourgeois revolution and capitalist modernization, and the new forms of social legitimation which these required. In other words, 'culture' takes on its modern sense in order to define who does or does not 'have culture', and to discriminate between the different forms of culture possessed by different strata of the population.

This modernizing project is continued, despite its revolt against bourgeois norms, by twentieth-century modernism, which in many cases incorporated popular or mass forms—one thinks particularly of the use of techniques derived from primitive art and cinema—but in so doing produced experimental works whose difficulty often restricted them to a highly educated public. For the avant-garde reaction against capitalism—whether from a left- or right-wing perspective—largely took the form of a rejection of cultural commercialization; in many cases, this served to reinforce the divide between high and low culture that itself had been manufactured by capitalism. The term 'avant-garde' implicitly supposes that the artist occupies a privileged, leading position. The incorporation of popular and mass cultural forms was, in fact, particularly marked in the case of the Spanish avant-garde; Ortega's establishment of an absolute divide between élite and mass culture (popular culture in its folkloric sense did not concern him) is not representative, and even he defined modernist art as a form of sport. The use of folkloric elements by Spanish avant-garde writers and composers is a particularly interesting case of this bridge but also division between élite and popular forms: for example, Lorca gave performances of his poetry and plays, which draw heavily on folk traditions, to educated audiences, but his touring theatre La Barraca took the Spanish classics—'high' art—to the rural population. The radicalization of culture by civil war would further erode the division between 'high' and 'low', effectively spelling the death of those forms of modernist artistic experiment that were felt to be élitist (something that cannot be blamed solely on Nationalist victory).

The major break effected by postmodernism has been the latter's positive revalorization of mass culture, and its refusal to respect modernism's rejection of cultural commercialization; hence the importance of postmodernist theory for cultural studies, which focus attention on culture as an industry. Postmodernist theory is mostly the product of advanced capitalist societies where, with the disappearance of a folk tradition, the terms 'mass culture' and 'popular culture' have become synonymous, producing a further slippage in the meaning of the latter term.[7] This ambiguity has been compounded by market ideology's definition of 'the popular' as that which appeals to a majority, creating a false sense of democratic neutrality to diguise the fact that 'popularity' is constructed precisely by marketing. But this increasing terminological ambiguity points to an important cultural shift, as 'high' culture is appropriated by the mass media—one thinks of Spanish state television's videos, available in department stores, on major Spanish artists, though it has to be said that the increasingly abysmal quality of Spanish television (state and private) makes this a relatively limited process—and mass culture is consumed, and often enjoyed, by all sectors of the population. This cultural pluralism is not, however, value-free: mass culture is construed as democratic and representative of the nation on the grounds that it is 'popular' (has high audience ratings), but inasmuch as it is produced for the masses it is still held to be the culture of the uncultured. And it should not be supposed that cultural pluralism, in allowing all sectors of the population access to the same range of cultural forms, produces cultural homogeneity: the audience's ability to participate in various cultural systems at once, cutting across boundaries of class, race, or gender, does not mean that everyone responds to this mixed diet in the same way. The case of Spain is again particularly interesting here: mass migration from the rural areas to the cities, and the extension of television and video to the remotest villages, has produced an intermingling of the popular and the mass imaginary which is begging for cultural analysis, as is the response of audiences with limited experience of other cultures to the increasingly high percentage of imported TV programmes (and films, but this is a process which dates back to the late 1940s).

The persistence in Spain into the modern period of strong rural cultural traditions means that Anglo-Saxon—and even French—theoretical models have to be applied with caution. First of all, the current English use of the term 'popular culture' as a synonym of 'mass culture' is less frequent in Spanish, where 'cultura popular' tends to be reserved for popular traditions (produced and consumed by the people, including both rural and urban lower classes since—with mass migration from the countryside continuing into recent times—the two are perceived as forming a continuum), as distinct from 'cultura de masas' (the mass media, consumed by the people but not produced by them). Secondly, the weakness of the central state (until the Franco regime's imposition of a monolithic state apparatus) and the strength of regionalist sentiment (reinforced in the post-Franco period by political devolution) has meant that the process of nation formation has continued longer than in most advanced capitalist countries, where it was completed before the growth of the mass media. As William Rowe and Vivian Schelling note in their book on Latin American popular culture: when the culture industry coincides with the process of nation formation, it takes on some of the aura of 'high' culture, further eroding the distinction between mass and élite cultural forms.[8] Thus the Spanish Republic would, through the Misiones Pedagógicas, use modern

technological forms of mass reproduction to take 'high' culture to the rural populace in the form of travelling exhibitions of prints of famous paintings, and concerts of gramophone recordings of classical music. A more recent instance is the
use of regional television channels, particularly—but not only—those transmitting
in Spain's minority languages, to construct a sense of micro-national identity: the
dubbing of an American soap opera into, say, Basque becomes a nationalist gesture reinforcing the authority of the autonomous regional government through
the use of imported mass culture, in a particularly complex blurring of categories.

It should be clear from the above discussion that cultural studies and modernity
go together, not just because of the discipline's interest in the modern mass media,
but because the term 'culture' first took on its current sense as part of the liberal
modernizing project. This project, with its emphasis on the extension of education
and culture to the masses, must be understood in the later nineteenth-century context of accelerated industrial expansion and the attendant social and demographic
change occurring in Europe. Like other political and philosophical currents before
and since, liberalism claimed to be universal, while its objectives were historically
specific and exclusive. Social improvement was being impelled not to promote some
abstract 'general good' but to protect the fortunes of the particular class most closely
linked with the expanding capitalist development of the time: the bourgeoisie.
Liberalism's stress on education and culture was integrally linked to emergent
ideologies of nationalism, through which the ascendant bourgeoisie sought to
integrate the rest of the population within the national territory into its own
project. By establishing common symbols of identity (in reality, its own) it would
be able to cement diverse interests in an apparent collectivity, thus deflecting social
discontents and the threat of revolution. Education—undertaken by the state
—was crucial both as a producer of labour and as an agent of nation-building/
homogenization to ensure the consolidation of the bourgeois social order and state.

In Spain, the successive generations of teachers, artists, and political reformers
educated by the Institución Libre de Enseñanza were the bearers of this liberal
modernizing project. But the persistence of the old regime of Church, army, and
landowners in late nineteenth-century Spain meant that, on the one hand, these
currents of liberal bourgeois culture existed partly against the state, operating at
its margins (quite literally in the case of Catalan nationalism), and that, on the
other, the state could not construct 'the nation' along liberal lines. The cumulative
effects of the underdevelopment limiting urban and industrial development in
Spain meant that by the twentieth century a still largely marginalized bourgeoisie
was moreover becoming increasingly internally fragmented as alliances attempted
between sectors of its industrial, commercial, and agrarian components failed to
cohere, in turn permitting the old regime to continue holding sway over what was
still a predominantly rural country.

Serious social cleavages manifested themselves after the First World War, in
the revolutionary crisis of 1917 and subsequent social strife in urban and rural
Spain. Indeed it was only its relative underdevelopment (change was accelerating

at a lesser rate than elsewhere) which made Spain a paler reflection of the latent civil war occurring contemporaneously in Italy and ending in fascist ascendancy. It was becoming apparent that nowhere in the Spanish bourgeoisie was there a minimally coherent class project for national economic development. As a result, the bearers of a progressive liberal culture became ever more peripheral to the perceived interests and outlook of their own increasingly fragmented class. This cleavage would culminate in the civil war (1936–9), which saw the final uncoupling of liberalism's cultural project from that dimension of 'modernity' understood as the imperative to capitalist economic development. In repudiating the former so as to facilitate the latter, Francoism set itself the (ultimately unachievable) goal of securing the permanent separation of cultural and political modernity from the modernization process.

The emergent 'modern' bourgeois social and political order in Europe can be said to have been forged out of the larger process of modernization which was gathering momentum by the last quarter of the nineteenth century. 'Modernization' is, in itself, a problematic term. In this volume it is used to denote a recognizable process of capital-driven social, economic, political, and cultural change occurring at differential rates over the past 200 years across Europe (and, of course, *par excellence* in the USA). Its main characteristics have been accelerated industrialization, urbanization, and secularization, agricultural rationalization, industrial growth and specialization, a more complex division of labour, increased social differentiation, an increased level of popular involvement (direct or indirect) in political life/the public sphere, the massive expansion of consumer industries (including culture), vastly increased access to goods and services, and an increasingly powerful state with a growing capacity for the institutional regulation of social and political conflict (failure to satisfy this last criterion being an important factor in the later demise of Francoism).

Use of the term 'modernization' is made particularly problematic—beyond a frequent lack of precision in definition—by the unacceptable normative and determinist baggage loaded onto it. Those espousing models of modernization often employ a notion of 'tradition' which oversimplifies pre-industrial and ritualistic societies, inadequately appreciates the persistence of traditional elements in 'modern' societies, and overlooks the mutual influence that old and new ways of life may exert on one another. Alternatively, modernization is seen as having a quasi-autonomic, self-sustaining quality verging on determinism. Or, as with post-1945 'modernization theory' (emerging from the unexpectedly successful western capitalist reconstruction and expansion in the post-Second World War period), its usage is blatantly ethnocentric and normative. Rather than being seen as a conceptual framework for investigating a specific period of western development, modernization is projected as something that will transform the non-European world in the image of contemporary western European and North American society (far-from-homogeneous societies and cultures in themselves) whereupon history will implicity 'end'.

We need, then, to be sensitive to the fact that some uses of the term 'modernization' amount to yet another incarnation of that universalizing discourse which runs from Renaissance humanism through Enlightenment 'progress' to the concept of bourgeois modernity (and from there into 'modernization theory'). All of these projects have used pseudo-universal rhetorics while in fact privileging specific dominant groups, classes, races—not to mention a specific gender, in that all have either excluded women from the frame or marginalized their experience. Modernity was most assuredly a gendered event. In sum, problematic analytical usage arises from a fundamental failure to historicize the categories in question.

The critical strategies and perspectives adopted in this volume seek precisely to unpack the problematic baggage of modernization and modernity: in particular, by deconstructing the false opposition of modernity and tradition, and by demonstrating how the gender- and class-specific construction of 'modernity' forms a major example of the way we successively construct and reconstruct values, reinforcing them through cultural practice. The essays that follow, then, provide inbuilt protection against possible misconstructions or misreadings of a term which throughout has been used in a circumscribed way.

It was capital-driven modernization which produced both modernity and modernism: modernity understood as the condition of life subjectively experienced as a consequence of the changes wrought by modernization, and modernism as an artistic/cultural response (across literature, theatre, painting, architecture, music, and later cinema and design) to that subjective experience.

People's sense of experiencing 'the new' or 'the modern' did not, of course, begin with the onset of the specific process of modernization described here. It had been a Renaissance convention to divide history into the ancient, medieval, and modern periods, and eighteenth-century Enlightenment literature already reflects a sense of the passing of old, established ways of life and the emergence of new social patterns, foreshadowing more formal concepts of tradition and modernity. In the specific case of the later nineteenth century, the newness was perceived as being focused on humanity's commitment—man's in the narrow sense is more accurate—to a scientific outlook, to social improvement, and to economic development. Moreover, crucially, 'modernity' here was permeated by a sense of accompanying crisis. From the mid-eighteenth century onwards the word 'modern' was being used to convey the subjective sense that the present was a time of incessant crises leading to new developments not comparable with any in the past, that something unprecedentedly new was coming to pass. While even this sense of crisis has a long history—Walter Benjamin noted that all epochs have felt themselves to be on the edge of an abyss—we can locate the specificity of late nineteenth- and early twentieth-century modernity by reference to two aspects. First, a changing perception of time (the time–space continuum) and an acute awareness of change and instability as the norm. Second, a sense of the fragmentariness of human life and experience.

The changes in time consciousness were closely related to capitalist development

—for example, the imposition of factory discipline as part of the process of rationalizing production and social relations—as was the sense of the fragmentation of everyday life. That fragmentariness was epitomized by the anonymous encounters and transactions of urban existence—modernity being fundamentally focused on the human experience of the city as the collective social product *par excellence* of nineteenth-century industrial development. Capitalist development was breaking down traditional, more fixed rurally based communities and forms of social organization. Urban existence was atomized. A rationalized and compartmentalized modern society was too big, and its processes too specialized, for the individual to comprehend their workings. Life was characterized by transitory, fleeting, and fortuitous interactions requiring only fragments of the individual personality to be involved. In sum, it was a potentially alienating experience in which feelings of loss of control and meaninglessness predominated. And even those who did not have direct experience of urban life and its trials came to feel threatened by the city and urban culture. Seen as a social dissolvent, its encroachment became the image of all that was felt to threaten their perceivedly stable, unchanging, and 'meaningful' rural existences.

The increasingly acute awareness that change is the condition we live by, that society and social relations exist in a constant state of flux, provoked all kinds of anxieties and insecurities, which fed into numerous forms of social, cultural and political expression in the period between the 1890s and the 1930s. While these modes of expression were hugely varied and often antagonistic to each other, they can all in some way be subsumed within the term 'modernism'.

Modernism (or 'the modern movement') is the name given to a wide range of experimental literary and artistic forms emerging in the period between the 1890s and the 1930s as a response to the experience of modern urban life. Fragmentation and a sense of crisis or watershed is the key linking processes and products/ artefacts in other ways quite distinct: for example, cubism and surrealism, which represented different formal articulations of the same sense of loss of wholeness and depth—whether of things or of the self. A classic, peculiarly Spanish case of the way in which different political contexts could inflect cultural movements that aesthetically had much in common is provided by the distinction between Castilian *modernismo*, with its retreat into an ostensibly apolitical if sexually dissident élitism, and Catalan *modernisme*, which directly expressed Catalan nationalist aspirations and in some cases—e.g. Gaudí's utopian projects for workers' colonies—had popular, if paternalist, overtones. Whatever the formal solution or political direction, all of this cultural work—across European national boundaries—was being produced with an awareness that art itself was coming hard up against a series of intellectual, social, and historical forces. Art, in short, faced the 'dislocation of the century'.

These experimental cultural forms—whatever the specific medium—signified a rupture with representationalism (realism/naturalism). They were abstract, substituting a multidimensional spatial sense for unilinearity, and with an ironic self-awareness of the process of creation (as in the use of collage). Their formal stylization was predicated on a heightened sense that the unproblematic solidity of things and of the self which realism/naturalism seemed to affirm no longer corresponded to human experience.[9] But this radical project was not necessarily allied to the political left: those artists who embraced communism, those who embraced fascism, and those who rejected politics altogether—to take only three of the many positions adopted—all saw themselves as radicals responding to the dislocating forces of the times. The political ambiguity of modernism is notorious, Ortega y Gasset being just one example of that élitist potential which sought to exclude the masses (equally a product of modernity) as a dangerous/'uncultured' other. Those of modernism's exponents who went as far as fascism did so in the name of a 'last-ditch stand against aesthetic barbarism' which in practice served to protect the old social order in new ways.[10] For others on the left, the central problem raised by the potential quietism of modernism's privileging of the aesthetic was how, if the aesthetic was the source of revitalization, could that same society be regenerated without the artist's active intervention?

The solution could not lie in individualistic rebellion or dissent, still less in the retreat into constructing or contributing to some new essentialist myth of wholeness and belonging (as offered by fascism), but in cultural engagement with social change in order not only to resolve aesthetic dilemmas but to go forward materially—not to mend the 'broken world' but to create a new order. This task was epitomized by the German art, architecture, and design school the Bauhaus, which sought to unify art and craft in pursuit of a positive, liberating modern vision that might serve humanity and heal the trauma of recent change. Walter Benjamin, the most important cultural critic of the late 1920s and 1930s, called for the left to politicize art in response to fascism's aestheticization of politics. Many intellectuals and avant-garde artists, in Spain as throughout Europe, were attracted to communism; those who joined the communist party found themselves torn between their belief in the subversive potential of creative autonomy and the realities of collective political organization, particularly when stalinization led to increasing party mistrust of artistic experiment, dismissed as bourgeois and élitist (which in some ways it was) and therefore lacking in revolutionary potential (which was not necessarily true). Some managed to reconcile party allegiance with artistic experimentation without too much apparent difficulty, as was the case (despite some embarrassing circumstantial poetry) with Rafael Alberti, who had however—like some other Spanish writers—initially wavered between radical options of the right and left. Others moved in the opposite direction, most notoriously Ernesto Giménez Caballero, editor of Spain's leading avant-garde magazine La Gaceta Literaria, who from having been a champion of modern film and art, and a surrealist poet and prose writer aggressively celebrating the dislocations of modern city life, became a founder-member of the Falange* and a virulent fascist propagandist. Curiously, Giménez Caballero was one of the very few Spanish modernists who whole-heartedly—in his surrealist phase—embraced the experience of modernity. The same can perhaps be said of Buñuel and Dalí; the political ambiguity of the latter is equally notorious.

The acute contradictions thrown up by Spain's belated, uneven development produced a particularly brilliant artistic, literary, and musical avant-garde. It has, in fact, been argued that the avant-garde occurred most characteristically in countries marked by uneven development, which exacerbated the experience of modernity as contradiction and crisis, rather than in the more advanced capitalist nations where modernity was less problematic.[11] This is borne out by the case of Spain, where the response of most modernists to modernization (most of them migrated to Madrid from underdeveloped rural areas) was one of trauma and loss. Valle-Inclán, who flirted with Carlism* and the Republic, moved from the depiction of rural barbarism to that of an urban horror lacking even the grandiosity of the former. Lorca made the reverse journey from horror at the dehumanization of city life (epitomized by New York) to the dramatization of rural repression, which allowed him to insert his subversive sexual politics into a network of organic—though by no means unproblematic—natural imagery. Lorca is in many ways the paradigmatic Spanish modernist: because of the ambivalence of his response to modernity, because of his inability to translate his political sympathies into direct political action, and because neither of these things prevented him from becoming a Republican martyr.

Although a sense of accelerated change and fragmentation was central to the experience of modernity, it was experienced differently and given different meanings by the different social classes. For both older élites and the bourgeoisie, the social and cultural anxieties of modernity were rooted in a fear of losing control. For the bourgeoisie especially, the paradox was that the process of capitalist economic development which had created them as a class had also unleashed other social dynamics producing stresses and tensions endangering their ascendancy. Bourgeois anxieties were rooted in fear of a working-class 'other' whose responses to modernity were unpredictable and perhaps not entirely controllable. These fears found expression as part of an existential crisis over 'the death of God', as an absolute value system rooted in religion came increasingly under threat from science and philosophy. The search for alternative values was first and foremost a search for structures that would contain change and stabilize society in ways that guaranteed their own social and economic position.

For the masses created by industrialization and urbanization, as the intended object of the liberal modernizing project's educational and cultural initiatives, modernity was experienced as material hardship, powerlessness, conflict, and often an acute sense of loss and alienation as the imperatives of capitalist production broke up old patterns of life (leading to new kinds of rural impoverishment and to migration), imposing new, alienating modes of existence (urban atomization, the strangeness of factory discipline, secularization experienced as a net loss of meaning). So while the liberal modernizing project, descended from the ideas of the Enlightenment and the French Revolution, with its focus on education and the dissemination of culture, could be seen to contain some egalitarian potential for the empowerment of the masses at whom it was directed (notwithstanding the class agenda it had acquired), modernity was in fact experienced by these masses as something quite different and negative. This explains why liberalism, with its ideal of 'progress', has so often failed to appeal to a working-class constituency. It simply did not accord with their lived experience of 'the modern'. The failure of modernity for workers shaped the construction and evolution of the cultures of labour, as well as the agendas of its unions and parties. Spain's anarcho-syndicalist movement is the example *par excellence* of the rejection of bourgeois modernity. This would lead it to resist—politically and culturally (and eventually with arms)— attempts to reconstruct the Republican state in 1936–7.

But given that only a small percentage of the masses were integrated into the social and cultural networks provided by labour organizations, the majority had less access to alternative structures of meaning and belonging. Thus popular cultural mediation of modernity—using 'culture' here in the broad sense, defined above, of the stories we tell each other to explain what and where we are—was dominated by a sense of fear, dislocation, and meaninglessness. The distance between the potentially liberatory project of progressive liberal educators and artists and the lived reality of modernity was the space where fascism's mass base grew.

The Spanish case confirms that it was often as much a fear of the unknown, of what might be lost, as direct experience which allowed popular constituencies to be mobilized behind conservative goals. Cumulative economic underdevelopment (and Spain's neutrality in the First World War) significantly limited the numbers and constituencies of the uprooted and alienated—although change was accelerating by the 1920s. As elsewhere, the rural and provincial lower middle classes— smallholders, tenant farmers, and so on—internalizing modernity as 'decadence' and a loss of wholeness, joined the ranks of the radical right.[12] Many (such as the peasant farmers of Castile) passed straight on to become the footsoldiers of Francoism, which promised a return to a simple world from which change and the 'enemy'—the bearer of difference—would be banished. (However, in the civil war the Basque nationalists, with identical objectives and a similar class base, would oppose Franco in the name of their right to secede from a secular, 'modern' Republic.)

In 1930s Spain, many of bourgeois modernity's contradictions and discontents converged and crystallized. A situation of acute national polarization was intensified by the Europe-wide tremors reverberating from the crisis of international capitalism. The conflict between Nationalists and Republicans was one of several sites in inter-war Europe where the cleavage within modernity between the imperative to capitalist economic development and the liberal democratic cultural project of national inclusion (i.e. building the nation to 'include' the masses, rather than constructing them as 'other') became a reality. In Spain, the process was clinched by the eruption of civil war: the cleavage was visible in the crisis of historic republicanism, a major part of its class base siding with the Nationalists, who rapidly came to represent and project a highly exclusive concept of the nation.

Inside Republican Spain another conflict was being waged. On the one hand, there were those who took up the remnants of liberalism's modernizing strategy in an attempt to remake it and, through it, the Republican state. This included part of the Socialist Party (PSOE*), but predominantly—given internal republican and socialist crisis—a much expanded Spanish Communist party (PCE*) which acquired a significant base among the middle classes (especially the professional classes) of the Republican zone. Opposing this Popular Front liberal-statist alliance was a more radical cultural project—although it only ever existed in fragments—which questioned and sought to go beyond the premises of bourgeois modernity. Its protagonists were predominantly an urban working class which had experienced 'modernity' not as a progressive project but as economic and cultural alienation. The struggle between the two is usually depicted in far too narrowly high-political terms as the clash between stalinist communists and anarchists (most notoriously in the Barcelona May Days of 1937). For the Popular Frontists, building the bourgeois state in the new wartime conjuncture posed certain strategic problems to which adequate solutions were never found. The 'heroic *pueblo*' long objectified in liberal mythology had become, of necessity, the historical subject, the only collective protagonist which could salvage the Republican state and with it the liberal cultural project. But the Popular Front—whose constituent groups, one must remember, had very little practical experience of power—were never able to elaborate a language—or indeed languages—of popular mobilization which could even begin to overcome the secular failures of nation-building. Nor can this be attributed to the always inchoate anti-statist challenge of libertarians and other radicals. It was, fairly and squarely, the last failure of a now bifurcated liberal modernity to connect with the constituencies to whom it claimed to offer emancipation and social reconciliation.

The international context too, as is well known, was unremittingly hostile to the Republic. For Europe's élites and the interests of capital, the Republic looked like a bad risk: the lateness and unevenness of Spain's development had provoked social stresses and radical potentials whose containment within a liberal democratic framework was seen as far from assured, and whose liberal democracy itself was perceived as a dangerously radical hybrid.

Victorious Francoism, by contrast, in jettisoning the 'dangerous' ambivalences and potentials of cultural modernity, would make Spain 'safe' for capitalist modernization. The fact that Franco never openly joined the Axis in the Second World War (and thus never directly threatened Allied imperialist interests) meant that, unlike the defeated German and Italian dictatorships, the Spanish regime was not militarily dislodged by the victors. Moreover, the subsequent escalation of the Cold War, in transforming Francoism into a useful western ally, enormously facilitated the regime's domestic consolidation. The strait-jacket provided over almost two decades by autarky, as a social and cultural practice, allowed state power to be built and bolstered on a rigid social hierarchy itself grounded in an anti-modern, anti-rationalist official culture. The cleavage within modernity thus became irreversible in Spain's case, indeed was institutionalized as the basis of the dictatorship. (There were, of course, worse cases of modernity combusting. But while the Holocaust would remain, in European terms, the unassimilable history *par excellence*, the Third Reich's defeat after a relatively short duration of twelve years meant that the cultural and economic facets of bourgeois modernity could be brought together, despite the fact that it would never really be the same again anywhere. For no amount of post-war economic miracle could erase the memory of the flaw in the project which genocide had opened up.)

By the 1960s, Spain too was a consumer society in the making. The Francoist political élite had correctly perceived the socially and politically pacificatory function of 'things' (consumer products), but some had also erroneously assumed this could be channelled to stabilize Francoism's authoritarian cultural project in perpetuity. In fact, as we know, the accumulated social and cultural change of the 1960s would create a complex, plural civil society whose mounting opposition to the anachronistic inflexibility of Francoism's political structures contributed significantly to the pressure which led to their dismantling.

But the process of democratic 'normalization' itself opens up crucial questions about the impact and legacy of Francoism—not least in cultural terms. The extremely compressed time period (less than thirty years) in which Spain's economic, social, and political European alignment has occurred amounts to the simultaneous experience of changes occurring elsewhere on the Continent much more gradually and sequentially. This makes it difficult to determine how much, for example, one might attribute the marginality of cultural alternatives in Spain (in terms of life-styles and ideas which counter or challenge the 'mainstream' of the consumerist nuclear family/couple) to the legacy of the dictatorship specifically and how much to the impact of mass commercial culture (the culture industry) and the neo-liberal project of the 1980s—neither of which is particular to Spain. More usefully, what we can say is that Francoism operated in different ways across a long period to reduce the extent of counter-cultural resistances—most crucially in depriving many young critical cultures of the public space in which to grow.

We need to remember this if we are not to fall prey to certain dangers and problems inherent in Spain's current enthusiastic celebration of postmodernist perspectives and practices. At one level these have brought in voices and experiences silenced and excluded by the cultural impact of Francoism which—together with the failure of the transition's transformative potential for the left—explains much of postmodernism's liberatory appeal. Yet, at the same time, postmodernism's emphasis on the irreducibility of the particular, on plural cultures 'at play', tends also to disguise precisely what this is symptomatic of: namely, the increasing concentration of economic power (multinational capital) which produces and reproduces the cultural jamboree.[13] This spectacle may disguise, but it cannot negate, the fact that the participating cultures continue to exist in hierarchical relationships to one another. While we play, power operates elsewhere. If some kinds of modernity 'excluded', postmodernism now merely disguises the continuing exclusions of power.

Also, the prevalence of pastiche can be problematic when it is used, not to ask questions about what is being legitimized by particular cultural representations, but to reduce history to a storehouse of exploitable images: as these become yet more commodities to be consumed, history is gutted of its dialectical power. Against this, our endeavour should be to uncover the complex interaction of cultural, social, and political alternatives which competed in the past: thereby opposing the retrospective operation of power—not least in the writing of history —which makes it appear as if the *de facto* outcome were the only one that was ever possible.

This is a process which reveals not a single, homogeneous 'modernity' but many potentials. In view of the evidently conservative readings and uses to which postmodernism is open, we should be careful not to jettison the radical, liberatory potential which cultural modernism itself contained, not least in its engagement with change and in its understanding of the need to assume its ever-recurring, exhilarating message: that of our multiple possibilities and our capacity for transformation. Postmodernism, while it operates against the homogenizing discourse of power, also operates against the powerless: by obscuring the commonality of their exploitation, it bars the route to solidarity and collective action.[14] It is strange that the only homogenizing discourse postmodernism has not relinquished is that which reduces modernity itself to one.

Notes

1 Brecht noted that Hitler's use of spectacle turned the people into a public (discussed by N. García Canclini, *Culturas híbridas: estrategias para entrar y salir de la modernidad* (Mexico, 1989), 154). It would be interesting to apply this notion to analysis of 1940s Spain, where political indoctrination concentrated on visual spectacle (though not in the form of mass political rallies). The Nationalist dramatist Torrente Ballester's advocacy of Greek drama on the grounds that it turned the masses into the chorus concurs with Brecht's analysis, suggesting that Nationalist intellectuals had a more conscious cultural policy than is often supposed.

2 For Gramsci and Italian neo-realism, see D. Forgacs, 'National-Popular: Genealogy of a Concept', in S. During (ed.), *The Cultural Studies Reader* (London, 1993), 177–90. Gramsci's prison notebooks, which elaborate his cultural theories, were published in Italy in 1948–51, the period when neo-realism was dominant.

3 See, in particular, the work of J. Martín-Barbero, N. García Canclini, and B. Sarlo. For an excellent overview, see W. Rowe and V. Schelling, *Memory and Modernity: Popular Culture in Latin America* (London, 1991).

4 See his important theoretical work, *De los medios a las mediaciones* (Barcelona, 1987), which discusses the role of the media in Latin America.

5 P. Bourdieu, *Distinction: A Social Critique of the Judgement of Taste* (Cambridge, Mass., 1984), 5.

6 See R. Williams, *Keywords* (London, 1990), 87–93. As Williams notes (87): 'Culture is one of the two or three most complicated words in the English language.'

7 For a useful discussion of the various meanings of the term 'popular culture', see J. Storey, *An Introductory Guide to Cultural Theory and Popular Culture* (New York, 1993), 6–17.

8 *Memory and Modernity*, 8.

9 See M. Berman, *All That is Solid Melts into Air* (London, 1983).

10 F. Jameson, *Fables of Aggression: Wyndham Lewis, the Modernist as Fascist* (Berkeley, 1979).

11 García Canclini, *Culturas híbridas*, 70.

12 For a European perspective, see G. M. Luebbert, *Liberalism, Fascism or Socialism: Social Classes and the Political Origins of Regimes in Inter-War Europe* (Oxford, 1991).

13 See F. Jameson, *Postmodernism; or, The Cultural Logic of Late Capitalism* (London, 1991). Also, Benjamin's observation: 'The mere experience of the ever-new forgets that its fundamental precondition is the ever-same reproduction of the social relations necessary for the ever-new to appear.' According to this view, postmodernity demonstrably belongs inside a modernist continuum. On this, see also F. Barker, P. Hulme, and M. Iverson (eds.), *Postmodernism and the Re-reading of Modernity* (Manchester, 1992).

14 Cf. Z. Bauman, *Modernity and Ambivalence* (Oxford, 1991), ch. 7.

Part I

Élites in Crisis
1898–1931

The basic requirement of an authentic, fully realized
Empire is internal political homogeneity. By
contrast, colonization supposes that the colonies and
the metropolis are heterogeneous. An Empire has
'provinces', not regions.

(Eugenio d'Ors,
'Colonial Empires do not Exist', 1938)

Editors' Introduction

Fin de siècle European anxieties about the decadence of western
civilization were experienced in a particularly complex form in
Spain, where intellectuals were divided as to whether or not
Spain should follow the European modernizing model, and as
to whether the problem in Spain's case was modernity or a
lack of modernization. The loss of Spain's last significant colonies (Cuba, Puerto Rico, and the Philippines) in 1898 not only
dealt the death blow to any pretensions of being a world power,
but also, in the context of growing demands for regional autonomy, exacerbated fears of Spain's breakup as a nation-state.
Cuba and Puerto Rico were constitutionally defined as provinces of Spain, which partly explains the ease of the converse
identification process whereby, for the post-imperial right,
peninsular Spain became the empire. The obsessive attempts at
redefining national identity which took place in this period
respond to a fear of the increasingly evident cultural pluralism
resulting from the modernizing process. This fear, articulated
in d'Ors's 'imperative of homogeneity' in the epigraph above,

would be adopted explicitly in 1939 by a victorious Francoism which had come to view Spain as the 'conquered territory'. During the early decades of the twentieth century, some—for example, the Church—would attempt to deny this pluralism altogether; others—intellectual reformers—felt the answer lay in the creation of cultural homogeneity through the 'civilizing' effects of education. However, as progressive liberals did not achieve power until 1931, and the state in any case lacked resources, no concerted attempt was made from the centre to develop such a strategy of nation-building. Artists divided into those who saw the incipient massification of culture as a threat to individual expression and consequently strove to reinforce the divide between high and low culture, and those who saw the contradictions of modernity as an opportunity for creating new artistic effects through a juxtaposition of élite, popular, and mass cultural forms that in its own way was also a reaction against cultural commercialization.

In all of these different cases, the question of intellectuals' and artists' relationship to the state, and to the public in the new form of an increasingly massified but also increasingly diversified market, is paramount: dissidence and conformism frequently blur into one another. Sexual rebellion, in particular, could combine the redefinition of gender roles with an élitist conception of the exotic, while the institutionalization and co-option through bourgeois patronage of literary and artistic modernism (in the broad European sense of the word) all too easily turned subversion into fashion. In a similar manner, bourgeois assimilation of mass cultural forms—for example, popular song—defused and sanitized their disruptive potential, while in a majority of cases artistic modernism offered an exclusively male perspective. The role of the artist in local nationalist projects—as in Catalonia—was especially fraught with contradiction, since rejection of dominant Spanish norms was inevitably the other side of the creation of a local cultural orthodoxy, additionally achieved through appeal to European models. The redefinition of national and local identities through the appropriation of international forms and trends is a constant; even the Church drew heavily on the ideas of the French Catholic revival and its agents in the form of the teaching orders displaced by late nineteenth-century French anticlerical legislation, while the construction of urban and rural labour cultures was a complex response to local needs and socialist or anarchist internationalism.

The relationship between popular and mass culture, and the relationship of both to hegemonic cultural processes, is especially complex. The politicization of rural culture that took place during this period is a sign both of incorporation into national life and of an attempt to create a contestatory counter-culture. And in a particularly interesting battle of meanings, the urban working classes were constructed as a public both by the cheap serialized fiction (mostly escapist but sometimes using melodrama as a vehicle for social protest) targeted at them by commercial publishers, and by the political novels distributed by labour organizations.

Another paradoxical constant found throughout the essays that follow is the interdependence of modernity and tradition, not just with the grafting of new ideas onto old, as in the influence of millenarianism on anarchist thought, but in the revival—by modernists (in the European, Castilian, and Catalan senses of the word) and traditionalists—of earlier cultural forms as a protest against a present that, for widely differing reasons, was found unacceptable (and one must remember that the bourgeoisie—far from culturally homogeneous, of course—was as unhappy about the modern age as everyone else). This period of Spanish cultural life shows that modernity is defined precisely by anxieties about modernization. It also sets the stage for what will be a central issue throughout twentieth-century Spanish history: the struggle between attempts—by right and left—to impose culture top-down and attempts to resist that process by creating alternative cultural spaces.

National Identities

SEBASTIAN
BALFOUR

ENRIC UCELAY
DA CAL

The Loss of Empire, Regenerationism, and the Forging of a Myth of National Identity

SEBASTIAN BALFOUR

In 1898 Spain lost the remnants of its empire after almost four years of colonial wars and a catastrophic military encounter with the United States. The Disaster of 1898 transformed the political climate in Spain. Criticism of the state of the nation previously levelled by a small minority of would-be reformers became a national polemic. From all sides, politicians, busi nessmen, writers, academics, officers, and a host of pundits and armchair philosophers joined in debate about the causes of Spain's decline and the remedies necessary to restore the nation's fortunes.

Encouraged by the prevailing intellectual fashion of positivism, most exegeses resorted to a pathology of the nation; Spain was suffering from a severe, if not terminal, illness and needed an immediate and radical cure. The deeply conservative view was that Spain had lost the empire because it had abandoned those virtues which had once made it great: unity, hierarchy, and militant Catholicism. Its decline had begun with the corrosive effects of reforms based on foreign models imported first by the Habsburgs, then by the Bourbons, and later borrowed from the French Enlightenment. Much more widespread was the view that attributed Spain's decline to its failure to modernize, for which blame was laid variously on incompetent politicians, the backward ideology of the ruling order, the corruption and clientelism of the political system, and the apathy of the masses. To recover health, Spain needed a vast programme of reforms modelled on those of the more advanced societies in Europe. These could not be carried out by the discredited politicians, who had to give way to the leadership of the 'vital forces' in Spain, the 'productive and intellectual classes' previously excluded from power.

Such demands found wide support, not just among the industrial bourgeoisie and the middle classes, but also within the establishment itself. For a while regenerationism, as this movement of opinion was called, became a catchword on everyone's lips, from elder statesmen to striking workers. The first government to be formed after the Disaster, under the dissident Conservative Francisco Silvela, fell in with the spirit of regeneration by calling for a 'revolution from above'. Its failure to achieve much beside balancing the nation's books—no mean feat given the colossal deficit created by the wars—led many to believe that regeneration could only be achieved outside the two-party (turno*) system of the Restoration regime.

The two organized movements for national regeneration which emerged after the Disaster crystallized around those economic interests most affected by the crisis following the loss of empire—the Catalan industrialists and regionalists who formed the conservative Catalanist party, the Lliga Regionalista, in 1901, and the nation-wide movement of the Chambers of Commerce and the Agrarian Chambers initiated by small businessmen and farmers in Castile and Aragon in 1898. In the vacuum of moral authority created by the Disaster, the latter movement gathered together a wide spectrum of support among the industrial bourgeoisie and the middle classes. In the space of two years, three widely reported assemblies were held in which the future of Spain was passionately debated and an immensely ambitious programme for its rehabilitation was launched. According to this programme, reforms were needed in education, health, and infrastructure, in particular in irrigation and communication networks; the civil service and the military had to be severely pruned; above all, electoral reform was necessary: although universal male suffrage had been law since 1890, elections were fraudulent exercises, openly manipulated by the two ruling parties through the prevailing system of patronage run by the caciques* or local political bosses. Together, these proposed reforms amounted to nothing less than a full-blown programme of modernization based on European models; hence it was described by some as the Europeanization of Spain.

Less clear in the regenerationists' programme was the means by which these reforms were to be achieved. What had brought the movement together were first a deeply felt grievance that industry and small business were having to pay an unfair burden of the war debts through tax increases, and a diffuse crisis of legitimacy in the immediate aftermath of the Disaster during which it appeared that the old political order was crumbling. However, the regime quickly recovered its balance. For all the anguish that it provoked, the loss of the colonies did not generate a severe economic or social crisis which might have threatened the regime. Only the textile manufacturers of Catalonia, for whom Cuba had been a major source of exports, and the wheat-growing regions of central Spain, where the loss of the colonial markets exacerbated a long-term agrarian decline, were seriously affected; it was from these two regions that the impetus for regenerationism was greatest. Neither republicans nor Carlists,* the old foes of the Restoration system, offered any threat. Indeed, in a largely traditional society with poor communications and a high rate of illiteracy, the old networks of social and ideological control ensured the continued stability of the ruling order dominated by the landed oligarchy.*

Beyond their immediate tax grievance, the Chambers movement was divided over what strategy to adopt in order to regenerate Spain. Its most charismatic leader, Joaquín Costa, a self-made intellectual from an Aragonese peasant family, sought to create a national party of the traditional middling classes, acting also on behalf of working people, which would sweep aside the parasitical oligarchy and modernize the country. In such an unevenly developed society as Spain, so marked by class and regional fissures, a strategy of this kind needed to take up the demands of a variety of constituencies. The Chambers' programme, however, did not address either the aspirations of working people, articulated in the mounting wave of strikes and urban riots, or those of the regionalist movements; nor, indeed, did it satisfy the demands of industrialists. Between Basque ironmasters and Catalan textile magnates, on one hand, and provincial shopkeepers and small farmers, on the other, there was a wide cultural and economic gap.

Within the Chambers movement, therefore, a range of different political agendas coexisted. Some sections were closely tied to the landed oligarchy and were vehemently opposed to political action of any kind. Most delegates were content for the movement to act as a lobby on the government and turned down Costa's proposal for a new political party which would challenge the hegemony of the reigning two-party system. Representatives of big business from Catalonia and the Basque Country withdrew when it became clear that their aims could be better achieved through their own resources. The Basques renewed their own effective lobby of the government and were rewarded shortly afterwards with a cabinet post. Catalan industrialists, on the other hand, having attempted unsuccessfully to change government policy through their cabinet allies, joined with the middle-class Catalanist movement to form a regional party (the Lliga) with the aim of breaking the local stranglehold of the Restoration parties and of regenerating Spain from a resurgent Catalonia. However, when doubly challenged by an emerging working-class movement and a newly mobilized republicanism under the populist leader Alejandro Lerroux, Catalan industrialists preferred to renew rather than break their links with their traditional Conservative allies in the state.

The Chambers movement, for its part, attempted to apply pressure on the government by using its only weapons; witholding tax payments and organizing nation-wide shop closures (the *tancament de caixes*). Its protest actions received unsolicited and unwelcome backing from masses of working people, who were themselves agitating against the heavy burden of indirect taxation on basic consumer goods. In many towns throughout Spain, workers went on strike and violent clashes took place in the streets between the popular masses and the forces of law and order, with the usual train of sacked tax offices and damaged public and clerical buildings. Embarrassed by the rough support of the crowd and unable to shift the government's resolution, the regenerationist movement was deserted by most of its backers. From a global challenge against the regime, it was reduced to a catalogue of grievances of the petty bourgeoisie in the area most affected by the post-colonial crisis.

Thus, in the agitated period that followed the Disaster, no nation-wide political alternative emerged to challenge the rule of the establishment. The disparate forces which had attempted to change the system were too divided by class and regional differences to unite. Moreover, they both underestimated the resilience of the regime and overestimated the depth of the crisis. In their frustration at the prevailing inertia, many regenerationists blamed the people. Yet contrary to most historical accounts, the masses were not uniformly passive. The rate of electoral participation was low and hence fraud continued to flourish, but there was a high level of mobilization around concrete grievances: landlessness, the price of bread, and the level of indirect tax. Riots against the clergy, military service, and the local authorities were also frequent and at moments of great tension spread across the whole of Spain. The middle-class revolt failed to gather together this diffuse protest or to join with left-wing, anti-dynastic forces because most of its base was too closely tied to the oligarchy or the bourgeoisie and fundamentally opposed to the independent organization of workers.

The lesson derived from the failure of the movement by many of the regenerationists, among whom were some of the outstanding intellectuals of the day, was one deeply pessimistic about the possibility of change. Some reiterated the view long argued by the influential, progressive Institución Libre de Enseñanza* that Spain could not properly modernize until the cultural level of Spaniards had been raised through the painstaking process of education. Others drifted back into the hegemonic sphere of the dynastic parties they had so vehemently denounced, encouraged by the emergence of new and more vigorous currents within them; some of the businessmen who had formed the base of the Chambers movement were lured by the corporatist seductions of the dynamic Conservative leadership of Antonio Maura, while an important nucleus of intellectuals collaborated with the progressive Liberal leader José Canalejas. Indeed, the Restoration system showed yet again its capacity to absorb tendencies to its left and right.

For his part, Costa turned to a desperate solution: if Spain were to avoid the calamity of social revolution, a leader had to emerge, an 'iron surgeon' who would operate on the sick body of the nation to restore its health. Although conservatives and the right would later claim his legacy, Costa's proposal was inspired more by a mix of republican Jacobinism and praetorian liberalism. But though the link between Costa's ideas and twentieth-century authoritarianism is problematic, it is true that some of the discourse of the disillusioned regenerationists seeped into right-wing ideology; in particular, the idea of Spain's spiritual mission, the distrust of parliamentary politics, and the belief in an essential, as opposed to plural, Spain whose roots lay in Castile and Catholicism.

For all the sense of inertia in the years following the Disaster, Restoration Spain was profoundly altered in its wake. It was not just the regime's legitimacy that was undermined. The wars and the loss of empire also deepened a crisis of identity which was to play a crucial part in political conflict in Spain. The Disaster subverted the complacent nationalism fostered by the establishment and much of the press; during the Spanish–American War, North Americans had been popularly portrayed as rapacious, amateurish, and cowardly, no match for the Old World valour of the Spanish soldiers and sailors. The ease of the American victory exposed the hollowness of this rhetoric. It also encouraged centrifugal tendencies in conceptions of national identity.

Spain's precarious unity between its different regions had been constructed around a common endeavour to extend its dominion and its religion to the empire and to extract the wealth contained therein. With the loss of the last colonies, the already fragile ideological ties binding the regions to the centre from which that empire had been run were put under even greater strain; this was particularly true of Catalonia because the ruling order had failed to retain the colonial markets which had absorbed so many of the region's exports. More importantly, rapid modernization, especially in Catalonia and the Basque region in the second half of the nineteenth century, had widened the socio-economic and cultural gap between the centre and the periphery. The sense of alienation towards the dominant oligarchic order felt by many Basques and their more outward-looking and cosmopolitan middle-class counterparts in Catalonia was merely heightened by the Disaster.

The crisis caused by the Disaster therefore flowed into a longer-term crisis generated by modernization. In many parts of Spain, industrialization, urbanization, migration, and the spread of communications networks and the media were undermining the social and ideological structures of the Restoration system. The change in values that ensued was quickened by the effects of the wars. During the period 1895–8, perhaps for the first time, deeply ingrained local identities had superimposed on them images of national identity conveyed through songs, speeches, and military ceremonies as well as the jingoistic articles and cartoons of the press. As the war with the United States approached, physical and ideological mobilization around national objectives had intensified, penetrating to the remotest areas. However, the terrible hardship of both families and conscripts sent to fight in the wars (many returning in piteous condition), combined with the catastrophe of the defeat, undermined the potential for the development of popular nationalism or social imperialism of the kind that was flourishing elsewhere in Europe; hence Spain's renewed colonialism in North Africa from the beginning of the century did not arouse popular enthusiasm and indeed would provoke ferocious protest in Barcelona in 1909. Thus the effect of the wars and to a greater extent of modernization encouraged the growth of a plurality of identities in more developed parts of Spain, replacing traditional self-images with new perceptions of regional, class, and gender identities.

In contrast, conservative opinion reacted to the twin crisis by raising ideological and cultural barricades. The pre-war debate over whether to grant autonomy to the colonies had created an extreme sensitivity about the question of regional devolution. The feeling was strong, especially amongst the military, that the concessions made to the Cuban autonomists had opened the door to independence. Hence, the regional movements in Catalonia and the Basque Country were viewed with deep suspicion. The growing alienation between centre and periphery found expression in chauvinist and even racist stereotypes on both sides which merely served to reinforce divisions and, amongst Spanish conservative opinion, to strengthen a monolithic conception of national identity constructed on a supposedly archetypal Castilian character. The failure of Christian democracy or liberalism to develop a mass base meant that the promotion of national identity became the preserve of deeply conservative forces such as the Church and the army and therefore served as a vehicle not of social integration and consensus but of division and exclusion.

Indeed, the Disaster and the challenge of modernization encouraged a renewal of traditional views about Spanish history and the nature of Spanishness. One such view laid stress on a universalist mission of Spain to bring spirituality to an increasingly materialistic world. According to this vision, the source of Spain's new resurgence lay in the Hispanic traditions it had created in its former empire; by increasing trade and cultural contacts with the ex-colonies, Spain could create a new cultural empire as a counterweight to the Anglo-Saxon world. Two icons above all were wielded in defence of this supposed vocation: Ariel, the symbol of the spirit as opposed to the capitalist Caliban, and Quixote, now ready to sally forth on a third voyage to bring spiritual values to a world losing its way. Other traditional images of national identity focused on the exceptional valour of Spanish men, their highly developed sense of honour, and their 'manliness', while Spanish women were portrayed as uniquely beautiful and devout.

A distorted and partial view of Spanish history, renovated by the historian Menéndez Pelayo in the latter part of the nineteenth century, was also mobilized to defend tradition against the inroads of modernization. The 'true' Spain was seen to lie in the spirit of the Counter-Reformation and in (a wholly conservative reading of) the Dos de Mayo (2 May) uprising of 1808 against the French invaders. The ancestral Castile of the Reconquest became a model for a renewed Spain. Castile exerted a fascination even among those regenerationist writers most critical of the supposed decadence of Spain. Their nostalgic musings over the medieval ruins and the harsh landscape of the *meseta* helped to nourish the conservative myth of national identity. The celebration of medieval Spain and of traditional rural life was, it can be argued, a flight from the dilemmas of modernization which increasingly threatened the autonomy of the petty bourgeoisie, caught between the revolt of the lower classes and the spread of capitalism. For more conservative sectors, such as the Carlists, the familiar social structures of the countryside, its rituals, the old paternalism of landlord and priest, were seen as bulwarks against the corrosive moral effects of industrialization and urbanization.

Conservative opinion, however, was not uniformly traditionalist. In the first two decades of the century, a new right-wing regenerationism emerged whose heart was the army. While this current of opinion shared the stereotypical view of national identity outlined above, it sought to sweep away the ineffectual two-party system of the Restoration regime and modernize the nation through an authoritarian state: by creating a strong economy, Spain could rebuild its military strength and recover greatness through imperialist expansion into Africa. The idea that the empire had been lost through the incompetence of parliament rather than through an international process of colonial redistribution became internalized among many army officers. As the twin challenge of regionalism and working-class agitation grew, this new nationalism combined with more traditional sectors such as the Church to impose its own solutions on Spanish society, first in 1923 and then in 1936. When the military rose against the Second Republic in 1936, they were able to draw on a coherent and exclusive myth of national identity and imperial greatness to legitimize their action, a myth shaped by the Disaster of 1898 and the parallel crisis of modernization in Spain.

Further reading
Alvarez Junco, J., *El emperador del paralelo: Lerroux y la demagogia populista* (Madrid, 1990), ch. 5.
Blinkhorn, M., 'Spain: The "Spanish Problem" and the Imperial Myth', *Journal of Contemporary History*, 15 (1980), 5–25.
Carr, R., *Spain 1808–1975* (Oxford, 2nd edn. 1982), chs. 9, 12, 13.
Costa, J., *Oligarquía y caciquismo como la forma actual de gobierno en España: urgencia y modo de cambiarla* (Madrid, 1902, available in modern editions).
Harrison, J., 'The Regenerationist Movement in Spain after the Disaster of 1898', *European Studies Review*, 9 (1979), 1–27.
Maurice, J., and Serrano, C., *J. Costa: crisis de la Restauración y populismo (1875–1911)* (Madrid, 1977).
Payne, S. G., 'Spanish Conservatism 1834–1923', *Journal of Contemporary History*, 13 (1978), 765–89.
—— *Politics and the Military in Modern Spain* (Stanford, Calif., 1967).
Ramsden, H., *The 1898 Movement in Spain: Towards a Reinterpretation* (Manchester, 1974).
Romero-Maura, J., *'La rosa de fuego': el obrerismo barcelonés de 1899 a 1909* (Barcelona, 1975).
Serrano, C., *Final del imperio: España 1895–1898* (Madrid, 1984).
—— *Le Tour du peuple: crise nationale, mouvements populaires et populisme en Espagne (1890–1910)* (Madrid, 1987).
Varela Ortega, J., 'Aftermath of Splendid Disaster: Spanish Politics before and after the Spanish American War of 1898', *Journal of Contemporary History*, 15 (1980), 317–44.

The Nationalisms of the Periphery: Culture and Politics in the Construction of National Identity

ENRIC UCELAY DA CAL

The rise of anti-Spanish nationalisms (i.e. those hostile to the central state) in the nineteenth and twentieth centuries is a complex process. To understand it one must make a preliminary distinction between regionalisms, which affirm local identity but accept some sense of common statehood, and nationalisms, which aspire at least in theory to achieve independence. In fact, none of these movements—whether nationalist or regionalist—has developed in ways consistent with its principles. It is also useful to remember that all contemporary nationalisms in Spain, including state nationalism, have so far failed in their explicit objectives.

Although the trend has been to study each movement in its own terms, isolated from other parallel nationalisms and/or regionalisms within Spain, this is a major conceptual error. All these movements were (and are) rivals for the same attention and the same resources. This means, ultimately, that anti-Spanish nationalisms and Spanish state nationalism are really one single social dynamic, not fully comprehensible if not understood as a whole. Understanding is not made easier by the fact that all these movements express themselves through arguments inherited from the past, in which the same terms are used again and again over time, but with changed meanings.

Spain's history, like many others, can be understood as a permanent tension between the pull towards centralization (centripetal) and the push towards fragmentation (centrifugal). The medieval Christian kingdoms expressed their political identity in terms of this duality. The crown (especially that of Castile) was legitimated by reference to a Hispanic 'imperial ideal' which blended the memory of Roman peninsular unity with dreams of religious unification, expansion, and chiliasm. At the same time, a strong, countervailing local patriotism, expressing the interests of the nobility or urban patriciates, was based on the affirmation of local institutions and common law, and of particularism against outside interference.

This duality between centripetal, imperial attitudes and centrifugal, localist sentiment remained visible in the gradual development of the Spanish state after the establishment of the unified Spanish Crown of the late Trastámaras and the Habsburgs in the passage from the fifteenth to the sixteenth centuries. Forged out of feudal civil wars, the identity of the united Crown was imperial (with a vast American empire as a sudden gift) and perceived as being guaranteed through religious unity (hence the importance of the Inquisition). Spanish imperial identity, waved as a banner by those social sectors involved in an expanding state service, was inevitably contradictory, sustaining as it did antiquated ideas and images as well as forward-looking ones. Accordingly, kingship was ultimately justified in neo-medieval terms by its apocalyptic or crusading nature. On the other hand, however, at the height of empire in the sixteenth century, royal administration was increasingly preoccupied with proving its efficiency, and, to this end, envisioned Castilian as the language of an absolutist state in the making. The inculcation in Spain of a sense of being a pioneer nation-state, together with the ideal of state service, had long-term effects in so far as, for example, it established the sense of administrative time, or of due protocol, or of the juridical corporativism of the bureaucracy, and many other micromechanisms of social practice that went beyond the broad process of élite legitimation and worked their way into the customs and hidden internal logic of a variegated society.

But this notion that imperial destiny and administrative cohesion were a historical necessity, a project in the making, was permanently offset by the call of localism: the component crowns with their particular laws and customs, municipal rights, and diverse social privileges were set against the greater whole, the latter never quite convincing to those sectors which did not derive immediate benefit from the imperial venture. From the uprising of the *comuneros* in Castile against Charles I (1520–2) to the revolt of the Catalans against Philip IV (1640–53), particularism kept resisting the expansion of the absolutist state. Even where no large-scale violence ensued, local patriotism was kept alive by the insistent respect for local law and opposition to bureaucratic fiat, summarized in the terms *fueros** and *foralismo*. By the seventeenth century, therefore, the discourse of Spanish politics was already patterned into a permanent and very legalistic debate between advocates of the state's relative superiority and defenders of local privilege, each accusing the other of perpetrating a selfish and exclusive form of abuse.

The struggle for succession to the Spanish Crown brought bitter civil war and invasion by foreign armies (1701–15). The victorious Bourbons further perfected the centralizing drive through the imposition of French-derived administrative reform, which included a far sterner insistence on the efficiency to be gained from the imposition of a single state language. By the time the reformist drive wound down at the end of the eighteenth century (with the reign of Charles IV), in spite of an eclectic and indeed contradictory array of popular resistances, the Bourbon dynasty was monopolizing the appeal to all things popular and local, usually referred to as *tipismo* [the typical], thereby absorbing the Habsburg inheritance of symbols and organizational habits. Despite its attempts at administrative centralization and establishment of far more effective fiscal foundations, Spanish state power under the Bourbons retained all the imperial claims of the past and remained identified with Counter-Reformation religiosity, maintenance of the Inquisition, and cultural isolationism in ways that scandalized 'enlightened' opinion at the French court. Throughout the Bourbon period right down to 1808, in the face of intermittent royal efforts to grant greater power to executive secretaries, the stubborn survival of the complex system of Spanish government—whose councils and hierarchies acted as a check on monarchical authority—was consistently defended in the name of 'national tradition', a process which kept the old arguments of particularist lawyers in circulation.

So, from the fifteenth to the nineteenth centuries, both particularist and national-state identities—never clearly differentiated—made use of a repertoire of aggressive images derived from external, expansionist imperial or missionary experience, alongside a sort of shared resistance to outside influences whose emotional core was expressed through the idealization of the local. These perspectives had much to do with the distribution of opportunities for social mobility within the various Spanish societies: those who could profit directly or indirectly from service to state and/or Church tended naturally to adopt national-state values and perspectives; those excluded tended to become caught up in petty disputes over local privileges ignored or trampled on by the centralizers. Castilian being the language of state bureaucracy, the remaining spoken idioms became vehicles almost exclusively of lower-class expression, of interest mostly to the clergy who were anxious to ensure doctrinal orthodoxy among the peasantry. Language was not the focal point of particularism. Thus, Catalan and Galician—previously rich literary languages—plus the multiple variants of Basque were consigned, along with local 'romance' variants such as Asturian Bable or Old Aragonese, to the margins of particularist and foralist discourse whose convoluted legalisms were still written in Castilian.

Modern nationalisms in the nineteenth and early twentieth centuries

The French invasion (1808–14), with its baggage of revolutionary and Napoleonic ideals, changed the nature of Spanish identity, though it did so in a cumulative way, reincorporating the inheritance of the past into a radically changing political framework. The Bourbon administration was fragmented into local juntas, which only came together in an effort to establish a political framework that could maintain the struggle against the outsiders who had kidnapped the dynasty. This meant the introduction of representative liberalism (embodied in the Constitution of 1812) even though, to cement the alliance between anti-French conservatives and liberals, it had to be presented as the recovery of local feudal parliaments suppressed by Habsburg and especially Bourbon absolutist centralism. Accordingly, one could argue that the impact of harsh foreign occupation and bitter internal strife (for many years the war was called 'our revolution') forged for the first time a real sense of Spanish nationhood, expressed as a mature nationalism, which combined the imagery of the past with a concept of citizenship and representation. Though liberals and neo-absolutists would battle over the significance of the changes wrought by the Napoleonic invasion for the following three decades (notably 1820–3 and 1832–9), both sides had essentially assumed a new national identification. Henceforward the debate would be about the form that political representation should or should not take. None the less, subsequent civil wars underlined the fact that the old tension between centralism and fragmentation was far from over.

By the mid-nineteenth century, under the influence of literary Romanticism, authors in Spain—as elsewhere—were recovering a mixture of political subjects and themes, resurrecting images and devices in order to construct a systematized nationalist discourse whose object was the discussion of the legitimate sphere of state power as against that of local administrations. With foreign attack still fresh in the collective memory, and civil wars omnipresent to keep the issue of identity simmering, the new mix of Spanish nationalism served all options, dominating literature, political rhetoric, and even street names and town planning. In 1868 the so-called 'Glorious Revolution', definitively introducing democratic principles into mainstream constitutional practice, fixed the institutional sense of Spanish nationalism and its associated imagery: even the Carlists* and the republicans accepted the liberal emblems of identity—the state crest and the flag—merely demurring over secondary aspects (the Carlists wanting to add a Sacred Heart and the republicans to remove the signs of royalty).

That the search to define and build the nation should pass from literature to politics must also be understood as a function of the failure of the nineteenth-century Spanish liberal revolution to provide effective public services. Liberalism was advocated by intellectuals (that is, lawyers and journalists) but implemented by army officers. Both groups were anxious for social promotion through a new kind of state service, but their rivalry also took its toll, particularly given the continued divergence between legal principles and effective action. The more inefficient the state was, the more it contradicted the vast promise of liberal modernization; and the more it failed its stated ideals, the more its lack of popular support (and thus legitimacy) made it defensive and vicious, especially to those who complained. At first, popular protest was channelled as usual via manifestations of local patriotism: Carlist foralism and republican federalism shared the conviction that national elections, even with universal manhood suffrage (nationality in Spanish law was transmitted through the male line only), were not as genuine as local politics. Both the republican experiment of 1873–4 and the Carlist insurrection of 1872–6, with its temporary regency, sought to guarantee the primacy of localism/particularism in the face of central state intervention and inefficiency.

Although defeated militarily as major political options after the 1870s, federalism and regionalism continued to offer idealized solutions to the problems of state organization. The formal, theoretical distinctions between the two options are less than clear at the receiving end. From the state side, however, the difference is evident. Federalism supposes the state to be composed of power granted upwards by the component parts, whereas regionalism accepts that power is devolved from a central power to new entities. Demonstrably, however, neither federalism nor regionalism was politically fixed beyond their opposition to unitary liberalism. Just as centralism could be reactionary or progressive so regionalism and federalism could be conservative or revolutionary. Ultra-conservative regionalists—for example the Carlists and, later, many Basque nationalists—saw the regions as bulwarks against the political and moral corruption of the liberal state; while federal republicans—and indeed, later, anarcho-syndicalists—dreamed of breaking the oppressive state by harnessing the revolutionary potential at the base of society against a liberal oligarchy.*

Ultimately, however, the civil war which most influenced the future was the so-called 'Long War' in Cuba (1868–78). Increasingly, the contradiction between the stated goals of liberalism and what was in fact delivered triggered a dynamic of mutual antagonism between the official discourse of Spanish nationalism and alternative nationalist projects—both on the mainland and in the colonies. This confrontation was clearly visible by the 1890s. The difficulty of crushing a colonial separatism which had the backing of a major power like the United States ended up dividing Spanish nationalism into two: an institutional nationalism was espoused by the professional classes which still adhered to the liberal ideal of the 1868 revolution, while the military increasingly invoked a new radical nationalism, based on unquestioning emotional identification with state symbols. As a result of this split, state nationalism could either be rigidly centralist or accept varying degrees of devolution in principle at least—although the latter was always understood as a ceding of power by the centre, which retained the ultimate authority. Despite the loss of empire in 1898–9, political expressions of militarism continued to emphasize the nation-building role of an imperial state in response to the threat of the new Catalan and Basque nationalist movements. These questioned the validity of both the liberal state as it came out of the nineteenth century and the heritage of the imperial past. Hereafter, Spanish and peripheral nationalisms have continued to feed off each other emotionally.

After the failure of federalism—with its descent in 1873 into uncontrollable cantonalism (a kind of extreme federal republicanism or particularism sometimes transmitting an inchoate social radicalism)—and the defeat of Carlist insurrection shortly thereafter, the 1880s were a period of renewed thinking about the territorial organization of the Spanish state. After the conservatives had re-established restrictive parliamentary government in 1876, based on the planned alternation in power (*turno pacífico**) of the two dynastic parties (Conservatives and Liberals), a prolonged period of government by the Liberal Party, notably in 1885–90, reintroduced the major reforms of the 1868 revolution, most importantly the abolition of slavery (1886) and universal manhood suffrage (1890). The question of what form to give to local administration was once more on the agenda, as almost everyone agreed that the provincial system introduced in 1833 was unsatisfactory. Basque foralism was again partially recognized after the restrictions imposed following the last Carlist outbreak, but the general discussion also opened the way for Catalan and Basque nationalism to develop and keep growing. But any form of peninsular devolution was bound to affect the military administration of Cuba, Puerto Rico, and the Philippines. By the time the Liberal government was prepared to offer autonomy statutes to the Antilles in 1897, Cuba was in open revolt, a conflict which ultimately involved the United States and brought the loss of all Spanish overseas territories outside Africa.

The major point to be made regarding the rise of anti-Spanish movements in the Peninsula is their relationship to urbanization and industry. Barcelona was from the mid-nineteenth century Spain's only metropolitan-sized city apart from Madrid, and was generally considered to be the economic centre of the country. No other city came close to competing with these two rivals for urban pre-eminence. The fact of urban concentration helps mark the very real differences between Catalan nationalism on the one hand, and the Basque and Galician movements—as well as other, more minor, regionalist currents in Andalusia, Aragon, Asturias, Extremadura, Murcia, and even Castile—in their development during the first three decades of the twentieth century. In Catalanism civic discourse predominated over rural nostalgia, in marked contrast to the other anti-Spanish nationalisms or regionalisms.

The two major nationalist movements in Catalonia and the Basque Country are best classified as, respectively, positive and negative forms of political dualism, in so far as both movements thought (and still think) of themselves as exceptional in the face of a more or less homogeneous Spain. However, unlike the above-described regionalism or federalism, which represented a regularizing solution for all the regions of Spain, dualism was a response to exceptional demands on the part of a single territory with allegedly specific characteristics setting it apart from the rest of the state—rather like the creation of Austria-Hungary in 1867. In the Catalan case, a number of factors converged: economic power and the metropolitan importance it conferred, cultural vibrancy (centred on Catalan as a working language), and the relative social cohesiveness of Catalan urban society helped to create a confident, outward-looking nationalism which sought a bi-national, bilingual system, a kind of partnership with the Spanish state; a positive dualism to give Catalans the recognition they felt they deserved and did not receive for their prestigious 'second city'. In the case of Basque nationalism, its negative dualism, persistently inward-looking, insistent on traditional religiosity, was expressed in the desire to cut itself off from Spain as a kind of protection from social change. Nor did the Basque language ever fulfil the role of its Catalan counterpart. This meant Basque nationalism was racially derived and exclusive, rather than linguistically based and therefore willing to assimilate immigrants, as was Catalanism. Galician nationalism, always much weaker than either the Catalan or Basque movements, remained half-way between an aspiring dualism and federal or regionalist schemes. All the other movements—from Andalusia to Castile—can be placed somewhere between the twin options of regionalism or federalism, but falling short of the dualism expressed in hard-core nationalist attitudes.

The colonial wars of the 1890s tended to polarize what had previously been a juridical debate about administrative organization pursued by politicians in parliament, transforming it into a controversial issue central to the rise of mass participation in Spanish politics. The subject of devolution was thus turned into a potentially violent conflict between the officer corps, viscerally unitarist after being defeated by Cuban separatists, and the new, alternative, non-Spanish nationalists in industrialized Catalonia and the Basque Country, who loved to bait centralist opinion with allusions to Cuba. The conflict remained a symbolic one until 1911 when the Catalanists sought to introduce legislation to consolidate administrative resources in the four provinces of Catalonia (something finally achieved by decree in 1913 with the creation of the Mancomunitat—an organ of administrative self-government). The emotions unleashed in 1911 were so powerful that this rather dull issue tore the two constitutional parties—first the Liberals and then the Conservatives—to shreds in 1912–13, after which parliament ceased to be an effective organ of government and the political system began to disintegrate. This situation was, moreover, exacerbated by the European war. One of the great themes of the First World War was the right to self-determination of small nations like Serbia or Belgium in the face of rapacious imperial powers. By the time of the armistice in 1918, Catalan opinion in particular was pushing for a full 'home rule' agreement. These demands were curtailed, however, as the Catalan élites drew back from political confrontation, faced by the abrupt outbreak of violent social conflict in the region—and especially in Barcelona—at the height of the parliamentary debate on Catalan autonomy at the start of 1919.

The last years of the parliamentary monarchy (1919–23) were dominated by military intervention in politics. Not surprisingly, throughout this period this centred on Barcelona as a particular social flash-point. The post-war years saw the splitting of both Catalan and Basque nationalism into moderates and radicals, the latter openly appealing for independence (much influenced emotionally by the Irish conflict of 1916–22). This process in turn encouraged other Spanish regions to follow suit—such as Andalusia, which had not previously experienced nationalist agitation. Finally, in 1923, it was a coup from the Catalan capital which established a military dictatorship in Spain. The new dictator, General Miguel Primo de Rivera, began with a pragmatic approach to all matters, whether the Catalan question or colonial problems in North Africa. However, intra-military feuding led him to espouse both a hard-line centralism and an equally conservative colonial policy. Soon his regime was obsessed with stamping out the Catalan 'threat'. While the Basque nationalists spent the years of dictatorial rule dedicated to cultural work, the tenor of government policy drew moderate and radical Catalanists to leading roles in the opposition to Primo.

In 1930–1, with the fall of the dictatorship and with subsequent transitional governments looking for a return to parliamentary 'normality', there was, logically, renewed speculation over regionalist solutions. The real beneficiaries were the republicans, who accepted an exceptional autonomy for Catalonia as part of their platform for an uprising in 1930. They were then obliged to honour their promise when the Catalan republicans united with the radical nationalists to proclaim the Second Spanish Republic in Barcelona after a general republican landslide in municipal elections throughout Spain in April 1931. Although there was much discussion about regional devolution during the years of the Second Republic, Catalonia remained the only region to be granted autonomy before the outbreak of civil war in 1936. The war itself cut off the prospects for Galician autonomy (since the intensely centralist military rebels conquered Galicia immediately), while it hastened Basque autonomy (and some other less explicit experiments elsewhere, notably in Aragon) until the force of 'Spanish nationalist' arms defeated the Republican army between 1937 and 1939.

Further reading
Barton, S., 'The Roots of the National Question in Spain', in M. Teich and R. Porter (eds.), *The National Question in Europe in Historical Context* (Cambridge, 1993), 106–27.
Diaz López, C. E., 'The Politicization of Galician Cleavages', in S. Rokkan and D. W. Urwin, *The Politics of Territorial Identity* (Beverly Hills, Calif., 1982), 389–424.
Giner, S., *The Social Structure of Catalonia* (Anglo-Catalan Society Occasional Publications, no. 1, 1984).
Fusi, J. P. (ed.), *España autonomías* (Madrid, 1989).
Heiberg, M., *The Making of the Basque Nation* (Cambridge, 1989).
Hernández, F., and Mercadé, F. (eds.), *Estructuras sociales y cuestión nacional en España* (Barcelona, 1986).
Linz, J. J., 'Early State Building and Late Peripheral Nationalisms against the State: The Case of Spain', in S. M. Eisenstadt and S. Rokkan (eds.), *Building States and Nations* (Beverly Hills, Calif., 1973), ii. 32–112.
Payne, S. G., *Basque Nationalism* (Reno, Nev., 1974).

3

FRANCES
LANNON

JOSÉ ALVAREZ
JUNCO

Ideological Tensions

The Social Praxis and Cultural Politics of Spanish Catholicism

FRANCES LANNON

In 1900 the Catholic Church in Spain was still benefiting from a religious revival that had begun in mid-century, and then been given institutional backing with the restoration of the Catholic monarchy in 1874. By the terms of the 1876 Constitution, which was not officially replaced until 1931, Catholicism was the state religion, and the state subsidized Catholic worship, and paid stipends to bishops and parish priests. Canonical marriage had full civil effects, archbishops sat as of right in the Senate, and the Catholic press and devotional associations flourished. Pilgrimages, processions, and missions became common features of a revitalized, populist Catholicism. The religious congregations not only recovered from the tiny base to which they had been reduced in mid-century, but expanded on a quite unprecedented scale. If there were fewer than 2,000 male religious and about 20,000 nuns in Spain at the end of the 1860s, there were approximately 11,000 and 40,000 respectively by the end of the century. And in 1930 these totals had surpassed 20,000 and 60,000.

Among all these reasons for celebrating the new century with confidence, none gave the Church more pleasure, nor filled it with more misgivings for the future, than the great expansion of Catholic education for which the religious congregations and their schools were mainly responsible. The Jesuits, Salesians, Escolapians, de la Salle Brothers, Marists, Ursulines, Sacred Heart Sisters, and many others opened numerous *colegios* [private schools] throughout the country, so that already by 1900 there was hardly a town of any size anywhere in Spain that did not have at least one. As many boys were prepared for the *bachillerato** and for technical and commercial qualifications in the Catholic *colegios* as in the state secondary schools, and middle-class parents preferred convent schooling to any other for their daughters. State provision of secondary education was woefully inadequate, and the Church stepped in to meet the need.

Church resources were not able to compete so successfully with those of the municipalities in providing basic primary education, but many of the municipal schools were themselves effective agencies of Catholic culture and Catholic faith. Public education was by no means associated with a proselytizing laicism, as it so frequently was in France from the 1880s onwards. Whether directly through its own schools, or indirectly through many of those run by municipalities and provincial authorities, the Catholic Church exerted the controlling ideological influence on the education of Spanish children that it had been assured of in the 1851 Concordat between the Spanish state and the Vatican.

Much less satisfactory from the point of view of the Church hierarchy was the situation in Spanish universities, where the struggle for Catholic control had been lost in 1881, and a measure of intellectual and ideological freedom established. Catholic initiatives at tertiary level, like the Jesuit University of Deusto in Bilbao, or the Augustinian college at El Escorial near Madrid, were on a very small scale in comparison with the numerous Spanish universities in which, although there were many Catholic professors, intellectual life was often dominated by deists and free-thinkers. Moreover, the respect for intellectual freedom and the consequent weakening of the imposition of Catholic orthodoxy showed every sign of trickling down to secondary schooling. In 1901, 1906, and 1910, liberal governments attempted—albeit with little success—to control the growth of the religious congregations and their cultural enterprises. In 1913 parents who did not consider themselves Catholic were allowed to exempt their children from religious classes in state schools. This was just the kind of trend that many Church leaders feared. They saw in it, rightly, the relativizing tendency of intellectual liberalism which Pope Leo XIII had warned against in his encyclical letter on liberty and liberalism (*Libertas praestantissimum*) in 1888. Any growth in freedom of the press, freedom of intellectual debate, or religious liberty necessarily clashed with the Church's continuing claim to be the unique source of truth in a world full of error and sin.

Some Catholic commentators took the matter further, and argued that behind intellectual liberalism there stood a whole range of earlier movements and traditions which were inimical to Catholicism. These included the Protestant Reformation with its exaltation of individual conscience, the Enlightenment with its emphasis on self-generating human progress, and the French Revolution which placed individual rights instead of religious obligation at the heart of its political theory. All of these were judged erroneous and foreign, and on both counts dangerous to the Spanish nation and its traditional values as well as to the Church.

Spanish bishops, no doubt with the Disaster of 1898 very much in mind, declared in a statement in 1899: '[w]e repudiate all those liberties of perdition, offspring of the so-called new rights, or liberalism, the application of which to the government of our fatherland is the source of so many sins, and which leads us to the brink of the abyss.' Equally catastrophist was a Jesuit commentator who wrote in the Jesuit intellectual journal *Razón y Fe* in 1903: '[t]his nation has Catholicism inscribed in its heart with letters of fire. Even more, Catholicism is so incorporated and connaturalized within its very being, that it cannot cease to be Catholic without ceasing, first of all, to be a nation.' For influential Catholic spokesmen like these, state, nation, and Church were inseparable. It was easy for them to trace a vibrant connection between Catholic orthodoxy and Spanish imperial expansion in the fifteenth and sixteenth centuries, and a destructive link between the growth of relativizing liberalism and national decline, culminating in the Disaster of 1898. What was to become of the Spanish nation, historically the 'hammer of heretics' as Marcelino Menéndez y Pelayo described it in the early 1880s, if religious error and infidelity were to eat away its very soul and destroy it from within?

Between 1900 and the shock of the fall of the Catholic monarchy in 1931, the Church in Spain continued to experience a degree of official state backing that was without parallel in contemporary France, Italy, Germany, or Portugal. To observers it seemed privileged and triumphant, but it feared change and looked to a past golden age with nostalgia. It entrenched itself in a highly defensive distrust of those it considered enemies of Church and nation, such as free-thinking Spanish intellectuals, political advocates of the separation of Church and state, or proponents of cultural and ideological pluralism. In its fear of intellectual apostasy, it relied heavily on the Catholic monarchy for protection, and was left exposed and vulnerable by its collapse in 1931.

The Catholic Church probably should have realized earlier the danger it would face from sectors of society which had gained very little from either state or Church during the current period of their close if sometimes tense interdependence. In 1900, notwithstanding the expansion of Church education, 60 per cent of the Spanish population was illiterate. Throughout large tracts of the southern countryside, and in the packed working-class areas of the large towns, lived millions of poor Spaniards who were both unchurched and unschooled, and for whom Spanish agriculture, industry, and commerce failed to provide either economic security in the present or hope for the future. The Catholic revival of the second half of the nineteenth century had flourished among many sections of the Spanish bourgeoisie, and in rural areas of traditional Catholic culture. But it had not reached the new industrial proletariat or the rural landless poor. If Spanish

Catholicism failed to inspire an intellectually lively high culture—as it undoubtedly did—it also failed to find a way over the class barriers between the propertied and the propertyless, between those identified with the political status quo and those intent on changing it.

Already back in 1891, Pope Leo XIII had focused attention on the burning issue of the age—the social question as it was called—in his encyclical letter *Rerum novarum*. He had urged modern states to protect the economically weak, and to ensure a just family wage to working men. He had called on employers to recognize their social responsibilities, and had acknowledged the legitimacy of class organization, even in some circumstances strike action, by workers' unions. At the time of its publication, *Rerum novarum*, the 'workers' charter', was leading from the front in Catholic social action, much closer to the social Catholicism of parts of the Rhineland than to more traditional, non-interventionist Catholic thinking in Spain. Unfortunately, Catholic social action in Spain never really caught up with it. Twenty years and more later, influential Catholic figures in Spain still resisted worker-only unions, clinging instead to the cross-class alternative of workers' associations under capitalist control, better known for piety and strike-breaking than for effective militancy. Moreover this social Catholicism was often as deeply marked by defensiveness as were Catholic attitudes to other elements of contemporary society and culture. More often than not, initiatives were taken because of a previous success locally by anarchist or socialist unions, and the emphasis was at least as much on keeping members uncontaminated by socialist ideas as on protecting their economic interests.

The frightening extent of the alienation of sectors of the Spanish masses from the Church was painfully revealed in the events of the Tragic Week in Barcelona in July 1909. Cuba, the Philippines, and Puerto Rico had all been lost in the calamity of 1898, but a decade later another colonial crisis in the one bit of the Spanish empire that remained, in North Africa, did indeed provoke the kind of conflict within Spain which had been so much feared but had barely materialized in 1898. After the call-up of Catalan conscripts in 1909 to fight in Morocco, infuriated workers began a general strike in protest, and then let loose a wave of violence in Barcelona which took five days to spend itself. To the genuine puzzlement of most Catholic observers, this violence was directed against churches, convents, and other Catholic centres, resulting in the destruction of about one-third of the ecclesiastical property in the city. It could hardly have been made more clear that, whether as an institution identified with the state or with the employers, the Church itself was in this crisis the prime target of extreme working-class disaffection.

There were lessons to be learned, but few understood them. One who did was Joan Maragall, who wrote a famous article in the Barcelona newspaper *La Veu de Catalunya* on 18 December 1909, arguing that the Catholic Church had associated itself too closely with the protection of property rights and should now address itself urgently to the need for social reform. But his call was not heeded by largely uncomprehending Church leaders. Those involved in the world of Spanish social Catholicism continued to worry far more about the religious orthodoxy and devotional life of Spanish workers than about their grievances against their employers and against the political regime. The exceptions—such as Father Maximiliano Arboleya Martínez in Asturias, and the Dominicans Pedro Gerard in Jerez and José Gafo in Barcelona—were willing to support militant action against industrial employers, but they ran into severe and effective opposition from the Church hierarchy.

The ecclesiastical authorities were more at ease with another section of Catholic social action, the Jesuit-inspired Acción Católica Nacional de Propagandistas (ACNP) of Ángel Herrera, founded in 1909. Communicating old truths in new ways was the speciality of these laymen, who ran local newspapers and a national daily, *El Debate*, from 1911, and organized networks of public speakers and activists. Their message of class harmony and interdependence was proclaimed with some useful results among peasant smallholders in northern and central Spain who benefited from the introduction of agricultural credit unions and co-operatives, often with the aid of larger-scale landowners. But such modest initiatives could do little or nothing to ease conflict on the great estates in the south, where landless peasants wanted a *reparto* [redistribution] of property from the landed élites to themselves. Nor did the emphasis on co-operation without a change in property relations make much headway among industrial workers who were already more impressed by the collectivist doctrines and proven militancy of anarchists and socialists.

The Church had no effective answer to the anticlerical violence in Barcelona in 1909, or to the waves of strikes, lawlessness, and killings that characterized Barcelona and parts of the rural south from 1916 onwards, as the social strains caused by the uneven impact of the First World War on the Spanish economy exploded into class war. In 1919 some Catholics took comfort in what seemed the culmination of the Catholic revival, even in these inauspicious circumstances, as the King himself ceremonially consecrated the whole of Spain to the Sacred Heart of Jesus. The Propagandists planned a showy but meaningless Great Social Campaign in 1922 to counter dangerous ideas and disorder. But it was beyond the power of piety and rhetorical campaigns to suppress a violence that frightened many.

In September 1923 General Miguel Primo de Rivera, Captain-General of Catalonia, took power in Madrid with the quiescence of Alfonso XIII, dismissed parliament, suspended the Constitution, outlawed anarchist organizations, and imposed social peace. The Church breathed a sigh of relief and praised the new dictator, knowing that he would control its enemies and protect its position. The sense of urgency and danger that had marked the previous few years disappeared. As the 1920s wore on, bishops criticized instead the short skirts and other immodesties of post-war fashion.

Archbishop Segura of Toledo convened in 1929 the first National Congress of Catholic Action, to co-ordinate the efforts of lay activists trying to construct a more fully Catholic society. It denounced blasphemy and immodest dress, and called for 'the defence of the sacred interests of religion, the family, authority, private property and the poor'. This congress revealed once again that Spanish social Catholicism was better at making statements and passing resolutions than at substantial organization and action. It also confirmed that the Church in Spain had still not recognized the insuperable problems inherent in maintaining an absolute defence of private property rights while also claiming to be defending the poor. In effect, even in social conditions as polarized as those in the rural south, the Church was unable to go much beyond a call to the rich to be charitable towards the poor. Pope Leo XIII had recognized in 1891 that this was not enough. It was certainly not enough in Spain forty years later.

As Pope Pius XI prepared his encyclical letter *Quadragessimo anno*, which was published in 1931 to commemorate the fortieth anniversary of *Rerum novarum*, the Catholic workers' charter, the Spanish Church was suddenly faced with the collapse of the Catholic monarchy and the Church–state alliance. Without these traditional supports, it had to face the consequences of the alienation and hostitility of two sectors of Spanish society which in different ways would help shape the new Republican regime, the intelligentsia and the labouring masses. The Church had long been unable to assimilate either of these into the culture of Catholic tradition.

Further reading
Andrés Gallego, J., *Pensamiento y acción social de la iglesia en España* (Madrid, 1984).
Aproximación a la historia social de la iglesia española contemporánea (Madrid, 1978) (collection by unspecified authors).
Benavides Gómez, D., *El fracaso social del catolicismo español* (Barcelona, 1973).
Botti, A., *Cielo y dinero: el nacionalcatolicismo en España (1881–1975)* (Madrid, 1992).
Cárcel Ortí, V. (ed.), *Historia de la iglesia en España*, vol. v (Madrid, 1979).
Lannon, F., *Privilege, Persecution, and Prophecy: The Catholic Church in Spain 1875–1975* (Oxford, 1987).
Payne, S. G., *Spanish Catholicism: An Historical Overview* (Madison, 1984).

Education and the Limits of Liberalism

JOSÉ ALVAREZ JUNCO

'Everywhere the same cry, the same challenge: everywhere pamphlets, memoirs, books are printed on the problem of education, that central problem of our national life.' This is how Luis Morote saw the issue in his book, *La moral de la derrota* [*The Lesson of Defeat*] of 1899. It was a typical response. In the months following the defeat of 1898, an entire intellectual generation set about analysing the qualities and defects of the nation's 'essence' in the hope of altering its future course. The aim was—as Antonio Machado aptly put it—to deal the death blow to the Spain that was 'worn-out and charlatan, quarrelsome and sad', so that a new Spain of 'chisel and mallet' might be born. In practical terms, this meant rooting out the causes of Spain's tardiness in coming to terms with the modern world. The key instrument for this mission of national regeneration was unanimously considered to be education. In 1900 the first 'regeneracionista' government responded to this universal clamour by establishing the Ministry of Public Instruction.

The idea of grounding the country's modernization in education was not new. Since the eighteenth century, reformers influenced by Enlightenment ideas had drawn up pedagogical projects aimed at reforming those habits held responsible for the decline dating from the Habsburg period, so as to turn the Spanish people into the hard-working, organized body required by 'progress'. The constitutional assembly of Cadiz began drafting a national education plan, based on a proposal by the poet Quintana, but this never progressed beyond draft stage and was inevitably abandoned in 1814 with the arrival of Ferdinand VII, representing the enthronement of political and cultural reaction. The 94 per cent illiteracy rate bequeathed by the absolute monarchy to modern Spain was no source of shame to the signatories of the 'Persian Manifesto' (conservative deputies hostile to the 1812 liberal constitution of Cadiz), who explicitly praised political systems which kept the people 'in the dark'.

The liberals in power from 1820 to 1823 (the 'liberal triennium') thought the opposite and revived Quintana's ideas, for the first time giving them the status of a legal document, one that was discarded with the return of absolutism in 1823. Nevertheless, the liberal revolution's education proposals acquired greater precision during its two periods of ascendancy (1808–14 and 1820–3), and commanded such support from the ruling élites that even the educational decrees issued by the Calomarde ministry, during the second period of reactionary government under Ferdinand (1823–33), were implicitly influenced by liberal ideas.

Despite the apparent emergence of some common ground, the set-backs suffered by the liberal revolution, combined with the administrative sluggishness and poverty of the Spanish state, made the creation of a stable Spanish education system a long, tortuous process. After the Duke of Rivas's plan in 1836, that of Pidal in 1845, and several feebler efforts, in 1857 the Minister of Development Claudio Moyano finally managed to get a law through parliament that was to provide the legal framework for the education system for over a century. This saw the division of public education into three levels (as envisaged in the proposals drawn up in Cadiz): primary education taught in municipal schools; secondary education taught in provincial institutes (or 'provincial universities' in the language of the debate); and professional or university education for which the state would be responsible. This was a straightforward plan, which was basically state-controlled ('doctrinaire, secular and royalist, unifying and hierarchical' in the words of the educational administrator Castillejo), though it was always assumed it would exist in tandem with private education.

With characteristic legalist naïvety, it was thought that once the law was approved the problem would be solved. But the real difficulties became apparent with the attempts to implement the decisions. Primary education, compulsory for all up to the age of 9, and free to those who could not afford it, was according to the Moyano Law to be paid for out of municipal budgets. Every municipality of over 500 inhabitants was to set up and maintain a school. This was completely unrealistic at a time when the municipal corporations were bereft of virtually all income in the wake of the nationalization and sale of common lands, and the centralization of taxation which typified the new state. Only in 1900, after decades of commentators condemning the scandalous situation, teachers being underpaid by a third, and the expression 'hungrier than a schoolteacher' having passed into popular parlance, did the state take responsibility for primary school teachers' salaries. This was one of the more tangible results of the 1898 colonial defeat.

Backwardness being a cumulative phenomenon, however, by that stage an even greater gap had opened up between Spain and the advanced European countries. Only 1.5 million out of almost 4 million children between the ages of 3 and 12 attended school in Spain. Some 30,000 municipalities did not have school provision of any sort; of the 30,000 public primary schools that existed on paper, barely more than 20,000 existed in reality. Equally disturbing was the poor quality of the education, in terms of both buildings and teaching staff. In consequence, some 60 per cent of the population remained illiterate,[1] and some even estimate a 70 per cent illiteracy rate which would make Spain an inverted mirror-image of France's 70 per cent literacy rate. Girls, for the most part, never even set foot in primary school, with female illiteracy possibly as high as 90 per cent.

Secondary education institutes were also public under the terms of the Moyano Law. But again the costs, instead of being borne by the central state, were derived from a variety of sources, mainly from provincial authorities. Despite the fact that this level of education was not compulsory and the number of students far lower than in primary education, the initial financial provision had been unrealistic and the system had to be abandoned in 1887, when responsibility for the salaries of secondary school teachers (catedráticos de instituto) was taken over by the central state. In the last decade of the century, the total number of secondary students in official public centres stood at around 12,000: approximately half the number in private schools. Significantly, in the first half of the century these two figures had been the other way round.

University was attended by around 15,000 students in all, way below the 18,000 seminary students in the country. Again, however, the main problem was the poor quality of the academic content and teaching methods. There were ludicrously few technical schools (and those existing attracted few students), while droves of students studied law and medicine. As regards gender differences, we do not have to calculate percentages: university was considered quite simply 'unsuitable for the female sex', and only in the 1890s did a woman, María Goyri, manage to assert her equality in this respect.[2] (Previously, women attending university— there were some—had been awarded certificates rather than degrees providing professional qualifications.) Neither scientific modernization nor the widening of access concerned the academic community. The big debates centred on the question of teachers' freedom from Church interference in their subject-matter or methodologies, or on the defence of their corporate privileges. This was often a response to the Church's attempts to secure official recognition for its own degrees, but sometimes the universities also rallied their defences against secular rivals as when, as late as 1918, Madrid University protested against the Instituto Escuela's encroachment.

In short, the early liberals' original good intentions were confounded over the subsequent hundred-year period by political instability, lack of state resources, and the reluctance of an obstinately conservative oligarchy which, despite political ups and downs, had retained overall control of the state for the greater part of the century. As a result, the educational legacy bequeathed to the twentieth century was discouraging. Total public expenditure on education in Spain was only 10 per cent of that spent on defence, and a quarter—per capita—of the amount spent in France or Italy, less than a fifth of that spent in Britain, and a tenth of that spent in the USA.

Faced with this situation in the public sector, private (overwhelmingly Catholic) education had expanded considerably during the course of the nineteenth century. It could be said that, after the sale of Church lands, the religious orders had redirected their activities from monastic contemplation to education. To do this, they had relied on favourable legislation allowing the Catholic Church to run schools which in effect were subject to virtually no state control beyond the fact that students from private schools sometimes had to sit general examinations in public institutes in order to have their qualifications recognized as the equivalent of those awarded by the state. Rather than state control over the Church, the reverse was more often the case. The Church claimed the right to monitor the general ideological line of state schools to ensure they did not deviate from Catholic dogma. This right gave rise to the famous 'university question' in 1865 and 1876, when the pious Minister Orovio sanctioned and expelled several notorious liberal Catholic professors from Madrid University. In 1881, the first Liberal government under Sagasta reinstated those expelled by Orovio, an action which marked the end of the Church's monopoly over university education. In the twentieth century, the battleground would shift to secondary education.

In 1900, aiming to put the entire public sector in order and rectify blatant errors and shortcomings, the newly established Ministry of Public Instruction began by assuming responsibility for paying teachers' salaries. Although this was motivated by a sense of fairness and concern for their plight (as such, it met with general public approval), it was also a political manoeuvre designed to undermine the local *caciques'** power. Subsequently, secondary education was reformed with an attempt to introduce technical training (another concern dating back to the eighteenth century). The attempt to institute an entirely vocational *bachillerato** was still-born through lack of funds. Given this failure, an attempt was made to upgrade existing schools, allocating different subjects to different times of day so as to facilitate part-time courses in, for example, teacher training, agriculture, manufacturing and retailing, liberal arts, and evening classes for workers. As for the universities, an attempt was made to modernize both the humanities and sciences. The arts were divided into three separate units—philosophy, literature, and history—and the social sciences separated from law. Physics and chemistry were created as separate units, and pharmacy degrees were brought up to date.

The achievements in higher education were the most successful, mainly due to the consensus here between the two government parties, reflected in the continuity of policy between the first two Ministers of Public Instruction, the Conservative García Alix and the Liberal Romanones. From 1901 the Ministry undertook a policy of active encouragement of study abroad, leading to the creation in 1907 of the Junta para Ampliación de Estudios. This was a measure which, from a long-term perspective, could be interpreted as a momentous break with the politics of isolation initiated under Philip II in 1559, seeking to counteract the deep-rooted Counter-Reformation mistrust of the modern world that had permeated Spanish attitudes for centuries. The short-term, but no less significant, aim was to redirect the 'middle classes' away from their notion of themselves as the 'ruling or affluent classes' towards a notion of themselves as the 'productive or useful classes'. The creation of the Junta para Ampliación de Estudios was followed by that of the Centro de Estudios Históricos in 1910 and the Instituto Escuela in 1918: all of these would form the political and intellectual élite that played a major role in the Second Republic.

However, this political consensus was limited to higher education. In primary and secondary education the problems were intractable, particularly because the Catholic Church had embarked on an all-out campaign to re-Christianize the nation, receiving substantial support from a contingent of French friars, ousted in the late nineteenth century by Jules Ferry's educational laws and the Third Republic's anticlerical legislation. The success of these French friars, who guaranteed an orthodox education, dyed-in-the-wool conservatism, and the acquisition of the language most esteemed in Spanish high society, was immediate. Their growth, however, alarmed the liberals, who saw them as a threat to the influence over the country's élites they themselves had so painstakingly won. The attempts at educational reform which followed the self-analysis and self-flagellation of 1898 were thus immediately tarnished by the heated debate over the clerical or anticlerical nature of the proposed reforms.

In particular, battle-lines were drawn around the Romanones ministry's proposals in four hotly debated areas: the limitation of the number of religious orders involved in education, the proposal to make religious education an optional subject, the requirement that teachers in religious schools have professional teaching qualifications, and the inspection of such schools by state functionaries. For the most part these requirements were already on the statutes, but the attempt to implement them brought accusations of sectarianism and Jacobinism, and led to a political squabble that nipped in the bud any attempt at reform, especially in secondary education. The difficulty of maintaining a coherent consensual policy between Liberals and Conservatives grew, particularly with the bad feeling between the parties in the Maura period and with the extreme government instability of the years 1912–23, ending with Primo de Rivera's coup.

The attempts at educational reform arising out of 'regenerationism' were thus blocked, and any success was limited to higher education and more particularly to postgraduate studies, available only to a privileged minority. The figures speak for the rest: 5,500 schools were created between 1900 and 1923 but in 1931 illiteracy still stood at 40 per cent. An effort had been made, but it was patently insufficient.

The leading role played by the Institución Libre de Enseñanza* in the renewal of higher education must be singled out. Founded in 1876 by Francisco Giner de los Ríos and a group of professors expelled in the aftermath of the second 'university question', its substantial prestige, maintained over the next sixty years, was due not only to its teaching but also to its teachers' interest in the complete overhaul of the Spanish system. This was expressed most clearly in the teachers' congresses held from the early 1880s. Such initiatives found their just reward in the major educational reforms of the Republic: both the proposals, and the individuals called upon to implement them, would be products of the Institución Libre.

It is true that, despite their insistence on the need to 'Europeanize' the country and to train its ruling class, the Institución's leaders were more interested in moral reform than in the technical content of their teaching. Nor did their moderation and pragmatism allow them to escape involvement in the anticlerical battle. It was probably impossible to avoid this, but its significance was largely symbolic and its benefits negligible. These inconsistencies were not serious, however, compared to the many others found in the complex world of Spanish education. In their defence of the idea of university autonomy, the members of the Institución Libre might find themselves sharing their platform with the most obscurantist sections of the Spanish Church, hoping to secure benefits for the Jesuit University of Deusto and the Augustine University at El Escorial. Opposing them were the 'liberals', long-time defenders of professorial freedom of speech but obstinately statist when it came to ministerial regulation, control, or monitoring of all forms of education or the granting of autonomy to state educational bodies.

As for the Conservatives, we must remember that the creation of the Ministry of Public Instruction and the extension of compulsory schooling to the age of 12 were measures taken by two of their most 'clerical' governments (Silvela in 1900 and Maura in 1908). This did not prevent them, in the name of educational freedom, from defending private schools and even universities. The first prize for inconsistency has to go to the Church spokesmen who, despite their inveterate anti-liberalism, invoked the principle of educational freedom to deny the state the right to inspect religious schools, while brazenly claiming their own right to intervene in private institutions whose teaching might contravene Catholic doctrine.

The contradictoriness of the situation was highlighted by Primo de Rivera's seizure of power. The dictator declared himself prepared to enforce state regulation of all educational institutions, including religious ones, thus showing a firmness befitting a soldier but also typical of the 'liberal' (statist) tradition. Primo was certainly a 'regenerationist' as far as school-building was concerned (2,000 new schools were built between 1923 and 1930, with a further 2,000 improved or entirely renovated), and in the emphasis on technical training in secondary education formulated in the Callejo Plan. The statism of the latter, however, reached quasi-fascist proportions, imposing the sole, compulsory use of ministerially approved texts in primary and secondary education. Curiously, it was not this which triggered Primo's confrontations with 'liberal' teachers and students, but his typically dictatorial lack of respect for professorial freedom of speech, which led to the disciplining of some highly influential dissidents such as Unamuno. Few of Primo's errors so tarnished his image during the dictatorship. But worse still was the fact that he granted official academic recognition to degrees awarded by Deusto and El Escorial, in response to pressure from the conservatives who were his political bedrock. The Spanish Church's achievement of its long-standing dream instantly aroused unanimous protest from students and lecturers at the state universities, a protest in which corporate interests no doubt took precedence over any genuine concern about educational quality. In short, the universities declared open war on the dictator, becoming one of the crucial factors behind his unpopularity and eventual fall.

The consequent declaration of the Second Republic gave the educationalists of the Institución Libre their long-awaited opportunity. At last Spanish liberalism was going to realize its dream of regenerating the country through education. Over and above any concern to balance the budget, priority was given to education funding, financed through special loans taken out by the state. A plan to create 27,000 new schools over five years was announced, teachers were trained, the Escuelas Normales were reorganized for this purpose, the Callejo Plan was jettisoned, the Misiones Pedagógicas (travelling teams charged with taking education and culture to the rural population) were created. There was so much to be done, the Republican regime could only scratch the surface of need. The problem, however, lay not so much in administrative deficiencies or financial shortfalls (despite the financial crisis of the 1930s which prevented the plans for funding new schools from being fully implemented). The real tragedy was that this generous-spirited education policy got bogged down in the usual squabbles over the removal of crucifixes from classrooms (something the conservative middle classes would remember as one of the Republic's most provocative acts), or the closure by decree of schools run by the religious orders. Education, itself a battleground, became the symbol of a wider conflict. It is no coincidence that teachers were among the main casualties of the victorious Francoist state's purges and executions.

Notes

1 59% according to M. Vilanova, *Atlas de evolución del analfabetismo en España, de 1887 a 1981* (Madrid, 1982), 167; 64% acccording to Enrique Guerrero Salom, 'La Institución, el sistema educativo y la educación de las clases obreras a finales de siglo', *Revista de Educación*, 243 (1976), 70.

2 See G. Menéndez Pidal, *La España del siglo XIX vista por sus contemporáneos* (Madrid, 1989), 292.

Further reading

Cacho Viu, V., *La Institución Libre de Enseñanza* (Madrid, 1962).

Castillejo, J., *Guerra de ideas en España (filosofía, política y educación)* (Revista de Occidente, Madrid, 1976) (trans. of 1937 English original).

Cossío, M. B., *De su jornada: fragmentos* (new edn. Madrid, 1966).

Guerrero Salom, E., *Historia de la educación en España: del despotismo ilustrado a las Cortes de Cádiz* (Madrid, 1979).

Medina Carrasco, E., *La lucha por la educación en España, 1770–1970* (Madrid, 1977).

Puelles Benítez, M., *Educación e ideología en la España contemporánea* (Barcelona, 1991).

Ruiz Berrio, J. (ed.), *La educación en la España contemporánea: cuestiones históricas* (Sociedad Española de Pedagogía, Madrid, 1985).

Viñao Frago, A., *Política y educación en los orígenes de la España contemporánea* (Madrid, 1982).

Modernismo and Modernisme

CHRIS PERRIAM

ARTHUR TERRY

EMMA DENT
COAD

Literary *Modernismo* in Castilian: The Creation of a Dissident Cultural Élite

CHRIS PERRIAM

The new writers of the turn of the century who soon became known (not always admiringly) as *modernistas* aspired to combine lived experience and the creation of art in a single, if complex, cultural process. Demonizing the dominant aesthetics of the last two or three generations, many found clumsiness and too much rhetoric in Romantic writing and developed a propensity for the elaboration of form and subtlety of expression which not only disturbed and transformed the established arts scene but led to new possibilities for ironic expression, to liberation from time-honoured notions of coherence, propriety, and intelligibility, and to a radical questioning of established canons of taste and of the very notion of taste itself. Others though—and *modernismo* was extremely heterogeneous—shamelessly plundered Romantic discourses, making imagination and the senses reign supreme in poetry, or, like Francisco Villaespesa (1877–1935) and Eduardo Marquina (1879–1946), bringing sumptuously exotic pseudo-history onto the stage.

A dissident taste for the exotic and a fascination with the ideal of Beauty marked many *modernista* texts, and it existed in a relation of dependence not only to many of the old literary practices which were supposed to be avoided but also to the workaday bourgeois world which the new discourse shunned. One needed the facilities of travel and commerce to acquire clothes, pictures, objects, rare books. To maintain a bohemian circle and keep up with the gossip on the shock of the new required leisure time. As with the *movida madrileña** in the early 1980s, *modernismo* depended upon personality cults, contacts, and networking to keep itself in a state of transformation. This élitist micro-culture could not but traffic intensely with the 'real' world.

A significant dialogue was established with those Latin American writers whose countries had a metropolitan core recognizable on European terms and who might bring into the dusty old warehouse of Spanish culture exotic new commodities for exploitation. Aspects of European cultural heritage (especially French and Italian) which sought to leave the old century behind and take up the banner of Art were greedily ingested, improved upon, simply copied, or exceeded and parodically exhausted of their possibilities. From sources as diverse as William Morris (whose urge to reconcile worlds of labour and creativity was also gaining favour with anarchist groupings in Spain) and Huysmans's and Wilde's decadentism, *modernismo* developed an insistence on the indivisibility of ethics and aesthetics which is seen in the *Sonatas* of Ramón del Valle-Inclán (1866–1936), in the triumphantly perverse prose fiction of Antonio de Hoyos y Vinent (1886–1940), and in a tendency— exemplified in poets like Manuel Machado (1874–1947)—to intermingle the lyrical and the autobiographical first person singular (the self-portrait with which Antonio Machado (1875–1939) commences his *Campos de Castilla* is a parodic recognition of the potency of this subgenre). Rebellious living and rebellious writing were linked also, and vitally, to the more intellectual forms of dissent associated with French *symbolisme*, with its famous avoidance of the obvious in literary expression. One of *modernismo*'s most powerful arguments was for radical formal change, for new rhythms, cadences, and suggestions in verse; new approaches to prose writing; a poetic, anti-realist theatre.

Its intense attention to form and surface and apparent evasion of social questions has meant that *modernismo* has had little appeal to conventional leftist critics, who have refused to recognize its subversive potential. Reactionary cultural historians, on the other hand, have constructed an opposition between a 'Generation of 1898' representing the solemn, austere, virile, and truly 'Spanish' (*castizo**) and a movement exclusively concerned with the literary, the frivolous, decadent, effeminate, escapist, foreign, and unwholesome: *modernismo*. Although Moorish, Asian, or Aztec palaces and princesses, enclosed worlds, and indolent enchantment frequently resurface, much of *modernista* writing rigorously deconstructs the very bases of the high culture it also seems to worship and, since the 1970s, it has begun to be recognized as a fascinatingly shifting example of culture in progress.

In particular, the *modernista* obsession with form frequently spills over into a fascination with the representation of transgressive desire. Naked flesh and sensually violent colour are to be found in early work by Juan Ramón Jiménez

(1881–1958); virginity, witchcraft, violent death, and violent desire permeate Valle-Inclán's *Comedias bárbaras* (1907–22) and early poetry; Salvador Rueda (1875–1933) transgressively links martyrdom, penitence, writing, and sex in 'Mujer de moras' [Blackberry Woman], where brambles whip and tattoo a willing man's flesh as he picks the berries which, tossed over the woman's breasts, form 'an exotic script | with rare letters the colour of flames'.

There is a radical openness in many of the 'exotic scripts' of *modernismo* to themes out of popular traditions such as the relationship between love and witchcraft, desire and submission, pleasure and pain (especially evident in rural folk cultures of the north and the *copla* [folk-song] and flamenco in the south). Similarly, their apparently highly literary preference for pastoral, courtly, and aristocratic scenarios can now be seen to link with major areas of fantasy in (mainly urban) popular cultural traditions such as the *zarzuela** and the popular novel, where working-class—or lower middle-class—protagonists dream of gaining access to a more utopian or exotic setting than the street where they live through romantic involvement with a 'better' class of person.

Modernismo's idolization of Form, Art, Beauty—its idealism—and its horror of the normal and exaltation of Experience—its dissidence—led it into an engagement with the world of sensations and sexuality, and with the complexity of culture beyond the pages of literature and the doors of museums. It can now be read as a cultural process which, while constructing itself as a closed system—an élitism—simultaneously and wilfully revealed its own incoherences and opened itself up to the very areas of reference—those of 'real life'—that it teases us into believing it was all along avoiding.

Further reading
Brotherston, G., *Manuel Machado: A Reevaluation* (Cambridge, 1968).
Cardwell, R., *Juan Ramón Jiménez: The Modernist Apprenticeship 1895–1900* (Berlin, 1977).
Gullón, R., *El modernismo visto por los modernistas* (Barcelona, 1980).
Litvak, L., *Erotismo fin de siglo* (Barcelona, 1979).
—— (ed.), *El modernismo* (Madrid, 1975).

Catalan Literary *Modernisme* and *Noucentisme*: From Dissidence to Order
ARTHUR TERRY

Catalan modernism—not to be confused with Spanish *modernismo*, whose context is quite different—was above all an attempt to create a genuinely modern, European culture out of what was felt to be a purely local and regional one. The immediate pretext was what Alan Yates has called 'the stagnation of official Spanish Restoration culture'; though it was already gathering weight during the late 1880s, it first came to a head in the year between September 1892 and September

1893 which saw the leading journal of the time, *L'Avenç*, intensify its campaign for modernizing the Catalan language and which ended with the first *Festa modernista* held at Sitges under the patronage of the writer and painter Santiago Rusiñol. This is also the year when the poet Joan Maragall begins to write for the *Diario de Barcelona* and when Raimon Casellas, later to write the first *modernista* novel, contributes his first piece of art criticism to *La Vanguardia*.

To call *modernisme* a 'movement' can be misleading; for much of the time, it seems more like a process than a deliberate movement, a matter of constant challenges and readjustments, many of which have to do with changing concepts of Catalan nationalism. Essentially, it is a version of late Romanticism in which questions of aesthetics engage at every point with the conditions of contemporary society. Thus, despite individual differences, a certain consensus emerges, which hinges on the relations between the artist and society. More specifically, the need was felt for a different, more professional, kind of artist: professional not in a commercial sense, but as someone totally dedicated to the pursuit of his art. And with this goes a new confidence in the value of artistic intuition: the writer or painter is now thought of as someone who conveys an individual vision of things, and who intervenes in reality in order to go beyond surface appearances.

As for what the *modernistes* regarded as 'modern', one can simply list the foreign writers and artists who most interested them: Carlyle, Nietzsche, Ruskin, Ibsen, Maeterlinck, and Wagner. As one might expect, these influences affected not only literature: the vogue for Maeterlinck and Wagner was used to justify the association of poetry and drama with the other arts, and the painting, like the architecture of the time, reflects the peculiar medievalism of the Pre-Raphaelites.

In practice, *modernisme* was faced with a paradox: if society is to be rejected for artistic reasons, how can this same society be regenerated without some kind of social intervention by the artist? It is this paradox which accounts for the two competing strands one finds in the early stages of *modernisme*: what one can roughly call the 'ivory tower' attitude which comes to be known as *decadentisme*, and the 'regenerationist' tendency which eventually becomes bound up with the politics of the turn of the century. And what keeps the paradox alive is the fact that *modernisme*, far from wanting to impose a superficial cosmopolitanism on a culturally backward country, is out to produce a genuinely Catalan culture: one which will be 'modern' in a European sense, but which will also take into account the traditions and pressures of its own society.

The example of the poet Joan Maragall is instructive here. Though still attracted by many aspects of *modernisme*, by 1900 Maragall is beginning to denounce some of its more 'decadent' manifestations and to work towards the conception of artistic wholeness which underlies the far greater achievement of his own later poems. One sign of this is that the cosmopolitan aspect of *modernisme* gives way to specifically Catalan themes, as in the poems of Maragall's 1900 collection *Visions i cants*. What Maragall is trying to do in these poems, though he might not have admitted it, is to create a new myth of the Catalan character at a time when Catalonia itself is going through a crisis of national consciousness. And this coincides with a major political shift: in the early 1890s *catalanisme*, though rather differently conceived, had been the main enemy of *modernisme*; now, however, the artistic and political fronts start to converge in the general swing towards Catalan autonomy—a movement which will eventually bring about the eclipse of *modernisme* itself.

What happens, roughly, is that, after the Spanish elections of 1901, the conservative Catalanist party, the Lliga Regionalista, comes to power under the leadership of Prat de la Riba, eventually to become the first president of a semi-devolved Catalan government. It is at this point that cultural life comes to be regarded officially for the first time as an essential component in the political future of Catalonia. Hence the emergence of *noucentisme*: a common, officially sponsored, cultural front with its basis in fixed institutions and with a corresponding stress on order and refinement.

It is, of course, likely that any new movement in literature or the arts will succeed only by doing a certain amount of injustice to what has gone before, partly to gain energy for its own purposes. In the case of *noucentisme*, this meant producing a polemical version of *modernisme*, oversimplifying its Romantic dimension in order to contrast it with a new 'classicism'. So various antitheses begin to take shape: 'classicism' versus 'Romanticism', urban values as against the so-called 'rusticity' of the existing literature, and, summing up most of these, 'objectivity' as opposed to 'subjectivity'. It is not difficult to show that most of these contrasts are exaggerated; more importantly, though much of the *noucentista* programme was admirable, like most official programes it involved certain sacrifices. Above all, there is a certain conservatism which underlies the *noucentista* call for order and which accounts for some of its more notorious exclusions, like its rejection of the *modernista* novel. And coming back to one of the central beliefs of *modernisme*—the idea that the artist is a creator who must intervene in reality—one can see how much *noucentisme* loses by refusing subjectivity as an aesthetic value and by excluding the whole individual, rebellious dimension of *modernisme*.

Noucentisme, then, is both a continuation and a reduction of *modernisme*. The real differences, in short, are political; or, to be more precise, they come from differing interpretations of what, for want of a better word, one calls *catalanitat* (what it means to be Catalan)—something which, as the *modernistes* clearly saw, involves the whole question of what it is to be a writer or artist in a society which is undergoing a crisis of national consciousness.

Further reading

Marfany, J.-L., *Aspectes del modernisme* (Barcelona, 1975).
Terry, A., *Catalan Literature* (London, 1972).
Yates, A., 'Catalan Literature between *Modernisme* and *Noucentisme*', in M. McCully (ed.), *Homage to Barcelona: The City and its Art, 1888–1936* (London, 1985), 253–63.

Catalan *Modernista* Architecture: Using the Past to Build the Modern

EMMA DENT COAD

As in all the various cultural manifestations of *modernisme*, Catalan architecture around 1875–1925 was focused on finding a regional identity. The group of architects whose work comes into the category of *modernisme* were extraordinarily prolific; this was made possible by a newly wealthy industrialist bourgeoisie who wished to signal their progressive, cosmopolitan outlook by emulating Europe, and who were reluctant to promote styles existing in the rest of Spain, particularly in Madrid. Wishing also to establish their new social status in the traditionally rigid structure of Spanish society, many members of this new class commissioned for their homes capacious apartments, grand mansions, or palaces. To mark this new phase, many of their architects began to move on from the 'aristocratic' and academic neo-Gothic and Romanesque aesthetic of early nineteenth-century religious architecture, taking their inspiration from contemporary European trends while at the same time stamping them with an emerging regional style.

Barcelona's position as a major trading city with Europe, Africa, and the Orient was reflected in the development of architectural forms. The last quarter of the nineteenth century saw the creation of fantastic buildings which borrowed Moorish, oriental, and North African features. Some architects retained a taste for the Gothic, but with exaggerated arches and asymmetric forms. Other recurrent motifs were carved stone or stucco swags of lush vegetation, sometimes forming balconies, window- and doorframes, or porticos. Shells and marine life were another source of curvaceous, organic forms which took shape as stained glass, ironwork, mosaics, and murals.

Like the concurrent Parisian art nouveau movement, German *Jugendstil* and English Liberty Style, *modernisme* not only allowed an upwardly mobile class to display its wealth and love of culture, but also represented its reaction against the excesses of the industrial revolution, which it feared was leading to the neglect of skills and the uniformity of mass production. Hence its patronage of luxury craftmade objects. Within its common bonds with art and design movements elsewhere in Europe, *modernisme* developed strong characteristics of its own: appreciation for the applied and decorative arts, and the emergence of the architect-craftsman and artist-craftsman, combined with vernacular references and a celebration of local craft specialities. Barcelona is pre-eminent in the number of buildings commissioned and in the number which still exist, immaculately restored; the same political forces that precipitated *modernisme* have ensured the survival of historical examples. Like the Viennese *Sezession*, *modernisme* was founded on a political platform which kicked against central government and attempted to escape formal classification by creating a new style without historical precedent, though based on the fusion of models borrowed from elsewhere. Bilbao, Valencia, and Palma de Mallorca were also touched by the vogue for *modernista* architecture, though generally tamer and more refined by *Jugendstil* influence: for example,

1 Contemporary photograph of first-floor landing of the Casa Batlló, Barcelona, designed by Gaudí 1904–6. Catalan *modernista* architecture was a protest against the standardization and dehumanization of modern industrial society, but depended on the Catalan industrial bourgeoisie who commissioned extravagant private residences—with everything, furnishings and fittings included, specially designed for them—to display their new wealth and cosmopolitan tastes, while at the same time affirming a nationalist sense of self-importance.

the prevalence in Valencia of brightly painted stucco murals for façades, as opposed to the more extreme textural treatment of exterior surface found in Barcelona.

Around the turn of the century, architects' disparate programmes began to form a recognizable movement, characterized more by dynamism, experimentation, and approach to form than by specific stylistic traits. Its battle-cry was 'novelty, freedom, and youth'.

Josep Marià Jujol, a student of Gaudí (see below), collaborated with him extensively from around 1905. His work combines many of the features emblematic of that of Gaudí—asymmetry, free-form ironwork, ripple plasterwork, broken plate mosaics, almost psychedelic murals—with the result that it is hard to say who influenced whom. Another of Gaudí's students, Francesc Berenguer, excelled in exaggerated Gothic styles which today look like cartoon witches' castles.

Josep Puig i Cadafalch, a co-founder in 1901 of the conservative Catalanist party, the Lliga Regionalista, specialized in vigorous medievalized forms. He had been one of the country's premier archaeologists before turning to the built form. His 1904 palace in the Gran Via, and his 1912 thread factory at Casarramona, celebrate Spanish medievalism in structures that are unmistakably nineteenth-century in scale and conception. The decorative work of Josep Grases Riera uses the infinitely plastic qualities of cement to create balconies, cornices, canopies, and architraves dripping with complex plant-like forms.

Lluís Domènech i Montaner is usually seen as the joint leader of *modernista* architecture with Gaudí, though some consider his potential to have been greater. He had a thorough understanding of medieval architecture and followed the theories of Viollet-le-duc, the influential nineteenth-century restorer and theorist, on the construction of Gothic architecture. He was passionate about Arab and Mudéjar decorative style, and, like many architects of this period, supported the politics and philosophy of the British Arts and Crafts movement. His few buildings—for example, the Hospital de la Santa Cruz, and the Ciudadela restaurant of 1888, subsequently converted into the Zoological Museum—are well known. The exterior of the latter is like a Moorish castle, build in plain brick though with exuberant decorative mannerisms. The interior shows his avant-garde treatment of structure: the roof exhibits its steel skeleton in a way which acknowledges his understanding of the formal simplicity and honest treatment of materials characteristic of contemporary architecture elsewhere in Europe. His Palau de la Música Catalana (1907), a large and highly decorated concert hall, has a very different visual language though its volumetrics and spirit have common bonds. Arguably the most successful *modernista* building, it combines the use of ceramic tiles, stained glass, ironwork, carved stone, mosaic, sculpture, enamel, and stucco in a way that is sensual and vital. Domènech's decoration is of primary importance, an intrinsic part of the architectonic scheme. He devoted much of his career to leading the Barcelona School of Architecture, and to writing and teaching, but never achieved the status of Gaudí.

There are a number of reasons why Antoni Gaudí is a key figure. His work became part of the popular culture of Barcelona, both as a highly visible and seductive expression of *catalanitat*, and because of its religious symbolism. Gaudí's buildings, furniture, and decorative motifs were inspired by the Romanticism of the art nouveau movement but were wilder and more assertive. A religious ascetic, celibate and reclusive, he was influenced by the philosophy and politics of John Ruskin and William Morris. The Sagrada Familia, begun in 1875 by Vilar de Pilar in the popular neo-Gothic style, was taken over by Gaudí in 1884: he intended it to be the centre of a complete environment including workers' housing, schools, and workshops—a self-contained community based around a forward-thinking Church.

The industrialist Eusebio Güell was patron of Gaudí's famous Güell Park, begun in 1900 and never finished. The 9.5-acre site overlooking the city was to have included a workers' residential estate, workshops, shops, and an open-air theatre for the people (the continuous curving mosaic bench that has become an emblem of Barcelona was to have been part of this). Gaudí's idea of providing colour and ornament for the common people, of working side by side with them in 'medieval' craftsmen's guilds and workshops, and of the dignity of physical work, is directly reminiscent of Morris.

Gaudí was equally daring and innovative in his approach to construction, using combinations of modern and historical techniques to compel his towers and arches to ever more improbable heights and contortions. His influence on architects since his death has been notable: for example, the work of Félix Candela (Republican period, later exiled in Mexico), Eduardo Torroja (Franco era), and more recently Santiago Calatrava—all gifted architectural engineers.

Like Morris, Gaudí suffered from the contradictions of his age. Both had idealized visions for the future in which the new bourgeoisie, sensitive both to the dangers of over-industrialization and to social need, would support the improvement of living conditions, education, and employment prospects for the working classes. The realities eventually led to disenchantment and cynicism about the possibilities for political change. Gaudí was not the first to discover that design and architecture alone cannot effect social change, and that, given the opportunity, the bourgeoisie would refuse self-sacrifice, forget their roots, and become what they had reviled: an isolated and self-centred élite like the aristocracy. Gaudí's political vision was eventually reduced, like that of Morris, to an episode in design history which will be remembered mainly for its original and dynamic visual impact.

Further reading
Antoni Gaudí (1852–1926) (Barcelona, 1985; 3rd edn. in Castilian 1989) (exhibition catalogue with important essays).
Bassegoda Nonell, J., *La arquitectura de Gaudí* (Madrid, 1982).
Collins, G. R., and **J. Bassegoda Nonell**, *The Designs and Drawings of Antoni Gaudí* (Princeton, 1983).
Domènech i Girbau, L., *Domènech i Montaner* (Barcelona, 1994).

Figueras, L., *Lluís Domènech i Montaner* (Barcelona, 1994) (bilingual English/Spanish).

Flores, C., *Arquitectura española contemporánea*, vol. i (Madrid, 1989).

—— *Gaudí, Jujols y el modernismo catalán* (Madrid, 1982).

Güell, X., *Antoni Gaudí* (Barcelona, 1992) (bilingual English/Spanish).

Hughes, R., *Barcelona* (London, 1992), chs. 7–8.

McCully, M. (ed.), *Homage to Barcelona: The City and its Art, 1888–1938* (London, 1985).

Mendoza, E. and C., *Barcelona modernista* (Barcelona, 1989).

Ràfols, J. F., *Gaudí* (Barcelona, 1929, new edn. 1960).

—— *Modernisme i modernistes* (Barcelona, 1982).

Solà-Morales, I. de, *Arquitectura modernista fin de siglo en Barcelona* (Barcelona, 1992).

—— *Gaudí* (London, 1987).

Tarragó, S. (ed.), *Antoni Gaudí: estudios críticos* (Barcelona, 1991).

The Avant-garde

SUE FRENK

CHRIS PERRIAM

MIKE THOMPSON

DAWN ADES

JULIAN WHITE

The Literary Avant-garde: A Contradictory Modernity

SUE FRENK, CHRIS PERRIAM, AND MIKE THOMPSON

Since the turn of the century, aspiring writers and artists from the more radical ranks of the liberal bourgeoisie had been faced with the dilemma of finding audiences for their work somewhere between the institutions of a reactionary state and the capitalist market-place. By the 1920s the dilemma had become the catalyst for contradictory cultural initiatives enmeshed in rapid processes of political and philosophical change. Whereas new images were flooding into exhibition spaces and onto cinema screens, the theatrical establishment was politically and artistically conservative, dominated by bourgeois audiences and their favourite authors, most of whose abundant output was written and staged according to well-tried formulas. However, a significant intellectual sector of the bourgeoisie was increasingly critical of the failure of established theatrical practices to meet the political and aesthetic challenges of the age. In prose narrative a complex dismantling and reconstruction develops as a response to the demands of a new, if limited, readership tired of romance and realism. In poetry a self-confident privileging of wit and taste and the idolization of publication itself—concerns of the intellectual élite—were countered by genuine attempts to record and disseminate popular forms of expression and to give a voice to marginalized cultures rural and urban.

If some of the most written-about figures—Dalí, Lorca, Buñuel—used the leisure and resources of such an exclusive space as the Madrid Residencia de Estudiantes (a kind of culturally vibrant Oxbridge college), other spaces colonized or created by artists and intellectuals were more in the public domain. In particular, the theorization of a social role for 'the artist' took place in the creation of clubs and regular gatherings (*tertulias*) held in selected cafés. As writings by Ramón Gómez de la Serna (1888–1967) on the Café Pombo suggest, these establishments provided a more or less open space for the holding of lectures, discussions, and readings, and competing notions of modern life and art were proclaimed and consecrated. However, the experience of the few women who can be discerned in contemporary photographs of these events is summed up by the novelist Rosa Chacel: 'I went occasionally [. . .]. Very occasionally [. . .]. It was like Chinese torture for me.' The marginalization of women in the secular and sacred spaces of the avant-garde prompts questions about its progressive credentials, as does the violence of its rhetoric, discussed later.

Linked to *tertulia* culture, probably the most crucial forums constituted by and for the avant-garde in Spain—as elsewhere in modernism—were the 'little magazines' which sprang up in the first decade of the twentieth century and proliferated in the 1920s. From *Prometeo* (1908–12), through the radical *Ultra* (1921–2) with its challenging graphics and polemical voice, co-edited by de la Serna, to the institutionalized *La Gaceta Literaria* (1927–31) and *Revista de Occidente* (1923–36), they cover a wide spectrum of cultural politics. The struggle for new meanings for art is played out with special vividness in *La Pluma* (Madrid, 1920–3). Like *Ultra*, it redefines the literary magazine (if less dramatically) but its content is contradictory, as in its rejection of cubism as a 'schizoid, dissociative disorder'. In questions of gender it is avowedly 'antifeminista': attention to women's artistic production is scarce and conceptualized in terms of 'maternal' and other 'natural' female instincts, as entertainment, or pale imitation of serious masculine models. Similarly, the influential *La Gaceta Literaria* is a curious blend of staid convention and pockets of excitement; élite critical discourse and sporadic engagement with popular culture; respectful attention to women artists like Maruja Mallo and Norah Borges; and more conservative literary coverage.

Theatre

Similar tensions affect theatre, which was extraordinarily busy and varied. In Madrid, some twenty venues offered 600–700 shows per season, up to 250 of these being premières. An elaborate infrastructure had been built up during the nineteenth century: Madrid and Barcelona were the main centres, complemented by provincial tours. Alongside the expensive city-centre theatres there was a range of cheap popular venues and a flourishing amateur sector. However, the social horizons of bourgeois drama and comedy were limited and their dramatic conventions stale, while the popular *género chico* (*sainete* or low-life sketch) had lost its earlier vitality and presented a view of working-class and rural life that was more sentimental and patronizing than ever. Since early in the century, Miguel de Unamuno (1864–1936), Ramón del Valle-Inclán (1866–1936), and others had railed against the closed circle of dramatists, impresarios, and actors who tailored shows to fit precise commercial specifications. The Spanish theatre seemed hopelessly mediocre and old-fashioned in comparison with developments elsewhere in Europe.

Some younger writers were beginning to make an impact in the theatre: Federico García Lorca (1898–1936), followed in the 1930s by fellow poets Rafael Alberti (born 1902), Pedro Salinas (1891–1951), and Miguel Hernández (1910–42); and Max Aub (1903–72). It would be misleading, however, to talk of the emergence in the 1920s of an organized avant-garde of new playwrights launching an assault on the theatrical establishment. Indeed, much of the most interesting work came from an older generation, born in the 1860s and 1870s, already well known as novelists, poets, and essayists, now writing with renewed energy for the stage: Unamuno, Valle-Inclán, Azorín (1873–1967), the Machado brothers (Manuel 1874–1947, Antonio 1875–1939), and Jacinto Grau (1877–1958).

Although these names, old and new, represent a great diversity of artistic practices, they were united by a passionate belief in the cultural importance of theatre and an awareness of working within a problematic space between the ambition to address new, wider audiences and the reality of appealing to an intellectual minority. In place of an institution that reflected the political agenda of the Restoration bourgeoisie by peddling complacency and nostalgia, they proposed radically unsettling kinds of theatre: aggressively satirical, philosophically anguished, or enigmatically poetic, and almost always self-consciously theatrical. The familiar focus on domestic situations and conventional morality was jolted both inwards (into dreams and the unconscious, problems of perception, and crises of identity) and outwards (towards wider social and cultural processes).

Established forms—*drama, comedia, tragedia, sainete, revista* [revue], *farsa* [farce], *zarzuela**—kept to recognizable patterns: audiences knew what to expect by reading the label. Experimental playwrights often made use of such conventions, but aimed to break down separations between genres and media. They playfully mixed elements of popular song, dance, and comic theatre with powerful intellectual themes; drew on circus and *commedia dell'arte* traditions; experimented with cinematic effects; collaborated with painters, musicians, and composers. They often sought to return to a pure essence of performance, to be found in the austerity of classical tragedy, in the physical expressiveness of dance and mime, or in the naïvety of farce and folklore.

Successful authors would be expected to write star roles for particular actors, especially women. The dissidents rejected this cosy arrangement, and many of their texts explode the ideal of rational, unified character and fixed social and sexual roles. Valle-Inclán's *esperpentos* [grotesqueries] and Lorca's farces explicitly represent human beings as puppets—grotesque archetypes of basic human desires, empty shells manipulated by social forces—while suggesting a tragic awareness of their own debasement. In Grau's *El señor de Pigmalión* (1921), lifelike dummies rebel against their tyrannical creator. The 'characters' of Lorca's *El público* (1929–30) metamorphose bewilderingly, their sexuality and their physical forms uncertain and unstable. In Unamuno's *El otro* (1926), personality is an agonizing mystery, while the Don Juan of *El hermano Juan* (1929) constantly creates his own personality as a performance.

Language was the other primary focus of experimentation. A desire to escape from deadening conventions was the immediate stimulus, but there was also a growing awareness of the essentially symbolic nature of language, and of theatre as a rich blend of multiple verbal and non-verbal sign systems. Aub's *Una botella* (1924) is a strange allegory on the emptiness of words. Unamuno developed a spare, cryptic language of metaphysical exploration, while Valle-Inclán created anarchic mixtures of the colloquial, the literary, the crude, the lyrical, and the parodic. Lorca's famous declaration that 'theatre is poetry that gets up from the page and becomes human' implied that everything—character, dialogue, staging, action—is shaped by a total poetic concept, which, in his work of the 1920s, varied in style from the cute symbolist fantasy of *El maleficio de la mariposa* (1920) to the startling surrealist images of *El público*.

The physical space of the stage began to be seen not merely as a familiar location in which dramatic business is carried out, but as a semiotic space, an expressive part of the overall symbolic structure. In some cases this meant schematic simplicity, in others, ambitious concepts far beyond the imaginative and technical resources of the theatrical establishment of the time.

Narrative

Ramón Gómez de la Serna's enthusiastic yet critical promotion of futurism, dada, and surrealism, his assimilation of constructivist aesthetics, and engagement with key figures of modernity (a brief encounter with Marx and a lifelong textual dialogue with Baudelaire, Nietzsche, and Freud) make his writings a key site for the avant-garde adventure. There are specifically Spanish pathways to be mapped in his route to the deconstruction of language, subjectivity, and narrative, in which Unamuno is a key figure, particularly in *Niebla* (1914). A precursor of de la Serna's *El novelista*, it is concerned with the tyranny of the author and the decoding of narrative conventions. Humour is central to both writers, in de la Serna's case ranging from playfulness to ironic distance, through the elaborate wit of the Spanish baroque, the dark satire of Goya, and the eccentric presence of his mentor from the 1898 group, Silverio Lanza.

The *greguerías*, begun around 1911 and refashioned incessantly up to his death, cross genre boundaries and rework fragments of everyday city life in a double process of defamiliarization: atomization (a 'microscopic' perspective), and strategies of linguistic disruption which anticipate surrealism. But they often depend on esoteric cultural reference and reveal a lingering nostalgia for the classical status of the élite artist. The larger scale *Cinelandia* (1923) marks a movement towards an increasing fascination with mass cultural forms which bridge the dichotomies of art and entertainment, particularly cinema and jazz, and establishes a multifaceted metaphor for capitalism and the modern state.

In the context of competing theories of gender and sexuality central to the various ideological struggles of the period, women writers explored the new relationships and dilemmas thrown up by social change and feminist activity, challenging the marginalization of gender issues in the major political movements. Carmen de Burgos (*c.*1870–1932) braved public scandal to divorce her husband and support herself as a single parent. An active suffragist, her influence can perhaps be detected, as a founding member and collaborator, in *Ultra*'s critical perspective on the misogyny of Italian futurism and in de la Serna's public support for egalitarian feminism during their long love affair. In *Ultra*'s 'Diálogos libres'— pre-surrealist free-associating conversations—her voice provides glimpses of a counter-discourse to the male avant-garde's celebration of 'darkness' over 'light' and their rejection of 'love'. Drawing on the legacy of naturalist and regionalist writing familiar to her intended readers, *La malcasada* and *Quiero vivir mi vida* (1931) are concerned with women's struggles with bourgeois institutions (including marriage) and establish an author–reader relationship very different from the often contemptuous dismissal by the male avant-garde of the presumed reading habits of a mass readership.

While women writers proved more willing to engage with the *folletín* [serialized melodrama] and the *novela sentimental* popular with female readers, male sexuality in the work of Benjamín Jarnés (1888–1949), de la Serna, and Aub confronts a female 'other', variously 'unreachable' or desirable only as fetishized body parts or as surrealism's violent 'convulsive beauty'—an indication of the gender trouble at the heart of Hispanic modernity. The reworking of 'sentiment', 'love', and desire by women writers, including poets such as Carmen Conde (b. 1907), can be read as an alternative discourse of gender relations, located in the struggles of everyday life. A truly innovative example is the Catalan writer Caterina Albert, who wrote for many years under the male pseudonym of Víctor Català. *Un film (3000 metres)* (1918) took off from the serial films then in vogue and played with the *folletín* from which they had developed. Anticipating the objectivist movement that would emerge after the civil war, the narration attempts to represent the eye of the camera. By downplaying plot and episodic structure, it participates in the dismantling of realist aesthetics.

Poetry

The radical alterations to cultural horizons of this period most famously gave rise to an upsurge in the production, exchange, and esteem of poetic texts. Not only was the range of aesthetic response in poetry expanded further than it had been by the *modernista* project but also, as in narrative, the interests of groups risking or already experiencing marginalization were firmly written into the scheme of things and straight representation of human experience written out. Above all, there are moments of abandonment to the irrational, the perversely erotic, to dreams and nightmares and experiences beyond the surface of capital-driven modernization.

Vicente Aleixandre's *Espadas como labios* (1932) and *Pasión de la tierra* (written 1928–9, published 1935) introduce long pulsing lines and poetry in prose to explore the irrational, the oneiric, and the erotic, partly in response to reading Freud, Rimbaud, and Lautréamont, partly out of a desire to escape the canon of 'great' Spanish texts and bring in the new. There are hallucinations, fragmented evocations of violent physical or mental pain, and damaging desires; there is also a strong nostalgia for the discourses of a more straightforward European Romanticism in which privileged perceptions and enhanced feeling might lead to a coherent sense of self, albeit a lost self. The same interestingly incompatible mix of the radically violent and the tender, the new and the established, is to be found in Rafael Alberti's *Sobre los ángeles* (1929) which depends on biblical and classical literary discourses quite as much as it reworks and transgresses them.

In Alberti, Aleixandre, and Lorca (especially in the poems of *Poeta en Nueva York* written in 1929–30) there is a tortured awareness of the body as poised hypersensitively on the edge of ecstasy and agony, given its specifically avant-garde edge by an insistence on severed or disconnected limbs, split eyeballs, close-up, and fetishization of separate parts of the body. In *Sobre los ángeles* the speaking subject is charred, burned out, while in Aleixandre the pain gets deflected onto the notional woman who is the object of desire in an increasingly misogynistic language of violent possession, penetration, and rawness. In *Poeta en Nueva York* culture shock, psychological distress, and a not entirely welcome sexual awakening combine with linguistic experimentation to turn the speaker into a martyr to perception and a stranger to himself. In the 'Poema doble del lago Eden' the perception is that 'era mi voz antigua | ignorante de los densos jugos amargos' [that voice of mine from long ago | knew nothing of these dense and bitter juices].

Unlike the young Pedro Salinas (1891–1951) and Jorge Guillén (1893–1984) or Alberti in *Cal y canto* (1927) and others impressed by futurism's bright and energetic visions of the modern metropolis, Lorca is repelled by the industrialized and crowded New York in the throes of a crisis of capitalism. Like Luis Cernuda, in *Los placeres prohibidos* (1931), Lorca finds that rebellion against the dominant culture brings with it inextricably a questioning of the sexual self and of the categories of sexuality. If representations of heterosexual desire in avant-garde poetry of this period leave hardly anyone in one piece, Lorca and Cernuda, paradoxically, find that the rebellious discourse and the unsettling possibilities of the new language can construct a coherent alternative culture in homosexuality. Both use the idealized male body as a focus for rebellion and dissent and underpin their linguistic adventurism with a potent myth of lost perfection. In *Poeta en Nueva York* a nostalgia for rural or pre-civilized simplicity is linked inextricably to another ideal world, one of same-sex relationships unsullied by commercialization (male prostitution and drag shows) and by the opprobrium of established culture. In Cernuda classical purity is given a similarly subversive turn.

The boom years for poetry had started with an unlikely combination of interests; in the autonomy of poetic creation and the supremacy of image over rational idea on the one hand, on the other in the links between poetry and certain, mainly historical, forms of popular culture. What was to be dubbed *poesia popular* frequently reveals the stresses which come of writing across class and cultural borders and there are many elisions, ignorances, and absences. Despite its zealous recreation of local histories and traditions and its closeness to popular musical and linguistic forms, cosmopolitan modes of expression (the daring metaphor, the sophisticatedly surreal turn of phrase) or bourgeois notions of 'human nature' frequently interfere. Lorca's *Romancero gitano* intercuts impressionistic evocations of popular and marginalized cultures with discourses more proper to the likes of the image- and wit-obsessed wing of *ultraísmo*, of Ortega y Gasset, or of Juan Ramón Jiménez, whose project in the 1920s emphasized 'the exaltation of the spirit and of intelligence' and promoted 'the taste for things of beauty'.

The institutionalization of these poets (particularly as a 'Generation') has led to a position in which most readers come to their texts as you might approach a museum exhibit; but the vitality of their circumstances of production is soon restored when they are read as part of a contradictory cultural process or in the context of recent poetry which builds on their more radical ideas. Similarly, in theatre there is today a process of rediscovery of texts and performance styles from this era, with Valle-Inclán in particular being often invoked or reworked. The possibilities for avant-garde narrative posited at the time returned in the 1950s and 1960s, and the deconstructive project continues (in the face of a generally conservative publishing industry). The position of the avant-garde is being radically reassessed in contemporary research into issues of gender. The disturbances and shocks of the 1920s still resonate.

Further reading
Concha, V. G. de la, *El surrealismo* (Madrid, 1982).
Molina, C. A., *Medio siglo de prensa literaria española (1900–1950)* (Madrid, 1990).
Morris, C. B., *Surrealism and Spain, 1920–1936* (Cambridge, 1972).
—— *The Surrealist Adventure in Spain* (Ottawa, 1991).
Ruiz Ramón, F., *Historia del teatro español: siglo XX* (3rd edn., Madrid, 1976).
Soria Olmedo, A., *Vanguardismo y crítica literaria en España* (Madrid, 1988).
Zavala, I. M., *Colonialism and Culture: Hispanic Modernism and the Social Imaginary* (Bloomington, Ind., 1992).

2 'Cartel literario' [literary poster] by Ernesto Giménez Caballero (founder of Spain's first cinema club and editor of the avant-garde literary magazine *La Gaceta Literaria*, who would in the late 1920s become a convert to fascism) dedicated 'To the poet Lorca' (shot by the Nationalists at the start of the civil war), showing how the avant-garde project could contain radically opposed political options. Giménez Caballero's collage highlights the coexistence in Lorca's work of avant-garde experimentalism (the manuscript drawing) and traditional elements drawn from popular culture (the *aleluya* [strip cartoon sold in broadsheet form], left; the fan and girl with mantilla, right).

Internationalism and Eclecticism: Surrealism and the Avant-garde in Painting and Film 1920–1930

DAWN ADES

The artistic avant-garde in Spain during the 1920s was highly eclectic but by no means simply marginal to, nor dependent upon, major centres like Paris. Several factors contributed to this paradoxical situation, including the relatively small number of artists actively engaging with the modern movements, who asserted their individualism in their own unique versions of modernist styles, the rapid proliferation of little reviews, and the dispersed and regional nature of cultural patronage and institutions. Barcelona, for example, the capital of Catalonia, had a thriving intellectual and artistic community, was in far more regular contact with Paris and avant-garde European movements in general than Madrid, but was also the centre of Catalan nationalism, whose influence on major artists like Joan Miró should not be underestimated. Miró solved the problem of being at one and the same time a committed anti-nationalist and a passionate Catalan by describing himself as an 'international Catalan'.

The situation was further confused by the almost simultaneous arrival in Spain, during the 1920s, of the major pre-war movements like cubism and futurism, and the post-war developments of purism, new objectivity, dada, the metaphysical painting of de Chirico, Carrà, and Morandi, and of surrealism. All these are not, of course, equivalent, in the sense that some were indeed movements, with a strong theoretical base, like futurism and surrealism which operated across a broad front involving both literature and the visual arts, while others acquired a name fortuitously, as a handy label for a distinctive and coherent style, like cubism, which was not, at least by its originators Picasso and Braque, intended to be a movement. It is notable that the critical debates in Spanish literary and artistic reviews of the time tended to discuss ideas, aesthetic qualities, and individual artists and works rather than the movements as monolithic whole; surrealism was the exception, and by 1927 the question 'What is surrealism?' was being regularly posed.

Post-war Paris still exerted a magnetic attraction on artists throughout Europe. It is obviously a key factor in the present story that three artists from Spain played major roles in the Parisian avant-garde and also dominated that of Spain during the 1920s: Picasso, born in Málaga, who first went to Paris from his Barcelona base in 1900, and was regarded by the surrealist leader André Breton as the most important artist for the surrealist movement; the Catalan Miró, who first visited Paris in 1919, belonged to the surrealist movement from its inception in 1924, and divided his time between the French capital and Catalonia during the 1920s; and Dalí, also Catalan, who joined the surrealist movement in 1929. Work by Picasso and Miró figured prominently in such reviews as L'Amic de les Arts, and both artists showed an interest in Dalí from the time of his first one-man show at the Dalmau Gallery in Barcelona in 1925, when he was only 21. The Spanish vanguard could thus be seen as enjoying a privileged position vis-à-vis Paris.

But other factors also distinguish Spain's relationship with the post-war modern movements in art. The Spanish ultraists had established a strong literary identity, and there was also Spain's American connection. A shared language and old cultural ties that independence from Spain had not wholly broken led to a lively exchange and made Spain a filter of artists and ideas from the New World. Several of the more exciting artists living and exhibiting at the time in Spain were from the Americas: Norah Borges from Argentina, Rafael Barradas and Torres-García from Uruguay. Linocuts and drawings in a broadly cubist style by Norah Borges were reproduced in the review *Horizonte* (Madrid, 1922–3) and in *L'Amic de les Arts* (Sitges, 1926–9). Barradas's vibrationism, a distinctive, dynamic urban style that combined futurist notions of simultaneity with cubist fragmentation, was the inspiration for Dalí's ink and wash drawings from his early student days in Madrid (1922–3). The Mexican David Alfaro Siqueiros, future muralist, launched his manifesto 'Three Appeals for a Modern Direction: To the New Generation of American Painters and Sculptors' in the Barcelona review *Vida Americana* (May 1921, single issue). This praised cubism's 'magnificent geometrical structuring of form', but called on his fellow Americans to look for inspiration in the comparable constructive vitality of the ancient art of the Maya, Aztec, and Inca. The review *Amauta*, founded by Mariátegui in Lima in 1926, was enthusiastically received in Spain. *Amauta* was eclectic, with a simultaneously international and indigenist outlook; it was sympathetic to surrealism and to the movement's revolutionary politics. Also influential in Spain was the creationism of the Chilean poet Huidobro, which asserted the independence and the objective value of artistic creation.

The proliferation of literary and artistic reviews was one of the characteristics of the post-war avant-garde; they provided the site for international communication and cultural and political argument. Such reviews were an important forum through which movements like dada, surrealism, or De Stijl disseminated their ideas, and presented the works of their poets and artists. If a movement was exclusive and tightly controlled from the centre, like surrealism in Paris, it would run just one journal at a time: through the 1920s this was *La Révolution surréaliste* (1924–9), succeeded by *Le Surréalisme au service de la révolution* (1930–3). Two reviews with a particularly strong international influence during the 1920s were *L'Esprit nouveau*, run from Paris by Le Corbusier and Ozenfant and propagating a post-cubist machine aesthetic, and *Valori plastici* (1918–21), lavishly illustrated with metaphysical paintings and also works by Picasso in his new, classical figurative style. Although Spain shared the explosion in literary and artistic reviews, they tended to be more eclectic in character, keeping an independent position across a broad spectrum.

The magazines in Spain during the 1920s could be roughly divided into the conservative, and those open to new ideas. Of the former, the Barcelona-based *Gaseta de les Arts* covered both 'Art antic' and 'Art modern', a section run by Rafael Benet, whose preference for naturalism in painting and dislike of cubism, abstract art, and other more radical tendencies like surrealism led to polemical exchanges with Dalí and Gasch. Of the more avant-garde in disposition, there were the relatively short-lived Madrid-based *Horizonte* (1922–3), Lorca's Granadan *Gallo* (1928), and the more encyclopedic *La Gaceta Literaria*. The later *Gaceta de Arte* (1932–6), published in Tenerife, was the most consistently sympathetic to surrealism and helped organize the International Surrealist Exhibition in Tenerife in 1936, but several reviews in the 1920s commented upon and included work by surrealist writers. Of these the most interesting was probably the Sitges-based Catalan review *L'Amic de les Arts* (1926–9), where Dalí published his first texts, and through which his trajectory towards a closer alignment with surrealism can be traced.

From 1923 Dalí, like Miró before him, entered into an idiosyncratic engagement with cubism before finding, in 1929, the unique style of the hand-painted dream picture which was one of his particular contributions to surrealism. Unlike Miró—who had found his distinctive spontaneous manner, with simplified forms on a freely painted colour-field, through automatism—Dalí, after one or two experiments with automatic drawing around 1927, was to reject what he saw as its passivity in favour of a more psychoanalytically oriented investigation, which was importantly influenced by his interest in film and photography.

The Dalmau Gallery had been active since before the war in stimulating local artistic activity and bringing art from abroad, including cubism. In 1922 it put on a one-man exhibition of Francis Picabia, prominent and notorious in Paris dada, on the occasion of which André Breton gave his important lecture 'Caractères de l'évolution moderne et ce qui en participe'. This was the beginning of Breton's attempt to salvage something positive from the ashes of dada, even if that something was rooted in the most apparently negative and nihilistic. Breton named Duchamp and Picabia as two of the most important figures: not just in their art but in their life, in their 'marvellous instability' and their challenge to the boundaries between art and life. There were other direct interventions in Spain of dada and surrealism: in 1917, Picabia launched *391* in Barcelona, meeting-place then—like Zurich—of artist-refugees of the First World War; and later Breton, Aragon, and Crevel all lectured in Spain, but these were sporadic occurrences and did not contribute to establishing an outpost of either movement there.

Dalí was later to claim that when he arrived in Madrid in 1922 his fellow art students were totally unaware of cubism, and indeed had only just discovered impressionism. This may well have been the case at the Academy, but cubism was by then a topic among the avant-garde. *Horizonte* published an extract from a lecture by the Polish painter Marjan Paskiewicz on 'Some Problems in Modern Painting'. Picasso's cubism was, he argued, a form of pictorial creationism that signified the end of painting, in that painting is inseparably bound up with representation and his cubism, while full of extraordinary plastic inventions, was essentially abstract and decorative. The key issue was the question of abstraction/representation; Dalí clashed with one of his teachers over this, maintaining that cubism was still an art of representation. His various pictorial experiments of

1923–6 confirm this anecdote; they engage in turn with Barradas's vibrationism, the analytical cubism of Picasso and Braque, the 'post-cubist' purism of Le Corbusier, the metaphysical style of Carrà, de Chirico, and Morandi, and finally, following a visit to Picasso in Paris in 1926, produced a massive form of neo-cubist classicism.

Paskiewicz's lecture on modern art had taken place at the Residencia de Estudiantes, an élite student hall of residence with an impressive lecture programme of its own, which played a very significant role in the literary and artistic vanguard. Here Dalí met the poet Federico García Lorca, the future film-maker Buñuel, and a number of others such as Pepín Bello who formed a group which, although unnamed, was the crucible of a new spirit of subversion and irony and an anti-creationist aesthetic informing Dalí's unique brand of surrealism. Among their inventions was the idea of the *putrefact*: sentimental, bourgeois, and conformist, epitomized for Dalí by the poet Juan Ramón Jiménez. Surviving fragments of a collaborative *Book of Putrefaction* by Dalí and Lorca reveal a dada-like satirical use of ready-made imagery and some of the seeds of Dalí's revolutionary pictorial style of 1927. A recurring motif in these paintings was the decaying donkey (which was to make a dramatic appearance in the film *Un chien andalou*).

One of the distinctive features of many of the reviews, including even *Gaseta de les Arts*, was the emphasis placed on cinema. In 1927 Buñuel became the editor of the cinema section of the lively *La Gaceta Literaria* (which described itself as 'Iberian: American: international'); at the time living in Paris, where he reviewed for *Cahiers d'art*, he sent articles on American, French, Spanish, and Russian cinema. Buñuel was then working with the French film-maker Jean Epstein, who also contributed to *La Gaceta Literaria*. Here, in December 1927, Dalí published his article 'Art Cinema Anti-art Cinema', one of the first texts in which he elaborated his idea of the 'anti-artistic'. Inspired in part by Miró's call to 'assassinate painting', he attacks what he calls the 'anti-cinematic methods' of art cinema and praises the directness of anonymous 'anti-art cinema', which, 'far from any concept of grandiose sublimity, shows us, not the emotion which comes from artistic delirium, but the completely new poetic emotion of all the most humble and immediate facts, which were impossible to imagine or predict before cinema'. He criticizes Man Ray and Léger, although the best of the 'artistic' film-makers, for relying on the world of invented forms—for being too abstract and manipulative in their films: 'The world of cinema and that of painting are very different: indeed, the possibilities of photography and the cinema reside in that unlimited fantasy which is born of things themselves.'

Dalí and Buñuel preferred Hollywood comedy to most other films, and Keaton and Langdon to Chaplin. Even Soviet cinema, whose methods of montage he admired, was 'literary and tendentious', Buñuel told Dalí in an interview in *L'Amic de les Arts* (April 1929). The ground was thus laid for their extraordinary film *Un chien andalou*, shot and first shown in Paris in 1929. This used film techniques like montage (or *découpage*), dissolve, and superimposition to create a dream narrative.

It was through film, they held, that surrealism would best be embodied, and at the same time surrealism was the natural mode for film: a belief which, even if he broke formally with the surrealist movement in 1933, Buñuel held in practice for the rest of his life. When Dalí returned to painting after the making of *Un chien andalou*, it was to a style that was profoundly influenced by the objective precision and the possibilities of fantastic juxtapositions and analogies of film. Nothing, he knew, so subverts 'reality' as the real itself displaced and uprooted, fragmented and re-combined.

In March 1928 Dalí, Lluís Montanyà, and Sebastià Gasch published the 'Catalan anti-art manifesto', first in pamphlet form, and then in April in Lorca's *Gallo*. This confirmed them as 'the most interesting faction' not only of Catalan youth but of the Spanish vanguard as a whole. The 'Manifest groc' [Yellow Manifesto] was pointedly and aggressively eclectic. It appealed to the 'most diverse tendencies', in a dada spirit, to unite against the conventional artistic and the picturesque with a striking combination of the hygienic objectivity of Le Corbusier, Léger's machine aesthetic, the futurists' embrace of modern technology and speed, naming in addition dadas and surrealists like Arp, Tzara, Miró, and Breton. They were for cinema, jazz, sport, modern dance, the gramophone, modern art, etc. Their eclecticism performed a double function: it robustly asserted independence from existing movements and was in itself a form of identity. Moreover, it was launched as a Catalan manifesto, against such representatives of Catalan culture as *La Nova Revista*, but from an internationalist perspective.

Dalí, Gasch, and Montanyà were all prominent contributors to one of the most important Catalan reviews, *L'Amic de les Arts*, itself an ecelectic review with a special interest in Catalan culture and increasingly in surrealism. Its attitude to the visual arts was symptomatic: it included woodcuts by Miró's friend Ricart and by Canyelles, which mingled pastoral Mediterranean, religious, and modern imagery, examples of Catalan Gothic and Romanesque art, and paintings and drawings by a range of contemporary painters, from classical naturalists like Togores to the more vanguard like Ramón Gaya and the cubist Papiol. The September 1928 issue included drawings by Lorca, and paintings by Maruja Mallo, who had been a fellow student of Dalí's in Madrid. Her paintings at this time were a unique blend of purism and surrealism. In the October 1928 issue J. V. Foix, one of the editors of the review, published an article characteristic of *L'Amic*'s attitude to surrealism: he argued that it was part of a long tradition, instancing Blake and Lautréamont, and revealed a somewhat sceptical attitude to automatic writing, just as Dalí did, finally suggesting that Paris surrealism was just a local phenomenon.

In terms of contemporary art, the review was dominated by Dalí and Miró; it favoured the latter's most recent, spare, and almost abstract paintings, and followed Dalí's development through cubism, and the sexual-biomorphic works of 1928, to his form of surrealism. The final issue of *L'Amic de les Arts*, in March 1929, was a pyrrhic victory for Dalí and the anti-art wing. Quite different in appearance from its usual format, the issue was illustrated exclusively with photographs,

3 Maruja Mallo, *La verbena* [*Carnival*] (1927). The avant-garde design celebrates popular culture in both its modern urban and traditional forms (the fairground and the strong, active women with short hair and short skirts in the foreground, juxtaposed with religious images). Mallo collaborated with Giménez Caballero as designer for his 1930 avant-garde documentary film *Esencia de verbena* [*Essence of Carnival*], again celebrating carnival as a popular cultural form, and using montage—like Mallo's collage of disparate images, many of them in movement, in this painting—to convey the fragmentation and dizzying speed of modern urban life.

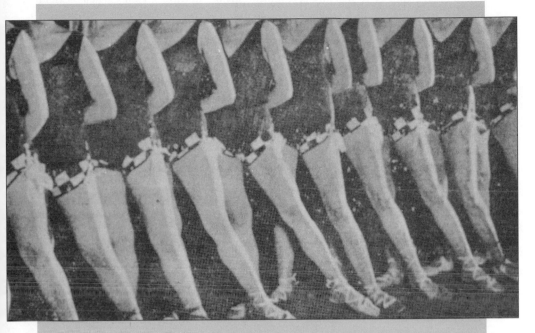

4 Photograph of chorus girls from the last 'anti-art' issue of *L'Amic de les Arts* (31 March 1929), accompanying an article by Sebastià Gasch, 'Vers la supressió de l'art' [Towards the Suppression of Art]. The caption reads: 'We propose these American "girls" and this anti-art magazine as a corrective to the almost narcotic artistic refinement of Diaghilev's ballets'. The serial image celebrates modernity by giving the female figures a mechanical quality (as Salaün's essay in this volume notes, the cabaret was a paradigmatic example of the shift from popular to mass culture); at the same time, this deprives them of any individualizing features or agency. Surrealism has been criticized for reducing woman to object status: here the cabaret dancers are presented as bodies without heads.

including cabaret girls, machinery, and the phallic thumbs of Dalí's article 'Liberation of the Fingers' which makes extensive use of Freudian ideas. Gasch, Montanyà, Foix, and Buñuel all contributed. A poem by Benjamin Péret, most admired of the surrealist poets, signals the close connection with French surrealism, but this issue is quite distinctive, with an aggressive, almost dada irrationality, and is in some ways closer to Georges Bataille's *Documents* than to *La Révolution surréaliste*. Perhaps only the rivalry between Bataille and Breton prevented Dalí, who required the platform the Paris group could give him as a painter, from forming closer ties with Bataille. By the time Dalí delivered his lecture on 'The Moral Position of Surrealism' at the Barcelona Ateneu on 22 March 1930 (published in *Helix*) he was not only the movement's acknowledged spokesperson in Spain, but had also already embedded himself at its Paris heart. The film he had made in 1929 with Luis Buñuel, *Un chien andalou*, the exhibition of paintings at the Goemans Gallery in November 1929, combined with his prolific writings and what Breton described as a permanent boiling of ideas, had rendered him indispensable to a movement in crisis. The 'heroic' period of surrealism, which since the first *Surrealist Manifesto* (1924) by André Breton had founded much of its creative activity on the idea of automatism, was more or less over; a number of artists and writers resented Breton's authoritarian attitude and several had begun to collaborate with Georges Bataille, whose review *Documents* became a rival to official surrealism; and there was internal conflict over the issue of political commitment, which came to a head in 1929. The arrival of the latest many-talented recruit was therefore of particular significance, and Dalí's lecture is revealing for several reasons, in terms of both his position and that of surrealism in Spain.

He starts by taking the line, laid down by Breton in the first and second *Surrealist Manifestos*, of rejecting the bourgeois social and moral order (ideas of family, nation, religion) and the value placed on logic and reason. He seeks to discredit conventional notions of reality with a campaign of demoralization and confusion, and the pursuit of irrationality. It is here that the originality of Dalí's contribution becomes apparent. He describes the paranoiac process he has invented, by means of which two or more images are seen in a single configuration by a process of imaginary construction akin to that of a real paranoid: a technique he characterized, in *La Femme visible* (1930), as active as opposed to the 'passivity' of automatism. This 'paranoiac critical' method was used in the paintings *Invisible Sleeper, Lion, Horse*, and *The Invisible Man*. Dalí stresses the importance of dreams, which, although already acknowledged as crucial to the surrealists' exploration of the unconscious, now found in his paintings a newly vivid representation. Dalí's familiarity with Freud, whose works were translated into Spanish from 1922, is evident, and he goes on to discuss other Freudian concepts: the opposition between the pleasure principle and the reality principle, and the death wish. Paintings such as *Lugubrious Game, Accommodations of Desire*, and *The Great Masturbator*, painted in Catalonia over the summer of 1929, were both his 'reception pieces' for surrealism and register in their imagery an enduring passion for the Catalan landscape. They fuse his debt to the surrealism of Ernst, Tanguy, Miró, and de Chirico with motifs that go back to the Residencia de Estudiantes collaborations with Lorca and to his fascination with film. It was Dalí's version of surrealism that, over the coming decade, was to fix that movement visually in the public domain.

Further reading
Breton, A., *Manifestos of Surrealism* (Ann Arbor, 1969).
Dalí, S., *The Secret Life of Salvador Dalí* (New York, 1942).
Ilie, P., *Documents of the Spanish Vanguard* (Chapel Hill, NC, 1969).
Morris, C. B., *Surrealism and Spain, 1920–1936* (Cambridge, 1972).
Raeburn, M. (ed.), *Salvador Dalí: The Early Years* (London, 1994).
Sanchez Vidal, A., *Buñuel, Lorca, Dalí: el enigma sin fin* (Barcelona, 1988).
Santos Toroella, R., *Dalí Residente* (Madrid, 1992).

The Musical Avant-garde: Modernity and Tradition

JULIAN WHITE

The late development in Spain of symphonic Romanticism and Romantic nationalism reflects the essentially anachronistic nature of early twentieth-century Spanish music. Its belated modernization after a long period of stagnation was largely due to the pioneering efforts of Felip Pedrell (1841–1922), the patriarch of the Spanish musical renaissance and mentor of two generations of Spanish composers. Pedrell exhorted Spanish composers to compose (in the words of Joaquín Turina) 'Spanish music geared to Europe', revealing the double heritage of Spain's popular and historical traditions on the one hand, whilst proposing a broadly European outlook on the other.

Pedrell's aesthetic principles—addressed specifically to the question of national opera in his 1891 manifesto 'Por nuestra música' [For a Music of our Own]—were clearly reflected in the music of his two early pupils—the pan-Hispanic nationalists Albéniz (1860–1909) and Granados (1867–1916)—who were the first Spanish composers to break with the distinctly parochial *zarzuela** tradition and gain international recognition in the twentieth century. However, their respective musical languages, whilst drawing on specifically Spanish models—those of the eighteenth-century *tonadilla* song tradition in Granados's idealized evocation of eighteenth-century Spain, *Goyescas* (1911), and the flamenco tradition in Albéniz's prolix *Iberia* (1906–9)—were clearly rooted in nineteenth-century European music and an anachronistic Romantic musical nationalism.

For the first truly contemporary and progressively nationalist musical language in Spain we have to wait until the works of a later Pedrell pupil, Manuel de Falla (1876–1946). Falla achieved a unique stylistic synthesis that encompassed French impressionism (*Nights in the Gardens of Spain*, 1916) and Stravinskian neo-classicism whilst referring to a wide range of Spanish folkloric and historical sources: flamenco *cante jondo* in the ballet *El amor brujo* of 1915; fifteenth-century Castilian folk-song, medieval liturgical music, Renaissance polyphony, eighteenth-century popular music in the *Harpsichord Concerto* of 1926; medieval canticles of Alphonso the Wise, Castilian Renaissance romances, sixteenth- and seventeenth-century court dances and Andalusian *pregones* [street cries] in *El retablo de Maese Pedro* (1923); and finally the traditions of the Calderonian *auto sacramental* [morality play] in the scenic cantata *Atlántida*. Falla succeeded in liberating Spanish music from the parochial, superficially picturesque style of much Spanish nationalist music, evolving a cosmopolitan musical style by delving into the totality of his national heritage and creatively transforming its basic musical materials.

Falla's achievement was built upon by the composers of the 'Generation of 1927', born around 1900 and beginning their careers in the early 1920s; particularly the Madrid-based Grupo de los Ocho who, under the aesthetic guidance of Adolfo Salazar (1890–1958), not only developed Falla's brand of Spanish neo-classicism, as in Ernesto Halffter's *Sinfonietta* of 1925, but also followed Falla's lead in forging friendships and collaborating with their literary contemporaries (Falla had collaborated with García Lorca in organising a *cante jondo* competition in 1922, and composed his *Soneto a Córdoba* for the 1927 tercentenary of the death of the poet Góngora, whose influence on Spanish avant-garde poetry was crucial; it was this commemoration which gave rise to the label '1927 Generation' applied to poets and composers alike).

But it is the career of the pioneering Catalan composer Roberto Gerhard (1896–1970)—retrospectively acknowledged as the principal member of the 1927 Generation and the most important Spanish composer since Falla—that perhaps best highlights the conflicting attitudes towards modernity and tradition during this period.

As one might expect from a pupil of Pedrell and Granados, it was the Spanish nationalist tradition that provided Gerhard with his initial musical idiom—his earliest compositions revealing the dual influence of Falla and Ravel. Highly self-critical, however, and acutely aware of the danger of succumbing to the kind of facile Spanish idiom associated with Albéniz, Granados, and early Falla, Gerhard embarked on an extended period of self-analysis. It was the *2 apunts* for piano (1921–2) and the *7 haiku* (1922) that signalled his first abrupt change in direction. Written following Gerhard's withdrawal from Spanish musical life, these aphoristic 'sketches' were symbolic landmarks not only in his own development but, retrospectively, in that of twentieth-century Spanish music. Their epigrammatic concision and proto-serial tendencies revealed a significant change in musical vocabulary (suggesting the influence of Schoenberg as well as Scriabin). Not surprisingly they were somewhat coolly received: Henri Collet, the French musicologist and champion of Spanish music in France, dismissed the *apunts* as 'torments like those of Scriabin, with an aggressive harmony', and hoped to see Gerhard return to his earlier style rather than moving 'into the worrying mazes of futuristic music'. Feeling the need to widen his artistic horizons, and having submitted the *Apunts* and *Haiku* to Schoenberg's scrutiny, an increasingly isolated Gerhard left Spain to study with Schoenberg in Vienna in order to receive the rigorous technical training unavailable in his homeland.

Gerhard returned to Spain in 1929 and immediately threw himself into the artistic, intellectual, and political activities of the Catalan avant-garde—promoting contemporary European music in general (and the music of Schoenberg in particular) in a series of challenging articles for the Catalan weekly *Mirador*. It was in its pages and those of the *Revista Musical Catalana* that a controversial polemic developed between the progressive young composer and the eminent Lluís Millet (1867–1941), following a concert (which almost ended in a riot) celebrating Gerhard's return to Catalonia and dedicated exclusively to his music. The *modernista* Millet—who in 1891 had co-founded, with Amadeu Vives, the cherished bourgeois Catalan choral organization the Orfeó Català—embodied the tradition-bound values of the Catalan cultural establishment. Gerhard's use of atonality was complete anathema to Millet, who encouraged the young composer to adopt a more 'popular' Catalan nationalist style. Gerhard, however, resolutely defended his aesthetic position. Whilst his post-Schoenberg 'Catalan' works hardly conformed to the conventional model of progressive modernism, and did in fact draw on Catalan folk music, folklore, and literature, it would be misleading to suggest that he capitulated to public taste. On the contrary, these works are particularly striking because of the way in which Gerhard adapted Schoenbergian 'modernist' techniques for his own ends as a means of breathing new life into Catalan musical traditions.

Further reading
Livermore, A., *A Short History of Spanish Music* (London, 1972).
Marco, T., *Spanish Music in the Twentieth Century* (Cambridge, Mass., 1993).
Martín Moreno, A., *Historia de la música española* (Madrid, 1993).
Ministerio de Cultura, *Poesía* 36–7 (1991) (Monograph on Falla).

JOSÉ ALVAREZ
JUNCO

SERGE SALAÜN

Popular Culture

Rural and Urban Popular Cultures
JOSÉ ALVAREZ JUNCO

The main difficulty involved in discussing this subject is its sheer diversity. For all that the political rhetoric of the period insistently referred to the 'pueblo español' [Spanish people], there were many *pueblos* and many cultures. This is especially true if we consider, in addition to regional differences, those between the different sectors and strata of labour.

There are, however, three essential statistics which provide a broad outline of the problem. In 1900, two-thirds of the Spanish working population was involved in agriculture (65 per cent in 1900, falling to 46 per cent by 1930). A similar proportion lived in rural or semi-rural population centres (those of under 10,000 inhabitants).[1] A slightly lower percentage was illiterate (59 per cent in 1900, 32 per cent in 1930).[2] A political consideration might be added to these demographic factors: this was a world excluded from the political sphere, from what Ortega called 'official Spain'.

Unwritten cultures and politically marginalized sectors of the population offer historians no recourse to their favourite sources: documents. Nowhere is this difficulty more evident than when we try to penetrate the closed world of rural Spain. There are of course literary accounts, for peasant life had from the middle of the nineteenth century appealed to *costumbrista** and 'realist' novelists, generally conservative in attitude (such as Fernán Caballero or Pereda). With the twentieth century, stories of a more modern style and a leftist tendency appeared (Blasco Ibáñez, Baroja). Both groups shared an image of the rural world as dormant, passive, and inward-looking, where the rhythm of life was punctuated by the tolling of church bells: a symbol of the parish priest's influence on rural inhabitants' consciences, but also of the continued operation of traditional agricultural cycles. In fact, it must be assumed that peasant culture reflected this rural world's economic stagnation: an agriculture based on time-honoured crops (vines, cereals, olives, pulses), with little need of skilled labour, using implements and techniques in some cases handed down from Roman times.

The absence of any widespread modernizing process in Spain left the rural world virtually untouched, an ocean with the industrial islands of Barcelona and Vizcaya standing out in its midst. The absence of a good communications system, preventing the emergence of a proper internal market, naturally created other handicaps. Traditional identities and links survived, and the new liberal-national identity, one of 'citizens' and 'Spaniards', was unable to impose itself on regional, local, and religious identities. As a result the revolutionary liberal measures, which had seen so much bloodshed, made little impact, while the administrative reforms providing a blueprint for a centralized state, made up of provinces administered by civil governors, and representing an 'indivisible national sovereignty' as in France, remained largely illusory. Those in government had no purchase on this rural world, and their reforms could not be implemented.

The political reforms of the nineteenth century did make some impact on rural life, but in a negative rather than a constructive sense. The large-scale disentailment [*desamortización*] and selling-off of common and private land, whose main purpose was to solve the problems of the Spanish treasury, left the coffers of local authorities bare. Total municipal income consisted of: 16 per cent land tax and a small percentage of industrial tax; 50 per cent of the revenue from identity documents (*cédulas personales*); 100 per cent of indirect taxes on alcohol and staple goods (food, drink, and fuel). The average income of a municipality with fewer than 2,300 inhabitants was calculated at some 5,900 pesetas per annum while its expenditure was around 9,040 pesetas per annum.[3] The centralized, conservative nature of oligarchic liberalism, which was in political control for most of the nineteenth century, also left the municipalities without the authority to elect their own officers, define their own functions, or find the resources to carry these out. Instead, as mere delegates of central government, the municipal authorities were lumbered with lesser administrative tasks, which were impossible to fulfil given the lack of resources and staff. The response of the provincial and central powers to this situation of perpetual and irredeemable illegality (i.e. the local bodies' inability to meet their statutory obligations) was one of tolerance in exchange for political favours. This was the source of *caciquismo,** which was perhaps the most notable characteristic of rural life in turn-of-the-century Spain.

Caciquismo—that inspired political term whose very utterance, as several commentators have pointed out, condemns a whole system—was not, as Costa or Azcárate maintained, a 'transformed feudalism'. *Caciquismo* was a new phenomenon, the product of the dual nature of both the socio-political structure and the system of social values. At its base was an overwhelmingly rural agrarian society, with all the fragmentation and local interests that entailed; onto this was grafted a still feeble centralized and urban political organization striving to impose itself. The *caciques* were not the established nobility, nor the *latifundistas* * nor the agrarian power bloc which had made its fortune with the land sales; they were a new political élite (albeit bound up with the old bloc), whose power derived not from its own resources but from its connections with the central state. These were individuals who exercised genuine political power over a locality both by controlling a network of patronage and through their ties (often informal, they did not necessarily hold political office) to local authorities and, through these, to a particular oligarch and a national political party. The key to their power was their role as conduits between the local community and national politics. Before the creation of the nineteenth-century centralized state, their existence would have been inconceivable.

Apart from the *caciques*, we know little regarding the repercussions of contemporary political skirmishes on rural life. Of course, the devastating effects of the Napoleonic invasion and war (1808–14), fought to a great extent in the countryside, were long-lasting. But to what extent did the subsequent attempts at political reform emanating from urban centres penetrate villages and rural communities? How were the ideologies and divisions of Moderates and Progressives translated into rural terms in the course of the nineteenth century? How was the triumph of a Riego or an Espartero (heroes of progressive liberalism) experienced in the first half of the century, or a government crisis around 1900? If we are to believe the poet Antonio Machado, who lived through this latter phase in Baeza (Andalusia), it was with scepticism and resignation, as if these political phenomena were akin to the weather or the human life-cycle—something beyond the control of those enduring them:

> Es de noche. Se platica
> al fondo de una botica.
> —Yo no sé,
> don José,
> cómo son los liberales
> tan perros, tan inmorales.
> —¡Oh, tranquilícese usté!
> Pasados los carnavales,
> vendrán los conservadores
> buenos administradores
> de su casa.
> Todo llega y todo pasa.

Nada eterno:
ni gobierno
que perdure,
ni mal que cien años dure.
—Tras estos tiempos vendrán
otros tiempos y otros y otros,
y lo mismo que nosotros,
otros se jorobarán.
Así es la vida, don Juan.
—Es verdad, así es la vida.
—La cebada está crecida.
—Con estas lluvias . . .

It's evening at the back of the chemist's shop and they're chatting. 'I don't know, don José, how those liberals can be so corrupt.' 'Oh, don't worry, my good friend. After the fiestas we'll have the conservatives back, and they know how to keep their house in order. And everything passes, you know: no government or misfortune lasts forever.' 'After these times are gone, there'll be other times and others after that, and others will moan like us. That's life, don Juan.' 'You're right, that's life.' 'The barley is growing nicely.' 'With all this rain . . .'[4]

But this was merely the beginning. It was specifically during the first third of the twentieth century that politics erupted in much of rural Spain. Not on account of new phenomena, but rather because the state's two traditional functions in relation to peasant communities were greatly intensified: on the one hand the extraction of resources (taxation for the Treasury and men for the army), due to regenerationist reform efforts and the Cuban and Moroccan wars; and, on the other, repression (the Civil Guard* for minor daily incidents, and the army in cases of exceptional strife), increasingly necessary because of the social tensions now extending into the countryside.

That the level of tension rose there is little doubt. Confronting the *cacique* and clerical control, there appeared for the first time such figures as the atheist doctor (depicted in Baroja); to be followed later by the syndicalist (as in Sender). There was a wave of strikes as early as 1904–5. Then, in the second decade of the century, the powerful FNAE (anarcho-syndicalist rural labour union which formally joined the CNT* in 1919) was the greatest source of CNT members who derived largely from Andalusia. Finally, during the Second Republic, the massive influx of the southern rural landless into the UGT* created a mood of radical expectation and confrontation in the countryside which was a crucial factor in the outbreak of the civil war. When and how this rural base passed across the political spectrum from Carlism* to anarchism—as it did in some regions—is perhaps one of the most fascinating areas of inquiry which the world of rural Spain in the period 1900–30 offers the historian interested in political culture.

When we come to urban culture, our starting-point also has to be fragmentation and diversity. First, because a slow and uneven industrialization process means we can talk of an industrial proletariat proper only in a few strongholds, such as the textile industry in Barcelona, the Basque iron industry, and Asturian mining. The rest of the 'working classes' were made up of a variety of artisanal trades and the service sector (maids and menservants above all). Politically, this diversity meant the predominance of anarchists in Barcelona or Cadiz, socialists in Bilbao or Madrid, and Catholics in Burgos or Valladolid (though there is no evident correlation between this political variety and different kinds of productive structure).

It is generally true that urban culture was becoming an increasingly important element in the life of the country as a whole. It was precisely in the first thirty years of the twentieth century that a great surge in the rate of urbanization occurred. This was especially true of the two major capitals, which had fewer than a quarter of a million inhabitants in the mid-nineteenth century, half a million in 1900, and about a million by the mid-1930s. While there were six cities with over 100,000 inhabitants at the beginning of the century, by 1930 these numbered eleven.

In the cities a whole new culture evolved. The historian is again tempted to begin with literary sources. However, direct descriptions taken from fiction prove particularly deceptive in this case. The *zarzuela*,* and popular entertainment in general, established a series of idealized and distorted 'popular characters', products of the imagination of middle-class writers (though there is always the question of whether this idealized image was then adopted by the object of the idealization—i.e. the popular classes—who might have gone on to imitate the stereotype).

Another literary source of greater interest is the novella. This did not attempt to portray the life of the popular classes but was aimed at such a readership. Widely distributed and cheap, these novellas were often published in weekly instalments. There were long runs, for example in collections such as *La Novela Ideal*, *La Novela Libre*, *El Cuento Semanal*, or *Los Contemporáneos*. This was a widespread phenomenon, with production on an industrial scale—one source traces up to 2,600 titles, estimating that the real figure would have been double this[5]— which reflects, at the very least, the decrease in illiteracy in the urban context. Alongside these texts there coexisted literary remnants from earlier times (often branded as subliterature), such as the *romances de ciego* (ballads traditionally sold by the blind), *pliegos de cordel* (broadsheets), and *aleluyas* (strip cartoons with words in verse, frequently satirical), all of which still enjoyed a considerable circulation in working-class districts in 1930s Spain.

As regards unwritten cultural forms, all the information on fiestas and other uses of leisure time confirms the persistence of an intense tavern life (cafés were for the middle classes), and the popularity of bullfighting, which became a mass entertainment at this time, built around the rivalry between Joselito and Belmonte. But it is also at this time that other mass sports/entertainments emerge; particularly football, which aroused passions by the end of the 1920s.

Sex and family life are areas which it is more difficult for the historian to open up. We know, by means of overall figures from medical and health records, that

La **Novela Semanal**

El artículo 438
— por Carmen de
Burgos "Colombine"
Precio 25 cts.—

LA NOVELA DE HOY

30
ctms

Devoradora

POR JUAN FERRAGUT

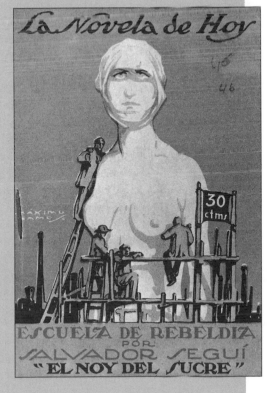

La Novela de Hoy

30
ctms

ESCUELA DE REBELDIA
POR
SALVADOR SEGUÍ
"EL NOY DEL SUCRE"

5 *a, b, c* Covers of three popular novellas published in small-format, cheap editions, (*a*) by Carmen de Burgos (1 October 1921), in the series *The Weekly Novel*; (*b*) by Juan Ferragut (11 July 1924), and (*c*) by Salvador Seguí (30 March 1923), both in the series *The Novel Today*. The title of Carmen de Burgos's novella refers to the article of the Penal Code sanctioning violence against an adulterous wife by her husband: the article (which prefaces her text) states that in such cases the punishment for murder shall be exile, while attempted murder or causing bodily injury are not punishable offences. (See p.67 for Carmen de Burgos's feminism.) The cover and title (*The Devouring Woman*) of Ferragut's novel evoke an image of modern woman as castrating vamp. Seguí, known by the nickname 'El Noi del Sucre' [Sugar Boy], was one of the top CNT* leaders in Barcelona, assassinated—like his protagonist, as the series editor's prologue points out—by hired killers on 10 March 1923, three weeks before the publication of this novella (subtitled *Story of a Trade Unionist*). All three novellas make use of the conventions of popular melodrama.

female prostitution remained widespread, as a generalized means of sexual initiation for males and an escape from, or tolerated addition to, later married life. But we have very little detailed information here. Nor do we know much about the lived experience of family life. Here, the occasional autobiography reveals grim scenes of traditional patriarchal tyranny, often expressed through violence towards women and, of course, towards sons whose bringing-up was geared to their being 'tamed'.[6] The 'new woman', who wore short skirts, and smoked, and danced the charleston, began to be seen among the urban middle classes, but the concept did not extend to the popular masses.

But there were changes. The most obvious was the widespread secularization of urban Spain, seen clearly in the figures for Sunday and Easter mass attendance. Although these were the years in which the Catholic Church became aware of its loss of influence in Spanish society and made an effort to organize a Catholic movement to form opinion, this was aimed at the middle classes (Acción Católica) or small rural landowners in the north of the country. Scarcely any efforts of this type—excepting worthy attempts such as Father Manjón's schools—were aimed at the masses. The abandonment of religious practice, and even of support for religious festivals of a folkloric and traditional nature, is particularly noticeable among men, who are also the ones occupying the public sphere and engaging in political action. Women, marginalized from this space and largely inactive politically, maintained closer links with the Church. This would seem to suggest a direct connection between secularization and political awareness and action. It is precisely in an urban milieu and in the first third of the twentieth century that political parties in Spain for the first time achieved mass levels of support (e.g. Blasco Ibáñez's Valencia, Lerroux's Barcelona, socialist Bilbao, anarchist Gijón, and many other cities and political tendencies during the Second Republic).

Apart from the decline of religious observance, it is difficult to know whether politicization altered behaviour patterns in any other way. Historians of workers' movements have, with unseemly haste, equated the institutional and ideological expressions of these politicized groups with an expression of the 'popular'. But, unfortunately, their representativity is highly questionable. To begin with, as the politicized themselves acknowledged remorsefully, they constituted only a small minority. The vast mass of working men and women did not embrace a fully-fledged political militancy nor belong to any union. The casas del pueblo*, worker ateneos, and Spanish rationalist schools were not comparable, in terms of their influence, to the party culture of the SPD in Germany, with its millions of 'cradle to grave' members. Nor was there political upheaval in Spain with a comparable impact to that of the First World War on the masses elsewhere in Europe. Only the Second Republic, and of course the civil war, would take politics to every corner of the country.

The question of the extent to which workers' movements were representative is, however, not so clear-cut. In a society accustomed to control by social and spiritual hierarchies, the fact that different cultural expressions appeared, no matter how small-scale, could provide enormous inspiration, through their example and their unexpected subversive effects, as with the innocent provision of fiction, which workers' organizations and centres distributed in quantities far superior to their own political propaganda. This indicates that the influence of politicized worker movements is hard to measure, and also that it was probably greater than their limited sphere of direct control might suggest. Despite being unable to achieve stable levels of high membership, they did after all achieve high levels of support in their most spectacular protest actions (e.g. the Tragic Week of 1909, the general strike of 1917, and the Canadiense strike in 1919).

Inevitably, these new political messages were interpreted in terms of old religious and redemptive mental schema. Even anarchists and socialists combined formal rationalism with evident millenarian remnants, expressed in the reduction of political conflicts to Manichaean categories, in the centrality of ethical judgments (formulated in traditional Christian terms),[7] and in an apocalyptic-redemptive message projected onto a *pueblo* seen as a Messianic force. This explosive combination explains some of the characteristics of the anticlerical outbursts of 1909 and 1931, and doubtless also those of the civil war.

Notes

1 27% in municipalities which were entirely rural, with fewer than 2,000 inhabitants (20.5% in 1930), and another 40% in centres with fewer than 10,000 inhabitants. Of the remaining 33%, some 6.2% lived in the six Spanish cities with more than 100,000 inhabitants each. The percentage of those living in rural or semi-rural areas would fall to 57% by 1930. See V. Pérez Moreda, 'Spain's Demographic Modernization, 1800–1930', in N. Sánchez-Albornoz (ed.), *The Economic Modernization of Spain 1830–1930* (New York, 1987), 30 ff.

2 According to M. Vilanova's thorough study in *Atlas del analfabetismo en España, de 1887 a 1981* (Madrid, 1982), 167; other sources give higher figures.

3 B. Vera y Casado, *La administración local* (Madrid, 1893).

4 'Poema de un día: meditaciones rurales' [A Day in Verse: Rural Reflections] from *Campos de Castilla*. A great deal is lost in translation, since much of the meaning is conveyed through the poem's rhythm and use of assonance.

5 J. I. Ferreras, *La novela en el siglo XX (hasta 1939)* (Madrid, 1978), 127–8. See also M. Bouché, B. Magnien, and S. Salaün, 'Les Collections populaires de contes et nouvelles au début du XXe siècle: *El Cuento Semanal*, 1907–1912'; and L. Urrutia, 'Una colección nueva: *Los Contemporáneos*, una revista de 1909 a 1912'; both in *Les Productions populaires en Espagne, 1850–1920* (Paris, 1986), 259–75 and 277–308.

6 See examples cited by A. Shubert, *A Social History of Modern Spain* (London, 1990), 134–44; for Lerroux's childhood see J. Alvarez Junco, *El emperador del paralelo* (Madrid, 1990), ch. 1.

7 See J. Alvarez Junco, 'La subcultura anarquista en España; racionalismo y populismo', in *Culturas populares: diferencias, divergencias, conflictos* (Madrid, 1986), 197–208; cf. by the same author, 'La cultura marxista en el movimiento obrero', in R. Reyes (ed.), *Cien años después de Marx* (Madrid, 1986), 469–76.

Further reading

Andrés Gallego, J., 'La iglesia y la cuestión social: replanteamiento', in *Estudios sobre la Iglesia española contemporánea* (El Escorial, 1979).

Arbeloa, V. M., *Aquella España católica* (Salamanca, 1975).

Casa de Velázquez/Universidad Complutense, *Culturas populares: diferencias, divergencias, conflictos* (Madrid, 1986).

Guereña, J. L., and Tiana, A., *Clases populares, cultura, educación: siglos XIX–XX* (Casa de Velázquez/UNED, Madrid, 1989).

Juliá, S., *Madrid, 1931–1934: de la fiesta popular a la lucha de clases* (Madrid, 1984).

Mainer, J. C., 'Notas sobre la lectura obrera en España (1890–1930)', in A. Balcells (ed.), *Teoría y práctica del movimiento obrero en España, 1900–1936* (Valencia, 1977), 173–239.

Monguió, L., 'Una biblioteca obrera madrileña en 1912–13', *Bulletin Hispanique*, 77 (1975), 154–73.

Pitt-Rivers, J., *The People of the Sierra* (London, 1971).

Centre National de la Recherche Scientifique, *Les Productions populaires en Espagne, 1850–1920* (Bordeaux, 1986).

Romero-Maura, J., '*La rosa de fuego*': el obrerismo barcelonés de 1899 a 1909 (Barcelona, 1975).

Sánchez-Albornoz, N., *Españoles hacia América: la emigración en masa* (Madrid, 1988).

Santonja, G., *La novela revolucionaria del quiosco 1905–1939* (Madrid, 1993).

Shubert, A., *A Social History of Modern Spain* (London, 1990).

Tuñón de Lara, M., and Botrel, J. F., *Movimiento obrero, política y literatura en la España contemporánea* (Madrid, 1974).

On caciquismo

Costa, J., *Oligarquía y caciquismo como la forma actual de gobierno en España: urgencia y modo de cambiarla* (the classic critique, first published in 1902. See edition published by Ediciones de la Revista de Trabajo (Madrid, 1975), with introd. by A. Orti.).

Tusell, J., 'The Functioning of the *Cacique* System in Andalusia, 1890–1931', in S. G. Payne (ed.), *Politics and Society in Twentieth-Century Spain* (New York, 1976), 1–28.

Varela Ortega, J., *Los amigos políticos (partidos, elecciones, y caciquismo en la Restauración, 1875–1900)* (Madrid, 1977).

The *Cuplé*: Modernity and Mass Culture

SERGE SALAÜN

The *cuplé* is a compendium of the contradictions that make up Spanish modernity, harnessing tradition and innovation, *casticismo** and cosmopolitanism, though it has always been seen as a specifically national genre.

The word first appears in *zarzuela** librettos around 1880—its spelling *couplet* making clear its debt to the French cabaret tradition—to refer to a *cantable* or song alternating with speech: these *couplets* had two or three verses and a refrain, with an average length of three minutes. Twentieth-century *cupletistas* or singers of *cuplés*—female till 1920 when a few male artistes appear, disguised first as women, then as Argentine tango singers—drew on the vast repertoire of the *zarzuela* [operetta] and *tonadilla* [lightweight song for theatrical performance, popular in the eighteenth century]. In effect, the *cuplé*—in its original theatrical (i.e. *zarzuela*) form and in its later music-hall varieties—continued both a popular tradition (rural, folkloric) and a learned tradition (the *tonadilla*), which explains why it caught on throughout the Peninsula at a time when Spain was embarking on a process of demographic, economic, and social change.

The virtual stage monopoly of the *zarzuela* till around 1900 created a resistance to foreign cultural forms, and the music-hall was notoriously slow to establish itself in Spain. Paradoxically, the *zarzuela* would end up facilitating the assimilation process, succumbing to the latest European and American musical crazes: the waltz, the polka, the mazurka, and the *chotis* (that ultra-*castizo** dance of the Madrid lower classes whose name is a corruption of 'Scottish'), all of them foreign imports.

The appearance in Spain of the modern *cuplé*—that is, as a free-standing, single-performer mode of entertainment—is traditionally dated at 1893, with a German singer Augusta Bergés and a song 'La pulga' [The Flea] based on an Italian or French original, which established itself in the repertoire of dozens of *cupletistas* till the late 1920s. It was only after 1900 that the music-hall (or *Varietés* as it was often called in Spain) began to flourish, with the creation of new venues more suitable than the traditional theatre; *Salones* of every possible denomination ('Blue', 'Red') sprang up everywhere. A reliable source gives a figure of 6,000 such cabarets in Spain in 1912, from the most chic (the *Salón Japonés* in Madrid) to the most disreputable. The highest concentration was in Madrid and especially Barcelona, but the phenomenon was nation-wide, including isolated villages. The expansion would continue up to the civil war. The *cuplé* responded to the cultural demands of the rapidly growing towns and cities, whose populations were receptive to a form of urban acculturation that was artistically and economically accessible (cafés are much cheaper than theatres).

From 1900 to 1912, the *cuplé* was a form of entertainment 'for men only', as posters at the door put it. The singers concentrated on witty, 'naughty' songs, full of *double entendre*, on the lines of 'La pulga'. Andalusian flamenco-based song also had its public and always would; some singers—Amalia Molina, Pastora Imperio—specialized in this genre but it figured in every singer's repertoire. The growing vogue for the *cuplé* allowed thousands of *cupletistas* to make a living by combining singing with more or less concealed sexual favours (if not outright prostitution), and also helped institutionalize a star system (La Fornarina popularized the term *vedette* around 1912), with stars with turbulent lives, rags-to-riches careers, exotic love affairs, and colossal fortunes which featured prominently in the specialized press, also expanding rapidly at this time. The songs became incredibly well known, invading not only the stage but every area of public and private life; one has to remember that the idea of copyright was not yet firmly established and singers poached material from each other freely. The most widely imitated stars were the 'naughty' ones like La Bella Dorita or Julita Fons, but 'dramatic' singers, such as Pastora Imperio, La Fornarina, or Amalia Isaura, were also hugely popular with songs like 'Luis', 'Clavelitos', 'El Polichinela', 'Ven y ven', etc.

After 1912, the *cuplé* as a song form and as a profession underwent marked changes. The comic-erotic strand did not die out (it remained a staple with provincial and lower-class audiences), but the sentimental *cuplé* became the order of the day: the moral order campaigns and the Leagues of Virtue had found a receptive

6 *a, b* Contemporary postcards of the *cupletistas* [cabaret singers] (*a*) La Fornarina and (*b*) Pastora Imperio. La Fornarina is depicted as the modern liberated women, smoking seductively. Pastora Imperio is portrayed against a painted backcloth, in exotic theatrical costume, illustrating the evolution of the *cuplé* into a self-contained dramatic performance. The manufacture of such postcards (enormously popular in the early decades of the twentieth century) shows the development of song into a mass cultural form, propagated by an organized publicity machinery through the promotion of a star system.

ear in the Canalejas government. The change is illustrated by the singer La Goya: less provocatively dressed (the 'naughty' *cuplé* went with a suggestive *déshabillé* and curvaceous forms), she revolutionized performance styles by emphasizing expressiveness, making the *cuplé* into a total art-form, a small one-act play. The triumph of the 'respectable' *cuplé* matches the profession's economic transformation as it becomes institutionalized on a national and international scale: directors, managers, agents with world-wide contacts are all signs of the commercialization of the performing arts, not forgetting the Society of Authors, founded in 1900, whose legal and administrative role was crucial. Raquel Meller is a good example here: a humble seamstress, in 1907 she embarked on a meteoric career that took her to Paris and New York, amassing an equally meteoric fortune. It was not her voice or looks that made her remarkable, but her performances: every song had its own costume, choreography, even lighting and décor. The success of numbers like 'La violetera' or 'El relicario', the two high points of her stage act, speaks to her talents as an actress-singer.

Between 1912 and 1925, the *cuplé* becomes a high-quality form of single-performer entertainment in cabarets and even in the theatre, where singers were billed for whole sessions. This conquest of respectability also permitted the *cuplé* to reach wider audiences: the middle classes and women. The *cuplé* was becoming a national cultural form, suitable for all audiences; in other words, a mass-marketable commodity.

The massification process represented by the *cuplé* is explained by commercial factors but also by its ability to absorb and disseminate a wide range of modern forms. The successive fashions over the period 1900–30 for North American rhythms (cake-walk, foxtrot, charleston, and jazz at the end of the First World War) and Latin American dance and song (rumba, tango, mambo, bolero), all coexisting with the perennial native Andalusian tradition, helped create a mental shift and facilitated the assimilation of foreign models (largely Anglo-Saxon). As for content, the *cuplé* never went in for social or even 'realistic' subject-matter; as time progressed, it became increasingly restricted to the sentimental conventions of passionate or tragic love. Another vein, the comic, continued the *zarzuela* tradition of word-play ('Las chicas del 17', 'Tadeo') on superficially modern topics (the motor car, sport, elevators).

Although the picture it gives of society is schematic, the *cuplé* reflects and indeed contributes to the technical and industrial modernization that typifies mass culture. As a form of entertainment and part of the collective memory, it is closely linked with the development of cinema (even before the advent of sound); its links with the 'talkies' are even stronger, with singers (Raquel Meller, Imperio Argentina) becoming film stars. The gradual development of radio from 1924 also owed much to song; while the introduction of records, the gramophone, and the microphone was entirely dependent on it. In turn these advances, still in their early stages, significantly modified the nature, consumption, and diffusion of oral culture, of which song was now a central element. The *cuplé* represents the preindustrial phase of mass culture, a crucial stage in the technological, commercial, and cultural changes that would culminate in the 1950s and 1960s.

After 1925, the *cuplé* reverted to the big stage, with the vogue for spectacular revues (the *revista de visualidad*), with semi-clad chorus girls and glamorous stars. Under the Republic, American influence increased its hold with Broadway-type musicals of an overtly titillating nature (*¡Cómo están las mujeres!, Las Leandras*).

After the civil war, the *cuplé* continued in the guise of 'Spanish song', with the same composers (Padilla), the same songwriters (León, Valerio, Quiroga), and sometimes the same singers (Celia Gámez, Conchita Piquer). The conventional, sentimental, patriotic tone reflects the type of cultural alienation favoured by the regime.

The *cuplé* corresponds to a key period—from 1900 to 1936—in the cultural history of Spain; it illustrates the effects on production and consumption of a new massification and industrialization, while remaining part of the collective and individual memory, in a complex dialectic of escapism and pleasure.

Further reading
Salaün, S., *El cuplé* (Madrid, 1990).
—— and **Serrano, C.** (eds.), *1900 en España* (Madrid, 1991) (in addition to the performing arts, this contains excellent essays on the press and publishing, education, and town planning at the turn of the century).

Part II

The Failure of Democratic Modernization 1931–1939

To articulate the past historically [. . .] means to
seize hold of a memory as it flashes up in a
moment of danger.   (Walter Benjamin)

Editors' Introduction

The 1930s was a period of increasing polarization but it is important to recognize that many cultural issues cut across political
and class divisions. Positions on gender, religion, and regional
autonomy did not correspond in a straightforward manner to
political or class allegiances: there were liberal Catholics, at
least to start with; bourgeois and working-class Catalan nationalists; clerical-conservative Basque nationalists who opposed
Franco's 'Crusade', and the right mobilized women to protest
against the Republic, while anarchist attempts to liberate women
did not always question traditional definitions of femininity,
and not all socialists supported giving the vote to women.

   This is a period when attempts at political reform, and ensuing civil war, initiated a radical restructuring of the public/
private division (readily measurable via women's experience), and
of the relations between centre and periphery. Both processes
were symptomatic of an underlying state crisis encompassing
both the means of capitalist production and the post-imperial
political legitimacy of Spain's national élite. Like many of the
other nation-state crises in 1930s Europe, its political, social,

and cultural materialization was closely bound up with the acuteness of international economic depression which, everywhere, had crystallized anxieties over the acceleration of modernity. But whereas élites elsewhere, with a greater degree of internal cohesion and in control of more powerful state apparatuses (especially in Germany), rapidly found authoritarian solutions to social situations perceived to threaten their hegemony, in the Spanish case the specific confluence of a relatively backward industry and weak central state, combined with a powerful military élite but an oligarchy* in political crisis and a highly fragmented bourgeoisie, brought about a temporary equilibrium of social forces which was the pre-condition for the outbreak of civil war (as opposed to the 'latent' varieties of civil war in post-1918 Italy or Weimar Germany). The ultimate stake in the civil war was control of the process of future change in order to determine how the dual crisis of the Spanish state would be solved. Crucially here, Republicans and Nationalists adhered to deeply antagonistic concepts of the nation and culture.

The tolerance or otherwise of cultural pluralism became literally a matter of life or death, as the Nationalists took up arms against the democratically elected Popular Front government in a bid to impose a monolithic model of culture, thereby removing the threat to a stable social hierarchy which the disruptive 'differences' produced by modernity had posed. What unified the Nationalists—initially a collection of right-wing factions—was a brand of ultra-traditionalist (Tridentine) Catholicism, profoundly hostile to difference and significantly referred to by one of its leading ideologues as Spain's 'true fascism'. Nationalist victory in the civil war would permit the implementation of one very particular kind of solution to Spain's regional crisis of modernity. As the defeated Republican project had envisioned, this too saw the extension of state power. But whereas the Republic—heir to the Enlightenment tradition—sought to democratize power in order to spread the cost of change, the dictatorship's object was to contain and neutralize the socially revolutionary potential present in Spain's late and uneven modernity (proof of which was found in the eruption of civil war) by imposing an authoritarian cultural/social framework in which economic change could safely be pursued.

The Republican centre-left parliamentary alliance which sustained the Popular Frontist war effort shared a fundamentally liberal humanist respect for individual rights and freedoms. This meant its reform programme also continued the liberal intellectual tradition of imposing reform from above: it was this top-down approach (in which liberal and stalinist approaches dovetailed), as well as the Church's enforcement of a single cultural model, that was resisted by the anarchists with their stress on grass-roots mutual aid and self-empowerment.

The political issues that destroyed the Republic—as well as those for which the civil war was fought—were, then, as much about conflicting cultural models as about conflicting economic ones. Indeed the two were inseparable. The Republic has been called 'the intellectuals' Republic', and the Spanish civil war 'the poets' war': education was at the centre of the Republican programme as the fundamental means of creating a civil society, by instilling the 'civilizing' values of liberalism's modernizing project into the populace as a whole. For the anarchists, therefore, liberation had to come through self-education, since the liberal state's efforts, no less than the Church's, were an explicit means of social control. Viewed with hindsight, in the knowledge of how many young cultures were stifled by Francoism, the Republican and anarchist faith in the power of culture to enlighten and transform is profoundly moving. The Republican case is, however, a tragic textbook example of the contradictions inherent in any cultural project based on the desire to empower the masses through culture without relinquishing cultural control. Neither the tensions between élite and popular culture, nor those between modernity's patrician reform and the politics of empowerment, were ever satisfactorily resolved. In the end, though, it was not these contradictions that defeated the Republic (though they undoubtedly sapped its wartime resilience) but Nationalist guns. Ironically, the Nationalists were right in foreseeing—in a way that many Republicans failed to do—that the logical consequence of giving the masses access to culture was popular power. The Spanish civil war was a time when, as has been said, 'culture mattered', for rarely have the links between culture and power been made more evident.

7

Sexual Politics

HELEN GRAHAM

RICHARD
CLEMINSON

Women and Social Change

HELEN GRAHAM

The birth of the Second Republic in Spain was both a symptom of and response to a national political crisis which mirrored the Europe-wide crisis of the 1930s. This larger crisis had been gathering pace since the turn of the century, being rooted in the clash between different ways of life: urban with rural, religious with secular, fixed hierarchies against the rise of new social movements (organized labour in particular). In sum, tradition was coming up against the social and cultural change deriving from a recognizable process of industrialization and urbanization, and the expansion of state power (i.e. the public sphere) occurring at differential rates across the European continent. The process of change had speeded up noticeably by the second decade of the century, social and cultural conflict being further intensified by the 1914–18 war experience and its outcome. European social, political, and cultural crisis was finally precipitated by the Wall Street crash (1929) and the ensuing world-wide economic depression. The capitalist system in crisis saw the collapse of pluralist democratic regimes across the continent and their replacement by fascist, quasi-fascist, or authoritarian dictatorships.

Whatever their political varieties, these regimes—in Italy,

Portugal, Germany, Austria, etc.—bore common social and cultural traits. Paralleling the attempts at political monolithicity, social and cultural conservatism was also in the ascendant. There was a marked hostility to all forms of experimental cultural expression, an (often literal) proscription of the avant-garde and of all social and artistic forms which challenged the established order. To understand the popular appeal of this conservatism (as opposed to its usefulness to political and economic élites), its attractiveness needs to be seen as a product of anxiety. Like the search for a political messiah, so the attraction of traditional cultural forms/patterns lay in the fact that, while scarcely amounting to a 'solution' to the crisis, for many people their familiarity did offer a comforting way of living through it. It is not unsurprising, but still highly significant, that the central impulse of this social-cultural conservatism was often directed at reimposing or reinforcing ultra-traditional gender roles on women—the social (and in particular reproductive) policies of Italian and German fascism being just the most widely known examples. Whether overtly articulated or not, the reinforcing of traditional gender divisions was clearly felt to be one of the keys to stabilizing societies in flux, along socially and economically traditional lines.

This is a pattern we shall see developing later in Spain too. However, at the outset of the 1930s, in spite of an inauspicious international environment, Spain was steering markedly against this rightward European drift. National political developments—namely the collapse of the Primo de Rivera military dictatorship (1923–30) and the consequent political disarray on the right—allowed a progressive democratic Republic to be born.

The motor of the new regime was provided by a reforming republican ideology, borne by the numerically exiguous liberal sectors of Spain's urban lower middle classes and the social democratic current within the Spanish Socialist Party (PSOE*), backed by the electoral muscle of its near million-strong trade union movement, the UGT.* The Republic's brief was to modernize Spain politically, economically, socially, and culturally: its tool would be the state, whose power would necessarily be extended. In 1931 this rationale took shape first in the new Constitution (December 1931), which borrowed ideas from those of previous radical republican experiments (Mexico 1917, Weimar Germany 1919), and then in a series of legislative reforms. Land and army reforms were designed to shift the balance of socio-economic power away from the oligarchy* and to build up the resources and political authority of the new state. The Republic's social/labour and educational/cultural reforms, including its controversial anticlerical legislation, were designed, in the immediate term, to create a social support base for the new regime and in the long term to forge a new mentality as a stable basis for the 'Republican nation'. But in fact quite often the extension of state power had an alienating effect among the popular classes, as we shall see in specific relation to some sectors of Spanish women. Ultimately, the Republic's blueprint for reform would be shipwrecked both by the right's political mobilization and by the consequences of economic crisis reaching Spain. Recession facilitated the conservatives' task, because in reducing the progressive Republic's economic room for manœuvre, it prevented it from significantly improving the lot of the socially and economically dispossessed. Without this, the Republic could not achieve the broadening of its support base crucial to consolidation. Instead the poor, unemployed, and unskilled would look increasingly to the extraparliamentary left, predominantly the anarcho-syndicalist movement (CNT*), which articulated a radical critique of the existing order that directly addressed their plight. In the process, the Republic was destabilized.

In 1931, however, optimism was to the fore, as the Republic sought to initiate social change via constitutional and legislative reform. An important part of this focused on women. In an astonishingly short time, in one of Europe's most backward societies and polities women became the *legal* equals of men. Under the December 1931 Constitution, they could vote and stand for parliament (the legal majority being set at 23 years for both men and women).[1] In addition, a package of progressive social reforms, including one of the most liberal divorce laws in existence (February 1932), significantly enhanced their civil and employment rights. For the first time women could legally act as witnesses and guardians, sign contracts, and administer estates. Nor were employers formally able to dismiss women merely because they had married. Yet formal equality was, inevitably, to be a far cry from real, lived equality, as we shall see.

The first point to note, however, is that women's formal political emancipation was being implemented in 1931 'from above' in order to deliver the principles of republicanism rather than achieved 'from below' by dint of women's grass-roots mobilization. The lack of this is scarcely surprising if we recall Spain was an unevenly developed country—its urban and industrial nucleii rising like islands out of a sea of rural backwardness. In consequence, until the second decade of the twentieth century there were relatively low levels of popular political mobilization *per se*, with structured labour organization being largely confined to the developed urban, industrial areas and to a male constituency. Women industrial workers, a small percentage of the total industrial labour force (though larger than the recorded statistics suggest), had begun to come together by the end of the nineteenth century to address their specific needs.[2] But women's unionization in urban Spain came up against the familiar obstacles. They were a fragmented labour force and thus difficult to organize (e.g. home workers, those in small 'sweated labour' units typical of the Catalan textile industry, domestic servants). Female workers had less time because of the 'double burden' of employment outside the home and domestic labour (to which unmarried daughters as well as wives were obligated). Female socialization too—including very low levels of education (often illiteracy) and cultural expectations—meant women so often excluded themselves. But even when urban working women did join unions, they faced incomprehension, when not downright hostility, from the male-dominated bureaucracy and/or membership (this was as true in the CNT as in the UGT). In spite of anarcho-syndicalism's abstract espousal of female equality the daily practice

of the vast majority of male *cenetistas* was as patriarchal as their non-libertarian*
counterparts: the anarchist utopia stopped at the front door. While from 1900 on
women's presence inside both wings of the labour movement did increase in
relative terms, only in exceptional cases did women achieve leadership positions
where they could influence policy or act on their own initiative. For most women
the labour sphere re-presented the subordinate role 'natural' to their gender which
they occupied in society at large. 'Women's "otherness" was as encoded into the
programs of socialist oppositional groups as it was into the policies of the capitalist
regimes they opposed.'[3]

The bulk of Spain's population was, however, not urban but rurally based,
living in what is termed 'la España profunda' [deep or submerged Spain]—in
small, atomized units. Willingly or otherwise they were confined, by custom,
culture, and/or material necessity, within a traditional social order whose relative
stability until the 1930s could be measured, not by the absence of social conflict
(e.g. landed versus landless) but by the relative ease with which this could be
contained within the locality (usually by the use of the Civil Guard*). The various
female constituencies within rural Spain were further even from systematic political mobilization than their male counterparts—whether landless peasants, tenant
farmers, estate bailiffs, shopkeepers, etc. Among male labourers and smallholders,
illiteracy was high. Among their wives, daughters, and sisters it was higher still.

Coexisting with these low levels of formally structured female political organization, however, and extending from the cities to provincial towns—and sometimes to smaller conurbations—there was a long tradition of 'spontaneous' female
mobilization across Spain which both expressed and tried to solve specific economic grievances and needs at times of acute social turmoil—for example in 1898
or 1909 when women initiated food riots or took the lead in peace demonstrations, rent strikes, or other sorts of public protests. Male labour leaders were
deeply disparaging of this practice as 'chaotic' and 'non-political'. But in fact, this
kind of action obeyed a rigorous logic. Women were taking action to alleviate
rapidly problems and needs which directly affected the quality of life in their
families and communities—the space to which the sexual division of labour had
largely confined them. Female direct action was conditioned, then, by their exclusion from other forms of political protest which rested on permanent structures—
i.e. unions. Moreover, as we have seen, these structures also failed to address the
specific needs of female proletarians and working-class mothers (i.e. equal pay,
maternity benefit, child care). In many ways the CNT, which espoused direct
syndical action, eschewing parliamentary politics, was closer than the UGT to this
kind of female mobilization. But until the 1930s combined new political circumstances and acute economic crisis, not even the CNT would be able to organize
among sectors of women involved in such protest actions—and even in the 1930s
the CNT was only intermittently successful.

In terms of feminism itself, its nineteenth- and early twentieth-century forms in
Spain, like the rest of Europe, were mainly conservative. Until the impetus given

by the 1930s political reforms, *autonomous* organization by women in Spain was that of an élite—often university-linked. They formed first around suffrage reform and then, in a more sustained fashion, promoted the cause of middle-class women's education. For socialist and anarchist women who defined themselves and their primary goal as the struggle for socio-economic—i.e. class—equality, feminism was therefore judged to be a blind alley, essentially conservative, concerned only to extend rights within an already privileged élite. Indeed, in spite of the uphill battle women on the left waged to change the male-dominated agendas of political parties and unions, only in the 1930s would some of them come to accept that autonomous organization by women might be the best way forward on the left too. This would lead to the creation of the libertarian-feminist initiative Mujeres Libres in 1936 (discussed below). But its activists would always defend a separate women's organization as a strategic and temporary measure.

This conservative tradition of minoritarian Spanish feminism goes some way to explaining the reluctance displayed in the 1931 Cortes debates by progressive republicans (including some women republicans, e.g. Victoria Kent) to accept the logical outcome of their liberal principles: the political enfranchisement of women. The fear was that the religious devotion/piety and familial role which were perceived as shaping the world view of most rural female constituencies of whatever socio-economic class (excepting the anticlerical proletariat of the 'deep south') would be translated directly into a clerical-conservative vote that—added to the rest of the conservative base—would kill the progressive Republic at birth. Ironically then, in spite of republicanism's abstract emancipatory principles, in reality Spanish women achieved the vote because of decisive pressure and persuasion applied by social democratic support for it evident in the PSOE. Although some PSOE deputies shared the republicans' fears (as did the prominent socialist leader and deputy Margarita Nelken), the party was significantly influenced by the social reform programme of Weimar (from which the Spanish reformers virtually copied the articles on marriage and the family). Spanish socialists were concerned both to educate (in every sense) and mobilize women politically as a crucial support base for the Republic.

The republican groups were also concerned to educate specifically middle-class women for the same reasons. However, this was not perceived as the antechamber to their political mobilization. Indeed the emergence of women as political protagonists, contesting power in public, was stubbornly resisted as those few women republicans—most notably Clara Campoamor—discovered as they battled throughout the early 1930s to change republican political culture from the inside.

Most centrists believed that existing gender divisions were natural and therefore not susceptible to reform. Within this logic, female education was to be for the recipients a passive process. Middle-class women had to have democratic, secular Republican values inculcated in them, not primarily for their own benefit, but to ensure that they would reproduce in their children new values to sustain and nurture the Republican order. There is an evident patriarchal continuity between this view of women's natural passivity and Francoism's: in both cases women were to be the ideological as well as physical reproducers of the nation.

Unlike the republican political centre, however, the right was prepared for a time (1931–3) to do all it could to mobilize women. The most visible losers in the immediate term here were the republicans. Their strategic limitations, exemplified by their attitude to female mobilization, meant an increasingly stagnant support base. But, more fundamentally, their lack of strategy, combined with the organizational fragmentation and policy antagonisms on the left, together profoundly and fatally destabilized the Republic itself.

Immediately women achieved the vote, the right looked to them as a valuable commodity to be mobilized in order to reverse the Republic's modernizing reforms. Thus, between 1931 and 1933, those female constituencies in which reserves of social conservatism and clerical sympathy could be found—primarily provincial/rural middle and lower middle-class women, formally uneducated, whose sociability (leisure) and cultural values were formed by religious and devotional activities—were 'pragmatically' mobilized, largely under Church or lay Catholic auspices, in order to guarantee both a politically and socially/culturally conservative order which would, supposedly, demobilize women, returning them to their allegedly natural domestic sphere: 'we believe that it is the women of Spain, as a block, who safeguard the traditions of our nation, all that is best in our race; [. . .] that they are a tremendous source of social continuity.'[4]

A variety of cultural initiatives were launched by both the Church and the clerico-monarchist and fascist right. The Church established organizations such as Juventud Católica Femenina (Catholic Girls' Association) and Juventud Agrícola Femenina (its rural equivalent) to offer a range of cultural, leisure, and educational activities, while the Madrid-based Centro de Cultura Superior Femenina was specifically geared to prepare a female élite to spearhead cultural 'counter-reform'. Also aimed primarily at middle- and upper-class women, the Asociación Femenina de Acción Popular was established early on (Acción Popular being the nucleus of the mass Catholic party CEDA*). Campaigning activities also grew up around magazines such as *Aspiraciones*, produced by and targeted at middle-class women. Apart from the general array of cultural activities (including evening classes in religious instruction and practical housekeeping for working women run by the AP group), women's political activities ranged from the prosaic (electoral propaganda and census preparation) to 'fronting' Catholic schools once the religious orders had formally been debarred, via street demonstrations against the Republic's anticlerical measures, to going to prison for repeatedly flouting the Republic's Press Law with their anti-Soviet (and even anti-Semitic) propaganda. Aristocratic women, organized around the magazine *Ellas*, also went to gaol for openly wearing monarchist insignia and refusing to pay the resulting fines.

These forms of female mobilization all occurred under male tutelage (e.g. the women who led the Asociación Femenina de Acción Popular were nominated by the male party leadership, the main criteria being their family connection to the latter). Equally, the specific type of activities women undertook—whether in Catholic groups, AP, or Falange*—reproduced the traditional sexual division of labour. They were largely employed in subordinate clerical, pastoral, or domestic tasks requiring 'sacrifice', 'service', and 'dedication', often presented to the women carrying them out as a continuation of the charitable work of previous decades. Nevertheless, these activities constituted a process which was, over time, genuinely transformative of gender categories.

Indeed, from 1933 the right demonstrated some instinctive awareness of the ultimate uncontrollability of this dynamic by seeking to halt the very forms of women's mobilization which they themselves had set in train in 1931–2. Propelled particularly by the Church hierarchy (under the new Primate Gomá y Tomás), late 1934 and 1935 saw the virtual disappearance of much of the Catholic/conservative press directed at women (all that remained being religious bulletins and magazines aimed at the family). The message was now unequivocally one of 'back to the home', perceived as a safe space where moral control could be assured. In itself this was, of course, deeply problematic since the Republican experience (including the political right's own practice) had accelerated the boundary-shift between public and private. The very act of mobilization had altered women's perceptions of their own roles. Moreover, for all the nostalgia of the 'sociological right' (male and female), the 'home' itself would henceforward be penetrated increasingly by the state—whether democratic or authoritarian. These contradictions are perhaps best illustrated by the fact that this political withdrawal of conservative women occurred virtually simultaneously with the creation of Sección Femenina* de Falange (June 1934).

Looked at 'from below', from the perspective of those women mobilized by or voting for the right, the appeal of its message is clear. It promised protection from the changes which threatened the security of their familiar world. For example, it is probably the case that a majority of Spanish women in the 1930s were hostile to the new divorce legislation—not because their confessors or parish priests told them to be (though they did), but primarily because it was viewed as eroding their economic security and the only social environment they had experience of. The right, on the other hand, proffered a vision of a separate sphere where the familial and religious values and structures which shaped women's identity would be cherished and perpetuated. (The CEDA committed itself to rescinding the divorce law in its 1933 electoral programme.)

Across Europe cultural anxiety and fear of change were common factors in the political mobilization of middle-class men and women in the inter-war period and Spain was no exception to the rule. The attraction of fascist or quasi-fascist formations to both genders lay in their nostalgia appeal and promise to 'turn the clock back'. (And here one must include some kinds of nationalist movement, including the Basque example, where race provided the 'immutable' building-block of traditionalist reconstruction.) It was in Germany where the most pronounced female conservative backlash occurred (general fears about social change being expressed as a rejection of the social and sexual radicalism at Weimar's margins, and in particular of the 'new woman'). But in Spain too, middle-class women went public in an aggressive way: boycotting 'communist' and even 'Jewish' shopkeepers (in the latter case imitating the European right's demonizing lexicon, for there were no Jews in Spain) and demonstrating in favour of 'lynching' those using violence against the Civil Guard (e.g. after the Castilblanco incident of December 1931). Their cultural and social anxieties were manifest in their repeated calls to 'cleanse' [barrer] Spain of 'undesirable' elements. Such fears, and aspirations to a protected separate sphere, explain why so many women collectively endorsed the clerical-conservative right's new demobilizing tack in 1934–5. Other tendencies which fit within the same explanatory frame are: the growing social and political conservatism (1933–6) of the largely middle-class Asociación Nacional de Mujeres Españolas (founded in 1918), and the attempt to create a separate political party for women in 1934 (Acción Femenina Independiente) and to circumscribe women's political action within the municipal framework (which was reminiscent of the Primo dictatorship).

In the general elections of November 1933, when Spanish women voted for the first time, specific female sectors' social conservatism was translated into a vote for the rightist bloc. However, it is not tenable to argue that this was the primary or decisive reason for the Republican centre-left's defeat at the polls. While we do not possess the statistics which would permit a comparative analysis of the impact of women's vote by province or region, in overall national terms, by far the most significant factor in centre-left defeat was its own disunity. Put at its simplest, the Republic's electoral law significantly advantaged coalitions. The right had one, the centre-left did not.

While the right was prepared to mobilize women as another weapon in its legalist/parliamentary armoury, the radical left—largely represented by the anarcho-syndicalist CNT—had from the start subjected the whole concept of the legal reform of women's status to swingeing criticism. As an integral part of their anti-parliamentary line, their press and propaganda exhorted women to eschew false legalism and join the revolutionary struggle. Two new series of 'instructional' novels appeared (La Novela Ideal and La Novela Libre) in which the heroines providing the role models won self-respect and true happiness through economic independence, 'amor libre' (personal relationships freely established and validated by reciprocal agreement rather than by state ratification), and by participating in the social struggle. The newspaper Tierra y Libertad established a page devoted to women which constantly emphasized the economic basis of women's oppression at home and at work, exhorting them to unionize. These initiatives did little to reduce the contradiction between libertarian theory and practice: on the one hand a relatively sophisticated critique of gender oppression, on the other, the fact that libertarian women bore the same domestic burden and experienced the same marginalization in the political and labour spheres as their non-anarchist counter-parts. But in spite of the fact that anarchist practice was patriarchal, the CNT was still able both to recruit significantly among women in the 1930s and also, more generally, to bring certain female sectors into its political orbit. In general terms, no doubt the anarcho-syndicalist movement gained support from women as well as men as the political credibility of the republican-socialist coalition government (1931–3) was eroded by the evidence of state violence against workers—which included female fatalities, for example the events at Arnedo (Logroño) in January 1932 and most notoriously at Casas Viejas (Cadiz, Andalusia) in January 1933. These kind of confrontations were themselves exacerbated by the 1930s economic crisis. As it began to bite and republican reform was undermined, the sectors of labour hardest hit were the already vulnerable and marginalized—the unskilled and casual labourers, among whom figured significant numbers of women work-ers. Just as the CNT became massively involved in organizing such male constitu-encies—e.g. the building workers of Madrid—so too it tried to create new unions in areas where the work-force was predominantly or exclusively female, such as textiles in Barcelona or domestic service. They organized strikes: for example, of female rural labourers, of fish processors and sellers, and large-scale work occupa-tions by telephonists (in 1931). The CNT could also appeal, more than any other group, to that female tradition of direct protest action in times of social conflict. There were hunger marches in Bilbao and Málaga, bread riots too in Bilbao where women swooped on the supply lorries and left them bare. Imprisonment as a result of popular (i.e. politically unaligned) protests often also initiated the process of an individual woman's politicization.

It can be argued too that because of their high-profile anti-statism, the anarcho-syndicalists also benefited from the deeply felt antipathy of sectors of working-class women to the Republic's social reforms. Rather than perceiving state-regulated maternity or old age benefits as a positive source of relief, many women resisted them because they were perceived as overt state encroachment on their own terrain and thus a violation of family and local custom.[5] Divorce reform elicited hostile responses, even among female constituencies where the confessional right's / Church's writ did not run. Women's resistance here was to what one might term the state's attempt to 'nationalize' them; although, in the Spanish case, it was a fairly piecemeal attempt (as indeed it would remain, relatively speaking, after 1939) because of the weakness of the state, compared to Nazi Germany's or fascist Italy's where, contemporaneously, much more thorough attempts were being made to achieve this end. Nevertheless, this provides a good example of how popular mentalities as much as articulated political opposition inhibited the Re-public's modernizing project. The progressive forces of the Republic lacked experi-ence of political power (and thus strategies) crucial if they were successfully to confront their political antagonists. In failing here, the Republic also lost the time which was vital—both for general popular 'acclimatization' and the implementation of specific educational and cultural programmes—in order to build the Republican nation. (A further attempt would be made during the civil war, but by then it was probably too late.)

Across 1933–4 tensions were mounting inside Spanish society as, in conditions of continuing economic crisis, the centre-right coalition put the reform programme into reverse. The clash came in October 1934 when CEDA Ministers entered the cabinet to claim, in a national climate of increasing protest and polarization, the three most sensitive portfolios: Agriculture, Labour, and Justice. This action triggered a general strike throughout Spain which largely failed, as did the Catalan Generalitat's* protest. But the northern mining region of Asturias exploded into rebellion. Its repression by the state left well over a thousand dead and 30,000 in prison. Although a defeat, the Asturian rising galvanized a fragmented left to organize around a concrete political programme whose unifying central demand was amnesty. This was the road which led to the Popular Front alliance that would win the February 1936 national elections. The intervening period saw unprecedented levels of women's mobilization by the left. Although some women were themselves political prisoners, many thousands more could be mobilized directly by the amnesty appeal to release their husbands and sons or other male relatives.

As well as joining existing parties and unions, many women became involved in the work of the umbrella organization, the 'Comité Nacional de Mujeres contra la Guerra y el Fascismo' [Women's Committee against War and Fascism] promoted by the PCE, under the leadership of Dolores Ibárruri, which was transformed for a time into the 'Organización pro Infancia Obrera' [Organization for the Welfare of Workers' Children] partly in order to avoid government repression, but also because it was seen as an 'appropriate' function. Women on the left—whether they were intellectuals or factory workers—were being mobilized, as they were on the right, according to conventional constructions of gender: in supportive, pastoral, or welfare capacities, helping prisoners and their families, dealing with propaganda and administrative work for parties, unions, and International Red Aid. As one historian tellingly records, women in the Socialist Youth complained of being required to do the collective laundry at the joint youth summer schools held throughout the pre-war Republican years.[6]

At the same time, however, in order to mobilize and sustain the support of these now visible female constituencies, the left political forces looking to their support had specifically to address their needs. Hence the increasing profiling of a programme. For example, the PCE, which was particularly concerned to expand its small membership, formed the Asociación de Mujeres Antifascistas (1933), popularly known as Mujeres Antifascistas (AMA), which attracted many middle-class women republicans from October 1934 onwards, presaging the general direction of PCE recruitment during the civil war. In the Popular Front period in early 1936 the PCE and its associate organizations clearly identified with a 'top-down', state-driven reform project. The AMA backed social reforms (e.g. via its paper *Mujeres*) including equal pay legislation, state nursery provision, equal access to the professions for women, and a quota system whereby a third of all seats on municipal councils would be filled by women. This statist rationale would inform all its policy during the civil war and bring it into direct conflict with anti-statist/anti-centralist tendencies mainly concentrated in the anarcho-syndicalist movement. In particular, the AMA would find its most influential rival in the anarchist-feminist nucleus, which first emerged in May 1936 around a journal of the same name—Mujeres Libres. In the civil war it would grow into a national federation (1937), whose theory and praxis were far removed from the statism of the PCE/AMA (see below).

From the discussion so far it is apparent that the impact of women's mobilization in the 1930s is open to various readings. On the one hand, from 1931 the Republic opened up public spaces previously debarred to women. Nor was it just for 'exceptional' women—parliamentary deputies like Margarita Nelken (PSOE) or the republican Victoria Kent (also Director-General of Prisons 1931–2), or the anarchist leader Federica Montseny, who as Minister of Health and Public Assistance (Nov. 1936 to May 1937) was only the second woman in Europe to occupy cabinet office (after Alexandra Kollontai). Women were publicly present from 1931 in greater if not massive numbers at lower levels too, in functions which were in part new ones: in political action across the ideological spectrum (electoral campaigning, meetings, demonstrations), in the labour sphere (union bureaucracies and state arbitration committees), in the press (both as subjects of features and as journalists), on the radio, in the university sector, and sometimes in the gaols too as political prisoners.

But this presence did not of course mean that women had 'conquered' the newly occupied space, transcending the patriarchal order thereby. Rather this was subtly readjusted to 'admit' women in capacities which accorded with a conventional understanding of gender role. For example, as we have seen, women were politically mobilized but as subordinates, often leading specifically 'women's sections' and ultimately responsible to a male leadership—whether left or right. In the progressive/left press, while women were depicted entirely favourably in their conventional roles (mothers or faithful wives), when the 'new woman' was featured (parliamentary deputy, political functionary, or—later—*miliciana*) these new functions were always made compatible with domestic and familial duties—thus demonstrating the patriarchal continuity underlying the new Republican order which cut across from the right to the radical anti-parliamentary left. Nevertheless, the material fact of mobilization had unleashed a dynamic of change, modernizing in its disruptiveness, which reached beyond republicanism's limited goals, beyond the political right's pragmatic manipulation, and which, during the civil war, would come to challenge—albeit fleetingly—the *de facto* patriarchal structures within the organizations of the left.

The civil war

The urgent requirements of war organization meant there was an unprecedented need in both zones for women to take on new public functions and social roles. In both Republican and Nationalist territory women responded instantly to that need—but in an instinctive way and from a perception of their traditional roles, not in a self-conscious attempt to change that status or role permanently. However, once women were mobilized, they became exposed to alternative experiences which changed them. This process was obviously more rapid and visible in Republican Spain which, qualitatively, provided a much more conducive environment for women to acquire critical consciousness and begin to question established gender roles—especially in the early stages of the war (until approximately spring 1937) while emergency defence needs and the crisis and fragmentation of the Republican state opened up significant mould-breaking possibilities and spaces for women's direct action and initiatives. The most striking example of this (though not necessarily the most significant in the long run) was that women went to fight (and sometimes die) at the front, a number also holding positions of command.

In Republican Spain large numbers of proletarian and middle-class women were also incorporated to war tasks—either directly to the workshops and factories (particularly metallurgy, chemicals, and textiles) of the Republican home front, or via the Popular Front organizations which provided a range of health and welfare services geared to the needs of home and military fronts. In both Barcelona and Madrid women ran much of the public transport systems. They worked both to replace men in some tasks and also—most specifically in the case of working-class women—to sustain their families while male breadwinners were absent.

In Nationalist Spain, there was no such industrial mobilization of women. (Axis aid meant the Nationalists never faced the dilemma of material war needs clashing overtly with ideology.) Nevertheless, as health and welfare services devolved to the competence of the Sección Femenina (SF), increasing numbers of lower middle-class women were involved in providing services which foreshadowed some of the post-war functions of that organization (i.e. the provision of primary health care and rudimentary social services). These tasks were represented via propaganda to the women mobilized—and indeed to the population of Nationalist Spain at large—as a continuation of women's traditional duties and pastoral/charitable work. It was stressed that the exceptional circumstances made women's presence in public life (albeit in a fitting manner) essential in order to win the battle to re-establish traditional norms and values which would allow them to return to the home. In fact, however, these circumstances were themselves part of a wider process of socio-economic crisis and change which was gradually altering women's perceptions of their function. The ambiguities of the SF's status and activities after the war attest to this complex dynamic. It would manifest itself from 1939 onwards as a dual process which shifted the boundaries of public and private: as the state expanded to regulate spaces previously defined as 'private'—such as child care and home management—this required the public-professional mobilization ('nationalization') of substantial numbers of (mainly middle-class) women. They were trained as SF cadres who, in a variety of capacities and forums (e.g. 'social service' instruction, health visiting (the *divulgadoras*), girls' education, and mobile rural schools (the *cátedras ambulantes*)), would provide the gender-specific instruction necessary to bring the state into the home.

In civil-war Catalonia, the epicentre of urban social revolutionary experimentation during the first phase of the conflict, women textile workers (historically the bulk of the labour force) were also subject to regulation via incorporation to factory production from home work or small workshops—this as part of the industrial rationalization process which often accompanied collectivization. As a result, piece-work was also abolished and women unionized by the CNT on a large scale and paid a daily wage. While conditions, hours, and pay were undoubtedly better in the factories, the situation was not one of net gain for women. The absence of child care, for example, made it difficult for women to fulfil the multiple roles still expected of them. Moreover, the reality of the collectives (urban or rural) was far from achieving—in terms of either gender or other criteria—the absolute equality striven for in theory. In practice, pay differentials remained—including, in most cases, those between male and female workers engaged on equal tasks. (The family wage also reinforced these differentials.) Women also remained largely on the margins of worker-management committees and union leadership cadres. For all that the CNT's male leadership professed (an undoubtedly genuine) concern for working women's conditions, devoting columns in their press to such questions, the real continuing absence of women's voices from union decision-making process meant the central problem of inequality—that of the pressures imposed by the 'double burden' (work plus domestic tasks and child care)—was never adequately addressed. One result of this failure was that large numbers of women, under increasing pressure on both 'fronts' during the war, became aware of gender contradictions which, in turn, opened them up to the ideas of Mujeres Libres (ML), inspired by libertarian ideas but organizationally independent of the CNT.

Much of ML's work was done in factories in the urgent task of providing a skills base for the newly incorporated female labour force. However, it was central to ML's ethos that both the practical skills training (*capacitación*) and general education which they imparted had as its principal object the cultural and human enrichment of individual women themselves—who were to be freed from their triple servitude: 'the enslavement of ignorance, enslavement as producers, and enslavement as women.' Indeed it was the need for this broad educational project as the pre-condition for working women's full and equal incorporation into social life which had impelled the establishment of ML in spring 1936.

The grass-roots focus on individual realization—rather than the specific range of activities/initiatives implemented—is what most clearly distinguishes ML from the other mass organization encadring women in Republican Spain—Mujeres

SE DEGAGEANT DE SON ENVELOPPE DE SUPERSTITION ET DE MISE-
RE DE L'ESCLAVE INMEMORIALE EST NEE **LA FEMME**
CAPABLE DE PRENDRE UNE PART ACTIVE A L'ELABORTION DE L'AVENIR

7 Exhibit from the Spanish Republican pavilion at the Paris International Art and
Technical Exhibition (1937), for which Picasso's *Guernica* was commissioned. The glass
show-case juxtaposes the image of a Salamancan peasant girl in traditional regalia—
literally laden with the past—with that of a Republican militiawoman. The triangular shape
of the ornately dressed peasant girl echoes that of popular images of the Virgin; the
militiawoman's uniform, by contrast, allows her to move freely. The label in French reads:
'Emerging from her shell of superstition and wretchedness, from the time-honoured slave
is born the WOMAN capable of playing an active part in the elaboration of the future': the
militiawoman is shouting, showing that she has a voice. The violent contrast between the
two images provides an uncompromising representation of the cultural and gendered war
between tradition and modernity being waged with arms as the Paris Exhibition was held.

8 Postcard issued in the Republican zone during the civil war, foregrounding a woman factory worker against a backdrop of male soldiers fighting at the front. The message is that women sustain the civilian front, which in turn sustains the war effort. At the same time, the depiction of a clearly gendered division of labour illustrates the way in which the restructuring of the Popular Front in wartime Republican Spain reimposed segregated gender roles, which had been blurred in the emergency stage of Republican defence (the Republic decreed the withdrawal of its remaining militiawomen from the front in March 1937).

Antifascistas. While both organized women engaged in war, welfare, and propaganda work as well as running health and educational services, cultural and recreational activities, ML concentrated on its *capacitación* mission, thus devoting itself mostly to the needs of proletarian women. The AMA was, by contrast, more clearly a Popular Frontist (i.e. inter-class) initiative, incorporating a very large constituency of middle-class women. Consistent with the PCE's functional 'top-down' statist approach, AMA (both larger and better resourced than ML precisely because of its state connection) viewed women's mobilization as primarily instrumental, the goal being shoring up the Republican state in order to win the war and then prepare for peacetime reconstruction. Victory in the war was of course crucial to ML too, but they focused on process (by taking on new roles in unfamiliar territory, women would acquire critical consciousness, a new sense of themselves) rather than product (a quantified contribution to the war effort) and on community and direct action rather than state and 'top-down' policy initiatives. For many of the women involved with AMA and ML the practical experience was no doubt often similarly liberating. Moreover, the differences in ethos were further blurred by the fact that, in practice, wartime priorities, along with the ML's need to engage with the existing cultural and educational level and needs of the women it mobilized, and also the hostility of their male libertarian counterparts, meant the ML's more radical sexual politics were never foregrounded during the war.

Female mobilization did differ, then, quantitatively and qualitatively in Republican and Nationalist Spain. This reflected not only contrasting ideological perspectives, but also the divergent material resource bases of the two war efforts (the Republican depended on mobilizing women as an industrial labour force in a way the Nationalist did not). Nevertheless, both Nationalists and Popular Frontists exhorted women, as wives and mothers, to defend their respective orders in what was a time of crisis precisely so there could be a return to 'social normality' which, in both cases, implied a return to gender norms built upon female subordination.[7]

But if the Republic was a more conservative environment gender-wise than we tend to think, conversely Francoism was less able than certain stereotypes imply to realize its professed policy of female demobilization. The existence and activities of the Sección Femenina, as we have seen, constitute a major example of this dialectic. The SF offered a new, public role for significant numbers of Spanish women—albeit in a mode conditioned by the prevailing social conservatism and the economic needs of an authoritarian dictatorship.

While Francoism was massively to delay, in the end it could not reverse, a process of modernization and cultural *aggiornamento* which eventually produced a dramatic evolution in the roles and lives of all Spaniards, women in particular. But one should never underestimate the material impact of Francoism on people's lives in that lengthy interim. In terms of political progress (legislative reform and constitutional emancipation) the Francoist victory in the civil war constituted a significant historical break. After 1939 women were deprived of the very legal/

political arena in which to mobilize. They could not even reach the starting line. Francoism, in its first phase, virtually obliterated an entire young culture of feminism (as it did so many other cultures). The regime also erased political rights and responsibilities women had gained under the Republic. It would take some two decades before the pressures of accelerated modernization and the interests of developing capital would oblige the state (via the SF) to table a variety of legal reforms improving the status of Spanish women.

Notes

1 Cf. Art. 25: 'None of the following may be the basis of special privilege before the law: inherited characteristics, family status, sex, social class, wealth, political or religious beliefs.'
2 Statistics for 1900–30 show an absolute decline in the proportion of women in the active population (from 18.32% to 12.65%), the steepest drop (from 18.32% to 13.51%) occurring 1900–10 (principally from the primary sector). See M. Nash, *Mujer, familia y trabajo en España 1875–1936* (Barcelona, 1983), 49–51. However, women's work is so often 'invisible', missing from the recorded statistics because it is located in irregular or marginal sectors of the economy.
3 M. A. Ackelsberg, *Free Women of Spain: Anarchism and the Struggle for the Emancipation of Women* (Bloomington, Ind., 1991), 170.
4 'creemos que la mujer española, su gran masa, conserva las virtudes raciales e históricas de nuestro pueblo; [. . .] que es magnífico elemento de conservación social,' *El Debate* (CEDA press) (11 Dec. 1932); cf. Pilar Primo de Rivera, 'a unity of criteria for generations', quoted in 'La mujer nacional-sindicalista', *Ciudadano Dossier* (May 1976), 73.
5 D. Bussy Genevois, 'El retorno de la hija pródiga: mujeres entre lo público y lo privado (1931–1936)', in P. Folguera (ed.), *Otras visiones de España* (Madrid, 1993), 122.
6 Ibid. 131.
7 Cf. E. Cabezali *et al.*, 'Myth as Suppression: Motherhood and the Historical Consciousness of the Women of Madrid, 1936–9', in R. Samuel and P. Thompson (eds.), *The Myths We Live By* (London, 1990).

Further reading

Ackelsberg, M. A., *Free Women of Spain: Anarchism and the Struggle for the Emancipation of Women* (Bloomington, Ind., 1991).
Bridenthal, R., 'Something Old, Something New: Women between the Two World Wars', in R. Bridenthal *et al.* (eds.), *Becoming Visible: Women in European History* (Boston, 2nd edn. 1987).
Capel, R. M., *El trabajo y la educación de la mujer en España 1900–1930* (Madrid, 1982).
Capel, R. M., Durán, M. A., *et al.*, *Mujer y sociedad en España 1700–1975* (Madrid, 1982).
Folguera, P., 'City Space and the Daily Life of Women in Madrid in the 1920s', *Oral History*, 13/2 (1985).
Instituto de la Mujer, *La mujer en la historia de España: cuadernos bibliográficos*, 2 vols. (Madrid, 1988).
—— *Las mujeres y la guerra civil española* (Ministerio de Cultura, proceedings of the III Jornadas de estudios monográficos, Salamanca, Oct. 1989) (Madrid, 1991).
Kaplan, T., 'Women and Communal Strikes in the Crisis of 1917–1922', in R. Bridenthal, *et al.* (eds.), *Becoming Visible* (Boston, 2nd edn, 1987).
—— *Red City, Blue Period: Social Movements in Picasso's Barcelona* (Berkeley, 1992), esp. chs. 4 and 5.
Kern, R. W. (ed.), *Historical Dictionary of Modern Spain 1700–1988* (Westport, Conn., 1990) (see entry on women).
Nash, M., *'Mujeres Libres': España, 1936–39* (Barcelona, 1976) (anthology).
—— *Mujer y movimiento obrero en España 1931–1939* (Barcelona, 1981).

Nash, M., *Mujer, familia y trabajo en España 1875–1936* (Barcelona, 1983) (editor's introd. plus anthology of texts).

Nuñez Pérez, M. G., *Trabajadoras en la segunda república: un estudio de la actividad extradoméstica (1931–1936)* (Madrid, 1989).

Various authors, 'What is women's history?', *History Today* (June 1985).

Memoirs/contemporary works

Campoamor, C., *El voto femenino y yo* (Barcelona, 1986).

Etchebéhère, M., *Ma guerre d'Espagne à moi: une femme à la tête d'une colonne au combat* (Paris, 1976).

Ibárruri, D., *They Shall Not Pass: The Autobiography of La Pasionaria* (trans. of *El único camino*) (New York, 1976).

Nelken, M., *La condición social de la mujer en España* (Barcelona, 1983).

Biographies and novels

Alcalde, C., *Federica Montseny: palabra en rojo y negro* (Barcelona, 1983).

García, C., *Las cárceles de Soledad Real: una vida* (Madrid, 1983) (novel about life of a communist militant during civil war and post-war years).

Beyond Tradition and 'Modernity': The Cultural and Sexual Politics of Spanish Anarchism

RICHARD CLEMINSON

In the 1920s and 1930s, against a backdrop of economic, political, and social backwardness, the Spanish anarchist movement drew up a social and cultural agenda intended to subvert contemporary power structures, dominant forms of culture, and, in particular, the influence of the Catholic Church. The anarchist—or libertarian—movement aspired to the creation of a new form of society that would be constructed by individuals acting free of external forces such as capitalism, state, and religion.

From its inception in the 1860s when the delegates of Bakunin set up the first organizations in Spain, Spanish anarchism had always concentrated on education as an enabling factor allowing the individual to create new forms of social organization and life-styles, based on the principles of self-management, democratic decision-making, and anti-authoritarianism. These principles were to inform all relationships in the anarchist utopia, whether economic, political, social, or affective.

In addition to its facility for organizing workers in different trades, it is this stress on discussion of the new society that characterizes Spanish anarchism best. The time spent on conferences and on the production of publications proposing blueprints for alternative forms of social organization was important in the establishment of a movement whose values went far beyond those commonly espoused by either the social democratic movement or revolutionary marxism—both of which were still primarily economistic in their outlook in the 1930s. Anarchist propagandists believed that, for any revolution to succeed in sweeping away capitalism, authority, social classes, and the state, it was necessary to win the minds (and hearts) of people, change their attitudes, outlooks, and actions, and empower them to take over the running of all areas of society by themselves, without the need for leaders.

By the 1930s most sectors of the broad anarchist movement, including the revolutionary unionist (or anarcho-syndicalist) CNT* [National Confederation of Labour] and the FAI* [Iberian Anarchist Federation], had defined their aims. Even though their ideas were not homogeneous in every sense, by 1936—with the outbreak of the civil war and popular revolution—the CNT was clear that what it was striving for was not the 'modernity' of bourgeois democracy, liberal land reform, and a *modus vivendi* between social classes; in short, not the cultural project offered by the Second Republic. The CNT had rejected the Republic in 1931 as being no better than the defunct monarchy and wished neither for a return to the past nor for the kind of future mapped out by the Republicans. As the CNT's National Secretary put it in his opening remarks to the May 1936 Congress: '[w]e wish this to be the last congress that the CNT holds under capitalism.'[1]

Anarchist cultural and sexual politics of the 1920s and 1930s, then, ran counter to dominant norms of both the left and the right. This means that the civil war which broke out in July 1936 was more complex than a straightforward conflict between 'Republicans' and 'Nationalists'. In those parts of the Republican zone which became anarchist strongholds (Aragon and parts of Catalonia and the Levante), anarchist thought and praxis was opposed to the values of Republican as well as Nationalist Spain. The fact that the anarchists were fighting for a new society that was different from both these options is shown by Buenaventura Durruti's reply in September 1936 to the journalist Pierre Van Paasen, who had remarked that even if the workers were victorious they would be sitting on a pile of ruins:

We've always lived in slums and holes in the wall. We'll manage. For you mustn't forget, we can also build. It was the workers who built these palaces and cities here in Spain, and in America and everywhere else. We can build others to take their place. Better ones. We're not in the least afraid of ruins. We're going to inherit the earth. That's a fact. The bourgeoisie may blast and ruin its own world before it leaves the stage of history. We carry a new world here in our hearts. That world is growing by the minute.[2]

Many in the anarchist movement believed that the war was a golden opportunity to attempt the libertarian* revolution that had been germinating for some seventy years.

The anarchists' emphasis on the needs of the individual and on personal change made their movement a unique forum for radical ideas on community organization, on the role of science, culture, and education, as well as on sexuality. Their belief in human beings as responsible for forming history and ideas contrasted with marxists, who saw economic factors as primary, and with the Church's faith in supernatural deities. This essay will outline the origins, evolution, and chief areas of debate of Spanish anarchist radical cultural and sexual politics across the 1920s and 1930s, stressing the link established between personal change and revolutionary transformation.

Culture, science, and education

Spain at the beginning of the twentieth century suffered from economic fragmentation and an enormous cultural divide between different sectors of the population, problems still unresolved in 1936. Given the failure of political liberalism to address these problems, and a landowning class and industrial bourgeoisie hostile to real change, for most of the populace culture and knowledge were often self-acquired or provided by radical or revolutionary workers' organizations. The role of anarchism, with its autodidactic tradition and schools established by pro-anarchist teachers such as Francesc Ferrer i Guardia, was vital in providing a basis for the acquisition of knowledge.

A common theme in anarchist journals and publications of the 1920s and 1930s was their criticism of the ignorance in which bourgeois capitalist society kept most of the population. This helped establish a tradition which exalted knowledge, science, and culture as liberating agents in the fight against exploitation, whether economic, political, or cultural. Culture and knowledge were sought for their own sakes, but especially as the key to liberation. Anarchists were aware that access to knowledge was often used by their bourgeois opponents to reinforce the supposed 'naturalness' of the status quo. For example, the Russian anarchist Kropotkin's analysis of the international debate on Darwinism in his *Mutual Aid*,[3] and discussion of this issue in Spanish anarchist journals such as *Natura* and *La Revista Blanca*, show an awareness of the fact that 'social Darwinism' had been appropriated by particular social groups to justify the triumph of the strong over the weak, thus serving their own class interests.

Of vital importance to education and cultural change in the anarchist movement were the hundreds of journals circulating, some more closely linked to the CNT than others, embracing topics such as vegetarianism and nudism. A key component of anarchist culture was the production of small pamphlets and novelettes which extolled non-authoritarian ways of living and relating to others. Issues such as marriage, free love, maternity, and chastity were dealt with, as, for example, in the *Novela Ideal* series published by the *Revista Blanca*. Hundreds of anti-religious novelettes were published, often focusing on love and sexuality, and they were extremely popular in libertarian circles. According to Federica Montseny, who was editor of this series and published stories in it herself, between 10,000 and 50,000 copies of such novelettes were printed weekly. As Montseny notes, the Franco regime held publications like these responsible for 'poisoning three generations of Spaniards'.[4]

More important still were the attempts to translate such anti-authoritarian values into reality. Here, I shall focus on some of the customs and practices promoted by anarchists as 'counter-cultural', as well as looking at the spaces where this culture was disseminated.

Essential to the production of anarchist counter-culture were the *ateneos* or meeting-houses which grew up in most cities and towns. Here, anarchist publications would be displayed and classes held. Indeed, for one woman anarchist, the *ateneo* was the place 'where we were formed, most deeply, ideologically'.[5] She does not appear to be alone in her judgement. Martha Ackelsberg has illustrated the key role of these cultural centres in providing the building for an organized community politics of empowerment, where education and discussion were viewed as essential for the development of free individuals capable of constructing a new society according to anarchist principles. (And in the anarchist *ateneos*, unlike their bourgeois counterparts, women were welcome.) The *ateneos* represented a unique forum where local people could come together to solve specific problems and broaden their horizons. The unions set up by the CNT also acted as conduits for analysis of issues relevant to the construction of the new society. Libraries were established in the union headquarters and a variety of classes held. The CNT unions also subscribed to anarchist publications which gave rise to regular informal discussion that also served an educative purpose.

Essential in anarchist cultural and educational endeavours were the rationalist schools established and inspired by the pedagogue Francesc Ferrer i Guardia and the French educationalist Paul Robin. In these schools, established where state schools were non-existent to give access to people unable to attend because of work commitments, the traditional rote-learning was abolished as was any kind of religious instruction. Education was coeducational and based on equality of the sexes. The schools taught rationalist interpretations of society and nature, encouraging students to think for themselves rather than submit to the authority of a teacher or of abstract ideas and religious dogma.

Counter-culture and sexuality

Anarchist attempts to educate workers and to create a counter-culture were part of a total programme for the reform of mentalities and material conditions. The anarchist cultural project was firmly linked to the wider connotations of general freedom and the right to act without the coercion of Church or state. In a society where the Church was omnipresent and omnipotent, anarchists believed that it was essential to create their own ethics beyond bourgeois moral strictures. This alternative moral system was seen as a mechanism for the subversion of existing power structures: not only was the acquisition of knowledge seen as important, but its use on a personal-political level was perceived as vital. Radical positions on education, diet, religion, and culture merge with an extensive discourse on how people should relate to one another, show love, and practise sexual relations. It is impossible in this short space to document the breadth and extent of anarchist attitudes to sexuality; this essay will outline the main anarchist views on sexuality, and illustrate the reforms which anarchists championed after July 1936.

From its beginning Spanish anarchism had severely criticized the moral code of the bourgeoisie, both for its insistence on compulsory marriage and for its attitudes towards sex. Anarchists, for the most part, rejected marriage by the Church

9 Cover of anarchist magazine *Estudios* (April 1931) illustrating the libertarian cultural critique of the repressive authority of the Catholic Church in shackling self-knowledge and self-expression, particularly in the area of sexuality. The Manichaean black/white design shows a vampiric, devilish priest restraining a blindfold youth, whose androgynous quality suggests a utopian desire to blur gender differences. In practice, anarchist efforts towards sexual emancipation in the 1930s, although remarkably radical, did not always manage to get beyond traditional constructions of masculinity and femininity as polar opposites.

as unnatural and restricting, shoring up a society based on inequality and power: the power of one sex over the other. Anarchists attempted to live as couples without being married, which in a society riddled with rigid concepts of 'propriety' and 'decency' was considered an overt attack on the Catholic Church and established norms. Subversive also, and viewed with constant disapproval by the Church, was the use of contraceptives, whether employed as a method of preventing venereal disease or as a form of contraception, thus separating pleasure from procreation. It was this that led to the persecution of the early twentieth-century propagandists grouped around the anarchist Lluís Bulffi and the first Spanish neo-Malthusian organization.

Anarchists' promotion of 'free love' as opposed to the marriage contract (the former understood as a freely established relationship validated by reciprocal agreement rather than state ratification) was seen by them as a way in which anarchist ideals could be put into practice under capitalism; it was thus central to the creation of the new kind of society. In marriage, they argued, the power of men over women in capitalist society was replicated, creating a kind of authoritarian mini-state in the worker's own hearth. Love, anarchists believed, should be given freely or not at all; marriage only sterilized love and sex, turning it into a relationship which was oppressive for *both* sexes. Anarchists also opposed prostitution, which they saw as a capitalist form of exploitation, demeaning to both parties. On occasion, as with the anarchist faith in the role of culture and science, it was suggested that love would in itself solve society's problems. Conversely, it was argued that without hate, exploitation, and competition, people living naturally and in harmony with nature would love in a fulfilled and fulfilling manner.

Anarchism and sex reform in the Spanish revolution

Although anarchists were promoting their new morality before the civil war and revolution of 1936, the latter was seen as an unparalleled opportunity to put their ideas into practice on a wider scale. In Catalonia, for example, Church weddings were abolished and the 'free union' was available to all those wanting it. While people were sometimes 'married' in the CNT offices with a short ceremony, the couple believed that their union was entirely different in nature from that endorsed by a marriage ceremony. Anarchist doctors, in publications such as *Generación Consciente* and *Estudios*, gave advice on child-rearing and how to avoid passing hereditary complaints on to offspring, in a kind of proletarian eugenics that was far removed from the nationalist 'race-hygiene' of Nazi Germany. As described in the previous essay, a specific anarchist women's organization, Mujeres Libres, was formed to address the problems of female emancipation.

In Catalonia, a decree allowing legal abortion for the first time in Spanish history was passed on 25 December 1936 by the anarchist-controlled Catalan Health Department (SIAS), and an order of 1 March 1937 established the norms regulating its provision by hospitals and clinics. Despite the enthusiasm of the SIAS for this provision, the curtailment of CNT involvement in SIAS in June 1937 meant that the impact of the decree—never openly publicized—was probably minimal. In addition to abortion on demand, anarchists planned to set up rehabilitation centres for prostitutes, sex counselling consultancies for young people, and an Institute of Sexual Science. None of these was in fact established because the period of radical social and cultural experimentation was relatively short-lived, eroded by the economic and political reconstruction of the bourgeois state.[6]

Beyond tradition, beyond 'modernity'

There are three major points that need to be drawn out from this brief discussion of Spanish anarchist cultural and sexual politics.

First, there are clear links between anarchist sexual politics and their discourse on the nature of culture. In this essay I have viewed 'culture' as a dynamic, active, and generalized system of customs and knowledge. Anarchists encouraged broad knowledge on many issues such as conception and contraceptive methods, as part of their attempt to educate people into more responsible and caring modes of sexual behaviour, and into learning about themselves and their own bodies through co-education in anarchist schools. Thus, prerogatives of health, knowledge, and sex appear bound together into an overall project for human empowerment and betterment. The anarchist cultural-sexual project was a multifaceted one which both participants and observers viewed as subversive of accepted cultural and moral norms.

Secondly, it is important to note that anarchists believed that it was necessary to change and empower people before the revolutionary event which was supposed to sweep capitalism away. Through education, anarchist militants were made aware of the need to alter ideas, life-styles, and behaviours so that the transformation from capitalism to a stateless society could be effected without the need for governmental or statist structures. Therefore, like many utopian socialists, living and loving were bound together in a coherent whole (or at least an attempt at one) in accordance with anarchist ideals of justice and fraternity.

Thirdly, we can now assess the cultural-sexual enterprise inspired by Spanish anarchists with the benefit of hindsight. While it is true to say that a culture of opposition and resistance grew up around the CNT, the *ateneos*, and the many anarchist publications which had a discernible material effect on people's lives, we may be more critical of a less successful sexual politics. Libertarians, while attempting to find solutions to problems of women's liberation, male domination, prostitution, and monogamy, often found their morality co-opted by traditional dictates on sexual morality. In general male attitudes towards women were still imbued with patriarchal overtones; heterosexuality as the only legitimate form of sexual expression was promoted by anarchist sexologists, even though by 1936 the question of homosexuality was increasingly viewed with a more 'comprehensive' eye;[7] puritanism with regard to 'promiscuous' sex still existed.

Although Spanish anarchism attempted a radical reform of ideology, behaviour, mores, and roles, and, within the context of 1920s and 1930s Spain, achieved much in this respect, nevertheless respectability, 'manliness', and 'femininity', inherited from traditional morality, were still exalted as the healthy norm. This tension between radical and traditional cultural and sexual models and aspirations was ever present in anarchists' minds.

We must be clear that the Spanish anarchists aspired to more than simply eradicating what they saw as the negative aspects of tradition: the moral code of the Catholic Church and the mean-minded morality of the bourgeoisie. They made it abundantly clear that what they were proposing was far removed from the system of values—economic, political, cultural, or sexual—of the liberal democratic Republic and its attempted reforms. Anarchists rejected the political pluralism and class 'harmony' espoused by the defenders of the modernizing capitalist bourgeois democratic Republic because they sought a society beyond classes and beyond bourgeois morality. What anarchists proposed was, needless to say, even further removed from the archaic morality of the Nationalists. When these mutually antagonistic forms of culture collided in the civil war, the anarchists believed that the Republican state's resulting collapse presented them with a unique historic opportunity to go beyond both archaism and 'modernity' into a future society where people could live and develop without Church, capitalism, or state. The advances made during the revolutionary period in the first months of the civil war were a testimony to this vision. With the take-over of fields and factories by workers, the chasm between Republican 'modernity' and an anarchist future became unbridgeable. At the time, with CNT membership standing at 1.5 million, that anarchist future did not seem unrealizable.

Notes
1 El Congreso Confederal de Zaragoza: 1936: CNT (Madrid, 1978), 10.
2 Cited in V. Richards, Lessons of the Spanish Revolution (London, 1983), 193, n. 47.
3 P. Kropotkin, Mutual Aid: A Factor of Evolution (London, 1987, orig. 1902).
4 F. Montseny, Mis primeros cuarenta años (Barcelona, 1987), 56.
5 Quoted in M. A. Ackelsberg, Free Women of Spain: Anarchism and the Struggle for the Emancipation of Women (Bloomington, Ind., 1991), 32.
6 See F. Martí Ibáñez, Obra: diez meses de labor en Sanidad y Asistencia Social (Barcelona, 1937).
7 See R. Cleminson, Anarquismo y homosexualidad: antología de artículos de 'La Revista Blanca', 'Generación Consciente', 'Estudios' e 'Iniciales' (Ediciones Libertarias Madrid, forthcoming).

Further reading
Ackelsberg, M. A., Free Women of Spain: Anarchism and the Struggle for the Emancipation of Women (Bloomington, Ind., 1991).
Alvarez Junco, J., La ideología política del anarquismo español 1868–1910 (Madrid, 2nd edn. 1991).
Cleminson, R., Anarquismo y homosexualidad: antología de artículos de 'La Revista Blanca', 'Generación Consciente', 'Estudios' e 'Iniciales' (Ediciones Libertarias Madrid, forthcoming).
Kaplan, T., Red City, Blue Period (Berkeley, 1992).
Montseny, F., Mis primeros cuarenta años (Barcelona, 1987).
Nash, M., 'Mujeres Libres': España, 1936–39 (Barcelona, 1976) (anthology).
Peirats, J., Anarchists in the Spanish Revolution (London, 1990).
Richards, V., Lessons of the Spanish Revolution (London, 1983).

8

ENRIQUE
MONTERO

CHRISTOPHER
COBB

Intellectuals and Power

Reform Idealized: The Intellectual and Ideological Origins of the Second Republic

ENRIQUE MONTERO

It can be asserted that the Second Spanish Republic was largely an ideological product of new liberalism. New liberalism was an ideology for mass politics that superseded traditional liberalism by being interventionist in social questions and by emphasizing the development of the so-called 'social organism' (civil society). In Spain the formulation of new liberalism was due principally to the work of the Krausist* philosophers of law. Karl Krause (1781–1832) was a post-Kantian German philosopher whose thought was introduced to Spain by Julián Sanz del Río, the first professor of philosophy at the University of Madrid, after a study tour in Germany in the early 1840s. One can only gauge the historical importance of Krausism for modern philosophical and scientific thought in Spain if it is borne in mind that Spanish philosophy in the 1840s was reduced mainly to theology and dry erudition. Several factors contributed to the remarkable impact the thought of this minor philosopher had in Spain. Undoubtedly much of the appeal of Krausism lay in the fact that it seemed to offer a practical means of regenerating the country. Thus, although its influence as a philosophy based on metaphysics was short-lived, it made a long-lasting contribution to Spanish culture by providing the modern scientific method of research that Spain badly needed. It offered above all a comprehensive and ample vision of modern science in which the various sciences emanated from philosophy and were interrelated. This vision provided the intellectual foundations which facilitated the assimilation of subsequent European schools of thought such as positivism.

The success of Krausism no doubt also owed a great deal to the high calibre of the men, including a number of leading university professors, who embraced it. These Krausists made important contributions not only in science but also in education and the philosophy of law. In the latter Krausism provided an all-embracing vision of society as made up of 'personas sociales' (social units) who functioned in a harmonious way and contributed to the improvement of the whole 'social organism'. Albeit in Krausist jargon, this was a description of the modern pluralistic, democratic society in the process of being created in western Europe. The moral values at the centre of the Krausist vision of the world were to provide the driving force behind the construction of the new society.

The key to the Krausists' success was a strong awareness of the need to allow their ideas to 'permeate'—to use a term coined in Britain by the Fabians—the educated élite of the country which in its vast majority was made up of law graduates. In this task they were helped by two factors. The first was the smallness of the Madrid intellectual and political world, centred on the cultural club the Ateneo. The second was the fact that all postgraduate law students in Spain were obliged to attend the courses given in the University of Madrid by the most distinguished Krausist law professors, Francisco Giner and Gumersindo de Azcárate. The Krausists also employed textbooks, the press, and politics to spread their ideas. In 1876 the Krausists founded the Institución Libre de Enseñanza* to protect academic freedom in the face of state attempts to curtail it. The Institución gathered together the first group of intellectuals who were aware of themselves as such and who had a sense of mission to modernize the country. They acted as contemporary Spain's first think-tank in matters of politics, educational reform, and the promotion of science. In politics, one can trace Krausist postulates in the views of many politicians and intellectuals of the Restoration monarchy: from those of the founder of the turno pacífico* system, the doctrinaire Conservative Antonio Cánovas del Castillo, to the Liberal Segismundo Moret, a disciple of Sanz del Río, instigator of the Commission for Social Reform (1883–9), Minister in numerous governments and Prime Minister in several at the beginning of the century. Important leaders of the twentieth-century Spanish right such as Antonio Maura and José Calvo Sotelo had been distinguished students of Azcárate. This gave rise to the peculiar scenario in which politicians of different ideological shades voiced similar critiques of the Restoration system, dominated as it was by an oligarchy* and caciquismo:* clearly it was only a matter of time before the system was either transformed or collapsed.

The Krausist influence was equally strong in republicanism. Nicolás Salmerón, a disciple of Sanz del Río and professor of philosophy, was one of the presidents of the First Republic of 1873 and leader of the joint republican movement, Unión Republicana, in 1903. Giner's brother Hermenegildo was a leading figure in Alejandro Lerroux's Radical Party, the most important republican party of the first decades of the century. Melquíades Alvarez, a professor of law at the University of Oviedo, one of the main centres of Krausism at the turn of the century, was leader of the Partido Reformista which he founded together with Gumersindo de Azcárate in 1912 and which survived until the Second Republic. One of the early members of his party, Manuel Azaña, who had attended Giner's lectures, became Prime Minister of the Republic in 1931 and later its President.

New liberalism is an ideology that under different names can be found in many European countries at the turn of the century. It is simply the replacement of the old model of individualistic liberalism by a more socially oriented brand in which state intervention plays an ever-larger role. Its driving force was a great emphasis on moral values. In England the best expression of new liberalism was the ideological movement behind Lloyd George's People's Budget of 1909. What distinguished Spanish from British new liberalism was the importance it attached to the development of society. In a country in which, as Sanz del Río had noted, the Church and the army seemed to be the largest and best-organized institutions there still remained the huge task of organizing a modern and complex society, a process which would eventually usher in mass politics. A significant aspect of Spanish new liberalism was the rejection of all forms of absolutism, and of the doctrinaire liberalism dominant in Spain at that time which accorded much importance to political forms but little to the reforms necessary for the organization of a modern society. It also opened the way to more modern forms of corporativism to fill the vacuum left by the abolition of the medieval guilds (gremios) in Spain in the 1830s. In Barcelona another version of new liberalism was developed in the 1880s which was at the heart of the nationalist revival of Catalonia. Its origins can be traced to the federal republican Francisco Pi y Margall. The main trait distinguishing the new liberalism of Madrid from that of Barcelona was the latter's identification from the start with the economic aspirations of the Catalan industrial bourgeosie and commercial middle classes. The founder of this Catalanist brand of new liberalism, Valentí Almirall, identified the economic protectionism that Catalan industry and commerce hoped to gain from Madrid with the essence of Catalan 'particularism'. Meanwhile, in Madrid, the centre of political power and the civil service, new liberalism became more an ideology for planning national growth and revival through education and the promotion of moral principles.

Central to new liberalism in Spain was the concept of an intellectual élite destined to rule the country. The notion was taken up at the turn of the century by a generation of young intellectuals imbued with the regenerationist ideas that swept the country after the loss of the last colonies in 1898. This group, known as 'the Generation of 1914', had its counterpart elsewhere in Europe. It developed an ideology of youth, making youth a specific value, and distinguished itself from previous generations of intellectuals by its strong sense of national mission to further Spanish science and to transform the country through political action. This new generation followed in the footsteps of a previous generation of writers, the so-called 'Generation of 1898' who had also been galvanized by the loss of the colonies. The older generation included, among others, Miguel de Unamuno, Pío Baroja, Ramiro de Maeztu, and Azorín. The 'Generation of 1914' criticized these older writers for their iconoclastic criticism and confused ideas. The younger generation had also been influenced by other senior intellectual figures, such as the hystologist Santiago Ramón y Cajal, whom the events of 1898 had turned into oracles of secular morality, science, and politics. Their careers were advanced by the boost Spanish science received after the defeat in the colonial wars—which many in Spain perceived as a triumph for American education and science. Many members of the new generation went to study abroad. Some of them, such as the philosopher José Ortega y Gasset (who acted as the leader and ideologue of his generation) as well as Azaña, Salvador de Madariaga, Marcelino Domingo, Luis de Zulueta, and Luis Araquistain would be key figures during the Second Republic. At the same time in Catalonia a new generation known as the *noucentistas* emerged, characterized by their emphasis on a knowledge of the classics and their profes-sional specialization. The importance of these groups was such that the Second Republic would be called 'the intellectuals' Republic'.

In politics the new generation distinguished itself by its criticism of the Restor-ation system for damming up the country's energies and preventing 'los mejores' [superior individuals] from coming to power. The new generation also conceived the national 'problem' in terms of the duality formulated by Giner between the 'estado oficial' [official state] and the nation; in Ortega's words, 'la España oficial' and 'la España vital'. In this formulation, if the official state was not capable of realizing the nation's aspirations to progress and social justice, then the nation was entitled to overthrow the state. These young intellectuals forged and projected an awareness of themselves as a group through *tertulias* [cultural gatherings] held mostly in cafés, through their activities in the Ateneo, and especially through the press, which was their chief instrument for popularizing their ideas and making themselves known nation-wide. The new generation benefited especially from the modernization and expansion of the press during the early decades of the century. In 1917 many of them participated in the foundation of *El Sol*—a milestone in the history of Spanish journalism. The aim of the newspaper, influenced by Krausism, was to educate readers in the complexity of the society in which they lived and thus to encourage them to support or promote the reforms necessary for the country's modernization. These intellectuals also popularized their ideas through lectures, theatre, serious literature, and popular novels—all of which formed part of a flourishing cultural industry. Eventually, the failure of the *turno* system, and the subsequent failure of the Primo de Rivera dictatorship to consolidate itself, meant that the organizational and ideological disarray of the Spanish right allowed this group of liberal intellectuals to come to the political fore as the natural rulers of the new Republic.

Intellectuals had always had very clear ideas about the need in Spain for an ethic of public service in political life and for more extensive cultural and educational policies, but, equally, they had always faced the problem of how to translate their prestige into a political vehicle. They founded groups of intellectuals such as the Liga de Educación Política in 1914 but their most important endeavour was the Agrupación al Servicio de la República created by Ortega y Gasset, Ramón Pérez de Ayala, and Dr Gregorio Marañón in 1931. The Agrupación was to show how impossible it was for a group of 'minorías selectas' [select minorities] to make the transition to a national party in an age of mass politics. It was clear that to become successful politicians intellectuals had to create, or at least participate in, mass political parties. However, in so doing, they put at risk the image of the intellectual that they had forged during the first three decades of the century: that of a person with a free, independent political and social conscience, and an educator of the nation. Another problem that the Republic brought to the fore was the rivalry between the 1914 generation of intellectuals who came to power with the Republic and a younger cohort. Many of the latter belonged to the student movement of the FUE (Federación Universitaria Escolar) which had sprung up during the Primo de Rivera dictatorship and whose members would soon swell the ranks of the fascist Falange* and of the radical wing of the Socialist Party (PSOE*). This younger generation had contributed to revamping new liberalism with the introduction into the political arena of new topics typical of the 1920s such as equality of the sexes, divorce, and eugenics. As part of this movement, women across the socio-economic spectrum began to play a more active role in society. Thousands entered university for the first time and demanded a more open and equal relationship between the sexes.

To understand the intellectual and ideological origins of the Second Republic it is also necessary to examine republican tradition and culture. First of all, Spanish republicans had been part of a culture that exalted the French Revolution and its democratic ideals. They were profoundly anticlerical, having abandoned religion for a typically nineteenth-century faith in science. They affirmed the superiority of a secular ethic over what they saw as clerical hypocrisy. Consequently, for many republicans the *raison d'être* of the Republic was to establish the lay state and curb the power of the Church over society. The cult of science and anticlericalism were the common denominators for republicans, socialists, and other elements of the left.

Another important ideological influence on the Republic was that brand of doctrinaire liberalism which placed great emphasis on political forms for their own sake. The most notable instance of this was the significance attached to legal forms and in particular to the Constitution of 1931. This was largely due to the symbolic importance that the Constitution of 1876 had acquired during the last years of the monarchy as a guarantee of national liberties. The 1876 Constitution had, in fact, scarcely excited much passion before 1923, when its suspension by Primo de Rivera helped to create the naïve conviction that a Constitutional Assembly was the magic formula for solving the country's problems and establishing mass politics at a stroke. In fact, the King's betrayal of the 1876 Constitution— when he backed Primo's coup—became the strongest argument against him, and united men as different as Sánchez Guerra, the former leader of the Conservative Party, and the Radical republican Lerroux. During the last period of the monarchist government under General Dámaso Berenguer (1930–1), the only change in the opposition's tactics was to demand a Constitutional Assembly under a Republic rather than the monarchy. The importance attached to legal forms was also encapsulated in a village's greeting of Republican campaigners shortly before the proclamation of the Republic: '¡Vivan los hombres que nos traen la ley!' [Long live the men who bring us the rule of law!]. Republicans were seen as those who would establish the legality on which the monarch had trampled. Intellectual élites with a predominantly legal formation and with little experience of political power advocated legality because they equated it with democratic reform and freedoms. Professional sectors believed democratic legality would provide the means through which they could secure the satisfaction of their demands. One can only surmise that the broader popular support for legal political forms derived from the fact that they had been associated with liberty and democracy since the wars for the liberal constitutions in the early part of the nineteenth century. The political life of the Republic would thus be shaped by this fixation with legal forms known as 'juridicidad', and also by the Constitution which embodied liberal and social principles such as the separation of Church and state, a divorce law, female enfranchisement, the investigation of paternity, free and compulsory primary education, the possibility of expropriating property according to its 'social usefulness', state intervention in industry, the protection of agricultural workers, and comprehensive social legislation.

New liberalism also influenced the corporative ideology of the professions which played a key role in the advent of the Republic. Professional groups such as teachers, post office clerks, and rural doctors had evolved during the latter part of the nineteenth and the first decades of the twentieth century, adapting themselves to the demands of the modern age with new methodologies and greater professionalism. They came to see themselves as groups contributing to the welfare of the nation as a whole. Some of them resorted to the glorification of science and technology to bolster their aspirations. During the period of Berenguer's government which followed Primo de Rivera's fall in January 1930, their accumulated professional grievances flared up and either put them on a collision course with the monarchy or at least disposed them to stand aloof from a regime unable to guarantee law and order. The republicanization of these professional groups is essential to an understanding of the monarchy's fall, to the extent that they played the role of opposition groups at a time when the republican parties were very weak. In Spain, therefore, while one can talk of the upsurge of mass politics with the advent of the Republic, it was in fact the professional groups which constituted its most organized sector. None the less, the role of the professional groups is difficult to quantify in terms of the ballot box. Given their important contribution to the fall of the monarchy, they should have played a major role during the Republic, but the republican parties were more interested in constructing a modern state and modern mass parties than in collaborating with such groups.

Among the professional groups which most influenced the development of the Republic were the conservative agrarian associations of medium-sized and small landowners and tenants prepared to support the new regime. The Republic could easily have assimilated these associations, which had a long history of combating *caciquismo* and in many cases had already organized to lobby for their economic interests. Such an assimilation should have been facilitated by the fact that the republicans had taken from the French Revolution a belief in agrarian reform as a means of constituting a power-base for the Republic: a peasantry which had acquired land or simply reinforced its position under a Republican regime would either actively support, or at least be unwilling to overthrow, the new order from which it had benefited. However, the first governments of the Republic failed to attract the agrarian associations since the Socialists made use of their position in the government to try to establish a political clientele among the rural landless at the expense of the conservative agrarian associations. This pushed the latter towards the Catholic-conservative CEDA* (Confederación Española de Derechas Autónomas), founded in February 1933 and led by José María Gil Robles.

The CEDA's ideology, which many—especially on the left in the 1930s—have equated with unfettered reaction, shared elements of a Krausist view of society with that self-same left. During the previous decades, encouraged by the social encyclical of Leo XIII, *Rerum novarum* (1891), there had been a determined effort by Catholic activists to come to terms with the social needs of the new times. This had led to the formation of a Christian democratic political current which culminated in the CEDA and, among other projects, in the foundation of the important agrarian lobby, the Confederación Nacional Católico Agraria (CNCA). The CEDA developed an ideology imbued with traditional Catholic values, such as the protection of property and the family, which they equated with 'Spain' itself. As in other European countries, this was partly a reformulation of a very traditional nationalism together with indisputable elements of democratic modernity such as the acceptance of the principle of parliamentary democracy. It is significant that, in his parliamentary interventions, Gil Robles started by invoking the most traditional values and ended up employing Krausist-like arguments in order to justify acceptance of the Republic's legality. However, some historians see the CEDA as fascist or pre-fascist—with its combination of a rhetoric of traditional values, the glorification by some party sectors of Gil Robles as the 'jefe' [leader], and the recourse to modern methods such as mass rallies. Certainly, the advances of fascism in Europe in the 1930s, with its combination of tradition and modernity, could not but have some bearing in Spain. It is important, however, to distinguish those of the CEDA's traits that could be described as pre-fascist (mostly external ones such as rhetoric and style) from its ideological foundations which were rooted in social Catholicism. Although some sectors of the CEDA were tempted by the fascist fashion, by far the greatest 'temptation' was the possibility of a conservative Republic. The coming of the Spanish civil war, however, frustrated the development of a successful conservative Christian democratic movement of the sort that flourished in other western European countries after the Second World War.

When one speaks of the ideological origins of the Second Spanish Republic the contribution of the Socialist Party (PSOE) must also be mentioned. Ideologically, the main contribution of the Socialists to the Republic was an emphasis on reformist social legislation. Inspired by the Weimar Constitution they championed the enshrining of social rights in the Spanish Constitution (1931). Another of the Socialists' significant contributions to the political culture of the day was the vision of a disciplined and well-organized national mass party, a phenomenon unknown in Spain. However, it can be safely stated that the PSOE's marxism, which was to influence the development of the Republic thereafter, had no immediate ideological influence on its origins. The marxism officially espoused by the party in its early days had become by the turn of the century a utopian ideal that in practice allowed all kinds of tactics, such as the out-and-out pragmatism of those socialists (associated predominantly with the trade union organization) who collaborated with the Primo de Rivera dictatorship. The marxist ideal did contribute, however, to making the Socialist Party the strongest and best-organized party of the left in 1931.

During the first three decades of the century, the PSOE's marxism had undergone revision. This was accelerated with intellectuals' entrance into the party, making the Spanish Socialist Party an example of new liberal permeation, a process which also occurred in other European countries. Since the death of the party's founder, Pablo Iglesias, in 1925, its leader until 1930 had been Julián Besteiro, one the first pupils of the Institución Libre de Enseñanza primary school. Another important leader was Fernando de los Ríos, a relative of Giner who had written in 1914 that all Spanish political thought had come from Krausism. These men were to play an important role during the first phase of centre-left government (1931–3). By the time the socialists had joined the republicans in the Conjunción Republicano-Socialista of 1909 there was already a predominant current supportive of a reformist republican vision. As Araquistain remarked, they had given up their ideal socialist city for that of the republicans. However, during the last years of the monarchy, small groups of intellectuals had shown an increasing interest in the Russian Revolution and in the revival of maximalist marxism. Some of them founded publishing companies such as Cenit which produced revolutionary literature and helped incorporate the image of revolutionary Russia into the concept of modernity held by contemporary youth. As one observer commented in 1927: Russia, together with other expressions of modernity such as 'aviation, the radio, telephone', gave life great interest. This new generation of intellectuals, together with those of the Generation of 1914 such as Araquistain, played an important role in laying the ideological foundations for the radicalization of one sector of the Socialist Party during the Republic.

Spanish anarchism seems to have contributed little directly to the ideological origins of the Republic. The anarchists, refusing all involvement in parliamentary politics, saw the Republic as the regime that would introduce a legal framework enabling the anarcho-syndicalist CNT* (Confederación Nacional del Trabajo) to flourish. During the Republic the CNT became the strongest anarchist-inspired working-class union in the Europe of the period. It was, however, one of the main focuses of social turmoil during this period. The repeated uprisings in the name of the libertarian revolution were a symptom of the political exclusion and economic hardship experienced by sectors of the CNT base under the Republic. The mounting internal divisions in the CNT over ideology and strategy saw the emergence of a syndicalist group—headed by former CNT leader Ángel Pestaña—which evolved during the Republic towards a parliamentary stance, leading to the foundation of the Partido Sindicalista. The ideology of this group shared with Krausism some aspects of the latter's organic model of society. In wider terms, however, the anarchists made a significant cultural contribution to the Republic. Many of them, especially the young, were (in Spain as elsewhere in Europe) exploring alternative cultural forms and modes of social organization: for example, they were interested in naturism, vegetarianism, oriental philosophies and religions, and they also questioned and explored issues of gender and sexuality. They adopted a life-style that in many respects anticipated the developments of later decades.

This brief survey of the ideological origins of the Second Republic illustrates the existence of important ideological common ground between the right and left. However, a number of factors made both right and left overlook in many cases what they had in common and instead emphasize what separated them. Since nineteenth-century debates on the question of science versus religion, Catholic and liberal circles had tended to be mutually exclusive and antagonistic. They competed vigorously to extend their influence and made no attempt to understand one another. There was, moreover, an important integrist sector of the Church opposed to all modernization which many on the left identified with the Church as a whole. This long history of misunderstanding was above all tragically compounded by the perennial absence of a culture of consensus and tolerance, which opened the gates to the confrontation culminating in the Spanish civil war.

Further reading
García Queipo de Llano, G., *Los intelectuales y la dictadura de Primo de Rivera* (Madrid, 1988).
López-Morillas, J., *El krausismo español: perfil de una aventura intelectual* (2nd rev. edn., Mexico, 1980); Eng. trans. *The Krausist Movement and Ideological Change in Spain, 1854–1974* (Cambridge, 1981).
Mainer, J. C., *La Edad de Plata (1902–1939): ensayo de interpretación de un proceso cultural* (Madrid, 1981).

Tuñón de Lara, M., *Medio siglo de cultura española* (Madrid, 1970).
Villacorta Baños, F., *Burguesía y cultura: los intelectuales españoles en la sociedad liberal 1808–1931* (Madrid, 1980).

The Republican State and Mass Educational-Cultural Initiatives 1931–1936

CHRISTOPHER COBB

The peaceful overthrow of the Spanish monarchy in April 1931 took place amidst scenes of popular rejoicing, a reaction in part inspired by the frustrations accumulated during the dictatorship of General Miguel Primo de Rivera (1923–30). Amongst the supporters of the new Republic in parliament there was a clear awareness of the nature and significance of the task before them. For the socialist Rodolfo Llopis, Director-General of primary education, the coming of the Republic had awakened the moral sense of the whole country and it would be the government's task to form the new citizens of the Republic. In the preamble to the legislation on the creation of new schools, Marcelino Domingo, the Minister of Education, proclaimed· '[t]he Republic aims to bring about a fundamental transformation of Spanish reality so that Spain may become an authentic democracy.' The legitimization of democratic, Republican values, and the change in public attitudes needed to achieve this, represented an enormous undertaking and, for Llopis, it would only become possible by transforming the state educational system. The school was to be the ideological arm of the democratic revolution: it would be the transmission belt, carrying 'modern', civic values to the furthest corner of rural Spain.

In modern Spain the socio-political dimension of education has always been particularly close to the surface. It has regularly served in a very evident way either to maintain and provide support for a given social order or, conversely, to promote change. In this respect it has constituted the battleground for deciding Spain's future direction, as the country proceeded slowly and intermittently with its industrial revolution and accompanying social transformation. The growth of urban centres of population had been seen as a significant threat to the broad cultural hegemony of the Catholic Church, still smarting from the forced sale of its lands in the mid-nineteenth century. Inevitably, its defensive alliance with the established social order was to grow and here its overpowering influence on the education system was to be seen as a guarantee of continuity by its supporters and a check on social and ideological pluralism by its opponents. Far from relaxing with the passage of time, the Church's intransigent position was to be stated with renewed vigour in response to Republican legislation on the future of the religious orders. Thus Pius XI, in his encyclical *Dilectissima nobis* (3 June 1933), spelt out uncompromisingly the fundamental principle of the Church's social stance: '[t]here is no more powerful barrier against social disorder than the Church.'

The socio-political importance of education was also reflected in the efforts of the various groups and organizations which sought to establish alternative systems to try both to make up for the inadequacies of state provision and to combat Church predominance. For the libertarians it was axiomatic to break with the existing structures by developing instructional activities within their own organization: Workers' Societies, Republican Fraternities, the Union of Free Thinkers, as well as a considerable number of Rationalist Schools. A similar process, albeit inspired by a different political ideology, could be observed within Spanish socialist ranks (PSOE* and UGT*). They ran Apprentices' Schools, Workers' and Union Schools and Centres, Popular Universities, together with the Secular Schools Organization for which, in the early years of this century, Juan Almela Meliá had produced a series of reading primers for basic literacy teaching 'in which the basic reading exercises were not to be based on the usual series of religious maxims'. Of particular importance was the New School founded by Núñez Arenas in 1910. Defining itself as a centre for socialist studies, it was to remain closely related to the Socialist Party until the advent of the Primo de Rivera dictatorship in 1923. As well as offering basic educational provision, it also sought to foster a greater political awareness among its members so they might 'avoid being persecuted and imprisoned'. A particular milestone was reached when the New School presented an education programme to the 1918 Congress of the Socialist Party. Nevertheless, the Party's relationship with the cultural and educational activities both of the New School and of the socialist youth movement was frequently lukewarm, a result perhaps of its strong working-class identity which resulted in a distrust of learning and intellectual pursuits. This relative indifference to the intensification of popular cultural activities was to place the Socialists at a disadvantage when, in the 1930s, they faced the rapid growth of more radical groupings.

Of all these alternative projects, the greatest influence was exercised by the group of educational reformers associated with Francisco Giner dè los Ríos and his Institución Libre de Enseñanza.* Founded in 1876, this has been described as the most coherent and sustained attempt to shape Spanish life according to the principles of modern European culture. The way of life of this group of educational reformers was recognizably that of the nineteenth-century middle class: their outlook was secular, their attitudes also displayed a concern for aesthetic refinement, a certain moral puritanism, and a definite élitism. The emphasis on the separation of Church and state and the insistence on ideological neutrality can be seen as a direct reaction to the Church's preponderance in the school system. Indeed, the Institución Libre's firm position here would see it become the major challenger of Church hegemony in education.

Many of these currents were to come together in the Second Republic's educational reform programme which blended the old principles of Spanish liberalism, the modern pedagogy of the members of the Institución Libre, and the educational ideas of the socialists. We can observe the symbolism of Rodolfo Llopis's office, from which he directed primary education, being dominated by portraits of Pablo Iglesias, father of Spanish socialism, and of Giner de los Ríos, founder of the Institución Libre.

As we have noted, the Republic had set vast and loosely defined objectives for the educational system, but in many ways the acute shortcomings which had accumulated over the years demanded attention first to more basic needs, such as the provision of schools and teachers. In 1932–3 only 51.2 per cent of school-age children were in fact on a school roll, a figure which would climb slowly to 52.9 per cent by 1934–5. The actual situation was even worse, since the attendance of those enrolled barely averaged over 70 per cent during the same period.[1] At a time of financial constraint the fact that 13,580 new teaching posts were created between April 1931 and November 1933 (when a right-wing government was returned to power) was one of the Republic's most laudable achievements. Amidst the considerable variety of professional training activities (e.g. pedagogical weeks) organized to prepare the new teachers, the socio-political importance of the educative task was not forgotten: special short courses were arranged in all provincial capitals to make them aware of the need to inculcate the Republic's democratic and secular values.

The number of new schools created by the Republic has been the subject of much discussion. Some of the higher estimates quoted (14,000 new schools during the quinquennium) may have originated in government propaganda: the reality seems to be nearer an annual average of 2,000 new schools.[2] Whilst this was one more indication of the commitment to education, it has to be noted that over 60 per cent of primary schools had only a single class, a consequence of the dispersed nature of the rural population.

Even the most cursory review of the situation is sufficient to show the intractable nature of some of the problems overshadowing ministerial hopes for a rapid transformation of Spanish society. The picture was complicated further in June 1933 by proposals to exclude the religious orders from teaching. Quite apart from the material difficulties which would soon make themselves felt as a result of the rapid timetable proposed, it also became apparent that the issue would strain relations between the different groups broadly supportive of the Republican project. In the parliamentary debate in October 1933, Azaña made plain the fundamental priority of this issue for many in the Republican bloc opposed to the Church: 'At no time and under no conditions will either my party or myself acting on its behalf accept a legislative clause making over education to the religious orders. Never. I regret having to say it, but this is the true defence of the Republic.'

For the liberal followers of the Institución Libre, the dilemma was profound. On the one hand, the elimination of the Church's educational influence was crucial, but many were perturbed that the liberty of the individual to teach should be categorically denied in the Constitution itself. The Institución Libre's members also saw this as a double-edged weapon which might be used (at a time of more conservative government, for example) to rule the Institución itself as unconstitutional. Behind these tensions loomed the even more significant differences of opinion between the liberal and radical elements among the government's supporters; differences which would keep reappearing, as for example in the debate on the 'escuela única' [single or comprehensive school], criticized by conservatives as the imposition of a 'totalitarian' model, or in the debates within the Federation of Workers in Education (FETE) over the identification of teachers with the working class. Llopis himself, clearly closer on these issues to the liberal 'institucionistas', neatly encapsulated the difference in his critical comment on Zinoviev's dictum: 'whatever the cost may be, we must take over control of the child's mind.' In the Spanish case, he suggested, this should be transformed to read: 'whatever the cost may be, we must respect the child's conscience.' For, he continued: 'the fact is that today, in Spain, as a result of the moral violence we had to endure under the monarchy and the persecution suffered by any dissident thinker, respect for the individual conscience still constitutes a splendid revolutionary virtue.'[3]

These were some of the awkward realities which were to hamper the realization of the government's ideals. Many of them were apparent in one of the Republic's most prestigious operations: the promotion of cultural activities. The aim of opening up Spain's cultural heritage to deprived sectors of the population, particularly in rural areas, was entirely consistent with the government's overall strategy. In its endeavour to achieve its objectives here, the Republic expanded the existing network of cultural agencies at its disposal by the addition of bodies such as the Council for the Exchange and Acquisition of Books, founded in November 1931. In Marcelino Domingo's words: 'a properly managed library can be just as effective a cultural medium as a school.' In order to reach rural areas efforts were concentrated on providing all schools with a library which was also to be open to the adult population.

However, the initiative most frequently regarded as the Republic's most significant cultural creation was the foundation in August 1931 of the Misiones Pedagógicas [Pedagogical Missions]. Article 1 of the ministerial decree creating them stated their objectives as 'the diffusion of general culture, a modern approach to teaching and civic education in small towns, villages and hamlets with special attention to the needs of the rural population'. The public imagination was caught by the spectacle of teams of 'missionaries' taking theatrical and musical performances to remote villages or organizing the showing of films and exhibitions of reproductions of famous paintings. Their work has not been without its detractors, however. First, because the approach adopted by the travelling 'missions' implied the existence of a certain passivity amongst the local population. The Missions were operating within a progressive yet distinctly paternalistic tradition 'which considered the people as a receptive being to whom culture is distributed as a work of charity'. Second, there were obvious limitations inherent in the fleeting nature of the contact. Moreover, there was very little inter-communication between purveyors and recipients. The playwright Alejandro Casona, himself a 'missionary', commented later: '[t]hey needed bread and medicine and we had only songs and poems in our bags.'

It may be the charismatic presence of García Lorca that has focused attention almost exclusively on the Missions' theatrical presentations, at the expense of their work in the area of civic education which, in many ways, made a more significant contribution to the government's objective of instilling Republican values. During the Missions' visits the evening would be devoted to meetings with the adult population: there would be lectures and readings on the organization of the new state, the Republican Constitution, and the rights and duties of all citizens in the new political context. It was small wonder that the conservative government elected at the end of 1933 cut back the Missions' budget in 1934 and 1935—fearful perhaps of their ability to mobilize popular support for the progressive Republic.

Another example of the Missions' work which has failed to attract the attention it deserves was the development of a considerable chain of libraries. By 1935 the Board of the Pedagogical Missions had overseen the setting up of more than 5,000 small libraries, all in centres with fewer than 200 inhabitants. According to their report for 1931–3, there were 269,325 child readers and 198,450 adults making use of these facilities. One of the reasons for their singular success could well have been the fact that, far from being an isolated event (as with the theatrical performances), the development of the library service was carried out in a more generally supportive cultural climate. Mention has already been made of the growth in the number of school libraries. All of this took place against the background of greatly increased editorial activity between 1929 and 1933. This campaign was not confined to developed urban centres: bearing the title of 'editorial missions', a fleet of lorries was organized to pass through poorer and more isolated rural areas. Considerable sales were achieved during these visits and, by persuading local individuals to act as the publishers' agents, continuity was assured.

Given the severe economic difficulties which the Republican government faced, no one can doubt their principled commitment to educational reform. Through it they sought to achieve a cherished objective: the eradication of illiteracy and the political and cultural dispossession it inflicted on large sectors of the population. Ultimately too it was understood that, without educational reform and cultural change, it would be impossible to transform—that is, modernize—Spanish society. Yet the progressive Republic was dogged by intractable problems such as the basic shortage of schools and teachers, as well as the unmitigated hostility of a Church opposed to any form of social progress. There were two pre-conditions for any successful reform programme. It would need first to take into account the high illiteracy rate in Spain's rural population, and second to enjoy a broad base of social support, as in the case of the campaign to extend public readership. Neither pre-condition could easily be satisfied within the Republic's short life. The utopian enthusiasm of 1931 always risked provoking disenchantment, since the realization of projects in the cultural field (let alone the creation of the new 'Republican citizen') would necessarily take significantly longer to achieve than some of the Republic's more concrete socio-economic reform projects. Sadly it would not be allowed the time that was so desperately needed.

Notes

1 M. Pérez Galán, *La enseñanza en la II República Española* (Madrid, 1975), 338.
2 For discussion of these figures see M. Samaniego Boneu, *La política educativa de la II República Española* (Madrid, 1977), 388; and Pérez Galán, *La enseñanza en la II República Española*, 342.
3 R. Llopis, *La revolución en la escuela* (Madrid, 1933), 19.

Further reading

Fernández Soria, J. M., 'Revolución versus reforma educativa en la II República Española: elementos de ruptura', *Historia de la Educación*, 4 (1985), 337–53.

Iglesias Rodríguez, G., 'Las Misiones Pedagógicas: un intento de democratización cultural', in C. Garitaonaindia (ed.), *Comunicación, cultura y política durante la II República y la guerra civil*, vol. ii (Bilbao, 1990), 337–65.

Krane Paucker, E., 'Cinco años de Misiones Pedagógicas', *Revista de Occidente*, 7–8 (1981), 233–68.

Luis Martín, F. de, 'Las Juventudes Socialistas como frente cultural pedagógico del socialismo español', *Historia Contemporánea*, 8 (1992).

Molero Pintado, A., 'La Institución Libre de Enseñanza y sus relaciones con la política educativa de la II República Española', *Revista de Educación*, 243 (1976), 82–90.

Otero Urtaza, E., *Las Misiones Pedagógicas: una experiencia de educación popular* (Corunna, 1982).

Puelles Benítez, M., 'El sistema educativo republicano: un proyecto frustrado', *Historia Contemporánea*, 6 (1991), 159–71.

Santonja, G., *La República de los libros* (Barcelona, 1989).

9

Monolithicity versus Pluralism: Political Debates

FRANCES LANNON

ENRIC UCELAY
DA CAL

The Political Debate within Catholicism

FRANCES LANNON

The departure of Alfonso XIII and the proclamation of the Second Republic in April 1931 filled many Catholics with fore-boding. So deeply identified had the Church been with the monarchical regime that when this regime collapsed the Church itself immediately looked vulnerable. Its natural political de-fenders had been conservative monarchists, but who would look after its interests now, in a suddenly transformed political world in which monarchism had been disabled? No one doubted that the Church would need vigorous defence, because every-one in Spain knew that the change of regime represented more than the replacement of a monarchical by a non-monarchical system. In Spanish political discourse in 1931, the term 'Repub-lic' signified a break with the past—not just with the monar-chy, but with the undemocratic politics and the cultural traditions it had embodied. The settled hierarchy of public values had been destabilized as mass politics erupted into national life. In this new situation, the Church could not hope to avoid sceptical, or even hostile, scrutiny.

The first sign of a new order in religious affairs, and one not at all to the Church's liking, was the proclamation of freedom of conscience by the Provisional Government on 15 April, just one day after the inauguration of the Republic. This was a small but sure indicator that the traditional Catholic claim to religious and cultural hegemony would no longer be upheld by the state. On 11 May, in an anti-monarchist demonstration in Madrid, churches and convents were burned down while the new government refused to use force against the demonstrators, whose exploits were then copied in some other Spanish cities. On 23 May the government decreed that religious symbols, including crucifixes, should be removed from state schools. While the two decrees clearly constituted the beginnings of the withdrawal of state support for Catholicism and its privileged position in national life, the failure to protect Church property and Church personnel from attack went further and showed that the Church might not always be accorded the normal safeguards that citizens and institutions usually expect from democratic governments.

This was an abrupt transition, and one which made it imperative for the Church to look to its own defences. As early as 9 May the Spanish archbishops, while affirming their complete separation from party politics, had called on Catholics to use their votes in the elections to the Constituent Cortes to elect deputies 'who offer full guarantees that they will defend the rights of the Church and of the social order'. This instruction to Catholics was followed on 3 June by a letter in the name of all the archbishops from Cardinal Segura, Cardinal Archbishop of Toledo, to the President of the Provisional Government, protesting vehemently at all of the changes already either introduced or threatened in the public role of the Church. The last such letters from the archbishops to the President of the Council of Ministers had been dated 16 and 17 October 1928, and had been concerned with routine ecclesiastical matters—the level of clergy stipends paid by the state, the control of immoral dress and behaviour, and the defence of Sundays as days of rest. There could hardly be a better demonstration of how radically the Church's perception of its priorities had been changed by just a few weeks of the new Republican regime. The issue now was how to salvage as much as possible from the old order in these new circumstances.

The best hope for the Church in the summer of 1931 was that the elections to the Constituent Cortes would produce a conservative assembly. But conservative forces were in disarray, the election results were unfavourable, and the Church could expect little sympathy from the majority coalition of Radicals, Socialists, and republicans which dominated the chamber. In different ways, the modernizing agenda of each of the groups on the left and centre-left included a radical redefinition of the public role of the Spanish Church. Secularizing initiatives were inevitable. The question was how far they would go, and how far Catholics could tolerate them.

In the very first weeks of the Republic, it was already clear that Catholic opinion was not uniform. Cardinal Segura's open mistrust of the Republic led to his expulsion from Spain, and eventually his resignation from the archbishopric of Toledo, but Miguel Maura, the Minister of the Interior in the Provisional Government who ordered his expulsion on 15 June, was himself a Catholic, as was the

President, Niceto Alcalá Zamora. On 25 July Segura published from his French refuge a pastoral letter in the name of all the Spanish bishops (though without consulting them), in which he roundly condemned the draft Constitution of the Republic for its laicism. He argued that its recognition of popular sovereignty was a form of 'official atheism', that the separation of Church and state was unacceptable, and that the liberty of thought, expression, and religion which it enshrined were contrary to Catholic teaching. But this constitutional draft, which the newly elected deputies to the Cortes were immediately to reject in its entirety as too moderate, was itself the work of a commission headed by the Catholic lawyer and politican Ángel Ossorio y Gallardo.

Alcalá Zamora, Maura, and Ossorio y Gallardo were all erstwhile monarchists, who now saw themselves as democratic, reformist conservatives. They represented one strand within Catholic opinion which saw that the Republic would necessarily take some secularizing initiatives, and that these would probably include the separation of Church and state, the extension of lay, state schooling, and the provision of civil alternatives to Church marriage and Church burial. Similar initiatives in other countries had not prevented the Church from flourishing, and it was not certain that they need do so in Spain. There seemed to be space for negotiation.

The history of the relationship between Church and Republic is essentially a history of how that space diminished and all but disappeared. Initiatives on both sides contributed to this. The Republic adopted in December 1931 a Constitution that was more radically anticlerical than Alcalá Zamora, Maura, or Ossorio y Gallardo could find acceptable. Catholic conservatives in the Spain of the 1930s, however democratic their politics, could not be expected to welcome civil marriage and divorce, but they might come to terms with them. They might consider the separation of Church and state unavoidable and yet fear the results of withdrawing state subsidies that helped maintain churches and clergy. But the Constitution went further than this. It dissolved the Society of Jesus (Jesuits), and forbade members of the religious orders to teach in Spain, even in their own schools. It would have gone further still, as its principal drafter, Luis Jiménez de Asúa, intended, and abolished all religious orders, had it not been for the intervention of Manuel Azaña. In the Cortes on 13 October 1931, Azaña argued that contemplative nuns should be left alone because they were harmless, and the religious orders engaged in health and welfare work should be tolerated because there was no immediate substitute for them in Spanish hospitals, orphanages, and old people's homes. On the other hand, he was adamant that the Jesuits must go, and that education given by the religious orders must cease. Recognizing the force of the arguments put forward by deputies who pointed out that such illiberal prohibitions curtailed individual rights that elsewhere the Constitution sought to defend, he none the less insisted that these measures should remain. His reason was chilling: '[w]e cannot put forward an eternal principle of justice when dealing with the religious orders, but rather a principle of social utility and defence of the

Republic.' Safeguarding the state from the unacceptable ideology propounded in Catholic education was more important than respecting the liberty of Spaniards to send their daughters to convent schools, or their sons to be educated by the Jesuits or Salesians or any of the other orders that ran hundreds of schools in Spain in 1931.

The Constitution's attack on the religious orders was more than Catholics could tolerate. Those who argued for it did so with a profound conviction that the religious schools were anti-democratic in ethos and a danger to the Republic. Even if they were right, it is probably the case that their own anti-democratic action was more dangerous to the Republic's long-term prospects, because it made it much harder for Catholics to be Republican, and left the small band of avowed Catholic Republicans vulnerable to charges of bad faith and treachery from their fellow Catholics.

Once the Constitution was adopted, the bishops under the leadership of Cardinal Vidal i Barraquer published in December 1931 a careful and critical analysis, addressed to all Spanish Catholics. They protested strongly against the 'vengeful' treatment of the Church, but called for Church–state dialogue, and for peaceful efforts to reform the Constitution, while keeping the Church free of identification with any political party. This stance was already quite irrelevant to many Catholic monarchists and Carlists and others on the right who found the Republic intolerable and beyond reform. Their pessimism was undoubtedly shared by many bishops, including Isidro Gomá, who was eventually appointed by the Pope to Segura's vacant see of Toledo in 1933, and therefore to the position of head of the Spanish Church.

The most important Catholic movement that claimed to translate the hierarchy's official line of offended but loyal criticism of the regime and its Constitution into politics was the CEDA,* led by José María Gil Robles. The roots of the CEDA lay in Acción Popular of 1931, and beyond that, in the network of Catholic activists, speakers, agrarian associations, and newspapers surrounding Ángel Herrera, who was the influential editor of El Debate and the central figure in the ACNP (Catholic Propagandists). CEDA declared itself uninterested in the outward 'accidentals' of the regime, that is, whether it was Republican or monarchist, but deeply interested in what was substantial and important, that is, policies. Its own policies included defence of the Church, private property, and the family, and promoting a centralist rather than devolutionary state. The CEDA had strong, even demagogic leadership in Gil Robles, effective propaganda, and the trump card of 'the Church in danger'. By the elections of 1933 it had become the foremost political vehicle of Catholic values and Catholic votes, and the election made it the largest party in the Cortes. Indeed, its success left little room for any Catholic competitor within the politics of the Republic, and it exposed the weakness of politicians like Maura and Alcalá Zamora who had no proper organization or popular mobilization behind them.

CEDA was openly committed to a root and branch reform of the Constitution and the state in a direction that would take both of them away not only from anticlericalism, but also from redistributive and reformist social policies, and probably far away from democracy as well, towards an authoritarian regime. CEDA deputies helped repeal the agrarian reforms of the early Republic, and replace them with measures that were much more protective of property owners and much harsher on tenants and agricultural labourers. With other Catholic deputies further to the right, like the Traditionalist landowner José María Lamamié de Clairac, many of them were quite untroubled when critics pointed out that their views seemed incompatible with the kind of reformist social policy on property and employment urged on modern states as far back as 1891 by Pope Leo XIII in his *Rerum novarum*. It was not surprising that groups on the political left had decided in October 1934 that the appointment of three CEDA deputies as Ministers in coalition government with the Radicals (and, notoriously, to the three most sensitive portfolios of Justice, Labour, and Agriculture) marked the end of the reforming Republic as it had defined itself in the first two years of its existence. The attempted revolution of October 1934 failed, and in itself clearly represented a loss of faith in the democratic process. But it also revealed the depth of antagonism to the CEDA, and often also to the Church, among some of the groups most closely identified with the early Republic.

Between them, the Republic's distrust of the Church and especially of Catholic schools, and CEDA's mobilization of the Catholic vote against the Republic's anticlerical measures and efforts to create a new social order, combined to eradicate the option of a genuine Catholic Republicanism. Catholics who approved of the Republic's employment and land reforms of 1931–3, and its democratic principles, had difficulty with its hostility to the Church, and lost credibility among fellow Catholics. Catholics who supported the CEDA's campaign to defend the Church often also supported its onslaught on other aspects of the Constitution. If it was possible to be Catholic and an enthusiastic Republican in the summer of 1931, it was much harder in 1933, and harder still by the spring of 1936. By then, Alcalá Zamora had been removed from the Presidency of the Republic—paradoxically, for having dissolved parliament and called the February 1936 elections rather than appoint his co-religionary Gil Robles as Prime Minister, so great was his distrust of Gil Robles's motives and intentions. By then, too, Gil Robles had failed in his task of gaining power for the CEDA by democratic means, when the February elections were won by the Popular Front, committed to policies very similar to those of the period 1931–3.

There were few Catholic voices to be heard in the summer of 1936 defending the Republic of the Popular Front, or protesting against the plots for its overthrow which everyone suspected. The CEDA leadership was moving towards support for military intervention. When the military coup was unleashed, in mid-July 1936, most Catholics found little to admire in the threatened Republic. There was certainly no official pronouncement from the bishops regretting the military takeover, or recalling the duties of allegiance to the constituted authorities. It soon became horribly clear that such regret was unthinkable, as a terrifying wave of anticlerical violence engulfed many of the areas where the coup failed and the Republic—or some semblance of it—survived. As the partially successful coup gave way to civil war, thousands of priests and religious were assassinated in acts of revolutionary violence behind the Republican lines (almost 7,000 by the end of the war, but most of them within the first few uncontrolled months), Churches were burned or closed, and Catholicism went underground. Faced with a terror unprecedented in western Europe in modern times, few Catholics could contemplate Republican loyalty. Ángel Ossorio y Gallardo was notoriously atypical in choosing to proclaim himself a Catholic Republican throughout the civil war and beyond it. He and a few others argued that the Church must itself accept some responsibility for provoking the hatred it experienced. Cardinal Vidal i Barraquer warned, from an exile made necessary first by anticlerical barbarity, and then by the Catholic saviour, Franco, of the dangers of identifying Catholicism with the anti-Republican side in the civil war. Many Basque Catholics fought for both Catholicism and a devolutionary Republic that belatedly conceded Basque home rule. But for most Catholics, Cardinal Gomá and the great majority of bishops who approved the pastoral letter he published in July 1937 spoke the obvious truth when they said the civil war was a struggle between Republican enemies of religion on the one side, and Catholics united by persecution on the other.

Further reading
Botti, A., *Cielo y dinero: el nacionalcatolicismo en España (1881–1975)* (Madrid, 1992).
Cárcel Ortí, V. (ed.), *Historia de la iglesia en España*, vol. v (Madrid, 1979).
Lannon, F., 'The Church's Crusade against the Republic', in P. Preston (ed.), *Revolution and War in Spain 1931–1939* (London, 1984), 35–58.
—— *Privilege, Persecution, and Prophecy: The Catholic Church in Spain 1875–1975* (Oxford, 1987).
Montero, J. R., *La CEDA: el catolicismo social político en la II República*, 2 vols. (Madrid, 1977).
Payne, S. G., *Spanish Catholicism: An Historical Overview* (Madison, 1984).
Raguer i Suñer, H., *La espada y la cruz* (Barcelona, 1977).
Sánchez, J. M., *The Spanish Civil War as a Religious Tragedy* (Notre Dame, Ind., 1987).

Catalan Nationalism: Cultural Plurality and Political Ambiguity

ENRIC UCELAY DA CAL

The subject of nationalisms in Spain in the years of the Second Republic and the civil war has been dealt with only in the most superficial manner. There has been a tendency to concentrate on descriptions of formal ideology or party politics, paying little attention to aspects of sociological, anthropological, or psychological interpretation which might more satisfactorily explain nationalist mobilization. Too often, the crudely ideological affirmations of contemporary politicians or commentators have been taken at face value. Rather than taking this kind of approach, swamping the reader in a sea of Catalan political parties and factions, and the often hairsplitting distinctions such groups make about themselves, we can better appreciate the nature of Catalan nationalism in the 1930s if we look at it from the general perspective of urban growth, and its subjective and objective effects.

In the 1930s, geographers and urban historians and planners across the globe elaborated the theory of the 'prime city' model, which assumed that an outstanding metropolis would in each country centralize political, economic, and cultural functions. It was a concept very much in line with planning ideals of the time. Nevertheless, it was recognized that there were numerous societies—Spain was often cited as a classic example—where such a clear metropolitan pre-eminence had either not developed or had failed, creating special problems.

From the mid-nineteenth century onwards, Madrid and Barcelona were locked in a bitter rivalry over urban size and the privileges allegedly deriving from demographic superiority. By 1930–1, Madrid and Barcelona were the only Spanish cities with a population of over a million, at the time regarded universally as the threshold level for metropolitan status. Madrid was the state capital, with all the advantages this represented. Barcelona, the outstanding economic centre, bitterly resented being relegated to provincial status, on a level with minor administrative capitals of 20,000 or 30,000 inhabitants.

Instead, Barcelona dreamed of leading the Mediterranean coast, with its concentration of larger cities with populations of over 200,000 (Valencia, with 341,000; Seville, with 236,000; followed by those centres with more than 100,000, such as Málaga, Zaragoza, Murcia, Granada, and Cordoba; only Bilbao, with 171,000, remained outside the Mediterranean urban arc; all the remaining provincial capitals and towns had less than 100,000 inhabitants). Accordingly, Barcelona was the historic reference point for Spanish federalism. All the so-called 'peripheral nationalisms' naturally looked to Barcelona's leadership. This in turn encouraged all manner of grand pan-Catalanist dreams among Catalan intellectuals, who dreamed of joining all the Catalan-speaking areas of Spain with the Occitanian south of France in a vast cultural revival with the Catalan metropolis as its hub. Within Catalan politics, this perception of, and appeal to, some sort of shared Catalan identity or communality meant that a basic substratum of 'Catalanism' (unproblematic only in so far as it was never subject to precise definition) was common to a large portion of the political spectrum, despite the variety of seemingly divisive or distinctive political labels such as federalism, autonomism, regionalism, nationalism, or separatism.

Barcelona, like Madrid, kept growing through immigration, attracted first by economic and secondly by state power. But Barcelona's bid for pre-eminence was not just derived from relative industrial prosperity or comparative political frustration. The city's progress fostered a new cultural market not just in Spanish but now also in the Catalan language. This is what the much-vaunted *fin-de-siècle* Catalan *modernisme* was all about. As elsewhere in cities that had no recent cultural significance, modernism (in the international sense, meaning anything from art nouveau to abstract expressionism) was a chance for a clean start, with monuments from the past being devalued as 'anachronistic'. A new cultural beginning in which everybody kicked off with the same resources, modernism in theory gave no lead or precedence to old established cultural centres as opposed to new starters. As a result, Catalan literature and art could be just as good as their Spanish counterparts and the Catalan capital just as imposing as the Spanish capital.

Such attitudes came easily in Catalonia, since the Spanish administration was traditionally inefficient and, precisely because it was inefficient, tended to be defensively overbearing, aggressive, far more preoccupied with maintaining order than with solving the conditions that nurtured disorder in the first place. Educational policy, or its absence, was a prime example of the general mediocrity of state services from the citizen's viewpoint, whereas the 'Benemérita' (the 'Meritorious' Civil Guard* or gendarmerie) served as a contrary example of one of the few areas of the state administration which worked outstandingly well. (But, of course, its repressive activities were scarcely designed to promote a sense of national integration, in the way an efficient state education system could have done.) With such anti-centralist attitudes widespread, Barcelona became the focus for all discontent, the 'big city' which challenged state omnipotence, as important a symbol to anarchists or republicans as to staunch Catalan nationalists. This meant Barcelona was characterized in a seemingly permanent way as a centre of pluralism. However this appearance of tolerance, in what remained in many ways a closed and conservative society, was only due to the fact that any political strategy —from socially conservative regionalism to libertarian social revolution—reflected the essential ambiguity of the city's status (i.e. the contradiction between its metropolitan scale and its flimsy political authority as a mere provincial capital). Being politically undefined, the Catalan metropolis seemed the key to any sort of large-scale change in Spain. But it was Barcelona's nature as a fast-expanding job market, promising rapid social promotion, which fed the dreams of both newcomers and the established population.

As if to boost the hopes pinned on the city by the discontented of all ideological shades, in the wake of colonial defeat in 1898 and the consequent repatriation of capital, reinvestment led to a socially broad-based dream of permanent economic take-off. Both conservative regionalists and republicans talked of relaunching the Catalan economy, propelling it to a higher stage of development through sustained urban growth, fuelled by a chain reaction of construction, full employment, and increased consumption. The large amounts of French money flowing through neutral Barcelona during the boom years of the First World War encouraged even bigger plans among Catalan economic and political leaders of the right and left. Systematic electrification and the consolidation of a basic communications grid (new railways, roads, and telephones), taking advantage of the demands generated by sustained metropolitan enlargement, were intended to expand the regional economy sufficiently so as to allow it to carry other weaker submarkets such as cultural production, thereby transforming Barcelona into the largest commercial centre on the western Mediterranean. For a time the plan worked: in 1900 there were almost nine times as many workers in textiles as in construction; by 1930 there would be more in construction than in textiles.

Urban expansion and economic growth, combined with Barcelona's rancour as a 'second city', led to a distinctive and highly divisive pattern in Catalan politics after the first decade of the twentieth century. There rapidly arose three rival projects—Spanish nationalism, Catalan nationalism, and a revolutionary working-class movement—all seeking political control of the city and its hinterland, and all of them basing their appeal on the promise of jobs for a clientele of new immigrants.

Spanish nationalism in Barcelona was ambivalent over the question of whether the expansion of state service jobs could be preserved for Spanish speakers by protecting the provincial apparatus of local government against any regionalist reform. Thus provincialism was a job guarantee for the better sort of non-Catalan immigrant to the city (white-collar aspirants and lower middle-class office-seekers), who in turn were supposed to offer social leadership to the rush of poorer, illiterate manual labourers. It became the political hallmark both of radical democrats (like Alejandro Lerroux) and of the increasingly restive army officers who were eager to intervene in local politics.

In marked contrast, Catalan nationalism appealed to internal migrants to the big city from the Catalan countryside, or to those outsiders who assimilated the language and prevailing social codes (above all, the distinctive patterns of sociability which made Barcelona's civil society outstanding in Spain). Contrary to what is often suggested, Catalanism was not led by businessmen but rather by liberal professionals, lawyers and doctors, anxious to define their creed in terms of protectionist social promotion for Catalans. Accordingly, the diverse strands of Catalanism all formulated some sort of dualism—that is, a division of the state into Spanish and Catalan parts, with Barcelona as the political capital of the latter. Barcelona's expanding private service sector would be channelled into a new bureaucracy (in education and other public services where the central administration's provision was inadequate), which would be linguistically defined as a job preserve for Catalan speakers.

Finally, the working-class movement, dominated by the anarcho-syndicalist CNT* and led by a welter of anarchist groups, avoided the debate between provincialism and dualism by harping on about federalism and pointing to the inevitable withering-away of the state. But the anarcho-syndicalists also promised a vague future of union-led, committee-run economic management, in which the least privileged sectors of working-class immigrants (i.e. poor and unskilled) would be running things over the heads of the rest, wherever they were from.

This triangular rivalry was defined between 1905 and 1909 and confirmed in the successive social and political crises of 1917, 1919–20, and 1923. No one corner was able to dominate the other two. The rise of labour protest encouraged the growth of military insubordination, while Catalan regional demands shattered the dynastic party system of the *turno** in 1912–13, stimulating the growth of extraparliamentary political alternatives. So, after 1919–20, anarcho-syndicalist revolutionary activity brought together the moderate regionalist leadership of the Mancomunitat (organ of Catalan administrative self-government) and the chiefs of the local military garrisons, while radical Catalan nationalists looked indecisively towards the CNT. In large measure, this convergence brought about the military dictatorship of General Primo de Rivera, with a coup based in Barcelona in 1923.

The long-term effects of the dictatorship were, however, somewhat paradoxical. After 1919, the clear positions of 1905–9 became increasingly confused, producing contradictory, explosive alliances formed in opposition to the regime —especially in 1924–6 (when the separatist leader Francesc Macià, exiled in France, established a revolutionary coalition with the extraparliamentary left) and again in 1928–9 (when a broad political front attempted to organize another Spain-wide revolt against Primo). In spite of their anti-parliamentary stance, the anarchists were drawn into political collaboration with the nationalists and the republican left. Thereby, a new generation of radical nationalist office- and shop-workers helped Catalanism lose its long-standing conservative, even clerical, tone. Republicans and Catalanists could finally mix successfully, going beyond their old meeting ground in federal ideology to join with the anarcho-syndicalists in the call for a new kind of social rule. By 1930, in the transitional period after Primo's fall, this new political blend was already visible both in the political amnesty campaigns and in the strong Barcelona connection in the last plots against the monarchy.

Thus the imposition of military dictatorship during the 1920s had a paradoxical effect on Catalan nationalism. Joint opposition to Spanish nationalist militarism permitted the development of an understanding between a service sector dominated by nationalists, an immigrant-dominated industrial unionism of anarcho-syndicalist hue, and left republicans with a support base in the peasant sharecroppers' movement (*rabassaires*). When the fall of the dictatorship dragged the monarchy down with it, this understanding allowed the formation in early 1931 of an unusual populist coalition, the Esquerra Republicana de Catalunya (ERC) (Catalan republican left), which joined urban and rural republicans and radical nationalists in a broad-based coalition which would dominate Catalan politics through to the civil war.

The ERC had a degree of social support far more wide-ranging than the rest of Spanish republicanism, while its grass-roots political organization and limited territorial extension facilitated a close relationship between rank-and-file and leadership. The difference can easily be seen by contrasting the style of its charismatic populist founder and leader, Macià, with that of the major Spanish republican politician, Manuel Azaña. Macià, one of the pioneers of personalized mass politics in Spain, was a poor public speaker but an accomplished manipulator of crowd sentiment through his warm personal touches; while Azaña, though a fine orator, lacked personal charisma. The ERC's unique political dynamism stemmed from the fact that Catalan autonomy (granted by the Second Republic in 1932) was to make Barcelona the centre of the only formal alternative political system to the central government. From the outset the Esquerra scored such an overwhelming victory, first in the municipal elections of April 1931 which ushered in the Second Republic, then in the voting for the Constituent Spanish parliament in June of the same year, that the party had absolute control of all Catalan institutions. Accordingly, the ERC scarcely distinguished between these formal institutions and its own role as ruling party. This trend was confirmed both by the hostile parliamentary debate in Madrid over the granting of the Catalan autonomy statute (finally promulgated after the failed conservative revolt of August 1932) and by the elections to the Catalan parliament in November, which once again returned an absolute majority for the ERC.

Dualism and Esquerra hegemony, however, did not favour stability in either Catalan or Spanish politics. The internal rivalry between republicans and nationalists within the ERC encouraged the growing breach in 1932–3 between the ERC and revolutionary anarcho-syndicalism. Since it proved impossible to control the urban unions, the concern to ensure a broad populist social base for the ERC led to an excessive attention to sharecropper demands. Inner ERC squabbles were papered over after the death in December 1933 of the much revered Macià. Sobered by the electoral losses of the November 1933 general elections, most of the Catalan left accepted a coalition headed by the leader of the ERC's republican wing, labour lawyer Lluís Companys. With increasing responsibility for day-to day services, as the central government transferred such delicate matters as public order to Barcelona's autonomous authorities during 1933–4, the Companys coalition found itself obliged to fulfil its political promises. An agrarian reform law passed by the Catalan parliament provoked a constitutional conflict with the centreright government in Madrid. The confrontation encouraged the regrouping of the Spanish left which had been divided since 1933. The result was ERC participation in the October 1934 revolt against the new right-wing governmental combination in Madrid. The overnight defeat of the Esquerra and its allies in Barcelona led to the extensive gaoling of the left, the suspension of autonomy such as it had been, and a temporary domination of Catalan politics by conservative regionalists, centreright republicans, and Catholics, who—in the short time during the second half of 1935 in which they had a serious opportunity to act—were unable to do much more than argue.

The radical Catalan nationalists' failure in the October 1934 insurrection broke them, but permitted the hitherto marginal marxist groupings to appeal to the radicalized political support base of nationalist-republican populism. The various small communist or extreme left parties came from the same social milieu in the urban service sector as the ERC militants. They used similar arguments, only they gave them a revolutionary gloss. But beneath this they attached the same importance to Catalan autonomy and, therefore, to the policy of creating an alternative bureaucracy. The resulting process of centre-left political reunification, in 1935–6, under the aegis of the Catalan Popular Front, favoured the rise of two rival communist parties, one stalinist and the other emphatically not so, both the product of the fusion of diverse smaller groups. Their expansion was at the expense first of the nationalists, and ultimately of the Esquerra. In the immediate term, though, the general elections of February 1936, which gave victory to the centre-left reformist Popular Front, permitted the re-establishment of the formal institutional and political situation prior to the October 1934 revolt.

On the outbreak of civil war in July 1936, Catalonia was somewhat removed from the front line of the fighting. This facilitated a variety of revolutionary experiments. With state authority gone, and power reduced to its most physical expression, there was a complete breakdown in social co-ordination such that normal production, transport, and communication became almost impossible to sustain in the face of an extreme particularism whereby each town (or, in the case of Barcelona, each neighbourhood) and factory was under its own revolutionary committee. However appealing in theory, the practice was chaotic. The anarcho-syndicalists attempted both to control the situation and to transform it into their ideal of a union-run, corporative industrial democracy; but they failed on both counts. Both radical nationalists and ERC tended to be relegated, and the central political conflict in the winter of 1936–7 was between the anarcho-syndicalists (CNT) and the rival communist groupings that had inherited the populist mantle. A confused revolt in Barcelona in May 1937 (the 'May Days') permitted the ERC government, with stalinist and nationalist support, to impose some sense of its own preferred order on the clutter of committees and particularist interests. With the May revolt, the central government (since November 1936 installed in Valencia) finally roused itself to intervene in Catalan affairs, and, some months later, in autumn 1937 transferred itself to Barcelona, thereby—in fact if not in theory— reducing Catalan autonomy to its most symbolic expression.

The 1936–7 revolution in Catalonia generated much comment at the time, as it has since, but the vast majority of this has been devoted to the theoretical merits of applied libertarian* theory (from differing viewpoints) as against the correct application of leninist principles by stalinist and anti-stalinist communists. Class realities, however, were considerably more complicated since both marxist groupings came from the same lower middle-class backgrounds (the leadership being primarily composed of schoolteachers, journalists, and clerical workers) and shared common values, while the anarcho-syndicalists represented a poorer outsiders' version of the same (i.e. schoolteachers in Libertarian Schools, journalists in the anarcho-syndicalist press, confined to the militant proletarian 'ghetto' rather than employed in mainstream bourgeois institutions). But whatever the case, the war represented the utmost expression of Catalan dualism. First, Barcelona managed, however chaotically, to subsist for almost a year without the tutelage of Madrid, something surprisingly satisfying even to some conservative victims of the process. Second, the arrival of the Republican government, however irritating to particularist sentiment (ranging from anarcho-syndicalists to the Catalan stalinists or the ERC), was none the less indirectly gratifying as it could be seen as representing an ultimate recognition of Barcelona's status as the real capital of the whole country, over and above Madrid.

At least until the second half of 1937, there was little sense of the proximity of conflict in Barcelona, beyond the growing stream of refugees from other parts of Republican territory and, of course, an omnipresent hunger. But by 1938 the war had come with all its force, subjecting Barcelona to fierce aerial bombardment and consuming cannon fodder through enforced conscription for the desperate Ebro offensive in the summer. The Francoist victory, however, by conquering all Catalonia between November 1938 and February 1939, wiped out everything save the memory of Catalan dualism.

The 1930s in Catalonia can thus be viewed as a succession of the three social options which had disputed control of the urban service market since the beginning of the century. First the Catalan nationalist option, with the ERC (during the war sustained by the stalinists), defined a new political space. Then the anarcho-syndicalists tried unsuccessfully to redesign that same space, literally from bottom to top. Finally, the Spanish nationalist option reimposed itself through military dictatorship, as it had in the preceding decade, but this time with far greater thoroughness and ruthlessness.

Further reading
Balcells, A., *El nacionalismo catalán* (Madrid, 1991) (English trans. forthcoming).
Fraser, R., *Blood of Spain* (London, 1979; new edn. 1994).
McDonogh, G. W. (ed.), *Conflict in Catalonia: Image of an Urban Society, 1840–1940* (Gainesville, Fla., 1986).
Nagel, K. J., *Arbeiterschaft und nationale Frage in Katalonien zwischen 1898 und 1923* (Saarbrücken, 1991).
Payne, S. G., *The Spanish Revolution* (New York, 1970).
Peers, E. A., *Catalonia Infelix* (Oxford, 1938).
Ucelay Da Cal, E. *La Catalunya populista (1931–1939)* (Barcelona, 1972).

ALICIA ALTED

JO LABANYI

The Cultural Politics of the Civil War

The Republican and Nationalist Wartime Cultural Apparatus

ALICIA ALTED

The ideological nature of the Spanish civil war was expressed in the confrontation of two conceptual models of reality, both of which used culture as a legitimizing weapon. On one side stood the popular revolution, the people rising up in arms against those social classes that for centuries had controlled all branches of political power and culture. On the other side were members of the military, waging a counter-revolutionary war with the support of those same social classes. The result was the subordination of culture to political and military interests, which meant the subordination of creative and critical freedom to the defence of the particular cause to which one was committed. This fact necessarily governed intellectuals' position with regard to the war.

Since the start of the century, intellectuals had played an increasingly central role in Spanish society and politics. In addition, the course of early twentieth-century European history had led to intellectuals' growing commitment to what they regarded as 'the people'; that is, the proletariat. The Mexican and Soviet Revolutions, the latter in particular, played a crucial role in politicizing intellectuals in a social scenario increasingly defined by the class struggle, economic crisis, and the rise of violent nationalist movements. Spain was no exception to this process, which coincided with an indigenous intellectual tradition going back to the Enlightenment and continued in the late nineteenth-century regenerationist movement and the Institución Libre de Enseñanza,* finding its clearest expression in the political formulations of socialists, anarchists, and communists during the Second Republic. At that time, it was bourgeois reformers who promoted culture as a means of transforming society. Once the war had started, it was the people who upheld the value of culture as a way of combating ignorance and class oppression, for—as a poster stated— 'culture will make you free'.

This championing of culture by and for the people was accompanied by the figure of the proletarian intellectual, and was the subject of a series of debates in the Republican zone on the political and revolutionary significance of the work of art. For example: the polemic between the painter Ramón Gaya and the poster artist Josep Renau (then General Director of Fine Arts) about whether art should be 'free, authentic, and spontaneous' or socially committed and in the service of political ideals. Underscoring this debate was the contradiction between intellectuals' political awareness and their inherently anomalous class position, divorced from their social roots by education. As José Bergamín put it in 1937: 'When those of us who are writers say we want to belong to the people, we are simply voicing the most deeply felt dictates of our conscience [. . .]. And this being and not being part of the people was and is the key issue in Spanish culture.'

In effect, the war produced a wave of solidarity among a majority of Spanish and European intellectuals, for whom—in both cases—the defence of the Republic was synonymous with the defence of freedom and democracy at a time when the dangers of fascism-Nazism were starting to be keenly perceived. The clearest expression of this commitment was the Second International Congress of Writers in Defence of Culture organized by the Alliance of Antifascist Intellectuals, held in Valencia, Madrid, Barcelona, and Paris 4–18 July 1937.

Obviously, the issues thrown up by intellectuals' commitment to a popular cause did not arise in the Nationalist zone. Here culture was used to legitimize the military struggle against a Republic dominated by international Bolshevik materialism, threatening national unity and the Christian way of life. The Church played a fundamental role in shaping the cultural model of Nationalist Spain, diluting the influence of totalitarian movements, as can be seen in the magazine *Jerarquía* [*Hierarchy*] which, under the editorship of the priest Fermín Yzurdiaga, elaborated the intellectual basis of what one can call Spanish fascism. This was grounded in the trilogy God–Caesar–Empire, and its point of reference was sixteenth- and seventeenth-century Spain which had exhausted 'its material strength in order to impose and defend a spiritual, religious view of civilization'. The goal was the restoration of this Spain 'which fell asleep two hundred years ago', to quote the poem by Miguel Martínez del Cerro included in the *Antología poética del Alzamiento* [*Poetic Anthology of the Nationalist Uprising*].

The differences in the institutional organization of culture by the two sides are glaring. In the Nationalist zone the military were in charge; consequently they stamped their hierarchical, homogenizing imprint on all forms of cultural expression. In the Republican zone, however, there was conflict between military and political interests, as well as disagreement between the various political and trade union groups, and between the central government and the governments of the autonomous regions, especially Catalonia. All of them wanted to take advantage of the war to carry out their own revolution, but the problem was that there had to be agreement on what kind of revolution this should be, and to put it into effect they had to defeat the enemy. The ideological differences and lack of political unity in the Republican zone were reflected in a consequent cultural diversity, with a proliferation of forms of expression sponsored by organizations of many different kinds.

By the end of August 1936, the situation in the Republican zone was chaotic, and the Communists in particular felt the need to form a strong government whose priority would be political and military unity, in order to win the war. With the formation on 4 September of the government headed by Francisco Largo Caballero, the Communist Party became the leading force. This had its cultural repercussions in the policies of the Ministry of Public Instruction and Fine Arts, from September 1936 under Jesús Hernández, editor of the Communist newspaper *Mundo Obrero* [*Workers' World*]. The goal of these policies was 'the immediate putting into practice of the principle of culture for the people'. To achieve this, he relied heavily on the Alliance of Antifascist Intellectuals which functioned as a public sector body, controlling the Ministry's Propaganda Section. As in the Nationalist zone, these cultural policies involved a strict process of political purges and highly sectarian attitudes. A major cultural and propaganda initiative was launched to save the artistic and historical heritage. In particular, valuable salvage work was done by the Junta Central del Tesoro Artístico [Central Committee for Art Treasures], responsible to the Ministry's General Directorate of Fine Arts. Also valuable was the Ministry's sponsorship of exhibitions, notably the Spanish Republican pavilion at the Paris International Art and Technical Exhibition of 1937. However, the defence of the national heritage in both the Republican and the Nationalist zones is a controversial and murky area, with the inevitable evacuation of art treasures, unofficial destruction of works of art, confiscations, pillage, and illegal export and sale abroad of art objects.

In the educational field, the principle of 'culture for the people' was implemented through the literacy campaign, the beginnings of primary school reform, and measures to increase the lower classes' access to all levels of a single, unified school system. These proposals had previously been mooted under the Republic but were now radicalized in the name of the people's control of cultural resources, to the detriment of the essential educational freedom and diversity that had marked the years 1931–6.

The government sworn in on 6 April 1938, under Juan Negrín, gave responsibility for Public Instruction and Health (as the Ministry was now called) to the anarchist Segundo Blanco, an Asturian construction worker whose name had been put forward by the CNT* executive. Under him the Ministry's activities were chiefly directed towards children evacuated to areas away from the fighting; the educational colonies set up to house them also provided an opportunity to put into practice the principles behind the reform of the school system.

In Catalonia, cultural policy was formulated by the Consell de Cultura, headed by appointees of Esquerra Republicana de Catalunya (Catalan republican left). Responsible to the Consell were the Comisariat de Propaganda and the Consell de l'Escola Nova Unificada (CENU), the latter responsible for educational policy. The Basque government of 1936–7 put José María de Leizaola of the Basque Nationalist Party (PNV*) in charge of Justice and Culture. One of his first measures was the creation of a University of the Basque Country.

Alongside these official bodies there existed a multiplicity of organizations linked to political or trade union groups, which undertook an intensive programme of cultural diffusion both on the front and in the rearguard, mostly with the support of some official body, usually the Ministry of Public Instruction. Some of these had existed before the war, others were created in the heat of the battle. Particularly important in the literacy campaign were the Milicias de la Cultura working with soldiers on the front, and the Brigadas Volantes de Lucha contra el Analfabetismo [Flying Literacy Brigades] working with civilians. The broader-based Cultura Popular was set up to co-ordinate the cultural activities of the various Popular Front bodies; among its different departments, the work of its Library Section (set up before the war started) deserves special mention. Its Theatre Section included the repertory and actors of the earlier touring company La Barraca. These organizations took over the role that had been played by Misiones Pedagógicas under the Republic, modified to suit the requirements of war. Among the various propaganda organizations, Altavoz del Frente should be mentioned. Also important were the Army Education Clubs set up by the Federation of United Socialist Youth, as was the continued work of the Popular Universities, Casas de la Cultura, Ateneos Libertarios, and the libertarian* women's organization Mujeres Libres.

The activities of these organizations spanned all branches of culture from education to literature, art, and the mass media. But magazines, theatre, posters, and poetry were the areas that most strongly expressed the principles behind the creation of the Republican Cultural Front. In poetry, for example, ballads and songs (both deeply rooted in popular culture) were the vehicles of the desired alliance between intellectuals and the people, in the double sense of integrating the popular into culture and of making writers' work available to the people. Poetic compilations published ballads and songs by Antonio Machado, Miguel Hernández, León Felipe, Emilo Prados, or Rafael Alberti alongside those by anonymous soldiers for whom poetry provided a way of conveying their own perceptions of a war fought with a gun in one hand and a book in the other. The best

10 Republican soldiers in a dug-out during the civil war, reading books from the Biblioteca del Combatiente [Soldier's Library] provided by the government-run Cultural Militias. For the Republic, widening educational and cultural access was integral to its struggle in the civil war. This democratizing project was however criticized by radicals on the left who argued that its emphasis on extending bourgeois 'high' cultural forms to the masses was a way of neutralizing the proletarian threat.

EJERCICIOS

Hacer multiplicaciones con números de dos o más cifras.

EJEMPLOS

		43105
	1000	× 319
	× 16	387945
24	6000	43105
× 10	1000	129315
240	16000	· 13750495

USAMOS LA MULTIPLICACION:

Para hacer un número dos, tres, etc., veces mayor.
Para saber el valor de varias cosas conociendo el de una.
Para convertir unidades de especie superior en otras de especie inferior: duros en pesetas, años en meses, etc.

EJERCICIOS

Hacer problemas sencillos aplicando la multiplicación en los usos indicados.

MULTIPLIQUEMOS
NUESTRO ESFUERZO HASTA VENCER AL FASCISMO

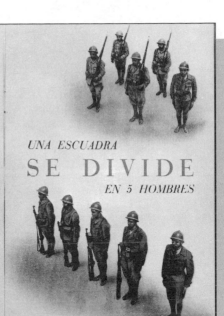

UNA ESCUADRA
SE DIVIDE
EN 5 HOMBRES

---

ejercicios: formar otras sílabas, palabras y frases con los elementos ya conocidos
ejemplos de sílabas

To, ta, dos, das, los, las, es,

as, fuer, zos, zas, ven, van, cer,

cir, car, cor, cur

ejemplos de palabras:

Tajo, tabaco, fuerte, fuero, fuego, cerca, circo,

venganza, venta, vanguardia, corte, curva,

Cervantes, Cartagena

La retaguardia debe colaborar con

la vanguardia

LUCHAMOS POR NUESTRA CULTURA

Lu-cha-mos por nues-tra cul-tu-ra

L-u-ch-a-m-o-s p-o-r n-u-e-s-t-r-a c-u-l-t-u-r-a

u, a, o, e

L, ch, m, s, p, r, n, t, c, l

11 *a, b* Anti-fascist primers issued in 1937 by the Republican Cultural Militias to teach literacy and numeracy to the troops at the front. The numeracy primer (*a*) reads: 'We must multiply our efforts till fascism is defeated', 'A squad is divided into 5 men.' The text of the literacy primer (*b*) includes the slogans 'The rearguard must collaborate with the vanguard' (illustrated by the visual collage of a co-educational class defended by front line troops), and 'We are fighting for our culture.' The militarized vocabulary drew on the troops' everyday experiences of war, stressing that the Republic was fighting to defend the people's right to culture and also that culture is itself a form of struggle.

12 Republican civil war poster issued by the Cultural Militias, promoting the value of literacy. The text reads: 'Illiteracy blinds the spirit. Soldier, educate yourself.' The effort put into encouraging newly literate troops to write their own poetry as a form of self-expression is here echoed by the emphasis on self-education. The mechanized image of the soldier is typical of the constructivist design favoured by Communist poster artists. Similar mechanized figures are found in German and Italian fascist art, but the visual and verbal stress here on self-education could not be more different from the Nationalists' anti-intellectual stance and their authoritarian view of education as propaganda. (In a famous incident at Salamanca in October 1936, the Nationalist General Millán Astray interrupted Unamuno's denunciation of Nationalist violence and philistinism with the cry 'Death to intelligence!'; the Spanish fascist propagandist Giménez Caballero defined fascism—echoing Goebbels—as 'the mysticism/mystique of anti-culture'.)

known of these collections was the *Romancero general de la guerra de España*, published in Valencia in 1937. One of the first magazines to print such poems was *El Mono Azul*, a weekly linked to the Alliance of Antifascist Intellectuals, a selection of which formed the first *Romancero de la guerra civil* published in 1936 by the Ministry of Public Instruction. Significantly, after May 1937 *El Mono Azul* stopped publishing ballads and restricted itself to poems and songs by 'learned' poets, responding to the above-mentioned debate between Gaya and Renau—published in the other major Republican cultural magazine, *Hora de España*—on the function of art. The question of artistic autonomy was explicitly raised by a 'group of young writers' in a joint paper given at the Second International Congress of Antifascist Intellectuals in July 1937.

As the war advanced, the institutional apparatus of an increasingly beleaguered Republic gradually fell apart, while the Nationalist zone saw the reverse process of the construction of a 'new' institutional framework under military cover, but headed by the civilian forces and organizations (Church and Falange*) that had backed the uprising. The first attempt to structure the 'New State' was the establishment, by a law issued on 1 October 1936, of the Junta Técnica del Estado [Technical State Command] comprised of a president and a number of sections, one of which was the Culture and Education Committee headed by the writer José María Pemán. He concentrated his efforts on drawing up guidelines for the purging of teachers (especially schoolteachers) and on getting classes going again at primary and secondary level. From the start of the war, the news media had been subject to strict military censorship. A 1937 directive placed them under the control of the newly established State Press and Propaganda Delegation, headed first by Vicente Gay and then by Manuel Arias Paz. The Falange and the Carlists* had their own parallel delegations which, with the unification decree of April 1937 merging the two organizations, joined to form the Delegación Nacional de Prensa y Propaganda de FET y de las JONS* under Fermín Yzurdiaga. The latter started to function—creating the beginnings of the Nationalist press (what later would be called 'la prensa del Movimiento*')—by taking over confiscated newspapers and printing presses.

It must be remembered that, at the start of the war, most printing presses were in the big cities which had remained loyal to the Republic and which saw an unparalleled growth of news publications, most significantly of mural newsboards (*periódicos murales*). By contrast, Nationalist propaganda mostly used the medium of radio, despite the fact that the main radio transmitters were also in the Republican zone. Radio Nacional de España first started to broadcast from Salamanca in January 1937. By that time, the Falange and the Carlists already had their own stations: FET-1 Radio Valladolid, famous for its 'Emergency Appeals'; and EAJ-6 Radio Pamplona, becoming Radio Requeté de Pamplona, on which General Mola frequently broadcast. But the most popular broadcasts by far were those of General Queipo de Llano from EAJ-5 Radio Sevilla. Every night since 18 July 1936, the 'radio general' had used the medium as a devastating propaganda weapon against the Republic, broadcasting news and rumours, occasionally true but mostly false or distorted, which made a big impact on listeners not because of their informational value (being largely misinformation) but because of his strident, pompous, ranting style.

As the war progressed and new territory was gained, there was a need for a more complex administrative structure; consequently in January 1938 a law was issued organizing the central state bureaucracy into ministerial departments. Everything to do with education and culture was put under the Ministry of Education where the Church's influence was paramount. However, the Falange was given control of the media, responsible to Ramón Serrano Suñer as Minister of the Interior; a National Press Service and Propaganda Service were set up under José Antonio Giménez Arnau and Dionisio Ridruejo respectively. The main contribution of the Press Service was the April 1938 Press Law, which remained in force till 1966, giving the state complete control of the 'organization, monitoring, and control' of the press. Ridruejo staffed his Propaganda Service with a group of writers and artists that would in time become (in his own words) 'an intellectual group defined more by generational than ideological ties'; their numbers included the poets Luis Rosales, Luis Felipe Vivanco, and Leopoldo Panero, the novelists Juan Antonio Zunzunegui and Ignacio Agustí, critics and writers like Antonio Tovar and Pedro Laín Entralgo, the painters Juan Cabanas and José Caballero, the musician Regino Sainz de la Maza, and the dramatist Gonzalo Torrente Ballester. It was members of this group who would in the 1940s, using the magazine *Escorial* as a platform, initiate the recovery of liberal thought, and who would form part of Joaquín Ruiz Giménez's team at the Ministry of Education in 1951.

Torrente Ballester was launched by Dionisio Ridruejo and Luis Escobar, director of the Theatre Department, as a promising young writer who would revitalize the Spanish stage by creating a new heroic, imperial theatre, as theorized by Torrente in his essay 'For a Theatre of the Future', published in the magazine *Jerarquía* in October 1937. His theories were put into practice in his play *El viaje del joven Tobías*, a 'morality play in seven conversations', based on the biblical story of Tobias. In Torrente's hands, however, the story underwent a metamorphosis thanks to the ironic and comic use of all manner of anachronisms. Although the play is overly rhetorical and full of the statutory references to order, hierarchy, and unity, it was a daring dramatic experiment anticipating formal and thematic elements typical of his later fictional work. The play was given a public reading, organized by Ridruejo's group. Its blithe treatment and symbolic distortion of its biblical material caused it to be immediately denounced, on publication in 1938 (by the Bilbao publishing house Jerarquía, with illustrations by Juan Cabanas), to the Church authorities, accused (among other things) of heresy and lack of respect in treating a biblical subject, using psychoanalytic theory as an excuse to dwell on incest between father and daughter, and defending pantheism and suicide. At that time Torrente also published *El casamiento engañoso*, in line with the official policy of reviving the sixteenth- and seventeenth-century *auto sacramental* [morality play], here turned into political allegory. Another example of the 'new' theatre was Rosales and Vivanco's historical drama *Spain's Greatest Queen*, based on Isabel la Católica.

Further reading

Alted, A., 'Poesía de guerra y "nueva" poesía durante el período 1936–1939 en España', in *Homenaje a Pedro Sainz Rodríguez, iii: Estudios históricos* (Madrid, 1986), 21–36.

—— *Política del nuevo estado sobre el patrimonio cultural y la educación durante la guerra civil española* (Madrid, 1984).

Alvarez Lopera, J., *La política de bienes culturales del gobierno republicano durante la guerra civil española*, 2 vols. (Madrid, 1982).

Bilbatúa, M. (ed.), *Teatro de agitación política (1933–1939)* (Madrid, 1976).

Collado, G., *El teatro bajo las bombas (en la guerra civil)* (Madrid, 1989).

Escolar, H., *La cultura durante la guerra civil* (Madrid, 1987).

Fernández Soria, J. M., *Educación y cultura en la guerra civil (España, 1936–1939)* (Valencia, 1984).

Gagen, D., and George, D. (eds.), *La guerra civil española: arte y violencia* (Murcia, 1990).

Gamonal Torres, M. A., *Arte y política en la guerra civil española: el caso republicano* (Granada, 1987).

García Lara, F. (ed.), *Literatura y guerra civil* (Almería, 1987).

Garitaonaindía, C., *La radio en España, 1923–1939: de altavoz musical a arma de propaganda* (Bilbao, 1988).

Grimau, C., *El cartel republicano en la guerra civil* (Madrid, 1979).

Hart, S. (ed.), *¡No pasarán! Art, Literature and the Spanish Civil War* (London, 1988).

Lozano, C., *La educación republicana, 1931–1939* (Barcelona, 1980).

Monleón, J., *'El Mono Azul': teatro de urgencia y Romancero de la guerra civil* (Madrid, 1979).

Mundi, F., *El teatro de la guerra civil* (Barcelona, 1987).

Pabellón español: exposición internacional de París, 1937 (Madrid, 1987).

Rodríguez Puértolas, J., *Literatura fascista española*, 2 vols. (Madrid, 1986–7).

Salaün, S., *La poesía de la guerra de España* (Madrid, 1985).

Santa, A. (ed.), *Literatura y guerra civil* (Barcelona, 1988).

Tiana, A., *Educación libertaria y revolución social: España, 1936–1939* (Madrid, 1987).

Tisa, J. (ed.), *The Palette and the Flame: Posters of the Spanish Civil War* (London, 1980).

Vernon, K. M. (ed.), *The Spanish Civil War and the Visual Arts* (Ithaca, NY, 1990).

Propaganda Art: Culture by the People or for the People?

JO LABANYI

The vast majority of Spanish civil war art was produced on the Republican side, most writers and artists sympathizing with the Republic because of its promotion of culture as an educational tool: the Republican cultural effort was actually stepped up during the war years. The privileging of art as a propaganda weapon was a natural extension of the ideals of the Institución Libre de Enseñanza,* which saw the diffusion of culture as a way of introducing reform from above, taking enlightenment—meaning bourgeois, liberal values—to the people. The anarchists and some socialists were concerned with developing proletarian cultural forms as a source of alternative values, but the socialists' belief in the importance of party discipline again tended to lead to a top-down approach which often conflicted with rank-and-file practice. Despite the best of intentions, most Republican intellectuals were unable to get beyond an implicit cultural paternalism, as evidenced by their overwhelming preference for the Romantic term *pueblo* (cf. German *Volk*) to the marxist term *masas*, whose use was largely restricted to grass-roots labour organizations. Even anarchists, despite their radical cultural project, tended to prefer the former term because of its sense of organic community, disliking the latter because of its anti-individualist connotations.

Republican propaganda art challenged basic cultural assumptions, blurring distinctions between the fine and applied arts, and attempting to get beyond bourgeois concepts of the individual artist and the original work. In the process, many contradictions emerged. Posters were produced in collective workshops but most were signed by individual artists. Performance of agitprop plays was necessarily collaborative but they were scripted by well-known individual writers (some did allow space for improvisation). Propaganda poetry was mostly published in collective form but the anthologies published by the Republican government limited themselves to work by established poets, as on the whole did the magazine *Hora de España*, edited by centre-left intellectuals. *El Mono Azul*, an organ of the Alliance of Anti-Fascist Intellectuals, whose editors were affiliated to the Spanish Communist Party, printed work by both established and unknown or anonymous poets (till May 1937, see essay by Alted above), whereas anarchist magazines and those produced by both anarchist and socialist trade unions printed only poems by amateurs, many newly introduced to writing by the Republic's pre-war or war-time literacy campaigns. The most democratic organs were the 'murals' where soldiers were encouraged to pin their poems, and the broadsheets printed at the front: many Republican battalions had their own printing presses, the most famous being that run by the poet Manuel Altolaguirre on the eastern front, which printed the first edition of Neruda's *España en el corazón* on paper manufactured from the debris of war. The concept of the original work of art was challenged both by posters, using modern technological means of mass reproduction, and by poetry recitals and theatre, drawing on a pre-literate tradition of oral performance (though poems and plays usually existed also as written texts). In both cases, the aim was to reach an illiterate audience through use of the visual image and the spoken word. Posters and performance were also ephemeral art-forms [*arte de urgencia*] with no pretensions to the 'eternal value' of 'great art'; the ultimate in ephemeral art was the 1937 Fallas Antifascistas (burning of grotesque papier mâché effigies) celebrated in Valencia, exploiting the subversive potential of popular carnival.

Republican agitprop was aimed chiefly at troops on the front, including the enemy (despite being in short supply, planes were used to drop poems behind enemy lines), and to a lesser extent civilians whose contribution to food and arms production was vital (street theatre was also used to recruit troops). Separate posters and art exhibitions rallied support abroad. The main objective was to raise morale or, in the case of the enemy and foreign powers, sympathy; but posters also had the prosaic function of warning against contaminated water or venereal disease.

As a mass-produced cultural object, the poster was promoted as a proletarian art-form, but its links with capitalist consumerism were uneasily recognized: several wartime poster artists had previously worked in advertising. Others had been newspaper cartoonists or illustrators of comics and drew on those traditions, as on the popular imagery of cinema posters (especially those for horror films). The influence of Soviet agitprop was strong on Communist poster artists, particularly Josep Renau, who in 1936 was named Director of Fine Arts, a post traditionally held by an art historian. Communist posters used constructivist design to celebrate an image of man as machine, depicted in non-individualized serial form, that sometimes coincided with the mechanized conception of the male body found in German and Italian fascist art; photomontage was also used, though in a fairly rudimentary way. Anarchist posters tended to be formally conservative, retaining an emphasis on the individualized human figure and using conventions of realism or melodrama. In particular, anarchist posters celebrated the peasant rather than the industrial proletariat, in an idealization of rural life bordering on sentimental nostalgia and overlapping awkwardly with the Nationalist stress on organic community (though what the Nationalists meant by this was a return to hierarchy, rather than collectivization). Some posters celebrated women's contribution to wartime production behind the lines—not, however, to the fighting at the front; the Republic ordered the withdrawal of its women's militia in March 1937—but others cast woman in the traditional role of national emblem. The poster was not developed as a mass art-form by the Nationalists since for most of the war the Republic had a virtual monopoly of print technology.

Agitprop theatre likewise reflected the tension between Soviet futurism (as in the plays of María Teresa León, director of Las Guerrillas del Teatro) and, more commonly, traditional or popular forms such as the Golden Age *entremés* [curtain-raiser] and the vaudeville sketch; in both cases, their one-act format lent itself to performance in difficult conditions. As in Golden Age drama, dialogue is frequently in verse (the popular *romance* or ballad form), and low-life humour and bawdy are used to produce a carnivalesque reversal of hierarchy—and sometimes of gender roles, as in Alberti's *Radio Sevilla* [1937]—though in most plays the image of the heroic mother or *novia* [fiancée] dominates. Texts by Cervantes (*Numancia, El retablo de las maravillas*) were rewritten (by Alberti and Rafael Dieste respectively) as exaltations of popular collective endeavour, continuing the practice of Lorca's touring company La Barraca which before the war had taken the classics (notably Lope de Vega's *Fuenteovejuna*) to the people. Ironically the Compañía del Teatro Nacional de FET y de las JONS,* set up in 1938 by Ridruejo as Nationalist Head of Press and Propaganda, took many of its ideas from La Barraca, appropriating *Fuenteovejuna* for its own conservative purposes (Lorca's production had suppressed the Catholic Monarchs' restoration of order at the

13 Poster issued by the Central Theatre Council of the Ministry of Public Instruction and Health probably in 1938, promoting the agitprop theatre group Las Guerrillas del Teatro, which under María Teresa León's direction performed at the front to raise the troops' morale. The text reads: 'The Theatre *Guerrillas* go into action against fascism for the victory of the people and for culture'; culture is seen both as a means of struggle and as its goal.

end). The Teatro Nacional specialized in adaptations of Golden Age morality plays staged spectacularly on cathedral steps, or of Greek tragedy which (paraphrasing the principal Nationalist dramatist, Torrente Ballester) gave the masses a corporate identity as the chorus.

Nationalist poetry consisted largely in epic panegyric or allegory (e.g. Pemán's *Poema de la bestia y el ángel*) replete with biblical and classical imagery. In his classic study *La poesía de la guerra de España*, Salaün counts 223 wartime magazines published by the Nationalists, compared with 1,376 on the Republican side: the latter contain some 8,500 surviving poems, mostly by unknown individuals including women and children. This 'poetic inflation' (as Salaün calls it) was a genuine attempt to give a voice to the people, producing an oral history of the war: the vast majority of poems, written for recital, are in the narrative ballad form. Irregular metre is rare, even relatively so in poems by established writers (the 1927 Generation, most of whose surviving members contributed to the Republican war effort, had always drawn heavily on popular forms), since oral delivery—often with musical accompaniment—required regular rhythm. Some poems draw on a burlesque tradition of popular song, or on parodic forms such as *poesía extremeña* which mimic dialect. Oral delivery also made immediate intelligibility a necessity; hence the generalized use, even in most poems by established poets, of traditional imagery which sometimes seems at odds with the Republic's political agenda: for example, the stress on Christian sacrificial imagery or on sacrificial female figures, contradicting attempts to create a secular society and to emancipate women. Even when women are depicted as agents—as in poems celebrating the legendary *dinamiteras* —they are still turned into objects of conventional gallantry. The overall emphasis on sacrificial victims reads like a desperate attempt to make a virtue out of necessity, attracting sympathy at the expense of stressing Republican losses. Further ambivalence is introduced through the general appeal—even by communist poets—to nature, legitimizing the Republic by equating it with the organic as opposed to Nationalist usurpation. This 'naturalization' of the Republic leads to an almost exclusive concentration on the rural, reflecting the Republic's concern with agrarian reform but leaving the industrial proletariat out of the picture, in what sometimes reads like a reaction not just against capitalism but against modernity as a whole.

Such contradictions do not devalue the Republic's wartime cultural effort, but point to the problems inherent in the attempt to harness artistic production to a popular tradition whose values (particularly with regard to gender) are not always progressive. Republican propaganda art was a genuine attempt to redefine culture in non-bourgeois terms; this inevitably came into conflict with intellectuals' desire to retain a leading cultural role (implicit in the term 'avant-garde'). The juxtaposition of popular traditions of oral performance with modern, technologically reproduced, mass cultural forms such as the poster points to the increasing ambiguity in the twentieth century of the term 'popular culture', which with the growth of the mass media has moved from its original sense of culture by the people to that of culture for the people: Republican propaganda art marks a mid-way point in this process. The tension between these two concepts—culture by the people and culture for the people—was fundamental to Republican politics, which foundered on the question of how and to what extent power should be put in the people's hands; it is a tension that is a fundamental issue in cultural studies.

Further reading
See items listed under the preceding essay by Alicia Alted.

Authoritarian Modernization

1940–1975

Part

III

14 Illustration from the Falangist magazine *Vértice* (February 1939, just before the end of the civil war on 1 April), contrasting the Nationalist victors (depicted symbolically on top) with a trail of defeated Republican refugees crossing into France. The stress on the victors' helmets and bayonets creates an image of invincibility but also of inhumanity and aggression, designed to inspire fear. The defeated are shown with their backs turned to the spectator; the following pages, showing Republican refugees in France, are titled 'La huida' [The Flight], implying that they are fleeing out of cowardice. The Manichaean contrast between the two images is typical of Nationalist discourse; the effect is somewhat undermined by the fact that the shadows in the top picture associate the Nationalists with darkness while the Republicans, in bright sunshine, are an image of light.

Section 1
Building the State and the Practice of Power 1940–1959

The reign of material truths
(Manuel Vázquez Montalbán)

Editors' introduction

Francoism represented the attempt to solve the crisis of the state by uncoupling economic modernization from cultural modernity and jettisoning the latter. This translated into the eradication of pluralism of any kind, in order to create a Spain that was 'one, great, and free'. But post-war Spain—plunged into impoverishment and repression—was patently neither 'great' nor 'free'; nor, despite the image of national unity conveyed in the officially controlled media, was it 'one'. As always, the attempt to deny contradictions led to their multiplication. While attempting to enforce homogeneity through education, censorship, and repression of the *guerrilla*,* the regime was also actively engaged in creating a Manichaean division of the nation into victors (the true Spain) and vanquished ('la anti-España') through political and economic repression, both of which turned the material practices of everyday life—the sheer task of survival—into politically charged instruments of resistance. The regime's dirty war was in effect waged not only against the *guerrilla* but against vast swathes of the civilian population. Censorship too was counter-productive in encouraging the public to read the political into everything; Spanish audiences became adept at the art of resignification so stressed in contemporary cultural studies.

The education system and indoctrination of women through the Sección Femenina* were explicitly divisive and classist. While SF cadres transmitted regime policies designed to stabilize social hierarchy on the basis of an 'ideal', closed family unit, exhorting women to 'make the nation', poor women—experiencing the most acute contradictions between regime ideology and material reality and at the sharp end of the battle for daily survival—concentrated their attention on 'making ends meet'. A further cultural divide was reinforced by censorship, chiefly concerned with driving a wedge between élite and popular or mass culture; at the same time the regime's promotion of ideologized versions of folklore, cinema, and sport gave certain versions of popular and mass culture something of the aura of high culture by co-opting them for the purposes of national unification. The promotion of cultural nationalism was accompanied by the encouragement of idealist art, whose apparent depoliticization was part of an explicitly political project. The obsession with controlling all forms of cultural expression inevitably served to give culture an importance beyond that assigned to it in most democratic societies (the Second Republic, as we have seen, was exceptional here); creative writers and artists found themselves at the forefront of an opposition that could not express itself in direct political terms. Most ironical of all, the protagonists of that opposition were largely sons and daughters of the victorious Nationalists.

There were, however, ways in which Nationalist ideology succeeded in leaving an indelible mark on the opposition, which only later would recognize that its 'cultural mandarinism' was the product of its élitist formation, and that in opting for neo-realism as a cultural weapon they were not just following Gramsci's directives but acquiescing in the regime's repudiation of artistic modernism. Today's reader is struck by the anachronistic and parochial nature of intellectual debate in 1950s Spain, whether among the regime's adherents or its opponents: this was the inevitable result of two decades of enforced cultural—and economic—isolationism, during which (especially in the 1940s) the exercise of critical reason was more or less banished from the public sphere, as the regime instrumentalized a return to cultural primitivism (Tridentine Catholicism, religiosity, Manichaeism, miracles, and mysteries) to bolster its power. This isolation would be mitigated by the influx from the late 1940s of Hollywood movies, and by the arrival in the 1950s of American aid, prefiguring the massification and Americanization of culture that would mark the regime's later decades. The reception of Hollywood movies in Spain is an interesting example of how the same cultural product will mean different things to different audiences, and of how the same response can be simultaneously conformist and contestatory: the escapist pleasure they afforded created, in the context of 1940s moral puritanism and economic hardship, a liberatory space in which things could be otherwise.

The same conformist-contestatory ambivalence is shared by other popular genres —notably song. These can be read at various levels, as the exorcizing of grievous loss, or as an ironic commentary on the irrelevance of official morality to a daily life dominated by the exchange values of the black market. But in the end, no amount of irony was sufficient protection against the harrowing experience of powerlessness and humiliation suffered by the dispossessed in a 'post-war' which, in its social and political institutionalization of a vengeful victory, really constituted the continuation of war by other means. The combination of savage material deprivation—administered daily by autarky—and the regime's demonization of the urban working-class, seen as the epitome of an alien and threatening modernity, would take its toll. Through the experience of daily life, defeat was internalized in its most fundamental terms as that of an entire social class and political/cultural project. Economic repression and social exclusion, as well as the regime's promotion of cultural primitivism, prepared the ground for a 'safe' economic modernization. The social threat had apparently been vanquished (not least in low expectations learned), and the remnants and echoes of modernism and the dissidences it allowed had been forced underground into the private spaces of the opposition's inner exile.

The Material Reality of State Power

MIKE RICHARDS

HELEN GRAHAM

'Terror and Progress': Industrialization, Modernity, and the Making of Francoism

MIKE RICHARDS

The idea of modernization used in relation to the early Franco regime might seem rather out of place. Francoism represented the total rejection of modern representative democracy. The 1940s in Spain saw widespread starvation and epidemic disease in the countryside and in the regime's prisons, and the use of extreme physical brutality and atavistic cultural forms—drawn from the mythology of Reconquest, Counter-Reformation, and empire—to repress sectors of the population. However, although repressive ideology and extreme violence appeared to conflict with 'pure' economic rationality, the actions of the Francoist 'New State' have to be evaluated as a reflection of the depth of the social crisis in Spain during the 1930s and 1940s and as a response to that crisis which laid a particular pathway towards what we might label 'modernity'. Indeed, as this essay will argue, the 'return to the past', represented by the primitive living conditions imposed upon the working class, together with the reconstruction of state authority, was, in some ways, the very basis for Spain's 'economic miracle' of the 1960s. Most importantly, early Francoism saw the re-establishment of a relatively stabilized bourgeois power-base as the foundation for the future.

Throughout the first three decades of this century, the twin processes of industrialization and urbanization in Spain produced a level of popular political mobilization which the exclusive, oligarchic system of the Restoration monarchy was unable to absorb. The result was sporadic but considerable social unrest. Moreover, as Spain's was a very uneven process of industrialization, undercapitalized, with poorly developed markets, reliant upon high tariff barriers and antiquated production techniques, the economic foundations of modernization were in themselves extremely shaky. The Spanish economy was highly sectoralized and economic élites were permanently engaged in internecine antagonisms. These élites possessed no agreed class project beyond that of subjugating the working-class. The civil war represented the culmination of this dual economic and political crisis. But the war itself did not automatically resolve Spain's crisis. The conflict saw the country's traumatized social élites delegate political power to other forces dominated by the military. Yet from this chaotic situation Spain's élites would influence the setting of the course for the transition from a traditional agricultural society to a predominantly industrial one. In the process, the state would be reconstructed in a way which confirmed the outcome of the war itself. The Francoist dictatorship functioned to control the potentially threatening consequences of social and economic change.

Industrialization was confirmed as the ultimate goal of development. But this transition was not achieved by sacrificing the social power of landed wealth. The civil war had partly been fought to avoid land reform. There would be no enforced restructuring of the agrarian sector to improve general living standards (thereby broadening the domestic market for industrial products), to direct investment towards industry or to develop agricultural exports. Instead, the inevitable tensions produced by the continued protection of an inefficient agricultural system simultaneously with an attempted development of the national industrial base would, in the first two decades of Francoism, be partly resolved by placing an enormous burden upon the working-class. The chosen strategy of autarky—in theory, industrialization through the exploitation of purely national resources—in practice promised a reconciliation of several demands. It was seen as allowing for industrial growth without the need for a structural reform which would damage existing interests and coincided with a desire to confirm the subjugation of the defeated. In the process, Spain's social élites would both support and participate in various forms of repression.

Francoism's protection of élite interests placed severe material constraints upon such economic development as could occur in the wake of the civil war. Indeed, for a time, and due to a variety of factors, little more than an abstract 'notion' of industrialization existed. None the less, with hindsight we can see that the way in which élite power was reconstructed during the first two decades of Francoism effectively made possible a particular form of modernization in Spain.

The shift towards an industrial society was slow and the pain which it entailed was borne disproportionately by the working-class. According to the Ministers of the regime itself, the rationalization of industry would take forty years. The mass of landless labourers, impossible to incorporate socially or politically as such, could, it was believed, be absorbed by industrial development over a similar time-span. Although under a liberal-democratic regime this increased proletarian-ization might have brought an intensification of class conflict, as the 1930s had witnessed, under Franco's 'strong state' this danger could, in the language of the regime, be 'neutralized'. Meanwhile, the landed oligarchy, which had helped finance the military rebellion in 1936, would become more closely fused with the industrial élite. This would happen because the agrarian élite was able to partici-pate on favourable terms in the financing of industrialization. In this way, the conditions for reinvigorated capital accumulation within Spain and participation in the world capitalist boom of the 1960s would be established. Modernization would be restricted and extremely gradual because it would be sternly controlled from above.

At the public level, the relationship of the regime to agriculture, on the one hand, and to industry, on the other, remained somewhat ambiguous. Spanish nationalism, as an expression of the ideology of the Spanish political right, was deeply rooted in a specifically agrarian notion of Spain. However, industrial capi-talism was constrained by this entrenched power of rural élites. At the same time, Francoist generals, ideologues, and economists resented what was seen as the international economic community's determination to keep Spain essentially ru-ral, destined only to supply the industrialized world with a few limited agricultural exports and to live with continued poverty and social unrest in the countryside. Within months of the final victory in the civil war, the regime had begun to put in place an industrial strategy designed to stimulate and supplement the activities of private industry. The autumn of 1939 saw the enactment of legislation designed to protect and stimulate Spain's industrial base. In September 1941 a state holding company, the Instituto Nacional de Industria (INI), was created with public funds, with the specific task of initiating industrial projects to boost national production in strategic sectors alongside the action of private capital. The industrialization process would be developed through drastic measures of state intervention, in-tended to channel national resources, control production, limit imports, regiment the work-force, and guarantee private property and profits.

Thus the 1940s and 1950s saw a process—albeit confused and often contradic-tory—whereby the conflict between agrarian and industrial society was mediated while the outcome of the civil war was confirmed. According to a future INI president, reviewing the years between 1939 and 1958, the image of an agrarian Spain had faded from the popular perception and been replaced by a different vision 'of smoking chimneys, mineworks and great industrial factories, a more modern concept, more in tune with the rhythm of our times, in short, more European'. Moreover, this change had occurred 'whilst substantially conserving the existing capitalist structure [. . .] Traditional juridical relations between the elements of production have not been altered.'[1] The maintenance of this structure, built upon capitalist economic and social relations, would be ensured during the early decades of the dictatorship through physical and economic repression.

Repression and the remaking of the state under Francoism

The basis of the Francoist 'New State' was founded on the systematic exclusion of what were seen as the socially unacceptable elements which had supported the reforming Republican Popular Front electoral coalition of February 1936. The state would be constructed in the image of the 'crusade'—the myth of the Nationalist civil war effort as a struggle against 'anti-Spain' as represented by the Republic.

Physical and economic repression in the wake of the Spanish civil war were used as a way of disciplining the lower orders of society and confirming their defeat. The political economy of the 'New State' was developed to maintain the basic features of existing social power while industrialization was taking place. In practice, the concept of autarky offered a potential way of achieving the essential aims of this brutal vision of modernity: repression, the concentration of economic power and industrialization. Indeed, in the 1940s, the Francoist state was made through economic, political, and cultural autarky.

Social 'purification' could, it was calculated by regime ideologues, be most efficiently carried out within a closed society. The 'modern state'—as represented by the dictatorial regimes of Italy, Germany, and Spain—was seen as reordering society in fundamental ways to face the challenges of the future. The basis was the harmonious organization of production—a fusion of worker regimentation and potential industrial modernization to achieve higher production. Work, national-ism, authority, sacrifice, 'austerity', and 'purification' provided not only a way out of economic crisis, but a means of reconstructing power. Accordingly, for the ideologues of the regime, the best thing about 'Hitlerism', for example, was its 'labour of political and moral cleansing'. Stalinist Russia was grudgingly admired. The tasks of economic development performed there, through the sacrifices of the working-class, were seen as similar to those which Spain faced. However, in Russia, the regime had forgotten about God and allowed communism to breed hatred and despair.[2] In Spain, on the other hand, the 'moral force' represented by the ideology of the Catholic Church was seen by the regime as offering a way of disciplining the work-force by granting the possibility of 'redemption' through total obedience to authority.

The notion of a kind of collective purging through sacrifice permeates Francoist proclamations concerning social relations in post-war Spain. The regime, inter-nally at any rate, reckoned that industrialization could take place on the backs of the population because the Spaniards were historically accustomed to making sacrifices. The purposes of the repression were summarized succinctly by Franco himself: only those 'capable of loving the Fatherland, of working and struggling for it, of adding their grain of sand to the common effort' would be tolerated. The

15 Still from Basilio Martín Patino's documentary film *Canciones para después de una guerra* [*Songs for after a War*] (1971, authorized 1976), showing a 1940s photograph of Republican prisoners with the slogan 'Redemption from (remission of) sentences through labour.' In the immediate post-war, Republican prisoners were formed into work battalions and used as free labour by the state and army, as well as being hired out to private capital. The Catholic rhetoric of expiation through suffering ('freedom' from guilt) is here used to legitimize the extraction of absolute surplus value (free labour) from the defeated, in a complex transaction whereby the return to traditional values facilitates capitalist modernization. This image also graphically illustrates the way in which the price of Nationalist victory was materially inscribed on the bodies of the defeated.

others could not be allowed back into 'social circulation [. . .] Wicked, deviant, politically and morally poisoned elements [. . .] those without possible redemption within the human order.' Salvation for such people could only come through labour.[3] In practice, this meant that repression was overwhelmingly targeted on the urban and rural working-class.[4] The claim that justice would be granted to those 'without blood on their hands' was meaningless in a situation where state violence was utilized to confirm the defeat of an entire political order and social class.

With no apparent sense of irony, the long series of dictatorial edicts issued by the Franco regime was initiated by a law against 'military rebellion', proclaimed just ten days after the illegal rebellion of July 1936 which was itself the first act of the embryonic Francoist state. Under this law, which was not rescinded until 1969, a series of ill-defined acts became illegal and the perpetrators deemed subject to trial by military court. During the civil war and in its aftermath this law gave a semblance of legality to the thousands of summary executions carried out as the Nationalist state was made. 'Power', from the beginning, was largely determined by the permanent threat and use of violence.

In September 1936 the military rebels declared illegal all the political organizations which had participated in the Republican alliance of 1936 and supported its social reforms. This was one of the first measures designed to help construct an organized power structure for the future. This structure was further formalized in April 1937 when the various political groupings of the Nationalist side were unified in an attempt to give greater coherence to the nascent regime. Anyone who did not integrate themselves into the new single party—FET y de las JONS,* later known as the Movimiento,* and based upon the Spanish fascist party, Falange Española—would be denied any political participation in the 'New Spain'. As well as an exclusivist political unity, enforced national unity was also a central element in the remaking of the Spanish state. As Franco's troops approached Catalonia in April 1938, for example, the statute of regional autonomy granted by the Republic was abolished.

Another of the foundation-stones of the repressive apparatus was the so-called Law of Political Responsibilities, proclaimed to provide a legal framework for the blanket repression imposed as Nationalist forces established their occupation of Barcelona in February 1939. This law was directed against those 'who by their actions or omissions' had supported the 'Red subversion' or 'hindered' or opposed the victory of the National Movement. This was the juridical basis for the 'purging' or 'purifying' of Spain's economy and society. It should be remembered that this law was retroactive—treating as crimes legal political or trade union activity going back to October 1934. The state redrew the boundaries of 'criminality' so widely as to make imprecise that which actually constituted a crime. Franco, in April 1939, explained: 'Of course, given the fantastic amount of criminality some mistakes are inevitable [. . .] But nobody could demand that in so vast a work of just redress everything would be perfect as if we were carrying out a task of archangels.'[5] However, so-called 'mistakes' were built into the mechanism of repression; they were inevitable and desirable since they helped produce an all-enveloping sense of fear from which none but the most highly placed could escape.

The most obvious form of repression was physical extermination. This did not cease when the war was officially over. It has been estimated that as many as 200,000 men and women were executed in the post-war period alone. Since many officially sanctioned executions took place outside the dictatorial legal framework we will certainly never know the true figure. The deprivation of liberty was also used to such an extent that the country's prisons were soon hopelessly overcrowded. In October 1938, in the midst of the conflict, the Nationalist authorities issued an order for prisoners to 'redeem' themselves through labour, and companies were authorized to apply for work detachments to be used as labour in factories. Within months of the formal cessation of hostilities, plans were put into operation for military penal colonies to be established under the authority of the regional divisions of what the regime itself called 'the army of occupation'. In 1939 there were officially more than 270,000 men and women held in the regime's prisons. The state had to act to reduce the unmanageable numbers it had condemned to incarceration. A system of 'conditional liberty' (libertad vigilada) was introduced, based on that operated in fascist Italy. The local authorities, normally consisting of representatives of industry or landowners, with senior figures from the local Falange and the Church hierarchy, would report on the behaviour of those selected. Political or 'moral' misdemeanours would be punished with a return to prison. Prisoners released under these stringent conditions were not permitted by the law to live in their previous place of residence but forced to search for work and a place to live miles away. This only increased the acute vulnerability of individuals in the labour market during the post-war era.

Economic repression: autarky, industrialization, and the black market

Economic repression became intimately linked to the autarkic strategy of industrialization. Industrial development depended largely upon cheap labour since autarky restricted access to imports of modern machinery. As we have seen, the state acted to guarantee low-cost labour. In the wake of defeat and under the provisions of the Law of Political Responsibilities, workers in industrial areas were compelled to reapply for their jobs. Securing them was dependent upon workers' ability to demonstrate their allegiance to the 'New State'. Those with 'proven' political or trade union backgrounds would be purged—condemned to a spell of imprisonment or enforced unemployment or to the margins of the economy where levels of exploitation were intensified and capital accumulation thereby facilitated.

This process was partly made possible by the state's exclusive control of labour. Production was to be maintained by the construction of a huge state corporativist structure—the basis of a modern bureaucracy. The resources of the democratic unions of pre-civil war Spain were handed over to the Movement which controlled this syndical system. The formal economic and social foundation of the 'New State' was the Fuero del Trabajo, proclaimed in March 1938—a sort of labour charter based upon the Italian fascist Carta del Lavoro and designed to regiment the work-force. The principles of private property and private enterprise were expressly maintained. While the rhetoric claimed that the law constituted the centrepiece of the 'National Syndicalist Revolution'—asserting a more just distribution of wealth and a harmony between the boss, technology, and the worker in the interest of increased national production—its real effect was to make strikes illegal, crimes against the nation, and strikers criminals to be tried by a military court.

At the same time, an inflationary strategy of industrialization was chosen. Taxes continued to be disproportionately levied on the poorest in society since the taxing of income remained largely unreformed. The black market which came to dominate the economy, and within which the state itself played an important role, effectively constituted a kind of punitive taxation upon the private consumption of basic necessities. Moreover, industries which were deemed to be of 'national interest' benefited from generous tax exemptions. National finances were put under the strain of the constant issuing of public debt, acquired largely by private banks which thereby safeguarded their virtual monopoly of the industrializing process. Autarky also made foreign investment difficult in Spain. Legislation of October 1939 specifically limited the level of foreign capital invested in companies in Spain to 25 per cent of the total, enabling existing economic élites to tighten their grip on the national wealth. Thus, inflation had specific class-based characteristics and consequences in a situation of unmitigated social domination which greatly exacerbated existing inequalities.

In the long run, of course, autarkic industrialization was hopelessly unrealistic since the country's only genuine substantial resources were the food-producing land and the people. While it lasted, however, since the established landowning structure was considered sacred, it would be the labouring population which would bear the burden of the state's strategy. Thus autarky contained within it the possibility of a society-wide repression. It allowed the country's existing economic élites to dominate each sector of production. At the same time, this drastic reduction in economic activity helped create a widespread scarcity which, in turn, increased society's dependence upon the action of the state.

Defeat defined the reality of everyday life for much of the population. Social control was based upon the distribution and manipulation of the most fundamental necessities for survival: food and work. The state colluded in the operation of a devastating black market which facilitated capital accumulation by landowners and meant desperation among the lower classes. Official rationing was hopelessly inadequate. In the 1940s there was starvation in Spain and malaria and typhoid stalked the countryside. The supply of food was influenced by political considerations. The provision of 'supplementary rations', which could mean the difference between life and death, was controlled by a local board made up of the mayor (usually a local industrialist or landowner), the parish priest, and the local head of the party. 'Acceptable behaviour' would be required before extra rations were dished out.[6] Indeed, the families of prisoners or of those in hiding or enforced exile were expected by the local authorities to suffer. There was much indignation within regional party hierarchies that, because of collections within the community, the so-called 'Red Aid' organized by the remnants of opposition groups, 'numerous families are able to lead normal lives'.

In reality, the black market, which was effectively the real economy in the 1940s, and the strategy of autarky which helped produce it, were used as a way of imposing power. FET y de la JONS and its battery of provincial offshoots, which came to be dominated by local social élites, was heavily implicated, along with the forces of public order, in the operation of the unofficial economy which ensured that the burden of the crisis was firmly placed upon the lower classes. The population understood through the material experience of daily life that the regime had come partly to define its power through the control of food. In the Spanish post-war popular political expectations were consumed by the reality of social brutality. Popular aspirations were reduced to a simple hope that, with a restoration of the monarchy, bread might again be sold without the intervention of the state.

The Spanish post-war years saw the rupture of social relations which had produced the civil war taken to its ultimate extreme. Whole sections of the population were seen by the dictator and his Ministers as infected by the corrosive influence of 'foreign' ideology. At the same time, the civil war experience seemed to confirm, at least to Franco and his generals, a sense of Spain's dependency and weakness, reinforcing in them the belief that the country needed to industrialize. But social élites could only countenance such a drastic reorientation after a period of 'social transition' during which a new basis for class domination could be established. The Spanish proletariat, in particular, it was claimed, was 'sick'— contaminated by Bolshevism. Autarky imposed a form of quarantine during which it could be 'treated'. The priority of the victorious regime was to carry out a purge at the very roots of society. This would form the basis for what was considered a 'healthy' road to modernity. In practice, this meant protecting the interests of Spain's social élites. Repression contained relatively novel elements drawn from the authoritarian corporativism of fascist Italy and Nazi Germany as well as other long-established means of class repression—the uncontrolled brutality of the forces of order and the manipulation of material resources. 'Progress' in the wake of the Spanish civil war entailed a terroristic reversion to primitivism.

Notes
1 F. Labadié Otermín and G. Cerezo Barredo, *Notas al futuro económico de España* (Madrid, 1958), 145–7.
2 See e.g. E. Montero, *Los estados modernos y la Nueva España* (Vitoria, 1939).

3 *La Vanguardia Española*, 4 Apr. 1939.
4 See J. M. Solé i Sabaté, *La repressió franquista a Catalunya, 1938–1953* (Barcelona, 1985); F. Moreno Gómez, 'La represión en la España campesina', in J. L. García Delgado (ed.), *El primer franquismo* (Madrid, 1989), 189–207.
5 *La Vanguardia Española*, 4 Apr. 1939.
6 F. Alburquerque, 'Métodos de control político de la población civil: el sistema de racionamiento de alimentos y productos básicos impuesto en España tras la última guerra civil', in M. Tuñón de Lara (ed.), *Estudios sobre la historia de España* (Madrid, 1981), 427.

Further reading

Abella, R., *Por el imperio hacia Dios: crónica de una posguerra (1939–1955)* (Barcelona, 1978).
Balfour, S., *Dictatorship, Workers and the City: Labour in Greater Barcelona since 1939* (Oxford, 1989).
Ellwood, S., *Spanish Fascism in the Franco Era: Falange Española de las JONS, 1936–76* (London, 1987).
Esteban, J., 'The Economic Policy of Francoism: An Interpretation', in P. Preston (ed.), *Spain in Crisis: Evolution and Decline of the Franco Regime* (Hassocks, 1976), 82–100.
Fontana, J. (ed.), *España bajo el franquismo* (Barcelona, 1986).
Harrison, J., *The Spanish Economy in the Twentieth Century* (London, 1985).
Preston, P., *The Politics of Revenge: Fascism and the Military in Twentieth-Century Spain* (London, 1990).
Reig Tapia, A., *Ideología e historia: sobre la represión franquista y la guerra civil* (Madrid, 1984).
Sevilla Guzmán, E., 'The Peasantry and the Franco Regime', in P. Preston (ed.), *Spain in Crisis* (Hassocks, 1976), 101–24.

Gender and the State: Women in the 1940s

HELEN GRAHAM

This essay will look at regime policies towards women in order to shed light on both the functioning of triumphalist Francoism as a system and the social history of various female constituencies in the 1940s. Gender politics are vital to our understanding of the efforts made at regime stabilization. To this end, Francoism projected (via both the Church and Sección Femenina* de Falange) an ultra-conservative construction of 'ideal' womanhood, perceived as the fundamental guarantor of social stability, or indeed stasis. But the regime's economic policies combined with its politico-moral/ideological framework to produce highly con-tradictory results. For all the Franco regime's aspirations to monolithicity, the socio-economic and cultural experiences of women's lives in 1940s Spain were complex, conflictive, and plural. Different female constituencies would contribute in varying degrees to regime stabilization, as we shall see. But even in its most overt and conscious forms, as with the social service and educational activities of the Sección Femenina's cadres, this contribution carried within it the seeds of social/gender change.

The experience of the civil war had left Spain with a shattered body politic and an atomized society. This fragmentation was intensified by the very policies im-plemented by the victors. Spain in the 1940s contained frighteningly separate worlds. Alongside the savage poverty and the widespread terror of the post-war repression unleashed against the defeated, there coexisted an upper middle-class milieu of ease, security, and order regained. As Republican women were being shaved and dosed with castor oil by the 'victors' of their villages, or transported with their children across Spain in cattle trucks in scenes of Dantesque horror, women in the Sevillian aristocracy or Salamancan bourgeoisie celebrated the 're-demption' of their private family sphere and revelled in the tremendous upsurge of public Catholic ceremonial—of religious processions in particular.

The sheer extremity of the times makes 1940s Spain a clear illustration of the axiom that there is no such thing as 'women in general' and no such thing as their 'typical experience'. Gender cannot denote a single experience because it is always bisected by socio-economic class and other competing cultural and political iden-tities. Women experienced both the civil war and the long aftermath of conflict in different geographical locations, as parts of disparate and often antagonistic political collectivities and cultural communities. Nor did socio-economic marginalization itself indicate a shared perspective: a female factory worker from Barcelona's urban belt would not have identified some primary commonality of experience with the wife or daughter of an impoverished Castilian smallholder just because they were both female. At the very least religious belief—whose meaning obviously varied according to the social context—as well as their experi-ence of work would have separated their world-views.

So the usual factors—wealth, status (including marital status), age, family cir-cumstances, socio-economic class (whether or not they had to work for a wage), and religious belief—mediated women's experience of: (1) the political conse-quences of Nationalist victory, (2) the resulting legal/constitutional restrictions affecting women, (3) state social policy towards women/the family (including its pronatalist policies, discussed below), (4) the demographic impact of the war, (5) the socio-economic disruption erupting into full post-war crisis (exacerbated by the regime's own disastrous economic policies), (6) the impact of (1–5) on women's own perception of their roles/identities. What was specific to the 1940s was the acuteness of the social differentials operating. This essay will look first at the regime's policies towards women, and then focus on those specific female constituencies on the 'fault line' who experienced the gender contradictions of triumphalist Francoism in their most acute form: predominantly urban working-class women and lower middle-class sectors, especially those encadred in the Sección Femenina.

'Making the nation': the Franco regime and the politics of gender

To seal victory in the post-war required the imposition not just of an authoritarian political framework and regressive economic policies, but also of a socially con-servative project. In general terms, the motivation for this was the same kind of 'politics of moral panic' which had operated elsewhere in Europe in the inter-war period, as a result of cultural anxieties produced by increasingly rapid socio-economic change ('modernity'). Women's changing identity and roles, symptomatic of these wider changes, were perceived by those sectors of society adversely affected as the *cause* of their personal problems and of 'falling standards/degenerating values' (which is how anxious humans generally read social change). Thus, reimposing traditional gender roles on women became at once a substitute for this lack of control in other areas and an (ultimately unsuccessful) bid to 'turn the clock back'. As a result, a whole pathology of modernity was written on women's bodies via repressive state legislation—in particular with regard to pronatalism.

In its bid to stabilize itself and to effect the social institutionalization of victory, the Franco regime targeted women because of the pivotal role they played within the family. The patriarchal family was seen as representing the corporate order of the state in microcosm. So, by reconstructing or reinforcing it, Francoism would, in theory, be able to operate on an atomized post-war society to build up the 'new order'. The family, as envisaged by the regime, was unthreatening because it connected vertically with the state rather than horizontally within society. Thus it reinforced the unity and power of the state, rather than challenging it as did the horizontal solidarities of civil society (other sorts of 'family'/affective ties, political parties, trade unions, and the traditions of civil associationism). One of the major functions of the civil war had been to annihilate these threats.

The regime promoted an 'ideal' image of womanhood as 'eternal', passive, pious, pure, submissive woman-as-mother for whom self-denial was the only road to real fulfilment. The many incarnations of the Virgin provided the perfect role model. But others too were provided by sanitized reconstructions of Isabel la Católica and St Teresa of Ávila. Church teaching on the irreducible nature of male and female, and the latter's exclusive fittedness for the home, received tendentious justification via pronouncements of the medical establishment which presented women as weak and emotional creatures, a miry mess of hormonally inspired conditions.

The Franco regime's object, similar to that of Italian and German fascism, was to obliterate women as independent social beings (hence the difficulty of unreconstructed versions of St Teresa/Queen Isabella as role models). Socially, 'woman' was to be an identity indivisible from 'the family'. Legally, there was a return to the 1889 Civil Code which enshrined women's juridical inferiority, married women becoming minors before the law.

Under the terms of the March 1938 Labour Charter (Fuero del Trabajo), married women were also to be 'free[d] from the workplace and the factory'. The Fundamental Law of 18 July 1938 (Ley de Bases) established the family subsidy (paid to the father) ostensibly so that women should no longer need to work to supplement low male wages. From 1942 onwards all labour regulations stipulated the dismissal of married women (*excedencia forzosa por matrimonio*) and on 26 March 1946 the Family Subsidy Law (Ley de Ayuda Familiar) deprived men whose wives worked of the state-paid family bonus (*plus familiar*).

16 Illustration from a children's book on St Teresa (c.1955). The Franco regime used sanitized versions of certain historical figures to legitimize its values; in particular St Teresa—'the saint of the race'—was pressed into service to exemplify ideal Catholic womanhood. In the process, the regime had to edit out certain awkward heterodoxies: in this case, St Teresa's possible Jewish ancestry, independent thought, and active role as a religious reformer. Her transformation here into a Snow White figure, demurely sewing indoors, shows how the regime promoted a version of popular culture steeped in retrograde archetypal imagery. This book appeared in a series of *Accessible Biographies of Great Figures*: series I (on great men) was published in the 1940s; series II (on great women) had to wait till the 1950s. All were written by men except, curiously, that on Isabel la Católica. The Francoist concern with forming the minds of the young—through its manipulation of children's literature and other forms of indoctrination—reflects a view of the populace in general as minors in need of supervision.

Removing married women from the workplace was closely linked to the regime's pursuit of pronatalism. Through a variety of legislative policy measures, involving both punishment and perks, the Franco regime sought to boost the birth rate. Twenty-five per cent of a state dowry loan could be written off against the birth of a child. And, again, as under German and Italian fascism, abortion and contraception were criminalized. Conversely, numerous schemes were implemented in the early 1940s to assist large families: including, in addition to extra family allowances, state payment of school fees, subsidized transport, and special credit terms. Francoism, like other authoritarian regimes, equated population levels with socio-economic and political strength. Moreover, the economic policy of autarky being pursued by the regime also demanded the maximum possible production of labour.

Autarky is a policy which, in theory, seeks to achieve total national economic self-sufficiency. As an extreme expression of economic nationalism it is most specifically associated with fascist regimes. In Spain's case, autarky was basically designed to cut Spain off from world trade and the international economy in order to protect the weak, antiquated (*latifundista**), agrarian sector. Autarkic controls and state intervention (two sides of the same coin in the 1940s) caused enormous stresses and problems in the economy, virtually creating the pre-conditions for the enormous black market which constituted the real national economy during this decade. One significant characteristic of the economic system was the labour force's subjection to extremely high levels of exploitation in order to try to make up for old or broken plant, a lack of foreign investment, and the dearth of raw materials consequent upon autarkic policies themselves. Wages dropped, until by 1945 they were frequently worth only a quarter of their pre-war value (and it was not until 1952 that they rose above half of this). The poverty consequent upon autarky forced workers into double or triple employment (although often in marginal activities and/or on the black economy). Inevitably this meant that proletarian women worked in whatever way they could (whether they were married or single, whether there was a male breadwinner or not). While this was an advantage to some sectors of capital (generally the larger concerns), especially since legal discrimination pushed women to the margins of the labour market, making them an even more pliant work-force, the intense poverty experienced by the working-class disrupted the regime's family policy and its pronatalist strategy. (Indeed, a primary indicator of massive economic crisis was the very high infantile mortality rate itself.) In order to contain the growing material crisis and to avert any wider political repercussions, the Franco regime was obliged to adopt a level of intervention in the private sphere.

This intervention, moreover, was also paradoxically generated by the very restorationist-patriarchal ideology underpinning the regime. On the one hand, it had sought to make a rigid division between public and private, closing down society (by ensuring the disarticulation of the aforementioned horizontal solidarities), promoting its 'privatization' or 'atomization' based on the 'haven' of the private household at whose centre was the 'mother'. Women were envisioned as the source not only of physical reproduction (i.e. babies for the *patria*) but also of 'correct' ideological reproduction via the socialization of children in the home—the goal here being the imposition of a social hierarchy. But, to ensure this outcome, the state could not really afford to let the private sphere remain entirely 'private'. Control, especially of women, had to be enforced.

Women thus became the target both of a cult of morality and of the educational and low-level welfare ministrations of state agencies. Although the Church should be included in this category, predominant here was the Sección Femenina de Falange (SF). Thousands of middle- and lower middle-class women were mobilized in its cadres to perform functions which signified the penetration of the private sphere by the state. In this way, middle-class women were being taken into the public domain and used to police other women—most overtly, the urban and rural poor. In the process, the rigid division between public and private was blurred and shifted.

As the transmission belt for state directives to women, the SF was involved in numerous different educational, cultural, and health/welfare initiatives. Most relevant here are its Social Service programme (Servicio Social (SS)) whereby unmarried women between the ages of 17 and 35 were encouraged (or required if they wanted employment) to provide six months' state service of which at least three constituted unpaid welfare work. Women served in schools, hospitals, orphanages, old people's homes, or else they helped in food kitchens, made up clothes and baby baskets for the poor in the SF's own workshops, or assisted literacy teachers and the SF's rural health visitors. Without this free labour, even a state as underdeveloped as Franco's in the area of social provision (whose population thus had correspondingly low social expectations) would have been in crisis as it sought to cover the minimum necessities for reproducing labour. Via the SF and SS, then, the Francoist state secured rudimentary welfare provision on the cheap.

This was particularly important in political as well as material terms in rural Spain. Throughout the 1940s a majority of the population still lived outside urban centres and were engaged in agricultural production of some kind. (Women in villages near provincial capitals or bigger urban centres would often combine this labour—unpaid if it was for a family concern—with some form of domestic service work.) At a practical level the SF cadres (via its rural section, the Hermandad de la Ciudad y el Campo) provided the *divulgadoras* [health visitors] whose major task was preventive health education—of crucial importance in a post-war society ravaged by malnutrition and contagious disease. Their immunization campaigns were an attempt to reduce Spain's very high infant mortality rate. Moreover, close contacts with families allowed the health visitors to exert moral control—for example ensuring children were baptized. But even the most practical aspects of their work ultimately need to be read politically. The *divulgadoras*, in effect, were controlling the social fall-out of economic policies whose rationale had been bitterly disputed on the battlefields in the civil war.

More generally in rural areas the SF was involved in providing a variety of services: from literacy classes and library facilities (provided by the *cátedras ambulantes*) to courses in a variety of agricultural and artisanal skills (including silkworm production, which seems to epitomize the bizarre economics of triumphalist Francoism). Behind these initiatives lay a typically fascist nostalgia for a self-sufficient peasantry. But while in material terms these rural projects remained marginal to Spanish development, they did serve a useful political purpose. Through them the SF ensured that the regime retained the support of impoverished smallholders and tenant farmers, the sociological bedrock of Francoism and a crucial part of its ongoing support base throughout the 1940s and early 1950s. By formulating policies which seemed to address their needs (the rural lower middle classes never having been the object of state attention previously), the SF camouflaged the real impact of state autarkic policies which meant the severe economic exploitation of the rural lower middle classes, despite the fact that they believed they had 'won' the civil war. The SF, by acting to contain material crisis and hold the social fabric together, and also as 'cheer-leader' to manage lower middle-class support, facilitated regime stabilization.

'Making ends meet': women, the family, and work in 1940s Spain

Against impossible odds, they administer the routine of millions of bleak, hungry and ignorant families; [. . .] the women of Spain make her a nation [. . .] [Their] daily striving and suffering make what little structure there is [. . .] Spanish men have built a state, but they have never built a society [. . .] that [. . .] is in the hearts and minds and the habits and love and devotion of its women.[1]

While the Franco regime institutionalized its victory 'top-down', power was also being restructured in Spanish society 'bottom-up'. Through its daily operation at the micro level—and predominantly through the regime's control of food and work—the defeated would learn the real meaning of their defeat, internalizing their lack of power. Culture, for the urban poor especially, came to revolve around the procuring of food and warmth: the basic necessities of life. In this social milieu the work of daily survival was in women's hands. Even if there was a male breadwinner, women too were forced to work—'officially' or otherwise—to supplement starvation wages. But very often the male family members were dead, or in work battalions, labour service, or prison.[2] (The post-war prison population in Spain reached astronomical proportions.) Moreover, the wives and mothers of those executed or imprisoned were frequently reduced to destitution—denied pension rights, subjected to economic penalties by Francoist courts or to the repeated raids of Falangist squads—all of which was permitted by the sweeping Law of Political Responsibilities. It has been estimated that at least half a million families were without a male breadwinner. Indeed the perspective of female community and solidarities seems to offer a promising way of researching the social history of Spain's urban poor in the 1940s. It might also be useful to explore the socio-cultural parallels between Madrid or Barcelona and Berlin in the 1940s during the decade of reconstruction and Allied occupation when a third of families were headed by women while men were prisoners of war, refugees, or political detainees. In Spain, however, the significant number of family units which did not conform to the state-projected norm were statistically invisible as well as culturally marginalized, making any historical reconstruction of this complex picture a difficult task.

The extreme nature of Spain's social crisis in the 1940s transformed the nature and significance of food procurement. Apart from their demonstrating great ingenuity in bartering, this situation inevitably involved women in buying and selling on the black market (*estraperlo*), usually at the lower levels where the risk was greatest. (Women were tried for buying as well as selling on the black market; both were illegal.) Thus poor urban female constituencies would experience in particularly acute form, as they struggled daily to ensure their own and their families' survival, how food was a key commodity in the reconstruction, operation, and circulation of state and élite power.

In these conditions of scarcity, hunger, malnutrition, and epidemic disease—which accelerated social atomization—one could argue that it was female solidarity, established around collective activities such as communal cooking or information networks to aid food procurement, which constituted a key part of the pockets and remnants of civil society. Equally, 'traditional' modes of female protest—such as bread riots and overturning market stalls to protest against black market prices—signified women's civil opposition to the state's strategies for extending its power. The domestic space too—even the family, despite the regime's ideological appropriation of it—was subjectively experienced as a haven against state persecution, in contrast to the street where 'defeated' workers could be subjected to humiliation or worse at the hands of agents of the victorious order (Falangists, police, etc.). But in this sense the family's function was complementary to the state's goals since it facilitated the imposition of 'order' and regime stabilization. In the same way, women's resistance to the state existed alongside their crucial role in holding together the social fabric and coping with vast material crisis.

'Women's work' took many forms in this impoverished urban environment: they were textile operatives, provided casual, unskilled labour (e.g. canning factories, fish processing), many worked in the domestic service sector as maids, laundresses, cooks, and dressmakers/seamstresses, or provided other services which paid (at least potentially) somewhat better, the most notable being prostitution.

In spite of the official puritanism of the New State's ideology, this was one economic activity from which women were not even legally debarred until 1956, when brothels (significantly known as 'casas de tolerancia') were criminalized, and prostitution further 'privatized' as a result. Comparative assessment of the quantity of prostitution occurring relative to the pre-war or wartime periods is fraught with difficulty because it begs some enormous methodological and conceptual

17 Still from Patino's documentary film *Canciones para después de una guerra* showing a postwar newspaper headline: 'A mother sells her daughter for 400 pesetas'. The text continues: 'The buyer, in a green coat, cannot be traced. The go-between refuses to talk.' This story—whether true or false—highlights the searing poverty which in the 1940s operated a brutal 'reign of material truths' as the market—in effect the black market—saturated all social relations and values. The Catholic moral values proclaimed by the Nationalists were a luxury for the defeated as they struggled to satisfy the most elementary needs; for the wealthy, moral values could be maintained only at the expense of turning a blind eye to the material truths around them or, as here, by demonizing the poor.

questions. The data are scarce—the statistics for controlled prostitution in Spain in the 1940s (i.e. within brothels) obviously being of little use.[3] But what is certain is that the particularly desperate economic straits of many lower middle-class and working-class women in the immediate post-war, and their need to support families (parents and aged relatives as well as children) in the absence (permanent or temporary) of male breadwinners, was the strongest motivation towards some form of prostitution—whether widely or narrowly defined. ('Widely' in the sense that many women would form relationships with men who had political or economic leverage—those with Falangist/military connections or black marketeers of various levels—in order to secure material support for themselves and/or relatives and children.) There was a close reciprocal relationship between the black market and prostitution in that fortunes were being made through *estraperlo* speculation of all kinds. And not only was there the economic opportunity but also a culturally conducive climate. Prostitution thrived on the rigid gender roles and sexual Manichacism/oppression which underpinned the state's efforts to stabilize itself on the basis of a closed family unit. At both the economic and cultural/ sexual levels, prostitution operated as a safety valve. But the highest price for that was paid by the thousands of women who experienced in their own lives the most acute contradictions between state ideology/policy and the material reality of autarkic Spain.

But in fact all poor urban working women—whether prostitutes or not—epitomized the vulnerability of the urban labour force. Legally discriminated against (either under the terms of the Labour Charter and Fundamental Law of 1938 or directly by the actions of the state security forces), they worked in the most irregular and semi-clandestine sectors of the labour market. They represent the 'marginal', not because they were few in number, but because of their position: first, in the urban world, the spatial location *par excellence* of Francoism's 'other'; and second, because they found themselves, in relation to official Francoist discourse, on a kind of 'fault line' where a complex social reality diverged sharply from the regime's projected images of women and their role. While we know, in theoretical terms, that 'women have always had to interpret their womanhood within the contexts and parameters of their lives',[4] to date we know very little about how these specific contradictions were internalized, shaping the very construction of gender identity itself. (For an English-language source conveying something of the atmosphere of these times, readers should see Richard Wright's remarkable, virtually contemporary account, *Pagan Spain*, parts of which evoke— albeit within the constraints of a 1950s male sexual sensibility—the diversity of women's lives in 1940s Spain and something of the struggle going on below the state's monolithic-mythic construction of gender, as 'real' women faced a communal life dominated by the brutal materiality of food, sex, and death.)

Certainly the opportunities to manifest any behaviour or attitude dissenting from the dominant discourse were few and far between for most working women—not least because there was so little physical or mental energy to spare. Commentators have read some of the most famous popular songs of the period as a form of female cultural resistance to both Francoist gender norms and the material misery inflicted upon them: in particular the quite extraordinary 'Tatuaje' [Tattoo], which tells of a woman searching desperately and endlessly in the bars of a port for her lost sailor lover whose name she bears tattooed upon her arm.

[Lines] sung by all those exhausted housewives and mothers doing shift work in the sweat shops of the textile industry. They sang it for whoever was listening beyond the wide open windows of the workshops, not as a commercialized popular song, but as a cry of protest against the human condition, against their own lot as the Carmens of Spain waiting for husbands on whom History had imposed too great a trial, they sang against the grinding routine of a life spent queuing in front of food shops, ration book in hand, day after day, with no chance of that sailor who had arrived one day on a ship and whom, who knows, they might have encountered in the port at dusk.[5]

These were women who had themselves been tattooed by history, by the searing experience of civil war, all their grief, frustration, and longing personified in the description of the inaccessible, impossibly tall, blonde, *foreign* sailor. 'Tatuaje' and other popular songs, as well as the myths of the 1940s, constituted a form of cultural resistance to the state, helping people in the enormous task of getting by in dark times. (Indeed, the contestatory power of 'Tatuaje' is evidenced by its rediscovered popularity, in a camp reading, during the *movida** *madrileña*.)

More quantifiably, we know that in the 1940s Spanish women had recourse to long-established socio-economic survival strategies (although the women concerned would not, for the most part, have interpreted this behaviour as protest or political resistance). Such indicators of the state's failure to construct woman in its image would include, most obviously, the downright failure in Spain, as in fascist Italy and Nazi Germany, of pronatalism. (Spanish birth rates would not reach 1930s levels until the economic take-off of the 1960s.) Poor, working women used whatever birth control methods they could gain access to—and abortion, as before—to exert some degree of control in order to protect their own health, and stave off economic disaster and family crisis—all of which were closely connected. No amount of persuasion on the part of the Sección Femenina's cadres could persuade them of the joys of prolific motherhood.

For the poor, the Francoist image of 'family' and women's return to the home, as preached by state agencies, was a myth—above all in an urban working-class milieu. Here the family was often an absence. The imperative of autarky meant women left their homes to work (and this included prostitution) so their families could survive—although they often did so within alternative structures not remotely resembling the Francoist 'model' family (e.g. children deposited with different relatives or those of women working as prostitutes looked after by a variety of 'grandmothers' and 'mothers').

Of the various sources of socialization where working-class women were concerned, probably the least influential was that occurring via the intervention of the

Sección Femenina. Working in marginal sectors as so many women did, they mostly avoided the six months' labour service (Servicio Social) required—theoretically—of all single working women and overseen by the SF. (Marriage, of course, provided universal exemption from SS.) Of those young, single, urban working-class women who might have been targeted, the decrees of 1944–6 released them from the labour requirement, at which not only they had balked but also their employers, most of whom saw it as unwonted state interference with their workforce and its productive capacity. (Henceforward working-class women had only to attend classes—which ranged from basic literacy to low-level domestic science, sewing, and etiquette, and some very elementary aspects of 'national history and culture'.)

In so far as the point of control for female mobilization was entry to the official labour market, and in that industrial workers were exempt from labour service proper from the mid-1940s onwards, then the majority of those 'drafted' were in fact single middle- and lower middle-class women. Indeed the SF was mainly a middle class affair in terms of both its cadres and those they mobilized. These were the women—above all the urban middle classes—who provided the free labour in hospitals, schools, food kitchens, old people's homes, orphanages, charity workshops, etc. so crucial to the containment of socio-economic crisis and thus to regime stabilization in the 1940s.

For the SF's cadres proper—those who organized SS or provided the SF's many other educational or cultural services—these activities meant more than just the provision of low-level welfare services gratis. For many urban lower middle-class women, of course, it meant the implementation of a conscious political project: they saw themselves as actively contributing in the great enterprise of building the 'New State' and nation. But perhaps for even greater numbers it came to mean a relative freedom, alternative life chances—albeit according to norms acceptable within a deeply conservative society and polity. Yet the SF's cadres were single, economically independent women with an unusually self-sufficient life-style. The discrepancy between this and the message they disseminated—of the virtues of female submission, subservience, and joy through domesticity—was remarkable. Of course the SF was in a sense itself a form of cultural control in that it permitted the appearance of female involvement in public life without giving women entry to formal politics. Nevertheless, the ambiguities and contradictions of SF praxis contributed to creating a new mentality for some younger urban middle-class women. In the end, the conscious political objectives espoused by the SF's cadres may be seen to be less significant in terms of what the organization ultimately 'meant' than the process of change of which it formed a part.

Conclusion

There are two conclusions underpinning this brief exploration. First, that the regime's project for Spanish 'womanhood' scarcely functioned as its ideological progenitors had intended. This was unsurprising as the Spanish state was poor (in both absolute and relative terms) and could devote few resources to back its social policies. As far as urban working-class women were concerned, social control came chiefly through their total absorption in the battle for material survival rather than by dint of any internalization of regime norms of 'womanhood'. While female resistance to the regime's natalist policy did contribute to the collapse of autarky, here again women were motivated more directly by imperatives of material survival rather than political opposition in the strict sense. By contrast, however, the thousands of middle-class women mobilized as providers of basic health and education provision in the cadres of the Sección Femenina were often much more consciously engaged on a project: sustaining the social fabric in the vast material crisis of the 1940s, helping to stabilize the regime in order to build the New State as a self-consciously middle-class enterprise. But here too an ambiguous dynamic was present. For the process and experience of SF mobilization played, over time, a not insignificant part in disrupting and dynamizing gender relations and thus formed part of a matrix of social/cultural change.

Notes

1 R. Wright, *Pagan Spain* (London, 1957), 160–1.
2 On the scale of the post-war repression generally, J. Fontana, 'Naturaleza y consecuencias del franquismo', in J. Fontana (ed.), *España bajo el franquismo* (Barcelona, 1986), 22–4; A. Reig Tapia, *Ideología e historia: sobre la represión franquista y la guerra civil* (Madrid, 1984), 25–6; also M. Richards's essay in this volume.
3 The only published studies are contemporary medical-moral ones focusing mainly on the spread of venereal disease. More usefully and accessibly, see the accounts in novels such as Luis Martín Santos's *Tiempo de silencio* (1962) and Juan Marsé's *Si te dicen que caí* (1973).
4 J. Scott, foreword to M. J. Boxer and J. H. Quataert (eds.), *Connecting Spheres: Women in the Western World, 1500 to the Present* (Oxford, 1987).
5 M. Vázquez Montalbán, *Crónica sentimental de España* (Barcelona, 1980), 25 (translation mine). For 'Tatuaje' and many more, see Basilio Martín Patino's remarkable film *Canciones para después de una guerra* [*Songs for after a War*] (1971, authorized for release only in 1976).

Further reading

Abella, R., *Por el imperio hacia Dios: crónica de una posguerra (1939–1955)* (Barcelona, 1978).
Balfour, S., *Dictatorship, Workers and the City: Labour in Greater Barcelona since 1939* (Oxford, 1989), ch. 1.
Boxer, M. J., and Quataert, J. H. (eds.), *Connecting Spheres: Women in the Western World, 1500 to the Present* (Oxford, 1987), 217 ff.
Espina, A., 'La participación femenina en la actividad económica: el caso español', in R. Conde (ed.), *Familia y cambio social* (Madrid, 1982).
Falcón, L., *Mujer y sociedad* (Barcelona, 1984).
Febo, G. di, *La santa de la raza: un culto barroco en la España franquista* (Barcelona, 1988).
Gallego Méndez, M. T., *Mujer, falange y franquismo* (Madrid, 1983).
Martín Gaite, C., *Usos amorosos de la postguerra española* (Barcelona, 1987).
Miguel, A. de, *40 millones de españoles 40 años después* (Barcelona, 1976).
Nash, M., 'Pronatalism and Motherhood in Franco's Spain', in G. Bock and P. Thane (eds.), *Maternity and Gender Policies: Women and the Rise of the European Welfare States 1880s–1950s* (London, 1991), 160–77.

Preston, P., *The Politics of Revenge: Fascism and the Military in Twentieth-Century Spain* (London, 1990), ch. 2.

Sánchez López, R., *Mujer española: una sombra de destino en lo universal (trayectoria histórica de Sección Femenina de Falange, 1934–1977)* (Murcia, 1990).

Scanlon, G. M., *La polémica feminista en la España contemporánea (1868–1974)* (Madrid, 1976), ch. 7.

Suárez, L., *Crónica de la Sección Femenina de Falange y su tiempo* (Madrid, 1993) (the 'official biography').

Vázquez Montalbán, M., *Crónica sentimental de España* (Barcelona, 1980).

Memoirs

Doña, J., *Desde la noche y la niebla: mujeres en las cárceles franquistas* (n.p., 1978, 2nd edn., 1993).

Falcón, L., *Los hijos de los vencidos 1939–49* (Madrid, 2nd edn., 1989).

García-Madrid, A., *Réquiem por la libertad* (Madrid, 1982).

Wright, R., *Pagan Spain* (London, 1957).

12

ALICIA ALTED

SHEELAGH
ELLWOOD

JOHN LONDON

JO LABANYI

Cultural Control

Education and Political Control

ALICIA ALTED

The Franco regime was the product of a civil war. Its defining characteristics became clear in 1938 with the setting up of the Burgos government, which shared political responsibilities out between the various civil factions that had supported the uprising. Education was put in the hands of a Church deeply imbued with the spirit of the crusade and backed socially by the traditional right. All educational activities were controlled centrally by the Ministry of Education, replacing the Republican Ministry of Public Instruction.

Because of its origins in a military revolt against a constitutionally elected government, the New State needed to find a way of legitimizing itself; the manipulation of culture offered itself as a tool: first, by controlling all cultural activities through advance censorship and the purging of cultural workers, and second, by creating a cultural model to shape the behaviour of Spanish citizens, thus guaranteeing the regime's stability and permanence. The basis of this model was the disqualification of those who had lost the war (the 'reds'), and the negation of everything the Republic had stood for (qualified with the prefix 'anti-'). The prime channel for instilling this model was, of course, the education system.

The regime's cultural apparatus was founded on two simple principles: the 're-Spanishification' and 're-Catholicization' of society. The exaltation of a seamless Spanish fatherland meant the persecution of all expressions of regional national identity, language in particular. And Catholicism became an essential element in reconstituting a social order eroded by the levelling policies of the Republic, aimed at promoting equal opportunities through the development of talent and access to culture for the disadvantaged. The new social order was based on the notion of the natural inequality of human beings, and their inherent wickedness as a result of original sin. Such notions served to justify class divisions and the need for differential forms of education. The regime's policies drew on the educational principles and systems of sixteenth- and seventeenth-century Spain, on nineteenth- and early twentieth-century Catholic educational theory, and on traditional Church doctrine on the Christian education of youth, formulated by Pius XI in his encyclical *Divini illius magistri* of 21 December 1929. The mentors of the new educational and cultural policies were Marcelino Menéndez Pelayo and Andrés Manjón, founder of the Escuelas del Ave María. The latter had been founded at the end of the nineteenth century to counter the 'neutral' stance to religion of Francisco Giner de los Ríos's educational activities, particularly the Institución Libre de Enseñanza* (ILE). However in other pedagogical aspects Manjón coincided with the ILE, since both were in touch with new educational ideas of the time. What made the Ministry adopt Manjón as mentor was his belief in a 'Spanish, Christian education'. Menéndez Pelayo was the major exponent of a humanistic and national Catholic brand of traditional thought. For him, Spain's greatness had to be sought in the sixteenth and seventeenth centuries; her decline had begun with the abandonment of that national Catholic tradition in the late eighteenth century, thanks to the influence of French Enlightenment thought.

This educational policy was based, then, on principles that implied the rejection of everything achieved by the Republican educational effort, as seen in the New State's appropriation of liberal organizations and bodies originally under the wing of the ILE and subsequently sponsored by the Republic: for example, the Junta para Ampliación de Estudios e Investigaciones Científicas [Council for the Promotion of Study and Scientific Research], the Instituto Escuela, the Residencia de Estudiantes, and the Misiones Pedagógicas. These bodies were reconstituted under a new ethos that made them look like a break with the past, as the Consejo Superior de Investigaciones Científicas,* the Instituto Ramiro de Maeztu, the Colegios Mayores, and the *cátedras ambulantes* set up by the Sección Femenina.*

The 're-Catholicization' of education meant compulsory study of sacred texts, and the subordination of all forms of teaching and student behaviour to Catholic moral norms. The social consequences of this were the predominance of private education (provided by the religious orders), and the provision of special education for women. The former was facilitated through the state's application of the principle of 'subsidiarity': that is, the primary educational agent in the regime's schema was the 'naturally Christian' family, which entrusted the education of its children to the Church. The state, in other words, delegated its responsibility to the latter. The principle of different education according to sex was based on traditional notions of the image and function of women, according to which women were essentially different from men for biological reasons. Woman's entire being was conditioned by motherhood, and her destiny was to live for home, husband, and family. Such thinking meant the abolition of coeducation for 'moral and pedagogical' reasons, the inclusion of domestic science in the curriculum as a compulsory subject for women, and restricting teacher training for women to primary and technical (i.e. non-academic) education. This process of ideological re-education was undertaken by Acción Católica, a secular organization dependent on the Church, and by the Sección Femenina of the Falange,* entrusted with teaching domestic science at the various educational levels and with indoctrinating women through a form of compulsory labour service (Servicio Social). The Church's control of education meant that the Falange took responsibility for extracurricular activities, run by institutions created for this purpose: the Sección Femenina for girls and women, the Frente de Juventudes charged with the 'formation and discipline of the youthful [male] forces of Spain', and the Spanish University Student Union (SEU). The Falange's contribution was confined to specialized subjects that were educationally marginal: domestic science as mentioned, political indoctrination ('Formation of the National Spirit'), and physical training and sport.

In this period, educational policy faithfully reflected the ideological bias of successive Ministers of Education and their closest associates. Pedro Sainz Rodríguez, Minister of Education from January 1938 to April 1939, was an Alphonsine monarchist from a conservative, Catholic bourgeois background. Under the Republic he had been a member of the group of intellectuals centred on the 'counter-revolutionary' journal Acción Española. His successor José Ibáñez Martín belonged to the influential, élite lay Catholic organization the Asociación Católica Nacional de Propagandistas (ACNP). Franco's longest serving Minister, he was replaced in 1951, after twelve unbroken years in service, by Joaquín Ruiz Giménez (a member of the same association) because of the need for 'new blood'. His successor in 1956, Jesús Rubio García-Mina, had connections with the founder members of the Falange and had served as Under-Secretary for Education in Ibáñez Martín's ministry.

The importance attached to education as a means of instilling principles and behavioural norms underlay the first attempts at reforming secondary education. Its fundamental mission was seen as that of forming a ruling class, divided—in the educational jargon of the day—into a 'select minority' centred on the universities, and the rest whose job was to guide the 'popular masses' by occupying key intermediary positions in the power structure. The regime's need to form a ruling élite explains why this reform of secondary education—then called 'intermediary education'; one of the regime's sociological quirks was the creation of a middle class that was entirely *sui generis*—started with the *bachillerato* *universitario* (the qualification leading to university). The law of September 1938 set up an élitist baccalaureate based on National-Catholic principles, heavily weighted towards a strongly ideologized version of the classical humanities. This idea of creating a 'spiritual aristocracy' was the guiding principle behind Ibáñez Martín's period in office; he continued his predecessor's reforms with the University Law of July 1943, which formalized a national university system in which all branches of knowledge were subordinated to the principles of Catholic dogma, with a pyramidal structure headed by a state-appointed rector. This notion that the role of the universities was to form 'select spirits'—as the Minister of Education put it, borrowing an expression used by Ortega y Gasset and other writers and intellectuals of the 1920s—was reinforced through the SEU, which all university students had to belong to. The 1943 law gave the SEU official status, turning it into an increasingly ineffective bureaucratic machine for the political indoctrination of the younger generation.

Paradoxically, the earliest student protests came from Falangist students whose combative spirit and revolutionary ardour soon clashed with the reality of what would become the Movimiento.* Other minor outbreaks of unrest in the mid-1940s were led by the sons of former Republicans. The majority of students stood somewhere in between, depoliticized and swamped by a political conservatism from which the lecturers were not exempt.

The most notable feature of the education system in the 1940s is that it was not till 1945 that norms were established for primary education and a budget earmarked for the building of schools, in marked contrast to Republican educational policies. Earlier efforts to achieve equal educational opportunities had been replaced by a classist concept of education geared to the formation of élites.

In the 1950s, the change of image made necessary by international recognition and the beginnings of industrialization started to shift the foundations of the educational structure erected in the previous decade. Under Ruiz Giménez as Minister of Education, a two-way process began that would underpin the formulation of all subsequent educational policies. First, it started to be accepted that education had a role to play in stimulating economic and social transformation. Secondly, it became clear that a degree of intellectual liberalization was necessary to promote such socio-economic change. Accordingly, Ruiz Giménez's team implemented a series of reforms with a significantly increased educational budget. For the first time since the Republic, the problem of the shortage of schools was recognized with the December 1953 law setting targets for school-building. But it was Ruiz Giménez's successor, Jesús Rubio García-Mina, who tackled the problem head on with his five-year School-Building Plan for 1957–61, which had an inadequate budget and did not sufficiently take into account the rapid increase in demand for school places during those years, both because of the birth rate and because of the beginnings of mass migration from south to north and from country to city.

In February 1953 a secondary education law was passed to deal with the serious problems created by the 1938 law setting up the *bachillerato universitario*, which had overlooked the need for secondary studies geared to economic development. As a preliminary measure, the *bachillerato* was divided into two levels: an elementary one, which provided school-leavers with basic academic and professional qualifications, and a higher one; in both, the balance was shifted slightly away from study of the classics towards more practical subjects. Things were taken a step further by the 1955 Law of Professional Industrial Formation, which accepted the latter as a 'branch of education' whose essential aim was to train skilled industrial workers. This law had been preceded by the Secondary and Professional Education Law of July 1949, instituting the *bachillerato laboral*, and the 1953 law encouraging the teaching of economics and business studies. Under Jesús Rubio, technical universities were finally given legal recognition in 1959. Both the technical *bachillerato* and the technical universities had full official backing, particularly from leaders of the state trade unions. Both were needed to meet the growing demand for skilled workers in industry, but the rhetoric of the regime justified the policy shift as an attempt 'to give the working class the opportunity to enter and lead the state'.

In the early 1950s, a generation mostly educated in religious schools in accordance with the principles of the 1938 law entered the universities. Their parents had fought the war mostly on the winning side but their frame of reference was repression, harsh living conditions, and a lack of freedom. At this time, encouraged by somewhat more liberal attitudes at the Ministry of Education, student groups started to organize against SEU and government controls on academic life. A leading role in channelling these early outbreaks of protest was played by the Communist Party. The demonstrations organized by a core of students linked to the Party, with the rector's approval in the case of Madrid University, attracted mass student support and led to the first anti-government protests and to clashes with Falangist students, which culminated in the events of February 1956, provoking a ministerial crisis in which both the Education Minister and the General Secretary of the Movimiento lost their jobs.

The education policies of Jesús Rubio García-Mina, who succeeded Ruiz Giménez at the Ministry 1956–62, represented a continuation of the reform programme initiated by his predecessor. In effect, this period was a pivotal one, marking the transition from the overtly ideological 'spiritual' model previously dominant to the implicitly conservative technocratic model that would prevail in the 1960s.

Further reading
Alted, A., *Política del Nuevo Estado sobre el patrimonio cultural y la educación durante la guerra civil española* (Madrid, 1984).
Carreras, J. J., and Ruiz Carnicer, M. A. (eds.), *La universidad española bajo el régimen de Franco (1939–1975)* (Zaragoza, 1991).
Cooper, N. B., *Catholicism and the Franco Regime* (Beverly Hills, Calif., 1975).
Crespo, J., et al., *Purga de maestros en la guerra civil (la depuración del magisterio nacional de la provincia de Burgos)* (Valladolid, 1987).

Lerena, C., *Escuela, ideología y clases sociales en España* (Barcelona, 1986).

—— (ed.), *Educación y sociología en España* (Madrid, 1987).

Mayordomo, A. (ed.), *Historia de la educación en España*, part v, vols. i and ii: *Nacional-catolicismo y educación en la España de la posguerra* (Madrid, 1990).

Navarro, R., *La enseñanza primaria durante el franquismo (1936–1975)* (Barcelona, 1990).

Puelles, M. de, *Educación e ideología en la España contemporánea (1767–1975)* (Barcelona, 1991).

Sáez Marín, J., *El Frente de Juventudes: política de juventud en la España de la postguerra (1937–1960)* (Madrid, 1988).

Sopeña Monsalve, A., *El florido pensil: memoria de la escuela nacionalcatólica* (Barcelona, 1994).

Suárez, L., *Crónica de la Sección Femenina y su tiempo* (Madrid, 1993).

Valls, F., *La enseñanza de la literatura en el franquismo (1936–1951)* (Barcelona, 1983).

Valls, R., *La interpretación de la historia de España y sus orígenes ideológicos en el bachillerato franquista (1936–1951)* (Valencia, 1987).

Vilanova, M., *Atlas de la evolución del analfabetismo en España, de 1887 a 1981* (Madrid, 1992).

The Moving Image of the Franco Regime: Noticiarios y Documentales 1943–1975

SHEELAGH ELLWOOD

The official film company of the Franco regime came into being on 29 September 1942, under the aegis of the General Secretariat of the Francoist single party, Falange Española Tradicionalista y de las Juntas de Ofensiva Nacional Sindicalista (FET y de las JONS*). The title of the new entity was Noticiarios y Documentales Cinematográficos (Cinematographic Newsreel and Documentaries), but it was to be known by its acronym NO-DO. Three months later, a decree was issued establishing the ground rules for newsreel production and projection. With effect from 1 January 1943, no newsreels other than those produced by NO-DO could be made 'in Spain, her possessions and colonies' and no film-maker except those employed or authorized by NO-DO would be allowed, 'under any pretext whatsoever', to obtain cinematographic reports. Equally, all laboratories were forbidden to handle any material which had not been filmed by NO-DO crews and were immediately required to inform NO-DO if approached by anyone with unauthorized film for processing. Furthermore, NO-DO would enjoy the monopoly of exchanges with foreign newsreel companies and, finally, the screening of NO-DO newsreels would be obligatory in all cinemas.[1] The regime thus exercised total control over news and information presented in the form of moving pictures, tightening still further the stranglehold it already had, through censorship and the state press and radio networks, on public knowledge and perceptions of national and international reality.

The research on which this contribution is based was carried out in 1987 thanks to a Senior Fellowship of the Vicente Cañada Blanch Anglo-Spanish Foundation. The opinions expressed here are the author's own and should not be taken as an expression of official government policy.

When the NO-DO slogan proclaimed that its newsreels put 'the entire world within reach of all Spaniards' it was, to say the least, being economical with the truth, given the limited nature of its sources and the effects of censorship on its production. Its manipulation of historical truth was not confined to what was excluded, but extended to how it treated what was included. Thus when, in 1959, NO-DO made the first Spanish documentary about the civil war which had given birth to the Franco regime, its title *El camino de la paz* [*The Path to Peace*] pointed to the fallacious message conveyed by the film: the civil war had been necessary and justified as the only way to restore peace and order, destroyed by the chaos of the Second Republic. NO-DO's picture of what life was like under 'Franco's peace' naturally did not include such realities as the rationing, repression, fuel shortages, and general misery of the early years, or the strikes, continuing repression, economic crisis, and political discontent of the later years. The occasional disaster had, inevitably, to be included but, for the most part, NO-DO portrayed contemporary Spain through images and commentary which exulted in the prowess of Spanish industry or agriculture, cheap housing for the working classes, the celebration of the regime's ritual occasions, roads and reservoirs inaugurated by Franco, and, of course, football. NO-DO's depiction of the outside world was more ambiguous, reflecting, as I have written elsewhere, 'the contradiction between the Franco regime's instinctive rejection of foreign influences [. . .] and its pragmatic need for foreign political and economic support'.[2] But if reporting of foreign events tended to oscillate between the purely frivolous (new hairstyles from Paris) and the conflictive (strikes in France or Britain), there was one constant feature: anti-communism. Thus the underlying message of news items—for example, on war in Korea and Vietnam or on 'starvation in China'—was that communist regimes brought conflict and misery in their wake.

As part of the Francoist propaganda arsenal, NO-DO newsreels were naturally used to remind audiences whom they had to thank for the peace and tranquillity in which *they* lived, while foreign contemporaries allegedly suffered all manner of deprivations. Between the first edition in January 1943 and the death of the Caudillo* in November 1975, Franco appeared in nearly 900 separate reports, which was equivalent to approximately 4 per cent of NO-DO's total production. This was far from a monopoly; but no other person or subject received such exposure. As one might expect, Franco's appearances became less frequent towards the end of his life, dwindling from a record 45 in 1965, to a mere 9 in 1974 and 2 in 1975. Yet it would be wrong to assume that the number of times cinema audiences were regaled with Franco's activities followed a steady pattern of decrease from the pinnacle of his achievement (winning the civil war in 1939) to his death. In fact, his cinema 'career' can be divided into phases, whose varying intensity was not haphazard but closely related to changes in the economic and political development of the regime. When it was in a 'positive' period of economic prosperity, international recognition, and internal stability, Franco appeared frequently in NO-DO reports. By contrast, when the regime was subject to economic crisis, international opprobrium, or domestic unrest, the Caudillo maintained a low cinematographic profile. The intention was clearly to enhance the association between Franco and prosperity in the popular mind, playing down negative associations or even eliminating them altogether.

It was appropriate that the man who had risen to professional prominence and political power by dint of military prowess, and who saw himself as a latter-day warrior king, should make his final newsreel appearance presiding over the annual Victory Day parade, in April 1975. Yet this was a relatively rare cinematographic reference to the military origin of his power. Despite his penchant for military uniforms, even on civilian occasions, the number of reports which featured him taking part in military events other than the Victory Parade was low: a mere 37, of which half were between 1943 and 1948. Similarly, he appeared in his role as National Chief of FET y de las JONS only 25 times, 21 of them between 1943 and 1951. And in spite of his belief in himself as God's emissary, his relationship with the Catholic Church was captured on celluloid only 40 times in thirty-three years (although these occasions were spread more evenly throughout his career).

The contrasting volume of Franco's appearances in political and propagandistic roles tell their own story (as, indeed, the images themselves were intended to) about how he wished to be seen and remembered by popular audiences. Between 1943 and 1975, he featured in 200 reports of a political nature and as the protagonist of a massive 529 propagandistic events (including 154 openings of factories, bridges, reservoirs, etc.). It was in these roles that his appearances remained steadiest throughout his life, tailing off significantly only from 1971 onwards. This constant association of Franco with political stability and material prosperity was part of the regime's efforts not only to rewrite its own history but also to guarantee its future. Thus, in its small but sustained and pervasive way, NO-DO too made its contribution to the longevity of the Caudillo's 'reign'.

Notes
1 *Boletín Oficial del Estado*, 356 (22 Dec. 1942).
2 S. Ellwood, 'Spanish Newsreels 1943–1975: The Image of the Franco Regime', in *Historical Journal of Film, Radio and Television*, 7/3 (1987), 234.

Further Reading
Ellwood, S., 'Spanish Newsreels 1943–1975: The Image of the Franco Regime', *Historical Journal of Film, Radio and Television*, 7/3 (1987), 225–38.
Gubern, R. (ed.), 'NO-DO: 50 años después', *Archivos de la Filmoteca* (Valencia), 15 (Oct, 1993), 5–59.
Sánchez-Biosca, V., and Tranche, R. R., *NO-DO: el tiempo y la memoria* (Cuadernos de la Filmoteca 1) (Madrid, 1993).

An anthology of NO-DO newsreels *NO-DO: una historia próxima* is available on video (Filmoteca Española/RTVE/Metrovideo, 1992).

The Ideology and Practice of Sport

JOHN LONDON

Falangist conceptions of sport developed in detail during the civil war. As such, they were antagonistic towards the preceding regime and constantly related to military endeavours. Hence, according to Falangist propaganda, the Second Republic became synonymous with an era of sporting weakness and disunity. Falangist sport was, in contrast, heroic, and commentators had no difficulty in viewing the national conflict in sporting terms: '[t]hose who demonstrate such a magnificent talent for that sublime and tragic sport which is war, should later find the aptitude to relax and build up their strength in the practice of ordinary sports.'[1] This military rhetoric led to the glorification of strategically important sports like skiing.

From the early stages of the Francoist regime, sports bureaucracy was dominated by the amalgamated version of the Falange* (FET y de las JONS*) created by Franco during the civil war. General Moscardó, president of the Consejo Nacional de Deportes (National Sports Council), fixed the tone at the outset by undertaking an official visit to Nazi Germany in April 1939. He returned with a special plan for Spanish sport, explained how the Consejo would have its headquarters in the capital, Madrid, and would be made up solely of military men so that Spanish sportsmen would be subject to military discipline. Moscardó became head of the renamed Delegación Nacional de Deportes [National Sports Delegation] which was founded by decree on 22 February 1941. Its first article entrusted the 'management and promotion' of Spanish sport to the Falange.

The repercussions of these measures were immediate. The suspiciously red football shirts of the national soccer team were replaced by blue ones (blue being the colour of Falangist shirts). The fascist salute became compulsory before the start of all football games and was used when medals were awarded for other sports events. As a reaction against decadent foreign influences, non-Spanish words were eliminated from official language (the football team called Sporting de Gijón, for example, became Deportivo Gijón). Moreover, state policy was distinctly anti-regionalist: Catalan and Basque groups in all sports were not allowed to use their own language to describe their identity or to function as teams. In the writing of the period, two elements surface as the essential values to be inculcated by both the participation in and attendance at all sporting events: patriotism and discipline.

To propagate these virtues a training camp for young Falangists was set up during the civil war. Called Campamento José Antonio after the founder of the Falange, it closely resembled Italian fascist training camps. Elsewhere, there were mass, open-air choreographed gymnastics exercises at Falangist gatherings. Sports activities such as *pelota* (a ball game of Basque origin) and swimming competitions were organized to raise money for the Blue Division which fought on the Russian front from 1941 to 1943. The Sección Femenina* of the Falange held its own large-scale gymnastics championships designed, alongside other activities, to inculcate

18 Gymnastics display of the Sección Femenina of the Falange in the bullring at Murcia, reproduced in the Italian fascist magazine *Legioni e Falangi* (1 June 1941). The caption reads: 'The Spanish coat of arms harmoniously composed by athletes of the Sección Femenina.' The national emblem (the imperial eagle) is in fact here composed by the female athletes lying on their backs: an apt image of the role Spanish women were called upon to play in constructing the New State. Although the mass political mobilization characteristic of fascist Germany and Italy did not occur in Francoist Spain, sporting events—and religious ceremonial—were used in a similar attempt to integrate the masses into a strictly organized hierarchical structure, reflected here by the vertical angle of the camera looking down on its diminutive, dehumanized subjects.

a specific ideal of feminine deportment. Patriotism was subsumed into neo-fascist solidarity in the majority of international sporting events in which Spain took part during the Second World War. The most significant of these were the football matches played in Berlin and Milan against Germany and Italy in April 1942.

Sports reporting supplied a suitably heroic treatment of official activities. The sports newspaper *Marca*, founded in 1938 by the Falangist Manuel Fernández Cuesta, after the war developed a daily circulation of up to 400,000. As well as providing a distinct political angle on events, it contributed to a sporting vision of Franco's political leadership. A front-page article celebrated *Marca*'s fourth year of publication on 25 November 1942. It bore the title 'A fascist salute to all Spanish sportsmen'. The Caudillo* was described as the 'captain of Spain', for it was to him that Spaniards owed 'the resurrection and noble guidance' of their sport. (The same spirit led a make of football to be called 'Invicto' [Unvanquished] in homage to the Generalísimo.*) At the same time, press censorship attempted to eliminate criticism of referees' decisions and the reporting of violence among crowds and participants. Of course, these restraints were relaxed for Spanish journalists reporting on international matches: when the national football team suffered a 4-1 defeat at the hands of Portugal in January 1947, a journalist claimed that the English referee must have been a Labour supporter who hated Spain. Likewise, Armando Muñoz Calero, head of the Real Federación Española de Fútbol [Spanish Football Federation], broadcast over Radio Nacional a notorious cry of victory after the Spanish defeat of England in the World Cup in Brazil in 1950: '[w]e have beaten perfidious Albion!'

Although an outline of Falangist predominance gives the impression of a thorough programme of indoctrination, the state invested very little in sport, particularly in comparison to the amounts spent on sports policies in fascist Italy and Nazi Germany. At a competitive level, Spain won only one gold medal in all of the six Olympic Games in which it participated. On a wider social level, the influence of the Catholic Church over mainstream education meant that politicized sports were not integral to schooling. Despite the existence of fascist trappings in sports stadiums, it is debatable exactly how many spectators were influenced in the way intended. After the end of the Second World War the fascist salute was abandoned at general sports events and, by the late 1940s, foreign trainers and players were working for Spanish football teams. Far from being subservient to nationalist authority, regional teams came, in the eyes of their fans, to represent independence. Especially when it was competing against Real Madrid, Barcelona Football Club (Barça) came for many of its supporters to symbolize the Catalan cause itself, just as support for Athlétic Bilbao provided an outlet for Basque aspirations.

If any government policy can be identified from the early 1950s onwards, it consisted in depoliticizing sport rather than allowing more space for the Falangist presence of the early 1940s. The change in attitude is well illustrated by Franco's personal stance. In May 1960 he personally cancelled the football match due to take place in Madrid between Spain and the Soviet Union in the quarter-finals of the European Nations Cup (the USSR thus automatically qualified for the semi-finals). One of the prime reasons for this action was his fear that there would be enormous popular demonstrations in favour of the Soviet team. The regime had begun by giving the Falangists the opportunity to manipulate Spaniards into fascist support. Not only had this strategy failed, but the regime had become frightened by the mass defiance occasioned by public events. The authorities logically concluded that sport had only one function that was both safe and useful: to serve as an escapist form of popular culture and thus divert attention away from political and social problems.

Note
1 Fex, 'Deportes', *Vértice*, 5 (Sept.–Oct. 1937), n.p.

Further reading
Alcoba, A., *El periodismo deportivo en la sociedad moderna* (Madrid, 1980).
Cazorla Prieto, L. M., *Deporte y estado* (Barcelona, 1979).
Fernández Santander, C., *El fútbol durante la guerra civil y el franquismo* (Madrid, 1990).
London, J., 'Competing Together in Fascist Europe: Sport in Early Francoism', in G. Berghaus (ed.), *Fascist Theatre: Comparative Studies on the Politics and Aesthetics of Performance* (Oxford, 1995).
MacClancy, J., 'The Basques of Vizcaya and Athlétic Club de Bilbao', in J. MacClancy (ed.), *Sport and Identity: Comparative Approaches* (Oxford, 1995).
Shaw, D., *Fútbol y franquismo*, trans. J. A. Miguez (Madrid, 1987).
Vizcaíno Casas, F., *La España de la posguerra (1939–1953)* (Barcelona, 1981).

Censorship or the Fear of Mass Culture

JO LABANYI

It is generally argued that, unlike fascism in Germany and Italy, the Franco regime did not mobilize the nation around a co-ordinated cultural programme, but was motivated by the negative project of suppressing the cultural values of the Republic. Yet in practice propaganda and censorship are hard to separate. From 1936 to 1951, censorship of all media other than the press came under the propaganda office. The censors did not just cut and suppress texts; they rewrote texts, added to texts, issued their own texts. Their interference in the trivia of everyday life—from menus (in the 1940s the Russian salad served in Spanish bars was renamed 'imperial' or 'national salad') to matchboxes (as late as 1972 Fosforera General Española was fined for a design that, upside down, could be read as a woman masturbating)—shows that they saw all forms of social communication as a 'text'. In this, and in their attention to issues of class, ethnicity, and gender, they can be said to have anticipated the insights of modern cultural theory.

During the Franco period, the censorship bodies underwent a series of restructurings that betray the regime's ideological tensions and shifts. I shall concentrate here on the period to 1962, when Manuel Fraga Iribarne became Minister of Information and Tourism, briefly outlining later developments.

The Press and Propaganda Office set up in 1936 at the Nationalist military headquarters in Salamanca was put under General Millán Astray, whose slogan 'Death to Intelligence!' made Unamuno break with the Nationalists. In 1937 censorship passed to the Press and Propaganda Delegation at Burgos, headed by Falangist intellectuals; film censorship offices were set up at Seville and Corunna, moving to Salamanca. Franco's first government of 1938 put the Press and Propaganda Delegation, now extended to cover radio (the main vehicle for Nationalist wartime propaganda), under control of the Interior Minister, Serrano Suñer. The 1938 Press Law (in force till 1966) put the press 'at the service of the state' and confirmed the obligation for all printed, visual, or broadcast materials to be submitted for censorship before publication (German correspondents were exempted).

The 1939 Law of Political Responsibilities 'purged' many cultural workers, particularly journalists. Advance censorship was extended to theatre, song, and music, and from 1940 all public lectures and talks required authorization. The Book Fairs of May 1939 and 1940 were celebrated with book burnings, to recital of the episode in the *Quixote* where the Canon purges Don Quixote's library. The confiscation of books from libraries (authorized since 1937) ironically gave the public access in the long run to many private collections, which ended up in the National Library. In 1940 postal censorship was ended at home but retained for overseas mail.

After Catalonia's fall in 1939 public use of Catalan was banned, adding to orders of 1937 and 1938 formally proscribing Galician and Basque (Nationalist military commanders had issued local orders banning Galician and Basque from the start of Nationalist occupation in July 1936 and April 1937 respectively). A 1941 decree, based on Mussolini's Defence of the Language Law, banned public use of all 'dialects' (minority languages), 'barbarisms' (foreign borrowings), and foreign languages (including song lyrics; all imported films had to be dubbed into Spanish). This law had massive repercussions on everyday life, requiring all place and Christian names to be Castilianized: Palace Hotels were renamed, and tombstones with inscriptions in Basque had to be replaced by the deceased's family.

In 1941 the censorship and propaganda office was put under the Falange* and renamed Vice-Secretariat for Popular Education, creating a more civilian image and showing that mass culture was the prime concern. In charge was Arias Salgado, who saw his mission as propagating a 'theology of information'; his Press Delegate was Juan Aparicio, creator of the slogan 'One, Great, Free Spain' and the yoke-and-arrows symbol. With the Falange's demotion on Allied victory in 1945, censorship moved to the Ministry of Education, completing the shift to a civilian image and giving control to the Church, in charge of education since 1938: Church appointees on censorship boards had a veto, and Catholic publishers, radio, and press were exempt (before 1941 pastorals and the Vatican press had been cut). The 1945 Fuero de los Españoles, aimed at giving the semblance of a constitution, merely ratified the 1938 military Press Law. Article 12—'All Spaniards may express their ideas freely provided they do not contravene the fundamental principles of the state'—was usefully vague; additionally all rights could be suspended by military decree. In 1951 censorship passed to the new Ministry of Information and Tourism (MIT), reflecting current concern with Spain's international image. The return of the Falangist Arias Salgado to head the MIT 1951–62 meant a reversion to hard-line policies, particularly after the 1956 student riots; the 1960 Banditry and Terrorism Decree made the spreading of 'false news' a military offence.

The practical work of censorship was mostly farmed out to freelancers, who had to report whether items offended Catholic dogma, morality, the Church, the regime, and its associates; and mark cuts or changes. The average workload was 500 books per month; a backlog of 6,000 films had accumulated by 1941. Censors' names were confidential; they comprised religious, military, and civilian personnel, including writers (Cela censored magazines 1941–5). In tricky cases Franco adjudicated, usually favourably. Books and films were sometimes authorized for export only; from the late 1950s double versions were produced for home and overseas. Even after publication, items could be denounced by individuals or institutions: the Church constantly banned authorized films, while the armed forces confiscated approved material. Provincial delegations dealt with the local press, cinemas, and theatres.

The press, with its mass readership, was the chief target. All newspaper and magazine editors were state appointees (the job included censoring one's paper) and had to be Falange members, as did trainees of the Official Journalists' School created in 1941. The state press agency EFE, with its subsidiaries, held a monopoly over news coverage; it, like the foreign press agencies, had to submit all reports for advance approval. Infringements were punished with fines, suspensions, or the editor's sacking. Control was also exercised through paper quotas.

The censors issued editors with directives listing banned topics or supplying reports of Franco's activities (often written in advance, sometimes by himself; during the 'years of hunger' banquets in his honour could not be mentioned). Franco's speeches, occasionally themselves censored, had to be printed on the front page with headlines of a specified size. No mention could be made of the following: individuals associated with the Republic; arrests, trials, executions; guerrilla activity, strike action; the Royal Family; crimes, suicides, bankruptcies; stock exchange falls, devaluations; food and housing shortages, price rises; industrial and traffic accidents; epidemics, droughts, flood or storm damage. Editors were encouraged to give coverage to sport, but could not report fouls and referees' errors, or 'exacerbate regional passions'. Illustrators were employed to touch up news photos, usually to fill in cleavages or lower hemlines. Advertisements too were censored, especially when containing female figures: publicity for gymnasiums, dancing schools, and marriage agencies was banned, and in the 'years of hunger' restaurant advertising was controlled. Most unprintable of all was mention of the existence of censorship.

In the performing arts, local delegates attended dress rehearsals and first nights, making later spot checks. Their reports took audience response into account when deciding what was risky. Chorus girls could show their legs in towns of over 40,000; luxury venues or theatre clubs had more latitude. The work of 'dangerous' playwrights—e.g. Beckett or Pinter—was sometimes authorized for one-off performances or book publication only. Music-hall, with its popular audience and topical satire, was scrutinized rigorously. Improvisation was banned: all scripts, including jokes and lyrics, had to be submitted for advance censorship, with drawings or photos of costumes, and performers' names (those with Republican associations might be authorized if omitted from posters). Carlos Barral recalls seeing La Bella Dorita, star of the Barcelona cabaret Moulin Rouge, visit the censor's office each morning, with mantilla and prayer-book, to sing that evening's *cuplés* (the audience frequently clubbed together to pay performers' fines so they could be 'naughty'). All 'decadent' or 'so-called black' music—i.e. jazz—was banned, though Afro-Cuban dance and song was allowed on the grounds that it formed part of the Hispanic imperial tradition.

In cinema, compulsory dubbing of foreign films facilitated censorship through mistranslation. In *The Snows of Kilimanjaro* a declaration of love became a prayer; in *Arch of Triumph* Ingrid Bergman, asked if her lover was her husband, was dubbed as saying yes while shaking her head. Great pains were taken to avoid female adultery: in *Mogambo* and *The Barefoot Countess*, to justify the wife's attraction to another man, husband and wife were made into brother and sister, and in *The Clay Idol* into father and daughter. *The Rains of Ranchipur* was rewritten to have Lana Turner's husband eaten by a tiger, to justify her passion for another man. Violence was not generally censored; sex was the problem. Censors' reports routinely included the phrases 'cut/shorten final kiss', 'cut thighs throughout'; even men's naked legs were unacceptable (as were shots including a Protestant Bible). All films from socialist countries were banned. Posters were also censored: Tarzan's Jane had her midriff painted over.

The popularity of US movies was used to control Spanish film companies by allocating import licence quotas according to the political orthodoxy of their own productions, the highest incentives being for the 'National Interest' category created in 1944. In 1952 import licence quotas were replaced with a sliding scale of subsidies according to rating; from 1958, films given low ratings could not be shown in major cities. Banned films were sometimes allowed one-off showings at film festivals.

Criteria for approving Spanish films were particularly strict. Till 1976, all scripts had to be approved before filming could start (Berlanga estimated that the censors frustrated 80 per cent of his projects). Mention of the civil war was taboo till 1948; in 1965, Saura had to cut references to it in *La caza*. Happy endings were enforced when social issues such as the rural exodus or housing shortages were involved, as in the Falangist Nieves Conde's *Surcos* (1951) and *El inquilino* (1957). Often (as with foreign films) a voice-over or title was added at the start or end to 'guide' the viewer or deny resemblance to Spain. There was a respite in 1951–2, when García Escudero as the new MIT's Director-General for Film tried to encourage a Spanish art cinema (a devout Catholic, he believed in controlling mass culture). His authorization of the First Italian Film Week and of *Surcos* led to his sacking, despite the film's personal authorization by Franco.

Literary censorship too was lenient with high cultural forms. Poetry became a vehicle for social protest in the 1950s because dissidence could be tolerated in a minority genre. A surprising number of 1950s social realist novels got through the censors: Ridruejo, Franco's first propaganda chief who broke with the regime in the 1940s, suggests that the censors knew the novels' pessimism would produce only inertia. Doubtful texts were often allowed in small print-runs or luxury editions. But popular romances and adventure stories were strictly controlled, as were historical and political texts in cheap editions. Penalties for publishers included closure, fines, withdrawal of passport, or the installation of inspectors on the premises. In the early years, paper quotas were also used as a weapon, as with the press.

Books in the minority languages began to be allowed in the late 1940s, restricted largely to religious texts and poetry. As late as 1957, comics in Catalan were banned. Children's literature was censored by a special office under Church control (in the 1940s *Little Red Riding Hood* became *Little Blue Riding Hood*). Propaganda comics were encouraged, such as *Juan Centella* (modelled on Mussolini's *Dick Fulmine*), and *El Guerrero del Antifaz*, set in Moorish Spain and sanctioning racist violence in the name of chivalry. *Batman*, *Superman*, and other foreign comics were allowed in bowdlerized form after 1944. Female writers were subjected to particularly strict moral scrutiny. Inoffensive texts by 'red' authors could be authorized but not displayed. Translations of foreign works were equally subject to censorship: books in 'unusual' languages often remained untranslated because no censor could read them. Latin American authors were treated leniently as their publication in Spain boosted exports (Borges was approved, despite his agnosticism, since only 'initiates' would understand him). But Spanish exile writers remained taboo: the National Library still lacks copies of their works published in Mexico or Argentina.

In 1960, 1,000 intellectuals petitioned the MIT to relax censorship. On appointment as Minister of Information and Tourism in 1962, Fraga initiated a process of cautious liberalization, contracting the US advertising agency McCann Erickson to improve Spain's image, and bringing back García Escudero as head of film censorship. In 1962 the first Spanish film showing a bikini was allowed, and audiences got their first chance to see many formerly banned foreign films, including Soviet films if set before 1917. Marxist texts were authorized in expensive editions if they did not mention Spain, the Cuban Revolution, or May 1968. Translations into the minority languages were also increasingly allowed. Fraga's 1966 Press Law, which operated till 1978, was as vague as its predecessor (Article 2 states that 'freedom of expression will have no limits other than those imposed by law'), but abolished

19 Sequence from the Nationalist comic *El Guerrero del Antifaz* [*The Masked Warrior*], from its first year of publication (1944). Set in the crusading Middle Ages, this comic licensed racist violence against alien (Arab) antagonists and, like most comics elsewhere, endorsed images of male aggression and female seduction/submission, implying a male fear of women. Here the text reads (in sequence): Shortly after, the Masked Warrior bursts into Harúm's harem to his wives' astonishment. | 'An intruder!', 'By Allah!', 'It's the Masked Warrior!' | 'By Christ! What have I got myself into . . .' | 'Intrepid Christian, how dare you . . . !', 'This looks like fun.' | 'I didn't mean to break in here, beautiful daughters of Allah, I just want to get out as quick as possible.', 'Go back where you've come from! There's no escaping the wrath of our lord and master!' | The Moorish princeling is beside himself with fury when he hears his enemy has entered 'the forbidden door'. | 'The mangy cur! Now he'll know my wrath!' | 'Shall we come in with you, lord?', 'No! . . . I'll get him out of there!'.

obligatory advance censorship and press directives. Anything could be published but it had to be deposited with the MIT, which could order confiscation or prosecution. This move, in line with economic moves away from state control, put the onus for censorship onto writers and publishers, who had to guess what was acceptable. Rather than risk confiscation, which could bankrupt a small firm, many publishers continued to submit works for 'advance consultation'. Prosecutions inevitably increased under Fraga's law (before, unacceptable material rarely reached publication); from 1963 to 1976 these came before the infamous Public Order Tribunals. Fraga exploited publishers' insecurities through methods such as 'administrative silence' (refusing comment on material submitted for advance consultation), telephone authorizations without written confirmation, or refusing to license publishers but letting them operate unofficially (Seix Barral and Edicions 62 were licensed only in 1968 and 1972). Several small publishers selling cheap marxist texts were closed; the popular satirical magazine *La Cordorniz* was fined six times in 1966–8. Liberalization was confined to minority publications. From 1969 the book censorship department, previously called 'Bibliographical Guidance Service', was renamed 'Popular Culture', showing where interests lay. Similarly, in 1964 García Escudero introduced incentives to experimental directors, and in 1967 created luxury Experimental Art Cinemas in cities and tourist areas, where foreign films could be seen undubbed.

In 1969 Fraga was sacked for allowing press reports of the MATESA scandal that brought down the Opus Dei* government, and replaced by a hard-liner. Confiscations, prosecutions, and closures increased with the 1969 State of Emergency and 1970 Burgos Trials, till in 1973 Ricardo de la Cierva took over Popular Culture, and in 1974 Pío Cabanillas became head of the MIT. For ten months, till Cabanillas's sacking by Franco in October 1974—among other things, for allowing news reports of Franco's illness—there was genuine liberalization, particularly in the press; confiscations stopped, even Lenin and Mao were authorized. The 1975 Prevention of Terrorism Act made infringement of the Press Law a military crime; confiscations and trials continued into 1977. Between 1971 and 1976 sixty-six attacks on bookshops, cinemas, publishers, and newspapers went unprosecuted. The Book Law and New Film Censorship Regulations of 1975 changed nothing, apart from authorizing nudes if they did not 'aim to arouse passions in the normal spectator'. In 1977 the MIT was replaced by the Ministry of Culture, under Cabanillas, and censorship effectively ended with the January amendment to the 1976 Law of Political Reform. Its abolition was confirmed by the 1978 Constitution.

Censorship was not passively 'suffered' by Spaniards; they developed strategies to counter its effects. Publishers would resubmit the same book with another title or cover; present dubious works in summer when senior censors were on holiday; or exploit the fact that military censors read German and were strict on politics while religious censors read French and were strict on morals, to submit morally tricky foreign texts in German translation and politically tricky ones in French. Sometimes refused books were published dated pre-1936 or with a foreign place of publication. The press commented on taboo issues through articles on other countries or past Spanish history. Talks and symposia secured approval by submitting anodyne titles. Saura's producer Querejeta worked with two scripts, one for the censor and one for the film crew, the results slipping through the net. The vogue for film adaptations of literary classics was another ploy for getting approval.

Writers and film-makers resorted to realism to replace a shackled press, but censorship also encouraged indirect statement (irony, symbolism, visual metaphor, the use of actors known for their roles in officially approved movies). Censorship was counter-productive in that it produced a hyper-politicization of culture, with censors, artists, and public keen to read the political into everything; but the recourse to techniques of allusion restricted appeal to a minority public. It is easy to dismiss the censors as stupid, but their tolerance of high art-forms suggests they knew what they were doing. It was not till the 1960s that intellectuals started to realize what the censors had always known: that élite culture is, sadly, not a political threat. If the censors distrusted mass culture, it was because they appreciated its importance; the other side of the tight controls was the management of popular culture for populist purposes, through the encouragement of folkloric spectacle and sport.

Further reading

On the workings of censorship
Abellán, M. L., *Censura y creación literaria en España (1939–1976)* (Barcelona, 1980).
—— (ed.), *Censura y literaturas peninsulares* (Amsterdam, 1987).
Cisquella, G., **Erviti, J. L.**, and **Sorolla, J. A.**, *Diez años de represión cultural: la censura de libros durante la Ley de Prensa (1966–76)* (Barcelona, 1977).
Gallofré, M. J., *L'edició catalana i la censura franquista* (Barcelona, 1991).
González Ballesteros, T., *Aspectos jurídicos de la censura cinematográfica en España, con especial referencia al período 1936–1977* (Madrid, 1981).
Gubern, R., *La censura: función política y ordenamiento jurídico bajo el franquismo (1936–1975)* (Barcelona, 1981) (mainly on film).
Sinova, J., *La censura de prensa durante el franquismo (1936–1951)* (Madrid, 1989).
Solé i Sabaté, J. M., and **Villarroya, J.**, *Cronologia de la repressió de la llengua: la cultura catalana (1936–1975)* (Barcelona, 1993).

On the cultural climate created by censorship
Barral, C., *Los años sin excusa* (Barcelona, 1978).
Goytisolo, J., *El furgón de cola* (Barcelona, 1976; orig. Paris, 1967).
Mangini, S., *Rojos y rebeldes: la cultura de la disidencia durante el franquismo* (Barcelona, 1987).
Martín Gaite, C., *Usos amorosos de la postguerra española* (Barcelona, 1987).
Ridruejo, D., *Escrito en España* (Buenos Aires, 1962).

Texts and film scripts submitted for censorship throughout the Franco period (whether authorized or banned) are now housed in the Archivo General de la Administración del Estado at Alcalá de Henares.

Cultural Nationalism

PETER EVANS

EMMA DENT
COAD

JULIAN WHITE

Cifesa: Cinema and Authoritarian Aesthetics

PETER EVANS

During the first decade of dictatorship, Cifesa (Compañía Industrial Film Español) was the regime's ideological standard
bearer, the 'eternalizer' (adopting a term used by Barthes), not
the transformer of realities, the purveyor of bourgeois myths
leading to the privation of history. Even if, at routine bureaucratic levels of contact, relations between the studio and the
regime's various functionaries lacked the cosiness of its owner
Vicente Casanova's friendships with high-ranking politicians like
Carrero Blanco, films made by Cifesa projected conformist
attitudes towards God, nation, and family.

All the films are imbued with conservative forms of Catholic
ethics. Indeed, even during the Republic, the studio's first film
was the religious narrative *La hermana San Sulpicio* (1931). While
Filmófono was identified with democratic, liberal tendencies,
and a more mature discussion of love, sex, divorce, and so on,
Cifesa had always inclined towards more conservative priorities.
After the war the impact of its conservative Catholic attitudes

I am greatly indebted to Leandro Martínez Joven, Departamento de
Difusión y Exhibición, Filmoteca Municipal de Zaragoza, and to Carmen
Solano (Departamento de Cultura, Ayuntamiento de Zaragoza), for en-
abling me to see all the Cifesa films referred to in this chapter.

not only determined a narrow range of film subjects on overtly religious themes, but also meant that even the patterns of secular narratives were vetted by those same values. At the most trivial level this led to a virtual prohibition on kissing. But the more serious implications of Cifesa's commitment to traditional forms of Catholicism led to a variety of films in which human behaviour was ultimately measured by the standards of religious dogma. So a Malvaloca or a Dolores finds salvation or self-fulfilment through devotion to the Virgin Mary; elsewhere, films carry effusive acknowledgements to ecclesiastical authorities, as in *Agustina de Aragón* (Juan de Orduña, 1950), where the ideological prejudices of the credits preface the drives of the narrative: 'to the most excellent Reverend Archbishop of Zaragoza [. . .] to the Religious Assessor, for his collaborations and facilities which have allowed us to film inside the Holy Basilica of Our Lady of the Pillar, national temple, and sanctuary of the Race.'

The concept of race, identifying Spaniards as of 'one blood, with one ideal and one noble purpose',[1] permeates all the films, as well as providing the title *Raza* of the notorious film scripted by Franco in 1941. As John Hopewell notes, Francoist notions of *raza* are not spared contradiction since 'any accurate emphasis on Spaniards' racial distinctiveness led to an admittance of partial Moorish and Semitic origins unacceptable in a supposed essentially Christian culture'.[2] Consequently, as in *Raza*, not a Cifesa product, so too in *Harka*, a film that was made by the studio, the Moorish army's alliance with the Nationalists earns a glowing tribute both in the narrative itself and, again, in the opening dedication to 'the splendid Hispanic/Moroccan brotherhood. Let this film be a homage to the memory of those who gave everything for Spain!'

In addition to these and many other calls to national unity, gestures to regionalist sensitivities also sometimes manage to acknowledge in suitably reductive terms the diversity of Spanish culture. The films abound with Aragonese, Andalusian, Galician, and even Catalonian elements and references, all gestures, paralleling the regime's policies of regionalist tokenism attempting to project an image of a country united through variety.

The process is exemplified in *Agustina de Aragón* where the *jota* (an Aragonese popular song and dance) sung in the background as a patriotic soldier breathes his last superficially pays tribute to regionalism, something ultimately undermined by a more powerful sentiment appealing to national unity: 'Aragon is Aragon. | Catalonia is Catalonia. | And Aragon is Aragon. | Let us agree from the start | They have an identical heart.' Despite its regionalist sensibility, the unambiguous meaning of the song, as of the dying soldier's last words, 'You no longer belong to me, now you belong only to Spain,' summarizes the regime's intractable sense of the country's unchallengeable homogeneity. Regionalist culture, especially in its folkloric elements, was promoted through a wide variety of state-approved events, the most conspicuous of which were the Sección Femenina's* *Coros y danzas* shows staged all over the country. Films like *La Dolores* (Florián Rey, 1940) seem in parts like screened versions of this type of extravaganza, often overlaid with crude jingoistic contempt for foreigners. Among Cifesa's trivialized figures of 'otherness', that process described by Barthes in *Mythologies* as transforming the foreigner into 'a pure object, a spectacle, a clown',[3] confined to the margins of humanity, a gauche female English tourist in *Currito de la Cruz* (Luis Lucía, 1948) becomes an easy target for the regime's contempt for 'perfidious Albion'. More seriously, the French in *Agustina de Aragón*, or the Flemish in *Locura de amor* (Orduña, 1948), reflect Francoism's less sophisticated forms of xenophobia. In *Agustina de Aragón* the French are ruthless enemies, with the Napoleonic troops burning buildings, raping and massacring Spaniards. These emotive images serve not only to provoke anti-Gallic feeling, but also to recall the events of the civil war in Spain, with the French here (as revolutionaries, appropriate symbols of Franco's Republican opponents) doubly vilified as figures of both internal and external otherness. Elsewhere, in *Locura de amor*, foreignness as represented by Philip the Fair signifies philandering and deception, Spain the realm of the truth.

But perhaps the film that strives most to project an image of Spain as a nation of honour and truth, an image designed to inspire nostalgia for a utopian past, a project according to Félix Fanés promoted by Carrero Blanco himself, is *Alba de América* (Orduña, 1951).[4] This was Cifesa's answer to Gainsborough's *Christopher Columbus* (1948), a film that succeeded in outraging the regime in a number of ways: the portrayal of King Ferdinand as a skirt-chasing buffoon, the liberal sprinkling of egocentric politicians, unflattering reference to disease, disorder, bloodshed, and chaos in the colonies, and the Catholic Monarchs' ungrateful treatment of Columbus himself, who utters the film's last, Hispanophobic line, 'People will remember me long after they [the Catholic Monarchs] are dead and forgotten.'

Alba de América sought to redress the balance, reasserting the country's heroic involvement in the discoveries, to create, again in Barthes's terms, a mythicized text naturalizing and universalizing the historical realities of fifteenth-century Spain. Here, Fredric March's tetchy, wheeler-dealer Columbus, struggling to convince the Monarchs to back his venture, falling foul of the King's weak, courtier-dominated personality, is transformed into a saintly, almost Messianic hero, only very occasionally slipping into less than Christ-like behaviour, as in his initial somewhat haughty treatment of Pinzón, an attitude perhaps ultimately attributable to chauvinistic convictions about Columbus's Italianness as invalidating any claims to the kind of perfection to which, after all, only Spanish heroes could aspire. The problem raised by this blemish of nationality or *raza* is elegantly solved anyway by surrounding Columbus with a crew of worthy Spanish sailors and sympathetic friars, one of whom also claims to be a navigator though of a more spiritual sort. The representation of the Catholic Monarchs' reconquest of Spain from the Moors parallels Columbus' annexation of the Americas, in the name of God's chosen, from the heathens. As Columbus sets sail, friars bless the ships, plainsong is chanted, and Columbus himself draws attention to his Christian name as 'Christopher, carrier of Christ'. When land is sighted cannons fire and a choir sings the *Gloria*. A very brief scene shows the landing of Columbus and his men, greeted by natives climbing up and down palm trees like wild marsupials, before the action shifts immediately back to Spain, with Columbus returning in triumph, accompanied by a troop of 'bring 'em back alive' partially naked former savages, one of whom in the presence of the Catholic Monarchs lifts his head heavenwards to recite the Lord's Prayer.

The film concentrates exclusively on Spanish involvement, a reminder to audiences at home and abroad of the traditional, pre-Republican values for which a civil war had been fought, an affirmation of national identity, partly achieved through the fulfilment of one of Hobsbawm's important criteria of nationhood, a 'proven capacity for conquest'. As Hobsbawm further remarks, 'There is nothing like being an imperial people to make a population conscious of its collective existence as such.'[5] Exhausted, poverty-stricken Spain had no intention of embarking on foreign imperialist adventures. Nevertheless, films like Alba, with their denials and grandiose evocations of imperialist history, helped sustain the regime's propaganda strategies of unifying the nation through memories of a glorious past. Alba's crude propaganda makes its ideological undercurrents unmistakable. But other historical films do sometimes unconsciously manage to create ambiguities that surprisingly expose the contradictions of the system. Perhaps the most interesting of these are Harka and Locura de amor. In both films, each crossed by the divergent tendencies of separate genres, the drives and rhythms of melodramatic form raise unexpected tensions with the norms of the epic, war, or historical biopic.

Of all genres, war films, epics, and historical biopics offer most potential for narratives about male bonding and identity, rites of passage, and physical or mental endurance. Harka's narrative embraces all these and more, exposing far more clearly than other films of the period the darker implications of authoritarian attitudes towards women. Content in the 1940s with definitions of women as home-makers and male supports, would even the Sección Femenina have tolerated the dismissive, castration-anxiety trivializations of the female characters in Harka? As in many other war films of the period where they are seen as threats to the male group, women are identified with frivolity and self-indulgence, compromising the masculinity of the virile male. A pattern of alternating syntagma intersects scenes of men fighting in the desert led by Carlos's mentor and homo-erotically defined Oedipal father-figure, the symbolically named Santiago Valcázar, with shots of the young hero himself, accompanied by his new girlfriend, seemingly renouncing the warrior world of the Harka for the elegant dance halls and restaurants of Madrid.

Domesticity and socializing may be admissible to the lesser man, but for the regime's élite, constructed by an ideology sympathetic to Nietzsche's concept of the higher man, the distinguishing feature of heroic masculinity is independence: 'Every superior human being will instinctively aspire after a secret citadel where he is set free from the crowd, the many, the majority [. . .] Few are made for independence—it is a privilege of the strong.'[6] In making its point about the superiority of the male, in describing the potential tenderness that exists in all relationships between higher types of men, the film strays into extremely danger-ous ideological territory where transference of the techniques and resources of melodrama—soft lighting, close-up shots of two officers bonding in the desert night—onto the conventions of the war film leads to the point where, inevitably, the excesses of the former overwhelm the austerities of the latter. The result is that the film astonishingly succeeds in apparently condoning homosexuality. The choice of Morocco as testing ground for heroic masculinity seems appropriate in the light of the desert's traditional parallel connotations (cf. T. E. Lawrence and others) of purification and desire. Tensions between dialogue and visual style reflect this duality of purpose with Carlos, the young officer, explaining his attrac-tion to the desert and to the company of soldiers with unsoldierly lyrical intro-spection: 'I came to Africa having recently left the academy, searching for what you have just described: risk, endurance tests. Gradually these people's customs began to interest me. I learned a little Arabic. I wanted to command them and now I am here, perhaps because I feel a little like them.' Santiago, the older officer, replies: 'I understand you perfectly, boy.'

The mode of address, 'muchacho' [boy], emphasizes the youthfulness of the junior officer, characterized in some scenes by an almost girlish demureness emphasized in the nocturnal desert encounter during which the soft lighting feminizes naturally androgynous features, especially long eyelashes often lowered in coyness born of a shared but unspoken secret mutual attraction. The term also draws attention both to the rites of passage to which the embryonic hero must submit and, unconsciously, to the latent, repressed homosexuality of the group, a sexual preference here seemingly arising naturally from an ideology at once marginalizing women, and celebrating the triumphant independence of heroic masculinity. *Harka*'s homosexual subtext, to which Fanés and Hopewell have already drawn attention, represents one of many occasions where a Cifesa film dramatizes the return of the repressed. Here the love that cannot be named does after all succeed in gaining recognition.

Elsewhere women, although in *Harka* more than usually trivialized, unexpect-edly find a voice with which to counteract the resonant prejudices of their social-ized definitions. The independent, self-assertive woman—Rocío, for instance, in *Currito de la Cruz*—enjoys moments of rebellion, but the film's closure sees her back in the family, once again reclaiming her place as the spiritualized, infantilized toy of her father's fantasy, replacing in her affections the swarthy sexual predator Romerita (Jorge Mistral) with the infinitely less phallic Currito (de la Cruz!), pro-totype of the chaste, sexless male of ecclesiastical approval. As one of Currito's concluding remarks makes clear, sacramental marriage tolerating sexual congress for the exclusive purposes of procreation reflects natural and divine harmonies: 'I shall be a bullfighter until I become rich and then only for you, Rocío, to enjoy with you our happiness in these Andalusian fields, pretty like your face, big like my heart that still seems to me too small for the amount of love I have for you.'

Yet when dialogue like this, paralleled by narrative closures restoring women to domesticity, is also linked to baroque framing devices of grilles and windows and doorway, literal constraints create through the processes of self-consciousness a distancing effect inevitably leading to reflection on the imprisonments of ideology. So, Dolores's framing in the film that bears her name, in the early scene where she is viewed from a house interior, through a window grille—a shot which also includes Palm Sunday branches significantly strewn across the bottom of the frame—ultimately works like the so-called hysterical *mise-en-scène* of Hollywood melodrama in highlighting the ideological pressures and constraints to which women in Spain during the 1940s and 1950s were subjected.

The use of *coplas* (popular song, of a folkloric nature), designed to promote further the ideology of the times, often creates similar tensions. Dolores herself seems at times unmistakably to represent tradition, scolding a 13-year-old girl, for instance, for talking to a young boy, singing religious *jotas* like 'For those who made your son Jesus suffer, Mother of the Pillar | Take pity on me', or endorsing traditional attitudes towards her own sex through approval of 'men who always slander the women they love'. But for all her subservience, the conventional woman (both as character in the narrative and as star-vehicle for Concha Piquer) is crossed over with contradictory elements complicating the wider significances of the representation of women in this and other films made by Cifesa. Like the framing devices, the *jotas* themselves, given a boost in sanitized forms by the regime, inevitably recall their alternative, more ribald traditions of pre-Franco times.

Even here, though, that bawdier tradition flickers on through the sexual innuendo in the lyrics of the film's unifying *jota*: 'If you go to Calatayud | Ask for La Dolores | For she's a very pretty girl | And likes to do you favours.' These lines, like others ('Carter halt your cart | drink my wine from a jug | For I'll drink first | If you're in pain | If you're bleeding from a wound | My wine from Cariñena will cure you in no time'), provide unexpected resistance to the film's ideological momentum, combining with the force of Concha Piquer's star presence, and her look of dark, brilliantined hair parted down the middle, virile eyes, and robust nasal features, in providing a strong contrast to the images of more docile femininity projected elsewhere in the film.

Not a studio regular, Concha Piquer does not look out of place among Cifesa's range of forceful actresses such as Amparito Rivelles, Luchy Soto, and perhaps above all Aurora Bautista, all rivalling the frothy, girlish stars like Josita Hernán also used in these films. Aurora Bautista's powerful presence (in looks and role she was Cifesa's Jennifer Jones) often drives her towards excess and kitsch, especially in *Agustina de Aragón*. In *Locura de amor*, helped by lines like 'I defended my rights as a woman, and they called me mad', and a narrative that in its exposure of male injustices to women lifts the film from epic to melodrama and the Cifesa equivalent of the Hollywood Woman's Picture, Aurora Bautista unexpectedly mediates through the representation of Juana La Loca the experience of ordinary women living under dictatorship.

20 Still from the film *Agustina de Aragón* (Orduña, 1950), one of the last (and best) of
Cifesa's big budget historical epics. Based on the siege of Zaragoza in the War of
Independence, the film was a pretext for anti-French sentiment (we never learn that the
city eventually fell to the French). Surprisingly, given the passive 'nature' ascribed by
Francoism to women, most of these historical epics had female protagonists who were
given highly active, if not masculine, roles: it is interesting to speculate on the kind of
audience identification such star roles may have permitted to contemporary female
spectators. Here, in the classic image from the film which would be reproduced on
calendars and postage stamps, Agustina (Aurora Bautista) fires the cannon to repel the
invading French, rallying the men who are failing to fulfil their masculine role.

This pattern of mediating rather than literally mirroring 1940s life in Spain characterizes the Capra-esque, sub-Lubitschean world of extremely popular Cifesa comedies (often carrying ambivalent titles like *Tuvo la culpa Adán*), a sometimes screwball-oriented, high-society world of fast dialogue, zany socialites, and expensive gowns and haircuts. As Fanés remarks, this was hardly how most Spaniards lived in the austere 1940s. Yet the comedies were enormously successful, distracting the population from the hardships of the immediate post-war years. Here again, though, there are patterns of contradiction and resistance. The hero may be a traditionalist (often Rafael Durán), though in a charming Herbert Marshall sort of a way; the heroine may be a fluffy version of Miriam Hopkins (often Josita Hernán); and—as in, say, *Bringing up Baby* (Hawks, 1938), *It Happened One Night* (Capra, 1934), or *Trouble in Paradise* (Lubitsch, 1932)—the male is not only gratified but also feminized through love: for example, in *Ella, él y sus millones* (Orduña, 1944).

Looking now at their attitudes towards sex, gender, and identity, these films are fascinating. By the end of the 1940s they had begun to seem to contemporary audiences less satisfying, cruder than they really are. In any case Vicente Casanova had fallen from the favour of his friends in high places, the studio continued to distribute but stopped producing films, and audiences were much more attracted by the flood of Hollywood imports, dubbed and censored though they were. The studio that in Spain approximated most to the Hollywood system (as regards its Paramount-influenced ethos, roster of stars, technical and creative personnel, etc.) was in the end defeated at the box-office by the real thing.

Notes
1 P. Besas, *Behind the Spanish Lens: Spanish Cinema under Fascism and Democracy* (Denver, 1985), 19.
2 *Out of the Past: Spanish Cinema after Franco* (London, 1986), 34.
3 R. Barthes, *Mythologies* (London, 1973), 152.
4 See F. Fanés, *El cas Cifesa; vint anys de cine espanyol (1932–1951)* (Valencia, 1989), 252.
5 E. J. Hobsbawm, *Nations and Nationalism since 1780: Programme, Myth, Reality* (Cambridge, 1991), 38.
6 F. Nietzsche, *Beyond Good and Evil* (Harmondsworth, 1984), 39.

Further reading
Besas, P., *Behind the Spanish Lens: Spanish Cinema under Franco* (Denver, 1985).
Fanés, F., *El cas Cifesa: vint anys de cine espanyol (1932–1951)* (Valencia, 1989).
Freixas, R., 'Cifesa: un gigante con pies de barro', *Dirigido Por*, 104 (May 1983), 16–27.
Hopewell, J., *Out of the Past: Spanish Cinema after Franco* (London, 1986).
Kinder, M., *Blood Cinema: The Reconstruction of National Identity in Spain* (Berkeley, 1993).
Méndez Leite, F., *Historia del cine español* (Madrid, 1965).

Constructing the Nation: Francoist Architecture

EMMA DENT COAD

Like Hitler and Mussolini, Franco understood the power of architecture as a collectivizing force and as a symbol of the supremacy of the state. He set up the Dirección General de Arquitectura (DGA), the body in charge of architectural policy and projects, in 1938 before the civil war had been won. The man chosen to head the DGA, Pedro Muguruza, was well versed in both the theory and practice of architecture. Both acknowledged that a building can have an underlying narrative, symbolizing social and political power struggles in all their complexities and subtleties. Franco also believed that, by establishing a unique architectural vision of Spanishness, he could bind the disparate regionalist and separatist factions within Spain.

During the Republic the government had embraced the modernist movement in architecture exemplified by the Bauhaus school in Weimar Germany. A school of design, architecture, and fine art run by a group of avant-garde and firmly socialist practitioners, the Bauhaus had sought, by the union of art and technology, to create modern architecture and artefacts which were socially beneficial, egalitarian, and directly addressed to human needs. Their rationalisation of human needs led to a revolutionary questioning of the basic principles of structure and interior design. As with other variants of European fascism, Franco and his architects chose to 'return to history' in a total rejection of socialist politics and modernist architecture (for a brief period after Nationalist victory, key modernist buildings in Madrid constructed under the Republic were boarded up), favouring the political certainty and familiarity of styles from the past. But the paradox of a revival of tradition is that, in trying to capture and repeat the 'real', the inevitable result is pastiche. Interestingly, the dangers of pastiche had been recognized by José Antonio Primo de Rivera, the founder of the Falange,* executed by the Republicans in November 1936: 'In a quest for elegance, some have turned their backs on the things that are our own; others have lapsed into the stupid nonsense of converting the delicate and precise substance of Spain into a blatantly jingoistic caricature.'

The return to historical models, and the rejection of foreign avant-garde influences, was seen as a way of restoring religion, the family, patriotism, order, and authority through a construction of 'Spanishness'. Many literary figures, artists, and architects began investigating medieval culture, seen as compatible with Nationalist values because of its association with unquestionable religious and hierarchical order. Roman classical themes were also investigated, and neo-classicism was revived in sculpture, painting, and prose as well as in architecture. This imitation of past models was seen as 'neutral' and 'above style'.

To the Republicans, architecture had been a celebration of the cultural richness and aesthetic diversity of a country with strong regional traditions. The leading Republican architect, the Catalan Josep Lluís Sert, had studied abroad with founders of modernism such as Gropius and Mies van der Rohe (both of the Bauhaus), and had brought the French modernist Le Corbusier to Barcelona to work on city projects. Sert contended that 'to apply historical styles nowadays is equivalent to perpetuating the conditions of the past and constitutes a denial of our times'. To the Nationalists, by contrast, 'Spanishness' was a unifying quality. In eradicating the ethics and aesthetics of modernism, they wished to create a new common architectural language based on traditional elements that for them represented the 'essence' of a united Spain. Functionalism in architecture was seen as a negation of 'beauty'. Instead buildings were to be based on 'the essence of the glorious century of the Spanish empire, creator of states in America, and creator of that profound and perfect symbol: the Escorial'. The sixteenth-century monastery of the Escorial by the architect Juan de Herrera was a key symbolic building for this period, also giving its name to an important Falangist cultural magazine. The emulation or 'reinterpretation' of Herreran neo-classicism in the 1940s was considered a patriotic act. The eternal values of beauty and well-proportioned form were contrasted with the 'paltriness' of modern architecture, while 'eternal' materials such as stone, brick, and wood were contrasted with 'impoverished' materials such as steel and concrete.

During the civil war, 192 towns lost more than 60 per cent of their total building stock. A major building programme was announced, plus a plan to establish Madrid as a major imperial centre. Existing public buildings were 'monumentalized' with the addition of porticos and grand entrances, monuments were erected, new squares were laid out, and traffic circulation was reorganized. The Prado was extended and given a grand driveway, supposedly in line with the architect's 'original intentions'. Countless buildings in Madrid and throughout the country copied the Herrera style, most notoriously the imposing Air Force Ministry and the Monastery-Mausoleum of the Valley of the Fallen, built by Republican prisoners and designated by Franco as his own future burial place. Whole towns or town centres were modelled on the Escorial or other Spanish Renaissance forms. But a number of failures to achieve a coherent Spanish style led, by the end of the 1940s, to a gradual rejection of historicist forms and to a reappraisal of the tenets of modern architecture, emphasizing its purely stylistic attributes—seen as representing not modernism (rejected for its radical political implications) but modernity (establishing Spain as a modern country).

In the course of the 1950s, both public and private architectural commissions began to show the imagination and creativity that are the hallmark of Spanish architecture today. A number of newly graduated young architects began to produce buildings inspired by modernist work in Italy, whose political connotations were safe since in some instances it had been commissioned by Mussolini. The majority of these young architects were Madrid-trained, and, whatever their beliefs, were more or less reconciled to living under the Franco regime. In 1949 Francisco Cabrero won a competition to build the headquarters of the official state trade unions (vertical trade unions*), modelled on Mussolini's corporativist syndicates. The building, located opposite the Prado, was modern in conception, construction, and interior layout, but its stone and brick materials, scale, and relationship between volumes matched those of its neighbour.

Two years later José Antonio Coderch and Manuel Valls won first prize at the 1951 Milan Triennale for their Spanish pavilion, putting Spanish architecture on the international map. Further awards followed: Ramón Molezún at the 1954 Triennale; Miguel Fisac for his religious architecture in Vienna the same year; Javier Carvajal and José Antonio García de Paredes at the 1957 Triennale; and the gold medal for José Antonio Corrales and Ramón Molezún for their elegant and innovatory prefab design for the Spanish pavilion at the Brussels World Fair in 1958.

Why were these architects singled out for recognition? What had begun to develop was a particularly Latin form of modernism, sometimes described as 'organic', less formal and rigid than that of Germany. The academic geometry of northern Europe was replaced by more eclectic forms and a less rationalist approach to human needs and living habits, coupled with appreciation of vernacular characteristics and the use of local building materials. Ironically, this was exactly the kind of architecture that Josep Lluís Sert had advocated twenty years before.

Further reading
Bohigas, O., *Arquitectura i urbanisme durant la Republica* (Barcelona, 1978).
Bonet Correa, A. (ed.), *Arte del franquismo* (Madrid, 1981).
Dent Coad, E., 'Constructing a Nation: Architecture and Politics in Nationalist Spain 1939–1949' (Royal College of Art dissertation, 1992).
Flores, C., *Arquitectura española contemporánea*, 2 vols. (Madrid, 1989).
Méndez, D., *El Valle de los Caídos: idea, proyecto, construcción* (Madrid, 1982).
Sust, X. (ed.), *La arquitectura como símbolo de poder* (Barcelona, 1975).
Ureña, G., *Arquitectura y urbanismo civil y militar en el período de la autarquía (1936–1945)* (Madrid, 1979).

Music and the Limits of Cultural Nationalism

JULIAN WHITE

The profound political and social changes resulting from Franco's victory in the civil war and the subsequent cultural vacuum significantly hindered the development of Spanish music, bringing to an abrupt halt the musical renaissance instigated by Pedrell and consolidated by Falla and his successors. The brutal repression and tight state control that characterized the first decade of Franco's dictatorship affected all the arts, with the imposition of censorship, discouragement of innovation in any form, and the prohibition of any expression of regionalist sentiment. In April 1936, three months prior to the military insurrection, Barcelona had been capital of the musical world as host to the prestigious International Society of Contemporary Music Festival; but on the city's 'liberation' in 1939 the activities of its leading musical organizations were severely curtailed: casualties included the Associació de Música 'da Camera', the Orquesta Pau Casals, the Associació Obrera de Concerts, and the Orfeó Català.

The composers of the 1927 Generation had joined the diaspora and were unable therefore to exert any decisive influence—Bautista and Falla in exile in Argentina (the latter having refused to compose an anthem for the victorious Nationalists), Bacarisse in France, Rudolfo Halffter in Mexico, Ernesto Halffter in Portugal, and Gerhard in England.

Two decades of isolation caused by the civil war, Second World War, and the United Nations blockade imposed on Spain meant that Spanish music was left to its own devices with disastrous consequences. Contacts between new Spanish music and the outside world effectively ceased, there was a loss of public interest in music, and music institutions themselves, many extensively damaged during the war, fell into terminal decline. Official organs such as the Orquesta Nacional de España and the Orquesta Municipal de Barcelona remained dedicated to the standard repertoire whilst contemporary Spanish and European music were neglected. Largely responsible for this lamentable state of affairs was the Comisaría de la Música, ostensibly created to promote the musical life of Spain and headed, after Joaquín Turina's death in 1949, by Antonio de las Heras, who became the arbiter of 'official' music.

Whilst the new regime rarely intervened in administrative affairs and was largely unconcerned with aesthetic and technical musical matters, the prevailing *casticista**nationalism, exemplified by the post-war composers Turina and Rodrigo, coincided—in its purist emphasis on a return to 'authentic', traditional roots—with official cultural ideology, even if it was not directly determined by it. As Tomás Marco has observed, 'the music of the post-Falla era belongs to the pre-Falla era, the lessons of his example not having been digested at all'.

This regressiveness is most strikingly highlighted by the case of Joaquín Rodrigo (b. 1901), whose celebrated *Concierto de Aranjuez* (1938–9)—performed in Madrid at the end of the civil war amidst feelings of great nationalistic fervour—is typical. His subsequent works repeat the Aranjuez three-movement concerto formula, lying squarely within the same nationalist *casticista* tradition and showing minimal stylistic evolution. Other composers whose works typify the prevailing official aesthetic include Muñoz Molleda (b. 1895), García Leoz (1904–53), Jesus Arámbarri (1902–60), particularly the heroic *casticismo* of his grandiloquent tone poem *Castile* (1941), and Carlos Suriñach (b. 1915), whose compositions such as the *Danza andaluza* (1946) display a superficial folkloric Andalusianism which, fostered by the regime, became extremely popular at this time.

It was not until the end of the 1940s that this long period of stagnation was brought to an end. Creative renewal was effected by the composers of the Generation of 1951, a term coined by one of its leading members, Cristóbal Halffter. This innovative generation was keen, for political as well as aesthetic reasons, to make a clean break with the *casticista* nationalism of the 1940s—to achieve, as

Ramón Barce revealed, a 'liberation from explicit nationalism' through the 'total elimination of folkloric techniques'. They also sought 'to accelerate the evolution of Spanish music in order to catch up with Europe'; thus the rapid assimilation of avant-garde trends such as atonal expressionism, Stravinsky, Bartók, total serialism, mobile and aleatory forms (the use of chance operations), and electronic developments. This coincided with an abrupt change in the direction of other arts in Spain, particularly painting and sculpture, and led to some fruitful associations between the composers of the 1951 Generation and both the Madrid group of painters El Paso and the painters of the Catalan avant-garde.

The first stage in this rejuvenation process was brought about in 1947 with the formation of the Círculo Manuel de Falla. This group of composers, who worked together until 1955, was supported by the French Institute and later Club 49 (a group of private patrons in Barcelona who presented the works of young avant-garde painters and sculptors). The group consisted of José Cercós, Ángel Cerdá, Alberto Blancafort, Manuel Valls, Juan Comellas, and Jose Maria Mestres-Quadreny. They sought new expressive means in the music of Bartok, 1930s Stravinsky and Hindemith, and late Falla.

The second stage was the formation in 1958 of the Grupo Nueva Música in Madrid which worked closely with the Juventudes Musicales Españolas and the Ateneo de Madrid. The members of the group included Antón García-Abril, Manuel Moreno Buendía, Manuel Carra, Enrique Franco, Ramón Barce, and, most importantly, Luis de Pablo and Cristóbal Halffter. Halffter's serial *Cinco microformas* (1960) was a key work. Its première, which caused a scandal, marked the real arrival in Spain of the music of Boulez, Stockhausen, and Nono—international avant-garde figures whose music had first been performed in Barcelona in 1955. De Pablo's early works were in the typical inter-war style, whilst his *Elegía* (1956) combined Bartókian techniques with free (pre-serial) atonality. His *Cuatro invenciones para orquesta* (1955–60) exploited serial techniques and his *Movil 1* for two pianos (1959) represented an initial experiment with aleatory forms.

Finally in 1959 Juan Hidalgo with Luis de Pablo, Joaquim Homs, Mestres-Quadreny, and José Cercós formed Música Abierta whose manifesto called for 'open music, active music, music of the immediate past, music of today and tomorrow'. Hidalgo was to become a seminal figure in the Spanish avant-garde. He was better placed than any of his Spanish contemporaries to keep abreast of international avant-garde developments having studied with Bruno Maderna in Milan and seen him present his electronically inspired, total-serial instrumental work, *Ubanga* (1957)—a work more advanced than anything being composed then in Spain—at the 1957 Darmstadt Festival. Subsequent compositions—*Offenes trio* (1958), *Ciu-Quartett* (1958)—exploited open, aleatory forms and betrayed the influence of John Cage, the experimental American composer.

Thus, by the end of the 1950s, Spanish composers stood once again on the brink of a new musical renaissance that was to prove as important to the future of Spanish music as that initiated by Pedrell at the beginning of the century. Their subsequent compositions reveal a striking plurality of styles and techniques: atonality in the music of Joaquim Homs (b. 1906); post-Webernian serialism in the music of Gerardo Gombau (b. 1906); universal eclecticism in the music of Xavier de Montsalvatge (b. 1912); indeterminacy in the music of Carmela Bernaola (b. 1929); electro-acoustic experiments in the works of Francisco Guerrero (b. 1942) and Eduardo Polonio (b. 1941); minimalism (or 'new simplicity') and action music in the compositions of Carles Santos (b. 1940); graphic notation in the experimental works of Jesús Villa Rojo (b. 1940); experimental neo-expressionism in the music of Francisco Otero (b. 1940); and music theatre in the works of Tomás Marco (b. 1942).

Further reading
Custer, A., 'Contemporary Music in Spain', *Musical Quarterly*, 43/1 (Jan. 1962), 1–18.
Livermore, A., *A Short History of Spanish Music* (London, 1972).
Marco, T., *Spanish Music in the Twentieth Century* (Cambridge, Mass., 1993).
Martín Moreno, A., *Historia de la música española* (Madrid, 1993).

Resisting the State

PAUL PRESTON

HELEN GRAHAM

BARRY JORDAN

The Urban and Rural *Guerrilla* of the 1940s

PAUL PRESTON

Despite the collapse of the Republican armies after the fall of Barcelona, despite the succession of victory parades organized in the spring and early summer of 1939 in Spain's major cities, and despite the boastful declarations of the new dictator, for many Spaniards the civil war was not over. Until the end of the 1940s, Franco's armed forces were obliged to undertake military operations against armed groups who were involved in a vain if heroic attempt to reverse the result of the war. In a sporadic way, the civil war, or violent resistance against the establishment of the Francoist state, continued until the withdrawal of the last guerrilla* units in 1951.

It is hardly surprising that, in the 1940s, the most serious opposition to the Franco regime was of a military nature and even less that the methods used to repress it should also have been military. What is altogether striking is that there was any opposition at all to the dictatorship other than the purely passive. The Spanish left had been militarily defeated and its most dynamic and representative cadres had been decimated during three years of bloodshed. Half a million survivors fled into exile where those who did not have the luck to escape to Latin America were quickly swept up by the whirlwind of war. Those who were left behind quickly realized that Francoist policy towards the defeated would be every bit as brutal as the repression implemented during the war as the Nationalists carried out purges of captured territory. On top of the repression, the anti-Francoist forces were hindered by their own internal divisions. The pre-existing conflicts within the Republican left were multiplied by the geographical dispersion which followed 1939 and even more so by the bitter mutual recriminations about responsibility for defeat.

In fact, the history of the anti-Francoist opposition in the 1940s is the story of continual fragmentation and of short-lived coalitions. For the majority, the constant internal wranglings were merely a source of sterility and impotence. Only the Communist Party (Partido Comunista de España (PCE*)), because of its hermetic internal cell-structure, because of its impregnably triumphalist ideology, and by dint of Soviet aid, was able eventually to ride out the debilitating consequences of theoretical divisions. Even so, between 1939 and 1947, the PCE was virtually torn apart by internal conflict. Within this gloomy overview, there were two groups of anti-Francoists who, for different albeit related reasons, managed to avoid the worst consequences of internecine hostilities and concentrate on a single primordial task, the struggle against the dictatorship. These two groups would be, the first 1939–44, the second 1944–51, the nuclei of the anti-francoist guerrilla forces. They were the so-called *huídos* or stragglers, Republicans separated from their units during the civil war who opted to take to the hills rather than surrender, and the Spanish *maquis*, the exiles who played a crucial role in the French Resistance and, with the gradual collapse of the Germans, were able to turn their gaze to Spain.

As far as the *huídos* were concerned, guerrilla war was the only possible response to the Nationalist repression. During the civil war itself and during the first three years of the post-war period, the new regime made a massive effort to eliminate not only the surviving cadres of the political parties of the Popular Front but also the leaders, middle-rank functionaries, and rank-and-file members of the socialist and anarcho-syndicalist unions—the Unión General de Trabajadores (UGT*) and the Confederación Nacional del Trabajo (CNT*)—as well as members of the liberal intelligentsia. To that end, the regime executed nearly 200,000 Republicans and imprisoned over 400,000. The great majority of the defeated had no choice but to accept their fate: at worst, prison or the firing-squad; at best, resigning themselves to life as second-class citizens unable to find work without certificates of political reliability and good conduct issued by parish priests and local Falangist* chiefs.

A few had the chance to go on fighting; others did not get the choice. After initially avoiding surrender by fleeing to the hills, and continuing the struggle against Franco in the same way as the anti-Napoleonic *guerrilleros* of the previous century, the *huídos* were convinced that, to avoid death or prison, they had to fight on. Within a few months of the end of the war, there was a significant number of *guerrilleros* in rural, and especially mountainous, areas. There it was easier to hide, to avoid the patrols of the Civil Guard,* and even to find the wherewithal to live, if not with the help of sympathetic peasants, at least by means of hunting and collecting wild fruit. As in other twentieth-century guerrilla wars, the principal activity of the *huídos* was defensive, their initial objective simply survival. Unlike their Chinese and Cuban counterparts, the Spanish *guerrilleros* had little possibility of establishing the *focos* (liberated zones) that might have served as bases for the future struggle against the regime. The only places sufficiently remote from the forces of repression to permit any contemplation of the establishment of autonomous revolutionary communities were, in Spain, in the most inhospitable parts of the Peninsula. Moreover, the depressed circumstances of the defeated Spanish left between 1939 and 1944 were hardly propitious for a revolutionary war. The repression, hunger, families destroyed by death and exile, and, above all, the intense weariness left by the titanic struggles of the previous three years ensured that there would be no popular uprising in support of the *huídos*, who were condemned to a hard and solitary existence.

None the less, on occasions they were able to emerge from their defensive positions. Attacks were carried out against Civil Guard barracks, local Falangist offices, and Francoist town halls. Although it is absurd to suggest, as the Communist leader Enrique Líster did, that the guerrilla war occupied sufficient troops to prevent Franco entering the Second World War on the Axis side, the activities of the *huídos* were a constant irritant for the regime. In so far as the controlled press mentioned their activities, it was to denounce them as acts of banditry and looting. However, in some rural areas, the activities of the *guerrilleros* had the effect of raising the morale of the defeated population until, that is, the savage reprisals taken by the authorities took their toll of popular support. In any case, in no way can the *guerrilla* be considered a threat to the dictatorship.

In the autumn of 1944, there came about an important change. Many Spanish *maquis*, after having played a crucial role in the French Resistance, responded to signs of German collapse by moving towards the frontier with Spain. In part, this was a spontaneous movement, but it also reflected the orders of the then *de facto* leader of the Spanish Communist Party, Jesús Monzón. It was his ambition to overthrow the dictatorship by means of an armed invasion which would spark off a popular uprising. Wartime circumstances, with communications rendered difficult by the rapid Allied advance, gave a certain *de facto* autonomy to Monzón, who was thus able to act without taking into consideration the strategic needs of the Soviet Union. It would be wrong to give the impression that the PCE was the sole component of the invasion or of the guerrilla war in general. Nevertheless, leaving aside the exaggerations of the Communists themselves or the obsessively anti-Communist accusations of the regime, there is no doubt that, for various reasons, the PCE enjoyed a certain pre-eminence within the *guerrilla*. The individual rank-and-file *guerrilleros* were socialists, anarchists, communists, or simply anti-Francoists. However, the anarchists in exile, loosely gathered in the Movimiento Libertario Español, were irreparably divided. The Socialist Party

(Partido Socialista Obrero Español (PSOE*)), was bitterly divided on geographical, and ideological lines. The PSOE's militant pro-Communist sections were in a minority and the majority leadership was naïvely assuming that Franco would be removed by a future Allied military intervention. In consequence, the senior Communist Party cadres in the south of France were readily able to fill the vacuum and simply assumed the leadership of the Spanish *maquis*. Moreover, the Communists' internal cell-structure and their Bolshevik traditions facilitated the transition to armed struggle. Accordingly, the PCE was the only political organization that, for a number of years, devoted the greater part of its human and material resources to the *guerrilla*.

The Communists took the initiative in constructing a national guerrilla organization on the basis of the vague structures created by the *huídos*. The spontaneous groups of Asturias and Galicia had already united as the so-called Federación de Guerrilleros de Galicia y León. This structure was adopted by the Communists. They created on paper a nation-wide network of divisions and detachments which often had no basis in fact. Where there were authentic units, they were under the command of a Communist general staff. The invention of the so-called Ejército Guerrillero (Guerrilla Army) was not just a symptom of Communist triumphalism but also a propaganda device to give the impression of greater strength and so perplex the Francoist authorities and raise the morale of the *guerrilleros* themselves and also of the sympathizers who, at enormous risk, gave them food and medicines.

In the autumn of 1944, the existing groups in the interior requested help from the exiled PCE leadership in France. They saw the opportunity to make a reality of Monzón's dream of an invasion and assumed that it would unite all those who had not accepted that April 1939 was the end of the civil war. Monzón himself was living clandestinely in Spain. None the less, once his subordinates in France had decided on the venture, it was organized virtually as a conventional military operation with little by way of security. Its preparation was an open secret. Before leaving for the south of France, some *guerrillero* units were the object of public tributes and large send-offs by the people of the French towns and cities where they had participated in the Resistance. The PCE ordered its organizations in the interior of Spain to prepare for an immediate popular insurrection. The regime was fully informed of what was imminent, proclaimed by Communist propaganda as 'the reconquest of Spain'.

The aspect of the events of autumn 1944 which most preoccupied Franco and his immediate entourage was the suspicion that the more or less open preparation of the invasion appeared to enjoy not only the support of the French Resistance but the approval of the Allies. In fact, Franco had reason to hope that both the British and the Americans were already thinking in Cold War terms and regarded Francoism as a better guarantee against communism than a restored Republic. However, the Allies' total absorption in the war against the Germans left the way open for the *guerrilleros* and gave the impression of tacit acquiescence in the invasion. Certainly, the enthusiastic co-operation of the French Resistance ensured that the invading forces were well equipped with supplies of food, fuel, light arms, ammunition, and vehicles, most supplied by the Allies.

Beginning on 9 October 1944, approximately 12,000 men of the invading army began to enter Spanish territory, principally through the Pyrenean Val d'Arán. Snow-covered for most of the year and sparsely populated, it was an area of shepherds and wood-cutters, a place barely appropriate as the *foco* of a popular uprising. Despite the ostentatious military structure set up by the Communist leaders of the *maquis*, the invasion appeared improvised and euphoric. It flouted the obvious fact that a conventional military incursion played into the hands of Franco's huge land forces. None the less, the invaders chalked up their successes, some units getting over 100 kilometres into the interior. In some individual actions, they roundly defeated units of the Spanish army and held large numbers of prisoners for short periods. In the last resort, however, the troops under the command of experienced Francoist generals, Yagüe, García Valiño, Monasterio, and Moscardó, were too much for the relatively small army of *guerrilleros*. The invasion's hopes of triggering off an uprising were always remote. It was launched at a time of massive demoralization on the Spanish left, which had still not recovered from the trauma of defeat, was ground down by fear of the daily repression, and, finally and most importantly, was only distantly and vaguely aware of what was happening in the north. The regime's iron control of the press and the minuscule circulation within Spain, at least, of the Communists' clandestine broadsheet *La Reconquista de España* ensured that the *guerrillero* invasion took place in a deafening silence.

In the last resort, it was the numerical superiority of Franco's forces which won the day. In most encounters, the *guerrilleros* of the invading force were outnumbered by at least four to one and, finally, forced to retreat. In giving the order so to do, the PCE leadership was assisted by the knowledge that a change of course accorded with the direction of Moscow's thinking. In the following weeks the PCE switched rapidly to an entirely different guerrilla tactic.

Monzón and the rest of the party leadership remained convinced that a popular rising was feasible if only the necessary spark would ignite it. It was now decided that a more realistic tactic was the gradual infiltration of small groups of *guerrilleros* across the French frontier after which they would link up with the existing groups of *huídos*. Arriving with food and arms, the ex-*maquisards* were able to organize relatively efficacious guerrilla units. Given the lack of any other leadership initiatives from anarchists or socialists, the PCE filled the gap, acting as the co-ordinator of these groups and sending in hardened militants trained in the French Resistance or even in the Ukrainian *guerrilla*. The idea pushed by the PCE at a plenary meeting of the Central Committee held in Toulouse between 5 and 8 December 1945 was that the *guerrilla* would be the catalyst of a popular struggle sufficiently broad-based to intensify international hostility against the Franco regime. This was a vain hope given the ever more anti-Communist attitudes of the Anglo-Saxon powers.

Civil Guard barracks were attacked, trains were blown up, and electrical power lines were brought down. The reactions of the peasantry appeared, at first, to be passively sympathetic, especially when the *guerrilleros* undertook specific actions by request, such as the burning of municipal archives to impede the collection of taxes. However, in general, the Spanish *maquis* followed the example of the French Resistance, rather than adopting the method of the *foco*, or the impregnable safe territory, a concept being used with great success by the Chinese at the time and later by the Cubans. The Spanish *guerrilleros* saw themselves as the vanguard of a future invading army and, therefore, did not devote much effort to sinking roots among the local peasantry. In any case, in the conditions of Spain in the 1940s, a *foco* tactic would have been extremely difficult to carry off. After three years of civil war and five more of state terror, the majority of the population had enough to cope with merely surviving the prevailing famine without in addition taking part in the great uprising which was the objective of the *guerrilla*. In the long term, the *guerrilla* was doomed to failure.

Nevertheless, for a few years, from 1945 to 1948, the *guerrilla* was a considerable irritant to the regime. Part of the Communist tactic was to inflate the importance of the *guerrilla* by inventing a national structure of guerrilla forces for each region of the country. It was thereby hoped to undermine both the fears of the civilian population and the belief of the repressive forces in the stability of the regime. In fact, the forces deployed in the anti-*guerrilla* struggle, primarily the Civil Guard but also regular units of the army, of the Spanish Foreign Legion, and of the colonial force recruited in Morocco, the Regulares Indígenas, were under the impression that they were fighting tens of thousands of *guerrilleros*. It is difficult, given the exaggerations of both sides, to calculate the exact numbers of the men and women who participated in the *guerrilla*. Once thought to be about 15,000, it may be as few as 3,000. The impression that they were more was created by the technique of striking in successive days in places 40 or 50 kilometres apart.

However, given the difficulty of establishing *focos* or liberated zones, it was not surprising that the peasantry began slowly to reject the *maquis*. When, as occasionally happened, the *guerrilleros* were able to capture a village and fly the Republican flag from the town hall, they invariably had to withdraw when Civil Guard reinforcements arrived. At that point, violent reprisals would be taken against villagers accused of giving succour to the *guerrilleros*. The brutality of the reprisals was linked to what amounted to a deliberate scorched earth policy with entire villages put to the torch to prevent the *guerrilleros* returning. The process of peasant rejection of the *guerrilla* was accelerated by another tactic used by the Civil Guard. It consisted of the creation of special units, known as *contra-partidas* (counter guerrilla bands), which looked, talked, and behaved like real *guerrilleros* but were really *agents provocateurs*. They would imitate the routine of the authentic *guerrilleros*, enter a village and, by asking for food and shelter, encourage sympathizers to come forward. Once support networks had been revealed, they would be dismantled with some violence. At other times, these fake or counter-*guerrilleros* would simply rampage through villages, raping and plundering. The combined effect of these special operations gradually made it impossible for the *guerrilleros* to return to villages where they had once been welcome. Once they could no longer count on peasant sympathy, which was the case by the late 1940s, the *guerrilleros* were obliged to steal simply to survive. That gave substance to the regime claim that they were never more than bandits.

In fact, it had become obvious by 1940 that the much-awaited uprising was not going to take place. With the French frontier subjected to military vigilance, it became ever harder to get supplies of food, weapons, and ammunition. Moreover, as they had in 1944, deteriorating conditions combined with wider Soviet interests in pointing to the need for withdrawal. Much has been made of a famous interview in Moscow between Stalin and a delegation from the PCE. According to the most reliable of several eye-witness accounts, that of Fernando Claudín, Stalin did not insist on the abandonment of the *guerrilla* so much as on the need for the PCE to widen its activities to include other forms of struggle, particularly the infiltration of the regime's own mass organizations. Objective circumstances inclined the PCE to renounce the guerrilla struggle but the final decision was not taken until the approval of Stalin was certain. That approval was never really in doubt. The deterioration of relations with the United States was sufficiently acute to incline Stalin to remove a gratuitous irritant in the form of the ever more unsustainable conflict in Spain. However, Stalin's principal motive in calling in the Spanish delegation was to clinch Spanish loyalty for the imminent conflict with the Yugoslavian Communist leader Tito. To do this, he chose to manifest a greater interest in the Spanish situation than he probably felt. The recommendation to the Spaniards to adopt a tactic of infiltration was suggested to him by one of his functionaries. In October 1948, a joint delegation of the PCE and the Soviet Union Communist Party executive met some leaders of the *guerrilla* to inform them of the decision. The *guerrilleros* themselves accepted the change of tactic grudgingly despite the fact that they were already fully convinced of the futility of continuing the armed struggle. It was hard to give up a way of life that some had pursued for over a decade and even harder to admit that the sacrifices of those years had been to no avail. The evacuation, which took the form of a long forced march, began in 1950 but the last units did not leave Spain until well into 1951.

There was also an urban *guerrilla* which went on sporadically until the end of the 1950s. In Madrid and its environs, a hero of the French Resistance, Cristino García, together with one of the PCE's earliest leaders, Gabriel León Trilla, headed a Communist guerrilla group. Trilla had been one of the founders of the PCE in the 1920s, was expelled from the Party in 1932 after a policy swerve by the Kremlin, and had returned to the ranks during the civil war. The activities of this group consisted of bank robberies and attacks on Falangist offices but they provoked waves of arrests on a scale which led to them being considered counter-productive.

Cristino García was captured at the end of 1945 a few weeks after Trilla had been stabbed to death in an abandoned cemetery known as the field of skulls, allegedly murdered because of discrepancies with the party leadership. After this sordid episode and the disappearance of Cristino García, the PCE virtually abandoned the urban *guerrilla*, which henceforth would be the exclusive terrain of the Movimiento Libertario Español.

The anarchist urban *guerrilla* which was centred on Barcelona ultimately experienced the same fate as that of Madrid although it lasted nearly fifteen years longer. Several libertarian* groups, such as Talión or Los Maños, and also some individuals acting entirely alone, such as Francisco Sabaté or José Luis Facerías, organized robberies of banks and factories, attacks on known police informers and torturers, and even attempts to free prisoners from Francoist gaols. Many of their actions were carried out with bravery and imagination, but even when successful, they were usually followed by brutal reprisals against those working-class elements known to be sympathizers of the CNT. It is difficult to believe that the achievements of the urban *guerrilla* could raise the morale of the population sufficiently to compensate for the damage that they provoked. Moreover, the possibility of linking up with the discontented masses was seriously reduced by a series of obstacles which arose within the leadership of the Movimiento Libertario Español exiled in France. Some anarchist leaders were hostile to the *guerrilla* for fear that it might cause difficulties with the French authorities and so provoke measures against the functioning of the CNT in France. Moreover, the ease with which the open structures of the CNT could be infiltrated by police spies and *agents provocateurs* soon provoked difficulties for the militant activists inside Spain.

Thus, the anarchist urban *guerrilla* was, just like its rural communist counterpart, unable to be the spark which would ignite a broad mass movement against Franco. In the 1940s, the *guerrilla* in its various forms was never really more than the rearguard of the defeated Republican forces. A resistance movement that would seriously challenge the survival of the Franco regime was not to come until the 1960s, with the rebirth of the labour movement and the emergence of the violent, direct action of the radical Basque nationalists, ETA.* But by that time, the conditions from which a new working class would emerge were also changing the nature of the dictatorship itself. In the event, it would not be overthrown by violent action but gradually dismantled by a complex process of political negotiation in a context of broad popular consensus.

Further reading
Aguado Sánchez, F., *El maquis en España* (Madrid, 1975).
Arasa, D., *Años 40: los maquis y el PCE* (Barcelona, 1984).
Cossías, T., *La lucha contra el 'maquis' en España* (Madrid, 1956).
Heine, H., *La oposición política al franquismo de 1939 a 1952* (Barcelona, 1983).
Ippécourt, P. V., *Les Chemins d'Espagne: mémoires et documents sur la guerre secrète à travers les Pyrénées 1940–1945* (Éditions Gaucher, Paris, 1948).
Pons Prades, E., *Guerrillas españolas 1936–1960* (Barcelona, 1977).

Sorel, A., *Búsqueda, reconstrucción e historia de la guerrilla española del siglo XX a través de sus documentos, relatos y protagonistas* (Éditions de la Librairie du Globe, Paris, 1970).

Téllez, A., *Sabaté: Guerrilla Extraordinary* (Cienfuegos Press, London, 1974).

Popular Culture in the 'Years of Hunger'

HELEN GRAHAM

The 1940s saw the making of the Francoist state. Power was reconstructed mainly through the exercise of autarky. The social/cultural dimension of autarky was no less crucial to the Francoist project than autarky's more obvious component—extreme economic protectionism. Autarkic structures and practices provided the means of social and cultural exclusion, and of physical and economic repression (explored in Mike Richards's essay). In the 1940s the regime attempted to exercise cultural hegemony through the dissemination of what could be called an archaizing vision. Through state and Church ceremonial; monuments to those fallen 'por Dios y por España' ('for God and Spain'—supremely, the Valle de los Caídos); in school textbooks; sanitized folklore (via the Sección Femenina* de Falange); comics glorifying 'heroic' crusaders against the Moors and the production by the national film industry of folkloric spectacles, religious dramas, and historical epics, the regime projected an idealized, highly tendentious image of Spain's imperial past as a model for its present.

The cultural myths of Reconquest, Counter-Reformation, and empire (most crucially, concepts of penitence/suffering and sacrifice) were used to repress the defeated sectors of the population. The 'return' to fifteenth-century values and the 'reinvention' of Philip II's sixteenth-century Spain, especially a militant, intolerant Catholicism, meant in fact the functional resurrection of its Manichaean moral categories (roughly analogous to the 'rediscovery' of 'Victorian values' in 1980s Britain). Work, nationalism, authority, purification through sacrifice not only provided a way out of economic crisis but were also a means of restructuring power. The ultimate value in the Francoist new order was the 'nation': constructed as 'a single, universal destiny' ('unidad de destino en lo universal'), it was projected as the antithesis of change. National identity was to be reinforced by the construction of an internal other: the industrial working class. Demonized by Francoism as the epitome of anti-Spain, its extreme economic exploitation was justified in terms of its being 'alien to the nation'. Indeed, the military forces detached to organize penal battalions and work brigades referred to themselves as 'the army of occupation'.

The reinforcement of national-patriotic values was also pursued via forms of mass commercial culture, such as musical comedies and popular song, which promoted the superiority and wholesomeness of all things Hispanic ('el culto a lo español'). (Spaniards were uniquely responsible, so it seemed, for the (often remote) prototypes of innumerable useful inventions—from the submarine and helicopter to nylon stockings, the latter springing from the fertile imagination of an eighteenth-century Jesuit.) All this was proffered as an 'epic consolation' for searing poverty —never directly referred to. This ultra-*casticismo** was a crucial part of the way Francoism developed the 'internalization of empire' central to the thinking of the twentieth-century Spanish right. *Casticismo* operated as an inverted form of social imperialism, projected inward to reinforce an exclusive construction of the 'nation' as a substitute for the external/geographic empire definitively lost with Axis defeat in the Second World War.

Commercial popular culture in all its forms was perceived as useful to the regime because, chauvinism aside, it was seen as pacificatory, offering malnourished and unhappy Spaniards a form of—ostensibly depoliticized—'escapist' entertainment. Among the forms susceptible to such use were: sport (most notably football, which spawned the pools as a further 'spectator sport'); bullfighting (more fleetingly); Hollywood films; kiosk literature of various sorts and drama serials and popular song—transmitted both by travelling singers/bands and the radio, a ubiquitous medium in working- and lower middle-class homes.

Articulating the regime's intent regarding such cultural forms is not, however, the same thing as ascertaining their impact on the constituencies of Spaniards consuming them. We can state—uncontentiously—that the regime's triumphalist discourse could not homogenize the disparate and highly contradictory social and cultural realities of 1940s Spain. Indeed, its own savagely discriminatory policies intensified difference, monolithic Spain existing primarily as a repressive cultural myth. Both the national-patriotic 'high' cultural material and the commercial kind met a variety of cultural resistances (the two forms overlapping considerably anyway, given authoritarian state control of the emergent culture industry in a period of nation formation). The more transparent the instrumentalization of cultural forms to transmit values which did not accord with the lived experience of the popular audience, the more people 'voted with their feet'. (And in the riven social milieux of post-war Spain, this was the experience not only of an urban working class already 'marked' by the regime, but of huge numbers of Spain's provincial lower middle classes also living the reality of a squalid, hungry 1940s.) Thus imperial/heroic cinema flopped whereas other kinds flourished, as did football, because it was possible to engage at levels unconnected with the overt national-patriotic message.

Beneath this pall of national-patriotic culture, the decade was dominated by what Manuel Vázquez Montalbán has called the 'reign of material truths'. Through the combination of sub-subsistence state rationing (in force in Spain until 1952) and the functioning of a black market (*estraperlo*) so enormous that it represented the real national economy, civil war victory and defeat were institutionalized. This occurred as much through a 'bottom-up' process of cultural internalization as it did through the operation of state power 'top-down'. On 1 April 1939, defeat had been an abstract concept for the Republican population. But subsequently, through the desperate and degrading experience of daily life—hunger, cold, homelessness, contagious disease (rife in the 1940s), economic penury/destitution, political persecution, and the thousand acts of abasement these dictated—many learned the real meaning of defeat, internalizing their powerlessness through its sheer overwhelming materiality.

The vast black market was the matrix both symbolizing and reproducing the class inequalities on which the Francoist social order was made. A mechanism for primitive capital accumulation based on the punitive taxation of the poor, the *estraperlo* represented the unfettered market red in tooth and claw. It saturated all social relations and value—not only did everything have its price, but the tags were all on display. In such an extreme situation all human interaction was reduced to the most primitive level of exchange. Material survival was the 'currency' of life, so we should not be surprised by the newspaper headline about the mother who 'sold her daughter' (relayed in Patino's remarkable 1971 documentary film *Canciones para después de una guerra*; see Plate 17). In conditions of such social brutality, culture for vast swathes of the population—but especially the urban poor—came to be synonymous with the struggle to achieve, by whatever means, the basic necessities of life: food, shelter, and work. The picaresque* made a dramatic return in the 1940s—in real life rather than literature. But the level of social brutality meant tragedy eclipsed earthy humour/farce.

It is this context of the brutal and brutalizing experience of daily life—1940s 'culture' in its widest sense—which, I would argue, provides the key to the reception of the popular songs of the period. Assessing their reception inevitably involves a certain amount of hypothesis—especially given the lack of work to date on the cultural and social history of the 1940s. The object here is therefore to pose some central questions, which as yet have scarcely begun to be addressed, as a stimulus to future investigation. How did the social institutionalization of civil war on which the Francoist state was built shape popular consciousness and identities? What psychological strategies of survival were employed to get by in dark times and with what effects? What was the relationship between the social dislocation, atomization, and disorientation which characterized the decade and the cultural forms it generated? One way of gaining an insight into the popular mentalities of the period, as expressed in its myths, rituals, obsessions, and conventional wisdom, is through a reading of the popular songs of the 1940s.

To appreciate the concentrated power of these songs—a mix of the trivial, sentimental, melodramatic, and sometimes surreal—one must understand what the Franco regime was doing culturally speaking. Defeat, decimation, and diaspora had seriously muted, when not reduced to silence, the cultural as well as political voices of opposition. 'High' culture belonged in the most overt way to the victors. Its inscription in the public space was theirs exclusively, condemning the memories and grief of their opponents to silence and oblivion: nowhere is this portrayed more clearly than in the scenes of mass 'evocación de caídos' (act of remembrance for the war dead) featured in Patino's *Canciones*. At the same time, the regime promoted a cult of the folkloric which magnified the parodic, kitsch, and sentimental in the products of mass commercial or 'low' culture. Yet, paradoxically, through the often deformed sentimentality of these commercialized songs it is possible to map the sensibility of the politically and culturally dispossessed. For 'popular culture is an inheritor of something else [. . .] cheap songs, so-called, actually do have something of the Psalms of David about them'.[1] Nor were these songs 'escapist' in any simple sense of blocking out a murderous and miserable reality. 'Escapism' is in fact a much more complex process.

One major function of popular songs was emotional catharsis. This, however, was provided 'by proxy', in so far as the real cause of the grief and loss expressed could not be named. Consider the extraordinary popular success of a song like 'No te mires en el río' [Don't look into the river], sung by Concha Piquer. With a clear debt to García Lorca's 'Romance anónimo', it tells of one who commands his *novia* (sweetheart) not to look out of the window into the river flowing by. But when he returns, bearing gifts, he finds her dead in the river, 'como el agua la llevaba | ¡ay, corazón, parecía una rosa! | ¡ay corazón, una rosa muy blanca!' [as the waters carried her away, she seemed a rose, a rose of purest white]. The song ends with a lament for his loss and his jealousy towards the river. At one level, it is a basic sentimental song—a pair of lovers and a tragic death foretold. But, at another, the song, like the river, is the medium which carries an overwhelming burden of emotion—pure anguish, desolation, loss, mystery. As Vázquez Montalbán suggests, its meaning is to be found not in the clichés of its surface form, but in 'una lógica subnormal' perceptible only to those with a highly developed sense of the 'abnormal':

y bien educado lo tenían aquellos seres de precaria épica, aquellos españoles de los años cuarenta que habían perdido en el río de acontecimientos incontrolables: novias, novios, tierras, recuerdos, dignidades, palabras sagradas, ideas, símbolos, mitos, la alegría de la propia sombra.

and finely attuned it was indeed in those vulnerable souls, the Spaniards of the 40s who had seen swept away in the torrential river of events: lovers, homes, memories, self respect, sacred truths, ideas, symbols, myths, peace of mind, the small pleasures of daily life.[2]

The need to express what was repressed made popular consciousness elliptical. In the songs, as in daily life, the meaning had to be sought not in the words, but in the tone or stress, or in the space between words (a good example of how tonality and phrasing can carry more of a song's meaning than the words themselves is to be found in Marifé de Triana's recording of 'Torre de Arena'). This ellipsis came to signify more than just a refusal to communicate certain feelings or memories to others: it meant their suppression below the level of conscious thought itself. This was something more than the phenomenon of 'inner exile'—understood as the conscious retreat into a private world in a society whose values are alien—which the sons and daughters of the defeated have recorded as the 'inwardness' of their parents, the sense that they were 'somewhere else'. Rather this ellipsis is connected with aboulia—where time and space are experienced as a void—a term which encapsulates the cultural disorientation of the 1940s as cinematographically distilled in Víctor Erice's 1973 film *El espíritu de la colmena* [*The Spirit of the Beehive*].

At the same time, there are popular songs which can be read as an ironic commentary on the enormous distance separating real life from the national-patriotic 'moral superstructure' of Francoism. Some songs might proclaim that true love could not be bought ('ni se compra ni se vende el cariño verdadero'), but all around daily experience acutely contradicted this. Indeed, as another song affirmed, it could be bought very nicely for a *topolino** (tiny SEAT car), especially if it was full of petrol—a substance scarcer than gold in the 1940s. In short, what was needed in these new times was 'cara dura' (cheek): 'Se acabó la valentía | el trabajo y la bravura | para darse la gran vida | es cuestión de cara dura' [The days of being honest, hardworking, and upright are gone, to enjoy the good life now what you need is cheek]. Songs with this coating of irony and self-knowledge, as well as the more strikingly contestatory—such as 'Tatuaje' [Tattoo] (discussed in the above essay on women in the 1940s)—can be read as a means of self-protection, a form of cultural resistance which helped people in the enormous task of 'getting by'. They signify a kind of affirmative cynicism in desperate times when so much human reciprocity had been reduced to the exchange value of the market. (One way of exploring this affirmative cynicism further—and indeed popular mentalities more generally—would be to look at the jokes circulating at the time. Although such an undertaking presupposes practical difficulties, it could offer extraordinarily valuable insights.)

While popular song performed a contestatory role—either through protest or the ironic debunking of official values—there was rather more ambiguity at another level. As we have seen, popular song also represented the way in which popular consciousness was being shaped by the material experience of the 1940s. The task of ensuring survival in such an atomized and deprived society was as crucially a psychological as a physical struggle—as the increased incidence of suicide suggests. (Official statistics show a rise in reported suicides for the 1940s, although, as with prostitution, the statistics fail to reflect the extent of its occurrence.) For many of the politically defeated and economically dispossessed who endured that war we call the post-war, psychological survival was achieved at a high cost: by jettisoning the ballast of a too painful, traumatizing memory—the personal and collective aspirations of 'before' were self-repressed because the memory of what had been lost was a hindrance, making unbearable all the petty acts of mediocrity and prostitution (literal or metaphorical) which survival inevitably entailed. (The above reading of 'No te mires en el río' is essentially about this process.)

The space left by the self-repression of personal and collective memory was filled by an alternative mythology of things—white bread, olive oil, meat, 'the food from those days before the war', soap, a good cut of cloth, housing—unsurprising in such a materially deprived environment. This substitution process is what Manuel Vázquez Montalbán has called the 'orchestrated depoliticization of social consciousness'. Whether or not the regime consciously utilized hunger and deprivation as instruments of social control, the fact remains that what was occurring here, rather than depoliticization, was a particular form of political formation which fed into regime attempts, at other levels, to eradicate unacceptable (i.e. collectivist) political and cultural values. In the unremitting harshness of life, popular energy was channelled towards the securing of small personal respites. People dreamed, but very often of 'material myths': from the most basic—food and shelter—to the pre-consumerism of the *chicas topolino** (the fashion-conscious young women who modelled their style on avidly consumed American movies). Above all, there was the sheer relief at being alive: in spite of all the trials of post-war life, its savage inequalities and institutionalized revenge, they had survived when so many had not. There was a desire, then, to make a life, to find a consolatory pleasure because there was ultimately no other option: 'se vive solamente una vez, | hay que aprender a querer y a vivir' [We only live once, we must learn to love and live life to the full]. These apparently clichéd sentiments would have had a very particular piquancy for a popular audience in Spain. The Sunday dances were full as a generation of ill-fed Spaniards learned to dance the 'bugui-bugui', one of the most well-known being 'Un bugui más . . . ¿qué importa?' [One more boogie-woogie . . . who cares?]—a gloss (typical of the language of allusion used in the period) on the well-known, sardonic last line of the Spanish Romantic poet Espronceda's poem on the death of his lover Teresa: 'un cadáver más . . . ¿qué importa al mundo?' [one more corpse . . . what does the world care?]. The reality of daily life was that people could not afford to care, nothing 'extraneous' could be allowed to matter: 'sobre las tumbas del recuerdo, del cerebro, del corazón, sobre las tumbas reales de más de media España muerta: un bugui más ¿qué importaba?' [on the grave of memory, intellect, love, on the real graves of more than half of Spain lying dead: one more boogie-woogie, who cared?].[3]

Autarkic Francoism was to produce a propitious social climate for the later implantation of the cultural values underpinning consumerist capitalism. People were not, of course, screens to be wiped clean and written on afresh according to the regime's political and cultural agenda. Still less is it my contention that the regime itself understood or consciously instrumentalized this process. Nevertheless, 'the years of hunger', far from being a blip on the graph before the Francoist project 'proper' began, were integral to it.

The way in which the combination of National-Catholic culture, social dislocation, and poverty fuelled a return to 'primitivism' also forms part of this picture of reducing cultural resistances. The regime's cultivation of the irrational (integrist Catholicism and public religiosity) found a popular response in an upsurge of miracles and visions (usually of the Virgin in her many incarnations). Such a hostile public environment saw the eclipse of critical reason itself—except for some small private spaces (see Elías Díaz's essay in Part III, Section 2). It also stifled those young pluralist cultures which had begun to make headway in the 1930s—not the least of which had been feminism. This return to primitivism provides the key to the Francoist project: the uncoupling of cultural modernity from the process of economic modernization.

And, paradoxically, in spite of the evident contradiction between authoritarian Catholic, national-patriotic culture on the one hand and the pre-consumerist values of much 1940s popular culture on the other, because the former impeded or atrophied independent critical thought, there is a sense in which it can be said to have facilitated the uncritical assimilation of new, consumerist cultural values—under the later guise even of rebellion against regime puritanism, or in some cases against the seriousness of the opposition.

The lines of analysis suggested here chart an intrahistory which is part of a larger picture. Elsewhere Paul Preston has written about the 'bankable' terror of the 1940s and the way in which it underwrote more than two decades of labour discipline and 'stability' in Spain, making the country a highly attractive proposition for foreign capital investment. Economic repression too taught workers to have extremely low expectations by western European standards—affluence, like poverty, being a relative value. The material deprivation of the 1940s had been culturally mediated. Republican defeat and post-war repression had violently broken the continuity of labour cultures. While a new workers' movement would emerge and grow, boosted by 1960s expansion, in the interim what was learned and transmitted across generations was precisely that workers should expect very little.

As the neo-liberal technocrats of the Opus Dei* presided over industrial take-off and accelerated economic growth (courtesy of European boom), the urban working class would experience the underside of the 'miracle', since the consequences of development remained largely unmitigated by any social budget or welfare net. Spaniards accepted the 'trickle-down' of televisions and other consumer goods, putting up with life in the shanty towns, devoid of minimal sanitation or other infrastructure, with high infant mortality and a lack of basic educational facilities for their children. They habitually worked longer hours than their western European counterparts and the industrial accident level was also significantly higher.

To understand how the 'economic miracle' was experienced by the workers who made it possible—to write its social history, as it were—requires us to go back to the 1940s to identify and articulate the links between autarky and development. Economic histories have tended to cordon off the autarkic phase of Francoism, treating it as a cul-de-sac whose policy failures were 'reversed' across the second half of the 1950s (and finally abandoned in 1959). Such studies miss the wider picture precisely because they define autarky in very narrow economic terms, measuring it via GDP (gross domestic product) levels (themselves highly problematic given the enormous scale of the black market). To date we have no study which explores autarky as the social and cultural process through which the Francoist state was constructed and the enduring power relations within it were made.

By defining autarky so narrowly—as an economic aberration generated by fascist mimetism but somehow anachronistically outlasting its Axis environment by some ten years—awkward questions about Francoism's function as a domestic fascism are avoided. According to this schema, Francoism 'proper' begins in 1957—the new 'first triumphal year'—with US loans under way, the arrival of the Opus Dei technocrats in power, and the fetishizing of macro-economic plans. The Franco regime is thus retrospectively transformed. As the 1940s are written out of the script, the awkard linkage between repression and economic development is blotted out. 'Terror and progress', with the political and cultural brutality Francoism inflicted upon other Spaniards (moving opposition critics to refer to the regime's 'cannibalism'), is too problematic a past to be assimilated as a 'usable history' by today's liberal democratic Spain.

In post-Franco Spain there has been no public polemic over questions of nationalism and historical memory such as those which occurred in the later 1980s in (the then) West Germany around the 'historians' dispute' [*Historikerstreit*]. (This dispute, while somewhat basic and unenlightening in its empirical historical content, is of interest because it represented an attempt to rehabilitate a conservative nationalism—and such a reading of German history—by 'uncoupling' Nazism as a mere 'aberration', an unfortunate wrong turning.) The similarities between this and the rather convenient view of autarkic Francoism as a 'dead end' are striking. The lack of public debate on such matters in Spain reflects the relative marginalization of historical work on the civil war and its aftermath. This marginalization itself must be read as part of the political logic of the democratic transition, with the so-called 'pact of oblivion' tacitly agreed between the Francoist élites and their opposition interlocutors. Accordingly, the regime would be dismantled as long as no one went picking over the entrails. Unfortunately, the resulting *desmemoria* [amnesia] has facilitated the emergence of a new conservative orthodoxy: that developmental dictatorship, rising from the ashes of the 1940s, authored the 'miracle' and through it the democratic transition itself. By this sleight of hand, political democracy and cultural plurality become the legacy of a benevolent dictator. By going back to the social history of the 1940s, however, we can identify quite a different legacy and tell another, very necessary story.

Notes
1 Dennis Potter's acute observation in 'Living for the Present: The Last Interview', *Guardian*, 6 Apr. 1994.
2 I wish to acknowledge my (evident) debt in this section to Manuel Vázquez Montalbán's resonant if brief analysis of Spanish popular song in *Crónica sentimental de España* (Barcelona, 1980)—p. 23 quoted here—and, by derivation, to Basilio Martín Patino's film *Canciones para después de una guerra* (1971).
3 Vázquez Montalbán, *Crónica sentimental*, 46.

Further reading
Abella, R., *Por el imperio hacia Dios: crónica de una posguerra (1939–1955)* (Barcelona, 1978).
Ilie, P., *Literature and Inner Exile: Authoritarian Spain 1939–1975* (Baltimore, 1980).

Martín Gaite, C., *Usos amorosos de la postguerra española* (Barcelona, 1987).
Morgan, R., 'Romper los moldes: implicaciones estéticas e ideológicas de *El espíritu de la colmena*', *ACIS* (Journal of the Association for Contemporary Iberian Studies), 6 (Spring 1993), 25–31.
Preston, P., *The Politics of Revenge* (London, 1990).
Román, M., *Memoria de la copla: la canción española de Conchita Piquer a Isabel Pantoja* (Madrid, 1993) (also deals with later periods).
Vázquez Montalbán, M., *Crónica sentimental de España: una mirada irreverente a tres décadas de mitos y de ensueños* (Barcelona, 1980) (covers 1940s, 1950s, and 1960s).
—— *Cancionero general 1939–71*, 2 vols. (Barcelona, 1972) (vol. i covers 1940s and 1950s).
—— *La penetración americana en España* (Madrid, 1974).

Memoirs and novels
Barral, C., *Años de penitencia* (Barcelona, 1975, new edn. 1990).
Marsé, J., *Si te dicen que caí* (Mexico, 1973, and later Spanish editions).
Martín Santos, L., *Tiempo de silencio* (Barcelona, 1962, and later editions).
Vázquez Montalbán, M., *El pianista* (Barcelona, 1985).
Wright, R., *Pagan Spain* (London, 1957).

The Emergence of a Dissident Intelligentsia

BARRY JORDAN

Over the years, a number of arguments have been put forward to explain the rise of a dissenting intelligenstia in the 1950s in Spain. First, there is the notion of a 'generation gap' which develops among the sons and daughters of families belonging to the winning side in the civil war, a gap which supposedly has its origins in the traumatic effects of the war itself. Secondly, critics regularly claim that new economic and political conditions prevailing at the turn of the 1950s facilitate the emergence of student dissidence, which gives way to a radical opposition cultural front. Thirdly, it is argued that many of the dissident intellectuals of the 1950s came from official organizations such as the Frente de Juventudes or the SEU (Sindicato Español Universitario [Spanish University Students Union]), that is, they received their initial political training and cultural formation within the Falange,* but because of subsequent disillusionments and ideological crises they moved towards the opposition. In other words, they underwent a process of ideological conversion. Fourthly, while many dissidents became politicized through their membership of official organizations, a number of writers and intellectuals reached opposition attitudes through other channels, such as a religious education or their own anti-Francoist family background. I should like briefly to consider each of these arguments in turn.

Generation gap/psychological trauma

José María Castellet, intellectual guru and leading dissident of the period, is one of the main proponents of this first argument, which can be summarized as follows: the so-called 'Generación del medio siglo', that is, the young writers, artists, poets, playwrights, film-makers, etc. who come to form the oppositional intelligentsia of the 1950s, were all marked, argues Castellet, by their common experience of the civil war. Unlike their elders, they took no part in the hostilities, nor did they take sides politically. They were thus innocent spectators and hapless victims of a monstrous, bloody, and damaging conflict. Moreover, their formative years, the 1940s, were conditioned by the tragic and repressive aftermath of the war, as well as international isolation, economic dislocation, shortages, rationing, and censorship. Since they were children at the time, the civil war and its effects are seen as having had a traumatic impact upon them. Such a harrowing experience, Castellet asserts, is translated into a wide-ranging condemnation of the older generation and this is expressed through a so-called 'generation gap'. Moreover, rather than take sides, the youngsters were apparently anxious to overcome the divisions created by the war, to heal the divide between winners and losers.[1]

On the surface, a degree of support for this argument seems to emerge in the early novels of writers such as Juan Goytisolo and Ana María Matute. These works deal with the theme of children whose lives are radically disrupted by the horrors of fratricidal war. Interestingly, however, this thematic focus does not enjoy wide currency since it tends not to be found to any great or enduring extent in the creative writing of the period. At a more general level, the above argument is perhaps too all-embracing and diffuse and relies more on an emotional and psychological appeal than on a solid body of evidence. It tends to regard the civil war as an abstract moral outrage, a wild orgy of blood-letting, whose appalling effects are visited upon a whole generation of innocent children, irrespective of social and class differences. While the very real horrors of civil war for all concerned cannot be overstated, Castellet's somewhat sweeping view tends to obscure the fact that the civil war in Spain was fought for very clear economic, social, and political reasons, the outcome of which produced a society divided into two opposing camps, winners and losers. Also, without recourse to reasonably sound sociological evidence, it is difficult to gauge the extent to which children were affected by hostilities more than adults and whether children of different social and class backgrounds experienced the war in rather different ways. In general, while there can be no doubt that a generation gap played an important role in the process towards intellectual and political dissidence for many of these young people, the question of whether it can be put down to a psychological trauma, caused by the war, remains open and unproven. Moreover, the notion of a generation gap need not rely exclusively on the idea of children traumatized by the war. We can posit other, equally persuasive, reasons for generational rebellion, not the least of which has to be that of 'mala conciencia' or class guilt, as Mangini quite correctly points out. In terms of social class, as mentioned earlier, the majority of dissident writers and intellectuals of the 1950s were drawn from the families of the winning side in the civil war, families which arguably coped rather better with the war and its consequences than those on the losing side. Indeed, the economic, social, and political disparities of post-war Spain became so acute that some of the more privileged offspring of the winning side felt compelled to assume responsibilities ignored by their parents. This version of the 'generation gap', the expression of an anxiety for responsibility in order to correct the errors of the older generation, might be a more appropriate framework within which to locate the early work of writers such as Goytisolo, Matute, Marsé, etc. Young writers thus began to call the older generation to account for their role in the war and their apparent indifference to the social and political inequities arising out of that victory. This questioning process perhaps forms the background if not the basis for the afore-mentioned 'generation gap'. In this regard, we might ask to what extent the emergence and public expression of this generational condemnation depended on changes in the political climate inside and outside Spain.

Liberalization

Most critics and commentators point to 'liberalization' in Spain at the turn of the 1950s as providing the appropriate conditions for the emergence of a dissenting intelligentsia and limited cultural renewal. They mention the consolidation of the regime, the slow transition towards a market economy, growing international recognition, the Concordat with the Vatican, and the famous economic/military pacts with the USA in 1953, as well as Spain's return to the United Nations in 1955. In short, the growing international legitimation of the regime leads to a conditional *apertura* [relaxation] in economic, diplomatic, and cultural terms and the re-establishment of contacts which had been severed for a decade.

To a large extent, this is the case. In the late 1940s and early 1950s, we certainly find a growing *rapprochement* between Spain and those countries which had been allies during the Second World War. This undoubtedly responded to the consolidation of the Cold War and the replacement of anti-fascism by anti-communism as the dominant ideology of the west. Spain was a direct beneficiary of these changes. Franco's earlier fascist connections were conveniently forgotten and his long-standing 'crusade' against communism (including his much-trumpeted role as prescient 'sentinel of the west') were amply vindicated by the Cold War. Of course, virtually all of these initiatives came from the outside. Other countries, particularly the USA, were beginning to appreciate the advantages Spain appeared to offer in military and economic terms. If this was liberalization, it was basically external and driven by changes in the nature and balance of international politics.

Inside Spain, liberalization, if such a term is appropriate, was arguably a side-effect, a corollary of these external developments, a series of fairly superficial and opportunist reponses by the regime. I should like briefly to mention three of them:

1. Compared to the dark days of the 1940s, by the early 1950s the regime could afford to be a little less repressive in its forms of political control. Given its con-solidation and recognition by the international community, there was simply less

need for the sort of overt large-scale purging and militarized policing of the previous decade. Also, if Franco was unlikely to be ousted through international pressure and his position was secure, then clearly the real, illegal, and still heavily repressed political opposition had to rethink their policies and tactics. In the case of the Spanish Communist Party (PCE*), for example, these changes led to the abandonment of guerrilla warfare in favour of attempts to infiltrate and work within the institutions of the state, especially the official unions (vertical trade unions*) and also the universities. In this connection, figures such as Enrique Múgica, Jorge Semprún, and Ricardo Muñoz Suay would act as Communist Party agents and organizers within the universities. Apart from recruiting members and gaining the support of 'fellow-travellers', such people would play a key role in mounting and at the same time redirecting official cultural events towards decidedly unofficial, oppositional goals. This was the case with such events as the 'Encuentros de Poesía con la Universidad' [Poetry–University Encounters] of 1954, the 'Conversaciones Cinematográficas de Salamanca' [Salamanca Film Conversations] of 1955, and the now legendary 'Congreso Universitario de Escritores Jóvenes' [Young Writers' University Congress] of 1956.

2. In the economic sphere, when specialists talk of the liberalization of the economy, they tend to refer, not to the abandonment, but to the 'freeing up' of the autarkic economic model adopted by the regime after the civil war. By 1950 this shift was translated into the adoption of more orthodox forms of capitalist exploitation, such as easing the rules on the entry of foreign capital, easing restrictions on tariffs and quotas to encourage foreign trade, bringing rationing to an end, and effecting a small rise in consumption. However, this process was highly uneven and uncoordinated, eventually leading to the inflationary crisis of the late 1950s and that famous austerity programme which gave rise to short-term recession, otherwise known as the Stabilization Plan of 1959.

3. In the cabinet reshuffle of 1951 (resulting from the regime's problems in coping with the brief strike wave of 1951), some of the pro-Falangist contingent (Suanzes and Ibáñez Martín) were removed in favour of a greater Catholic presence, including the appointment of Joaquín Ruiz Giménez as Minister of Education. This was an important development and indeed during the new Minister's term of office (1951–6) a number of reforms at the secondary and tertiary levels were enacted. At the same time and apart from increasing the number of scholarships and travel grants to university students, Ruiz Giménez made two crucial appointments to the rectorships of two major Spanish universities, Madrid and Salamanca—assigned to Pedro Laín Entralgo and Antonio Tovar respectively. Though still members of the Falange, Laín and Tovar were, by the early 1950s, undergoing a process of political reassessment which made them rather more receptive to the radical demands of their students.

The extent and nature of the above reforms are debatable, but as far as the universities were concerned there was certainly a noticeable change in the atmosphere on the campuses, thanks to which cultural events (lectures, poetry readings, film shows, debates on literature, etc.) impossible a few years before were given permission to go ahead. As already noted, many of these events were infiltrated, if not directly mounted, by members and sympathizers of the Communist Party. Following the critical student disturbances of 1956 and vociferous demands for a democratic student union, Ruiz Giménez was sacked. The reformist Minister had presided over a period that had seen something of a flowering of student rebellion during which student dissidents seized the opportunities granted to them for 'instrumentalizing' and exploiting cultural events for anti-regime purposes. We should not forget, however, that, in the same year that Ruiz Giménez was given the education portfolio, Gabriel Arias Salgado was appointed Minister of Information, responsible among other things for the press and the cinema. Salgado's activities were draconian and ruthless, making it virtually impossible for the media to be at all critical or inquisitive about social issues. By implication, one has to take into account the strong likelihood that this repressive regime imposed on the print media may be just as important a factor as liberalization in the universities in accounting for the rise of a new dissident intelligentsia and the role of 'high cultural' forms as substitutes for the media.

Ideological conversion

Given the fact of political and ideological repression and the general situation under Francoism of enforced depoliticization, the question arises as to how dissident writers and intellectuals of the 1950s arrived at their nonconformist, anti-regime attitudes. As previously noted, since the majority of the oppositional intelligentsia of the 1950s were sons and daughters of the winning side, the development of political dissent in their case would depend primarily on a process of disenchantment and ideological transition or conversion. Clearly, this would not happen out of the blue but would require some sort of agency. The obvious vehicle, of course, would be the Falange, or, to be more precise, organizations such as the Frente de Juventudes and the SEU. These organizations were important in the 1950s in that they were virtually the only available ones which offered young writers, intellectuals, and politicians platforms and publication outlets through which to develop their craft. Indeed, some commentators, particularly Martínez Cachero, take the view that Falangist cultural activities and youth publications were remarkably open for the times, and actively fostered discrepant and dissident views.[2] In short, they were the repository of liberal opinion and culture in the 1940s.

However, such a view, while having certain merits, needs to be seriously qualified, particularly the notion of 'liberal'. Though often seen as synonymous with the Movimiento* and while being a significant part of it, the Falange was not the only strand within it. Moreover, let us not forget that during much of the 1940s, and even allowing for the fact that there existed varying degrees of militancy and commitment to the Axis cause, members of the Falange were fascists. They were used by Franco to manage the state bureaucracies, especially the official trade unions, as well as to give ideological direction and legitimation to the regime. Right from 18 July 1936 the Falange was the regime's faithful and well-rewarded servant, as well as implacable enemy of communism, socialism, liberalism, republicanism, and freemasonry. And though the organization was often at loggerheads with other members of the regime's 'families', such as monarchists or Catholic groups like the ACNP, such disputes were hardly signs of liberalism or some inherent tendency towards political pluralism. It would thus be a serious mistake to view the Falange or its broad membership as 'liberal' in any conventional political sense. Indeed, those people who did in fact show tendencies towards ideological discrepancy and dissent were not Falangists in general but certain highly committed militants, that is, a very small number of Falangist academics and intellectuals, such as Pedro Laín Entralgo, Antonio Tovar, Juan Antonio Maravall, Dionisio Ridruejo, etc. These were the very people who had been instrumental in providing the Nationalist cause with its anthems, slogans, mythologies, and its combative ideology of counter-revolution.

Of course, once the civil war was over this sort of ideological work was no longer needed. Except for the period 1939–42, the post-war regime demanded a rather different form of dominant ideology more suited to the requirements of repression, control, and shifts in international opinion. So, while it retained much of the Falange's programme, the regime gradually drew more heavily on Catholic conservatism and traditionalism. Consequently, the Falange's revolutionary posturing became surplus to requirements. Of course, it did fulfil a post-war role in fashioning the theoretical and doctrinal legitimation of the new regime. But on the whole, the Falange increasingly adopted a technical, bureaucratic repressive outlook and though deeply embedded in the state administration was kept in a weak, subservient position and played a largely decorative role. For the vast majority of the membership, many in lucrative jobs in the various branches of the administration, this loss of status, prestige, and ideological edge would not matter at all. A few, however, especially those most highly politicized members who had once harboured illusions of creating a fascist state and who were dismayed at Franco's growing reliance on the Church and the monarchist option, would and did feel acutely resentful and their sense of betrayal would act as a basis for dissent. Perhaps one of the most striking cases in this regard is that of Dionisio Ridruejo, co-author of the Falangist anthem 'Cara al sol', head of Press and Propaganda in the early 1940s, and veteran of the civil war and the Blue Division. One could not find a truer, bluer, more committed Falangist. Precisely because of his Falangist 'purism', on his return from Russia in April 1942, and in the face of the increasing institutional domestication of Falange, Ridruejo dared to voice his disquiet in a letter to Franco in which he pointed out the following:

The Movement cannot be regarded merely as a group of people united by certain common concerns but as a strong, homogeneous and resolute militia [. . .] This view is almost totally contradicted by reality [. . .] To be a Falangist nowadays means virtually nothing

[. . .] Because, of course, 'it seems' that the Falange is in control but at the same time it also 'seems' that Your Excellency is making a mockery of Falange [. . .] This is not the Falange that we wanted nor the Spain that we need.[3]

As a result, Ridruejo was punished with loss of post and privileges and subjected to almost a decade of internal exile in Ronda and then in Catalonia. It was probably his support for the student disturbances of 1956, as a result of which he spent six weeks in gaol, which at last brought his own ideological crisis to a head and which resulted in the launch of his Partido Social de Acción Democrática in 1957.

The case of Ridruejo is perhaps one in which an 'old guard' fascist, a member of the Falange's originating 'front line', eventually catches up with and taps into more radical developments taking place among members of the younger generation, youngsters whose ideological reassessment was rather more rapid than his own but who were none the less attracted to Falangism. As Manuel Sacristán has argued, in Spain in the 1940s Falangism was the only available ideology, the only vehicle which satisfied desires for youth revolt.[4] Falangism made a very strident appeal to the youth of the nation, stressing the moral bankruptcy of the older generation and the role of young people in the political vanguard; though hollow and virtually meaningless, the Falange's slogans still managed to capture the imagination of certain types of youngsters, especially those imbued with notions of militancy and revolution. The trouble was, of course, that the Falange's leading, vanguard role and its radical ideological outlook were contradicted on a daily basis, with the revolution always being indefinitely postponed, always remaining 'pendiente'. As mentioned earlier, for most Falangists, including those who received their political training in the higher reaches of the bureaucracy, such as Manuel Fraga Iribarne, Adolfo Suárez, and Rodolfo Martín Villa, such contradictions presented no problem at all. These people quickly adapted to being administrators, technocrats, and in a sense became 'apolitical' in relation to the more 'purist' of Falangist sentiments. For a few militants, however, such contradictions had to be resolved.

Of course, the articulation of disenchantment with the Falange was only possible in real terms outside the organization. One could not be a committed Falangist and be anti-regime in any real, practical sense. One either ignored the contradictions, kept one's head down, mouthed the appropriate slogans at the right time, and kept one's job or one left the organization. And as Ridruejo has often argued, Falangist militants disenchanted with the system were as likely as not to latch onto other, alternative ideologies which still stressed notions of revolutionary transformation. They thus transferred their ideological militancy intact to creeds in many ways opposed to Falangism. This usually meant the adoption of some form of marxism. Here, the process of adaptation is interesting in that the disaffected Falangist had to come to terms with the idea that social and political change depended on class struggle and class-consciousness, concepts which the Falange's founder, José Antonio Primo de Rivera, had banished from its credo.

However, the idea of revolution from above, the élitist cornerstone of Falangism, would in some senses be preserved in marxism-leninism by the leading role assigned to the Party and Party militants and intellectuals. The cultural mandarinism so characteristic of official Francoist activities would thus be recycled, so to speak, within the ranks of the opposition intelligentsia.

As the cases of Castellet, Sacristán, Sastre, Aldecoa, and possibly Sánchez Ferlosio and others have shown, there is no doubt that this type of development, though involving relatively small numbers, constituted a major channel for the creation of a dissenting intelligentsia. Indeed, as products of the system, dissident young Falangists would be well placed to exploit the opportunities, the publications, platforms, and cultural activities provided by the SEU and other organizations to promote alternative, anti-regime views. As I have shown elsewhere, student magazines, journals, and reviews such as *Laye* in the early 1950s, and *Acento Cultural* later in the decade, were important sites for the development of intellectual dissidence. Often as a result of ecclesiastical pressure or the threat to introduce censorship into their day-to-day operation, these magazines were closed down and many of their circle of contributors invariably passed over to the Communist Party or became fellow-travellers. We need to take into account of course that the manipulation, infiltration, and exploitation of official outlets was to some extent tolerated by the regime's administrators, who were under pressure to show to their superiors a vibrant official youth culture and present it as a product of Falangist initiative. As Ridruejo again points out and he should know:

The rebellious generation has been formed in the very bosom of the system and it was necessary to greet this fact with applause in order to conceal the break [. . .] To absorb, neutralize, take control, boast of having created the rebellious generation was undoubtedly a far more subtle move than to bar its way.[5]

It would be a mistake of course to overestimate the importance of Falangist organizations as a channel for dissent. Just as important perhaps, even more so in certain cases, was the experience of a religious education in the 1940s and 1950s.

Politicization through reaction

While not all offspring of the Francoist bourgeoisie would enter Falangist youth organizations, most of them would spend their primary and secondary education at orthodox religious schools. Unlike Falangist organizations, in religious schools a political education was likely to be rudimentary, to say the least. In fact, such schools stressed the desirability of keeping politics out of school life altogether and indeed keeping politics out of the home as well, as Giner and Maravall have shown (see further reading below). Thus, for many children, their formative years would be characterized by a deliberate process of depoliticization, through school and family, a process cleverly recaptured by the poet and publisher Carlos Barral in his memoirs. He recalls, in grisly detail, the repressive, puritanical nature of his

Jesuit education, blaming his family for abandoning him to those religious educators who were determined to rid him of any wayward ideas and completely destroy any semblance of a legitimate, healthy sexuality. Needless to say, Barral was quick to reject Catholicism and formal religion and his experience taught him also to question and reject authority. His 'generational revolt' found him adopting a vague anti-Francoism and, though desultory, a strong emotional attachment to the losing side in the civil war, a mythified image which initially provided him with an oppositional identity:

In our earliest political passions, ideas were not as important as the feeling of disgust, a strong, healthy repugnance, for the world they tried to impose upon us. The crassness of Fascist rhetoric and the mediocrity of its lies transformed us into irreconcilable enemies of that discredited power, of that order imposed by force; and the nostalgia for a Republic we had never known and about which we had never heard one objective judgement, turned us into pseudo-marxists or anarchists.[6]

It is not difficult to detect Barral's contempt for official propaganda and the cultural activities which underpinned it. Moreover, in his adoption of a position of cultural and moral superiority to the regime, we find once again the sort of cultural élitism and mandarinism which would permeate much of the oppositional intelligentsia's work in the 1950s. Indeed, the very youngsters who might well have formed the élite cadres of an official culture, had that been historically possible, ended up running the publication houses which promoted the cultural activities and products (novels, plays, poems, etc.) of the opposition.

Clearly, apart from the Falange and negative reactions to a Catholic education, there were also other factors involved in pushing the privileged youth of the winning side towards opposition views, among them the direct contact with 'the other Spain' which Juan Goytisolo has recorded so poignantly in his novels and memoirs. For example, Goytisolo reports: 'I was from a bourgeois family, I was brought up in a traditional way and I had absolutely no idea of the existence of suburbs, the working class or social problems.' The chance discovery of the *chabolas* [shanty towns] on the outskirts of Barcelona had a very powerful effect on the young Goytisolo: 'It both fascinated and horrified me. My disenchantment with the social class to which my family belonged, my political radicalization—the negative view of the regime which had allowed such a situation to arise—start from there. I was 22 years old at the time.'[7]

A further channel of dissent, which feeds into the above, though from a different social category, is that of those people from the lower middle-class and working-class families of the losing side, the resistance families, in which the parents pass on their anti-Francoism to their offspring. This sort of development would involve such writers as Juan García Hortelano, Alfonso Grosso, and José María Caballero Bonald, people who did have the chance of obtaining a university education and achieving a professional training. There are of course other writers in this category, the non-university, autodidact, working class who received their anti-Francoism within the family and social milieu, such as Antonio Ferres, Armando López Salinas, and Juan Marsé.

To sum up: the radical, opposition intelligentsia in Spain in the 1950s and beyond was largely led by the well-heeled, well-educated offspring of the upper middle classes of the winning side. This was not surprising. Given their massive defeat in the civil war, the sheer weight of the repression meted out in the 1940s, and the time needed to rebuild the working-class movement, Spain's proletariat was in no position to challenge the regime seriously until the 1960s. So, as Barral says, it was within the ranks of the victorious bourgeoisie, for whom Franco had won the war, that we find the first splits and defections, mainly arising from those too young to have been actively involved in the war and thus be affected by its political divisions. Here, I refer to the students of the late 1940s and early 1950s, the vanguard of intellectual and cultural dissent under Franco.

Clearly, for many youngsters, opposition student politics was a romantic, voluntaristic, and even frivolous affair and many would find it extremely difficult to resolve the contradictions between their class background and their radical politics. Also, the penalties for student dissent were as nothing compared to the punishment meted out to those clandestine opposition party workers and militants unfortunate enough to be arrested. Yet, it was the same bourgeois youth who organized the lectures, poetry readings, film clubs, discussions, conferences, etc. These were activities which were quite successfully (though quite subtly) appropriated by the real political opposition, especially the Communist Party, and channelled into a broad democratic opposition front against the regime. The effects and efficacy of the politics of the oppositional intelligentsia of the 1950s and 1960s are clearly relevant issues but ones which are beyond the scope of this essay.

Notes
1 See J. M. Castellet, 'La novela española quince años después (1942–1957)', *Cuadernos del Congreso por la Libertad de la Cultura*, 33 (1958), 48–52, and 'La joven novela española', *Sur* (1963), 48–54.
2 J. M. Martínez Cachero, *La novela española entre 1936 y 1980: historia de una aventura* (Madrid, 1985).
3 Cited in J. Rodríguez Puértolas, *Literatura fascista española*, vol. i (Madrid, 1986), 466.
4 Interviewed by S. Vilar in *Protagonistas de la España democrática* (Paris, 1969), 266.
5 D. Ridruejo, *Escrito en España* (Buenos Aires, 1962), 225.
6 C. Barral, *Años de penitencia* (Madrid, 1977), 17.
7 Cited in A. C. Isasi Angulo, 'La novelística de Juan Goytisolo (entrevista con el autor)', *Papeles de Son Armadans*, 75/226 (1975), 69–70.

Further reading
Blaye, E. de, *Franco and the Politics of Spain* (Harmondsworth, 1976).
Giner, S., 'Power, Freedom and Social Change in the Spanish University: 1939–1975', in P. Preston (ed.), *Spain in Crisis: The Evolution and Decline of the Franco Regime* (Hassocks, 1976), 183–211.
Jordan, B., *Writing and Politics in Franco's Spain* (London, 1990).
Lizcano, P., *La generación del 56: la universidad contra Franco* (Barcelona, 1981).

Mangini, S., *Rojos y rebeldes: la cultura de la disidencia durante el franquismo* (Barcelona, 1987).

Maravall, J. M., *Dictatorship and Political Dissent: Workers and Students in Franco's Spain* (London, 1978).

Riera, C., *La escuela de Barcelona* (Barcelona, 1988).

Section 2
Developmentalism, Mass Culture, and Consumerism 1960–1975

'With too much memory we cannot live', but
without remembrance we cannot live justly.
(Michael Newman, glossing a phrase
by Nietzsche)

Editors' introduction

The later part of the Franco period needs to be seen in the context of 1960s
affluence, consumerism, and cultural massification in the western world generally; and reactions against this in the form of 1960s youth protest, and the
radicalization of Vatican policy and development of liberation theology initiated
under Pope John XXIII. The fundamental shift in collective identities that took
place during this period represents a kind of 'normalization', in that the national
once more becomes inseparable from the international. It represents a 'normalization' also in the sense that the period sees the emergence of a new civil society;
but it must be remembered that this was still operating under the 'abnormal'
circumstances of enforced clandestinity, with periods of return—particularly in
the regime's last years—to hard-line repression. The rapid economic changes at
this time also produced massive enforced social dislocation in the name of a
'normalizing' modernization—particularly in the internal and overseas migration
underpinning the economic 'miracle' for which the rural and urban proletariat
paid so heavily. This dislocation would in its turn, however, contribute to Spain's
cultural *apertura* or liberalization.

This is the period when Spain makes the decisive transition from a predominantly rural, agrarian society to an urban, industrial nation: the Francoist project of
national unification is completed by the incorporation of all sectors of the population—albeit at differential rates—into a nationally integrated consumer-capitalist

economy: a process facilitated by the accompanying development of the modern mass media. This multi-speed transition produced a paradoxical mix of increased standardization and increased cultural diversification. The pleasures afforded by the new consumerism also encouraged a complex combination of conformism and new demands, the latter exacerbated by the evident contradiction between increased opportunities for material satisfaction at a time when intellectual and creative freedom was still denied. In particular, the development in this period of new youth cultures—especially around popular music—was the result of consumerist massification but nevertheless provided a channel through which demands for freedom of expression could be voiced. Consumerism's own momentum of ever-increasing material and political demands revealed the fallacy at the heart of the regime's game-plan: that things would replace ideas, thus leading to a 'post-ideological', conflict-free society.

Writers and artists responded to cultural massification by incorporating mass cultural forms into their work, in many cases opting simultaneously for a language of cultural allusion accessible only to an educated minority. Nevertheless, this language of allusion constructed the public as an agent actively engaged in the production of meaning, encouraging the development of independent, critical thinking. The role of opposition culture in this period was vital for paving the way to the transition to democracy, by encouraging pluralism and debate, and by connecting the present not only with the memory of previous progressive intellectual and artistic traditions but also with their contemporary, transformative potential. Culture—in this form of collective memory, at both popular and intellectual levels—was thus central to the construction of the future.

Adapting to Social Change

BORJA DE
RIQUER I
PERMANYER

ALICIA ALTED

FRANCES
LANNON

Social and Economic Change in a Climate of Political Immobilism

BORJA DE RIQUER I PERMANYER

The years between 1960 and 1975 were riddled with contradictions and contrasts. This period saw the most accelerated, deepseated social, economic, and cultural transformation in Spanish history—in stark contrast to the arthritic grip of the Franco dictatorship. In little more than fifteen years, Spain went from being a backward agrarian country on the periphery of international capitalism, to one which could be considered fully industrialized, with a strong service sector, fully integrated into the global economic system. However, this radical economic turnaround and social modernization should not be attributed to any inspired policy on the part of the dictatorship, but rather should be seen as the consequence of pressures and conditions at home and abroad, beyond the control of the Francoist authorities. The conjuncture with a period of unparalleled growth in the western world was the principal external factor, and to this should be added the pressure from and capacity of Spanish society to emerge from the isolation and underdevelopment brought about by the Franco regime's autarkic fantasy. This made the growth of the Spanish economy incoherent to the point of chaos, prone to sharp imbalances, tensions, and deficits.

And it was these tensions and inadequacies which created the conditions for the growth of new and significant mass movements, whose increasingly politicized action would undermine the regime's prestige and solidity, rendering its continuation inconceivable after Franco's death in 1975.

The economic development model 1960–1970

The inevitable starting-point for this discussion is the failure of the post-war economic policy of autarky. This produced a sharp fall in output and living standards for over a decade. It was not till 1953–8 that output and income levels returned to what they had been in 1935. This represented a disastrous hiatus lasting over twenty years.

Towards the end of the 1950s the Spanish economy was in an extremely precarious situation, with the state faced with bankruptcy as it remained unable to curb inflation (12 per cent in 1958), reduce its trade deficit, or attract foreign investment. The Stabilization Plan of 1959, introduced despite Franco's reservations, reflected the decision to opt for a market economy and to end government interference. Backed by the World Bank, the OECD, and the IMF, foreign and domestic trading was liberalized, a policy aimed at attracting foreign investment was implemented, and a more orthodox financial policy adopted—entailing a 50 per cent devaluation of the peseta—along with a programme for the development of public services.

Coinciding with the period of greatest capitalist growth, these economic decisions were a great success. Spain imported machinery, technology, raw materials, and energy resources on a massive scale, and was able to pay for these thanks to the foreign capital from tourism, remittances from Spaniards working abroad, and foreign investment. The industrializing impetus was remarkable, and it is from this point that we can speak in terms of a complete industrial cycle—one which was diversified and intense, involving the development of vital new sectors such as cars, household appliances, engineering, chemicals, pharmaceuticals, plastics, shipbuilding, and steel. The Spanish industrial sector in this period grew from 25 per cent to 40 per cent of the gross domestic product (GDP), rising in the 1970s to over 60 per cent of total exports.

The service sector underwent an even greater transformation, accounting for 48 per cent of the GDP. This was due largely to the tourist boom. The 6 million visitors in 1960 rose to 30 million in 1975, when they contributed $3,000 million to the Spanish economy. Along with tourism, property and construction were the principal growth sectors. This was due primarily to the phemonenon of *urbanización*—housing construction in the major cities—and to public works projects—reservoirs, motorways, etc. By the same token, the public sector experienced considerable growth as the state was obliged by glaring inadequacies to invest heavily in education, health, and social security. The number of workers in the public sector doubled, with the latter rising in just over ten years from 15 per

21 Cover of the satirical magazine *La Codorniz* (26 February 1961), sending up the new economic policy of fast-track modernization introduced by the 1959 Stabilization Plan. The technocrat (note his gangster-like colleague in the background) asks the shepherd: 'And what about you? What kind of working hours would suit you best, the ones you've got now or the American system?' As implied here, there was no place in the new industrialized economic order for large numbers of rural workers. The magazine's slogan (bottom right) 'The more daring magazine for the more intelligent reader' points to its role in testing the limits of censorship; it was frequently fined and banned.

cent of the GDP to over 25 per cent. The financial sphere also underwent a transformation, with a reduction in the number of banks, significant penetration of the industrial and service sectors, and the marked involvement of foreign capital.

The transformation of agriculture was as spectacular as that of industry and the service sector. Here, however, restructuring was accompanied by a notable reduction in the work-force. This fell from 42 per cent of the population in 1960 to 20 per cent in 1976, halving the rural population. The adoption of new eating habits and productivity requirements led to significant growth in animal husbandry, market-gardening, and the food industry (farming and fishing) in general. This involved a reduction in grain production, and brought about the concentration of farms in larger commercial units.

The result of these economic transformations can be summed up by four sets of statistics. Between 1960 and 1974 the average income per capita trebled, rising from $400 to $1,350 per annum. The GDP grew during the 1960s at an average of 7.5 per cent per annum, a rate surpassed only by Japan. Growth in industrial output in 1960–7 was the fastest in the world at 10.5 per cent per annum. And real industrial wages increased by 40 per cent in this period.

These factors represented a radical redistribution of the Spanish working population: the number working on the land fell by half, a reduction of 1,500,000; the industrial sector took on 300,000 more workers, while the tertiary (service) sector provided 1,500,000 new jobs in services, and 500,000 in the building trade.

However, this accelerated economic growth hid numerous weaknesses, while simultaneously being dependent on external factors and exacting a high social and ecological price. It also reflected the peculiar character of foreign capital entering Spain. This was not a 'colonial' penetration—where foreign capital and domestic capital remain separate. On the contrary, foreign investment was carried out in close association with the Spanish banking system, which benefited greatly. Foreign investment in the 1960s was considerable—accounting for 25 per cent of total investment—and was motivated by low Spanish labour costs (the result of the labour discipline imposed by the dictatorship), and by the rapid expansion of the domestic market. The end result was that large Spanish companies, established as well as new, passed into the hands of foreign and domestic bank-controlled capital. Hence by 1974, out of the 100 largest Spanish companies—comprising electrical companies, engineering, petro-chemicals, insurance, property, construction, etc.—Spanish banks had capital invested in 83, foreign interests in 28, the state itself in 20, and private investors in only 5.

Dependence on foreign investment in the Spanish development model was extremely high if the accompanying emigration of Spanish workers to other European economies is taken into account. (The danger of such a level of dependency was revealed in the economic crisis of 1974 when the variable nature of that foreign investment became clear.) This reliance on external conditions was also evident in the tourist industry. It was built on cheap package holidays—seasonal (summertime) and localized (coastal)—which were controlled by the big foreign tour operators.

To this we should add the economic imbalances brought about by the dictatorial nature of Francoism. It was politically impossible to carry out a rigorous and progressive tax reform to increase the financial resources of the state, as this would have aroused the anger of the upper classes. The implementation of a policy of agrarian reform involving any form of land redistribution was also out of the question given wholesale opposition from the large landowners. And finally, relaxation of labour and trade union legislation was ruled out by fear of a resurgence of the labour movement. So economic growth did materialize but it was largely conditioned by the limited financial capacity of the state, the limited internal dynamism of the agrarian sector, and the increasingly confrontational and politicized nature of labour relations.

Despite its Development Plans, the government had limited planning capacity and control over growth. Additionally, the absence of a genuine regional and urban policy, alongside the political impunity of many municipal authorities which pandered to dominant economic interests, led to large-scale speculation and substantial damage to the countryside and the environment in the large cities and tourist centres. To this should be added the class bias of government policy, which tended to underwrite those sectors of the economy which suffered substantial losses—coal-mining in Asturias, steel, transport, endangered banks, etc.—and to leave in private hands those which made profits.

A radical transformation of society

The greatest social phenomenon of these years which needs to be borne in mind was the increased mobility of the population. Between 1955 and 1975 6 million Spaniards—20 per cent of the population—moved province. Two million migrated to Madrid and 1,800,000 to Barcelona. (Moreover, it should be remembered that in that period nearly 1,500,000 Spaniards emigrated to Europe in search of work.) Consequently, there was rapid urban growth which saw the expansion of the established metropolitan centres—Madrid, Barcelona, Seville, Bilbao—and the emergence of new large cities—Zaragoza, Valladolid, Málaga, Corunna, Vigo, Pamplona, Vitoria, Las Palmas, etc. The number of cities with populations of over 100,000 rose from twenty in 1960 to forty in 1975.

The rapid rise in the urban population was accompanied by the growth of enormous dormitory suburbs, ghettos for the new arrivals. This highlighted the inadequacy not only of public housing provision but of every aspect of public services—education, sanitation, medical facilities, parks and gardens, sports facilities, etc. The public authorities almost immediately proved incapable of coping with the increased demands placed on them by the new city-dwellers. Substantial increased investment in education, for example, could not compensate for long-term underfunding; in 1960 there were still 3 million illiterates in Spain, 15 per cent of the population over the age of 8. In that same year, the shortfall of available class-room space across the country was estimated at 20 per cent, rising to 30 per cent in the larger cities. By 1975 education extended to virtually the whole population, with 90 per cent of those of school age covered by compulsory education, and the number of university students had quintupled since 1960. As regards health, despite the extension of obligatory health insurance to over 80 per cent of the population, there continued to be significant inadequacies: while the World Health Organization recommended a minimum of 10 hospital beds per 1,000 members of the public, in 1970 Spain could manage only 7, falling to 5 in the larger cities.

Generally speaking, although the formation of a more modern consumer society during these years meant the creation of genuine public services reaching the bulk of the population, these services were of low quality, cumbersome, inefficient, and often defective. Similarly, though the improvement in quality of life was substantial and widespread, there continued to be extreme inequality of income distribution between social classes. While the upper classes benefited from the lowest tax levels in Europe, the working class suffered extreme exploitation. In 1969, a worker in Spanish industry worked an average of 55 hours per week, compared to a European average of 44 hours, while earning just half the European average.

Perhaps the most progressive feature as regards income distribution was the impact on regional differences. These tended to diminish as a consequence of the migration of low-income groups towards zones where there was better-paid work. Hence, in 1960 the income differential per head between Spain's richest province, Vizcaya, and its poorest, Lugo, stood at 81 points—138 as compared to 57—taking the national average to be 100. By 1975, however, the richest province, now Madrid with 125, only stood 45 points above the poorest, Cáceres with 80. Income differentials had been reduced by almost half.

But the social transformation was qualitative as well as quantitative. As mentioned above, the Spanish countryside had changed dramatically. Through emigration and/or financial ruin, 60 per cent of small farmers and 70 per cent of day labourers disappeared from the land. A new urban bourgeoisie emerged closely linked to the world of new banking interests, the service sector (tourism, property, construction, etc.), and foreign capital. The greatest fortunes made in these years were amassed by figures such as Areces, with El Corte Inglés; Koplowitz, with Construcciones y Contratas; Banús, with Puerto Banús on the Costa del Sol; Barrié de la Maza, with Fenosa; Meliá, with hotels; Barreiros, with road haulage; or Ruiz Mateos, with banking and wine.

Similarly there emerged a new urban middle class made up of professionals and technicians with university qualifications, who acted as managers or qualified administrators in the financial and service sectors. In addition to this group, which also constituted a significant route of social advancement for the old middle classes, we should note the emergence of a new working class. This was made up of young people, largely of rural origin, with few professional qualifications and little trade union or political background, living in the dormitory suburbs of the large metropolitan areas and working in the new industries or the service sector.

Towards a consumer society and the making of a mass culture

Spain in the 1960s was quickly absorbed into consumer society. Purchases of consumer durables soared. The speed of this process is exemplified by the impact of television. Spanish Television did not begin broadcasting regularly until 1959, but by 1974 70 per cent of homes had a TV. The same year saw 85 per cent of households in possession of a washing-machine and a fridge. Car ownership rose even more rapidly. The SEAT factory in Barcelona, which turned out 30,000 saloon cars in 1960, produced over 360,000 by 1972. Spanish levels of car owner-ship rose from 500,000 (one car for every fifty-five inhabitants) in 1960, to over 3,300,000 (one for every nine) in 1974.

The kind of mass culture establishing itself in Spain in these years had several features distinguishing it from other European countries. The process of cultural massification was extremely rapid, highly superficial, and rife with contradictions caused by the country's peculiar political situation and by the substantial cultural shortfalls which existed. The spearhead of the phenomenon was television, popu-lar music, and film. Spain passed rapidly from high levels of functional illiteracy to TV saturation without passing through intermediate stages of cultural develop-ment. This contributed to low levels of book and newspaper reading, still notice-able today.

Television, despite the rigid political control to which it was subjected, turned itself into a genuine window onto the world, indirectly helping to break the stran-glehold of the cultural and informational 'autarky' enforced by the regime. Simi-larly, the youth culture of the 1960s had a startling impact on the rigid social world of Franco's Spain, where enthusiasm for the Beatles or Bob Dylan, or emerging Spanish protest singers, represented a more overt political statement than in democratic societies.

The worlds of books and film also came into conflict with the regime, in a more directly political way. The emergence of an innovative and politicized publishing sector surprised the Francoist authorities. The publishing boom in cheap paper-back editions not only made Spanish and Latin American new writing widely available; it also saw the emergence into the public domain of previously unthink-able works of social comment, history, politics, even translations of Karl Marx. This caught the regime's censors on the hop. Their cosmetic attempts at *aperturismo* (liberalization) were shown up as window-dressing. The most famous example of the regime's confusion and increasing tendency to become a laughing-stock was Buñuel's film *Viridiana*, which, after having been the official Spanish entry to the Cannes Film Festival, where it won an award, was banned in Spain.

Newspapers and other publications considered hostile to the regime were vigor-ously prosecuted despite the supposed softening of censorship under the dynamic

Minister of Tourism and Information, Manuel Fraga Iribarne (for example, the cases of the newspaper *Madrid* or the magazine *Triunfo*).

Changes in attitudes and behaviour

The economic, cultural, and social changes described above naturally created a new mood and what might be termed an increasingly alienated public opinion. This was seen particularly in the younger generation which had not lived through the civil war. This increasingly critical attitude was based on two fundamental principles: better information about world affairs and the decline of traditional religious values.

Greater public awareness of how democratic societies functioned revitalized democratic values to the detriment of traditional Francoist attitudes which identified democracy with civil war and communism. The new world situation, with the thawing of the Cold War, also led to a questioning of the unthinking anti-communism peddled by the dictatorship. The huge influence of the new mass media—television, cinema, and the press—and even the social impact of tourism helped end the news isolation imposed on Spaniards since 1939.

Possibly even more important was the profound crisis affecting the chief ideological bastion of Francoism, the Catholic Church. The iron moral grip which the Catholic Church had on Spaniards during the 1940s and 1950s, and its desire to justify and legitimize the dictatorship, lessened as a consequence of the *aggiornamento* undertaken by the Second Vatican Council and the wholesale transformation of Spanish society. The change in the younger generation's mentality and behaviour coincided with the severe internal crisis which Vatican II provoked in a Church which had spent nearly thirty years linked to the Franco dictatorship. The rupture between the pro-Franco and anti-Vatican II Church hierarchy and the rank-and-file priesthood was radical. According to a survey of Spanish clergy carried out in 1966, 80 per cent of priests under the age of 45 disapproved of the political stance of the episcopate and rated their leadership as extremely poor. It is not surprising that the seminaries soon emptied and attendance at Sunday mass fell drastically. In 1972 this stood at 24 per cent of the population, but in cities like Barcelona it was no higher than 8 per cent. By the end of the 1960s the Church, Francoism's principal instrument of legitimization, was immersed in an acute internal crisis, exacerbated by the Vatican's support for the reformers over hardline traditionalists.

These factors doubtless contributed to the development of a critical mood, which would eventually erode the legitimacy of the Franco system itself. The official political discourse of the regime, including the utterances of *aperturistas* such as López Rodó and Fraga Iribarne, who made much of the achievements of Francoism and the 'Spanish miracle', was always undermined by the statutory requirement to refer to the 'unalterable principles of the Movimiento', to justify the civil war, and to harp on about the 'crusade against communism'. This discourse was not only ineffective by the mid-1960s, it was counter-productive. While the government veered between nods at reform and knee-jerk appeal to the values and attitudes of the civil war, the new Spaniards were beginning to think of the civil war as something of the past. They were immune to the outdated Falangist rhetoric, and did not accept that the political choice was between 'Franco and communism'. Little by little, the powers of persuasion of the ultra-Catholic Opus Dei* technocrats, despite the dictatorship's much-vaunted 'efficiency', were enfeebled by their insistence that Spanish society was 'not ready' for democracy.

Official political immobilism persisted, despite campaigns attempting to project a more attractive image of the dictatorship. The political changes introduced in the 1960s were modest and revealed the regime's incapacity to reform itself politically from within without changing its whole character. Despite the claims to reform, the repressive nature of the system persisted, though with different legal instruments—in 1963 the Tribunal de Orden Público (civil court) replaced military jurisdiction. The ignominious campaign celebrating '25 years of Peace', organized by Fraga in 1964, coincided with the state execution, or judicial murder, of Julián Grimau. The referendum on the Organic State Law in December 1966 was shamelessly manipulated by the authorities, who engaged in all sorts of duplicity and coercion: one locality saw the electoral miracle of a vote in favour from 126 per cent of the electorate.

The states of emergency of January 1969 and December 1970, together with the serious disturbances following the Burgos trial of ETA members and violent police action against the emergent labour movement, clearly showed the Franco regime's continued use of repression. The authorities themselves were conscious of the fact that any substantial reform could lead to loss of political control and so constitute a threat to the regime. A clear example of the ceiling imposed on the reformist tendency was the Press Law of 1966 which broadened freedom of expression to such an extent that it led to Fraga Iribarne's fall as Minister of Information and his replacement by the hard-line Sánchez Bella (1969–73). The smallest concession led to demands for still greater freedom, for freedom of information and political pluralism and democratization, demands which the regime could not satisfy without changing beyond recognition. This explains why the Francoist authorities clung whole-heartedly to *continuismo*. When in June 1973 Admiral Carrero Blanco, the leading figure of anti-reformist orthodoxy, was named Prime Minister, he uttered a significant phrase: 'my programme can be summed up in one word, *continuar*.' After his death—assassinated by ETA in December 1973— the new Prime Minister, Arias Navarro, was unable to reverse the regime's loss of prestige and political weakness.

The points of conflict and political erosion of Francoism had increased over the years. In the mid-1960s the dictatorship showed itself increasingly incapable of coping with the new conflicts that were emerging, such as strike action—only to be expected in what was now an industrial society—or the demands for democracy on various fronts. In the course of the 1960s new social conflicts emerged, some as a result of the increased importance and social impact of the universities and the cultural sphere; others as a result of the emergent labour movement or the crisis of the Church, while the nationalist clamour from the Basque Country and Catalonia became ever louder. As these conflicts grew and spread further afield, Francoism seemed to the dominant social sectors to be losing its most characteristic and convincing features: its capacity to guarantee social order and general political control. On the contrary, there was a growing sense that it was the dictatorial nature of the Franco regime itself, its total immobilism, which deepened the social conflicts and politicized them further by denying them a legal outlet.

The role of the opposition in the crisis of the Franco regime

There has recently been a tendency among academics to diminish the role and scale of the new movements of opposition to the dictatorship. Historians such as Javier Tusell consider the anti-Francoist opposition to have had a token signifi-cance, never having represented a genuine alternative to the regime. According to this historian, Spanish society was all but politically inert under the dictatorship, and additionally the deep divisions within the opposition prevented it from having a decisive role in the final crisis of Francoism. There are even those, like Santos Juliá, who maintain that social and political unrest between 1960 and 1975 was relatively low because there was a widespread conviction that the dictatorship would disappear on Franco's death and so it was not necessary to struggle against it.

It seems to this writer to be undeniable that there was increasing mass oppo-sition and that its influence and activities grew. Though it is true that the oppo-sition did not succeed in toppling the regime, it did manage to weaken it politically to such an extent that its continued existence after Franco's death was unthink-able. The strength and growing presence of the opposition developed and ex-panded a democratic culture among a broad sector of society. That is, it created a constantly increasing popular demand for democracy. The activities of the op-position created severe tensions and problems for the Franco regime, accelerating its internal collapse and radicalizing its external tensions by politicizing conflict of every type. The labour movement succeeded in showing up the inadequacies of Francoist labour legislation and unmasking the official syndicates. The strength of the student movement—demanding democratic students' unions—revealed the utter incapacity of the Francoist authorities to engage in genuine reform. Neigh-bourhood associations led to denunciation of municipal authorities' involvement in property speculation. The press itself, despite rigid ministerial control, began to report the occasional corruption scandal, such as the MATESA affair, implicating members of the government.

This led to explosions of protest, unrest, and criticism, which rapidly became politicized in the absence of legal outlets through which they could be channelled, and the invariable recourse of the authorities to outright repression. This is not the place for detailed analysis of the scope and scale of the opposition movements, but some key features need stressing. These include the extent and visibility of the student movement in 1966–7 and its subsequent ideological radicalization in the wake of May 1968, an indication of opposition to the regime by a significant proportion of the children of the bourgeoisie. Of possibly even greater importance was the emergence of a new labour movement, based on wage claims and working conditions, built up and spearheaded by the Workers' Commissions (Comisiones Obreras*) in the wake of the destruction of the established pre-war workers' organizations (CNT* and UGT*). Despite Comisiones' limited presence (in the work-force taken as a whole), their dispersal, and the relatively spontaneous character of much strike action, the new labour movement won substantial concessions over pay and conditions in the early 1970s. the strikes at El Ferrol, Vigo, Bilbao, Barcelona (SEAT), Madrid, or the Lower Llobregat signalled the start of an ever larger and better-organized worker offensive.

Of similar importance was the simmering political and cultural unrest born of nationalist grievances in the Basque Country and Catalonia. National identity in these two regions became a force for political cohesion, consensus, and unity. The example of the Assemblea de Catalunya, set up in 1971 by almost fifty political, social, and cultural organizations, or the great movement of solidarity with ETA members in the dock during the Burgos trial (December 1970), came to show that demands for autonomy were a key political feature, generating a broad cross-class anti-Francoist consensus.

The radical nature of the Church's internal crisis, outlined above, provoked acute tensions, such as the dissolution by the Church hierarchy of the Juventud Obrera Católica [Young Catholic Workers] and the Hermandades Obreras de Acción Católica [Catholic Action Workers' Brotherhoods] between 1966 and 1968, in the face of evidence that it no longer exercised control over these grass-roots organizations, or the famous conflict over Añoveros, the Bishop of Bilbao, which almost provoked the severing of diplomatic relations between the Vatican and the Franco regime.

As one would expect, the range of conflict was largely conditioned by the internal renewal of the political opposition. Due to the effective disappearance of certain historic organizations (such as the CNT and the republican movement), and the weakness of others (such as the UGT and the PSOE*), the great surge of opposition in these years was the result of communist action (the PCE* and PSUC*) and, to a lesser extent, of a new independent socialism of a Christian hue (the Frente de Liberación Popular (FLP) and its Catalan counterpart, the Front Obrer de Catalunya (FOC)), and the Catalan and Basque nationalist movements. The political success of this new opposition lay in its understanding of the country's new social and political situation and its ability to adapt to it. In effect, this opposition was able to take advantage of the economic, social, and political tensions which arose from the transformations of the 1960s, mobilizing the new social movements and channelling them towards the formulation of democrat-ically oriented political proposals. This opposition's most obvious weak points were, perhaps, its simplistic analysis of the nature of the Franco regime itself, leading to exaggeration of possible internal contradictions between hard-line *ultra* sectors and the reformers, plus the fact that their vision of the end of Francoism—the notion that the strength of the masses would provoke the dictatorship's col-lapse, as had happened with the monarchy in 1931—was an illusion. Another weakness was the deep divisions within the opposition, brought about by the anti-communism of the more moderate sectors and by the absence of a shared alter-native programme. There was no agreement as to whether the historic republican institutions should be restored, or whether a new democratic constituent process should be set in motion, or even whether a democratic monarchy might be a possibility.

Despite these deficiencies and weaknesses, the activities of the political oppo-sition and mass movements significantly eroded the Franco regime, challenging its legitimacy and establishing a culture of democracy to such an extent that the continuation of the dictatorship was rendered untenable. The opposition's strength and activities forced both a negotiated political transition after 1975 and a clearly democratic eventual resolution. Hence, the credit for the peaceful transition from dictatorship to democracy should by no means be attributed to the Franco re-gime, as the historian Stanley Payne appears to imply when he states that Franco had foreseen and paved the way for the transition. Nor should it be seen as the result of the modernization of Spanish society, as if it were merely a question of economic determinism. The transition to democracy was fundamentally a conse-quence of internal social pressure, of an ever-increasing desire to emerge from the political eccentricity which the Francoist regime had imposed on the country. It was the tensions brought about by 'modernization without change' which created the wide popular consensus that Francoism had to die with Franco.

It might be useful to end this brief overview of the developments of the final years of Francoism with a glance at the legacy of the dictatorship in Spanish society. The chaotic, *ad hoc*, and dependent character of economic growth ended by rendering the effects of the world economic crisis of 1974 particularly severe in Spain. Inflation soared, reaching 22 per cent in 1977; unemployment was the highest in Europe at 21 per cent in 1982; foreign investment fell considerably at the same time as the Spaniards laid off in the factories of Europe flocked home-wards. Additionally, the nature of the 'Spanish miracle' caused substantial damage to the environment: the absence of legislation to restrict pollution or property development has irreversibly damaged the Spanish coastline and the major cities. Examples such as Benidorm or the outskirts of Barcelona have become textbook cases of the ravages of unfettered capitalism. Mention should also be made of the significant cultural and political deficit left by the Francoist years. The superficial and accelerated cultural integration of much of the population; the profound ignor-ance of Spaniards regarding the nature and origins of the country's cultural and linguistic diversity; the absence of a genuine democratic tradition of citizenship; the reliance on an overstrong state, responsible for everything and expected to solve everything: these are just some of the consequences which need to be considered.

Further reading
Arango, J., 'La modernización demográfica de la sociedad española', in J. Nadal, A. Carreras, and C. Sudrià, *La economía española en el siglo XX: una perspectiva histórica* (Barcelona, 1987).
Balfour, S., *Dictatorship, Workers and the City: Labour in Greater Barcelona since 1939* (Oxford, 1989).
Carr, R., and Fusi, J. P., *Spain: Dictatorship to Democracy* (London, 1979).
Carreras, A., 'La industria: atraso y modernización', in J. Nadal *et al.*, *La economía española en el siglo XX* (Barcelona, 1987).
Casanova, J., 'Modernization and Democratization: Reflections on Spain's Transition to Democracy', *Social History*, 50/4 (1983).
Fontana, J. (ed.), *España bajo el franquismo* (Barcelona, 1986).
García Delgado, J. L., and Segura, J., *Reformismo y crisis económica: la herencia de la dictadura* (Madrid, 1977).
Heine, H., *La oposición política al franquismo* (Barcelona, 1983).
Juliá, S., 'Transiciones a la democracia en la España del siglo XX', *Sistema*, 84 (1988).
Maravall, J. M., *Dictatorship and Political Dissent* (London, 1978).
Molinero, C., and Ysàs, P., *El règim franquista: feixisme, modernització i consens* (Vic, 1992).
Payne, S., *The Franco Regime, 1936–1975* (Wisconsin, 1987).
Preston, P., *The Triumph of Democracy in Spain* (London, 1986).
Tusell, J., *La dictadura de Franco* (Madrid, 1988).
Vázquez Montalbán, M., *La penetración americana en España* (Madrid, 1974).

Educational Policy in a Changing Society

ALICIA ALTED

At the end of the 1950s, the Spanish economy was in a critical situation that made it necessary to seek foreign aid. Its arrival produced the policy changes reflected in the Stabilization Plan of July 1959, designed to 'modernize' society and 'rationalize' the public sector. This triggered a process of rapid industrial growth that would radically change the structure of Spanish society, as a result of mass migration from the countryside matched by a corresponding population explosion in the outlying areas of the big cities, a shift from the agricultural to the industrial and service sectors, and the increasing influence of other life-styles with the growth of tourism and emigration of the surplus work-force to the more developed countries of western Europe. The improved living standards resulting from these changes led to demands for goods and services that could not be catered for by existing state provision.

This state of affairs created constant tensions aggravated by the underlying premisses of 'developmentalism'. For the technocrats linked to Opus Dei,* economic growth meant social modernization and prosperity (development) as the best way of guaranteeing the regime's survival and continuity, whose political principles they never questioned. But economic growth and social development were only possible if the education system adjusted to the requirements of this double process. This was a basic point made by the international bodies who gave the Spanish government aid in the form of credits and advisers: specifically, Unesco, the OECD, and the World Bank. As a result, in 1961 Spain joined the General Mediterranean Plan set up by the OECD to promote educational reform in six Mediterranean countries. Additionally, the World Bank report *Spain's Economic Development*, which appeared in August 1962, stressed the fact that an economy cannot function without a skilled labour force and laid down educational guidelines for the government to follow. The ongoing recommendations of these bodies were incorporated into the Economic and Social Development Plans of 1964–7, 1968–71, and 1972–5.

This period saw four successive Ministers of Education. The ministerial reshuffle of July 1962 brought in Manuel Lora Tamayo, closely linked to the group of scientists working under José Albareda at the Consejo Superior de Investigaciones Científicas* (CSIC). His concern for science and research led to the Ministry's renaming as the Ministry of Education and Science. Endemic student unrest led to Lora Tamayo's resignation and replacement, in April 1968, by José Luis Villar Palasí, responsible for drafting the 1970 General Education Law (LGE). In June 1973 he was followed by Julio Rodríguez, who put the brakes on the reform process initiated by the LGE. A few months later, in January 1974, the job was taken over by Cruz Martínez Esteruelas, who previously had opposed the tax reforms proposed in the LGE.

In line with the recommendations of the international aid bodies, Lora Tamayo's team took a series of measures to meet changing socio-economic circumstances, though he held back from the thorough overhaul of the education system demanded by social needs. Obviously, educational development depended on the budget available. Increases here were considerable and sustained, to the extent that in 1972 for the first time expenditure on education outstripped that for the military; nevertheless, it was inadequate and extremely low compared to that of other European countries. During his time at the Ministry, Lora Tamayo had to confront a number of problems at the various educational levels, and his response was uneven. One of his biggest successes was the Literacy Camapaign started in 1963 to tackle two of the major problems holding back the Spanish economy: the high level of illiteracy and the majority of the working population's relative or total lack of professional qualifications. The same objectives lay behind the priority given to primary education: in 1964 this was made compulsory to the age of 14 (at 10, students had the choice of continuing primary studies and leaving school at 14 with a Certificate of Primary Studies, or opting for the *bachillerato**). To make this possible, in 1965 primary education was made free of charge, with qualifications for private schools; the *bachillerato superior* (equivalent of British A levels) was also made compulsory as a qualification for teacher training.

There was also an attempt to increase school provision, but measures here were overtaken by internal migration: schools were built in traditionally neglected areas like Andalusia, Extremadura, and the two Castiles, progressively abandoned by workers settling in the outskirts of the industrial conurbations of Catalonia, the Basque Country, or Madrid where there was a demand for school places the Ministry could or would not satisfy. This problem would be dealt with only under Villar Palasí. In 1975 school provision was more or less adequate in terms of the number of school places, but the state of buildings, provision of materials and of school transport, and class sizes were still far from satisfactory.

Numbers of students at secondary level also outstripped all expectations. More state schools were built catering for the elementary *bachillerato* than institutes dealing with the *bachillerato superior*. To cope with the demand, evening classes and distance education by radio and television were introduced. But neither the curriculum nor the number and training of teachers were adequate, leading to a high failure rate. One important change was the move to a single first level of secondary education with the abolition in 1967 of the elementary technical *bachillerato*, but there was no attempt to end the discrimination resulting from the streaming of students from the age of 10 into either the *bachillerato* or continuing primary studies.

Concern with the technical skills required by economic and social development had led Jesús Rubio García-Mina during his time at the Ministry to take a series of measures governing the regulation of technical colleges (Escuelas Técnicas de Enseñanza Superior), including a more even geographical distribution and the abolition of restricted entrance. This latter measure produced disquiet in professional quarters since engineers had traditionally been regarded as members of a privileged social élite. These reforms culminated in the 1964 Law reorganizing technical education, which merged the Escuelas Técnicas with the Technical Universities.

In the university sector, the influence of Opus Dei was evident in the policies adopted by Lora Tamayo's team towards those universities run by the Church. The long-standing Pontifical Seminary of Comillas at Santander, under Jesuit control, had in 1904 been granted the status of Pontifical University. The Pontifical University of Salamanca was set up in 1940, and its courses validated by the state in 1963; in that same year, degree-level courses at the Jesuit University of Deusto were also granted official recognition. Opus Dei's direct involvement in the university system was through the University of Navarre, the Barcelona Business School (Instituto de Estudios Superiores de la Empresa), and the Hispano-American University at La Rábida. This was apart from its running of a large number of student halls of residence, and its influence on research through the CSIC. The University of Navarre, first created as a college of education in 1952, had been recognized as a Church university in 1960 and its courses validated in 1962, allowing Opus to achieve one of its most cherished dreams: its own educational centre for the formation of professional élites. This same role was fulfilled by the Barcelona

Business School, set up in 1958 as a subsidiary of the University of Navarre; through its contacts with Harvard Business School, it became the nexus between Opus and the world of business, finance, and top management.

The favouring of Church universities set many Falangist students against the government and was one of many factors fuelling university student protest throughout the 1960s. This protest movement can be understood only in the wider context of current social restructuring. Increased prosperity and consumerism changed universities from élite institutions oriented mainly towards the humanities, to mass institutions geared to science and technology, with the additional growth of the social sciences. International events also left their political mark, particularly the decolonization process in various parts of the globe, the Vietnam War, the Cuban Revolution, Latin American guerrilla warfare, or communist China. Mao Tse-tung, Che Guevara, and Fidel Castro became the leaders of the so-called 'New Left'.

The student protest movement falls into two clearly distinct phases. The first, lasting till 1965, was focused on opposition to the Falangist Spanish University Student Union (SEU) and demands for an independent, representative student union. It is worth noting that university students were the only social group successfully to bring down one of the regime's political institutions during its lifetime, with the government's abolition of the SEU in April 1965 and creation of the Professional Student Associations (APE). This was complemented by the University Education Law which proposed 'radical' changes to the university system but in practice met with criticism from its inception. The second phase, lasting till the early 1970s, was in its early stages marked by open student opposition to government attempts to impose the APE, and by the creation of alternative free unions, the Democratic Student Unions (SDE). These permitted the development of an increasingly radicalized political culture, putting students at the forefront of opposition both to the regime and to the United States' imposition of neo-capitalism. This attitude of revolt and revolutionary protest, which erupted most spectacularly in the May 1968 events in Paris, led in Spain to serious confrontations between the police and student extremists. The government responded with a return to hard-line measures. In the early 1970s the student movement lost its impetus, having 'peaked ideologically' without having achieved a revolutionary transformation of society. Protest was now taken up by non-tenured lecturers (*profesores no numerarios*).

On his appointment to the Ministry, Villar Palasí realized immediately that the 'university problem' was the result of serious defects in the education system, requiring a complete overhaul of the kind attempted by Moyano's Education Law of 1857. This attitude represented a notable advance, as did his first step of publishing, in February 1969, the White Book on education, which provided a detailed, realistic analysis of the current situation, proposing solutions. The aim was to sensitize the public and the media to the need for reform, but the problem was that there were as yet no channels allowing them to participate in the political decision-making process. To get his reforms through, Villar Palasí had to rely on credits from the World Bank and advice from Unesco and international experts, some of whom he brought into his team, as was the case with Ricardo Díez Hochleitner. So, in August 1970, the Law on General Education and Financing of Educational Reform (LGE) entered the statute books.

This Law was a continuation of efforts since the late 1950s to reform Spanish society 'from above', in the best regenerationist tradition. Despite its first article stating that it was inspired by 'the Christian way of life and national traditions and culture', it adopted an innovative, modernizing, technocratic approach far removed from the regime's ideological principles, which had compromised earlier attempts at reform. One of its principal achievements was the institution of a single educational tier, the EGB or General Basic Education, from the age of 6 through to 14. This was compulsory and free, and replaced both the previous primary education and the elementary *bachillerato*, ending the above-mentioned discrimination against underprivileged students and establishing the basis for an equal educational opportunities policy. On completing the EGB, students would go on to either Level 1 Professional Formation (FP1) or the Single Polyvalent *Bachillerato* (BUP).

Professional Formation came under special scrutiny. The LGE defined it not as an educational level but as a post-education option which could be entered at various levels: Level 1 after EGB, Level 2 after BUP, and Level 3 after university first-degree level. Its stated objective was to give students the necessary skills 'to exercise the profession of their choice while continuing their overall education'. This formulation produced many practical problems owing to the mismatch between the excessively 'academic' subjects prescribed and the requirements of the labour market, and also because FP1 became the only option for less-gifted students who failed to get the school certificate required to go on to the BUP. This effectively turned it into what it was supposed not to be: an inferior educational tier parallel to the BUP. Level 2 Professional Formation was more successful in practice; Level 3 barely got off the ground.

Taken as a whole the LGE, despite its sound aims and proposals, met with serious problems in practice because of inadequate financial provision (the necessary tax reforms were never tackled) and an over-theoretical approach and lack of precision in certain areas. Its imposition 'from above' meant that the various social sectors involved in education had no direct input into its drafting, which in turn meant that it lacked the public support or pressure to make its application a success. The new regime that took over after Franco's death thus inherited a series of unresolved problems: serious infrastructural deficiencies, a shortage of teachers and insufficiently high standards of teacher training, the inferior social status of Professional Formation, unsatisfied demands for 'democratization' on the part of the various educational bodies, and, in the area of relations between the state and private education, the perennial issue of educational freedom: that staple of the Church's battle with the state over education.

Further reading

Carreras, J. J., and **Ruiz Carnicer, M. A.** (eds.), *La universidad española bajo el régimen de Franco (1939–1975)* (Zaragoza, 1991).

La educación en España: bases para una política educativa (Libro Blanco) (Madrid, 1969).

Foessa, *Informes sociológicos sobre la situación de España* (Madrid, 1966 and 1970).

Lerena, C., *Escuela, ideología y clases sociales en España* (Barcelona, 1986).

—— (ed.), *Educación y sociología en España (selección de textos)* (Madrid, 1987).

Navarro Sandalinas, R., *La enseñanza primaria durante el franquismo (1936–1975)* (Barcelona, 1990).

Sociedad, cultura y educación: homenaje a Carlos Lerena (Madrid, 1991).

Vilanova, M., *Atlas de la evolución del analfabetismo en España, de 1887 a 1981* (Madrid, 1992).

Catholicism and Social Change

FRANCES LANNON

In the 1960s and 1970s, the Catholic Church in Spain became, to the astonishment of many observers, a force for political change. In response to changes in Spanish society and new trends in Catholic theology, many priests, lay leaders, and eventually bishops publicly distanced themselves from the Franco regime. Yet, for many years after the Spanish civil war, Church and regime had been inseparable. Franco had rescued the Church from one of the most sustained and violent persecutions of modern times, and it was grateful. Moreover, he gave it a position of privilege and security greater than it had known for generations.

Catholicism was recognized as the established religion of the Spanish state, and alternatives were not tolerated. State payment of clerical stipends was restored, together with state subvention of cathedrals and parish churches. Education and censorship were based on Catholic values. The ideological purging of Spanish society was undertaken methodically and ruthlessly by the new regime, not least among the ranks of university lecturers and schoolteachers. Thousands of teachers were found to be ideologically unsound and were dismissed, transferred, or suspended from their posts, often with the active involvement of local priests who were asked to report on their reliability. At the same time, the trade unions and political parties of the left were abolished, and their activists punished.

The Church found itself given a position of ideological hegemony, untroubled by its erstwhile enemies—the free-thinkers, atheists, laicizers, and modernizers, whose various plans for the cultural, social, and political transformation of the country had finally been defeated, along with the Republican army, on the battlefields of the civil war. These enemies had been killed, imprisoned, forced into exile, or effectively silenced. The Church itself, after the terrible massacres and destruction of the war, was filled with a missionary determination to make Spain once more a truly Catholic country. It was an extraordinary opportunity, and one greeted with energy and even exultation by large numbers of priests, religious, and laity. New recruits flooded into the seminaries and novitiates, devotional associations of the laity flourished, and catechism classes, missions, and processions once more claimed Spain for Catholicism.

This reclamation was, none the less, a difficult task. It was unclear how a Church that had been so loud in the support of one side in a bitter civil war could successfully preach the good news to its recent enemies and opponents in Spanish society. The nuns who ran the women's prisons and reformatories in the Franco regime were unlikely to win the hearts of their charges. The same was true of the parish clergy in poor areas of town and country, where the Church was often regarded as a class enemy actively engaged in repression. The Church had to find a way—if such a thing were possible—of speaking to the Spanish population without immediately being heard by great swathes of it as the oppressive voice of the dictatorship.

Nor were Church–state relations devoid of difficulty—even in the extraordinary circumstances the Spanish civil war had created. Archbishop Gomá of Toledo, who had done so much as an international propagandist for Franco during the conflict, was shocked when Franco's government banned his pastoral letter *Lessons of the War and the Duties of Peace* at the end of the war because of its criticism of unlimited state power and its vision of the Church as a monitor of the government's religious orthodoxy. The Church was favoured by the regime but would not be allowed to usurp it and create a theocracy in Spain. However, it is going much too far to suggest, as some historians have recently done, that 'the Catholics' formed only a small and distinctive component of Francoist politics, struggling for place and influence. There were indeed some politicians in the early Franco regime who were members of a powerful Catholic lay association, the Propagandists (ACNP). In the 1950s members of another Catholic association, the Opus Dei,* also rose to political prominence. But it is inaccurate to regard the other political factions as somehow not Catholic. The entire regime, from Franco downwards, was committed to an authoritarian political model in which Church and state stood together against all subversive alternatives. The undoubted fact that there were policy disagreements within the narrow range of conservative, authoritarian options should not obscure the massive solidarity against everything that had been defeated in the war. In a very real sense the politics of Catholics, and of the Church, was Francoism. In the years immediately after the war it could not be otherwise.

There were, of course, politicians who were 'Catholic' in the sense that they were particularly identified with the promotion of Catholic values. One example is José Ibáñez Martín, Education Minister 1939–51, who was determined to reconstruct state education in a Catholic mode; another is Alberto Martín Artajo, who resigned the directorship of Catholic Action in 1945 to become Foreign Minister, and was centrally concerned with the negotiations leading to the 1953 Concordat between the Spanish state and the Vatican. There were also many Catholic politicians who would have preferred some other regime to Franco's military dictatorship, whether an Alfonsist or Carlist* monarchy, or a peculiarly Spanish fascism, or—at least by the 1960s, and increasingly in the early 1970s—some more democratic system. None of this, however, alters the fact that, for a very long period after the end of the war, Catholic politics meant in practice Francoism. Equally, the Franco regime could rely until the 1960s on the close relations with the Catholic Church formalized in the 1953 Concordat which, for example, gave the dictator an important and direct part in the choice of bishops for Spanish dioceses. Culturally and politically the dictatorship and the Church were interdependent.

The Church preached religious renewal while simultaneously identifying the Franco regime as the true current embodiment of Spanish Catholic traditions, in a potent combination that some historians and disaffected theologians later called 'National-Catholicism'. It was to be many years before a few individuals and small groups within the Church, then some bishops, then eventually, in the very last stages of the Franco regime, a majority of the hierarchy, argued openly that such close identification with the dictatorship was more of a hindrance than a help to the Church's mission in a changing Spanish society.

Many different influences were responsible for this gradual disengagement. Some of these were elements within Spanish Catholicism that had been largely silenced by the civil war and Franco's victory, but who eventually re-emerged, such as Basque and Catalan nationalists, and Christian democrats. Others were created by the very success of the Church's post-war initiatives among urban and rural workers, when Catholic workers' associations came to criticize the Franco regime for disregarding their rights and demands. Others again were Catholic intellectuals and politicians who increasingly saw both National-Catholicism and the dictatorship as inadequate responses to the social and economic changes of the 1950s and 1960s, when Spain experienced rapid industrialization, the onset of consumerism, and an influx of foreign tourists, all of which opened Spain to wider European influences. Finally, the Vatican itself, and the bishops and theologians from all over the world that Pope John XXIII summoned to the Second Vatican Council in 1962, demolished the theological and ecclesiastical underpinnings of National-Catholicism and state confessionalism, as they plotted a new, more liberal, and more tolerant course for the Church. This radical change left Catholic authoritarians in Spain, including Franco himself, disconcerted and suddenly displaced from the orthodox centre they were sure they had always occupied.

This final influence is the easiest to trace, because it was clearly expressed in documents published by the Vatican. First came two notable encyclical letters from Pope John XXIII, his *Mater et magistra* (1961), on social justice, and *Pacem in terris* (1963) on human rights. These letters were widely distributed, read, and studied in Spain as elsewhere. Between them they depicted Pope John's vision of a just and Christian society, and it bore little resemblance to Franco's Spain. In this new model, human rights such as the right of association and freedom of worship were scrupulously respected, wealth was redistributed down the social scale by progressive taxation and social insurance, and citizens participated in the affairs of the state. The clear implication was that participatory democracy was closer to the new papal ideal than Franco's dictatorship. Bishops of the whole Church assembled in the Vatican Council (1962–5) repeated the same message in different forms, as they agreed a series of documents that defended human rights, demanded religious liberty, and assumed political pluralism. There is no doubt that these documents undermined in theory the Franco regime's claims to be, from a Catholic point of view, a desirable polity. The regime reluctantly incorporated the new line on religious liberty into its own legislation in 1967, but it could not embrace genuine pluralism without ceasing to be what it was, a dictatorship. At the same time, it became possible for Catholic and clerical critics of the regime to express their criticism, embarrassingly, in quotations from unassailable Council documents and papal letters. This possibility was exploited by Basque nationalists, by trade unionists, and even by bishops. Finally, in January 1973, the Spanish bishops voted to publish a long statement, *The Church and the Political Community*, which for the first time formally committed them to political neutrality, independence of the state, and respect for political pluralism. The Church–regime symbiosis of National-Catholicism was shattered.

If it is easy to trace the destabilizing influence of the 1960s Vatican on the Franco state, it is more difficult, but equally essential, to follow the varied developments within Spanish Catholicism that contributed to the same end result. These in turn require an awareness of wider social change. The development of Catholic Action was a particularly interesting phenomenon that sprang as much from the special circumstances of the post-war economy and society as from religious devotion. Lay Catholic associations of all kinds flourished in the 1940s and 1950s, but by the late 1940s two vigorous associations rooted in the Spanish working class were combining spirituality with labour activism in a new way that distanced them from the more traditional piety of most of Catholic Action. Juventud Obrera Católica (JOC) [Young Catholic Workers], and Hermandades Obreras de Acción Católica (HOAC) [Catholic Action Workers' Brotherhoods], aimed respectively at young workers and at workers in general, defended the position of employees in industry, criticized employers' policies, produced publications that displeased both employers and government, and assumed many of the roles usually associated with independent trade unions, which were banned in Franco's Spain. JOC and HOAC had full-time officials, training sessions, and confidence. Their outspokenness, and suspected willingness to support illegal strikes, led them into open conflict with both the government and the Church authorities by the late 1950s and throughout the 1960s. The religious motivation of many of their leaders was undoubted, but so too was the legal umbrella that JOC and HOAC provided for some participants whose primary interest was in labour relations or even politics.

It is instructive to note that these associations were vitiated in the mid- to late 1960s, not directly by government repression, nor even by the emergence then of semi-tolerated unions, the Comisiones Obreras,* but by the determination of the Spanish bishops to rein in their 'secular' activities, and bring them organizationally under closer episcopal control. A generation of lay activists burned itself out, along with many of the young priests who were their chaplains, in a conflict that was full of danger signals for Spanish Catholicism. The ability of JOC and HOAC to engage with the real problems of workers had been their great strength, but it was difficult for the Church to contain them within its own religious sphere. But then, outside the special circumstances of a dictatorship that made ordinary labour unions illegal, why should workers need or wish to defend their position through religious associations? This was the dilemma that the Church was to face more generally in the late Franco regime. Some Catholics—both clerical and lay—put added hope in the Church as it tentatively responded to grass-roots pressures and moved away little by little from the National-Catholic model, opening up new channels of change and protest. Yet this movement itself pitted Catholic against Catholic and, in the longer run, fundamental political change after Franco's death would remove the need and opportunity for Church associations to function as the defenders of civil and labour rights.

A similar pattern was displayed in other areas. Three hundred and thirty-nine priests in the Basque Country wrote a letter of protest to the four bishops in Basque sees in 1960, listing state infractions of human rights in the area, and calling on the bishops to protest. This letter and all the others that followed in defence of Basque language and culture, and in protest at repression and torture, revealed and created as many tensions within the Church as between Church and state. And while some priests in the name of Catholic faith shielded members of ETA from police action even after 1968, when ETA embarked on terrorism, others were appalled at what they saw as the intrumentalization of the Church for political ends. The dilemma was inescapable. The clergy could not ignore the hostility of many of their parishioners to the dictatorship, yet giving this hostility ecclesiastical leadership—with many a quotation from *Pacem in terris* on the rights of ethnic minorities—created other problems of clerical identity, and eventually left many priests alienated from the Church as well as the state by the time of Franco's death.

Parallel but not quite such dramatic conflicts were very evident in Catalonia, where, for example, 400 priests and religious had written a letter to their bishops in 1964, arguing that the suppression of Catalan culture by the confessional Catholic state endangered the faith of Catalan Catholics. In both Catalonia and the Basque provinces, the determination of priests to express the economic and cultural, as well as religious, aspirations of their parishioners led to confrontation with the police, arrests, and imprisonments. These extraordinary, highly publicized events, including television coverage of priests in Barcelona being beaten up by the police in 1966, chipped away at the Catholic legitimacy of the Franco state. But they also—not least by exhaustion and attrition—eventually left many priests, religious, and lay activists outside the Church altogether.

The cultural, economic, and political demands of various sections of Spanish society in the 1950s and 1960s could hardly fail to find Catholic expression. This was true not just of industrial workers and Basque and Catalan autonomists, but

22 Cover of the satirical magazine *El Hermano Lobo* (1 December 1973), commenting on the political radicalization of sectors of the Catholic Church in the later stages of the Franco regime. The text is a retake of the children's bedtime prayer 'There are four little corners to my bed, four little angels guard them for me'; here the 'four little angels' have become 'four sergeants'. Like the slogan of *La Codorniz* (see Plate 21), this magazine's subtitle—'Satirical Weekly within the Limits of the Possible'—reminds readers of the existence of censorship (which could not be mentioned directly) and of the need to read between the lines.

also of students' and intellectuals' demands for greater freedom in the universities, and the insistence by entrepreneurs, writers, and politicians on opening up contacts with the rest of western Europe. In many respects, the Church had become by the late 1960s a modernizing influence. Its younger lay leaders, priests, religious, and bishops had struggled to respond to grass-roots desires for civic liberty and material security, and in effect to champion these against the state, Catholic though it was. The Church's contribution to the peaceful disappearance of the Franco regime was enormous.

This modernizing revolution, however, took a heavy toll on the Church itself. It ultimately redirected a good deal of Catholic energy and commitment away from religious reconstruction—which had been the project of the post-war years—to civic and political reconstruction. Paradoxically, the crisis and end of the Franco regime, which the Church helped bring about, also marked the end of the Church's period of extraordinarily dominant influence in Spanish society. The two had proved strangely interdependent at the end, as at the beginning. As democracy was established and a new agenda emerged in Spain, dominated by Europeanization, capitalist growth, cultural experimentation, and the transformation of women's roles and family structure, Catholicism found itself just one influence among many in the new pluralism.

Further reading
Alvarez Bolado, A., *El experimento del nacional-catolicismo 1939–1975* (Madrid, 1976).
Botti, A., *Cielo y dinero: el nacionalcatolicismo en España (1881–1975)* (Madrid, 1992).
Cárcel Ortí, V. (ed.), *Historia de la iglesia en España*, vol. v (Madrid, 1979).
Cooper, N., 'The Church: From Crusade to Christianity', in P. Preston (ed.), *Spain in Crisis* (Hassocks, 1976), 48–81.
Hermet, G., *Les Catholiques dans l'Espagne franquiste*, 2 vols. (Paris, 1980–1).
Lannon, F., *Privilege, Persecution, and Prophecy: The Catholic Church in Spain 1875–1975* (Oxford, 1987).
Payne, S. G., *Spanish Catholicism: An Historical Overview* (Madison, 1984).
Ruiz Rico, J. J., *El papel político de la iglesia católica en la España de Franco* (Madrid, 1977).

Opposition Culture

ELÍAS DÍAZ

CATHERINE
BOYLE

The Left and the Legacy of Francoism:
Political Culture in Opposition and Transition

ELÍAS DÍAZ

Viewed with hindsight, the close links between opposition
culture under Franco and the progressive culture of the democratic transition are evident, as this essay will demonstrate.
The contours of opposition culture were more clearly defined,
unity being provided by a common enemy: the dictatorship.
After its disappearance, the progressive culture of the democratic transition emphasized instead a plurality of viewpoints
and the need for self-criticism. Nevertheless the two cultures
remain inextricably linked, and elements of each blend in the
intellectual currents of the new democratic Spain—some of
these being highly critical of the new pluralism's limitations.

   To have some understanding of what has transpired politically, socially, and culturally in Spain since Franco's death, it
is crucial to appreciate the slow, painstaking conquest of democratic space over the long years of dictatorship. Partly, this
space was conquered during the social struggles of the 1960s.
Socio-economic transformation gave rise to new collective identities: a new labour movement was at the core of a new civil
society. It was in this civil society, growing within professional
and neighbourhood associations, student, Church, and women's
organizations, that the struggle to open up democratic spaces

took place. In these spaces, democratic habits and culture were acquired. But alongside this material struggle, crucial intellectual work of a deeply political nature was also under way (as it had been in some shape or form since 1939) in the fields of the creative arts, philosophy, and social science—with the similar aim of preserving and consolidating liberal, rationalist thought and the pluralist currents vital to the rebirth of a democratic society.[1]

This story of economic and social transformation in the 1960s and of the ensuing social conflict between the dictatorship and the new, demanding, upwardly mobile technical and professional middle classes on the one hand, and the labour and student movements on the other, plus the intellectual/cultural task of recovering a liberal tradition crushed with Republican defeat in 1939, is, in effect, the story of the long-term gestation of Spain's democratic transition. In highlighting the key role of social conflict and—particularly important here—cultural dissidence, one must not ignore other factors crucial to the achievement of a peaceful, negotiated transition, bringing the first free elections of June 1977 and the democratic Constitution of 1978. The role of the monarchy, the evolution of the Catholic Church, and the support of Europe and the USA were clearly important. For nothing about the transition was preordained and the new democratic Spain-in-waiting needed all the help it could get. What I want to stress here, however, is that an equally essential though not exclusive pre-condition of the democratic transition was a *cultural* transition which, understood in its widest sense, had in fact begun many years before 1975–6. This cultural transition was wholly dependent on the cultural process created by the resistance and opposition currents found in a variety of forms and milieux in Francoist Spain, and on the political demands they subsequently formulated.[2]

Indeed one can trace the cultural transition right back to the clandestine culture of resistance sustained, often at terrible personal cost, by the defeated opposition through the dictatorship's darkest years in the 1940s. In the 1950s a new opposition culture—its democratic colours somewhat muted—emerged from within the ranks of the privileged, as the sons and daughters of prominent Nationalist families turned their backs on a would-be totalitarian regime which they found politically appalling and culturally false, in the sense that it represented a negation of ethical, humanist civic values. Their opposition culminated in the well-known events of February 1956 at Madrid University. These multiple currents of political, cultural, and ethical resistance—great and small—kept alive an idea of freedom and, however imperfectly, a corpus of liberal, rationalist, humanist traditions which the victors had sought to obliterate in April 1939. (As historians know, nothing is ever totally obliterated.) If we do not remember this legacy and its impact through into the 1970s, the transition is simply incomprehensible or we can succumb to the neo-Francoist apologia which erroneously writes the anti-Franco opposition out of the script by claiming the democratic transition as its own political sleight of hand, organized from above by regime *apparatchiks* (Opus Dei* technocrats) as Franco's last 'bequest to the nation'.[3]

The excavation of the long process of democratic cultural renewal which made the transition possible thus involves a fundamental recuperation of historical memory. This will be one of the main themes of this essay, which outlines the principal features of progressive opposition culture and tries to show how this legacy has informed the political culture of the democratic transition.

The recovery of an intellectual space

From the dictatorship's start, one of the main goals of intellectual activity was to recreate a space—however minimal or marginal—in which individual freedom could literally be reclaimed. In the immediate post-war period, those involved in any kind of dissent ran considerable risks: one has only to remember the vast number of political prisoners in the prisons and labour camps. But those risks were necessary, not only for seasoned political opponents but for artists and intellectuals of all kinds. Nor was this a narrowly professional demand in the sense that, without intellectual freedom, production of any kind must be impaired. Rather, a free space beyond the regime's reach was a kind of ethical necessity for all those whose critical consciousness distanced them from the ruling order. Of course real freedom has always been won rather than bestowed by those in power, whether the state in question is a liberal democracy or a dictatorship. Francoism, precisely because of its stultifying cultural and political dogmatism, sharpened the critical edge of new, emergent currents of thought and generated significant cultural and political forms of resistance among writers, poets, philosophers, and scientists. These were more visible and numerous as time went on, the first major wave appearing in the 1950s as a group of politically engaged intellectuals sought indirect routes to a measure of freedom of expression and creative pluralism denied by official censorship (including the authorial self-censorship this induced).[4]

The transition, of course, brought both formal democratic liberties and freedom of expression. But as one battle was won, so new political and cultural conditions produced different dangers. In the 1980s and 1990s, an ultra-conservative neo liberalism has prevailed throughout Europe and beyond, which defines all 'freedom' in terms of the market and the extent to which state (i.e. public sector) expenditure can be reduced. In practice, this rhetoric of liberty means slashing the tax bills of the wealthiest at the expense of the poorest, most powerless members of society. Against this rampant and profoundly anti-social individualism, the new project of a left alliance—in Spain as elsewhere—must be to champion an alternative positive 'freedom', defined by policies that shift the balance of social and economic power, improving the lot of the majority.

The reconstruction of 'reason'

Opposition culture during the dictatorship was importantly engaged in what one could term the reconstruction of 'reason' (i.e. rational discourse/thought). The war had ravaged Spain not only materially but also culturally and even spiritually. Indeed the very construction of Francoist state power was dependent on the degradation and systematic daily humiliation of the defeated population. Against the massive material distress of the 1940s, the power of abstract 'reason' could bring little direct relief. But it was cherished within small, private liberated spaces, at a time when the whole of public life was swamped by an archaizing tide. The major components of this fifteenth-century Catholic revivalism were a rabid anti-intellectualism, and the concomitant privileging of all kinds of superstitious myths, dogmas, and irrationalism. In reality, the Manichaean moral categories of the fifteenth and sixteenth centuries were resurrected under triumphalist Francoism to legitimize its treatment of the defeated.

Later, in the 1960s, this reconstructed, questing 'reason' would again provide a critique of the technocrats' supposedly 'post-ideological', politically 'neutral' model of economic development (still a prevalent fallacy), exposing its profoundly élitist, conservative agenda.

It is useful at this stage to outline the different stages of opposition activity under the dictatorship. The first phase (1939–45) was the bleakest, with the destruction and diaspora (cultural-intellectual as well as physical) following Republican defeat and the imposition of the victors' triumphalist-totalitarian-imperialist discourse. Then, following Axis defeat in the Second World War, a second phase (1945–51) saw the briefly isolated regime make self-interested attempts (the first of several) to reclaim some of the 'safer' cultural currents and intellectual figures of liberal Spain, with an eye to hastening incorporation into the western bloc—inevitable given the logic of the Cold War.

This minimal 'cultural thaw' was extended during 1951–6 by the policies of Ruiz Giménez as Minister of Education. The 1956 student rebellion halted this timid liberalization from above. But grass-roots opposition culture was growing broader and stronger. Moreover, it was difficult for a regime attempting to make itself more acceptable to the western nations by erecting a cosmetic façade of 'organic democracy' to repress such oppositional manifestations with its previous 'totalitarian' thoroughness. The years 1956–62 saw the intensification of this confrontation between the representatives of a liberal, pluralist opposition culture (writers and scholars) and the political class, now composed of a strange mix of Catholic traditionalists and Opus Dei technocrats. But the latter, though advocates of economic liberalization, were as hostile as the traditionalists to any form of cultural pluralism or political liberalization.

The rapid economic growth of 1962–9 is undeniable, but so too is the less palatable reality that underlay the bonanza: the structural weakness of the Spanish economy; the high social cost of the boom, disproportionately paid for by the poorest; and the lack of freedom (except for capital), which seriously impaired the quality of life. In this context, the regime's attempt to gain institutional legitimacy behind a façade of 'constitutional legality' (the so-called 'Estado de Derecho') was a deeply cynical exercise.[5] But Francoism was to end as it began: badly. The sixth and final stage (1969–75) saw the regime collapsing under its own contradictions, triggered by an economic crisis both national and international. Under threat, the regime reverted in Pavlovian fashion to hard-line repression. But it could not reverse the progress towards political and cultural freedom that had been pains-takingly made by its opponents in the course of the 1960s. At that time, the regime no doubt appeared to have the advantage. But in fact it could not with-stand the pressure of a civil society growing more forceful, conscious, and insist-ent in its demands for democratic reform: constitutional guarantees, trade union rights, regional autonomy, and a recognition of linguistic and cultural pluralism. The Franco regime was ultimately defeated by a civil society which owed its health and strength to the ideas and practices nurtured by the political and cultural left.

The recuperation of historical memory: pre-civil war culture

One of the left's most important tasks in consolidating democracy has been to continue the recovery of progressive, critical political and cultural currents from pre-civil war Spain—a process begun under the dictatorship. In re-establishing the continuity between these liberal or social democratic cultures and opposition culture under Franco, the left has been instrumental in the crucial recovery of historical memory. In fact the regime, in its selective, limited engagement with the products and figures of pre-civil war liberal culture, was also an actor in this recovery process, which consequently has two strands.

For the regime's purposes, some elements of Spanish liberal culture were, of course, more readily recuperable than others. Joaquín Costa and his disciples could easily be recycled. The 'Generation of 1898' was much more heterodox and criti-cal, and thus problematic. Only opposition culture reclaimed it in its entirety. Ortega and his disciples also had to wait a while, and the 'Generations of 1914 and 1927' even longer. Most problematic of all was anything connected with that Francoist bugbear: the progressive, secularist Institución Libre de Enseñanza.* This had to wait till well into the 1960s. A genuinely open debate on the Second Republic and the civil war was only possible after Franco's death. Thus it was only during the transition and under democracy that Spain saw the full recovery of the best of progressive liberal or Catholic thought (Azaña and Bergamín respectively); the same holds for the socialist tradition of Besteiro, de los Ríos, Prieto, Araquistain, Negrín, and Largo Caballero, as well as for other currents on the left, whether libertarian or marxist.

With the return of democracy, it was evident that much of what had seemed irretrievably lost with defeat in 1939 had in fact been successfully recovered, slowly and painstakingly, in the search during the dictatorship for 'marks of cultural identity' (to use a common expression). Today we must ensure that this recupera-tion process continues without any slackening of rigorous, critical inquiry. In contemporary liberal democratic Spain, there is a perceptible lack of academic interest in areas of the recent past still desperately in need of research and critical analysis. Of course, after the highly charged atmosphere of political inquiry during the transition years, such a reaction is natural. But there is also a certain official reluctance, even political opportunism, operating here which seeks to promote a collective amnesia (*desmemoria*) *vis-à-vis* the recent past. At best, this stems from the well-intentioned if mistaken idea that 'consensus' depends on the obliteration from memory of past divisions, seen as irreducible. At worst, it is a politically interested denial of the past. Either way, the repression of the past is no basis on which to build a healthy, participatory democracy.

The recuperation of historical memory: the intelligentsia in exile

As we have seen, this recovery process involved establishing a dialogue across time with past traditions. But it also, equally crucially, required a dialogue in space: between the culture of the 'interior' (inside Franco's Spain) and the intellectual community in exile, putting an end to the stupidly sectarian, wasteful, Manichaean myth of 'la anti-España' propagated by the regime. But this dialogue was problematized by the distorting mirror of exile itself. If the routes and products of exile had to be learned by those in Spain, an even greater challenge awaited the exiles (though many, the most significant, only returned after Franco's death). For they came back not to the mythological, ahistorical Spain that lives in the exile's memory but to a real country they did not know. Since the 1950s, however, intellectuals in Spain had been increasingly influenced by the 'lost culture' of exile, as the exiled novelist Max Aub termed it. Of course, a full recuperation was only possible in democratic Spain. While some things had been definitively lost, the European and Latin American cultural traditions which the exiles brought back with them had an invaluable renovating effect.

Intellectual and cultural integration into Europe

Isolation, more than anything else, defines the impact of Francoism. Surmounting it, intellectual isolation in particular, was always the chief goal of those in Spain who espoused democratic, pluralist values and attempted to set up an essential dialogue with the outside world, Europe in particular. Things became relatively easier with the country's opening up in the 1960s, as tourists flocked to Spain and economic migrants and students left for northern Europe and America. But we should remember that until the very end of the dictatorship (and in some cases beyond) there was still rigorous censorship and many topics, authors, and works remained taboo.

In democratic Spain today, affected like other nations by the globalization of communications, the cultural dilemmas are the exact reverse. Our own identity risks being swamped by the excessive influx of cultural goods imported by US or other multinational purveyors of dominant western, capitalist culture. Even so, it is better to seek positive ways to control this tide than to take refuge in the promotion of a spurious, folkloric localism or anachronistic *casticista** pride. That way only cultural stagnation lies.

Of course, in signalling this danger one is not denigrating the entirely positive recovery in democratic Spain of cultural, linguistic, and political plurality evidenced in the regional autonomy movements. But even here there is a danger worth pointing out. As with sterile cultural localism, so too political diversity can end up as (at best) parochialism dressed in mystical rhetoric and (at worst) violent, xenophobic populism. It is to be hoped that a plural Spain—like a plural, united Europe—can provide a sane alternative to the false solutions currently so prominent: the glorification of tribal, even racial, loyalties that have made us blind to the value of collective solidarity and so degraded our common humanity.

From transition to democracy

In the first years of the transition, there occurred a process of popular political education and a consequent notable expansion of political culture. As the population had greater access to more information, they participated in discussions previously the preserve of minorities. There was a flood of enthusiasm for knowing and discussing a wide variety of political issues (e.g. the relative merits of different electoral systems, the differences between regionalism and federalism, various constitutional problems) which was bound to lose momentum. This is the source of the often misrepresented *desencanto** (political disillusionment/disappointment) of Spaniards after the transition. For good or ill—often the latter —many issues came to be discussed and resolved mainly by legal experts and professional politicians, apart from such exceptional moments as the attempted coup of 23 February 1981, the NATO referendum of 12 March 1986, more recently the general strike of 14 December 1988, and to a certain extent at election times (1977, 1979, 1982, 1986, 1989, 1993) when there has been a return to the wide public discussion of key political issues which a healthy democratic political culture should always foster.

Among the political issues and debates of current concern in what is a situation of significant flux in Spain, the following might be singled out: the evolution of constitutional debate and conflicting interpretations of the Constitution's application; nationalisms, autonomies, and the central state (including the impact of terrorism on the latter's functioning, abuses of power, etc.); the subordination of the army and state security forces to the constitutional authority of the elected government; civil rights (including those of conscientious objectors); economic problems, unemployment, the emergence of a new urban underclass, acute social inequalities, and the need for a new 'social contract' to remedy the worst of these; the negative impact of multinational capital (e.g. economic parasitism, unaccountability to democratically elected authorities); market ideology, economic individualism, and extreme competition fostered by the 'new' right; the impact of new technologies; neglect of the Third World (especially attempts through new, strict, racist immigration controls to create a 'Fortress Europe', holding out the possibility of a new apartheid); the politics of the post-Cold War era, the collapse of the USSR and the end of 'real socialism' in the east, and the corresponding renewal of the left with the creation of new democratic socialist projects; the future of Europe as a political, social, and cultural unit; the influence on civil society of 'new' social movements (ecology, feminism, pacifism) and their enhancement of participatory, representative democracy.

Many of these debates are common to other European nations in the 1980s and 1990s, while some are of special relevance to continuing democratic consolidation in Spain. Most vital of all in this respect is the ongoing recovery of that historical memory with which this essay has been concerned, as the only rational basis for a sober, critical assessment of Spain's achievements to date—and of what remains still to be achieved.

Notes
1 E. Díaz, *Pensamiento español en la era de Franco (1939–1975)* (Madrid, 1983).
2 R. Morodo, *Por una sociedad democrática y progresista* (Madrid, 1982), 13.
3 For a critique of this and other perspectives on the transition, see E. Díaz, *La transición a la democracia: claves ideológicas (1976–1986)* (Madrid, 1987) and *Ética contra política: los intelectuales y el poder* (Madrid, 1990).
4 See Díaz, *Pensamiento español en la era de Franco (1939–1975)*.
5 For a critique of this, see E. Díaz, *Estado de Derecho y sociedad democrática* (Madrid, 1966, new edn. 1991).

Further reading
Work on the transition had, in a sense, already begun during the dictatorship. On the one hand there was scholarly material which specifically exposed the regime's spurious attempts at democratic legitimation (e.g. critiques of 'organic democracy', the Francoist 'constitutional order' [Estado de Derecho], and the so-called 'social state'). In addition, many of the general ideological and institutional questions concerning the transition from dictatorship to democracy were debated (some of this work was also comparative). See:

Aranguren, J. L. L., *Ética y política* (Madrid, 1963).
Tierno Galván, E., *Humanismo y sociedad* (Barcelona, 1964).
—— *Escritos (1950–1960)* (Madrid, 1972).

Journals
Boletín Informativo de Derecho Político
Cuadernos para el Diálogo
Triunfo

On the transition's completion, more detailed, empirical studies (albeit of variable quality) appeared: for example, studies of individual political parties and the various political tendencies within them, or of ideological and electoral programmes and party leaders. See:

Esteban, J. de, and **López Guerra, L.**, *Los partidos políticos en la España actual* (Barcelona, 1982).
Juliá, S., García Delgado, J. L., Serrano Sanz, J. M., and **Mainer, J. C.**, *Transición y democracia*, vol. x of *Historia de España*, ed. M. Tuñón de Lara (Barcelona, 1991).
Morodo, R., *La transición política* (Madrid 1984, 2nd rev. edn. 1993).
Tezanos, J. F., Cotarelo, R., and **Blas, A. de** (eds.), *La transición democrática española* (Madrid, 1989).

Works in English
Carr, R., and **Fusi, J. P.**, *Spain: Dictatorship to Democracy* (London, 1979).
Giner, S., and **Sevilla, E.**, 'From Despotism to Parliamentarism: Class Domination and Political Order in the Spanish State', in R. Scase (ed.), *The State in Western Europe* (London, 1980).
Heywood, P., *Spain's Next Five Years: A Political Risk Analysis* (London, 1991).
Maravall, J. M., *The Transition to Democracy in Spain* (London, 1982).
Preston, P., *The Triumph of Democracy in Spain* (London, 1986).

The Politics of Popular Music: On the Dynamics of New Song

CATHERINE BOYLE

The Catalan singer-songwriter Lluís Llach performed for the first time in Britain at the 1993 Edinburgh Festival. Mishaps beset the concert: leads for instruments were missing, the sound was dodgy, and things finally came to a halt when the pedals of the grand piano disengaged themselves. As technicians besieged the stage, Lluís Llach set up in a corner and sang the song that has come to be his anthem: 'L'estaca' [The Stake]. With this song he won over the audience. Yet, in essence, audience and performer were at cross purposes: the audience saw a singer bravely weathering adverse circumstances; Lluís Llach was finding force in one of the key songs of resistance to Franco, whose words and music denoted the belonging to a living community of resistance. 'L'estaca' tells of a young man asking his grandfather how people tied to a stake can free themselves if they are to walk. The grandfather's answer is one of communal resistance: 'If I pull hard this way | and you pull hard that | the stake will surely fall | and we will all be free.' This moment illustrates the complex dynamics operating when artistic expression crosses cultures, allowing divergence in performance and reception to find a creative meeting-point. Put simply: music of resistance, written for specific purposes, can have an artistic, expressive life beyond the limits of the context in which it was written.

Lluís Llach is one of the leading protagonists of the Catalan New Song (*nova cançó*) movement. *Nova cançó* emerged in Catalonia in the early 1960s around a group of writers and artists who called themselves Els Setze Jutges [The Sixteen Judges]. The members of the group met regularly to exchange poetry and music, initially in small, exclusive meetings, but gradually opening up to present their work all over Catalonia. Primary among the aims of the group was the rescuing of Catalan language and culture, silenced under the Franco regime in the enforcement of a unitarian state. Alongside this was the desire to create an expression in song that would be a real alternative to commercialized (mostly anglophone) music, and whose themes would engage with the social and political realities of the time. Raimon, the most important early protagonist of *nova cançó*, talked of it as being something more than merely singing in Catalan, saying that it was about personal and collective dignity and identity, and about active participation in the life of the country.

In their recitals Els Setze Jutges appeared as individual artists, each member presenting his or her own work, and so even within the group there was a sense of diversity. The idea of diversity is extremely important, since *nova cançó* sought to bely the image of a monolithic culture presented by the regime. And from the outset *nova cançó* went beyond Catalonia and Spain to join an international community of artists, each rooted in a specific culture, vindicating that culture yet reaching across geographic frontiers to artists and peoples in similar positions elsewhere. So, Els Setze Jutges looked to France, particularly to singers such as Georges Brassens and Léo Ferré, while in Latin America the seeds were being sown for the new song movement there with the pioneering work of Violeta Parra, Atahualpa Yupanqui, Víctor Jara, among others. This highlights a crucial point: that *nova cançó* was not a movement in artistic and cultural isolation, even though it was marginalized within Spain.

The presence of New Song in Catalonia grew throughout the 1960s, largely through the immense popular appeal of Raimon. In 1963 he won the Mediterranean Song Festival with a song in Catalan, which was unprecedented. But like so many other seeming advances in the history of *nova cançó*, this was a first and a last. In subsequent years there was a blocking of Catalan songs in the selection process for international festivals. In the media, television appearances would give a glimpse of an opening but they were generally not repeated, and songs were pronounced 'no radiables' (unfit for radio transmission) for fear of popularizing a potential medium of protest. Artists were required to present lists of songs before performances, forbidden to appear in certain places, or indeed in Spain at all. And censorship was at times so arbitrary that the apparently ludicrous situation of the audience singing songs the artist was prohibited from performing became a common feature of concerts.

The movement reached a crisis point in 1968 when Joan Manuel Serrat was chosen to represent Spain in the European Song Contest. His records had been selling all over Spain, and his decision to sing in Castilian as well as Catalan was to give him access to television and radio. He looked to be an ideal candidate for the Eurovision, but stepped down when he was not allowed to sing in Catalan, and the Contest was won that year by the singer Massiel, singing in Castilian the song Serrat had refused to sing.

The Eurovision Song Contest may be looked upon with derision in Britain, but the Serrat incident is key to an understanding of what was happening in New Song at the end of the 1960s. Serrat had begun to take the dubious road of bilingualism, he had sought and won an audience inside Spain beyond Catalonia. This road of bilingualism and commercialization came to be the crux of a series of disputes and splits within the movement. If the 'establishment', as they called the dominant culture, feared the popularization of *nova cançó*, then so did the purists in the movement. For how does such a movement gain new and wider audiences through media controlled by the dominant culture without betraying its most basic principles?

23 Concert by the Catalan protest singer Lluís Llach in Barcelona, January 1976 (two months after Franco's death, at a time when the future evolution of the regime was still unclear). The audience continues the traditional gesture of holding up lighted candles and cigarette-lighters in the dark, as a symbol of hope, resistance, and solidarity. Llach was the only singer of the *nova cançó* to survive the transition to democracy, singing in Castilian as well as Catalan and opting for a more commercial style, with lyrics focused on individual sentiment rather than collective issues

In its maturity, *nova cançó* had entered the ground of debates that had plagued other performing arts, notably theatre. The well-rehearsed arguments of 'possibilism' in the theatre—the question of what it is possible to say on stage while still dissenting and showing a committed opposition to the regime—were to be part of the dynamics of New Song in its last moments. The movement as such came to an end in the late 1960s with the disintegration of Els Setze Jutges. But individual singers sang on, with continuing prohibitions—like that of Lluís Llach, banned for five years from performing in Spain—until after Franco's death.

Nova cançó was not only an act of artistic expression, it was an act of community. Between audience and performer coded languages of communication, of shared unease, and of social and political preoccupations were created: encoded languages, accessible to those with a will to understand, which, in the best spirit of 'possibilism', tested the bounds of what it was possible to say, when and where. During concerts the audience would light candles, matches, cigarette lighters in a simple symbol of hope and anticipation of the end of the long period of dictatorship, which found an easy and communicable symbol in darkness.

Yet this is a language whose codes are fluid. Talking of his music now Lluís Llach says that young people are still seeking freedoms of different types, within their own restraints, prohibitions, and possibilities, but always pulling at the stake to see if it can be toppled and its captives allowed to walk free. That is the lasting quality of New Song, be it in Spain or, for example, in Latin America where, during the authoritarian regimes of the 1970s and 1980s, singers such as the Argentine Mercedes Sosa could sing the songs of Chile's Violeta Parra or Víctor Jara knowing that the audience would join in, word perfect, and would light up the venues in the same way as in Spain. In these audiences too, a rich interplay is enacted, using by now truly international codes.

While *nova cançó* suffered as a result of the political and creative dynamics of the song, the 1960s and especially the 1970s saw the growing popularity in Spain of Latin American New Song (*nueva canción*), building on the foundations laid by *nova cançó*. It produced a new communication with an audience now ready to become part of an international community of song whose initial primary linking theme was solidarity: with the Cuban revolution, with those suffering under the new Latin American dictatorships, particularly of the Southern Cone countries, and with those struggling to win the most basic human rights. Among others, audiences shared the musical inventiveness and lyricism of Cuba's *Nueva Trova* through Silvio Rodríguez, and the dramatic and imposing style of Chilean *nueva canción* was introduced by the groups Quilapayún and Inti Illimani, in exile after the military coup of 1973. Political circumstances meant that the boundaries crossed artistically by New Song were being tested by geographic proximity, and the result has been an enriching of the medium. *Nova cançó* was the result of a need for expression, and has evolved to give a voice to successive expressive needs. The performance of 'L'estaca' in Edinburgh proved that the spirit is in the song and that at its strongest the song will survive.

Artistic Experiment and Diversification

JO LABANYI

EMMA DENT
COAD

PETER EVANS

Literary Experiment and Cultural Cannibalization

JO LABANYI

By the end of the 1950s, writers were starting to have doubts about the ethics and the efficacy of what Muñoz Suay, the Communist Party delegate responsible with Semprún for channelling cultural dissidence, ingenuously called 'Operation Realism'. Guilty consciences about the right of bourgeois intellectuals to speak for the working classes were temporarily assuaged in the late 1950s and early 1960s by what was called 'objectivism': an intensification of realism in which the narrator disappeared to let events 'speak for themselves'. As theorized by Castellet (*La hora del lector*, 1957) and Juan Goytisolo (*Problemas de la novela*, 1959), 'objectivism' was an incompatible amalgam of Italian neo-realism and the 'rejection of depth' of the French New Novel. The objectivist novels published 1959–62 (notably those of García Hortelano, one of the few writers from a working-class background) replaced earlier working-class characters with the new rich, recognizing the reality of incipient economic growth and abandoning the pretence of writing for a working-class public; even the earlier social realist novels had rarely sold over 2,000 copies, mostly bought by like-minded dissident intellectuals. Such small print-runs signalled the failure of the realist novel's aim of replacing a shackled press; the greater latitude given to the press after Fraga's appointment to the Ministry of Information and Tourism in 1962 made it increasingly pointless for fiction to simulate reportage. It has been noted that, in the second half of the Franco regime, the leading dissidents were no longer creative writers but journalists.

This sense of redundancy was compounded in the 1960s by various crises of the left. Under Carrillo, the Spanish Communist Party opted for a policy of 'national reconciliation' on the assumption that the regime would collapse under the weight of its own contradictions. In 1964 Claudín and Semprún (both close to literary circles) were expelled from the Party for insisting that, far from collapsing, the regime would be buoyed by the new economic growth. Juan Goytisolo (*El furgón de cola*) has described intellectuals' sense of futility as they realized the country was progressing without their intervention. In 1968, the Soviet invasion of Czechoslovakia plus the growing stalinization of Cuba made political alignments increasingly less clear-cut (many writers and publishers had visited Cuba in the 1960s, but severed links when the novelist Padilla was put on show trial in 1971 and information emerged about labour camps for homosexuals). In 1966, the International Association for Cultural Freedom, whose Spanish Committee under Ridruejo ran a dissident magazine and had organized a conference on realism in Madrid in 1963, was shown to be CIA funded. The 1963 conference on realism marked the beginning of the end, with Spanish writers and critics ridiculed by visiting foreign writers for adhering to an outdated realism, yet attacked by the Communist Party for aestheticism.

Also crucial was the publication in Spain, from 1962, of the new Latin American novel: publishers leapt at the chance to break into the international market, deserting the realist cause. The Latin American novel's international success offered a model for Spanish writers aware of their enforced provincialism, reminding them that revolutionary content needed to be matched by radical form.

In the mid 1960s many Spanish novelists (even conservatives like Delibes and mavericks like Cela) fell silent for some years, re-emerging between 1966 and 1969 with a dramatically changed experimental form of writing. In most writers, political comment became more overt in response to Fraga's abolition of advance censorship; but novelists' and critics' increasing insistence that the writer's duty was to revolutionize language implied that no other revolution was possible; indeed, it became fashionable to praise writers for the suicidal act of 'destroying language'. Influential here was the current French vogue for structuralism, which argued that texts have no direct link with the world but generate meaning through their internal organization plus their relationship to other texts. The experimental novels produced in the late 1960s and early 1970s are immensely demanding, with their lack of conventional punctuation, interminable monologues verging on solipsism, and intertextual references accessible to the few, as if writers were venting their anger at not reaching the masses by trying to alienate readers altogether.

However, the best of these experimental novels are on a par with their Latin American counterparts. The crisis of the left created an awareness of political contradiction that expressed itself through irony; a consequence was the rediscovery of humour, largely lost since the civil war. The recuperation of the European modernist tradition led to an obsession with time which—as in modernism—manifested itself in a tendency to incorporate history into the transcendental realm of myth, while at the same time demythifying the past through memory: Benet's *Volverás a Región* (1967), Cela's *San Camilo 1936* (1969), and Marsé's *Si te dicen que caí* (1973) return to the civil war and its aftermath, viewed through the modernist prism of multiple perspective. *San Camilo* and *Si te dicen*, plus Juan Goytisolo's *Reivindicación del conde don Julián* (1970) and *Juan sin tierra* (1975), also show a decidedly postmodernist interest in mass culture: Hollywood in Marsé and Goytisolo, and 1930s Spanish radio, press, and advertising in Cela. Curiously, the two writers who concentrate on transnational cultural models use them to empower their characters or narrators, while Cela's collage of Republican mass culture imprisons his characters in its mediocrity.

The paradox of a highly aestheticized form of writing which derives its inspiration from mass culture is the salient feature of the new generation of writers that emerged around 1970: the date of Castellet's seminal anthology *Nueve novísimos poetas españoles*. From around 1972, Barral also started to promote the New Spanish Novel, commissioning manuscripts from young arts graduates most of whom had lived and taught abroad (Molina Foix, Azúa, and Marías succeeded each other as *lectores* at Oxford University); Azúa and Fernández de Castro worked on Barral's editorial staff. Azúa and Molina Foix were also among Castellet's *novísimos*, whose other members were similarly young, cosmopolitan, and the product of 1960s university expansion. In short, a highly educated literary in-group, cultivatedly iconoclastic in their rejection of their elders' concern with national politics and in their rejection of seriousness for style. The influence of the new consumerism is obvious: in the way these new writers were marketed; in their cult of youth, novelty, and fashion; and in their appeal to technologically reproduced forms of mass culture, largely of US origin: Hollywood, but also pop music, comics, and poster art (a key novelist here, slightly pre-dating the New Novelists, is Terenci Moix writing in Catalan). The new camp sensibility (Sontag replaced Lukács as the guru) may have been escapist but it was making some important points. First, that contemporary Spain was part of the developed world, and foreign critics should stop expecting Spanish writers to conform to the Eurocentric model of the politically worthy 'Third World writer' (Barral criticized French publishers for taking up Spanish social realism as a kind of 'revolutionary indigenism'). And second (here the influence of May 1968 and Marcuse is evident), that Francoist authoritarianism had imposed itself even on its opponents by normalizing sexual puritanism: in early 1970s Spain, pop—and even advertising—offered a vision of sexual gratification that could be read as a sign both of late capitalist manipulation of consumer demand and of long denied individual self-expression. This duality is expressed in the new writing by the mixture of deconstructive ironic posturing and increasingly open celebration of sexual plurality: in poetry, Villena (not included in Castellet's anthology); in fiction (apart from the older Juan Goytisolo), Terenci and Ana María Moix, and Molina Foix. Interestingly, the young women novelists who emerge at this time eschew the appeal to mass culture: in this sense, Ana María Moix's novels are very different from her pop-art poetry.

In fact, the cult of pop went together with an array of references to high cultural forms (mostly foreign), in a deliberately incongruous intertextual collage. In poetry Pound, Yeats, Céline, Hölderlin, Cavafy, Ibn Quzman, Beardsley, Watteau, Sade, Virgil, Ovid join hands with Bob Dylan, Marilyn Monroe, Pink Floyd, Carnaby St., tango, jazz, Walt Disney, Dashiell Hammett, the Lone Ranger. Novelists shift between pastiche of mass cultural forms and abstruse intellectual discourse (exemplified by the trajectory of the young Javier Marías): influence of the French New Novel plus that of Benet, whom the New Novelists turned into a somewhat reluctant mentor, led to the provisional triumph of the latter trend; the former triumphed in the long run as Anglo-Saxon cultural models became dominant.

In a sense, this indiscriminate cultural cannibalization allowed the *novísimos* and the New Novelists to succeed where their more political literary elders had failed in breaking down the barrier between popular and élite culture. But in no way can they be called popular writers: their collage of intertextual references becomes a metafictional game in which texts refer only to other texts (the art of the epigraph is taken to its limits). Mass culture is turned into a collector's item: the word 'museum' recurs in the title of several poems and novels. The references to pop culture are part of the same exoticist exercise in cultural appropriation as the coincident cult of the Gothic, the oriental, and the Byzantine (also referred to as 'Alexandrianism' or 'Venetianism'). Poets celebrate an élitist concept of the artist as marginalized initiate, while novelists cultivate depersonalized interior monologue, reflecting what Soldevila sees as the double alienation of a generation denied social participation but sceptical about opposition politics (Barral criticized the older cultural opposition, himself included, for degenerating after 1968 into a *gauche divine*). However, it could be argued that the young writers of the early 1970s fulfilled the necessary role of cultural mediators (several were translators), putting Spain in touch with that part of world culture, past and present, that had been declared taboo or sanitized, whether by the regime or by an opposition ruled by duty rather than pleasure. The cultural indigestion resulting from this cannibalization process mirrors the incongruities of late Francoism, which subjected young intellectuals to an antiquated university curriculum (giving them their impressive command of classical references) while exposing them to growing US cultural hegemony. Such incongruities were compounded by the opposition's insistence on seriousness at a time when the regime was increasingly promoting consumerist fun. In Castellet's 1970 anthology, Ana María Moix tells how her brother Terenci gave her the banned works of Sartre to read wrapped in comics: she, like her brother, preferred the comics.

Further reading

Barral, C., *Cuando las horas veloces* (Barcelona, 1988).
Castellet, J. M., *Nueve novísimos poetas españoles* (Barcelona, 1970).
Goytisolo, J., *El furgón de cola* (Barcelona, 1976; orig. Paris, 1967).
—— 'La novela española contemporánea', in *Disidencias* (Barcelona, 1967), 153–69.
Labanyi, J., *Myth and History in the Contemporary Spanish Novel* (Cambridge, 1989).
Mangini, S., *Rojos y rebeldes: la cultura de la disidencia durante el franquismo* (Barcelona, 1987).
Moix, T., *Los comics, arte para el consumo y formas pop* (Barcelona, 1968).
Moral, C. G., and **Pereda, R. M.** (eds.), *Joven poesía española* (3rd edn., Madrid, 1982).
Soldevila Durante, I., *La novela desde 1936* (Madrid: Alhambra, 1980; rev. edn. in press), ch. 3.

Painting and Sculpture: The Rejection of High Art

EMMA DENT COAD

The period from the end of the civil war to around 1960 saw a number of major reversals in the development of art. The politicized, abstract painting of the Republic was rejected. The criteria for inclusion in the annual exhibitions of the Instituto de Bellas Artes in Madrid in the 1940s (Franco wrote some catalogue introductions himself) were strict: painting and sculpture should be figurative, and should 'celebrate' the life of 'ordinary people' (idealize the life of the peasantry) or deal with heroism in the war. Painting and sculpture became romanticized and sentimental, or heroic and neo-classical.

The movement in painting called *paisajismo* had been founded in the 1920s by Alberto Sánchez and Benjamín Palencia (a former member of the 1927 Generation, who had painted sets for Lorca's travelling theatre company La Barraca), but this passive, contemplative view of the countryside was now developed into a more dynamic vision. Around the early 1960s, Palencia began to view his subjects proactively, using startling colour to create recurring patterns in landscape, emphasizing the highly contrasted effects of the sun, and appearing to paint spontaneously with a raw edge very different from his earlier reflective work.

In the majority of cases, formal experimentation was accompanied by political theorization. Also in the early 1960s, a group of left-wing artists in Barcelona began to form itself around Ángel Ferrant, now in his seventies, who had stayed in Spain through the conflict and was now starting to re-examine pre-war avant-garde tendencies. Ferrant and Antoni Tàpies, the latter aged 37 in 1960, were founder members of a group of surrealist artists, Dau al Set, established in 1948. Salvador Dalí, who returned to Spain also in 1948, was largely shunned for his right-wing sympathies. Ferrant's series of organic sculptures and mobiles, begun before the war, attracted interest and were compared to those of Alexander Calder. His earlier theoretical writings were also reinvestigated, as were his experiments in transience and in transformable art which could be made in non-precious materials such as wood, steel, mud, found objects, or tree roots. The objectives behind this aesthetic were anti-establishment, a reaction against the politics of sentimental art.

The Dau al Set group included Modest Cuixart, Joan Ponç, and the writers Joan Brossa and Arnaldo Puig, but it was Antoni Tàpies who was to make the most impact. While his work evolved from surrealism and imaginary landscapes to totally abstract forms without figurative reference, his guiding principles remained constant: to 'look into the depths' for hidden meanings in everyday objects. From 1970, he wrote a number of theoretical articles, including those originally published in the newspaper *La Vanguardia* and printed in book form in *El arte contra la estética* (1974): these comprise his mission statement. Art, he declared, should not be approached intellectually but 'from degree zero', without preconceptions; it should be 'felt' rather than 'thought'. He also challenged the notion that art was 'dead' because it was irrelevant to everyday life, insisting on the contrary that ideas were a constituent part of art, and that it should be a vehicle for moral and political meaning and lead to action. The artist, he maintained, is not just the intermediary between content and form but an active participant relaying cogent meanings. Tàpies himself put these theories into practice more thoroughly than any other artist.

The late 1950s and early 1960s were a period of considerable change and dynamism in Spain, and many avant-garde groups and movements were set up despite official hostility. The Informalist group El Paso in Madrid included Antonio Saura, Rafael Canogar, and Manuel Rivera. The Experimentalist group Equipo 57 included José Cuenca, José Duarte, and Agustín Ibarrola. More blatantly political, José Ortega and Ricardo Zamorano were the artistic counterparts of the so-called 'realist generation' of writers and film-makers. Like the latter, they insisted that the aesthetically pleasing work had no place in a socially unjust world; art should reflect life in its raw, unaestheticized form and, more importantly, must force social and political change.

The politicization and intellectualization of art by these three movements— Informalismo, Experimentalismo, and Realismo Social—must be seen as the expression of a growing culture of insurrection and protest as, in the late 1950s and the 1960s, Spain embarked on a period of rapid industrialization, with the consequent depopulation of rural areas as a result of migration within Spain and to other European countries. With foreign travel becoming easier and with rapidly increasing numbers of tourists coming to Spain, outside cultural influences inevitably made an impact on the art world. The major focuses of interest were France and the USA, as artists reconnected with the pre-war Spanish Parisian group centred on Picasso and Miró (the latter had returned to Spain in 1940), or looked to the work of Jackson Pollock and De Kooning, and of pop artists Lichtenstein and Oldenburg.

A recurrent theme was the rejection of the art gallery dealing system. The Informalist Manuel Millares created sculptural installations of scrap and found objects. The narrative underlying this kind of work is the democratization of beauty, which is—or should be—available and free to everyone, not just to the frequenters of galleries. Eduardo Chillida began a lifelong examination of the qualities of space within and without his sculptures, using mainly wood and steel, in abstract and complex geometric forms which have no 'front' or 'back' but contrive different meanings on every side, with a rejection of anthropomorphic reference. As in much work of the period, the aim was to encourage the questioning of all 'givens' by turning the work of art into a metaphorical statement of ruthless self-criticism, contemporary political comment, and rejection of the élitist world of fine art.

These years were characterized by a number of artists working in collectives. The anonymity of group work was supposed to reduce 'selfish' individualistic drives, favouring the process of experimentation and analysis. These utopian attempts at creating 'non-gallery' art sadly backfired: avant-garde work was highly valued, fetching high prices in Spain and abroad, and inevitably joined the body of work—and the capitalist dealer system—against which it was protesting.

In the early 1970s this led to a questioning of the élitism of politicized and intellectualized art, seen as incomprehensible and of minority interest. To escape this culture of meta-meta-metaphor, so removed from its object as to be unintelligible, the 1970s were marked by the wish to create new languages, often playing on artistic clichés and demystifying history by reworking historical events and paintings. The Equipo Crónica group in Valencia (founded 1964, functioned till 1981) showed the influence of popular comic strips in their versions of canvases by Velázquez (for example, *Las meninas*) and El Greco. This was both a sarcastic comment on artistic clichés and emblems, and a reclamation of the historical past, associating their apparently ephemeral work with that of the old masters. Rafael Canogar worked in relief, sometimes using real objects or clothing in sinister, nightmare images of everyday life. Antonio López García's images concealed no metaphorical meaning but looked at ordinary details of daily life, presented as dead, meaningless, and nihilistic.

This movement, Realismo Crítico, includes elements of pop in its juxtaposition of everyday objects, especially in the work of Juan Genovés. Other images showed the helplessness of the human condition, in paintings or screenprints simulating news footage, with figures running across the canvas from some threat, unseen or seen, such as a soldier with a gun. In some cases, series of pictures representing a struggle created the impression of images captured but not analysed, as if recorded impassively by a camera.

By the mid-1970s, art seemed to be in crisis. Artists were openly criticizing not only the world in which they lived but also the market in which they disdained to work. Many critics suggested that art was dead, superseded by poster art, graphic design, and photography. As always, this crisis signalled the beginning of a new artistic period as the sense of helplessness was replaced by the prospect of real political and cultural change.

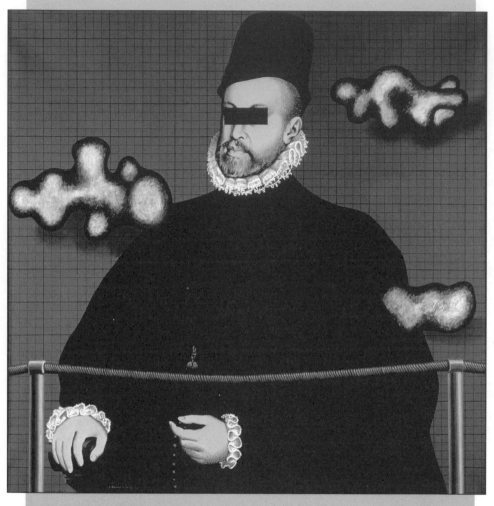

24 Equipo Crónica, *Tres nubes sobre el imperio* [*Three Clouds over the Empire*] (1973). (© DACS 1995.) A pastiche of a well-known portrait of Philip II (the king who presided over the peak period of Spain's imperial expansion) in the Prado, previously attributed to Sánchez Coello and in 1985 re-attributed to the Italian woman painter Sofonisba Anguissola, invited to the Spanish court by Philip II as lady-in-waiting. The metaphor of 'clouds looming on the horizon' is here literalized with the clouds superimposed on Philip's official image; his visionary gaze is likewise blocked by a patch over his eyes. A cordon is painted over the bottom of the portrait, highlighting its status as an exhibit and commenting ironically on the 'don't touch' attitue to high art traditionally encouraged by museums.

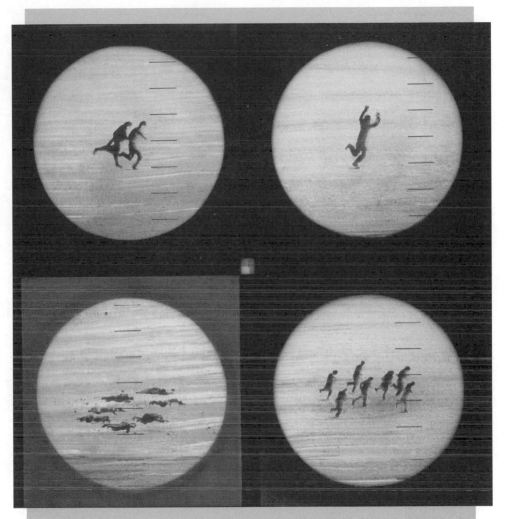

25 Juan Genovés, *Uno, dos, siete, siete* [*One, Two, Seven, Seven*] (1968). (© IVAM, Instituto Valenciano de Arte Moderno, Generalitat Valenciana.) An example of Critical Realism, depicting a sequence of running and falling figures, as if seen through the sight of a gun. The sense of menace and dehumanization provides a clear critique of political repression, without specifying—for reasons of censorship—where the scene is taking place or who is behind the gun. The anonymity of the picture, compounded by the 'objective' style, can however also create a feeling of impotence in the spectator. Franco's first head of propaganda, Ridruejo, later argued that much opposition art was permitted by the censors because they recognized that its stress on helpless victims would encourage fatalism.

Further reading
Bozal, V., *Historia del arte en España*, vol. ii (Madrid, 1991).
Cirlot, L., *El grupo 'Dau al Set'* (Madrid, 1986).
Tàpies, A., *El arte contra la estética* (Barcelona, 1974).
Toussaint, L., *'El Paso' y el arte abstracto en España* (Madrid, 1983).

Cinema, Memory, and the Unconscious

PETER EVANS

When, in Saura's *Ana y los lobos* (1972), Ana (Geraldine Chaplin) is disturbed from her sleep by Fernando (Fernando Fernán Gómez), the 'mystical' brother who has been attempting to cut off her hair, he tries persuading her that she has only dreamed the assault: 'It's a dream, a nightmare, sleep, sleep peacefully.' Full of castration anxiety provoked by the spectacle of female independence, his remark defines not only the narrative of this and many other films made in the 1960s and 1970s (the period of the so-called New Cinema and the 'estética franquista') but also the dictatorship's entire ideological project—rooted in regression, fetishization, and various forms of denial—to create a nation of somnambulists, film-goers content with ideologically tame, soporific, but also highly popular musicals, Alberto Closas melodramas, or Paco Martínez Soria *paleto* (country bumpkin) comedies.

Significantly, many of the more serious films made at this time rely on dream imagery to confront audiences with the numbing realities of officially sanctioned cinema. Film is anyway especially suited to reproducing the phantasmagoria of dreams. The processes of condensation, displacement, distortion, symbolism, and so on of dream imagery lend themselves easily to film narratives, particularly in a period when serious directors were obliged to make their statements in code, circumventing as best they could the prohibitions of state censorship.

These dream narratives are often less significant at manifest than at latent levels, since Spanish cinema of this period expresses the silences and protests of the unconscious, its history becoming inseparable from discreet triumph over censorship. Film censorship in Spain dates from 1913, although of course the post-civil war period presided over the enforcement of its strictest codes. These were not, however, free of contradiction. In 1951, for instance, Spanish cinema came under the control of the Ministry of Tourism and Information, one of whose main tasks was to combat opposition to the regime while simultaneously targeting tourist interest in Spain, something that could only reasonably be done through the projection abroad of a more liberal, democratic image of the country. The contradiction was partly resolved through the decision to make Spanish films available in two versions: one, fully censored, for local consumption; another, less mutilated, for foreign markets. Additionally, a whole series of popular films, including perhaps most crudely those starring the desexualized Spanish Lolita (Marisol), all of them brilliantly parodied by Berlanga's *Vivan los novios* (1969), were produced as propaganda for an 'España de charanga y pandereta' (folkloric Spain) of never-setting holiday sun.

From 1952 onwards all films made in Spain would be categorized, their sub-sidies depending on classification. At various times, though, the censors' zeal slackened, above all during the two periods in which José María García Escudero was Director-General of Cinematography: first, six months in 1951; then, 1962–7, to coincide with a period of 'posibilitismo' (possibilism), and a revised code of censorship and Fraga's appointment to the Ministry of Tourism and Information. Even so, little could be done outside state control, with the so-called Barcelona school (though it did produce Vicente Aranda) and other independents having little impact, above all because their films were denied public exhibition. As re-gards mainstream films, it was only much later on, in the early 1970s, that a limited degree of tolerance prevailed, due in part to the realization that many of the films falling foul of the censor's standards attracted only minority audiences, and in part because of a fear that strict censorship would only lead to negative repercussions abroad.

At the height of censorship Bardem's *Calle Mayor* (1956) could not be released without this prologue:

Here below, is the city. A small, provincial city. Any city in any province in any country. The story about to unfold does not have any specific geographical context. The colour of people's hair or the shape of the houses, the notices on the walls or a specific way of smiling or speaking should not be a flag in which to enfold these men and women about to become alive before us.

The censorship mechanism's work here succeeds in creating one of Spanish cin-ema's most ridiculous moments, a disclaimer failing to destroy the reality that everything in the film, from the language itself of course down to the RENFE insignia on the ticket seller's collar at the railway station, is unmistakably Spanish.

The work of Bardem, Berlanga and, to a slightly lesser extent, Edgar Neville and Nieves Conde, was to be enormously influential over the next two decades, especially as regards the borrowings and Hispanicizing of Italian neo-realism, bend-ing the mode's characteristic drives and strategies to the needs of Spanish realities in a process almost as significant as Garcilaso's adaptation of Italian metres to Spanish poetry of the sixteenth century. As exemplified by the work of Rossellini, De Sica, Fellini, and others, Italian neo-realism was a product of the end of the Second World War, an attempt to liberate Italian films from the cultural heritage of fascist Italy. The term neo-realism escapes easy definition, although it can loosely be described as a desire to represent ordinary human reality, with a marked pref-erence for the primacy of visual language and location shooting. Its subject-matter derives from the routine experiences of daily life, and Spanish films made in this mode, Neville's *El último caballo* (1950), Nieves Conde's *Surcos* (1951, one of the main reasons for García Escudero's first removal from his post), Berlanga and

Bardem's *Esa pareja feliz* (1951), Berlanga's *El verdugo* (1964), and so on, very much reflect this practice.

All these films depend on location shooting and authentic interiors, avoiding the studio look of contemporary commercial products. Nevertheless, the visual effects are extremely stylized. For instance, in *Muerte de un ciclista* (Bardem, 1955, a title echoing De Sica's *Ladri de biciclette*, 1948), the opening shot of the car carrying the adulterous lovers on the fateful journey leading to the accident that will change their lives, through its stylized rendering of bleak, misty landscapes with skeletal, leafless wintry trees, creates an atmosphere of gloom and menace with resonances beyond the immediate constraints of the narrative. In *Calle Mayor* the characters discuss self-consciously, and in a way the film surveys critically, the inferior though more seductive Hollywood *mise-en-scène* style of consumerist 'clean, white kitchens', so attractive to the Betsy Blair character because, as she says, 'it's so pretty, even though it's a lie'. Betsy Blair's very presence represents an ironic reminder of the Hollywood style, something to a limited extent reproduced by the popular state-approved films of the time (Sara Montiel/Joselito musicals, *comedias rosas*, etc.), and contrasted here with the harsher, more sombre, often nocturnal, grainy *mise-en-scène* of neo-realist urban settings.

Mise-en-scène as symbol of constraint or powerlessness characterizes the work of most 1960s and 1970s directors. From the early Rossellini and De Sica-inspired monochrome images of urban claustrophobia, such as at the beginning of *Los golfos* (Saura, 1959), where a credit actually states the film has been shot on location, to the end-of-dictatorship films like Saura's *Ana y los lobos* (1972), *La prima Angélica* (1973), *Cría cuervos* (1975), or Erice's *El espíritu de la colmena* (1975) and their colourful phantasmagoria of institutionalized repression, *mise-en-scène* regularly expresses over two decades the muted protest of dissident film-makers. The projection of bleakness, control, and repression through squalid interiors, or, as in *Los inocentes* (Bardem, 1962), grey, mist-shrouded exteriors reducing almost to insignificance, like the Rossellini films, characters dwarfed by vast skies, seas, or urban landscapes all carrying social as well as metaphysical meanings, finds its equivalent in the patterns of ellipsis, transference, or silence in the dialogue of these films.

In *Habla mudita* (Gutiérrez Aragón, 1973) the title itself reflects on silence, as the urban man of letters Ramiro (played by a central figure in the films of this period, José Luis López Vázquez, his simian face already identifying him with instinct and a partial rejection of rationality) attempts to give the mute girl (Kitty Manver) a voice. But for all its desired repudiation of the dominant values from which he is in flight, Ramiro's teaching is still vestigially traced over by convention as he seeks to turn the rustic maiden into a *señorita*.

This pastoral *éducation sentimentale* relies on a two-way process, the urban Franco-oppressed male discovering lost instincts in the course of his attempted socialization of the country girl. As this is 1970, not 1975, and as Gutiérrez Aragón prefers realism to idealism, the experiment on both sides is only a partial success, Ramiro hounded out of the country by the villagers, returning to Madrid and all he had hoped to leave behind, the girl falling back on her friends and family, only partially rescued from backwardness.

Resistances to silence elsewhere in the films of this period include discreet references to a pre-dictatorship past, the civil war itself, the use of children, animals, and foreign settings. In *Cría cuervos* another character has again been symbolically silenced by the regime. Stubbornly refusing to speak its platitudes, becoming animated only by the sights and sounds of her past, the mute granny loses herself through obsessive engrossment in her old photographs, postcards, and records (especially a favourite pre-war song, 'Mari-Cruz') in an interiorized world of the past. In *La caza* (Saura, 1965), *La prima Angélica*, and *Ana y los lobos*, for instance, the civil war is either symbolically restaged or recalled. When in *Ana y los lobos* another granny (Rafaela Aparicio) significantly comments on the greater order of her house and garden before the civil war the audience knows her remarks carry more than literal significance. Equally, as John Hopewell, Marsha Kinder, and others have pointed out, children or animals and related symbolism confer metaphorical significance ultimately subverting flatly literalist meanings. The animals and insects of, for instance, *La caza*, *Stress es tres tres* (Saura, 1968), or *Furtivos* (Borau, 1975) all refer codedly to the victimizations and cruelties of the regime.

Of the 'children of Franco' narratives, *La prima Angélica* ranks among the most powerful and, for all its condemnation of fascist tyrannies and absurdities, among the most optimistic. In a crucial scene Angélica, the young girl, is flanked by her liberal uncle and despotic father. Saura isolates all three characters in individual frames: the liberal uncle Luis, significantly at left of frame; the camera cutting from one to the other as Angélica listens to each in turn. Eventually the three are grouped together in the same frame. This time Luis on the left, the father in the middle and Angélica on the right. The difference is we see Luis's smiling face, not the father's, who has his back turned to the camera. Luis's smile is partly attributable to his reaction to Angélica's remark that she likes reading, especially poetry, in reply to her father's earlier comment about the general public's aversion to reading, now that there is only time, he states, for glancing at TV or magazine digests. Listening to Angélica, Luis knows the future is in safe hands. So Angélica at right of frame, significantly illuminated like her uncle by the lamp just behind her, not caught in the mirror of fascist ideology, performs the equivalent of Rossellini's children, who actually bomb their Nazi oppressors in *Roma, città aperta* (1945), in preparing for tomorrow's resistance to Franco.

As for other child-centred films, many have singled out Ana Torrent's baleful presence in two of the most richly textured films of this period: *El espíritu de la colmena* and *Cría cuervos*. Her silent glare as she surveys the moral squalor of the adult world around her manages more powerfully than words to condemn the regime's autocratic values. If *Ana y los lobos* and *La caza* perhaps more systematically than most films of this period interrogate the origins of state-approved authoritarian forms of masculinity, the Ana Torrent films are only two of several films primarily concerned with the depiction of women's experience during this period.

Even a film like *Hay que matar a B* (Borau, 1979), not primarily concerned with questions about women and social constructions of femininity, has a woman character (Patricia Neal) attempt the moral education of the male (Darren McGavin), who at one point is significantly seen in a shooting gallery aiming at the hearts of tin cut-outs of partially naked female targets. This vignette of gender relations, with its suggestions of authoritarian, victimizing attitudes born of conservative ideology, is symptomatic of film-makers' interest in the socialized constructions of subjectivity, especially of female subjectivity, an issue treated with great complexity in *La tía Tula* (Picazo, 1964), based on the novel by Unamuno. Like all those already mentioned, and countless others besides, this film focuses on the pressures and constraints of family life, with characters struggling for authenticity under the pressure of fascist ideals of individual or family identity. But while elsewhere the stress lies on male introspection (a fine example is *La prima Angélica* where the thematics of memory trace the main character's involuntary, often flawed Proustian recollections of a Nationalist family childhood) *La tía Tula*—like *Mi querida señorita* (Armiñán, 1971) and other films—concentrates on female questions. In *Mi querida señorita* ambiguities of gender are mainly in view. In *La tía Tula* the prototype of the Virgin Mother appears in a narrative readable against the background of conflict between traditional and feminist notions of femaleness and femininity. Ironically, Tula is played by an actress, Aurora Bautista, very much identified with highly traditional Cifesa roles, her appearance here seemingly referring back to and questioning ideologized versions of female subjectivity.

In Spain traditional constructions of femininity stretch all the way back to Luis Vives, Fray Luis de León, and, before them, to patristic and classical texts. More immediately relevant to post-civil war ideology, however, according to Geraldine Scanlon, were the writings of Ramón y Cajal, Ortega, and Marañón.[1] All in their own way relied on religion or science, or both, to confine women to lives of primarily domestic fulfilment. Whereas in the early stages of dictatorship state laws reserved the public arena for the male, later on economic circumstances, the increasing availability in Spain during the 1960s of American feminist texts, and greater contact with the outside world led to ideological shifts which meant women were now no longer identified so much with inferiority as with difference. Even the Sección Femenina,* keeping up with the times, began to support a policy if not actually of *feminismo* then at least of *promoción* (new opportunities for women).

In the Unamuno and Picazo texts, Tula struggles against purely sexual definitions of her subjectivity. While other women—e.g. Ana in *Cría cuervos*—sacrifice careers for domestic security, Tula seeks maternal fulfilment through surrogate motherhood, refusing to bear an intolerable burden of sexual intimacy. Across the rhetoric of the film's historically coded sexual politics, her refusal to marry her brother-in-law seems less a rejection of his individual qualities than a challenge to a system's failure to recognize women's rights. Storming out of the confessional, Tula informs the priest that she has refused Ramiro's offer of marriage 'out of respect for myself'.

These images of disinheritance belong to wider patterns of betrayal, repression, and denial, nowhere more vividly elaborated than in Borau's *Hay que matar a B*, where the endless twists and betrayals to which the protagonist is subjected formulate through the creative processes of generic intertextuality indirect statements about political realities in Spain. At one level the film belongs to a tradition, of which Saura was the master, that either theatricalizes or distances contemporary political realities. *Cría cuervos*, for instance, dramatizes the thematics of repression partly through the *mise-en-abîme* of domestic 'plays' staged by the children; *Llanto por un bandido* (Saura, 1963), on the other hand, makes its Casablanca-style statement about political engagement through historical detachment. Equally, *Hay que matar a B* relies on the generic patterns and drives of Hollywood films, especially the political thriller and *film noir*, adding an exotic Latin American setting as an extra measure of self-protection to make its various points. As in *El espíritu de la colmena*, where through allusions to foreign film traditions, especially Hollywood horror and German Expressionism, Erice broke free of formal and ideological constraints, so here in *Hay que matar a B* Borau liberates the narrative through gesturing to Hollywood genre films. The hired assassin, Pal Kovak, is an outsider caught in webs of intrigue and deception, victimized by the very system through which he had been offered salvation. Even though played by an American impersonating an eastern European *émigré*, Pal is Borau's contemporary Spaniard, in exile from himself, seen from a distance, traumatized by the past, and too easily compromised by a seductive ideology. The country's fortunes would change in due course but for the moment, as exemplified by Pal's compromises, its history was still inseparable from a collective unconscious and memory awaiting a more politicized return from repression.

Note
1 See G. Scanlon, *La polémica feminista en la España contemporánea, 1868–1974* (Madrid, 1986).

Further reading
Besas, P., *Behind the Spanish Lens: Spanish Cinema under Franco* (Denver, 1985).
Caparrós Lera, J. M., *El cine español de la democracia: de la muerte de Franco al 'cambio' socialista (1975–1989)* (Barcelona, 1992).
D'Lugo, M., *The Films of Carlos Saura: The Practice of Seeing* (Princeton, 1991).
Fiddian, R., and Evans, P. W., *Challenges to Authority: Fiction and Film in Contemporary Spain* (London, 1988).
García de León, M. A., 'El paleto, un estigma del mundo rural', in *La ciudad contra el campo* (Ciudad Real, 1992).
Gubern, R., *La censura: función política y ordenamiento jurídico bajo el franquismo* (Barcelona, 1981).
Heredero, C. F., *Las huellas del tiempo: cine español 1951–61* (Valencia, 1993) (traces beginnings of opposition cinema).
Higginbotham, V., *Spanish Film under Franco* (Austin, 1987).
Hopewell, J., *Out of the Past: Spanish Cinema after Franco* (London, 1986).

Kinder, M., *Blood Cinema: The Reconstruction of National Identity in Spain* (Berkeley, 1993).

—— 'The Children of Franco in the New Spanish Cinema', *Quarterly Review of Film Studies*, 8/2 (1983), 57–76.

Méndez Leite, F., *Historia del cine español* (Madrid, 1965).

Molina Foix, V., *New Cinema in Spain* (London, 1977).

Sánchez Vidal, A., *Borau* (Zaragoza, 1990).

—— *El cine de Carlos Saura* (Zaragoza, 1988).

Part IV

Democracy and Europeanization: Continuity and Change 1975–1992

It had all changed so much, so fast [. . .]. What was happening to them in real life was like when they were watching a movie and lost the thread [. . .] and couldn't work out how much time had elapsed in between the frames or connect the immediate past with the present racing past them.

(Antonio Muñoz Molina, *El jinete polaco*, 1991)

Editors' introduction

All the essays that follow stress that the post-Franco period has been one not only of extraordinary change but also of some occasionally surprising continuities: the cultural—and even in some senses the political—transition to democracy began some years before Franco's death; and the last twenty years have seen the consolidation of the process of capitalist modernization begun under the dictatorship. At the same time, some of the more unfortunate legacies of nearly forty years of dictatorship have proved resistant to change or resurfaced in a different guise, particularly in the degree of state control over the media and the arts; and, while the devolution of power to seventeen autonomous regional governments has meant decentralized cultural control, the 'top-down' approach to culture which has been a constant issue throughout this book remains a problem.

But state and local government control have also been used to facilitate cultural production, as indeed—to a surprising extent—has the new enterprise culture promoted by the PSOE* government since it came to power in 1982. However, this has been at the cost of institutionalizing cultural experiment—even that on the fringe—with the consequent risk of co-opting it into stabilizing political projects, as in the use of culture to reinforce a sense of regional identity in the new autonomies. Youth culture—even, or perhaps especially, as represented in the wilder films of Almodóvar—has become the official image of Spain.

The cultural pluralism of contemporary Spain owes much to the accelerated change of the last two decades which has obliged Spaniards to live in different time frames at once: that is, to experience simultaneously what in the rest of Europe have been successive stages of development. It is also the consequence of two complementary developments: recognition of Spain's regional—and linguistic—diversity, and an increasingly diversified, and internationalized, market economy. Globalization of the media, however, means both awareness of cultural diversity and the erosion of that diversity through imitation and pastiche, which provide the dominant note in current Spanish culture in its double sense of artistic production and life-styles. At the same time all this is fun: something there was not a lot of in Spanish culture under the dictatorship (and it was largely confined to establishment culture for the opposition had to be in earnest). The licensing of fun under democracy has however been accompanied by a political apathy new in Spain, though not of course exclusive to it.

The term *desencanto** (disenchantment/disappointment) used to describe this sentiment in fact covers a set of different, albeit interrelated, responses to developments in Spain since the end of the dictatorship. Most usually it denotes a general sense of disappointment with the reality of the liberal democratic system in action. Partly this has been the result of impractically high popular expectations that democracy—for so long the striven-for, almost mythic goal—would provide a panacea for all national problems. Partly it has been the unfortunate result of democracy and economic recession coinciding—as they did in the 1930s. While one should not exaggerate the significance of this parallel, the contemporary cycle of recession has certainly fuelled political disenchantment since existing democracy—in Spain as elsewhere—is visibly failing to deliver even minimally adequate life opportunities for the millions suffering the social disenfranchisement and attendant humiliations of long-term unemployment. The degree to which this has affected young people in Spain reflects a Europe-wide problem. But the impact of this democratic deficit is potentially even more damaging in a country where the social and cultural rooting of democratic practice is itself relatively recent. This said, the Spanish right has not derived any substantial political benefit from Francoist nostalgia. Quite the contrary in fact: the main conservative formation, the PP* [Popular Party], is above all concerned to present a 'new', youthful profile. What this suggests, however, is the degree to which the outcome of the transition has primarily met a neo-liberal market agenda rather than the left's social democratic one. As awareness of this grew, so did one major form of *desencanto*—that affecting the left in the post-transition period.

The left's *desencanto* was rooted in an awareness of the discrepancy between the enormous energy invested over the long years of the anti-Franco struggle and the minimal concessions to levelling social and economic reform gained as a result of the transition. For many men and women who had devoted the prime years of their adulthood to a cherished collective goal, making enormous sacrifices in their personal lives in the process, this realization was a bitter blow. In some cases the reaction was violent: there were suicides. But for many more the response was a withdrawal from political activism in search of compensatory fulfilments from a private life that had been for so many years 'on hold'. Some would return to other forms of political activity afforded by the new circumstances, but many never did.

The role of culture in keeping alive the collective memory remains paramount as Spaniards continue to rediscover the past that was taken from them under dictatorship; but it coexists with a converse urge to amnesia (*desmemoria*) which can be both a liberation from past traumas and a refusal to face them. Where the new hedonism has, however, been genuinely liberating is in the area of sexuality, with the erosion of fixed gender roles and increasing acceptance of sexualities in the plural. But the rapidity of the change, coupled with the plunge since 1992 back into economic recession, has also brought confusion—the rate of drug consumption among young people is particularly high. The resulting cultural anxieties—readily exploitable by the political right—could produce attempts to return to a repressive essentialism such as threaten elsewhere (cf. 'back to basics' in Britain). In Spain, as in the rest of western Europe, cultural anxieties have been fuelled by the erosion of collective values consequent on the ascendancy of market economics and enterprise culture. The resulting 'privatization of the social' is potentially even more damaging in Spain, with its younger and therefore more vulnerable civic culture. The media are a major site of struggle: in the face of ever more powerful vested commercial interests there is a bid to define, legitimize, and develop a notion of public service and civic responsibility which cannot be reduced to the imperative of audience ratings. Failure here would directly threaten both cultural and political pluralism, as the worthwhile came to mean only the popular and the popular exclusively the profitable.

Democracy and Cultural Change

ROSA MONTERO

ALICIA ALTED

PETER EVANS

Political Transition and Cultural Democracy: Coping with the Speed of Change

ROSA MONTERO

I should like to start with a bald statement: the changes that have taken place in Spain in the last twenty years are staggering. We have moved successfully, without bloodshed, from dictatorship to democracy. With four official languages and a variety of regional cultures, we have managed to free ourselves from totalitarian rule without breaking up the nation-state. We have made the long journey from underdevelopment to development in a short space of time, without too many casualties. In twenty years we have experienced in concentrated form what for other nations has been a century of social change. While other countries like the former Yugoslavia have failed to adapt to new contingencies and are locked in a horrific self-destructive spiral, Spain has successfully extricated itself from centuries of isolation and boarded the train of history.

The incredible speed of these changes is perhaps the most striking feature of modern Spain. Some idea of the abruptness of the transformation is given by the following statistics. If in 1950 almost half the working population (48 per cent) was engaged in agriculture, in 1990 the figure was 12 per cent; today the vast majority of Spaniards live in cities (84 per cent). The eternal rural Spain, with its old women in black and its old men with their berets and sticks, is dead. More incredible changes: in 1970 the overwhelming majority of Spaniards regarded themselves as practising Catholics (87 per cent), while in 1991 the figure had fallen to less than half the population (49 per cent). Spain is no longer the classic ultra-Catholic country of the past. The changes have been equally startling in education: it must be remembered that it was not till the 1970s that universal education was achieved in Spain, but now we have a higher percentage of the population in education than most other countries in Europe.

These dramatic changes of life-style and values began a few years before Franco's death, but it was only after his demise in 1975 that the normalization process really started. It can be divided into four phases. First the obvious change of political system from dictatorship to parliamentary democracy. Then legal change, with the new Constitution and the reform of statutes and administrative codes of practice. Of course all these huge legal changes did not take place overnight, the result being that for two or three years in the late 1970s there were some anomalies, with newly passed democratic laws coexisting with old Francoist laws not yet rescinded. It was this kind of jurisdictional conflict, typical of such transition periods, that gave rise in 1978 to the case of Els Joglars, a Catalan theatre group that put on a satirical play consonant with the level of freedom of expression of the new democratic Spain, but was tried for disrespect and sentenced to prison by a military court that was a relic of the old Francoist structures.

The third phase was one of generational change in the sense of a change of political personnel: political parties and trade unions were restructured as young people who had not fought in the civil war moved up the ranks. This phase meant the definitive loss of power for the Francoist establishment, and not everything went smoothly: it was at this juncture that the attempted coup of 23 February 1981 (popularly known as 'el 23-F') took place, led by the most reactionary sectors of the Civil Guard,* army, and political right. The failure of the attempted coup marked the end of the transition: a year later the PSOE* came to power, bringing an influx of new political blood untainted by involvement in the Franco regime. With the access to power of this new political class, the risk of a coup receded: democracy was finally established, if still in its infancy and in need of consolidation. This brings us to the fourth and current phase, marked on the one hand by economic change, with the creation of a new affluent class backed and encouraged by the PSOE in power, and on the other hand by the substantial shift in social values referred to previously.

There are however some constants in our society that have proved resistant to change: one inevitable statistic is that Spain has 133,000 bars, more than the total number for the other eleven EC countries put together. This astonishing excess no doubt says something about our national identity: joking apart, it points to a certain life-style and *Weltanschauung*. For, together with the Swedes, Spaniards spend more time socializing and being with their friends than any other people in Europe: a minimum of 2.5 hours a day. But while the Swedes also spend a lot of time reading, going to the cinema or theatre, or practising sport, we are way below the average when it comes to these more active forms of cultural participation. Because we meet our friends in bars. Sadly we seem not to be a very cultured country. It was only in 1992 that we reached the minimum level of newspaper readership for a developed country, estimated by Unesco at 100 copies sold per 1,000 inhabitants. The 105 copies currently sold in Spain for every 1,000 inhabitants is still well below the European average of 232; with Portugal, we occupy the bottom place. This is no coincidence for Spain and Portugal share a recent past of long dictatorships; and, as everyone knows, dictatorships lower the cultural level of the press, undermining its credibility and discouraging regular readership. This is illustrated by the fact that in 1900 2.5 million newspapers were sold every day, exactly the same figure as for 1980 except that in 1900 Spain had a population of 18 million of which 65 percent were illiterate, while in 1980 the population stood at 36 million with an illiteracy rate of only 6 percent. Which means that at the start of the century there was an extremely active intellectual minority which later succumbed to the vicissitudes of our recent history. The return of democracy has been accompanied by a revitalization of cultural activity. Although the cinema is in dire financial straits, among other things because of the stranglehold of the big US distribution companies, new directors have emerged: apart from the obvious success of Pedro Almodóvar, names to look out for include Fernando Colomo, Fernando Trueba, and the young Juanma Bajo Ulloa who in 1990, at the age of 24, won first prize at the San Sebastián Film Festival with his first film *Alas de mariposa*. The theatre too, despite even worse financial pressures, has seen the appearance of some exciting new companies, particularly Catalan groups like La Fura dels Baus and Els Comediants (which took part in the opening and closing ceremonies of the 1992 Barcelona Olympic Games), or Dagoll Dagom.

This cultural renewal has been felt particularly keenly in the literary field, with the so-called *boom* of the New Spanish Novel. Under the dictatorship Spanish writers, regardless of their quality, lived virtually on the margins of society; with few exceptions, they were largely ignored by the Spanish reading public. With the arrival of democracy a large number of new writers, male and female, started to publish, each writing in his or her own individual style rather than forming a coherent movement; and they were discovered by the reading public, who identified with them as *their* writers. At the 1988 Madrid Book Fair, of the ten best-selling novels seven were by Spanish authors aged under 45. This re-establishment of contact between writers and public—which we can call a kind of cultural normalization, because it is normal for a society to prefer its own authors—has produced a particularly rich moment in our literary history, with established writers still producing (e.g. Marsé, Carmen Martín Gaite, Delibes), the 'New Novelists' now reaching maturity (e.g. Javier Marías, Alejandro Gándara, Lourdes Ortiz), and a constant stream of promising new young writers (e.g. Luisa Castro, Francisco Casavella, Belén Gopegui).

In the media, the change from dictatorship to democracy is less of a success story. Television remained a state monopoly, as it had been under Franco, until the early 1990s when private channels were franchised. The two continuing public sector channels, despite the fact that all political tendencies are represented on their governing body, in practice are still too dependent on the government; while the new private television companies have led to a shocking lowering of standards. In addition Spain, like the rest of the world, is suffering from a dangerous concentration of the media in the hands of a small number of giant conglomerates, who have bought up radio stations, publishing houses, TV companies, magazines, and newspapers.

If, despite this cultural renewal, Spaniards do not seem to be a highly cultured nation, it is not only because we spend our free time with friends in bars, but also because we watch a lot of television and base our lives on the family. The family is what matters most to 83 per cent of Spaniards, followed by work (64 per cent) and then friends (44 per cent). And the Spanish divorce rate is the lowest in Europe. Apart from which only one Spaniard out of every ten lives alone, while the European average is one out of every four. In this sense traditional values have not changed that much. The family has adapted to new times, but it is still fundamental. And it is not just the family but the group, the clan, the tribe, the horde. It seems that Spaniards still care much more about their own kind—the friends, neighbours, and relatives who comprise their tribal network—than they do about the common good of society and the state (Gerald Brenan had noted this in 1943, in *The Spanish Labyrinth*). For the common good to be regarded as genuinely common, long-term experience of democracy is necessary. Our lack of this explains the existence in our society of discrepancies between the legal framework, which is perfectly democratic, and certain social customs and basic values left over from the old authoritarian Spain. We are still not entirely convinced that the state belongs to all of us. It is as if we had not quite managed to get the abstract notions of the collectivity and citizenship into our heads, with the result that everything that is perceived as not being our particular tribe is by definition perceived as being an enemy tribe. This explains why we keep our homes spotlessly clean but pile the pavement with old sofas, empty detergent cartons, and every conceivable kind of rubbish; though it seems that this barbaric kind of individualism is starting to change, despite being so ingrained in our mentality, because we are learning to stand patiently in queues: something that, however trivial, for us represents a major apprenticeship in collective responsibility.

Most of the changes we have experienced are, without doubt, positive. For example, Spain is no longer a fiercely *machista* society: our level of sexism is now comparable to that of any other EC country. And democracy is taking root for the first time in our history: in 1984, only 43 per cent of Spaniards were quite or very satisfied with the way democracy worked; in November 1992 this had gone up to 67 per cent, despite the current economic crisis and resulting gloom and fear of unemployment. The possibility of a military coup is now definitively behind us.

As a result Spaniards are losing their ancestral fear: that fear of citizens bludgeoned into submission without knowing their rights because they have not had them for centuries. In addition, we are learning tolerance and we have broken out of our century-old isolation. It is probably because we know the price of being isolated that Spain is strongly pro-Europe, despite the fact that joining the EC has meant a big economic readjustment. Indeed, at the time of the 1986 referendum on whether Spain should remain in NATO, the PSOE won a yes vote for our continued membership, despite strong anti-militarist feeling, as the result of a publicity campaign that equated leaving NATO with putting democracy at risk and returning to the ill effects of isolationism.

However, such vertiginous change leaves its marks and not all the changes are for the best. For example, we are losing the old sense of solidarity with the tribe, of loyalty to family and friends, without a corresponding gain in citizenship or respect for the common good. We no longer feel entirely at home in the tribe but neither do we feel entirely at ease in modern society. Spanish society today is much more competitive, aggressive, and stressful. We have lost much of that unhurried love of the present moment that was disastrous for business but made life pleasant, without—it seems—an equivalent gain in efficiency. We can organize magnificent peace congresses, a dazzling Olympic Games, and a successful World Exposition, but the phones still do not work, letters get lost, and it takes an average of eleven months to complete the paperwork to set up a new business.

Apart from this, the country has in the last few years experienced a veritable obsession with money. The streets seemed to be paved with gold: in 1992, Spain was 40 per cent wealthier than in 1980, if one takes into account the real value of the increase in gross domestic product (GDP). Another spectacular indication of economic and mental change connected to this is the fact that, in 1982, only 23 per cent of the population defined itself as middle class, while in 1992 54 per cent of Spaniards regarded themselves as such.

The day before yesterday we were poor and now we are not, and the bonanza seems to have gone to our heads, bringing out in us all the defects of the new rich: pretentiousness, ostentation, superficiality, selfishness, and a rejection of the poor worthy of the new convert, manifested in an increase in xenophobia and racism. And the combination of easy money with the current loss of values, and the fact that we have acquired wealth before acquiring culture, provides a perfect breeding ground for one of the most glaring and harmful features of Spanish society today: corruption, and that climate of general cynicism which makes people think that anyone who does not dip his hand in the coffers is a fool.

However, what most concerns Spaniards at the present time is not corruption but the economic crisis. We have known briefly what it is to have money, and now we can see poverty once more looming on the horizon. If a couple of years ago we were proudly parading our new European identity and modernity, now we feel plunged back into doom and gloom, though it is probably true to say that today's pessimism is as exaggerated as yesterday's optimism. But we are a country of extremes: a very old society and a very young democracy. And nothing has been more extreme than the recent changes. It was all going too smoothly.

Further reading
Folguera, P. (ed.), *Otras visiones de España* (Madrid: Editorial Pablo Iglesias, 1993).
Miguel, A. de, *Sociedad española 1992–3* (Madrid, 1993).
Pérez Díaz, V., *La primacía de la sociedad civil* (Madrid, 1993).
Tezanos, J. F., Cotarelo, R. and Blas, A. de, *La transición democrática española* (Madrid, 1989).
Tuñón de Lara, M., García Delgado, J. L., Juliá, S., Mainer, J.-C., and Serrano Sanz, J. M., *Transición y democracia (1973–1985)*, vol. x of *Historia de España*, ed. M. Tuñón de Lara (Barcelona, 1991) (has sections on society, politics, the economy, and culture, with wide-ranging bibliographies).
Zaldívar, C. A., and Castells, M., *España fin de siglo* (Madrid, 1992).

Educational Policy in Democratic Spain

ALICIA ALTED

It was only after 1975 that the practical effects of the 1970 General Education Law (LGE) started to make themselves felt, as much due to the economic crisis of 1973 as to the change of regime. The former led to modest growth if not actual cutbacks in educational expenditure, except in 1978 when a special quota for education was included in the Moncloa Pacts signed on 25 October 1977. The political process of transition to democracy resulted in constant turn-abouts in educational policy by successive governments from 1976 to 1982.

The transition was made possible by a consensus between a government made up of former Francoist politicians and representatives of the various opposition groupings. The government appointed on 8 July 1976 under Adolfo Suárez got the last parliament of the dictatorship to approve a Political Reform Law allowing elections to be held for a new parliament whose job would be to draw up the Constitution. The elections of 15 June 1977 gave a majority to the electoral coalition UCD* [Union of the Democratic Centre] headed by Suárez and formed from a mixture of liberals, Christian democrats, and social democrats, with the PSOE*-PSC [Spanish and Catalan Socialist Parties] forming the opposition, both representing moderate tendencies pushing for change from within the system with the monarchy's backing in the person of King Juan Carlos. Between July 1976 and March 1979 Suárez, with the support of the various political families comprising UCD, presided over a politics of consensus necessary to consolidate democracy. After the second general elections of 1 March 1979, again won by UCD, who formed a government in April, Suárez abandoned the earlier consensus politics for party rule, UCD having now been constituted as a political party. This new phase was plagued by problems stemming from the permanently precarious balance of forces within the Party, producing a swing towards the Socialists, who won the general elections of 28 October 1982. Since then the PSOE has governed with an absolute majority until the last general elections of June 1993 which it won with an overall majority.

The ten clauses of Article 27 of the 1978 Constitution, dealing with education, were the product of the above-mentioned consensus between UCD and the PSOE. The PSOE's main concessions to UCD were: recognition of educational freedom, the right of parents to give their children a moral and religious education in keeping with their convictions, the freedom to set up educational establishments, and public support for private educational establishments. UCD compromised by agreeing to universal access to education 'through a general restructuring of the education system', and obligatory monitoring by the relevant bodies of those establishments receiving public funding. The main point is that the Constitution laid down a set of educational norms basic to a democratic society: educational freedom, obligatory basic school education free of charge, freedom to set up private schools or colleges, university autonomy, and the 'democratization' of educational institutions, as well as other rights set out in clause 1 such as academic freedom, ideological and religious freedom, and the right of all Spaniards to culture.

Article 27 came under what was called 'the domain of responsibilities of the state' (Article 149.30). At the same time the Constitution stipulated that the autonomous communities, as laid down in their respective autonomy statutes, could assume all educational responsibilities that fell outside this domain. The autonomous communities divide into those with devolved responsibility for education (Andalusia, the Canaries, Catalonia, Galicia, Navarre, the Basque Country, Valencia) and those without such devolved responsibility (Aragon, Asturias, the Balearic Islands, Cantabria, Castile and León, Castile and La Mancha, Extremadura, La Rioja, Murcia). In the former, educational activities are run by an Education Council organized into departments replicating those of the Ministry of Education and Science (MEC), represented at provincial level by an Office of Education and Science. The latter, known as 'MEC territory', have Education Departments responsible to the Ministry through its Provincial Directorates. At local government level, municipal Education Offices are responsible for the upkeep of state schools from nursery to EGB (General Basic Education) level.

UCD's precariousness as a political grouping was reflected in the changes at the Ministry of Education 1976–82, which saw six successive Ministers, all Christian democrats. In an attempt to implement some of the educational norms and rights enshrined in the Constitution, two laws were drafted for parliamentary debate: the Institutional Law on School Statutes (LOECE) and the University Autonomy Law (LAU). The latter was withdrawn by the government after committee stage. The former led to angry exchanges between socialists and members of the political centre over the issue of educational freedom and its attendant rights, especially the right of school authorities to draw up their own educational guidelines. Apart from this, the LOECE set out the educational responsibilities of the autonomous communities within a nation-wide educational framework.

In marked contrast to the financial cut-backs in state education, this period saw considerable increases in financial support for the private sector. With most private schools belonging to the Church, this added to the clashes between socialists and centrists. While the latter argued that the state should play a supporting role in education, the former recognized the existence of private educational establishments but prioritized state education. This increased expenditure on private education was not matched by any requirement to introduce democratic management structures or to improve teachers' terms of employment in the private sector, which differed hugely from those of teachers in state schools.

By the time the PSOE came to power in 1982, the EGB was fully operative but problems remained at the level of infrastructure and, at curriculum level, in notable shortcomings in teaching of the creative arts, prerequisite subjects for technology courses, and foreign languages. An important factor, contrasting with expansion at other levels, was the continued (and continuing) decline, with the falling birth rate, of the school population at nursery level (from the academic year 1984–5) and EGB level (from 1985–6). However, there would still be a shortage of school places in certain city areas as a result of escalating migration from the countryside. The PSOE's long period in office has permitted sustained educational planning with undeniably positive results, despite acknowledged problems and question marks over the extent of its application. Four successive Ministers have continued the reform programme initiated by José María Maravall: after him, Javier Solana, Alfredo Pérez Rubalcaba, and at present (May 1994) Gustavo Suárez Pertierra.

From the start, the PSOE set out to tackle a range of issues: making access to education a reality; eliminating the problems stemming from inadequate schooling; improving teaching standards; countering lack of equal opportunity with adequate grants provision and increased attention to special educational needs, integrating handicapped children into the school system; facilitating university autonomy and research; and harmonizing national educational structures with those of the autonomous communities. To tackle the necessary reforms, increased funding was necessary. Educational expenditure has consequently gone up from 542,329 million pesetas (2.8 per cent of the gross domestic product (GDP)) in 1982 to 2,777,500 million pesetas (4.7 per cent of the GDP) in 1992. With current economic recession, a minimal budgetary increase is forecast for 1994, affecting the two major reforms in train: implementation of the Institutional Law on the Overall Structuring of the Education System (LOGSE), and university tenure. Despite the budgetary increases, education expenditure is still below the European average. Numbers in education have now reached European levels; the problem lies in teaching standards.

The principles behind the PSOE's educational reforms were formulated in the Institutional Law on the Right to Education (LODE) of 3 July 1985, the University Reform Law (LRU) of 25 August 1983, and the LOGSE of 30 March 1990.

The LODE regulates the right to education and to educational freedom laid down in the Constitution. In respect of the latter, it sets out the procedure for agreements with private schools, stipulating requirements with regard to their organization and operation, with both private and public sectors involved in their management and monitoring. The intention here is to allow the creation of a 'mixed educational network' under state control, in which state schools will co-exist with approved private schools partly funded by the state in exchange for observing a number of conditions set out in the Law. Outside this network will be those private schools regulated by the market.

Since the early 1960s, numbers of university students have continued to rise sharply. This massification process—an uneven one, with marked differences across subject areas and between the various autonomous communities—had created serious resourcing and staffing problems not tackled by the LGE or successive UCD governments. On taking over in 1982 the PSOE found itself faced with a university system at breaking point. Consequently its first educational reform measure was the LRU, designed to put the principle of university autonomy into effect. This involved a division of responsibilities between the state, the autonomous communities, and the university bodies, at the levels of statutes, management, academic activities, and funding. As envisaged by the LRU, universities will be based on a departmental structure with tenured lecturers and close links with the community, meaning that course content should correspond to social and professional needs.

An important point considered in the LRU is the existence of private universities. The LGE had not touched on this issue, though it had been raised by university unrest in the 1960s and early 1970s. At that time the Church universities, being identified with the regime, did not fit the image of a private university. It was only with the Royal Decree of 20 April 1991, stipulating the minimum requirements for setting up a university, public or private, that private universities could start to function. One of the main obstacles in their way is staff recruitment, since lecturers transferring to them from the state universities lose their right as public sector employees to return to their previous tenured post at a later date. The key to their success thus lies in the superior support services they can offer and the incentive of higher salaries than those offered in public sector institutions.

Despite the major changes introduced, the LRU has not solved certain problems and has created others: staff–student ratios are still high in some subject areas, too many students are doing courses that currently have low or virtually non-existent job outlets, the conversion of non-tenured into tenured posts has favoured in-house appointments sometimes at the expense of merit, internal promotion procedures are still unsatisfactory, and salary scales are still not on a par with those for equivalent public sector posts. The mismatch between course content and professional requirements leads to a high drop-out and failure rate, exacerbated by reduced job prospects. High unemployment increases the demand for university places, but is particularly damaging to graduates trying to find a job with no previous work experience.

Reform of non-university education, culminating in the LOGSE, had started some years before with pilot schemes testing methods and curricula in various schools under MEC and autonomous community control. In 1987 the PSOE government introduced its educational reform bill for discussion by the relevant parties, complemented in 1988 with a technical and professional education reform bill. The results of this debate were published two years later in the government's White Book on the reform of the educational system. The LOGSE translated these proposals into law. Its aim was the double one of remedying the defects inherited from the LGE, and adapting the system to the needs of 'a rapidly modernizing society moving ever more clearly towards a common European future', as stated in its 'List of objectives'. It tries to put these aims into practice at all the various educational levels.

Nursery education is seen as optional, with specifically defined activities. It is divided into two phases: 0–3 years and 3–6 years. Numbers at this level have grown slowly but steadily. It is now becoming a social necessity as more women join the job market and because it favours equal opportunities by encouraging the child's early 'socialization'.

The former EGB is, in the new system, replaced by Primary Education, 6–12 years, and Compulsory Secondary Education (ESO), 12–16 years. Both are compulsory and free. School-leavers receive a Secondary Education Graduation Certificate, which qualifies them to go on—if wished—to the second stage of Secondary Education, 16–18 years. This comprises the *bachillerato** and Intermediate Professional Formation. The *bachillerato* is broken down into four options: Arts, Humanities and Social Sciences, Natural and Health Sciences, Technology. The graduation certificate of *bachiller* allows direct access to Higher Professional Formation; those wanting to go on to university have to sit an entrance test. The Law also allows for access to Professional Formation without the required certificate if applicants demonstrate competence by sitting an entrance test designed and marked by the educational body concerned.

There has been widespread criticism of the proposed assessment system, which connects directly with the question of teaching standards, and of the reduction of the *bachillerato* to two years, supposedly devaluing studies traditionally seen as a university qualification. The LOGSE does not envisage any form of examination external to the individual school (such as the former state-run examinations held during or at the end of primary and secondary education), and also scraps the old marking system. All assessment is to be continuous at all levels, and is to be non-subject-specific at primary level. If pupils' performance fails to satisfy the stated criteria at primary or compulsory secondary level, they may repeat one year at each level. The Law does not consider the possibility of a student failing to satisfy the stipulated criteria even after this repeat year. In principle, all students are supposed to reach the required level. This is none too logical but at least provides a subtle way of disguising failure and of making compulsory schooling up to the age of 16 (18 with two repeat years) a reality.

The LGE had failed in its attempt to turn the *bachillerato* and Professional

Formation into a concluding stage of school education leading directly to employment for most students: the *bachillerato* continued to be seen as a route to university, and Professional Formation as an option for low achievers. The LOGSE's restructuring of secondary education into two levels was an attempt to deal with this, especially the stigma attached to Professional Formation. The Law's chief aim is to turn the latter into an alternative to university education, with teaching methods and curricula closely geared to the world of work: placements with a company are now an obligatory part of the course, and continuous Professional Formation is planned for the unemployed or workers needing specific skills.

It is obviously too soon to pass judgement on the practical implementation of the LOGSE. What is clear is that, as with the LGE, there has been no accompanying law guaranteeing specifically earmarked financial resources. Economic recession has already put the brakes on some of the initial measures proposed: for example, the new system was supposed to come into operation in years 3–6 of primary education in the current academic session 1993–4, but in May 1993 it was decided to implement it only in years 3–4. Curiously the new system is being introduced piecemeal, since in this same academic session 340 secondary institutes under MEC control are teaching all four years of the ESO syllabus, although a revised timetable issued in December 1993 proposed that the first year be introduced in 1996–7. Despite this, the LOGSE is one of the most ambitious attempts at adapting the educational system to the needs of a modern society, albeit one in which the welfare state is in crisis. That is precisely why it represents a challenge

Further reading
Fernández Enguita, M., *Educación, formación y empleo en el umbral de los 90* (Ministry of Education/ CIDE report) (Madrid, 1990).
González-Anleo, J., 'La enseñanza en España: el desafío de los noventa', in J. Vidal-Beneyto (ed.), *España a debate*, ii: *La sociedad* (Madrid, 1991).
—— 'La educación: logros y fallos de la gestión socialista', in J. Tusell and J. Sinova (eds.), *La década socialista: el ocaso de Felipe González* (Madrid, 1992).
González Blasco, P., 'La ciencia y la investigación en España', in J. Vidal-Beneyto (ed.), *España a debate*, vol. ii (Madrid, 1991).
Foessa, *Informe sociológico sobre el cambio social en España, 1975–1983* (Madrid, 1983).
Ministry of Education, *Libro Blanco sobre la reforma del sistema educativo español* (Madrid, 1983).
Nogueira, R., *Principios constitucionales del sistema educativo español* (Ministry of Education report) (Madrid, 1988).
Ollero Tassara, A., 'La educación: desahogo para reformadores', in J. Rupérez and C. Moro (eds.), *El decenio González* (Madrid, 1992).
Perspectivas actuales en sociología de la educación (Madrid, 1983).
CIDE/Instituto de la Mujer, *La presencia de las mujeres en el sistema educativo* (Madrid, 1988).
Sociedad, cultura y educación: homenaje a Carlos Lerena (Madrid, 1991).
Solana Madariaga, J., 'La educación en España en el decenio 1982–1992', in A. Guerra and J. F. Tezanos (eds.), *La década del cambio: diez años de gobierno socialista, 1982–1992* (Madrid, 1992).

Back to the Future: Cinema and Democracy

PETER EVANS

In the widest terms the post-dictatorship cinema in Spain succeeded in repoliticizing film language. No longer looking over their shoulders after the abolition of censorship in 1977, Spanish film-makers rushed to speak the unspeakable, confronting the realities of everyday living, acknowledging the inseparability of art from the frameworks of history and tradition. At one level this meant an avalanche of *destape* [nudity] films satisfying the curiosity of viewers deprived in prim dictatorship times of the spectacle of naked human flesh, a genre of films soon waning after exhaustion of its novelty value; at another, it meant direct engagement with issues previously ignored, displayed, or allegorized. More recently following its own spectacular return of the repressed, the Spanish cinema has finally settled down, less hysterically than in the first flush of post-dictatorship freedoms, to pursue its own slightly more relaxed struggles with the pervasive issues of a widespread postmodernist consumer culture exemplified, above all, by the colonizing drives of American film and TV norms.

As everywhere, the Spanish cinema imitates American products, but at least in Almodóvar and one or two others (e.g. Colomo, Trueba) it has directors whose postmodernist parodies of the values they themselves vampirize succeed in providing a historical awareness of a seemingly inevitable process.

The triumph of consumerism at the box-office has not dimmed the memory of that rage for straight-talking that gripped the earliest moments of the post-censorship period. Above all, for the first time in thirty-five years, questions of history, politics and government, religion, ethnicity, regionalism, family, and sexuality could all be discussed openly and directly. Films on religious themes, for instance, like *Padre Nuestro* (Regueiro, 1985), in which a cardinal has an illegitimate prostitute daughter, or, more comically, *Pan de ángel* (Bellmunt, 1984), subject the Catholic Church to scandalous, quasi-blasphemous criticism. On historical themes (in contrast, say, to *Alba de América* where Cifesa had represented the discoveries as an indisputably noble enterprise in the service of God and his chosen representatives, the Catholic Monarchs), films like Saura's *El Dorado* (1987) provide an opportunity through complex deconstructions of masculinity for explorations of the origins of male violence. In *El rey pasmado* (Uribe, 1992), produced at a time in which only the corrosion of all sources of authority could command any ideological respectability (in *Las cosas del querer*, Chávarri, 1989, Franco's very voice is mocked by an irreverent partygoer), the King of Spain no longer assumes the hushed tones and saintly postures of Francoist imagination, becoming instead, as played by the rubber-faced Gabino Diego, the awkward, sexually repressed, and obsessive monarch whose overwhelming passion is not some complex matter of state business but the transgression of his entourage's prohibition on seeing his queen unclothed. The film's ironic tone, sanctioning the coexistence of detached, humorous Grand Inquisitors and clerics (Fernando Fernán Gómez among them) with more familiar traditionally fervent and inflexible ones (e.g. Juan Diego, still the sexual neurotic of Saura's *La noche oscura*, 1988), emphasizes the cooler treatment of what once epitomized the country's bewitchment by dogma. The alliance between the Devil and the Jesuit smacks of liberal settlings of old scores as, at the end of the film, the former heads for Rome via Barcelona, while the latter makes for London via Paris, neither pilgrim apparently seeking new dominions to colonize, only the comforts of already requisitioned spiritual homes. Their friendship perhaps confirms the fascist *ancien régime's* suspicions of the evil influence of Catalan, Italian, French, and British cultures, as the ravens of post-dictatorship realities return to peck out the eyes of their former ideological masters.

The Devil has done his worst in the political reconstruction of the country in democracy. Spanish films now openly attack surviving *fachas* (fascists)—as in Antonio Giménez Rico's *El disputado voto del Sr Cayo*—and the military—gently in *Mi general* (Armiñán, 1987), roughly in *Soldadito español* (Antonio Giménez Rico, 1988)—and directly reflect progress towards an ideal of fragmented regionalist cultures and structures. *El Lute II* (Aranda, 1988) discusses gypsy issues beyond the patronizing or folkloristic norms of the 1940s and 1950s. *La muerte de Mikel* (Uribe, 1984) takes up the more political implications of Basque separatism. And not shying away from the representation of Civil Guard* cruelty, and regional and rural neglect under Franco, *Tasio* (Armendáriz, 1984)—like *Vacas* (Medem, 1991)—concentrates, as John Hopewell notes, on confirming the survival of different traditions: 'Under Franco the relation of the environment to the individual was repressive; now it is far more symbiotic.'[1] But if, at least, for all their infinite capacity for natural as distinct from social disasters, pastoral settings offer characters the traditional consolations of the wilderness, beauty, tranquillity, peace of mind, etc., the city, released from political and moral repression, has become a place of new post-dictatorship pleasures and dangers.

The city often provides the setting in the 'films of democracy' for an overt representation of sexuality. Perhaps still recovering from the effects of past repression, the Spanish cinema seems less affected than others by the post-AIDS realities of modern life. Almodóvar, Aranda, Bigas Luna, and their disrobed stars (e.g. Victoria Abril, Antonio Banderas, and Javier Bardem), repeatedly show explicit sex scenes. It is not surprising that their films are box-office successes in a country where, without decoders, more people watch scrambled sex films on Canal+ than those who are actually subscribers. In this explosion of interest in screen sex, gay as well as heterosexual desire finds its explicit representation in these films, a trend exemplified above all perhaps by the films of Eloy de la Iglesia.

In their discussion of drug-related questions, these films also invariably surround their liberated city-dwelling characters with an ambience of seediness and menace, a characteristic wholly at odds with the parodic, cheery representation of drug culture in films like Colomo's *Bajarse al moro* (1989). As Paul Julian Smith has shown, for all their tacky aesthetics, these films at least address head-on urban social and sexual realities. If Almodóvar's films, so much in thrall to camp sensibility, often seem, with some exceptions and perhaps above all in *La ley del deseo*, to hystericize or to theatricalize sexuality, Eloy's appear more consistently realistic. In a film neither by Eloy nor by Almodóvar, but also dealing like theirs with homosexuality, Chávarri's *Las cosas del querer* (1989), a biopic loosely based on the life of the singer Miguel de Molina, homosexuality seems less an opportunity for the representation of same-sex relationships between men than for exposure of the cruelties and indignities to which in repressive times (the film is set in the 1940s) homosexual men have been subjected. The film is a reminder of Francoist Spain's banishment of homosexuality. The *maricón*-hating conformists speak for an outmoded age when one of their number accompanies the conclusion of his own part in the beating of Mario the homosexual with these words: 'This is a warning to you to leave Spain and not to return.' Elsewhere the film transgresses Francoist film norms by specularizing the male, as Mario (Manuel Banderas) lies back on his bed, naked from the waist up (though the towel around his midriff will later be removed by his aristocratic would-be male suitor) his arms behind his back, smooth pectorals in sharp focus, adopting a voluptuous pose reminiscent of some of the Hollywood beefcake publicity stills of, say, Tony Curtis, Victor Mature, or Jeff Chandler, 1950s stars whose thick, curly eyelashes and glycerined, hairless chests caused many matinée hearts to flutter. Besides Eloy's films, many others, not preoccupied with homosexuality, like *Demonios en el jardín* (Gutiérrez Aragón, 1982), *Don Juan en los infiernos* (Gonzalo Suárez, 1992), *El Dorado*, or *Tata Mía* (Borau, 1988) with its thematics of positive/negative modes of regression, a witty flashback to 1930s/1940s Hollywood screwball comedy, are all engaged in the project of the deconstruction of Francoist versions of masculinity.

This project has also appeared high on the agenda of work by women directors like Pilar Miró, Josefina Molina, Rosa Vergés, and Ana Belén. In *Lo más natural* Lucía (Viviane Vives) remarks, 'I've known a lot of women. They all wanted to be one thing and ended up being another. Why? Because of a man. It's always the same.' In the same film Clara (Charo López), abandoned by her successful, conservative middle-aged husband (Patrick Bauchau), replaces him with the much younger, pop music-identified, ecology-conscious, loosely clothed, and flexibly minded 'New Man' Miguel Bosé, unable nevertheless to liberate herself entirely from the rougher appeal of the former as, even though she is by now Bosé's mistress, a torrid sexual encounter with him reveals. The title *Lo más natural* [*It's Only Natural*], a constantly recurring phrase in the film, questions assumptions about normality or naturalness, highlighting the arbitrary motivations of agreed social conventions.[2] The Francoist mother-in-law, still wedded to notions of sexual difference and propriety rooted in patriarchal conditioning, seems terminally incapable of engagement with feminist arguments, explaining male drives for control over castration-threatening women as serving the interests of male self-protection: 'Men have their nature. We have ours. A man with a young girl at worst makes a fool of himself. A woman with a young man is pathetic. [. . .] One should go through one's menopause with more dignity.' In the 1990s ethos of freely available toy boys and hormone replacement therapy, the mother-in-law's strictures seem out of step with modern realities, her essentialist views of subjectivity incompatible with this and many other contemporary films' redefinitions of femininity and awareness of socialized norms of role and gender. These films dramatize female desire, but they stop short of the Almudena Grandes-inspired *Las edades de Lulú* (Bigas Luna, 1991), in which the specularization of the female of more traditionally minded films is reversed, the woman here appropriating the power of the look and paying for the spectacle of sexually desirable copulating males.

Far less savage than Pilar Miró's *La petición* (1976), in which a woman's frustrations with men lead to two murders, *Lo más natural* shares with Miró's *Gary Cooper que estás en los cielos* (1980) a conviction that, even if utopian constructions of the self are ultimately as elusive to men as to women, it may be possible for women to reconcile themselves to those men at least prepared to recognize and condemn traditional prejudices and tyrannies, establishing with them working relationships based on equality. But *Gary Cooper* above all recognizes that the more seductive credentials of equality of the 'New Man' (Jon Finch) frequently offer no compensation for the older man's more restrictive yet also perhaps more reliable, chivalrous instincts of respect and protectiveness, even if these are sometimes the companions of mystification and dominance.

Addiction to the rougher forms of supremacist masculinity, and adherence to patriarchal norms, even in the liberated climate of post-dictatorship Spain, do not only fascinate women directors. They are also the focus of interest of some of Spain's more dynamic male directors, especially Bigas Luna in *Lola* (1986), *Bilbao* (1978), and *Jamón, jamón* (1993) (a film that also reconsiders the deeper cultural traditions and rituals of country life), Bajo Ulloa in *Alas de mariposa* (1992), and, above all, Almodóvar in most of his films, but perhaps especially in *Mujeres al borde de un ataque de nervios* (1988).

Pilar Miró, Josefina Molina, Rosa Vergés, and Ana Belén—whose one Carmen Rico Godoy-scripted excursion into film-directing carries the significant title *Cómo ser mujer y no morir en el intento* [*How to Be a Woman and Come out of it Alive*] (1991)—struggle as women to find an authentic voice in the commercial cinema of this period. Equally, Almodóvar also seeks, from the male perspective, one admittedly governed by gay priorities, to highlight the predicament of women caught in the various traps of socialized constructions of subjectivity. As well as recuperating and reversing the repressions of male homosexuality, Almodóvar's interest in sexual politics sets out to explore the contradictory impulses of female desire.

In *Mujeres al borde de un ataque de nervios* all the women progress from passivity to activity, refusing victimization, self-assertively taking the initiative in pursuing their own destinies. Like the Joan Crawford of Nicholas Ray's *Johnny Guitar* (1954), whose lines she dubs into Spanish, Carmen Maura, in common with Laura del Sol, Ana Belén, Assumpta Serna, and others—all filmic prototypes of the Spanish 'New Woman'—is career-oriented, projecting fire and energy as well as passion.

Neither fey nor fragile, she gives as good an account of herself as any male in the hottest battles of the sexes. Yet not all the battles are won by the 'New Woman', and Almodóvar at his best, like the men and women his films satirize, keeps shifting his ground. The somewhat caricaturesque, rather moralistic, representation of the vicissitudes of male heterosexuality in *Mujeres* is reworked in *Tacones lejanos* to take account brilliantly of the contradictory urges of all forms of sexual relationships, making of all women, New as well as unreconstructed, as of all men, straight or gay, the playthings of desire.

Almodóvar's antics enjoy the licence of postmodernist convention. Other directors approach their subjects less anarchically. All more or less liberated from lingering post-civil war obsessions, now more relaxed, less morally and politically neurotic, even allowing space for criticism of the new liberal attitudes (as in *Pan de ángel*), they have to a larger or lesser extent returned to more intimate questions of psychology, explorations of modernity, or experimentations in form, struggling to acquire authenticity in a consumerist, America-dominated world of mass culture. While *Carmen* (Saura, 1983) is Spain's reconciliation both with its European and internal, heterogeneous culture (especially its gypsy and Moorish elements), *La línea del cielo* (Colomo, 1983), by taking its disoriented hero to New York, concentrates on reintegration after the years of wilderness into the mainstream preoccupations of the wider world. Even though the film's comedy springs in part from the Antonio Resines character's awkwardness and failures abroad, his return to Spain at the film's closure also represents a warning against beguilement by American values.

Postmodernist directors like Colomo and Almodóvar, whose comedies reflect the cannibalizing aesthetics of the times—bearing out a remark by one of Colomo's characters: 'We live in a cannibalistic society where, if you're not careful, you'll be devoured'—have successfully undermined hierarchies and traditions of all kinds. Through pastiche and parody, the decentring of the subject, insistence on provisionality, the fictionalization of experience, and the questioning of all realities, these directors have at least challenged—helped by one or two other dissenters like Erice in *El sol del membrillo* (1992) from outside the postmodernist ethos—what is fast becoming the universal law of American film and TV banality. These, and the neat narratives of Gonzalo Suárez, at least offer an alternative to the continuing box-office popularity of traditional fare such as, for instance, *folklóricas* starring Isabel Pantoja, or comedies with Fernando Esteso or Sazatornil, emphatic signs of the resilient pleasures of pre-democratic aesthetics.

Notes
1 *Out of the Past* (London, 1986), 235–6.
2 For discussion of the myth of 'naturalness', see R. Barthes, *Mythologies* (London, 1973).

Further reading
García de León, M. A., and Maldonado, T., *Pedro Almodóvar: la otra España cañí* (Ciudad Real, 1989).

Gómez de Castro, R., *La producción cinematográfica española: de la transición a la democracia (1976–1986)* (Bilbao, 1989).
Hopewell, J., *Out of the Past: Spanish Cinema after Franco* (London, 1986).
Kinder, M., *Blood Cinema: The Reconstruction of National Identity in Spain* (Berkeley, 1993).
Longi, P., 'El sexo en los 90: ni tanto ni tan poco', *Fotogramas*, 46/1 (1993), 92–101.
Monterde, J. E., *Veinte años de cine español: un cine bajo la paradoja (1973–1992)* (Barcelona, 1993).
Smith, P. J., *Desire Unlimited: The Cinema of Pedro Almodóvar* (London, 1994).
—— *Laws of Desire: Questions of Homosexuality in Spanish Writing and Film 1960–1990* (Oxford, 1992).
Vidal, N., *El cine de Pedro Almodóvar* (Madrid, 1988).

ANTONIO
ELORZA

CLARE MAR-
MOLINERO

JOSEP-ANTON
FERNÁNDEZ

XELÍS DE TORO
SANTOS

JESÚS MARÍA
LASAGABASTER

Regional Autonomy and Cultural Policy

Some Perspectives on the Nation-State and Autonomies in Spain

ANTONIO ELORZA

Inspired by an extreme brand of Spanish state nationalism, the Franco regime sought to eradicate every last trace of cultural difference, including the use of the vernacular in the supposedly 'separatist' regions—predominantly the Basque Country and Catalonia. Paradoxically Basque nationalism, though less politically developed, proved more resilient, cocooned inside Church and family. Catalan nationalism less so, since it customarily found expression in more overtly political forms which could be more readily repressed. But already by the 1960s the failure of the Francoist project was evident. Moreover, in the Basque case, state repression had only served to bring to the fore a radical form of nationalism in the shape of ETA,* employing terroristic methods, diametrically opposed to the political passivity of the PNV.* Indeed ETA came into being as the response of young Basques angry at the PNV's seemingly complacent policy of biding its time (in the full knowledge that it had no serious political challengers inside the Basque Country) and of looking to external democratic aid rather than becoming actively involved in the anti-Franco struggle. The founder of Basque nationalism, Sabino de Arana, once described Euskadi [the Basque Country] as a nation militarily occupied by Spain—which was manifestly untrue until the Franco regime turned this occupation into a reality. Indeed the sheer immensity of the state repression at its height (1965–75) legitimized ETA and its violent counter-response in the eyes of very large sectors of Basque society which, through a kind of collective complicity, provided a very real social support base for ETA. Basque terrorism is, thus, the most problematic element of Francoism's legacy to Spanish democracy. Indeed, even the very idea of 'Spain' became tainted by its connection with the dictatorship's attempt to obliterate every vestige of regional cultural difference. With the transition, it was necessary to find a rapid solution to the problem of nationalist demands, in order to avoid repeating in an intensified form the sort of tensions and frustrations which so damaged and destabilized the Second Republic. In the mean time, the economic development of the 1960s had finally laid the foundations for a Madrid-based Spanish state nationalism which fused political authority and economic power. But even though the economic pre-conditions for the peripheral nationalisms no longer existed, the cultural/historical fact of nationalist consolidation in the regions, and especially in Catalonia and Euskadi, meant that no simple centralizing solution was feasible, still less politically defensible. Spain's new democracy had to respond positively, fostering the means for diverse cultural traditions to affirm themselves and develop.

The Constitution of 6 December 1978 sought to offer a solution to the myriad demands for self-government which had intensified across the transitional process, all the while retaining such unitary or centralist elements as could serve to dispel the anxieties of the Crown and of the so-called 'de facto powers' (*poderes fácticos**)—namely the army. Thus Article 2 begins by affirming 'the indissoluble unity of the Spanish Nation', as the premiss for then recognizing 'the right to autonomy of the nationalities and regions of which it is composed'. The primacy of the 'Nation' does not, then, exclude acceptance of the idea that beneath its unifying mantle there coexist a number of nationalities and regions, each with the same rights as all the others. Spain is not a multinational state, nor a unitary one in the sense that the Second Republic was. Indeed the latter's successes and failures doubtless informed the decisions of those who drafted the new Constitution. Its defining feature is the inclusion of this new, second level of self-government which any centralist state model would explicitly exclude. The 'state of the autonomies', as the new democratic Spain is called, is also explained in the Constitution which establishes different levels of 'national/regional identity', and, accordingly, two possible routes by which regions could acquire autonomous status. The first, a more rapid route which envisaged a greater degree of self-government, was designed particularly for the 'historic nationalities', i.e. Euskadi and Catalonia, although it did not exclude other regions from applying. (The case of Andalusia, which also acceded via this first route, is an example of the potential for democratic mobilization offered by the Constitution.) Overall, this part of the constitutional process went smoothly, the only obstacle being the deadlock with the PNV,

which, taken together with the opposition from the more radical Basque nationalist sector, tends to give the impression that Euskadi was an exception to the
wide national consensus over the new form of state organization. In fact, at the
beginning of the 1980s the chief opposition to it derived both from the political
right, linked to sectors of the military, and also from the centralizing ambitions of
the national (i.e. state-wide) parties who, together, tried in vain to enact legislation
(LOAPA*) which would have curtailed the autonomy process.

The 'state of the autonomies' has certainly experienced some technical problems, but in some fifteen years of existence, it has overall been a notable political
success. One major shortcoming has been the fact that the Senate—by definition
the 'chamber of territorial representation' (Article 69.1)—has so far failed to function as such. In consequence, there is no institutional mediation between the
autonomous governments and central government. This has meant all sorts of
tensions which have pitted Basque and Catalan nationalists in particular against
the Madrid administration—with the nationalist politicians as usual loading the
blame onto 'Madrid'. But their proclaimed persecution rings a little hollow, given
that these self-same Basque and Catalan nationalist formations (PNV and CiU*
respectively) are in fact allied with 'Madrid' in the form of the PSOE* government
and its general political programme—including here its autonomy policy. Indeed,
for the past seven years in Euskadi the PSOE and PNV have been governing in
tandem. Nevertheless, in both the Basque and Catalan cases, the accusations of
political abuse levelled against Madrid undoubtedly serve a useful purpose in distancing the PNV and CiU from the PSOE and allowing political discontent to be
channelled safely towards the latter. Other criticisms of the practical operation of
the 'state of the autonomies' concern the increase in bureaucracy and thus public
expenditure involved. While this was tolerable in the boom years of the 1980s,
this now constitutes another facet of the state's financial crisis.

Nevertheless, these disadvantages have to be weighed against a series of advantages which more than compensate. For the 'state of the autonomies' has achieved
a workable division of powers between the central and regional governments. It
has, moreover, had a salutary effect on public perceptions and has managed to
balance centrifugal and centripetal tendencies in Spain. The scale of the achievement is evident in the fact that the plural reality of Spain is now part of mainstream national political discourse. So too is the ambiguity of her status as a
'nation of nations'. This results from the convergence of two distinct projects of
national construction: first that of the Spanish nation, once the difficulties originating in the nineteenth century had been overcome, and, second, that of the Basque
and Catalan nations, channelled via their respective political subsystems. An example of this new, relatively harmonious coexistence would be the joint public
affirmations of Spanish and Catalan national identity made on the occasion of the
1992 Olympic Games in Barcelona—something which would have been unthink-
able not so long ago. Again, the major obstacle remains ETA's enduring terrorist
activity in Euskadi, backed by a deep-rooted radical nationalism of populist protest:

this is a political culture which, like other populist nationalisms elsewhere in Europe, directly expresses the socio-economic malaise of a society in crisis.

To speak of a positive political balance-sheet for the new constitutional order is not, of course, the same thing as a definitive solution. In particular, it is crucial that the autonomous governments are made to feel that they have a greater stake in the viability of the central state. To take just one issue (though a vital one) as an example, one could cite the way in which the central government made transport policy in 1992 virtually a *golpe de feria*, by taking unilateral action to prioritize its 'show-case' developments connected with the Barcelona Olympics or Seville Expo, such as the AVE [Madrid–Seville high-speed train link]. This *ad hoc* manner of proceeding revealed the total lack both of an integrated national transport plan and of any concerted consultation between central government and the regions. Such *ad hoc*-ness is inappropriate in an advanced industrial democracy. Moreover, it is also irresponsible in a country like Spain which still has serious defects and inequalities in the fabric of its transport network. The lack of consultation between centre and regions brings us back to the point made earlier about the failure of the Senate to function as a 'chamber of territorial representation'. Yet a better integration of the component parts of the 'state of the autonomies' is essential to the consolidation of the state fabric as a whole. If this is not achieved, it augurs ill for Spain's political future. The central state will be placed under increasing strain as the autonomies become rebellious forces competing with each other for a 'slice of the state'. The recent Italian débâcle ought to provide the Spanish polity with a salutary warning here.

The current fluidity of Europe's borders will inevitably have repercussions in Spain, lending credibility to the aspirations to independence of some nationalist sectors in Euskadi, especially after the example of Slovakia striking out alone and with recent negotiations over Ulster's future. Economic and cultural trends may operate in the same direction. But it will be a good while before we know the consequences of the education systems in Euskadi and Catalonia which foster vernacular culture and contribute thereby to a distancing from the rest of Spain. The increasing integration of Catalonia into the Mediterranean axis of European development and the Basque economy's lengthy crisis, characteristic of those regions whose prosperity was based on heavy industry and iron and steel in particular, is another factor to be kept in mind. In Catalonia's case, the strength of nationalist feeling is generated by the optimism of potential growth—which could lead to her incorporation into a supranational network of economic production and distribution. In Euskadi, by contrast, nationalism is being fuelled by economic discontent. (Deindustrialization has meant a population shrinkage which has already seen Vizcaya and Guipúzcoa lose two parliamentary deputies in the 1993 general elections.) A prolonged crisis would see Basque society fragment further, allowing the entrenchment in the most economically blighted and thus politically dispossessed sectors of a radical nationalism favouring independence and prepared to employ terrorism to achieve it. For though ETA has come increasingly to be the target of critical public opinion in the Basque Country, the continued popularity of Herri Batasuna, the radical political party closely associated with it, should be noted.

Once again, nothing is certain about the outcome for Spain. The solution adopted during the transition of a 'state of the autonomies' was possible because of the process of economic growth (or 'modernization' in official—i.e. PSOE—terminology) begun in the 1960s. It was this process which effectively integrated the economic interests of Spain's various regions, facilitating thereby the articulation of previously disparate and often antagonistic political perspectives. In the last analysis, economic integration made possible the reciprocal concessions on which the new constitutional order is based. Precisely because of this, the Spanish state, unlike its French counterpart, played the Maastricht card for all it was worth. The process of European union was gradually resolving the internal tensions between nation-state and peripheral nationalisms in Spain, by defining for both a common European framework envisaged as a source of material support to promote further economic growth. Conversely, the blocking of European union and a prolonged economic crisis in Spain could operate in the opposite direction. We need also to remember the sheer velocity of change in Spain since the transition; from economic crisis to boom and now to recession again. This see-saw effect could have dangerous political consequences. As we can readily see elsewhere in Europe, nationalism has many potentials, not all of them positive. Tensions could intensify, thereby increasing the likelihood of Spain's disintegration as a nation-state. For this has been exactly the process (i.e. that of economic crisis eroding the legitimacy and fabric of existing political structures) which, since 1989, has led to the real or virtual breakup of several states on our European continent.

Further reading
Balcells, A., *El nacionalismo catalán* (Madrid, 1991).
Elorza, A., *Ideologías del nacionalismo vasco* (San Sebastián, 1978).
'La España de las autonomías', *Historia 16*, 200 (Dec. 1992).
García de Enterria, E., *Estudios sobre las autonomías territoriales* (Madrid, 1991).
Jáuregui, G., *Ideología y estrategia política de ETA* (Madrid, 1981).
Martín Rodríguez, M., *et al.*, 'Dinámica espacial de la economía', in J. L. García Delgado (ed.), *España: economía* (Madrid, 1989).
Solé Tura, J., *Nacionalidades y nacionalismos en España* (Madrid, 1985).

The Politics of Language: Spain's Minority Languages

CLARE MAR-MOLINERO

Article 3 of Spain's 1978 Constitution has been heralded as a radical new recognition of linguistic rights and cultural pluralism by many commentators. However, careful analysis of this article suggests that the politics of language in Spain remain contentious and ambiguous, in part because of the very language of politics itself.

This essay will look at the pull between consensus and ambiguity underpinning the present linguistic legal framework in Spain, and at how, as ever, this represents the tensions between the core and periphery of the Spanish state in its efforts to define nationhood and collective identity. It will emphasize, too, the fact that there exist many differences between the various minority language groups in terms of the successes or failures in their language planning efforts. Additionally, all such discussions have to be seen against the backdrop of so-called European unity and its possible effects on the promotion of linguistic minorities and their relationships with dominant language groups.

The first clause of Article 3 states: 'Castilian is the official Spanish language of the state.' The use of the term 'Castilian', and not 'Spanish', makes an important statement acknowledging the existence of various 'Spanish' languages, a statement that has been bitterly disputed by many not only on the political right.[1] It is significant, too, that 'state' and not 'nation' is used, given the delicate and complicated relationship between language and national identity which is only too evident in the Spanish context. Political boundaries of a state are more easily defined than those of a nation. This clause, however, goes on to say: 'All Spaniards have the duty to know it [Castilian] and the right to use it.' Immediately the radical tone of the first sentence is counteracted with a starkly prescriptive directive in the second. It is difficult to find any national constitution world-wide which prescribes the duty to know a language. And what is meant by 'know'? Something purely passive requiring no active competence? How can it be demonstrated that a citizen does or does not 'know' a language? This is highly ambiguous and awaits legal interpretation and clarification.

Clause 2 declares that 'The other Spanish languages will also be official in the respective autonomous communities in accordance with their statutes.' Once again a refreshingly enabling definition of Spain's minority languages, never tolerated in the previous forty years, is qualified by the highly prescriptive constraint of limiting their official status to their own territorial space. This clear geographical limitation means realistically that the future role of the minority languages will always take second place to Castilian. It could even be argued that it contravenes the spirit of later articles of the Constitution which claim equality for all Spanish citizens.[2] Those Spanish citizens whose mother tongue is not Castilian could argue that they do not have equal linguistic rights to those who are Castilian mother tongue speakers. A native Catalan speaker cannot insist on the right to use Catalan in official contexts in, for example, Madrid. Native Basque speakers cannot expect the Spanish state to provide Basque teaching to their children if they happen to live in, for example, Seville. On the other hand, throughout the Spanish state Castilian may be used and must be provided for. What seems a benevolent policy to promote linguistic pluralism in fact creates linguistic reservations and supports the subordination of the peripheries to the Castilian core.

As if to counter the potentially negative sense of the second clause, the third one confirms a belief in linguistic plurality when it states: 'The richness of Spain's different linguistic varieties is a cultural heritage which shall be the object of special respect and protection.' Fine words which may facilitate real action but which are unhelpfully vague: legal interpretation of such concepts as 'respect' or 'protection' is needed.

However, it is probably fair to say that this final clause has permitted a new and imaginative understanding of Spain's linguistic map. It allows autonomous communities to define their local linguistic variety and, even when this is not considered a discrete language separate from Castilian, its own particular features can be recognized and protected. This has inspired work on lexical and phonological features in, for example, Andalusia and the Canary Islands in order to draw up guidelines on what constitutes these regions' respective language varieties. The implications of this for education and the media in particular are highly significant, raising issues of standard versus local language varieties, and of forms of acceptable literacy: issues which have constantly plagued educators and language planners, not to mention politicians.

Despite these ambiguities in the constitutional framework, there is no denying the substantial advances that have taken place since 1978 in the promotion and status of Spain's minority languages. It is notoriously difficult to agree a definition for the term 'language' but, most usefully for this discussion, it can be equated with the linguistic code of a speech community of a significant size and with, therefore, some political influence. In this sense it is generally accepted that Spain contains four such 'languages': Castilian, Catalan, Basque, and Galician, although arguments in favour of Asturian and Aragonese, for instance, or for Galician to be a 'dialect' of Portuguese, will always remain. Significantly Francoist ideology termed Catalan and Galician 'dialects' in a clear attempt to downgrade their status to a category normally considered inferior to a language.

It is in the regions where the three non-Castilian languages are spoken—the so-called 'historic' communities—that the greatest activity in terms of language planning is taking place. These efforts are supported not only by Article 3 of the Constitution but also by the relevant Autonomy Statute and, in particular, by the local Linguistic Normalization Laws. There are many similarities between the various regional legal frameworks and the areas of linguistic activity through which they are being implemented, but there are also important differences, which is not surprising given that the various autonomous communities display marked differences.

By far the most active and apparently successful language promotion programmes are taking place in Catalonia, the largest and wealthiest of the three relevant communities. The autonomous community of Catalonia has more than 6 million inhabitants, of whom approximately 90 per cent claim to understand Catalan, whilst over 60 per cent admit to speaking it in some form.[3] As in the Basque Country and Galicia, the local government has set up a directorate to co-ordinate language promotion programmes and is encouraging the teaching of and through the medium of Catalan, the development of modern terminologies in

Catalan, and the use of the local language in all government, administration, and official public use, as well as in the media. The results are spectacular: the rise in the number of schools offering some or much of their curriculum through Catalan is sharp; most public notices, street names, menus, bank cheques, entrance tickets, etc. are in Catalan (sometimes exclusively, sometimes bilingually). There are two daily papers in Catalan in Barcelona and one in Gerona, two television channels solely in Catalan and a third offering some programmes in Catalan, plus numerous Catalan local radio stations. Theatre, cinema, and publications flourish in Catalan. Significantly, much of this includes translations from languages other than Castilian (*Neighbours* or *The 'A' Team* dubbed into Catalan; Marx or Proust translated).

Catalan has always been the language of the whole Catalan population including, significantly, the upper and middle classes; in this sense, it is different from Basque and Galician, and in fact from most comparable socio-linguistic situations. As a result, the language can serve as a symbol of social mobility and acceptance, producing consequently favourable attitudes to its use and teaching. This has undoubtedly helped overcome the single greatest obstacle, which is the large non-native-Catalan-speaking economic migrant population now resident in Catalonia. This has obviously diluted the spread of the language, especially in the urban industrial areas where these immigrant groups are concentrated. However, unlike Basque but like Galician, Catalan's accessibility to Castilian speakers has helped provide a very high incidence of passive knowledge of the language by the region's population.

At the same time, like Basque and Galician (and many other minority languages), Catalan faces the challenge of mass communications in modern technological societies. Satellite television, international travel, computer technology, multinational business creating the so-called global village inevitably weaken the role of lesser-used languages and strengthen the position of world languages, above all English. Castilian is, of course, a widely spoken world language, and to compete with it or aspire to equal bilingualism (as stated in the declaration of aims of the respective autonomous communities' language laws) is arguably an impossible goal.

With less than 2.5 million inhabitants, the Basque community is the smallest of the three autonomous communities in which a minority language is being promoted. Fewer than 25 per cent of this population claims to speak Basque, reflecting the inaccessibility of the language which—unlike Catalan, Galician, and Castilian—is not part of the Romance language continuum. The language has considerably less prestige and status than Catalan within its community, and significantly has not until recently been seen as an essential core value of Basque nationalism. Although during the 1960s and 1970s the language was given an increased symbolic status by the nationalist movement ETA.[*4] Another positive development dating back to the 1960s was the introduction of Basque schools, teaching Basque and providing a curriculum through the medium of Basque.

These schools, known as *ikastolas*, were an important attempt to promote Basque identity, originally as largely clandestine groups, then increasingly in the 1960s and 1970s as private organizations, often working as non-profit-making parental co-operatives. However, there is no strong literary tradition in Basque, and the codification of the language and selection of a standard variety from various competing dialects is very recent. All of this has made the teaching of Basque and the use of it in public life very much more difficult. The Basque Country also has an important non-Basque immigrant population which has been slow to want to learn Basque, particularly since, unlike Catalan, it has been associated with rural areas and backward traditionalism. There have been improvements and successes as Basque is promoted through the education system (there are now state-funded *ikastolas*) and used in local government wherever possible. But the obstacles to the learning of Basque create the sense that its promotion is more symbolic than practical.

Galicia, like the Basque Country, contains a small population (just under 3 million), but by contrast has not been affected by immigration; thus a very high percentage of the population—90 per cent—speak the language. However, Galician lacks status and as a result does not serve as an instrument for social advancement, and is used for more educated literate purposes only by a tiny minority of middle-class intellectuals. The language planning activities, similar in conception to those in Catalonia and the Basque Country, are attempting to counter these attitudes. Another important difference in the case of Galician is the tradition of large-scale emigration, tending to produce a conservative 'holding' mentality, particularly with womenfolk waiting for the return of the perceived head of the family. In such a predominantly rural society, belief in cultural independence and confidence are not strong. The changes now taking place as a result of the new language policies must also be seen in the context of a counter-movement by the so-called 'reintegrationists', a small but vociferous group who romanticize the need to return Galicia and Galician to the fold of Mother Portugal. Neither the reintegrationists nor the isolationists (those who see Galician culture and language as separate from either of their larger neighbours) are able to counter substantially the influence and dominance of Castilian.

Clearly issues of national and group identity are present in all these activities to promote and protect minority language rights in Spain, as they are also in the Castilian centre's determination to allow linguistic independence only up to a certain point. By limiting the promotion of non-Castilian languages to discrete geographical areas, the continued domination of Castilian as 'national' language is ensured. The minorities' cultural identities are acknowledged only when they are linked to territorial identities. In a world of increasingly mobile populations this is a questionable principle.

In analysing the linguistic map of Spain, two further factors need to be borne in mind: the role of an increasing variety of immigrant groups; and the effects of a more closely integrated European Community. On the one hand, likely changes in political power structures within the Community seem to point to the emergence of a 'Europe of the regions', in which direct links between the supranational European power centres and the local regional centres will increasingly bypass the central administration of the nation-state. This is seen by Catalans, Basques, and Galicians as a real chance to strengthen their particular cultures and languages, and to some extent is backed up by Community resources such as regional aid or initiatives like those of the European Bureau for Lesser-Used Languages and the Mercator Project. These last two projects aim to improve knowledge of and research into Europe's minority languages, to sponsor the teaching and learning of these languages, and to foster relations between the groups using them.

On the other hand, a major premiss of the European Community is the encouragement and right of the freedom of movement of persons within the member states. This policy is bound to have language implications, above all challenging the notion that linguistic and cultural identity can be tied to a particular geographical space. Added to this is the situation of significant numbers of non-European immigrants, many of whom do not speak as their mother tongue the language of any member state. Spain has only recently begun to experience the social and cultural effects of such immigration, largely with groups from North Africa and Latin America. In the case of the latter, language is obviously not an issue, but it is becoming a very serious one in the case of the former. If Spain is to honour the spirit of the EC's 1977 directive encouraging all member states to provide at least some mother tongue education for the children of immigrants, this will put a strain on the delicate balance reached between the present national language and the minority languages: a balance which not everyone sees as ideal, and which highlights the fraught relationship between language and constructions of national identity.

Notes
1 See e.g. G. Salvador, 'Lenguas de España, autonomías y fronteras lingüísticas', in *Lengua española y lenguas de España* (Barcelona, 1987).
2 e.g. Art. 14 states: 'Spaniards are equal in the eyes of the law, with no form of discrimination being allowed to prevail for reasons of birth, race, sex, religion, opinion, or any other condition or personal or social circumstance.' (Translations of all quotations from the 1978 Spanish Constitution are the author's own.)
3 For statistics on who speaks or understands what in six different regions of Spain and in Spain as a whole, see the 1990 EC Commission report, *Linguistic Minorities in the European Economic Community*, 8.
4 See D. Conversi, 'Language or Race?', *Ethnic and Racial Studies*, 13/1 (1990).

Further reading
Conversi, D., 'Language or Race? The Choice of Core Values in the Development of Catalan and Basque Nationalism', *Ethnic and Racial Studies*, 13/1 (1990), 50–70.
EC Commission, *Linguistic Minorities in the European Economic Community: Spain, Portugal, Greece* (Luxemburg, 1990).
Jardón, M., *La 'normalización lingüística', una normalidad democrática: el caso gallego* (Madrid, 1993).

Ninyoles, R., *Cuatro idiomas para un estado* (Madrid, 1977) (dated but provocative and much quoted).

Salvador, G., *Lengua española y lenguas de España* (Barcelona, 1987).

Siguán, M., *Multilingual Spain* (Amsterdam, 1993; trans. of *España plurilingüe*, Madrid, 1992) (good introductory text giving an overall view).

Woolard, K., *Double Talk: Bilingualism and the Politics of Ethnicity in Catalonia* (Stanford, Calif., 1989).

In addition, the Generalitat in Catalonia, the Basque Government, and the Xunta in Galicia all have useful official publications.

Becoming Normal: Cultural Production and Cultural Policy in Catalonia

JOSEP-ANTON FERNÁNDEZ

To understand developments in Catalan cultural production in the post-Franco years and cultural policy in this period, it is crucial to remember that military defeat in 1939 meant the practical disappearance of the cultural infrastructure that had been created over a century. As part of the victors' attempt to return Catalonia to the fold of the 'true Spanish soul' (*reespañolización*), the Catalan language was banned from public use and from education, and practically all signs of Catalan identity were outlawed. Most of the intellectual élite was forced into exile or was repressed and silenced, and all Catalan-identified cultural activity had to go underground. As Albert Manent has pointed out, the underground cultural resistance managed to maintain a precarious yet effective network of activists which enjoyed the support of some sectors of the Church and the bourgeoisie.[1] However, it was not until 1946 that books in Catalan could be legally published; even then no translations from foreign languages were allowed (this prohibition would be lifted in the early 1960s), and in any case all publications were subjected to severe censorship. It was also in 1946 that, for the first time since the end of the war, plays in Catalan could be staged; this renewed public presence of Catalan culture was followed in 1947 by the institution of the first post-war literary prize, something that would later become a successful formula for the promotion of Catalan books in times of political hardship. Throughout the 1950s the readership was slowly increasing, and with the regime's modest liberalization in the early 1960s some expansion was possible: new publishing houses were founded, as well as associations for the promotion of culture and the teaching of the language, and the songwriters' movement of the *nova cançó* achieved important popular success. All these initiatives involved significant growth, but the impossibility of teaching the Catalan language in schools (or Catalan literature and history, for that matter) and the virtual absence of the language from the press and audio-visual media, made it impossible to rebuild a proper, functional cultural market; most cultural enterprises, especially those in the publishing sector, were heavily sponsored by sympathetic sectors of the bourgeoisie, or financed through popular subscription. The aims of such efforts in the 1960s and early 1970s were mainly political: to maintain the prestige of Catalan as a language of high culture, to prepare the ground for expansion in the post-Franco period, to maintain a minimum level of cultural production and consumption, and to guarantee the visibility of Catalan culture.

The precariousness of this situation is clearly shown by the fact that it was not till 1976 that the number of books published in Catalan per year reached the same figures as in 1936 (around 800 titles), and that the first newspaper in Catalan since the end of the war, *Avui*, appeared. However, the presence of the language on radio and television was limited to a few hours a week; and, most importantly, the great waves of immigration from other parts of Spain between the 1950s and the 1970s meant that almost half the population could not speak Catalan, while the ban on education in Catalan during the dictatorship had made most of the Catalan-speaking population illiterate in its own language. This situation was widely recognized as 'abnormal'; and, with the advent of democracy, there was a consensus among the democratic forces that a state of linguistic and cultural 'normality' (*normalitat*) was essential to the full recovery of Catalonia's national identity. This was the conclusion reached by the Congrés de Cultura Catalana (1976), which set the agenda for subsequent years. The Congrés—which created an impressive popular mobilization over the whole of Catalonia and achieved a broad political consensus—argued in its mission statement that a return to self-rule was necessary in order to 'normalize' the use of the Catalan language and restore its official status, and in order to reinstitutionalize and promote Catalan culture.[2]

The creation of the Departament de Cultura of the Generalitat* de Catalunya after the first elections to the Catalan parliament in 1980 was the first major step to implementing this programme, and has been central to the dramatic growth of the Catalan cultural market since then. The promotion of Catalan culture is inseparable both from the policies of 'linguistic normalization' undertaken by the authorities, and from the discourse of political nationalism.[3] 'Cultural normalization', the cultural policy of contemporary Catalan nationalism, aims at constituting Catalonia as a 'normal' society: that is, a society in which Catalonia's own language would be hegemonic, in which citizens would share a common sense of (Catalan) national identity based on their cultural traditions, and which would be comparable to any other modern European society in terms of cultural infrastructures, habits of cultural consumption, and the balance between high and mass culture. The specific goals of 'cultural normalization' are the institutionalization of Catalan culture and the construction of cultural infrastructures, the consolidation of a media industry in Catalan, and the extension of habits of cultural consumption in the Catalan language. The final goal of this process is to reach a situation of *de facto* cultural independence, the old aspiration of nationalism; as Joan Guitart, Culture Minister of the Generalitat de Catalunya, has claimed: 'in cultural matters Catalonia should be equivalent to a state.'[4]

The efforts invested in the audio-visual field have met with by far the greatest success. The demand for mass media in Catalan headed the cultural agenda in the early years of the democratic regime, and became a priority of the autonomous government. As Josep Gifreu argues, the creation of an audio-visual space in Catalan has been vital for the '(re)construction' of national identity, and indeed for the progress of 'linguistic normalization'.[5] The regional centre of Televisión Española in Catalonia was already broadcasting in Catalan in the 1970s, but only for a small number of hours a week, outside prime time, and the schedule did not include foreign films or series dubbed into Catalan. Likewise, in 1976 the state radio company, Radio Nacional de España, created a station in Catalan, Ràdio 4, but it could be heard only in parts of Catalonia. This situation changed in 1983 with the institution by the Generalitat of the Corporació Catalana de Ràdio i Televisió (CCRTV), the body responsible for public broadcasting in Catalan. CCRTV controls four radio stations—one of which, Catalunya Ràdio (1983), has the biggest share of the overall Catalan audience—and two TV channels, TV3 (1983) and Canal 33 (1989). TV3 has had a tremendous impact on Catalan society; it broadcasts entirely in Catalan and from the start was designed to compete directly with TVE1 and TVE2, the Spanish public television stations. Although it has never overtaken TVE1, by 1990 TV3 had achieved a 40 per cent share of the overall Catalan audience, and has been largely responsible for the significant increase in knowledge of the Catalan language in recent years.[6] In Valencia, Canal 9, the public television channel owned by the Generalitat Valenciana, broadcasts partially in Catalan. A lively movement of local TV and radio stations, usually run as co-operatives, also exists.

The publishing market has also experienced spectacular growth: from just over 800 books published in 1976, the figures for books in Catalan have rocketed to almost 4,500 in 1990. This increase has been favoured by the extension of Catalan language teaching, and by the official policy of financial support for publishing in Catalan. The former has boosted the production of textbooks and children's literature, whilst the latter has made it possible to publish costly works such as dictionaries, and to start collections devoted to western literary classics or philosophical texts, for example. During the 1980s Catalan publishing houses, most of them small-scale, turned to popular genres such as crime fiction or erotica to increase their readership; they also set out to compete with their Spanish counterparts by publishing contemporary foreign narrative.

The poor reading habits of Catalan society, however, constitute a major drawback which also affects the press. Six daily newspapers are published entirely in Catalan—two of them, *Avui* (1976) and *Diari de Barcelona* (1986), based in Barcelona—but their circulation amounts to a mere 12 per cent of the overall daily press available in Catalonia. Of the four weekly news magazines launched in the 1980s, only *El Temps* (1983), published in Valencia, has survived. There are also a number of specialized journals and magazines covering high culture or academic writing (*Serra d'Or, Els Marges, L'Avenç*) which, despite their small circulation, have a well-established readership.

Cinema and popular music have perhaps been the most problematic areas of cultural production in recent years. Catalan cinema shares the structural problems of the Spanish film industry as a whole, compounded by the Catalan authorities' lack of a clear policy towards the film industry. As Miquel Porter i Moix points out, despite the financial support of the Spanish and Catalan authorities and the collaboration schemes between television and film producers, the presence of the Catalan language and of Catalan films in cinemas is minimal.[7] This is due partly to the fact that watching films in Catalan has never become a habit, but especially to the attitude of the commercial distributors, who regard the Catalan language as a marketing handicap; there is also a generalized feeling that the Catalan film industry has not succeeded in attracting viewers' interest.

Popular music suffered a serious decline in the 1980s, but it has recently seen an important recovery. Of the singer-songwriters of the *nova cançó* who in the 1960s and 1970s, following the prestigious model of the French *chanson*, combined literary and musical quality with political resistance, attracting large audiences, only a few managed to survive the climate of political disenchantment in the 1980s. This, together with the Catalan authorities' apparent lack of interest in popular music, turned cultural production in this area into a virtual wasteland, despite the success of the new TV and radio stations; the only two labels publishing music exclusively in Catalan disappeared. The late 1980s, however, have witnessed a blossoming of pop and rock music in Catalan, which has been able to create an audience for itself.

The process of 'cultural normalization', as this account shows, is far from harmonious, and there are several good reasons for this. Catalan culture has to face the objective limitations of its reduced dimensions and its minority status; as the most recent attempt at modernizing Catalan culture, 'cultural normalization' is taking place in an international context marked by globalization. Young intellectuals have pointed this out, and have started to develop an analysis of Catalan cultural dynamics which is highly critical of the present situation.[8] The Catalan government has also been criticized for imposing a traditionalist version of national identity through its subsidization policies (hence, among other things, its failure to support contemporary music).[9] Other problems derive from the collision of two cultural markets (Spanish versus Catalan) in the same territory, which places Catalan products in a position of inferiority; this has been aggravated by the introduction in 1989 of the three private television channels, which broadcast exclusively in Spanish. Finally, the conflict between Spanish and Catalan nationalisms remains, leading to hostility on the part of the Spanish state towards the development of an audio-visual space common to the Catalan-speaking territories in their entirety.[10]

Notes
1 *Escriptors i editors del nou-cents* (Barcelona, 1984), 215–26.
2 See J. Fuster, *El Congrés de Cultura Catalana* (Barcelona, 1978), 193–206.
3 See A. Balcells, *El nacionalismo catalán* (Madrid, 1991).

4 J. Guitart i Agell, *Cultura a Catalunya anys noranta* (Barcelona, 1990), 17.
5 J. Gifreu, 'Els *mass-media* i la identitat nacional', in J. Termes (ed.), *Catalanisme* (Barcelona, 1986), 20.
6 See M. Leprêtre, *The Catalan Language Today* (Barcelona, 1992), 40.
7 'Situació i previsions del cinema a la Catalunya Autònoma', in J. Puy (ed.), *La cultura catalana recent* (Barcelona, 1993), 67–73.
8 See O. Izquierdo, 'Una autocrítica', in A. Broch (ed.), *70–80–90* (Valencia, 1992), 91–112; and S. Peradejordi, 'Dues o tre coses que sé d'ella', *1991 Literatura*, 1 (1992), 71–80.
9 See J. Lorés, *La transició a Catalunya* (Barcelona, 1985), 180–2.
10 See Gifreu, 'Els *mass-media* i la identitat nacional', 297–9.

Further reading
Balcells, A., *El nacionalismo catalán* (Madrid, 1991).
Fernàndez, A., *Una experiència de normalitzáció lingüística: el Pla de la Dirección General d'Administració Local* (Barcelona, 1993).
Fuster, J., *El Congrés de Cultura Catalana* (Barcelona, 1978).
Gifreu, J., 'Els *mass-media* i la identitat nacional (Catalunya, 1939–1985)', in J. Termes (ed.), *Catalanisme: història, política i cultura* (Barcelona, 1986), 285–99.
Guitart i Agell, J., *Cultura a Catalunya anys noranta*, and M. Reniu i Tresserras, *Un nou impuls a la política lingüística* (Generalitat de Catalunya, Barcelona, 1990).
Izquierdo, O., 'Una autocrítica', in A. Broch (ed.), *70–80–90: Dues dècades des de la tercera i última* (Valencia, 1992), 91–112.
Leprêtre, M., *The Catalan Language Today* (Barcelona, 1992).
Lorés, J., *La transició a Catalunya (1977–1984): el pujolisme i els altres* (Barcelona, 1985).
Manent, A., *Escriptors i editors del nou-cents* (Barcelona, 1984).
Marí, I., '1960–1988: l'evolució de la llengua', in J. Puy (ed,), *La cultura catalana recent (1960–1988): cicle de conferències fet al CIC de Terrassa, curs 1988/1989* (Barcelona, 1993), 27–50.
Peradejordi, S., 'Dues o tres coses que sé d'ella', *1991 Literatura*, 1 (1992), 71–80.
Porter i Moix, M., 'Situació i previsions del cinema a la Catalunya Autònoma', in J. Puy (ed.), *La cultura catalana recent (1960–1988)*, 59–76.

Negotiating Galician Cultural Identity

XELÍS DE TORO SANTOS

Torrente Ballester's classic novel *La saga/fuga de J.B.* (1972) provides an apt image of the ambiguous position of Galician identity in the contemporary period: the mythical city of Castroforte de Baralla levitates and disappears into the clouds, in response to the collective anxiety of its inhabitants. This image can be used to illustrate two points. First, that Galicia has in some senses been obliterated from the cultural map, due to the failure to create a cohesive and integrated national identity. As a result, Galicia continues to be characterized in the rest of Spain by a series of clichés and stereotypes. Second, the image can be taken to illustrate the marginal position of Torrente Ballester's work within Galician culture, as 'a Galician who is a writer but not a Galician writer', having written exclusively in Castilian.[1] Yet the works of Torrente Ballester have created the most complex and positive literary representation of Galicia during the Franco period.

Historically, there have been various attempts to resolve these issues. The most determined was made by Galician intellectuals in the 1920s, who created a defi-nition of Galician cultural and national identity based on the language and Celtic roots, elements of which could be used to distinguish Galicia from the rest of Spain. In this essay, however, I wish to arge that Galician culture and identity constitute a historical process in which definitions and parameters have always to be renegotiated. Galician intellectuals and artists after Francoism have attempted to put Galicia on the map by offering new perspectives on its culture and identity.

The major feature of the transition from dictatorship to democracy was the recognition of Catalonia, the Basque Country, and Galicia as historic cultural en-tities. The introduction of the Autonomy Statute following a referendum in 1981 meant a radical change in the relationship between culture and politics in Galician society. The defence of Galician identity had played an important role in the resistance to Francoism, focusing opposition to centralization and asserting Galicia's position as a distinct cultural entity. However, Galician culture is no longer a cul-ture of resistance since it has become an official culture in its own right. This change in function has given rise to contradictory and sometimes uneasy relationships.

On the one hand, Galician culture was institutionalized for the first time. Hopes that the lack of cultural infrastructure would be overcome were raised by the inauguration of Radio and Television Galega (RTVG) in 1985;[2] the promotion of the Galician language through its introduction into the curriculum at the same time as it became the official language used in the regional government adminis-tration; and the beginnings of a policy to support culture and the arts. On the other hand, the success of these policies is highly questionable. The number of Galicians who use Galician as their mother tongue continues to fall and the media available for disseminating the language are minimal.[3]

With the final removal of censorship, Spain in the 1980s saw an explosion in the arts marked by the attempt to break with the past, projecting the idea of a new young Spain closer to Europe. Galician culture played an important role in this period. During the first half of the decade, Galician artists were a constant focus of attention in the Spanish media. In consecutive years film-makers such as Villaverde and Reixa were awarded the most important prizes for experimental film in Spanish competitions. The work of fashion designers such as Adolfo Dominguez received international recognition, paving the way for the emergence of new designers; and bands like Siniestro Total and Os Resentidos suggested new forms of expression in pop music, influencing new bands in the rest of Spain. Other artists who received important prizes were: Pepe Barro for graphic design, Miguel Anxo Prado for the design of comics, and Luisa Castro for poetry. We could further mention innovative magazines such as *Tintiman* and *La Nabal*, and the recognition achieved by the visual arts group Atlántica. This explosion of the arts in Galicia was known as the *movida* galega*. Behind this label, coined by the Spanish media, lay many different phenomena and ideas, and a broad range of artists with differing aesthetic aims and viewpoints. In its totality, this cultural explosion created a new image of artistic vitality and innovation challenging the stereotypical view of Galicia as a cultural backwater, reinforced for decades by the Spanish media.

Although it is difficult to identify groups or artists with a clear agenda regarding new representations of Galicia, I shall try to outline some ideas and positions emerging and becoming established during this period. These fall into three main groups.

The first position could be characterized as an attempt to link Galician tradition to the new circumstances. The idea that Galician culture could survive only if it was able to modernize was common. Modernization was understood in two senses: first, as an attempt to incorporate new aesthetic tendencies; and second, as the production of work in fields such as film which till that time had remained virtually virgin territory. The terms 'tradition' and 'modernity' were the keywords of the major intellectual debates in the mid-1970s and throughout the 1980s. The first clear statements of this position were made at the Encontros de Sargadelos, a series of summer conferences organized by the Laboratorio de Formas de Galicia. These were forums intended to encourage debate about the future of Galician culture. To some extent, this position has been incorporated into Xunta de Galicia policy. It is summed up by a quotation from the graphic design group Re-vision:

In Galicia, a small but significant cultural sector is working doggedly and consistently to re-invent this old country [. . .] Re-vision is conscious of its task: to invent [. . .] the new images needed by a Galician society that will see out the twentieth century and face the twenty-first.[4]

A second position emerged through youth and urban culture, promoted through magazines, pop music, and experimental film-making. This clearly rejected Spanish stereotypes while affirming a Galician identity; but it did so by exploring and challenging the contradictions and limitations of traditional forms of identity. Full of self-criticism and irony, it played with juxtapositions of those traditional images and symbols of Galician identity that had found their roots in the Celtic heritage, Galician language, and rural tradition. The attempts to project Galicia as avant-garde and innovative were also satirized. A quotation from the catalogue of the visual arts exhibition held during a week dedicated to Galicia at the Universidad Internacional Menéndez Pelayo Summer School at Santander provides a useful illustration:

A pitiless country needs a pitiless flag. Thirty Galician artists are taking part in this first encounter aimed at re-designing the present Galician flag, with its white, spiritless ground and thin, pale diagonal which seems to have been conceived more to separate bilingual texts than to provide a powerful representation of our national obsessions.[5]

It is in this spirit that phenomena such as the magazine *La Nabal*, the song 'Miña terra galega' by Siniestro Total, the lyrics of Os Resentidos, and the work of film-makers such as Reixa have to be understood.

A third position rejected innovation and sought to maintain a concept of Galicia

26 Design for an 'alternative' Galician flag by Antón Reixa, from the exhibition *Semana de las fuerzas atroces del Noroeste* held at the Universidad Internacional Menéndez Pelayo, Santander, in 1986. The design provides a witty comment on the pursuit of an essentialist national identity, by proposing as Galicia's national symbol the cow that reproduces the region's traditional image as a rural backwater devoted to dairy production, but representing this in a form obviously reminiscent of the label of a well-known brand of French (i.e. foreign) processed (i.e. not natural) cheese (La Vache qui rit: i.e. a joke, we are invited to laugh too).

as it had been traditionally understood. For those who adhered to this position, the debate centred on national oppression, with the aim of revealing the 'essential' nature of Galicia. The cultural explosion of the 1980s was interpreted as an artificial product of the Spanish media, unrepresentative of the 'true' Galicia. The main target of such criticisms was the marginal role that Galician language and traditional culture played in this explosion.

To turn now to Galician literature: broadly speaking, we can accept the criteria used in current Galician studies which define Galician literature as literature written in Galician, but there are some issues that require discussion. First, it must be stressed that the precise standardization of linguistic norms remains contentious. The position held by the majority and supported by the Xunta is that Galician should be regarded as a language in its own right within an Iberian context. The alternative 'lusista' position asserts that Galician should be located within a Luso-Brazilian framework and emphasizes the linguistic parallels with Portuguese. This latter version has been less widely disseminated because works published in lusista have not received official subsidies. Second, one cannot dismiss the fact that Galicia has contributed significantly to Spanish literature through the work of Galician authors writing in Castilian. While such writers have started to receive recognition in Galicia, for example through the newly established Cela Foundation and Torrente Ballester Prize, to include them in the concept of Galician culture would require a redefinition of the parameters used to describe Galician culture and identity. However, the vitality of the publishing world in this period must be stressed. The number of books published in Galician increased greatly. In 1972, 78 books were published; in 1980, a year before the Autonomy Statute was introduced, the figure had gone up to 303; and in 1989 it had gone up to 637.[6] Publishing houses headed by Edicións Xerais have launched new collections of popular literature, including detective novels and new journalism. At the same time, the work of new young writers such as Antón Reixa and Suso de Toro, have addressed from a radical and controversial viewpoint questions of identity, representation, and the function of literature, seeking to incorporate strains of postmodernism.

To conclude, the first half of the 1980s saw a powerful upsurge of creativity which put Galicia back on the cultural map. A flood of new ideas challenged stock images of Galicia as well as the basis of traditional Galician identity. This cultural explosion was encouraged by the Xunta's policy of cultural subsidies. The Xunta's cultural policies have not, however, been conducive to the creation of a long-term cultural infrastructure; the ambiguity of such policies is exemplified by attitudes towards the film industry: almost all of the film and TV series broadcast on TVG are imported and dubbed, leaving little space for domestic production. The second half of the 1980s was marked by a decline in artistic production. Neither the attempts made by the Xunta to project an image of Galicia,[7] nor the policy of providing support for the arts, can disguise a fundamental lack of vitality in current Galician cultural production. As the concept of Galician identity becomes increasingly part of an institutional culture, there is a progressive loss of self-awareness and self-criticism. Once again, the image of Castroforte de Baralla levitating into the clouds provides an insight into the current uncertainty of Galician identity, still searching for a way to ground itself.

Notes
1 R. Carballo Calero, *Historía da literatura galega contemporánea* (Vigo, 1981), 17.
2 RTVG was inaugurated on 25 July 1985, Galicia's National Day, though it started transmitting a year earlier. It consists of a TV channel and a radio station broadcasting exclusively in Galician, thus showing a commitment to the normalization of the Galician language.
3 Until 1993 the only press published in the Galician language was the weekly *A Nosa Terra*. In Jan. 1994 the first daily paper in Galician was launched.
4 P. Barro, X. Díaz, and L. Santana, 'Un raio de luz', *Luzes de Galicia*, 5–6 (1987); originally published in the Barcelona magazine *On/Diseño*, 80.
5 Catalogue of the exhibition *Semana de las fuerzas atroces del Noroeste*, 1986.
6 See M. D. Cabrera, 'A empresa editorial e o mundo do libro', in M. Rivas and X. López (eds.), *Informe da comunicación en Galicia* (Corunna 1993).
7 e.g. three exhibitions of Galician artistic production—*Galicia no tempo*, *Galicia: tradición e deseño*, *Bienal de arquitectura española*—mounted to present Galician culture to a wide audience both inside and outside Galicia.

Further reading
Actas: Congreso Internacional da Cultura Galega (Vigo, 1992).
Alvarez Cáccamo, X. M., 'As revistas literarias e culturais de 1975 a 1985', *Grial* (Vigo), 89 (1985), 340–53.
Dirección Xeral de Política Lingüística, *10 anos da Lei de Normalización* (Vigo, 1992).
Hernández Borge, J., *Tres millóns de galegos* (Santiago, 1990).
Jardón, M., *La 'normalización lingüística', una normalidad democrática: el caso gallego* (Madrid, 1993).
Luzes de Galicia (1985–) (magazine).
Maneiro Vila, A., and **Cabaleiro Durán, A.**, *A TVG: unha institución pública imprenscindible para Galicia* (Santiago, 1993).
Tarrío, A., 'Dez anos de narrativa galega', *Grial* (Vigo), 89 (1985), 309–36.

The Promotion of Cultural Production in Basque

JESÚS MARÍA LASAGABASTER

In 1976, 95 books were published in Basque [*euskara*];[1] by 1992, the figure had gone up to 980, of which 755 were first editions and 225 re-editions, with 459 written originally in Basque and 328 translated into Basque. Even more spectacular than this quantitative leap is the qualitative advance over this fifteen-year period. Of the 95 titles published in 1976, 22 were in literature and literary criticism, 15 in children's and teenage literature (including comics), 12 in linguistics (including grammars and language primers), 8 in geography, 7 in religion, and 7 in history. Only 1 or 2 were scientific texts. Of the 23 subject areas listed in Unesco's classification scheme, only 14 were covered (in comparison with 4 in 1961, and 10 in 1974). The subject areas not represented were in the main those corresponding to science, philosophy, medicine, law, government, and political science. In other words, in 1976 book production in Basque was concentrated mainly on literature (adult and juvenile) and the teaching of the language. Public life and science were largely alien territory. One could almost say that the Basque language was confined to the private sphere.

In 1992 not only had the number of books published in Basque increased ten-fold, but practically all the Unesco subject areas were represented; more important still, books in Basque now had a firm footing in education (at all levels), scientific research, government, and politics. Of the 980 titles published that year, 134 related to literature, 75 to the Basque language, and 372 were textbooks in practically all subject areas, from primary through to university level,[2] which gives the lie to those who persist in regarding *euskara* as an archaic, rural language, incapable of representing the modern cultural and scientific world. It is true that Basque emerged late as a literary language—the first known literary text is dated 1545—and that it was slow to gain currency in the cultural, scientific, and political spheres. But literature, the media, the performing arts, and education provide abundant evidence that the Basque language today has the status of a normalized educated language, despite the obvious socio-linguistic limitations to its usage.

Crucial to the changes that have taken place over this fifteen-year period are the Spanish Constitution of 1978, the Autonomy Statute of 1979, and the Linguistic Normalization Law approved by the Basque parliament in 1989. As the official language—jointly with Spanish—of the Basque Autonomous Community, *euskara* has legal access to all areas of public life, education, government, political institutions, research, sport, and cultural production. Institutional support for the *euskaldunización* [Basquification] of Basque life continues to be important, and is channelled mainly through the Secretariat for Linguistic Policy, responsible to the Presidential Office of the Basque government.

Publishing was the first and most obvious—but by no means only—area of cultural production affected by the Basque language's new legal and socio-cultural status. The impact was less strong on literature—literary texts had been available, if not exactly abundant, since the 1950s—than on scientific, educational, and technical book production (law, the professions, etc.), which previously had been virtually non-existent in *euskara*. There was an immediate and sustained increase in the issue of Basque texts—including oral forms of reproduction—right across the spectrum.

Nevertheless, literature remains the paradigm of cultural production in Basque. Not so much because writers are writing in Basque as because of the institutionalization of literary life stemming from *euskara*'s new status. Although literary quality is not directly related to quantity, the normalization of literary life obviously tends to normalize writers' working conditions, indirectly affecting the quality of what is written. This 'normalization' includes an increase in the number of publishers for works of literature (these have recently been hit by economic recession), the appearance of literary magazines (some short-lived), the emergence and relative consolidation of critical activity, and the laying of the foundations of a solid academic criticism of Basque literature through the three university faculties of Basque [Facultades de Euskal Filologia] currently existing in Euskadi [the Basque Country].

The award of the 1989 National Prize for Literature to the Basque writer Bernardo Atxaga for his book of stories *Obabakoak* not only shows that, in this case at least, Basque literature can produce writing of the highest quality, but also that literary creativity, publication, and consumption have become relatively stabilized. Yet the language's minority status necessarily makes literary production precarious, despite the subsidies, writers' bursaries, and literary awards offered by various Basque institutions (the Basque government, provincial and municipal governments, savings banks) in a somewhat hectic 'literary fair' that sometimes seems to have more to do with publicity than with culture.

Also crucial to cultural production in Basque are the mass media, and of course television in particular. Basque Television (Euskal Telebista) has two channels, one of which—Euskal Telebista 1—broadcasts entirely in *euskara*, providing its own news bulletins and sports coverage, and producing (as opposed to buying) an increasing percentage of programmes. The second channel broadcasts solely in Castilian; paradoxically, this justifies the existence of an all-Basque channel against arguments that the ratio of Basque to Castilian on television should be proportionate to the respective number of language users. For the Basque government—or rather for the Basque Nationalist Party currently forming a ruling coalition with the Socialist Party of Euskadi—a TV channel in *euskara* is basic to an individual and collective sense of Basque identity and is not negotiable.

As for the press, with the transition to democracy the Castilian-language dailies started to print a small but growing number of columns in Basque, and one newspaper—*Euskaldunon* EGUNKARIA [*Basque People's Newspaper*]—publishes entirely in *euskara*, with average sales of 15,000 copies.

Although a few radio stations broadcasting in Basque already existed under the dictatorship, these were of necessity privately owned and reached only a very restricted, highly localized public. The creation of Euskadi Irratia [Radio Euskadi], transmitting entirely in *euskara* throughout the whole autonomous community from its studios in San Sebastián, has established radio as a major cultural force, not only because of its news coverage and current affairs programmes but also because of its contribution to science and the arts.

Finally, the performing arts. Cinema is, beyond any doubt, the flagship of recent Basque culture, with directors and films receiving awards in Spain and abroad, to the point that the existence of a 'Basque cinema' is frequently talked about. Established directors like Pedro Olea and Imanol Uribe, or younger ones like Juanma Bajo Ulloa and Julio Medem (with films like *La madre muerta* and *La ardilla roja*, to mention two recent examples), demonstrate the importance of Basque cinema within the overall framework of Spanish film production. Or perhaps one should say 'films by Basque directors' since—with very few exceptions—Basque films are made, distributed, and shown entirely in Castilian. But this has not stopped people using the term 'Basque cinema'; language has not been felt to be the key criterion, as it has in literature where hard-liners have argued that Unamuno, Baroja, Celaya, Otero, and other major figures cannot be called Basque writers—despite the fact that they were born and saw themselves as Basques—because they wrote or write in Castilian. This restriction of Basque literature to that written in Basque is now less prevalent, and the two literatures produced in the Basque Country—that in *euskara* and that in Castilian—coexist without undue friction.

In the theatre, by contrast, the Basque language is much more in evidence. Independent theatre groups put on a considerable number of productions in *euskara*; however, these are mostly works translated into Basque from other languages. In this sense it has to be admitted that drama in *euskara* is still sadly lagging behind poetry and fiction, in terms of quantity and quality. There are practically no playwrights writing in *euskara*, and when authors who have made their name in another genre—Gabriel Aresti in poetry or Atxaga in fiction—have ventured into the theatre, the results have been disappointing. Several of the literary prizes offered by Basque institutions are open to all genres—plays as well as novels, short stories, poetry, and essays—but the dramatic entries are the least impressive. Drama prizes are frequently not awarded for lack of sufficiently high-quality entries, and the few plays that do receive awards are often undistinguished.

Any discussion of cultural production in Basque must include mention of the role played by translation, particularly in book form. Generally speaking, translation has been practised particularly in literature and is especially common in children's and teenage literature, understandably since the publication of literary works in Basque has always had the educational aim of furthering knowledge of the language. (There is also now a substantial output of children's and teenage literature written in Basque, and many established authors contribute to the genre, often for financial reasons since this kind of book, for the educational reasons mentioned above, is the most likely to sell.) The Basque government is currently supporting a major translation programme, with the aim of translating into *euskara* the major or most representative works of world literature, plus classic philosophical and scientific texts.

A further issue that needs raising here is that of the standardization of the language. Until relatively recently, the Basque language was geographically fragmented into five leading dialects and a proliferation of local variants, with no standard form to provide cohesion and act as a model. If Basque was to become a means of public and private expression for all Basque speakers, allowing them to 'live in Basque', there was an urgent need to create some kind of linguistic uniformity, even if this meant sacrificing the wealth—often more apparent than real—of dialectal and local varieties. This process of linguistic standardization—through the development and promotion of *euskara batua* [standard Basque]—has been championed by the Academy of the Basque Language [Euskaltzaindia], particularly thanks to the efforts of the eminent linguist Koldo Mitxelena. In 1968 the

Academy drew up a standardized linguistic model, based mainly on the Guipúzcoan dialect (the most widely spoken) with elements drawn from other dialects, intended at least for written usage. *Euskara batua* has been—and still is—criticized by hard-line defenders of the various dialectal forms, but in practice it has been accepted by virtually all writers and all the mass media (printed and spoken). This does not mean that the problems of linguistic standardization have been resolved. Languages are not made by academies. The success of the Basque Academy's initiative depends ultimately on those who speak the language, and here writers and cultural workers can play a vital role.

The opposition between standard Basque and its dialectal forms raises the issue of a possible split between two parallel cultural forms: that of a popular culture which continues to express itself in the various dialects, and that of a more restricted élite culture which uses the standardized model. In practice, it is more a matter of two forms of cultural expression which may be different in the sense that a literary or scientific text written in *euskara batua* differs from a deeply ingrained, highly popular cultural phenomenon like that of *bersolarismo*,[3] but which nevertheless coexist unproblematically in the minds and cultural practice of all Basques. The conflict is not between two forms of cultural expression but between those who defend and those who reject the notion of a standardized model of the language. The latter are increasingly less vociferous as the reasons for attacking a necessary and irreversible cultural process prove unfounded. For linguistic standardization does not—and must not—mean the death of the Basque dialects. The Academy of the Basque Language is fully aware of this and, while encouraging standardization in written usage, continues to defend traditional dialectal forms.

Notes

1 *Euskara*, the eastern dialectal form of the word, is regarded as more authentic than the alternative *euskera* and is now more common, particularly in written and educated usage; *euskera* is, however, still frequently used orally.

2 For the history of book production in Basque, see Joan Mari Torrealdai, *XX.mendeko euskal liburuen Katalogoa (1900–1992)* [*Catalogue of Basque Books in the Twentieth Century (1900–1992)*], published by the Departmento de Cultura, Diputación Foral de Gipuzkoa.

3 Improvisations in verse, customary at popular festivals or other celebrations, and today frequent on television shows and in competitions organized in theatres or in courts where the Basque ball game *pelota* is played.

Further reading

Haritschelhar, J. (ed.), *Être Basque* (Toulouse, 1983).

Intxausti, J., *Euskera: la lengua de los vascos* (Castilian trans. of Basque original) (Donostia [San Sebastián], 1992).

—— (ed.), *Euskal-Herria*, i: *Historia y sociedad*; ii: *Realidad y projecto* (Mondragón, 1985) (collective volume; most of the contributions are in Basque, some are in Castilian).

Lasagabaster, J. M., *Contemporary Basque Fiction* (Reno, Nev. 1990; Spanish original *Antología de la narrativa vasca contemporánea*, Barcelona, 1986).

The magazine *Jakin* publishes an annual list of all books published in Basque during the year, with critical commentary (in Basque).

ENRIQUE
BUSTAMANTE

BARRY JORDAN

AUGUSTO M.
TORRES

EMMA DENT
COAD

The State, Enterprise Culture, and the Arts

The Mass Media: A Problematic Modernization

ENRIQUE BUSTAMANTE

To talk of a mass communications sector or market in the late Franco years can be misleading. The dictatorship had imposed a primarily political function on the press, radio, and television which affected the way they, and almost all interested parties, worked. The press was subject to official sanction and advance censorship, and to Consejos de Fundadores (state-appointed management boards) instituted to keep an eye on political correctness rather than on market forces (prices were set officially); unofficial groupings, constituted by common shareholders or front companies, also existed within the press, largely representing financial and industrial groups using the press as a public platform in the in-fighting between the regime's different families, even if this meant considerable financial losses.[1]

In radio, Spain was unique in Europe with three private networks (SER, COPE under Church control, and CRI) which, despite legal restrictions on news coverage, enjoyed a politically tolerated joint monopoly from the mid-1950s. The rest of the news media—the newspaper chain controlled by the Movimiento;* state radio and television; the news agencies Pyresa and EFE; the press and radio run by the vertical trade unions* (especially the newspaper *Pueblo*)—comprised a formidable pro-dictatorship apparatus in the hands of the state. By and large, the private media and commun-ications groups coexisted happily with the interests of the political system.

The Spanish media would themselves later put about the myth of 'the press' as a force generally in favour of change, if not a vital factor in securing democracy. Future historians researching the newspaper libraries will find ample evidence to the contrary. Those of us who lived through that period as active members of the broad democratic front of journalists which flourished particularly in the big cities, usually within the Press Associations, know from painful experience that the articles supporting change we fought so hard to get through constantly came up against the watchful eye and ultra-conservative attitudes of the vast majority of the public and private media.

In fact only a tiny, relatively marginal section of the media had from the 1970s openly lobbied for democracy. This consisted largely of magazines formed from various opposition alliances—including the legendary *Cuadernos para el Diálogo* and *Triunfo*—which paradoxically folded during the transition. To be fair, there were some daily newspapers—*El Alcázar* despite its name, *Madrid* which was closed down, *Informaciones* till the April 1974 Portuguese Revolution—that clashed with the regime over political issues or because reporting restrictions undermined their business dynamic. The intensification of repressive measures against the press in the dictatorship's last phases, or in the early stages of the inappropriately termed 'transition' under UCD,* indicates assorted managerial or professional conflicts of this kind, but not that the communications network was predominantly in favour of democratic rule.

The new press media created in response to the climate of change almost all (with the exception of *Cambio 16*, founded in 1971) started up in the first years of the transition (*El País* and *Interviú* were founded in 1976), and made relatively small inroads into the market. It was in the 1980s and 1990s, thanks to commercial successes at the centre of big communications groups, that they increased their profile.

A similar picture applies when we turn to the growing globalization of commu-nications and of the culture industries generally. The Franco regime declared a no-go area all those sectors assumed to have immediate political influence—the press, radio, publishing, etc.—but opened up to foreign capital those cultural sectors felt to be of purely economic or entertainment value. In this way several big Euro-pean groups got a foothold in the press and publishing by taking over the distri-bution networks (Hachette, Bertelsmann), and even covertly in actual magazine publication (Bertelsmann with *Selecciones del Reader's Digest*); by contrast, at the height of the Franco period, they swept the board with the record industry, film distribution, and advertising, acquiring a virtually irreversible degree of control over important sectors of the Spanish culture and communications industries.

This almost entirely political, instrumental conception of the media, divorced from any kind of cultural policy or objective, would leave its mark on the com-munications industry under democracy to the present day. Thus the neo-liberal, mercantilist wave of the 1980s would invade Spain, as it did western Europe generally, without there having been a preceding experience or concept of the mass media as a mouthpiece of society. This is particularly worrying in television and radio where, contrary to the rest of Europe, deregulation and commercialization would occur in the absence of any concept of public service broadcasting.

Government-led concentration

The 1980s, especially after the PSOE* came to power in 1982, saw a number of fundamental structural changes in the Spanish media; in particular, a new concordance between political influence and the maximization of profits, through the introduction of market mechanisms automatically encouraging concentration and globalization. The communications policy of successive Spanish governments—never a coherent whole but manifest in their actions, laws, and omissions—acted as a trigger enabling the industry to restructure roughly on the lines of the more developed countries of western Europe.

Thus the dual process of lateral concentration within the same media, and of diversification across a range of media, was marked by a series of developments resulting from political decisions. First, the selling off in 1984 of the state-owned newspaper chain Medios de Comunicación Social del Estado started a rush to set up big regional press groups. Second, the concession in 1981–2 of 300 new FM radio stations consolidated the old radio groups of the Franco period, generating two new networks Antena 3 and Radio 80 which merged shortly after. Third, the concession in 1988 of three private television channels, despite the imposition of a ceiling on shares of 25 per cent per person or company, ended up benefiting existing big press groups and facilitating their links with international consortia (Telecinco, Antena 3, Canal+). Fourth, the concession in 1993 of television transmission franchises for the Spanish satellite system Hispasat gives a preview of the kind of configuration that is likely to be produced by new television markets.

At the start of the 1990s, the effects of these developments on the mass media are clear.

In the daily press, five groups own over 40 papers, amounting to roughly 55 per cent of registered sales. Apart from these, plus *ABC* and *El Mundo* (the latter a creation of the 1980s), there are 75 other daily papers with a total circulation of barely half a million. In the national press this concentration of the market in a few hands has not yet reached levels comparable to those of other European countries, but in the regional press four groups (El Correo, Prensa Ibérica, Zeta, and Grupo 16) have in recent years triggered an escalating cycle of mergers and take-overs (wiping out competition in some regions) which is reaching danger levels.

In radio, two networks with common shareholders—SER and Antena 3—own 417 out of a total of 800 commercial stations, claiming 58 per cent of the audience and 63 per cent of profits for the commercial sector. These two networks plus two others—COPE and Onda Cero—account for 80 per cent of the total radio audience, including that for the state-controlled sector.

In television, two Spanish groups—El País-PRISA and ZETA—control two of the private channels—Canal+ and Antena 3—while the third is controlled by Berlusconi's Fininvest. Stock market dealing resulting from unstable share prices has made it impossible to determine the identity of a significant number of shareholders, despite the fact that all transfers of holdings require state authorization.

This recent pattern of take-overs has created a situation in which a tiny number of companies control a large chunk of the news media. Despite widespread use of the term, the number of Spanish multi-media groups can effectively be reduced to two, PRISA and ZETA; joint operations are, however, mainly restricted to finance, with little evidence of genuine collaborative practice or substantial savings.

PRISA, whose leading partner has beyond any doubt been the newspaper *El País*, has a majority holding in the biggest private radio network in Europe, SER; a significant holding in Antena 3 Radio; 25 per cent of holdings in the subscription TV channel Canal+ (jointly with French Canal+ and other Spanish financial groups); and close links with the book publishing chain Timón. In addition, through its subsidiaries, it has moved into audio-visual products, audio-visual copyright and advertising, and most importantly (together with Carat) into the area of holding companies. It is the only Spanish-backed group that has embarked on modest overseas expansion, with the *Independent* in the UK, *Publico* in Portugal, the radio network M-40 in France, *La Prensa* in Mexico, among others.

ZETA, which grew out of the success of the magazine *Interviú*, owns a wide regional press chain, notably *El Periódico de Cataluña*; and has diversified laterally by taking over a broad range of general- and special-interest magazines, subsequently launching into a vast range of economic sectors from construction to tourism and food. In initial partnership with Rupert Murdoch (who later denied collaboration beyond publishing) and with one of the biggest Spanish banking groups (Banesto), it now controls the television channel Antena 3 TV.

However, if one takes the term multi-media group to mean simply financial involvement in various media, the biggest Spanish multi-media groups by far turn out to be the four big banks. Banesto, the Banco Central-Hispano, the Banco de Bilbao-Vizcaya, and the Banco de Santander have in recent years gained key positions in the press, radio, and television by putting a significant amount of money into the big communications groups. In addition, they already have a foothold in the leading companies preparing bids for cable television franchising in 1994, strong holdings in companies competing for the value-added services market in telecommunications, and have even started to move into specialized communications networks (the Banco de Santander-British Telecom and BCH-ATT partnerships) despite being shareholders in, and on the board of directors of, the Compañía Telefónica which has monopoly control of the Spanish telephone system.

Selective globalization

The globalization of communications and culture has followed a similar course, marked since the transition period by the lifting of legal obstacles to foreign investment in practically all sectors of the economy.

Between 1982 and 1986, the press was opened up to foreign capital. The Regulation of Telecommunications Law of 1988 also allowed investment in television and radio. Legal adjustment to the European Community will extend the process. But even with the single market, foreign groups have been signally cautious in their investments, consolidating established positions or building on their specialist expertise. With few exceptions (e.g. Hersant), moves into new sectors have been made in partnership rather than competition with Spanish groups.

The picture in the early 1990s is uneven but with enormous repercussions for the Spanish culture industries.

In the record industry, 5 international groups control 85 per cent of the market.

In book publishing, 2 of the 5 biggest groups (Springer, Bertelsmann) are foreign, between them controlling 57 per cent of sales.

In cinema and video, the biggest distributors are now appendages of the US giants, with just 4 of them (Warner, UIP, Fox, and Columbia Tri Star) taking over 50 per cent of box-office receipts, which partly explains why Spanish film companies get barely 12 per cent of takings. In video, 7 US distributors control 70 per cent of sales.

In advertising, the 'top 40' agencies consist almost entirely of multinational groups and megagroups, only 3 being Spanish. In particular, the proliferation of holding companies has given the multinationals a lead in advertising investment in the media, especially in television.

In television, the legislation setting up private channels has directly encouraged partnerships between Spanish and multinational groups: French Canal+ has holdings in the similarly named Spanish channel; News Corporation Int. (Murdoch) in Antena 3 TV; while three-quarters of the shares in Telecinco are (to date) held by Berlusconi, Kirch, and the Bank of Luxemburg. Even as minority shareholders, the foreign partners' technical input and control over programming gives them considerable leverage.

In the press and radio, foreign capital has only just begun to make inroads, but even these two sectors are no longer entirely under national control, as demonstrated by the holdings of Hersant in Grupo 16, Agnelli in *El Mundo*, and Hachette and even Televisa (Mexico) in Cadena Ibérica.

'Big is beautiful'

The Spanish communications and culture industries—never sound, even financially—have, then, been catapulted into 'modernity'. The mass media have in recent years popularized a dominant discourse that equates the big with the modern and with competitiveness in the international market. The praise which the media themselves heap on small and medium-sized businesses—seen as paragons of flexibility, growth, and increased employment—inexplicably stops when it comes to the communications and culture industries. Here 'atomization' has come to be synonymous with backwardness, and bigness tends to be uncritically equated with having an independent line and even with pluralism.

Some academics and management theorists have compounded this obfuscation by reviving the ideas of US thinkers like Benjamin Compaine or De Sola Pool, now some fifteen years out of date, in order to pin our hopes of pluralism and democracy on that 'other world' of the new technology. However, the immediate picture is dominated by the big groups, Spanish and foreign, using their established positions in the traditional communications market to expand still further, for example into the satellite and cable sectors. The close links of some of the above-mentioned media groups with Spanish banks and electricity companies, and with French or Belgian banks and water companies, are sufficient evidence.

'Postmodernization' is, for the time being, taking place on a purely economic level, with a singular lack of cultural and social innovation. And there is no sign on the horizon of any 'national champion' ready to defend Spain's colours in the great global tournament the media moguls keep announcing.

Note
1 A 1976 survey showed that 22 groups publishing 32 newspapers were closely connected through common board members or subsidiary companies to the biggest financial and industrial groups in the country. See E. Bustamante, *Los amos de la información en España* (Madrid, 1982).

Further reading
Alvarez Monzoncillo, J. M., and Iwens, J. L., *El futuro del audiovisual en España* (Madrid, 1992).
Bustamante, E., *Los amos de la información en España* (Madrid, 1982).
—— and Zallo, R. (eds.), *Las industrias culturales en España: grupos multimedia y transnacionales* (Madrid, 1988).
El sector cultural en España ante el proceso de integración europea (Madrid, 1992).
Timoteo Alvarez, J. (ed.), *Historia de los medios de comunicación en España: periodismo, imagen y publicidad (1900-1990)* (Barcelona, 1989).
Zallo, R., *El mercado de la cultura* (San Sebastián, 1992).

Redefining the Public Interest: Television in Spain Today

BARRY JORDAN

In early 1994, public television in Spain—Televisión Española (TVE)—adopted a new strategy which appeared to reaffirm its public service role and distinguish it from its increasingly aggressive private competitors. Both state-run channels TVE1 and TVE2, as well as TVE's international satellite channel, refashioned their news and current affairs output and from mid-April 1994 began offering a greater number of slots designed to give their coverage more immediacy and relevance to the viewer (for example, more on-site reports on traffic and transport problems). TVE1's flagship current affairs programme *Informe semanal* was also given a harder, more investigative, more international profile, beginning with an analysis of the role of Chinese mafia gangs in Spain. Such changes seemed to suggest that TVE was at last responding to widespread concern and taking its public service obligations more seriously. These adjustments have to be seen in the context of a particularly intense and acrimonious period of competition for market share between the state-run provider and the three main private channels.[1] TVE has also been under extreme political pressure to account for significant debts and losses.[2] Moreover, the attempt to revarnish its public service image through the vehicle of current affairs has come only after mounting criticism of scheduling decisions which reflected a managerial priority with ratings over programme quality. For example, the prize-winning thirteen-part documentary series *Mujeres de Latinoamerica* [*Women of Latin America*] had to wait well over a year for its first screening in January 1994, when it was given a 10.00 p.m. Sunday-night slot on the minority channel TVE2; in protest, its director Carmen Sarmiento called on TVE's management to respond more robustly to the need for peak-time quality programming.

The above media stories highlight the many contradictions and dilemmas faced by Spain's national public television provider. In the context of the increasing deregulation of broadcasting and rapid development in cable and satellite channels, public television outlets are under greater pressure than ever to compete for audiences. This essay seeks to determine the extent to which, under a pluralist, democratic, and increasingly deregulated Spanish system, the definition of the public interest has become a matter for the advertisers and the conglomerates rather than the official authorities, regulatory bodies, and audience pressure groups.

Television in Spain

One of the key terms underpinning the public service television debate in the UK is that of the licence fee. Since the Spanish viewing public does not pay a licence fee, it does not have a direct contractual relationship with the national supplier of television output. As all television services in Spain are funded predominantly by advertising revenue, the notion of public service is problematic and the defence of the public interest tends to be left to the government of the day, its monitoring committees, and, to a much smaller extent, audience pressure groups.

With regard to government influence in broadcasting, it is now widely acknowledged that the acquisition in 1990 of the franchise for the private channel Canal+ by the media and publishing conglomerate PRISA (plus its take-over of Antena 3 Radio) owed much to the group's political affinity to the PSOE* government in power. Also in 1992, at the height of the financial crisis suffered by Antena 3, it was again the PSOE government which allowed new entrants into the company

(Murdoch's News International, Banesto, and Grupo Zeta publishers) in exchange, it is said, for a less critical attitude towards government policy.[3] TVE is rarely out of the media spotlight and its operations, the role of its managers, and the behaviour of its political masters are constantly under scrutiny. In July 1992, for example, Pilar Miró, ex-Director-General of TVE, was finally cleared of the charge of restocking her wardrobe through the unlawful appropriation of public funds. At the same time, Javier Arenas, media spokesman for the conservative Partido Popular (PP*), accused the present Director-General of TVE (Jordi García Candau) of engaging in more than thirty instances of financial irregularities.[4] Such accusations form part of a long-running campaign by PP to embarrass the governing Socialist Party.

Corruption, malpractice, alleged embezzlement, theft, political control, and bias are hardly news when it comes to the operation and management of Spanish television. In this sense, little seems to have changed in TVE's internal functioning or public image since the dictatorship. During the transition and after, successive governments have been unwilling to sacrifice the considerable advantages of political patronage they inherited from the dictatorship over appointments in the television industry. In other ways, of course, things have changed quite fundamentally since the dictatorship and although the two main national television channels remain the effective fiefdom of the party in power, Spain has become a diverse, competitive, multi-channel and indeed multi-media broadcasting arena. If anything, these developments have complicated the terms of the debate concerning the relationship between television as public service and the pressures of commercial imperatives.

Television and dictatorship

Needless to say, during the Franco dictatorship the media were without exception controlled by the state through laws, regulatory measures, and frequently through direct state ownership of outlets, such as newspapers and radio stations. Private companies wishing to establish press or radio outlets had to apply for administrative licences, a bureaucratic exercise invariably facilitated by the working of *enchufe* (old-boy network, political contacts) and bribery. When the first official broadcasts began in Spain on 28 October 1956, the service was established as a public state monopoly dependent on the government and funded by the state from its General Budget. What is perhaps less well known is that, right from its inception and unlike most other European services, Spanish television followed the American example by accepting advertising, and from around March 1958 began earning revenue from the primitive *rótulos* or *cartones* [posters, placards] used in its incipient advertising spots. Absent from the Spanish experience under the dictatorship would be any attempt to foster an educated, well-informed, and demanding viewing public. Indeed, the regime required the exact opposite and this repressive, xenophobic, and paternalistic legacy would permeate attempts, after the dictatorship's fall, to disengage broadcasting from the apparatuses of central state control.

Television after Franco

The main reference points for the post-dictatorship debate over the nature of television services in Spain are provided by the 1978 Constitution which, in Article 20, guaranteed freedom of expression for all, freedom of the press, radio, and television, and the dissemination of ideas, in and out of the country, without censorship. It also recognized and protected the rights of the different linguistic communities, foreseeing their eventual access to the media. At the same time, however, Article 38 recognized and protected the exercise of free enterprise, an obligation which would have far-reaching consequences in the broadcasting sphere. And finally, in Article 128, clause 2, the Constitution defined broadcasting as an essential public service requiring governmental regulation if not financial support. It is the apparent contradiction in the Constitution between the protection of free enterprise and freedom of expression on the one hand, and the designation of public broadcasting as an essential public service on the other, which has led to severe legal confusion ever since and numerous appeals to the Constitutional Tribunal, especially from interested parties in the television business wanting to establish their own channels.

Perhaps the most important move in the regulation of the media was the Radio and Television Statute of 1980. This reasserted the right of government to control the media through various committees. However, the new law said nothing regarding the rights of private enterprise and the eventual introduction in Spain of commercial television. Under the terms of the 1980 Statute, Radio Televisión Española (RTVE) was established as a public corporation providing television and radio services to the country through Televisión Española (TVE) and Radio Nacional de España (RNE). RTVE was given a monopoly over the two existing television channels, TVE1 and TVE2. RNE had one AM network and four FM networks, one of which would broadcast different programmes in the regions. Both TVE and RNE would be governed by an Administrative Council comprising twelve members, including parliamentary deputies chosen proportionally according to relative party strengths. The role of the Administrative Council would be to approve plans regarding the general principles and policies to which all broadcasting should broadly adhere. Separate advisory councils for television and radio were also established: these would present opinions and reports to the Administrative Council regarding programming policies. Ultimate responsibility for the service rested, however, with a Director-General who appointed the chief executives of TV and radio services. The post of Director-General, needless to say, was a highly sensitive political appointment made by the party in power; if and when parliament were dissolved, the incumbent would cease to hold office. As regards policies for the regions in each of the (now seventeen) autonomous communities, there would be a regional advisory council of RTVE which would advise and report to the regional RTVE executive. In practice, neither the national nor the regional advisory councils appear to exert much influence on the management of television and radio services.

The 1980 Statute also foresaw the need to allow the autonomous communities to express their regional identities through the establishment of their own television services. To this effect, in December 1983 under the new PSOE government, a law was passed providing the legal basis for the establishment of the so-called 'third channel' in the various regions. This new law was curiously pre-empted by almost a year in the Basque Country, where Euskal Telebista was set up in January 1983. In January 1984, Catalonia developed its own third channel TV3, followed in July 1985 by Galicia's TVG. Since then, other third channels have come into being: Andalusia (Canal Sur), Valencia (Canal 9), Madrid (TeleMadrid). Moreover, both the Basque Country and Catalonia have created their own fourth channels, without any clear legal basis, it seems, and other regions are in the process of negotiating their own third channels. Let it be remembered that these third (or fourth) channels are dependent on the authority as well as financial support of the parliaments of the autonomous communities and thus, not unlike the national channels, subject to political pressures.

In 1988, after a long period of debate and numerous opposition amendments, the Spanish parliament finally passed a law allowing the PSOE government to grant licences to three private TV channels. Their remit would be national although the terms of the licence would require them to provide parallel regional programming. Virtually all opposition parties argued that the limitation on only three commercial channels be rescinded. The government refused any change here, conscious of the potential pressure on advertising revenue these new operators would exert.[5] Ownership of the private channels had to be predominantly Spanish (an initial suggested limit of 15 per cent on newspaper ownership of the new channels was raised to 25 per cent after successful lobbying by groups such as PRISA and La Vanguardia). Foreign entrants would be allowed a maximum 25 per cent shareholding in any one company. Moreover, an emphasis was placed on domestic output; 15 per cent was supposed to be produced 'in-house' and at least 40 per cent drawn from Spanish or EC production. Initially, the PSOE government bill also included the provision of a supervisory body for the new commercial stations but this was later dropped. The licences were awarded in 1990, initially for a ten-year term, to: Telecinco (in which Berlusconi's Fininvest has a 25 per cent holding, Anaya Publishers and Spain's National Organization for the Blind (ONCE) also having 25 per cent each), Antena 3 (intially controlled by La Vanguardia, who lost their controlling position in 1992 when News International, Banesto, and Grupo Zeta took holdings), and Canal+ (the French-owned subscription TV and film channel, in which the PRISA group, which includes the national daily El País, has a major holding). These commercial channels, like their national cousins, would be obliged to observe the same fundamental principles outlined in clause 4 of the 1980 Statute. Save for the subscription-based Canal+, all channels depend financially on advertising revenue. It is worth recalling that, up to 1991, TVE was virtually the only public European television service to be financed almost exclusively by advertising and not dependent officially on the General State Budget (in practice TVE continues to receive government hand-outs, though these do not figure in the official accounts). In the regions, as previously mentioned, television financing derives from a mixture of commercial advertising and subsidies from autonomous community budgets.

Public service versus private enterprise

During the period of debate over the introduction of private television (1978–88), the PSOE—with the Communist Party—consistently rejected demands for the establishment of a National Commission for television, preferring parliament to be the controlling body; during the 1980s, it has maintained this position. Not surprisingly, the main opposition parties and pressure groups have claimed that the government has effectively 'nationalized' the main national services. This 'top-down' management style also affects the regional channels' operations, since they are subordinate to RTVE in Madrid and cannot act independently when Madrid demands priority in transmission. Notwithstanding such political interference, there are numerous legal norms and official guidelines governing the operations and output of all broadcasting services, which spell out the obligations of the broadcasters towards the public and the public interest. These deserve consideration.

According to the Preamble to the 1980 Statute, television and radio are regarded as essential public services on two main grounds. First, they are seen as essential vehicles for the provision of information, participation of citizens, formation of public opinion, access to and advancement of the educational system as well as of the languages and cultures of Spain's regional communities. Second, they are viewed as an essential means for protecting the rights and freedoms of minorities as well as those of women. Such ideas clearly endorse civic values, national and regional identities, and the protection of minorities. Drafted over the period 1977–80, these norms were no doubt inspired by the desire to consolidate democracy in Spain. Article 4 of the Statute presents a series of recommendations applying to programming content and policy. It proposes the following principles: information should be true, objective, and impartial; information should be distinguished from opinion, and where necessary the opinion holder's identity should be revealed; there should be respect for social, cultural, political, and linguistic pluralism; respect for individual privacy and reputation; protection of minors; respect for the principles of freedom and equality as outlined in Article 14 of the Constitution. Underlying these principles, there is clearly a desire to break with the past, to separate the operation of the media from the state, and to make them more responsive to the needs of the individual, the regional communities, and the various minorities, thereby enhancing their democratic and pluralist outlook.

In 1981 the RTVE Administrative Council produced a further series of Principles and Guidelines. Paramount among the general guidelines was the media's active promotion of the democratic, civic values underlying the 1978 Constitution. Also important was the need to foster national unity and solidarity among all Spanish citizens while respecting the linguistic, cultural, and political rights of regional communities. The media were also encouraged to promote dialogue and debate as a means of settling disputes, to encourage a respect for the authority of public institutions, to explain to the public the problems of the national economy (so as to avoid the association between democracy and economic instability, a serious problem in the early 1980s), and to reflect life as well as promote citizens' participation and cultural enrichment. Again we find the broadcasting services being involved in a pseudo-political role, that of disseminating the Constitution's pluralist, civic, democratic ethos. The statements of principle informing the establishment of regional television services largely repeat the above guidelines; most refer specifically to the protection and promotion of regional languages and cultures and to the goal of reinforcing regional identities.

Other rules and guidelines have been produced with regard to advertising. Till 1988, advertising in Spain was regulated by the General Advertising Law (LGP) first promulgated under Franco in 1964 and designed largely to protect the regime's institutions, its notions of good taste, and standards of good conduct. The LGP was modified in 1988, and in 1990 was complemented by a series of norms on advertising produced by TVE's Administrative Council: the latter are the main guidelines regulating television advertising in Spain. Apart from condemning the use of advertising to incite or promote bad behaviour, disorder, and violence, and protecting standards of good taste, especially in regard to language, these recent norms have imposed a series of restrictions on presenting alcohol in advertising in terms of personal, physical, and particularly sexual success. There is, in fact, little or no legislation or formal guidance regarding the portrayal of sex and violence on the small screen (unlike film where legislation passed in 1977 and 1982 controls the exhibition of films whose main subject is sex or violence). The only guideline on the regulation of pornographic material in relation to young people is Article 20.4 of the Constitution, which recognizes the need to protect the public against the corrupting effects of material which undermines 'the basic principles of collective sexual morality'. The fact that there is no specific rule book on the broadcasting of pornographic material on TV has allowed both the national and commercial channels, aware of the need to capture audiences for the advertisers, to broadcast material bordering on the pornographic.

Spanish broadcasting, then, is not short on legislation and sets of norms to provide a framework within which broadcasting activities ought to take place. However, these norms and guidelines mostly operate only at the level of general principles and have not been elaborated into more specific commitments and policies. So far the Spanish system has not been able to create an effective method of regulating programme output; nor has it managed to redefine the notion of public service in relation to the more complex multi-channel and multi-media situation. Machinery to police the system and to provide an independent voice in defence of the public interest is either too politicized or simply unavailable. In principle, the Administrative Council of RTVE has considerable authority and wide-ranging powers to oversee the operations of the national channels. However, because a substantial number of its members are drawn from the political parties, its activities tend to focus on the politics of broadcasting rather than on programming standards. And as previously mentioned, the advisory councils linked to state and regional television have failed to step into the breach. The introduction of commercial television in Spain should have been a golden opportunity to take a serious look at programme standards and introduce some form of regulatory machinery. Where the government seems reluctant to get involved, Spanish people themselves are beginning to develop their own organizations and pressure groups in order to monitor and improve programme quality and standards. Indeed, a National Federation of Viewers' Associations has recently emerged as an umbrella organization whose aim is to press government and the commercial operators to be more accountable on specific programming issues. The demands of the Federation include: exclusion of programmes dealing with sex and violence from prime-time scheduling; the exercise of more control over the use of obscene language; the need to avoid promoting certain stereotypical images as desirable role models; the non-exploitation of women as advertising stereotypes and sex objects. Other bodies, including the Catholic Church, are also beginning to throw their weight behind this viewers' movement—which of course has the capacity to reinforce conservative as much as progressive values—with a view to putting pressure on advertisers and their sponsors.

Notes

1 *El País* (23 Apr. 1994), 56. In the ratings war with the private channels—esp. Antena 3, which has almost caught up with TVE1 in terms of audience share, see *El País* (5 Jan. 1994), 50— TVE1 and 2 have engaged in a highly aggressive programming policy: for example, the last-minute peak-time scheduling of blockbuster films (*Lethal Weapon, Batman*) against popular, weekend variety shows (Antena 5's *Noche noche*, Telecinco's *Querida Concha*), resulting in startling shifts in audience participation in favour of TVE.
2 In 1992–3 TVE committed large sums to extremely generous redundancy/early retirement packages, adding to an already sizeable financial deficit, recently criticized by TVE's Administrative Council, see *El País* (23 Apr. 1994), 56.
3 A. Sánchez Tabernero, *Media Concentration in Europe: Commercial Enterprise and the Public Interest* (Manchester, 1993), 162.
4 *El País* (25 May 1992), 88.
5 The PSOE's assumption that expansion in the number of broadcasting outlets would increase competition against a limited amount of advertising revenue was not borne out, since TV advertising expanded in the 1980s at the expense of advertising in other media, such as the press. However, in the 1990s the amount of TV advertising has remained virtually static, at *c*.200,000 million pesetas annually, though the number of advertisements shown has more than doubled, indicating greater competition and lower prices. See *El País* (28 Feb. 1993), 46.

Further reading
Aguilera, M. de, *El telediario: un proceso informativo* (Barcelona, 1985).
Bustamante, E., and Zallo, R. (eds.), *Las industrias culturales en España: grupos multimedia y transnacionales* (Madrid, 1988).
Equipo Reseña, *Doce años de cultura española (1976–1987)* (Madrid, 1989).
Hooper, J., *The Spaniards: A Portrait of the New Spain* (London, 1986; rev. edn., *The New Spaniards* (1995)).
López-Escobar, E., 'Vulnerable Values in Spanish Multichannel Television', in J. G. Blumler (ed.), *Television and the Public Interest: Vulnerable Values in West European Broadcasting* (London, 1992), 161–72.
Macía, P., *Televisión hora cero* (Madrid, 1981).
Mateo, R. de, and Corbella, J. M., 'Spain', in *The Media in Western Europe: The Euro Media Handbook* (London, 1992), 192–206.
Maxwell, R., *The Spectacle of Democracy: Spanish Television, Nationalism and Political Transition* (Minneapolis, 1994).
Sánchez Tabernero, A., *Media Concentration in Europe: Commercial Enterprise and the Public Interest* (Manchester, 1993).
Sinova, J., *La gran mentira* (Barcelona, 1983).
Vázquez Montalbán, M., *El libro gris de televisión española* (Madrid, 1973).

The Film Industry: Under Pressure from the State and Television

AUGUSTO M. TORRES

From cinema's beginnings, politicians have capitalized on its ability to influence the masses by appearing in news features and instituting controls to regulate production, distribution, and viewing, and (more positively) to protect domestic production from overseas competition. Mussolini, Hitler, Stalin, Perón, Mao, Castro all took an interest in their national film industries; Franco, who had a film shown for him every night at the Pardo Palace, was no exception. For many years his protectionist film laws allowed most Spanish films to recoup their costs before being shown (though foreign films were made more popular by compulsory dubbing). This, together with censorship, created a dependence on the state which made the industry vulnerable.

In the two years after Franco's death, new freedom plus the continued existence of the old structures produced a number of films unthinkable before, but which still had problems with the censors. This period also saw a revival of the documentary genre, almost non-existent under the dictatorship for obvious reasons, with new films and the release of others previously banned (e.g. Patino's *Canciones para después de una guerra*). This was also a time when Spanish cinema started to make its mark abroad, winning several prizes at international festivals.

On 1 December 1977, new legislation abolished film censorship, setting up a board of classification (with three ratings: adults only, general release, and S for pornographic or violent movies). Controls on importing foreign films were scrapped, but a quota system required distributors to show one day of Spanish films for every two of dubbed foreign films. Additionally, shorts became entitled to automatic subsidy.

In 1978 the Ministry of Culture passed an overspend of 2,000 million pesetas, the result of bad arithmetic, on to film companies at a time when average production costs stood at 20 million pesetas. This, plus difficulties in adapting to a free market economy, brought production to a virtual halt. In the same year, automatic monitoring of box-office returns was introduced to avoid future miscalculations, but in practice the collecting of official information on box-office takings in Spain is still a cumbersome, inaccurate process open to fraud. To make matters worse, in 1979 distributors obtained a High Court ruling declaring the current quota system unconstitutional; in 1980 the ratio was reduced to one day of Spanish films for every three of foreign films, increasing the hold of the US distributors. In addition, during this period Spanish cinemas were flooded by foreign films previously banned.

The only films banned after 1976 were Pasolini's *120 Days of Sodom*, Oshima's *Empire of the Senses*, and Pilar Miró's *El crimen de Cuenca* (1979), which depicted a nineteenth-century judicial error in which the Civil Guard* extracted confessions from innocent victims through torture; after eighteen months the threat of court martial was overruled and the film authorized with an S rating.

No longer needing import licences, most production companies severed links with the big US distributors, allowing them to work more freely. Several film co-operatives also emerged around 1979–80, making some interesting avant-garde productions on a shoestring budget; this experiment, whereby technicians and actors invested their salaries in the production, was short-lived for economic reasons. Such new production modes combined with the problems mentioned above to bring down the annual output of feature films from 108 in 1976 to 89 in 1979.

In 1980 Spanish Television signed a collaboration agreement with the film industry, putting 1,300 million pesetas into the production of films that, after two years' cinema screening, would be broadcast. After various hitches, this scheme bore fruit with several popular TV series plus some top-quality films based on works by Spanish writers. The original scheme developed into a more flexible arrangement whereby Televisión Española bought the broadcasting rights for films it wanted. The disadvantage of this collaboration was that it excluded controversial projects on contemporary issues, without the economic benefits derived from the TV connection being sufficient to compensate for what amounted to an indirect form of cultural control.

After the 1982 elections, the PSOE government named Pilar Miró Director-General of Film. For the first time the post-holder was someone in the profession, who had directed and produced films and worked in television; some important long- and short-term changes were mooted to tackle the industry's problems. Since domestic production comprised one-third each of S-rated movies, fraudulent co-productions with foreign companies made to secure dubbing permits, and potentially high-quality films, Miró decided to support the last, tightening up on co-productions, and creating 'X'-rated cinemas to show pornographic or violent films, making classification redundant. Subsidies for shorts became discretionary as for feature films, bringing production of the former down from 286 in 1983 to 81 in 1984.

In 1984 the so-called 'Miró Law' was passed. Based on the French *avance sur recette* system, it introduced subsidies (up to 50 per cent of total costs) in the form of an advance on the 15 per cent of box-office takings for Spanish films which since 1965 had reverted to production companies. The aim was to promote successful high-quality, big-budget productions, but nowhere did the law tackle the basic, sensitive issue of increasing production companies' cut of takings. The 'Miró Law' did however facilitate some excellent productions, several winning major international prizes, and encouraged a brief come-back by several middle-aged directors (Picazo, Olea, Patino, Camino, Regueiro).

In the same period, the new autonomous governments had a significant impact on the film industry, varying from region to region. These mostly funded the production of regional films that in many cases, being made in the respective 'dialect' banned under Franco, were reasonably successful with local audiences but made little impression in other regions where they were dubbed into Castilian. The Catalan autonomous government went so far as to subsidize the dubbing into Catalan of major US productions, to promote the language. The Basque government has adopted the most intelligent, effective criteria, subsidizing up to 25 per cent of the budget for productions made in Basque that treat regional subjects and use Basque technicians and actors.

In 1985 Miró resigned after increasing criticism from those who had been refused subsidies at a time when rising costs and the drop in cinema audiences made state funding vital. Unfortunately she did so without having pushed through a restructuring of the distribution and exhibition networks, increasingly dominated by the big US distributors, domestic production for 1984 having fallen to 75 feature films. Her successor Fernando Méndez Leite, also a film and TV director, continued the policy of subsidies in the form of advances, fighting for increases in state funding and fending off EC attacks on alleged excessive protectionism. He also abolished the requirement for cinemas to show a short with every feature film, killing off a useful low-cost form of apprenticeship.

In 1986 Spain joined the EC. The conditions, negotiated by the previous centre-right government, were disastrous for the film industry. Overnight, EC films qualified for inclusion in the screening quota for Spanish films; this, plus the fact that many US films masqueraded as British or Dutch productions, drastically reduced the proportion of Spanish films exhibited.

Accused of favouritism and serving vested interests, Méndez Leite resigned in 1988. In 1989 his replacement Miguel Marías, whose knowledge of cinema was purely theoretical, was forced under government pressure to dismantle the system of advance subsidies instituted by Miró, who meanwhile had been discredited as Director-General of Spanish Television. With cinema audiences dwindling (in Spain particularly), and the expansion of regional television and franchising of private TV channels offering the public an increased diet of films at home, domestic film production continued to plummet, falling from a 1981 peak of 137 films to 48 in 1989. Several talented producers moved to television, reduced their output to one film every four years, or stopped making films altogether, as did some directors.

In 1990 Marías was replaced by a civil servant, Enrique Balmaseda, in a return to the Francoist tradition of appointments. The PSOE's policy towards the national film industry looks increasingly like one of concerted rationalization. Miró's argument that funding should be concentrated on high-quality films was used as an excuse to reduce output, and in subsequent years funding was cut back further. Some subsidized films were undeniably poor, and during Méndez Leite's period in office the press put about the notion that money was being wasted. Miguel Marías was then given the job of stabilizing production at almost a quarter of previous levels. Meanwhile the US distributors are taking over, and soon TV companies will not be able to comply with the broadcasting quotas for Spanish films (whose audience ratings are curiously rising) for lack of material.

The predictable take-off of private television has caused a big drop in advertising income for state-owned Televisión Española. The latter's first measure, in 1990, was to cancel its collaboration agreement with the film industry, while also cancelling most of its own productions. As a result, television no longer offers a haven for refugees from the film industry.

Relations between cinema and television have always been fraught. When commercial TV first caught on in the USA at the end of the Second World War, politicians realized its hold over the masses was potentially greater than that of cinema, and the power struggle began. It was not till the mid-1950s that television made inroads in Spain, and only in the late 1960s that there were enough private sets for it to become a political weapon. Under the dictatorship this power could not be contested; but with the advent of democracy it was up for grabs, the result being the franchising in 1990 of three private TV channels: Antena 3, Telecinco (strongly Italian-based), and Canal+ (a subscription channel modelled on the similarly named French channel). These years saw a proliferation of news programmes, while competition produced a notable drop in average programme standards. Figures are not available for the first few years of the private TV channels' existence, but they seem to have turned initial losses into modest profits. Whereas in 1991 the two state-owned channels run by Televisión Española declared losses of 35,000 million pesetas, and the regional television channels (TV3 and Canal 33 in Catalonia, Canal Sur in Andalusia, TeleMadrid, ETB1 and ETB2 in the Basque Country, TVG in Galicia) sustained combined losses of 50,317 million pesetas. The entire deficit of 85,317 million pesetas has been written off by the respective political authorities on the sole condition that they be given prominent coverage on news programmes.

Set against this sum, the total subsidy to the film industry of 4,000 million pesetas (the figure at which funding has been pegged for several years) seems ludicrous. It seems equally unfair that there is no current collaboration between the various state and regional television companies and the film industry—the private channels are now starting to fund productions—when, out of the total of 112 films broadcast weekly, 23 (i.e. 21 per cent) are Spanish and among the most profitable because of the low prices paid for broadcasting rights plus their high audience ratings.

Further reading
Gómez, B., and de Castro, R., *La producción cinematográfica española: de la transición a la democracia (1976–1986)* (Bilbao, 1989).
Torres, A. M., *Diccionario del cine español* (Madrid, 1994).
Vallés Copeiro del Villar, A., *Historia de la política de fomento del cine español* (Valencia, 1992) (covers pre-war and post-war periods, up to 1990).

Artistic Patronage and Enterprise Culture
EMMA DENT COAD

During the dictatorship, there were varying degrees of control over the visual arts—as in all areas of culture—ranging from official support for exhibitions showing the 'right' sort of art to the blatant censorship of certain types of architecture. The nation-wide reconstruction scheme of the 1940s and 1950s employed hundreds of architects in the building of schools, sanatoriums, housing, and churches, but high-quality work was limited to that commissioned by private clients, mainly banks and private homes. Artistic innovation took place in spite of, and not because of, government attitudes.

When democracy was established, the new Ministry of Culture (created in 1977) set itself the task—particularly after the PSOE* came to power in 1982—of promoting the arts both through state support and by encouraging private sponsorship for art-related areas. The latter was done on a grand scale. Tax incentives were offered and the arts became big business. Interestingly though, in a 1992 survey companies listed their prime incentive as being a desire to improve their corporate and public image, followed by publicity and the satisfaction of serving the community. Tax relief was listed eighth, just ahead of 'altruism'.

Throughout the 1980s, commercial sponsors and the Ministry of Culture embraced the arts—and the visual arts most obviously—with unprecedented enthusiasm. In 1982 the Ministry set up the ARCO (Arte Contemporáneo) project, consisting of a government-sponsored annual art fair in Madrid and the Fundación Arco. This foundation's brief is to build up a collection of world-wide contemporary art, with an annual buying budget of 29 million pesetas. It also organizes educational events and advises commercial concerns on prospective purchases: for example, in 1994 it advised the Coca Cola Foundation on how to spend its annual 20 million peseta art budget. Also in that year, the Fundación Nat West spent part of its annual 5 million peseta cultural budget on sponsoring Foto ARCO, a major international fine art photography fair. It was in the 1980s, thanks to this and other exhibitions, that photography became a high-art form in Spain.

The pension fund La Caixa de Pensions became a high-profile sponsor, among other things setting up its own photography gallery in Barcelona. La Caja de Madrid, with a similar remit, has a 6 billion peseta cultural budget. Other major investors in this field are the Banco de Bilbao Vizcaya (BBV) with a staggering 14 billion peseta cultural budget, and Banco Central Hispano with a budget of nearly 6 billion. The fashion house Loewe makes two annual awards totalling 10 million pesetas (one of which is for poetry).

The results of this overwhelming support for cultural activities—covering fine art, public installations, theatre, music, museums, and architecture (the last being the most popular, taking 33 per cent of sponsorship)—have been well documented in the international press, as journalists responded to the orchestrated publicity campaigns. This 'discovery' process was given a particular boost by the publicity around the various cultural events hosted by Spain in 1992 (the Barcelona Olympics, Expo in Seville, Madrid Cultural Capital of Europe), leading to concurrent or subsequent exhibitions of Spanish painting, sculpture, and photography, festivals of Spanish cinema, theatre, dance, and music, and tours of Spanish writers throughout Europe (for example, the massive Spanish Arts Festival organized in the UK in 1993 with a mixture of state and private sponsorship).

By this date, most of the autonomous regions had opened brand new or impressively refurbished art centres, by local architects—most notably the Centro Reina Sofía in Madrid, and the Instituto Valenciano de Arte Moderno (IVAM) in Valencia, both opened in 1986. The arts—architecture in particular—became assimilated into popular culture as waiters and taxi drivers argued for and against the new public buildings. The initial refurbishment of the Centro Reina Sofía, with the intention of turning it into a national centre housing the best Spanish art from around the country, divesting regional galleries of their finest pieces, produced a major controversy. An uneasy compromise was reached—and Madrid kept *Guernica*—but the actual refurbishment was unsuccessful and had to be redone at tremendous cost in 1992. All this activity led to a terrific rise in the consumption of art, but there was no corresponding increase in analysis, research, cataloguing, archive work, and the various academic activities which the arts rely on for their interpretation and appreciation. The legacy of the lack of a critical forum during the Franco years was no doubt partly to blame. But far from seizing the opportunity to correct this lack, the Ministry of Culture treated art like a natural resource or product, to be promoted nationally or for export.

Paintings of the *movida madrileña*,* for example, were collected assiduously by wealthy patrons who stockpiled work, raising prices dramatically. But much of it was so closely linked with the ephemeral world of fashion and personality cults that its value was doomed to drop and not recover in the short term. Sponsorship of fringe artists and movements thrust experimental art directly into the mainstream. With so little critical analysis or guidance, the tendency towards support of personal favourites further unbalanced the normal progression from avant-garde marginalization to mainstream popularization. It was hard to know any more where the avant-garde was. By definition, it had always represented rebellion against the establishment. But, once democracy was established, art was put to the task of political propaganda, as an emblem of Spanish youth, energy, diversification, creativity, and tolerance. This process coincided with the rise of market ideology in the 1980s generally, intensified in Spain by the process of integration into Europe in the second part of the decade. In addition to being taken up by big business in a previously unprecedented fashion, art was reclaimed by the state and the establishment. As Mar Villaespesa wrote in 1989: 'this collaboration is the golden dream of any dictatorship.'[1]

Autonomous government support of the arts was similarly criticized. In 1989 Juan Gracián said in an article on the growth of art galleries in Andalusia: 'it is quite clear that the main concern is to imprint a political stamp on a building. No thought is given to creating an intelligent space in Seville or Granada where artistic events can flourish. What matters is to appear intelligent by creating a centre that provides monumental evidence of the way political developments are flourishing.'[2] In the 1990s, regionalist policies have come under discussion. For example, a crisis in regionalist architecture was caused by the insistence on distinct vernacular features, with many autonomous regional governments providing funds expressly for this purpose. There was a huge increase in research into and promotion of regional cultural heritages. For example, of thirty non-government-funded cultural foundations in the Basque Country in 1994, over half were devoted to regional history, language, music, and ethnography. In particular, research into historical and folkloric architectural styles was undertaken by regional architectural schools (for example, in Pamplona), to produce sets of variations on prevailing forms in a self-conscious postmodern mix which was often arbitrary. It could be argued that here sponsorship has been counter-productive.

In 1993, in a new climate of economic recession, Carmen Alborch Bataller was appointed to the Ministry of Culture. Among her proposals were major cut backs in foreign promotions and the encouragement of further private investment in the arts. More positively, she put forward plans for setting up debating forums for the arts, and for improving the level of cultural awareness. But the problem remains that, in Spain today, art is publicly seen as an item of consumption, a highbrow, élitist activity where connoisseurs, intellectuals, and patrons mingle: coverage in the gossip magazine *Hola* of the Thyssen entourage epitomizes this phenomenon. The PSOE government's negotiations to secure the Thyssen collection for Spain resulted in considerable publicity—the opening of the Thyssen-Bornemisza Museum coincided fortunately with the 1992 cultural bonanza—at the expense of striking a deal that was singularly advantageous to the collection's owner. Unfortunately many choose to ignore the tremendous interest in the arts of the Spanish general public, as shown in the wide-ranging survey published by the Ministry of Culture in 1992 to attract sponsorship. But most investment was going to high-profile, élitist projects of a short-term nature. Little was being invested in middle- or lowbrow cultural activities or in long-term research and education.

Notes
1 'Absolute Majority Syndrome', *Arena Internacional del Arte*, 1 (Feb. 1989), 86.
2 'The New Institutional Activity in Spain', *Arena Internacional del Arte*, 1 (Feb. 1989), 14.

Further reading
Jiménez-Blanco Carillo de Albornoz, M. D., *Arte y estado en la España del siglo XX* (Madrid, 1989) (on creation of state—including regional—museums of modern art from 1894 to present).

The Ministry of Culture produces regular reports on cultural activities, financing, and consumption. The following are particularly useful:

Equipamientos, prácticas y consumos culturales de los españoles (Madrid, 1991).
Fundaciones culturales privadas 1993: registro y protectorado del Ministerio de Cultura; registro y protectorado de las Comunidades Autónomas (Madrid, 1993).
Memoria anual '92 (Madrid, 1991).
El patrocinio empresarial de la cultura en España (Madrid, 1992).

Designer Culture in the 1980s: The Price of Success

EMMA DENT COAD

During the Franco regime the design of innovative products was officially deemed to be a subversive activity, too strongly linked to individual or regional expression, both of which were controlled by the censorship laws (these particularly affected cultural production in Catalonia). In the 1940s and early 1950s, the policy of autarky meant that industry was geared towards import substitution, which in practice meant that foreign products were copied, usually in an inferior manner to make them cheaper. It was thus virtually impossible to get original ideas manufactured.

Since no new organizations could be set up without government permission, it was also impossible for designers to form any kind of mutual support group or lobby. From the start of the 1950s, some designers made use of existing organizations mainly connected with the fine and decorative arts, such as El Foment de les Artes Decoratives (FAD, founded in Barcelona in 1903), setting up groups within their structures which met to discuss issues. Towards the end of the 1970s, the lack of manufacturing capacity led a number of designers to set up small manufacturing units themselves. Among them were BD (Barcelona Diseño) and Vinçon (also of Barcelona), which had their own retail outlets, together with a small number of furniture and lighting companies. With the arrival of democracy, Spaniards wishing to celebrate their new sense of cultural identity began to buy these locally made products in large numbers; in Catalonia it became a way of expressing regional pride. A combination of political and cultural freedom, increased personal income, and the desire to break with the past of a new generation born in the 1950s and 1960s, created a market hungry for new aesthetic ideas.

This phenomenon was first identified in Madrid, where underground rock bands suddenly became folk heroes. The bars and clubs where they performed served as a focus for a new, young, active, articulate avant-garde. Film-maker Pedro Almodóvar was a linchpin, using many of its protagonists as actors and as set and costume designers. Painting, sculpture, fashion, jewellery, film, music, theatre, and dance blossomed overnight and were quickly hailed as the new hope of a new Spain. One of the hundreds of foreign 'style' journalists—which one is a matter of dispute—christened the movement *la movida*.* Journalists and artists fed off each other in a mutual admiration society that had its own magazines, its own clubs, and its own galleries and shops.

Barcelona saw a similar explosion, which found concrete expression in the creation of new interiors both for clubs, restaurants, and bars, and for the shops where those benefiting from the new affluence could buy original, exciting products. While Madrid excelled in avant-garde fine arts and music, Barcelona specialized in fashion, furniture, and accessories. By the mid-1980s Barcelona had over twice as many design shops (30) as the entire British Isles (12). Large stores like BD, Vinçon, and Pilma sold furniture, lighting, accessories, and kitchen equipment. They were also the first to sell Italian goods, which became highly influential in the design world. These same stores—like the large number which sprang up nation-wide to satisfy the demand for designer objects—also sponsored designers to produce limited editions, and had fine-art galleries within the store (Vinçon in Barcelona, Lluís Adelantado in Valencia), firmly placing art and design in the same cultural category. Architecture enjoyed a similar vogue. The demand for designer products in the domestic market took everyone by surprise: by 1986, for example, production of furniture was doubling every year, demand coming almost entirely from the domestic market.

The cult of the designer bar began in Barcelona, spreading throughout Spain. As a meeting-point for architecture, interior design, fine art, fashion, and socializing, designer bars epitomized the spirit of the age: a coming together of culture, commerce, and, most important, youth. The celebration of youth was the starting-point for style in this period. It made fun of authority (whether Franco, parents, religion, or local government); it used and abused cultural clichés such as bulls, flamenco dancers, bourgeois taste; and it imbued a sense of meaning—real or imagined—through the use of metaphor and irony.

In 1978 Fernando Amat, together with a young designer/artist Javier Mariscal, had created Merbeye, arguably the first designer bar: avant-garde, built in a warehouse, characterized by visual jokes and the subversive treatment of materials and surfaces. Architect and designer Alfredo Arribas, in collaboration with Mariscal and/or others, created more designer interiors—shops, restaurants, but especially bars—than any other in the course of the 1980s. Arribas's style was rich in metaphorical references, employing the colours and materials of seduction—deep blues and reds, purple, velvet, suede, billowing curtains, opaque glass—and pounding music. His inspirations were a postmodern mix of 1950s design (the Italian Carlo Mollino), American-style movies (*Bladerunner*, *Blue Velvet*), and a local fascination

27 Interior of the designer bar Las Torres de Ávila, created in Barcelona in 1991 by Javier Mariscal and Alfredo Arribas, showing the 'female' tower in which tables and stools, arranged in a circle under a rising-and-falling canopy, look down through a hole on to the bar itself. (The 'male' tower has a piston travelling up and down it, in a deliberately vulgar joke.) This totally designed environment constructs a typically postmodernist self-contained, parodic space that turns everything into play and representation: a world with no 'outside'.

with necromancy. This was the ultimate designer experience, with everything—from décor to toilets, menus, logos, and even the music—designed by Arribas: in short, a totally designed environment, offering the youth of Barcelona release from their crowded family apartments and—above all—fun.

This movement reached its climax in 1991, when Arribas and Mariscal designed their most ambitious venture, Las Torres de Ávila. Over the past years, each successive bar had achieved new decorative excesses; Las Torres outdid them all. But it was the last bar of the 1980s rather than the first of the 1990s. Unlike its predecessors, it failed. For, located at the gates of the touristic Pueblo Español, Las Torres de Ávila played on the very clichés that Arribas himself had created, reducing itself to self-parody in a self-conscious reconstruction of the mottoes and motifs of the design world. It was not so much a designer bar as a simulation of a designer bar. Almost immediately it became the place where businessmen would bring overseas clients to view the cream of the city's youth, but not enough young people came. It marked a crisis point in the history of designer culture.

Another problem was that, once the dynamism and originality of Spanish design had been acknowledged, government policy did its best to promote it abroad. A wide-reaching, costly marketing strategy was implemented, sending Spanish designers on subsidized trips to foreign fairs, and bringing journalists to Spain by the planeload. The strategy was highly successful and the image of Spanish design prospered. But, without the corresponding investment in industrial modernization and management training, many of these organizations could not cope with the enquiries and orders that flooded in. Most designers had never worked in mainstream industry and had little business acumen. Some companies had no foreign-language speakers; some had only small manufacturing units which could not cope with increased orders. Others used a number of different manufacture or assembly studios, making quality control a nightmare. Orders were late and clients began to send products back.

In short, it all happened too quickly. There was a constant flurry of new shop openings, new bar openings, new exhibition openings, fashion weeks, furniture weeks. The spur of the 1992 Olympics—and the government and corporation money it attracted—set the machine of designer culture working at ever greater speed. What got lost in this orgy of cultural consumption were the ideas, ethos, and originality which had brought Spanish design to prominence in the first place.

The year 1992 was a tough one for Spain. Recession was beginning to hit tourism world-wide, and financial institutions—banks, savings banks, and investment foundations—were suffering. The Seville Expo, the celebrations for Madrid European Capital of Culture, the Barcelona Olympics went ahead with almost enough visitors who spent not quite enough money. In the aftermath, the design community paused to take stock. Bars are still opening and new furniture is still being launched, but at a much less frantic pace than previously. In this relative lull, the design community is learning from the mistakes it made in the 1980s, and refocusing on self-reflexion and theory.

Further reading
Dent Coad, E., *Spanish Design and Architecture* (London, 1990).
—— *Javier Mariscal: Designing the New Spain* (London, 1992).

Gender and Sexuality

ROSA MONTERO

ANNY
BROOKSBANK
JONES

CHRIS PERRIAM

The Silent Revolution: The Social and Cultural Advances of Women in Democratic Spain

ROSA MONTERO

The cliché of Spanish *machismo* is clearly outdated. Sexism still exists in Spain, of course, but no more so than in neighbouring countries; statistics indicate that the level of discrimination is comparable to the EC average. It is however true that, until very recently, our cultural traditions have discriminated heavily against women. The influence of Catholicism, for which sexual difference is divinely ordained, plus the legacy of eight centuries of Arab occupation laid the foundations for a sexism that the Franco period would only aggravate.

Forty years of dictatorship did more than halt the process of women's emancipation; the imposition of a traditionalist National-Catholicism and ultra-reactionary social norms set the clock back dramatically for Spanish women. Francoism cannot be understood without taking into account the fact that until 1975, the date of Franco's death, a married woman in Spain could not open a bank account, buy a car, apply for a passport, or even work without her husband's permission. And if she did work with her husband's approval, he had the right to claim her salary. On top of that, for the whole of the forty-year period contraception, divorce, and abortion were illegal. In addition,

Gender and Sexuality   381

adultery was a crime for which a woman could be sent to prison, while concubinage (male adultery), though a criminal offence, was treated more leniently.

Despite such handicaps, the position of women in Spain has changed drastically in the last twenty years. The process started before Franco's death: between 1970 and 1974, a key period of economic growth, 1.5 million Spanish women who had never worked before entered employment, radically altering the role of women both in and outside the home. The female working population has gone on increasing by leaps and bounds: in 1980, 27 per cent of the work-force was female; by 1991, the figure had risen to 35 per cent. This despite the very low employment rates for women aged 50 plus, who belong to a generation that is inevitably more *machista*. In the EC overall, women make up 41 per cent of the working population.

With the advent of democracy, legal guarantees against sexual discrimination came into operation, as stipulated by Article 14 of the 1978 Constitution plus the articles on marriage and divorce. Also in 1978 adultery and concubinage were decriminalized, as was the sale of contraceptives. The legalization of divorce met with greater opposition from the Church and the right but was finally approved in 1981. The real sticking point was abortion, a subject which created huge debate and disagreements which still have not been resolved. With the PSOE* in power, after an active pro-abortion campaign during which hundreds of thousands of women and men signed declarations that they had either had or participated in an abortion, the latter was finally legalized in 1985 in three circumstances: where there is danger to the mother's physical or mental well-being; where the foetus shows signs of physical or mental defects; and in the case of rape. At the time of writing, a Special Abortion Law has been announced for 1994 which apparently will increase the mother's say in the decision to terminate her pregnancy.

The fact that the social and cultural advances gained by women in Europe over the last fifty years (since the Second World War) have, in the case of Spain, been compressed into the last two decades has created a very special situation. First, as we have seen with regard to women entering employment, there are two Spains: the 50+ age group (male and female) tends to have much more traditional values and life-styles. Given this it is not surprising that, overall, Spain has the lowest figures for men helping with the housework of any country in the EC: 8 out of every 10 men make no contribution whatsoever (incidentally, the figures for the UK are 7 out of every 10), while Spanish women going out to work spend an average of three extra hours a day on housework.

Secondly, since the changes have mainly taken place since the 1970s—that is, at a time when the international women's movement was entering a period of crisis—activist groups have never been very strong. This, together with the general weakening of public debate under the dictatorship, helps explain why Spain has produced very little by way of feminist analysis and theory. The same holds true for feminist magazines, which have not achieved significant circulation figures or influence. The best known was probably *Vindicación Feminista* at the end of the 1970s but even this failed to make a mark outside activist circles, which have always been a minority. At present about twenty such magazines exist, many of them published by local government or official bodies, such as *Mujeres* issued by the Instituto de la Mujer; none of them can however be said to have a significant social impact.

A much greater impact has been made by women's bookshops, which have been extremely active. Their financial position has always been precarious and some have gone under, but there are three long-standing survivors which themselves publish, award literary prizes, organize meetings, and act as specialist libraries giving information and guidance: the Librería de Mujeres in Zaragoza and in Madrid, and the Librería Sal de Casa in Valencia. Finally, there is the Instituto de la Mujer, set up by the Socialists in 1983, originally under the Ministry of Culture but now under the Ministry of Social Services. This has done a great deal to normalize the situation of Spanish women, funding and supporting a range of services, associations, and social centres specifically for women. Particularly important are its research role, the many extremely interesting studies it has published, and the two Equal Opportunities Plans it has drawn up, which provide a genuine framework for the political and administrative changes affecting women in recent years.

Women provide a particularly good illustration of the speed of change in recent Spanish society and of the unique vitality that has resulted. The first bastion to be stormed was the media: twenty-five years ago this was a virtually all-male preserve; now there are roughly equal numbers of women and men on the editorial staff. Of course managerial posts are still largely held by men but here too there have been significant changes. There are now women heads of radio stations, of TV news, and of magazines; *El País*, the best-selling and most important national newspaper, has had a woman executive editor for the last 3 years, and the number of women deputy editors and chief subeditors in the national press generally is huge. This female conquest of the media shows no signs of abating: in 1988, for example, 58 per cent of students of journalism graduating were women.

This does not mean that there is no sexist bias in the media but it is much subtler than it used to be, especially in the news, where women are clearly more visible and treated more fairly. When we turn to the full range of TV broadcasting, however, things are not so rosy. With the licensing of private channels in the early 1990s, and the Italian model of junk TV imported by Berlusconi, there has been a marked decline, with women being exploited *ad nauseam* as sexual objects of the crudest kind.

The other cultural sector where women have made spectacular incursions is that of literary production. It is logical that women, in leaving the confines of the home for the public sphere, should have opted for the media and fiction, both of which give them a public platform.

The Franco years produced a select number of important women writers (e.g. Ana María Matute, Carmen Martín Gaite, Elena Soriano), but one of the most impressive socio-cultural features of the *boom* in new Spanish fiction after Franco's death has been the emergence of dozens of new women writers (e.g. Montserrat Roig, Esther Tusquets, Carmen Gómez Ojea, Soledad Puértolas, Lourdes Ortiz, Carme Riera, Cristina Fernández Cubas), many of them reaching the best-seller lists. If initially, especially in the late 1970s, their work was mostly concerned with depicting women's experience and problems (building on the efforts at a feminist —feminine?—realism of earlier writers like Martín Gaite), it soon started to branch out into different areas, becoming as eclectic and diversified as that of their male counterparts. Which does not mean that they have imitated male writers (they write as women in the same way that men write as men), but simply that their imaginative scope has broadened.

Spanish women novelists are now developing a personal style or cultivating a range of literary genres: fantastic literature (Cristina Fernández Cubas' *Mi hermana Elba*, Carmen Gómez Ojea's *Cantiga de agüero*), the chivalric romance (Paloma Díaz-Mas's *El rapto del Santo Grial*), the historical novel (Lourdes Ortiz's *Urraca*), metafiction (Nuria Amat's *Todos somos Kafka*), the Gothic (Ana María Moix's story in the anthology *Doce relatos de mujer*), etc. Some have taken up the subgenre of erotic or pornographic literature, with great commercial success, occasionally falling into the trap of imitating male models (Almudena Grandes's *Las edades de Lulú*).

Spanish women novelists have, then, conquered the market as well as their creative freedom. But, as in the rest of Europe, cultural officialdom is still reluctant to give women writers full recognition. We are still inadequately represented and treated dismissively in encyclopedias, anthologies, the Royal Academy, and other institutions. This discrimination is being contested, in Spain as elsewhere, by the increasing number of women reviewers and academics. An important role has been played here by the creation over the last ten years of a number of women's research centres and groups, such as the Instituto Universitario de Estudios de la Mujer at the Autonomous University of Madrid, the Seminario Interdisciplinario de Investigaciones Feministas at the University of Valencia, the Seminari de Estudis de la Dona at the Autonomous University of Barcelona, or the Asociación de Estudios Históricos de la Mujer at the University of Málaga. Altogether there are some twenty such academic research programmes in the country.

To turn to other cultural forms, we again find that, if women started to make an impression in the 1970s, it was in the 1980s that they consolidated their position and increased their numbers. In cinema, for example, old hands such as Pilar Miró and Josefina Molina have been joined by half a dozen new women directors. In the theatre, traditionally an impenetrable terrain (the only woman playwright worth mentioning in the last two decades is Ana Diosdado, whose conventional dramas have enjoyed considerable box-office success), there are now a number of female dramatists: well-known figures such as María Manuela Reina, or newcomers such as Paloma Pedrero, Maribel Lázaro, and Marisa Ares. There are female rock stars like Luz, female photographers like Ouka Lele, female designers like Sybila, female symphonic composers like Marisa Manchado.

In general terms it can be said that the incorporation of Spanish women into the world of work, including that of art and culture, is on a par with other European Community countries: in other words, we are no longer the exception in practically every field, and this gives us more room for manœuvre. Because when women are the exception at work, as in the early stages of integration, it is hard to do more than adapt to traditional male values; but once there are a considerable number of women at all levels it becomes possible to establish new ways of working, organizing, and relating. This is the exciting stage we are at now.

To conclude, perhaps the most spectacular and revealing statistics of all are in education. It was not till 1985 that the numbers of women in education equalled male levels and reached the European average; but since that date advances have been prodigious, to the extent that Spain now ranks third (after France and Denmark) in the EC league tables with regard to the percentage of women studying at university. In Spain today, there are more female than male students at all levels of education, and they do better. If in 1980 only 42 per cent of graduates were women, in 1990 women outstripped men at 54 per cent. Moreover, there has been a dramatic increase in the numbers of women in traditionally male disciplines: for example architecture, where in 1980 12 per cent of graduates were women and in 1990 25 per cent, and agriculture, where in 1980 women formed 10 per cent of forestry graduates and in 1990 33 per cent.

Spanish women are, then, increasingly well qualified, educated, and competitive. Hence their rapid incorporation into the work-force. If in 1988 only 5 per cent of architects and engineers were women, four years later in 1992 the figure had risen to 9 per cent. Over the same period, in business, the number of women directors went up from 6 per cent to 9 per cent, and the number of women managers from 8 per cent to 13 per cent. The number of women economists and lawyers went up from 20 per cent to 30 per cent, the number of women chemists and physicists from 26 per cent to 38 per cent Nothing less than a silent revolution, achieved through perseverance and hard work.

Further reading

On women and social change
See items listed under the following essay by Anny Brooksbank Jones.

On women's writing
Levine, L. G., *Spanish Women Writers: A Bio-bibliographical Source Book* (London, 1993) (basic reference for Spanish women writers generally).
Manteiga, R. C., Galerstein, C., and McKerney, K. (eds.), *Feminine Concerns in Contemporary Spanish Fiction by Women* (Potomac, 1988).
Nichols, G. C., *Des/cifrar la diferencia: narrativa femenina de la España contemporánea* (Madrid, 1992).
Ordóñez, E., *Voices of their Own: Contemporary Spanish Narrative by Women* (Lewisburg, 1991).
—— 'Inscribing Difference: "L'Écriture féminine" and New Narrative by Women', *Anales de Literatura Española Contemporánea*, 12 (1987), 45–58.
Pérez, J. W. (ed.), *Contemporary Women Writers of Spain* (Boston, 1988).

Work, Women, and the Family: A Critical Perspective

ANNY BROOKSBANK JONES

The dramatic acceleration of the modernization process following Franco's death in 1975 has had major repercussions for Spanish women at home and in paid employment. Increased life expectancy and falling birth rates, the extension of educational opportunities, the expansion of the state and the progressive erosion of its moral authority and that of the Church, the continuing decline of domestic in favour of state and private production, the foreshortening of men's working lives by longer studies and earlier retirement, and EU-imposed economic restructuring have all influenced women's participation in the public and private spheres. This essay examines some of the effects of these changes, women's responses to them, and the extent to which those responses are contributing to further change.

Although many rural and working-class women in particular still retain (often invisible) reserve labour roles, the last thirty years have seen the progressive integration of women into the labour market, assisted by the expansion first of secondary and, from the 1980s, of tertiary education. From 1961 (with the introduction of the *Ley de derechos políticos, profesionales y de trabajo de la mujer* [Women's Political, Professional, and Employment Rights Law]) the dynamic of the development process had begun to overturn the restrictions that had circumscribed women's work since 1939, and in the next twenty years women rose from around 14 per cent to 25 per cent of Spain's working population. Throughout the 1960s much of this increase was concentrated in the service industries, particularly tourism, which were deemed appropriate to women's social role and segmented enough to fit around their domestic commitments. At the same time expanding industrialization and demand for consumer durables saw the numbers of women in (largely unskilled) factory work increase—particularly in textiles and garment-making, chemicals, footwear, and hides, where they were already most strongly represented—while remaining the lowest in Europe. By the mid-1970s this work was being disproportionately hit by progressive technologization, the consequent labour reductions, and a shift away from consumer durables. During the economic crisis of 1973–82, as traditionally male sectors like industry and construction continued to decline, women turned progressively to the service sector, where they made up over 50 per cent of education and health care employees. Throughout this period women's employment grew along with the areas in which they were concentrated, chiefly the service sector and public administration. Since 1985 and the start of the economic recuperation women's representation has grown across all sectors, most notably—with their (albeit unevenly) increased access to higher education—in business and technology and in professions such as the law, pharmacy, and economics. A proportion of these enjoy job stability and working conditions comparable with those of male counterparts. Many do not, however, and labour market reform and other economic restructuring measures designed to promote European convergence have contributed to the climate of socio-economic instability that is driving ever larger numbers of (particularly, though not exclusively, young and less well-educated) women into the black economy which produces an estimated 30 per cent of Spain's domestic product. Employed chiefly in home working, sweatshops, seasonal agricultural work, subcontracting in various forms, prostitution, or domestic service, these women can expect high levels of job instability, little hope of career development or status, poor working conditions, and contracts which (where they exist) are unregulated and disadvantageous.

Associated with these shifts in women's socio-economic roles are significant changes of consciousness, particularly among women most exposed to the competing demands of public and private spheres. Tensions between and within so-called traditional (patriarchal, Catholic, and family-centred) and modern (feminist, career-minded, or liberal individualist) values are played out not only in the workplace but in the home. While formal education remains a function of the state, the broader socialization of the young—for conditions which can no longer be predicted with any certainty—is increasingly the responsibility not of the school or the Church but of parents who may be divorced, separated, unmarried, and/or have major extradomestic commitments. Their experience of the conflicting hours, time-scales, and (nurturing/affective versus productive/effective) priorities of home and workplace, of the percolation of feminist assumptions through key areas of Spanish society (and the apparent imperviousness of other areas), and of more equitable access to higher education has been accompanied in many younger women by an increased sensitivity to unequal social relations, and this in turn has helped unsettle the traditional association of progressive values with men and conservative ones with women. Today (particularly younger, middle-, and upper-class) women on the ideological centre or left are increasingly assumed to be more progressive than their male counterparts, while women in general are represented as the motor of contemporary social change.

Such generalizations obscure considerable variation in women's life experiences—as inflected by age (for example, in the generally very different attitudes to work among women who grew up under the Franco regime and those who did not), class, education, location, and ethnicity—and the range of values and priorities associated with them. They nevertheless underline changing perceptions of women's social roles and integration. In practice it is difficult to say to what extent women's changing consciousness is a cause and to what extent an effect of increased integration in the workplace, for example, and how far that integration is a result of transformations that lie beyond their control. The feminist explosion of the 1970s and the subsequent social and politico-juridical institutionalization of some of its less controversial assumptions have undoubtedly helped shift the focus of (especially younger and middle-class) women from family to career over the last twenty years. At the same time, many women's early experience of precarious employment and conflicting domestic commitments has pre-adapted them to the complex uncertainties of today's job market. In the context of the economic and broader social repercussions of current economic restructuring, a history of unstable employment looks rather like training for the new, flexible, working patterns. In ways feminists could not have predicted the playing field is gradually becoming more even, as the traditional precariousness of women's work is extended increasingly to men's.

According to official statistics, a third of the adult female population of Spain was officially seeking or in work in 1992, compared with almost two-thirds of men. However, this statistic obscures massive disparities: in the 25–9 age group, for example, there were 105 working women for every 100 men, while work rates for women over 50 remained close to 1976 levels. Throughout the years of economic and employment development and crisis (roughly 1964–84) women tended to be overrepresented in the least-skilled, worst-paid, and lowest-status areas of the sectors in which they participated, while their entry into and exit from the workplace were key factors in the ebb and flow of labour supply. Under Franco only permanent full-time jobs could be created; redundancies had to be government approved and attracted the highest compensation rates in Europe. By contrast the 1980s saw the introduction of new redundancy provisions and early retirement incentives, and increasingly (from 1984) of part-time contracting and so-called flexible working practices. Despite fairly concerted union resistance, these were supplemented in December 1993 by a new labour reform law with provisions for temporary job placement, apprenticeship, and other forms of temporary and part-time contract to be paid at 60–75 per cent of standard rates, offering reduced social security payments for employers with reduced protection for employees. At around 10 per cent, Spain's part-time employment rate is less than a third of Denmark's, for example, but women already make up two-thirds of this number and this proportion is increasing. Unemployment is also disproportionately high among women, particularly among those seeking their first job and—highlighting the persistent 'glass ceiling' effect—the best educated. Although almost twice as many men as women figure in the official active population, slightly more women than men are currently registered as unemployed. Unlike their counterparts in the development period, however, most women no longer see the home as their natural base or retreat; when expelled from the formal economy today they are more likely to register as unemployed, with a significant proportion disappearing into the black economy or other casual work in the interim.

The complex and mutually determining relations of economic and broader social change are played out not only in the workplace but in the homes and on the bodies of women. This is reflected in increased state provision for women's health training and monitoring as well as in greater demand for and availability of abortion and contraception. It is also increasingly visible in the so-called crisis of the family. Although there has never been a single, uniform Spanish family the dominant model throughout the Franco years was the extended household, which persists today, especially in northern rural areas (largely as a result of the prevailing inheritance system), and which offers women more opportunities to share domestic responsibilities, while ensuring there are more to share. Throughout the development period more women undertook paid extradomestic work in order to produce and be able to buy the new consumer durables. With more money and labour-saving appliances but less time they helped precipitate the displacement of the extended (productive/reproductive) family in favour of forms of nuclear consumer unit, particularly in more economically and demographically dynamic urban areas. Today both models persist alongside a range of non-institutionalized households. In 1993, although 64 per cent of families were of the two-generation nuclear type (parents plus one or more children), 16 per cent were couples without children or lone-parent families. As in Britain, the enormous majority of lone heads of family are women. Of these around one-third have no job, while many of the remainder are forced (by their need for paid employment to meet outgoings, the difficulties of finding it in a contracting labour market, and, once found, of reconciling it with child care) into some of the most precarious and worst-paid positions.

Spanish children have traditionally lived with parents for longer than most of their European counterparts and, despite a move towards earlier marriage in the development years, by the late 1970s the familiar pattern was reasserting itself. By 1990 a combination of longer studies, later entry into work, and better relations with their parents (particularly among the middle and upper classes) was leading young women to leave home on average at $25\frac{1}{2}$, and young men at 28. During the 1960s and early 1970s married women had tended to work after having children: today the increasing availability and acceptance of contraception enables them to delay childbearing to 30 or beyond (as they seek to establish themselves in their profession or support partners who are finishing their studies) and to end increasingly early. These shifts have contributed to one of the lowest birth rates in the world, currently at 1.36 per cent and prompting talk of a return to post-war childbirth incentives. Combined with Spain's increasing secularization, greater access to and acceptance of contraceptives, and the increased state role in child education and health, they have made young people less likely to marry on leaving home than to form (relatively) stable unmarried couples.

Associated with this gradual prolonging of single status and childlessness and women's more equitable access to educational opportunities is the decreasing significance since the mid-1980s of sex distinctions in sociological data, as the values and opinions of young men and women (especially in the middle and upper classes) become progressively less differentiated. The separation of sexuality and procreation as represented in the trend towards cohabitation, and the increasing acceptance (especially among the young and the better educated) of premarital sex, have led to a very different response among Madrid's 15–19-year-olds, however, in the form of a spectacular increase in the extramarital birth rate. Yet at 10 per cent overall this remains less than half the British figure. Couples who do marry do so progressively later, often on the point of starting a family, and usually in a civil ceremony—although the 18–24 age group is more likely to express a preference for a religious ceremony. Divorces (more usual among the working class) and separations (commoner among the middle and upper classes) have increased by 23 per cent and 52 per cent respectively since 1984. Despite gradual politico-juridical recognition of a European trend towards non-traditional households it can be difficult to communicate with the Spanish state except as a member of a family. As a result many such unions, including growing numbers of lesbian and gay couples, are demanding family status in the public as well as the private sphere—that is, for legal and economic motives (including pension and inheritance rights) as well as reasons of affectivity and intimacy. This does not simply reinforce the claims of the traditional family, however; it has already precipitated a substantive extension of its legal scope in asylum, habeas corpus, and adoptions cases, for example, while inheritance and pension rights are currently under consideration.

Most of the tensions arising from the so-called crisis of the family nevertheless relate to the fact that (despite significant politico-juridical liberalization since 1975) the existing social contract is still in the process of adapting to these new relations, and to the enlarged sense of equality and justice (particularly among women under 40 and the young) to which they appeal. As recently as the early 1980s, over one-quarter of women felt that a woman's first duty was to tend her family: by the early 1990s the figure was no longer significant. If traditional beliefs promoted by Church and state under Franco are losing their force, however, new ones can claim no equivalent source of legitimation. The resulting value disorientation—which underlies a growing tendency among the young to describe themselves as Catholics, albeit non-practising—compounds stress arising from the fact that women's education currently prepares them for work more efficiently than the Mediterranean tradition of sex segregation prepares men to help at home. The notoriously inequitable distribution of domestic responsibilities is slowly breaking down, particularly in young and middle-class couples, where the woman may well be of a similar age to and have a higher educational level than her partner. This has had little impact so far however—particularly for women who struggle to keep their job for social reasons—despite the fact that motherhood tends to come, where it comes, in the period of greatest professional development for both women and their (increasingly similarly aged) partners. In such circumstances women with sufficiently well-paid jobs may call on (usually working-class) casual domestic help, particularly as state child-care provision remains unavailable for children under 3 years of age—in Britain, under 5 years—and, like that of state-funded elderly daycare centres, has not kept pace with demand.

Prompted by feminist lobbies and funding from a number of EU initiatives (including the current New Opportunities for Women programme), national and regional politico-juridical measures have done much to reduce, although by no means eradicate, the most overt forms of direct sex discrimination. These measures have been institutionalized in the 1978 Constitution, subsequent amendments, and laws—including a 1989 law shifting the burden of proof in sex discrimination cases from the accuser to the accused, and a statute of the same year formally outlawing forms of sexual harassment—and since its inception in 1983 in the work of the Instituto de la Mujer [Institute for Women's Affairs]. Indirect discrimination remains rampant, however, not least in the institutionalized androcentrism of the educational system, for example, the judiciary and the political sphere—where women deputies currently comprise only 16 per cent of the parliamentary total and continue to suffer working conditions designed for men. The unsocial hours, tokenism (or ghettoization in areas of traditional overrepresentation), the likelihood of a 'second shift' of domestic responsibilities when they get home, exposure to forms of sexual abuse and harassment, disproportionately low chances of high office, and senior staffs' tendency to demand more of women than men—to treat women's absenteeism or lower productivity less leniently, for example, especially if child-care is a factor—are all broadly in line with what women can expect elsewhere in the labour market, where women's average wage is moreover around 30 per cent below men's.

Union affiliation in Spain is low overall—14 per cent in 1991 compared with 46 per cent in Britain—but particularly so among women. This partly reflects Spanish unions' own fairly unimpressive record on anti-discriminatory measures but also their strength among higher-level staff and in companies with over 1,000 employees, while women are concentrated chiefly in smaller companies and in middle-range posts. For example, one-sixth of the capital's labour force and a third of its unemployed women are to be found in the service sector, where mostly small and non-unionized offices provide precarious, non-standard, and low-grade work in poor conditions, and where record unemployment levels impact critically on pension and other employment-linked rights. For the 14 per cent of women on part-time, temporary, seasonal, or home-working contracts these conditions are generally compounded by even lower wages and reduced job security.

Although it is bearing the brunt of current changes, negative side-effects for women of the current economic restructuring are by no means restricted to the service sector. At the other end of the employment spectrum, for example, women agricultural workers are being exposed to a rural modernization process which is drastically reducing the work-force while exacerbating the sector's premodern and unequal social relations. There has been gradual change but no real agrarian reform in Spain and rural women continue to bear heavy domestic and productive responsibilities (often also working on neighbouring smallholdings on a reciprocal basis) with little or no payment or recognition. As European integration brings progressively lower profits and thus lower social status, however, women's responsibilities have come to seem increasingly secondary, particularly as new technology—the most valued part of the agricultural modernization process—is seen as an exclusively male preserve. In these circumstances younger rural women are increasingly rejecting their mothers' way of life and competing with their urban counterparts for professional salaried posts in industry, the professions, and technology and, as vacancies continue to shrink, continuing in the interim to substitute for men in informal seasonal labour pools. A return to the massive rural depopulation of the development years seems unlikely, however, not least because they are seeking work in or close to the rural home base.

These and other rapid changes in the workplace and the home since 1975 have been accompanied by no less significant changes in women's social roles, values, and relationships. Newer forms currently interact with more traditional ones in complex and unpredictable ways and in a climate of intense social and economic uncertainty. More experienced than men in the negotiation of such uncertainties, women have figured as the main beneficiaries of labour market changes. Many who would once have stayed at home with their children have taken advantage of flexible working patterns to join other women in the homogenizing structures of the workplace, in which inequitable treatment can be recognized as a shared rather than an individual issue, leading to demands for changes in both workplace and home. However, flexible working patterns as currently and increasingly constituted also entail negative side-effects for many women. If the political will existed, the most pernicious of these effects could undoubtedly be palliated; in practice, most recent government reforms suggest that the trend is towards compounding them.

Women are thus not the motors of social change in any simple sense, but nor are they its victims. They respond often innovatively to rapidly changing situations and with their responses—the increasing rejection of traditional roles at work and at home, for example, the postponement of childbearing, the redefinition of the family, and the refusal to return to the domestic sphere on becoming unemployed—modify the context for future changes. After generations of supposed conservatism their designation as a progressive social force marks not only a perceived change in women's consciousness but also a significant shift in the perception (among men as well as women) of their wider social possibilities. Moreover, unlike the boom/bust cycles experienced by women workers in the development years, the combination of technological and structural changes required by the globalizing labour market and the ideological shifts institutionalized in national educational, judicial, and other systems since 1975 makes these changes apparently irreversible.

Further reading
Amaranta: Revista de la Asamblea Feminista de Madrid (Dec. 1993) (special issue on women and work).
Brooksbank Jones, A., 'Feminisms in Contemporary Spain', *Journal of the Association for Contemporary Iberian Studies* (forthcoming, Sept. 1994).
Carrasco, C., *El trabajo doméstico y la reproducción social* (Madrid, 1991).
Casas, J. I., *La participación laboral de la mujer en España* (Madrid, 1987).
Centre d'Estudis Demogràfics, *Estructuras familiares en España* (Madrid, 1990).
Durán, M. A. (ed.), *De puertas adentro* (Madrid, 1987).
Folguera, P., 'De la transición política a la democracia: la evolución del feminismo en España durante el período 1975–1988', in P. Folguera (ed.), *El feminismo en España: dos siglos de historia* (Madrid, 1988), 111–31.
Garrido, L. J., *Las dos biografías de la mujer en España* (Madrid, 1993).

Gil Calvo, E., and Luzán, J., 'Mujeres: asalto al poder', *Semanal El País*, 121 (1 June 1993), 16–29.

Instituto de la Mujer, *El trabajo de las mujeres a través de la historia* (Madrid, 1992).

—— *Mujer, trabajo y maternidad* (Madrid, 1992).

Miguel, A. de, *La sociedad española 1993–94* (Madrid, 1994).

Poder y Libertad, 23 (1994) (special issue on women and the family).

Rubery, J. (ed.), *Las mujeres y la recesión* (Madrid, 1993; rev. and updated version of *Women and Recession*, London, 1988).

Gay and Lesbian Culture

CHRIS PERRIAM

Spanish gay culture after 1975 manifests itself in terms of an accelerated continuity rather than as sudden emergence, not least because Francoism had always half-tolerated those sexual differences it could safely label or caricature (transvestism, harmless effeminacy in men, comic manliness in women). An already coherent counter-cultural discourse can be seen emerging around 1975 in radical magazines like *Ajoblanco* and *Bicicleta*, and contacts with exiles in Europe and North America as well as alternative tourism into Spain (notably at Sitges and Ibiza) meant that the exchange of new ideas and life-styles was not limited to print. Action and discussion groups have been influential since the early 1970s in Valencia and Barcelona (originally the sexual political front line), in Madrid (a gay leisure culture growing up around the *movida**), and in Bilbao (perhaps the most radical of the centres today). Most university towns now have at least one organization which acts as a focus for a young lesbian/gay community, though the number of active members appears to be generally small. AIDS- and HIV-related issues are reconfiguring and revitalizing sexual politics for the urban young and all the big cities have produced a small-circulation gay press, with extensive coverage recently of debates concerning homosexuality and military service—also treated in the mainstream media—and the advantages and disadvantages of local authority registers of cohabiting couples.

As in the rest of western Europe, lesbian voices have been particularly silenced, lesbianism remaining 'invisible' even for otherwise progressive-thinking leftists in Spain today (although following an outbreak of images of lesbian chic in glossy magazines—as elsewhere in the west in the early 1990s—the up-market media have begun to chronicle lesbian—as well as gay—lives and to give a higher profile to the basic issues). *Nosotras*, the magazine of the Madrid Colectivo de Feministas Lesbianas, is one of a small number of publications which struggle to redress this (although the anti-heterosexist tradition started in the mid-1970s continues in the non-lesbian or gay alternative press). While *Nosotras* has been especially concerned to translate women's (theoretical) writing from other countries, the government-sponsored *Sol . . .* (a magazine for 'women's liberation and equality') offers space—from a centre-left and middle-class position—to non-lesbian but anti-heterosexist discourses from throughout Spain. Few bars and discos offer women-only space and outside the commercial scene alternative space is scarce.

Youth unemployment, a lack of local authority provision, and strong lasting echoes of the old morality (especially concerning the family) have restricted the possibilities for independent alternative living. But subversion of the iconography of the old regime is widespread, especially in camp manifestations, as is amply attested in the films of Pedro Almodóvar. The homo-erotic *pietà* which concludes *La ley del deseo* (*Law of Desire*, 1987), a film which strongly deconstructs the traditional family, is fondly but devastatingly iconoclastic. Almodóvar's use of popular song—especially the *bolero*—to camp effect is part of a wider reclaiming in gay cultures of popular music once associated with myths of quintessential *latinidad*. The soft flamenco rock of Azúcar Moreno is recognized in and beyond Spain as a camp gay favourite amongst those in their twenties to forties; it is matched, for an older generation, by an abiding adoration for the 1950s revival of interest in the *copla* (folkloric popular song) by singers such as Sara Montiel and Concha Piquer. Looking outside Spain, Eduardo Haro Ibars's *Gay Rock* (published in May 1975) engaged early on with rebellious discourses of the Gay Liberation Fronts in Europe and North America, and emphasized the importance of Glam Rock to experiments in constructing new identities. Indigenous pop and rock have continued to supply iconic figures around which gay fantasies and sexual political awareness have been able to develop, such as the Bowie-like Miguel Bosé who stars in Almodóvar's *Tacones lejanos* (1992).

Despite the much-vaunted opening-up in matters of sexual politics and behaviour, there has been little space for alternative sexualities in the traditional media. The scarce record left in written narrative, though, is a varied and lively one. Valencia is represented in Lluís Fernández's *L'anarquista nu* (1978), a radical and scandalously funny rewriting of sexual politics in transition which questions not only straight bourgeois culture but also emergent gay life-styles themselves. There are similar representations of early gay counter-culture in Barcelona and its relation to homosexual cultures outside Spain in Alberto Cardín's *Detrás por delante* (1978) and activist Jordi Petit's poems *De hombre a hombre* (1984). Also coming out of Catalan cultures, Esther Tusquets (b. 1936) and Juan Goytisolo (b. 1931) have used radical textual strategies to enact the disturbances of homosexual desire, although in a much less street-wise and more consciously literary and difficult way. Luis Antonio de Villena's *Chicos* (1989) centres on Madrid between 1974 and the early 1980s, representing it as a scene of dissidence and sexual adventure, rewriting the city many of us know from reading realist and neo-realist novels, albeit in an unashamedly élitist manner.

There is as yet very little cultural production about, by, or for ordinary lesbians and gay men. Even the otherwise down-to-earth and classless magazine of the Colectivo de Gais y Lesbianas de Madrid (COGAM), *¿Entiendes . . . ?*, heads the selection in its new mail-order book service (in the June 1993 issue) with Villena's exotic stories of obscure decadent lives, *Para los dioses turcos* (1980).[1] Although

Petit and others celebrated a new sexual politics of equality, a major theme throughout the period has been inequality in power relations, these being problematized in film by Eloy de la Iglesia's *Los placeres ocultos* (1976) and *El diputado* (1978) and in Manuel Vázquez Montalbán's novel *Los alegres muchachos de Atzavara* (1987), scandalously celebrated in the works of Terenci Moix (b. 1943), and both bravely normalized and conservatively idealized in poetry by Villena and Francisco Brines (b. 1932). Apart from what films and foreign serials have brought to the small screen (including the mixed blessings of *Brideshead Revisited* and *Another Country*) television has kept largely to the familiar stereotypes and has eschewed positive images. Alternative theatre in the university towns has kept a radical space for gays and (less so) lesbians, but only in the 1990s have established theatres been prepared to go further than Lorca. Gay culture, or 'el *mundo* gai' as it more commonly names itself, variously sustains a revolutionary distrust of static categories and a reactionary evasion of politicization while lesbian culture is still struggling to form itself, though now from a position of strength.

Note
1 COGAM now run a large bookshop in Madrid, Berkana, and informal reports suggest that it may well prove to be an important new resource and a focus for dialogue and support.

Further reading
Mirabet i Mullol, A., *Homosexualidad hoy: ¿aceptado o todavía condenado?* (Barcelona, 1985).
Smith, P. J., *Laws of Desire: Questions of Homosexuality in Spanish Writing and Film 1960–1990* (Oxford, 1992).

The magazine *Ajoblanco* is preparing a 'Dossier sobre la homosexualidad', due to appear in the January 1995 issue.

JO LABANYI

HELEN GRAHAM

ANTONIO
SÁNCHEZ

Conclusion: Modernity and Cultural Pluralism

Postmodernism and the Problem of Cultural Identity

JO LABANYI

Post-Franco Spain (almost twenty years after Franco's death, it is hard to avoid the expression) is marked by a sense of catching up with the future but also of being an irremediable postscript: a contradiction captured by the label *postnovísimos* given to poets of the transition period. The postmodernist sense of living after the 'end of history' was expressed in the *desencanto** years from 1979 to PSOE* election victory in 1982 by the *pasotismo* [dropping out] that succeeded the immediate post-1975 political and sexual euphoria. The initial demand for historical and political publications (and pornography) gave way to a new demand for fiction, with its stress on representation rather than reality: from around 1980, new series titled Narrativas Hispánicas, Narrativa Joven, Última Narrativa, Nueva Narrativa blossomed. The libertarian cultural magazines that had sprung up in the transition (*Ajoblanco* 1974, *Ozono* 1975, *El Viejo Topo* 1976) folded (*Ajoblanco* and *El Viejo Topo* were later revived) and were replaced by the purely literary *Quimera* (1980), *Anthropos* (1981), *Cuadernos del Norte* (1980, funded by the Caja de Ahorros de Asturias), *Fin de Siglo* (1982, funded by the Diputación de Cádiz, Junta de Andalucía, and Ayuntamiento de Jérez), *Las Nuevas Letras* (1984, funded by the Diputación de Almería), and by multinational glossies like *El Europeo* (1988). This sense of an 'end of history' was a response to a lack of clear-cut political alternatives, articulated by the left's ironic catchphrase of the *desencanto* years 'Things were better against Franco', and reinforced by the PSOE government's subsequent adoption of monetarist policies, blurring traditional left and right. These monetarist policies encouraged take-overs and multinational investment particularly in the media. If, as has been said, postmodernism is an expression of political impotence resulting from loss of belief in the master narratives of liberalism and marxism, and from the media's monopoly control of the images of reality available to us, then Spain is suffering from a bad attack: not now of a mythical 'national disease' of the kind diagnosed by the 1898 writers, but of the latest international fashion. Spain is no longer different.

And yet, as is often said, Spain is now a 'culture of heterogeneity'. The Franco regime tried to unify the nation by projecting difference outside its borders, or confining it to internal exclusion zones, in the form of otherness: *la anti-España*, necessarily equated with foreign influence. Postmodernist theory deconstructs the concept of unity—and by extension that of identity, in its sense of 'sameness'—exposing it as a political manœuvre designed to suppress recognition of difference within. It is because Spain has now recognized its cultural plurality that it is no longer possible to make clear-cut distinctions between what is and what is not Spanish: both because incompatible cultural forms may be equally Spanish, and because cultural forms found in Spain are found elsewhere. The loss of distinctions resulting from a multinational economy and from the 'global village' created by world-wide access to the media goes together with the recognition of internal differences: to be Spanish is to be Spanish and international at the same time; the Manichaean thinking that enabled Francoism to argue that everything that was not Spanish must be anti-Spanish no longer holds. Some Spaniards—and foreign tourists—lament this loss of Spain's 'differentness' as if it meant the loss of 'Spanishness' itself. But the postmodernist deconstruction of identity does not mean that one has to abandon all attempts at definition: rather, it means recognition of the fact that 'Spanishness' is a shifting concept, encompassing plurality and contradiction. And, above all, that identities are strategic constructions: neither inherent nor imposed, but negotiated.

Spanish cultural studies can learn from the more established discipline of Latin American cultural theory where, in the last two decades, emphasis has shifted from concepts of national identity to that of cultural hybridity. The notion of acculturation, whereby foreign cultural influence is seen as an alien imposition, has been replaced by that of transculturation, whereby the indigenous cultures respond to hegemonic imported cultural models by creating new hybrid forms that are neither local nor foreign but both. García Canclini has related this concept of hybrid cultures to that of uneven development, arguing that Latin America is characterized by the interaction of cultural forms corresponding to what, in conventional linear models of history, are regarded as different stages of historical development: thus, despite its disadvantaged position, tribal art can respond to

Modernity and Cultural Pluralism 397

tourism and mass production, and co-opt avant-garde forms (and not only vice versa, though of course this process takes place in a context where some art-forms have more prestige—and economic backing—than others). García Canclini stresses the importance of such cross-cultural formations in societies where accelerated development has led to 'modernity without modernization': that is, technologically advanced cultural forms without a corresponding economic and social infrastructure.[1] Of course, Spain is an ex-colonial power with a relatively homogeneous ethnic mix even by the standards of most modern European countries; but since the eighteenth century its dominant cultural models have been imported, and its recent history is one of both uneven and accelerated development. McHale has suggested that the anachronistic juxtaposition in Latin America of different stages of historical development has led to a postmodernist fascination with the coincidence of different worlds, putting an 'end to history' in the sense that linear time is experienced as synchronicity.[2] Best and Kellner argue that the debate on postmodernism began in France because the post-war period saw rapid change from an archaic rural economy to late capitalism, with industrialization taking place at the same time as the shift to a post-industrial economy.[3] The experience of anachronism and acceleration is even more acute in the case of Spain, which in the 1940s experienced a retrograde attempt at re-ruralization and the imposition of obsolescent Catholic moral values, followed from 1959 by vertiginous economic take-off and modernization, and since 1975 by even more precipitous change not only at the economic but also at the political and cultural levels. As a result, travelling from village to city is like travelling through time; conversely both worlds are exposed to the same mass media. The sense of cultural anachronism represented by writers' and film-makers' reversion to realism in the 1950s, and their belated assimilation of modernism in the 1960s, becomes acute in the transition period: as Acín notes, post-Francoism began about four years before Franco's death; the post-1975 climate of political and sexual liberation was a replay of a May 1968 not experienced at the time; and overnight the public was exposed to the whole backlog of previously banned works by foreign and Spanish exile writers and film-makers.

This experience of history as synchronicity did not produce a body of postmodernist theory, as in France; but it did produce a body of creative writing that was postmodernist before the term became current, with the *novísimos* and the New Novelists' pastiche of mass cultural forms and conversion of world culture into a museum, blurring the boundary between 'high' and 'low' culture. The pastiche science fiction novels of Mariano Antolín Rato, incomprehensible in the 1970s, when read in the retrospective light of postmodernist theory become paradigmatic expressions of the postmodernist replacement of linearity (time) with simultaneity (space). His first novel *Cuando 900 mil mach aprox* (1973) opens: 'here is once upon a time, then and now, all articulations between different points of time vanish, everything is held in suspension in a space that far from grounding itself calls itself into question'; his preface approvingly quotes the *novísimo* Leopoldo

María Panero: 'I inhabit the paranoid fantasy of the end of the world.' Science fiction, which turns travelling through time into a space trip, has been called the classic postmodernist genre: comics, the chief medium for science fiction, have acquired a cult following in post-Franco Spain, including the reissue as collectors' items of early Francoist comics such as *El Guerrero del Antifaz*, which made its readers travel backwards in time to the Middle Ages. This sense of accelerated motion going in all directions at once is captured by the term *la movida** applied to the Madrid cultural scene from 1975 to the mid-1980s, and in particular by the hysteria of Almodóvar's films, presented as a response to the attempt to live simultaneously in the old-fashioned world of sentimental kitsch and the modern world of information technology. Cristina García Rodero's photographs of village *fiestas* similarly show the anachronistic survival in contemporary Spain of cultural relics from the past, in this case freezing time to turn reality into a slick art object.

Indeed, the main reason why postmodernism has been seen as an 'end of history' is its stress on representation, reflecting the 'death of the real' produced by the mass media's conversion of reality into images and its replacement in information technology by simulated models. Cultural theorists are divided as to whether this emphasis on 'hyperreality' or 'virtual reality' implies a cynical rejection of history or a critical deconstruction of the ways in which reality is packaged for our consumption. This ambivalence is evident in the contemporary Spanish cultural scene. Perhaps the ultimate postmodernist product was Ventura Pons's film *Ocaña, retrato intermitente* (1978), which documented the popular Barcelona *loca* [transvestite] of the transition years, known for parading up and down the Ramblas dressed as the Virgin and for installing him/herself in a gallery as a living exhibit: the film is both a celebration of the conversion of life into performance and—as its subtitle implies—a subversion of the realist documentary genre, deconstructing fixed gender identities. The stylish films of Almodóvar are similarly examples of, as well as critiques of, designer culture, their characters empowered and trapped by media images. Saura's flamenco trilogy *Bodas de sangre* (1980), *Carmen* (1983), and *El amor brujo* (1986) can be seen as both the reduction of Spanish culture to folkloric cliché and an exposure of the constructed nature of the cliché as we are taken backstage to see the dancers putting on their make-up. His recent *¡Ay, Carmela!* (1991) reduces the civil war to a series of theatrical performances (the protagonists are music-hall artistes performing first for the Republicans and then for the Nationalists), but history interrupts the performance when Carmela is shot dead by a Nationalist officer in the audience. Fredric Jameson, who criticizes postmodernism for reducing history to representation, reminds us that the effects of history are all too real: 'history is what hurts.'[4] Like Saura, Almodóvar makes this point in a later film, *Kika* (1993), a celebration/critique of TV 'reality shows' in which, again, reality kills.

This idea perhaps underlies the popularity in post-Franco Spain of the thriller, traditionally centred on a murder. This vogue has been seen as a return to realism, but it is equally a continuation of the early 1970s obsession with pastiche of

28 Still from *La ley del deseo* [*The Law of Desire*] (Almodóvar, 1987), showing a detail of the kitsch altar constructed by Carmen Maura, playing the role of a transsexual. The postmodernist combination of heterogeneous images—the popular religious prints and 3-D image of the Virgin in a plastic sphere (centre left, far right); the porcelain Marilyn Monroe (right); the doll-like figurine made of shells and Muppet-like frog (centre right)—illustrates the hybridity of contemporary Spanish culture, fusing popular and mass culture, the religious and the secular, the traditional and the modern, the indigenous and the foreign. It is possible to read this frame as a critique of Catholicism and of mass culture, but it can also be experienced simply as fun; as with all kitsch, the pastiche contains a high degree of nostalgia.

29 Still from the documentary *Ocaña, retrato intermitente* [*Ocaña, an Intermittent Portrait*] (Pons, 1978), depicting the Barcelona transvestite Ocaña parodically assuming the stock image of Spanish womanhood with carnation, mantilla, and fan that was consecrated by the 1940s and 1950s cinematic genre of the *folklórica* (folkloric musical comedy, typically in an Andalusian setting). Ocaña's female/male gaze is both seductive and defiant, reproducing but also subverting traditional gender roles. The contrived nature of her/his pose also makes the point that gender is a construction which perhaps cannot be escaped but can at least be manipulated at will..

Anglo-Saxon mass cultural forms. Eduardo Mendoza's *La verdad sobre el caso Savolta* (1975) was a highly political historical thriller but also an exercise in styles; Manuel Vázquez Montalbán's *Galíndez* (1991) is likewise a historical thriller, while his Pepe Carvalho series combines pastiche—to the extent that in *Asesinato en el Comité Central* (1981) his detective hero attends seminars on detective fiction—with left-wing politics. The detective genre is used both to dramatize and to problematize the recovery of the real.

This ambivalent attitude to history as something to be recuperated but also something unknowable except in mediated form is illustrated in the work of Antonio Muñoz Molina, whose first novel *Beatus ille* (1986) starts as a seemingly conventional modernist recuperation of the past through memory, with the protagonist researching the biography of a fictitious member of the 1927 Generation, Solana; but in a final twist the protagonist discovers his story is being written by Solana: his historical investigation is only a literary text. Muñoz Molina went on to write a series of overtly postmodernist pastiches of the thriller genre, with abundant references to mass culture in the form of jazz and *film noir*; but in *El jinete polaco* (1991) he travels full circle back from postmodernism to modernism, as his protagonist renounces his 'postmodern' existence as an international interpreter endlessly reproducing the speech of others, and returns to his Andalusian home town (the fictional Mágina of *Beatus ille*) to reconstruct its historical past, in a modernist exploration of the passing of time through the medium of individual consciousness. Even Luis Landero's brilliant postmodernist celebration of the construction of false identities *Juegos de la edad tardía* (1989) punctuates its language games with references to Franco's presence; it ends with its protagonists embracing new bucolic aliases as Franco lies dying. Identity is a series of fraudulent constructions, but history is still there. (Though Barral's memoirs remind us that the interminable TV reports on Franco's artificially prolonged last moments turned his death into a classic postmodernist·spectacle.)

Vázquez Montalbán's recent novel *Autobiografía del general Franco* (1993) exploits the ambiguity of the autobiographical genre—half-way between fiction and documentary—to turn Franco's life into a literary spoof while at the same time exploring the historical collusion that made Francoism possible. The transition period saw a flood of autobiographies (a genre previously rare in Spain) as former Francoist political figures brought out their memoirs in a further ambiguous excavation of the past that was also an exercise in simulation. Recent years have seen something approximating to a 'recuperation industry', with the refurbishing of museums, restoration of municipal theatres, vogue for local history, and reissue of forgotten women writers: in one sense this is an example of the commercial packaging of the past that typifies contemporary postmodern cultures generally, but in another more important sense it represents a specifically Spanish need to salvage a history previously suppressed or neglected. Muñoz Molina has related the jumble of cultural influences found in Spanish writers born after the war to the fact that, because of censorship, they had to invent a literary tradition, making use of whatever was at hand (in his case, the half-burned library his grandfather salvaged from his landowning employer's house during the war, with its mix of the *Quixote*, *Orlando furioso*, Jules Verne, and penny dreadfuls).[5] This need to 'invent the past' is perhaps more than anything else what gives contemporary Spanish culture its affinity with postmodernism, while at the same time giving it a particular historical urgency.

The heritage industry has flourished especially in the regions, with autonomous governments and local savings banks subsidizing the arts, often—but not always—on condition that the content be of local interest. In many cases the results have been impressive: for example, the promotion of the Andalusian novel from 1974, and the boom of Valencian fiction from around 1980 supported by a flourishing local publishing industry. However, the sheer number of regional publications—and prizes; Catalonia alone has over 300—has produced a 'minifundismo editorial' (Acín's term) that risks promoting mediocrity and provincialism. All forms of nationalism, regional or otherwise, require the 'invention of a tradition'; the current use of culture to manufacture forms of regional identity comes close to replicating its manipulation by early Francoism to fabricate an 'essentially different' Spanishness. Recent developments in Basque culture are interesting here, with the local, national, and international success of Bernardo Atxaga's *Obabakoak* (1988), the first work of prose fiction in Basque to abandon the depiction of regional culture for a slick postmodernist collage of false identities constructed out of intertextual references. As Atxaga says in his postscript: 'Nothing today is uniquely characteristic. The world is everywhere.' Julio Medem's first film *Vacas* (1992)—like most Basque cinema, made in Castilian—reproduced the typical Basque rural saga format, only to subvert it by stressing asphyxia, madness, and the need to escape. His second feature *La ardilla roja* (1993) celebrates liberation from the past through amnesia, parodically recasts the return to natural roots as an outing to a campsite dominated by a cardboard cut-out of the indigenous red squirrel, and sends up the 'invention of tradition' with the promotion video of the hero's former Basque nostalgia band, dressed in cowhides on a mountain top, overlaid by the music playing on the campsite juke-box. This regional appropriation of postmodernism to expose the constructed nature of all identities offers a way out of the trap of essentialism.

The same tension between postmodernism and essentialism is found in recent women's writing. Some feminist theorists have argued that postmodernism's deconstruction of identity is unhelpful to women trying to create an identity for themselves; others argue that its stress on identity as a construct provides a useful antidote to fixed gender roles. Spanish women writers seem to divide into those concerned with specifically feminine forms of experience, who have opted for the modernist novel of consciousness (Montserrat Roig, Esther Tusquets), and those interested in the falsity or instability of identity (Soledad Puértolas, or Cristina Fernández Cubas, who uses the horror story to undermine the opposition between self and feared/desired Other). Up to a point these two tendencies correspond to

30 Still from *La ardilla roja* [*The Red Squirrel*] (Medem, 1993), sending up the 'back to roots' strain in Basque nationalism. In this parody of a rock video (itself a classic postmodernist product), the protagonist's Basque nostalgia band The Flies plays a mixture of traditional and modern instruments in thick fog on a mountaintop, dressed in cowhides and writhing as if in excruciating pain. The dirge-like quality of their music contrasts violently with the film's fast-moving images of modern life. The plot of the film undermines the notion of the need for a 'myth of origins' by insisting on the advantages of feigned amnesia.

successive stages, postmodernist play becoming possible once some form of feminine identity has been established; but both tendencies continue to be found. It has to be said that the writers in the latter category do not seem much interested in relating the postmodernist deconstruction of identity to gender issues. In this sense, there is a clear divide between gay writers and film-makers, who have embraced postmodernism as a release from fixed identities, and their feminist counterparts—in film, Pilar Miró—who seem more concerned with uncovering some kind of authentic female self. Perhaps the only successful feminist appropriation of postmodernist pastiche is the performance art of the singer Martirio, who sends up traditional images of Spanish womanhood by mixing punk with 1940s sentimental song and *folklóricas*, while wearing an exaggeratedly phallic model of the Giralda on her head.

Postmodernism has been linked to the erosion of the nation-state produced by increasing globalization, and by the converse shift to micropolitics (mobilization around local issues plus specific-interest lobbies such as feminism or the environment) that has resulted from disillusionment with the old political master narratives. The coexistence of the internationalist and the micropolitical—in the sense of local politics; participatory democracy is still too new for Spain to have developed a sophisticated lobby system, and sadly the environment is still barely an issue—typifies contemporary Spain, as in current Catalan and Basque moves towards economic collaboration with their respective French neighbours, setting up supranational regional groupings within the framework of the EU; or in the currently buoyant publishing industry, by 1987 occupying fourth position in world book production as a result of the combination of multinational take-overs and the boom in local publishing. It is worth noting that the current postmodernist emphasis on representation joins hands with the emphasis in 1940s Spain on spectacle, at that time used by the regime as a tool for instilling nationalist values into the unlettered masses. Sectors of the population have passed directly from a preliterate culture to one dominated by the visual and oral mass media. Visual or oral cultural forms such as the comic and song, or film which is both, have mediated the transition. The influence of film on fiction is noticeable, both in 1950s realism (aimed at an uneducated audience) and in 1970s and 1980s pastiche (aimed at mass media addicts). It is because of its stress on spectacle that 1940s Spanish culture lends itself so well to postmodernist pastiche. But the appeal of 1940s kitsch is also that its reproduction in a modern internationalist context deconstructs the essentialist concept of national identity that such cultural images were originally designed to promote. The Spanish nation-state may have been eroded but it is not under threat, precisely because contemporary Spaniards do not have to renounce their Spanishness to be simultaneously cosmopolitan and (say) Aragonese. What has been done to death—through parodic repetition—is the concept of a unified national identity that politicians and writers—originally liberal, subsequently reactionary—have attempted to impose since the Romantic period.

Notes

1 N. García Canclini, *Culturas híbridas: estrategias para entrar y salir de la modernidad* (Mexico, 1989).
2 B. McHale, *Postmodernist Fiction* (London, 1987).
3 S. Best and D. Kellner, *Postmodern Theory: Critical Interrogations* (London, 1991).
4 *The Political Unconscious* (Ithaca, NY, 1981), 21; see also *Postmodernism; or, The Cultural Logic of Late Capitalism* (London, 1991).
5 Lecture by Muñoz Molina at the Instituto Cervantes, London (17 June 1993).

Further reading

Acín, R., *Narrativa y consumo literario (1975–1987)* (Zaragoza, 1990).
Amell, S. (ed.), *Literature, the Arts, and Democracy: Spain in the Eighties* (London, 1990).
Letras españolas 1976–1986 (Madrid, 1987).
La literatura española actual, special number of *Cuenta y Razón*, 48–9 (July–Aug. 1989) (excellent though not widely available).

On detective fiction

Hart, P., *The Spanish Sleuth: The Detective in Spanish Fiction* (Rutherford, 1987).
Rix, R. (ed.), *Leeds Papers on Thrillers in the Transition: 'Novela negra' and Political Change in Spain* (Leeds, 1992).

On women's writing

See items listed under Rosa Montero's essay, 'The silent revolution', in Chapter 21 above.

The Politics of 1992

HELEN GRAHAM AND ANTONIO SÁNCHEZ

In 1992 Spain celebrated its new international status with a series of public events: the Olympic Games in Barcelona, the quincentennial commemoration of Columbus's voyage to the Americas, the World Fair in Seville, and Madrid's designation as 'European City of Culture'. The function of these events was perceived in Spain and abroad as both cultural and symbolic. They were explicitly intended to celebrate Spain's coming of age as a modern, democratic European nation-state, marking the end of a period of political transition (and uncertainty) and the completion of an economic, political, and social process initiated in the 1970s. These events proved to be highly successful in terms of the mass participation of Spanish people and the international publicity accorded to Spain.

But these popular celebrations of Spain's new status tended to neglect the past and glorify the present. Indeed this seemed to be part of an official attempt to represent Spain's new, 'modern', democratic national identity as if it were built on a *tabula rasa*, thus avoiding confrontation with the cultural, social, regional, and political tensions that have plagued Spain since its emergence as a nation-state. But it is only possible to understand this new national identity in the light of the historical conditions which have handicapped Spain's development to date.

History and underdevelopment

Spain's historical experience has tended to reinforce centrifugal tendencies, thus preventing the emergence of an integrating national identity. In fact, in the 1992 commemoration of Columbus's voyage, one could argue that modern European Spaniards were celebrating the very event which began the process of empire inextricably linked to the failure of metropolitan development and national integration. The civil war of 1936–9 in many ways represented the culmination of the tensions resulting from Spain's chronically uneven development. The war saw the confrontation of two deeply antagonistic models of socio-economic change, for Republicans and Nationalists had diametrically opposed views of what the Spanish nation-state should be. Franco's victory provided the space and time for the implementation of one particular programme of national modernization, which attempted to construct and impose a claustrophobic model of national identity grounded in the fifteenth, sixteenth, and seventeenth centuries (the age of medieval 'Reconquest', Counter-Reformation, and empire). This monolithic identity was to be the centre of a socio-economic project based on strict social hierarchy and reinforced by an anachronistic Catholic ideology which provided the regime with a highly effective means of repression, facilitating the exploitation of the social class defeated in the civil war. It did this by demonizing these sectors—constructing both the defeated working class and all bearers of pluralist cultural and political options as an internal 'other'—thereby consolidating (or such was the intent) the national identity projected by the regime. Spain's international isolation was also manipulated ideologically to the same end (a case here of Francoism making a virtue out of necessity), reinforcing the notion of Spain's national identity as 'other' than European liberal democratic 'decadence' and, of course, superior to it. And, later, the 1960s tourist slogan 'Spain is different', while intended to appeal to a desire for the exotic 'other', also referred back ambivalently to the idea of a national identity threatened by outside forces. The slogan, of course, also conveniently ignored the way the regime was seeking to impose an artificial unity on the different fragments of Spain by means of a monolithic, Castilianized construction of national identity.

From 1959 onwards, economic modernization started to erode what little meaning there was in the official notion of Spain's 'difference' as the basis for a national identity. The rapid introduction of consumer capitalism and its attendant cultural values—by the regime's own economic policies—transformed Spain, making redundant the official ideology which had prevailed to date. Economic development in the 1960s was followed by the rapid political changes of the 1970s and the social transformation of the 1980s. It is scarcely surprising, then, that Spain's most recent history and contemporary national identity are defined as the products of hugely accelerated development. It is precisely the breathtaking speed of many of these changes which accounts for the uneven results and the 'schizophrenic' tendencies in contemporary Spanish culture.

Accelerated development and social 'schizophrenia'

To describe Spanish culture as schizophrenic is not mere postmodernist affectation, but an attempt at defining the disorienting effects on Spaniards' consciousness of the speed and the complexity of the changes that have radically altered their society over the last thirty years.

The most specific characteristic of this process of change, apart from its singular rapidity, has been a confused (and confusing) hybridity, since it is a process which amalgamates the modern and the postmodern. For Spain's modern history has been out of kilter with that wider European process of modernization involving agricultural rationalization, industrialization, urbanization, secularization, greater social differentiation, the extension of central state power, and an increased capacity (although this varied considerably) for the institutional regulation of social and political conflict (including that achieved by franchise reform). The cultural modernism which emerged from and represented such changes in Europe at the end of the nineteenth century and during the early decades of the twentieth was limited in Spain initially by the unevenness of material development. Subsequently it was repressed by victorious Francoism, seeking (ultimately in vain) to separate a 'healthy' and 'necessary' process of economic modernization from the socio-cultural project of modernism. Thus in recent times, accelerating after 1978, Spain has experienced a rapid process of belated modernization (political democratization and the social-infrastructural development of civil society), but at the same time—precisely because this modernization process has necessarily meant assimilation to a wider European economic and cultural environment—it displays all the social and economic decentring and cultural fragmentation typical of the postmodern era. Indeed, the very speed of change in Spain provides the rest of Europe with a kind of technicolour close-up of a world-wide cultural and economic process.

The case of the 1978 Constitution is paradigmatic. Symbolizing a radical rejection of the centralist nation-state's authoritarian associations, it organized Spain into a series of autonomies with regional governing bodies envisaged as an institutional framework for accommodating cultural differences ('el estado de las autonomías'). It was a solution appropriate to a pluralist democracy, responding as it did to the real political demands for cultural self-determination coming from substantial sectors of the population. However, it was also in a sense an anachronistic solution, in that the economic imperatives which had historically given rise to powerful regional nationalist sentiments no longer obtained (Spain had achieved an integrated national economy well before the end of the dictatorship). This undoubtedly innovative and highly democratic solution to a historic problem may well itself prove to be a time bomb, given the particular conjuncture at which it has been implemented. For there are certainly serious question marks over the future of the nation-state *per se*, as a unit increasingly ill-fitted (neither large nor small enough) to the production categories of late capitalism which shape

31 Photograph by Cristina García Rodero, 'Eleven o'clock in El Salvador' (Cuenca, 1982), illustrating the temporal dislocation and sense of anachronism that characterizes contemporary Spain, where accelerated development—particularly since 1975—has produced a sense of living in different time frames at once. This process has been particularly traumatic for elderly people, made redundant by the stress on youth culture while also offered increased life expectancy by improved social welfare: mass emigration to the cities has reduced many village populations to those too old to find employment elsewhere. Photography became a 'high' art form for the first time in Spain in the 1980s (see the reference to García Rodero on p.399).

postmodern forms. The speed of change, too, is a potentially destabilizing factor. In Spain the regionalization of the state has taken a mere five years (1978–83), while the comparable process in Italy occurred over some three decades (1947–77).

It is precisely this rapidity, alongside an increasing heterogeneity, that gives Spanish society its vertigo-inducing postmodernist identity. It is a world where the archaic and the modern coexist; a society in which overt forms of male dominance and sexual prejudices are still prevalent but where certain recognizable 'others' are increasingly being represented as part of Spanish identity. For example, there is the startling popularity of the actress and occasional television presenter Bibi Andersen, a transsexual with a foreign name who embodies an ambiguous sexuality and has an undefined social status, yet projects a quintessentially Spanish female identity. We are in a world where social and national boundaries dissolve or coexist with new emerging forms, accentuating the tendency towards cultural and social dislocation.

The film director Pedro Almodóvar has often claimed that it is impossible to understand 1980s Spain without looking at his films. While there is a clear element of self-promotion in this assertion, his films convey precisely this schizophrenic dislocation—the 'fall-out' from the dual process of fast-track modern and postmodern transformation—which typifies contemporary Spanish identity. Almodóvar's films constantly juxtapose sophisticated, cosmopolitan, modern forms with highly traditional Spanish ones. In *Women on the Verge of a Nervous Breakdown* (1988) modern life, represented by airports and a skyscraper penthouse, is set against that archetypal Spanish dish *gazpacho*; but the *gazpacho* has been spiked with sleeping pills by a heroine desperate to escape the stress and emotional exhaustion of late twentieth-century life and love. Almodóvar's films constantly expose traditional female dependency on men while simultaneously representing women as the real protagonists; traditional family structures too are present but dysfunctional, and it is the loneliness of the modern individual (the price of a greater relative autonomy) that ultimately prevails. Almodóvar's films exemplify the apparent contradiction between being genuinely 'national' and, at the same time, modern European. It is precisely this juxtaposition which explains a significant part of Almodóvar's success. His films speak with a healthy irony from the verge of social schizophrenia, celebrating the simultaneous arrival of modernity and postmodernity as well as the continuing presence in Spanish society of certain archaic cultural forms.

Constructions of Europe

Despite a lingering tendency to see themselves as 'different', the contemporary cultural trend is for Spaniards to adopt 'modernity' as their mark of identity. This has been underlined by overwhelming popular support for Spain's integration into Europe. While the concept of 'modernity' is problematic—as the essays throughout this book have sought to elucidate—Spaniards have essentially associated it with 'being European', which progressives have regarded as a 'good thing'. It could be argued that the fundamental appeal of Europe for Spaniards today is that it apparently offers an easy way of unifying an otherwise fragmented and always problematic nationhood. Closer European integration is greeted enthusiastically because it provides a temporary safe structure for a historically fragmented national identity. However, this illusion of coherence breaks down as soon as one poses the question, which Europe? For there are, and have always been, many different Europes, often mutually incompatible.

Throughout the dictatorship, Europe was perceived by the forces of opposition (understood in its broadest sense) as a symbol of democracy and social and economic progress, the collectivity which Spain aspired to join. In reality, however, 'Europe' has always been somewhat more complex and contradictory than the one constructed by the anti-Franco forces in the image of their own democratic aspirations. Moreover, the idea of Europe lying 'beyond' is illusory. In spite of all Spain's historical specificities (the immense, lasting impact of the Counter-Reformation or the cumulative impact of the failure to modernize social and economic structures), the dominant intellectual and social models since the eighteenth century have been European ones. The notion of 'fortress Spain' is, as this volume has endeavoured to demonstrate, a significant cultural metaphor rather than an accurate reflection of a cultural reality. Spain has so often in its past embodied European conflicts, refracting them in extreme form, while European models have defined the political, economic, and cultural parameters of Spain's internal debates on national identity and modernization; for example, in the War of Independence (1808–14) or the destruction of the liberal triennium in 1823, or the civil war of 1936–9. In its most isolationist phase, the Franco regime itself was, Canute-like, defining as 'other' ideas and traditions which already were worked deep into the cultural fabric of Spain. Damage was done, of course: cultural repression had material effects. In the end, though, as we know, the 'other' is never beyond but inextricably linked to the dominant, ostensibly 'rejecting' culture itself.

But just as Spain remained a far more complex and plural entity than the Francoist agenda recognized, so too Europe was a more ambiguous, multivalent construct than the anti-Franco opposition perceived. When we speak of Spain joining Europe, we should be clear that, rather than an abstract democratic ideal, what Spain has joined is a specific political and economic entity which has at its centre (both commercially and ideologically) the market.

Economic integration

For all the participating countries, Spain included, it is ultimately an economic rationale that has driven the project for closer European integration. Since the 1970s it has been evident that only EC membership could guarantee Spain access both to European markets (for its agricultural exports) and to vital new technology.

With the end of the Franco dictatorship, the Spanish right recognized the crucial need to join this 'Europa de los mercaderes' (that is, Europe as an economic project based on the primacy of the market). This economic course led in the 1980s to the PSOE* government's implementation of a series of policies geared to completing Spain's integration into Europe's economic institutions, ensuring the country's complete assimilation to western capitalist practice.

The PSOE's 'conversion' to neo-liberal orthodoxies shocked the Spanish left. But it was not a national traffic accident attributable to some ideological or organizational 'flaw' in the party, but rather part of a pattern across 1980s Europe as social democratic governments with reforming agendas and reflationary economic strategies—such as those in France and Greece—performed U-turns, under pressure from industrial and financial capital (which exported or withdrew funds, as in the French industrialists' 'investment strike'), precipitating falling exchange rates and stock market crises. Sophisticated information technology means that increasingly multinational capital can move resources across national frontiers virtually instantaneously and, with this, the international financial institutions (the IMF, etc.) have come to act more and more as the real arbiters of 'acceptable' national macro-economic policy (meaning that based on strict monetary regulation), while the function of national governments seems to be reduced to the 'pragmatic management of GDP [gross domestic product] growth'. This is precisely the measure of the left's own economic crisis.

While Europe is a site where various political options dispute the terrain, this demonstrates the problem inherent in the left's strategy of building a hegemonic European option capable of circumventing national conservatisms, and ultimately providing a third way between the US capitalist and former Soviet models. For the process of European economic integration is not now primarily driven by the agenda of national polities, but is already operating beyond them. Moreover, economic neo-liberalism has already produced social policies and cultural reactions that are inimical to the collectivist values of the left.

Not all of the political options looking to Europe for a 'solution' are on the left, however. In Spain, regional nationalists of distinctly conservative hue (CiU* in Catalonia or the PNV* in the Basque Country) look to European integration as a source of greater independence from central government, via a 'Europe of the regions'. But there is a contradiction here too, because a closer relationship with Brussels means accepting a macro-economic system of production which no more requires or respects regional identities *per se* than it does the cultural needs and values of the nation-state itself. The dynamic of European integration has an ambiguous potential, then, in terms of all our political and cultural futures.

For Spain as a nation-state this is true not least because of the uncertain effects of the economic cycle of crisis–boom–recession experienced over the last twenty years (looking back from 1994). This dramatic see-sawing may well erode its coherence further, as the 'historic nationalities' in particular (Catalonia and the Basque Country) seek unilateral economic solutions—whether to stimulate future growth in the case of the former, or in a bid to stem or reverse decline in the latter. So while the 'estado de las autonomías' may seem a fitting conclusion to the story of Spain's democratic transition, in fact it should be seen not so much as a national resolution but rather as a staging post, or moment of equilibrium, in a wider process of European socio-economic and cultural transformation.

Between 1986 and 1989 the Spanish economy grew in spectacular fashion, outpacing its larger Community partners and expanding at an average of 5 per cent a year. But the costs were also considerable. Unemployment soared, in a sense an integral part of the boom, since a significant amount of it was generated by Spain's industrial restructuring of its primary sector. Foreign interests pumped some $30 billion in direct investment into Spain and more than $300 billion into its debt and equity markets, while the government also took out public sector loans to finance infrastructural modernization—often with a view to 1992. These public works were undertaken on a significant scale and, in their intent, owed more than a little to the ghost of a reflationary economic strategy.

But by the time 1992 arrived, the economic horizon was closing in. Indeed the events themselves epitomized the resulting 'present-centred' focus of both polity and populace. One day soon the party would be over, but meanwhile carnival would provide an effective distraction from what had been the negative consequences of the PSOE's economic policies for many, and also from the gathering gloom of inescapable oncoming recession. Indeed one could argue that the 1992 celebrations were a quite conscious attempt (and a reasonably successful one at that) to boost state prestige/legitimacy and national morale in the face of that recession.

Unfortunately this objective was undercut to some extent by polemics such as the one surrounding the construction of the AVE, the high-speed train link from Madrid to Seville. A prestige development designed to be one of the highlights of the World Fair in the southern city, the AVE was one of the most expensive projects undertaken by the Ministry of Transport. But critics have argued that neither its general social/economic utility, nor its impact on the quality of the national transport network, justifies the financial outlay. In its current state, the AVE also stops significantly short of Spain's nearest European frontier. The counter-argument posits that in facilitating communications between the south of Spain, the centre, and the more economically developed northern regions, the project will improve the quality of national economic integration and therefore be of net social benefit. The relative merits of these arguments will become clearer over time. Certainly the AVE's genesis had much to do with the fact that Andalusia is a major stronghold of the ruling PSOE and Seville in particular the base of some of the party's leading figures. Instead of symbolizing a project of national modernization, then, the AVE could be read as the outcome of a kind of neo-clientelist approach to the state where political power signifies, first and foremost, access to a spoils system which is then used to broker power, thus perpetuating the sustaining system of patronage. This impression is only reinforced by the wave of corruption scandals which have recently rocked public life in Spain. At the time of writing (September 1994) the jury on the AVE is still out.

New anxieties, old prejudices

Spain's transformation into a modern consumer society over the last thirty years has meant the erosion of traditional forms of social and political solidarity and the predominance of money in a hierarchy of social values. This shift is clearly reflected in the obsessive cult of designer culture and consumer values. While these are central characteristics of a Europe-wide (and beyond) enterprise culture which has developed alongside free market economics, they appear perhaps more accentuated in Spain because of the greater marginalization of counter-culture, itself a legacy of the dictatorship. 'Monetarized' cultural values inevitably translate human worth into pure exchange or production value. This, in turn, has had an impact on emergent forms of social prejudice, such as the growing racism towards migrant workers in Spain. While there is never necessarily a direct relationship between the dimensions of a migrant presence and the incidence of racist attitudes, the tangibility of the latter is significant in view of the smallness of the former in Spain. (Although there has been an increase in the number of foreign residents in Spain—from 200,000 in 1981 to 400,000 in 1990—the total migrant population still represents only 1.5 per cent of the total Spanish population.)

Discrimination against Spain's gypsies, as the 'foreigner within', has long been a matter of heated debate. But while the gypsy community has organized to campaign for its civil rights, now new racial conflicts have emerged. Migrant workers from North and Central Africa have come to be the particular targets of racism in Spain, even though they are a minority (only 25 per cent of the migrant population, the rest being constituted by Latin Americans together with Europeans and North Americans). But anti-Latino racism, of which there is a significant amount, has now also broken surface violently: in 1993 the first overtly racist murder in Madrid claimed as its victim a Dominican woman.

In many respects, the environments conducive to the growth of racist attitudes (economic recession, social and cultural anxieties, political demagoguery) and their forms of expression seem not to differ greatly between Spain and the rest of Europe. According to a survey carried out in 1990 by the Centro de Investigaciones Sociológicas (CIS), 64 per cent of those interviewed believe that their jobs and economic status are threatened by foreign migrants, 45 per cent associated their fear of urban crime with migrants, and 57 per cent perceived them as being involved in drug dealing. The same survey reveals these attitudes to be founded on prejudice, given the total lack of information on immigration matters freely admitted by those interviewed: 63 per cent did not follow the news on the topic and 90 per cent had never had any contact with migrant workers. But in spite of the similarities between Spain and the rest of Europe here, we still need to understand much more about the precise impact of the cultural specificities of Francoism's founding myths on how Spaniards deal with the issue of race today.

Throughout Europe, immigration policy (made as much through private protocols as 'open' legislation) is geared to creating a security cordon and internal controls to 'manage' the supply of migrants from the 'South', which exists in this scenario as a provider of cheap labour for Europe. In March 1991, the Spanish parliament approved new immigration legislation with no votes against and only eleven abstentions (Izquierda Unida*). Its object was declared to be: to establish a controlled recruitment of legal migrants, to regularize the situation of those currently in Spain illegally, and to clarify the procedure for obtaining refugee status. But the singular lack of clear guidelines here has, if anything, only empha- sized that it is the immigration authorities who define such status, while the absence of stated criteria means it is difficult to challenge their decisions. Although the immediate focus of this legislation was the national arena, its promulgation indicates the Spanish government's willingness to align with EC immigration policy. And given Spain's geographical position on the frontier between 'First' and 'Third' worlds, that alignment is crucial to the working of Europe's 'security cordon'.

So Spain, in spite of its own long and painful history of underdevelopment, economic emigration, and otherness, far from recognizing a commonality and attempting to integrate the experience of the marginalized into its own self- proclaimedly pluralistic culture, has instead assumed the stance of 'First World' Europe. It is almost as if constructing and adopting the same 'others' or outgroups as the rest were considered the hallmark of Spain's membership of the 'club'. (Perhaps too, in some oblique way, such status is perceived as a belated compen- sation for loss of empire.) But in opting for assimilation on these terms, Spanish policy is contributing to the build-up of a social and political climate which en- courages racism and xenophobia. For in Spain, as elsewhere, it is precisely that migrant minority which is paying most heavily, with its health, and increasingly its lives, for the modernization process.

But not all of Spain's new others can be perceived as belonging 'beyond', and therefore susceptible to being 'sent back'. Of the groups one could discuss here, the particular situation of HIV/AIDS sufferers in Spain provides an instructive example. In 1990 Spain had the second highest recorded number of AIDS-affected people in Europe. Moreover, the rate of contraction has been increasing exponentially. HIV/AIDS incidence in Spain is mostly located in the lowest social classes, and particularly among the young and the unemployed. Some 66 per cent of those diagnosed are intravenous drug-users—which is double the figure for most other European countries. The precise reasons for this difference remain unclear, although part of the problem is certainly to do with the difficulty of reaching and changing the behaviour patterns of marginal groups because of cultural and social barriers attributable to three and a half decades of dictatorship. The fact that central and regional government initiatives have come up against public apathy and prejudice (for example, the notion that gay men and drug-users are suffering the self-induced consequences of their aberrant behaviour) is scarcely specific to Spain. But the high incidence rate of HIV/AIDS and the difficulty in controlling the rate of increase does indicate some specific problems which throw into relief certain infrastructural inadequacies and democratic deficits consequent on accelerated modernization: for example, the inability of a hierarchical health system to provide the flexibility and innovation required to tackle the problem and the significant influence of the Catholic Church in reinforcing conservative attitudes in ways which directly obstruct policy implementation—one example of which would be the storm of protest from Church and Catholic circles over the preventive public health campaign encouraging the use of condoms with the slogan 'Póntelo, pónselo' [Put it on yourself, put it on him].

Perhaps curiously, Spanish attitudes and policies towards HIV sufferers bring us to the crux of the politics of commemorating 1492–1992: the relationship between a nation's encounter with its imperial past and its current political, social, and cultural practices. Critics of the quincentenary have pointed to its theme-park vacuity, its failure to confront the realities of genocide and racism either then or now; and to the way Spain's continuing historical 'amnesia' prevents the assimilation of the meaning of empire—in terms of the devastating experience of otherness visited not only on the colonized, but also on those cultures expelled from peninsular Spain (Arab, Jewish, and—later—Morisco). Both of these processes had profound consequences for metropolitan Spanish identities and mentalities which need to become the object of a new historical-psychological 'voyage of discovery', this time into the interior. Without this, the opportunity will be lost for Spain to become a real economic, social, and cultural bridge between the 'First' and 'Third' worlds, just as many Spaniards will be deprived of a real knowledge and understanding of the sheer range and diversity of their own history and culture. (Unfortunately, Almodóvar's popularity cannot be taken unproblematically to mean that his audiences are seriously prepared to 'live with difference'.) The real challenge of the quincentenary lies not in performing ritualized *mea culpa* for 'past wrongs', but in transforming present political and cultural processes into 'practices of freedom'.

And it is the cultural production coming from the AIDS/HIV battle front—that defining end-of-the-century crisis—which often best illuminates the route. The work of the Cordoban sculptor Pepe Espaliú (who died of AIDS in November 1993), recently exhibited at the ICA in London, conveys particularly rich insights. In his 'Carrying' (sedan chair) sculptures and performance we see culture as a process at work, making sense of emotional and existential states, constructing affirmative values from disorder and, in this case, quite literally from dis-ease. The carrier bears the virus and his own particular fear and suffering, but in the process acquires new perspectives, insights, and relates in new ways to those who, in their turn, 'carry' him (metaphorically, but also quite literally in Espaliú's performance piece where, in the course of 1992, in a number of Spanish cities including Madrid, Barcelona, and San Sebastián, the sculptor was carried barefoot down the street along a human chain, passed from couple to couple who supported him so that his feet never touched the ground). Carriers—in both senses—learn or relearn through reciprocity to reinterpret the social as a different set of values: to take possession of ideas like solidarity, community, love, and devotion, and to abandon those which represent humans as atomized 'islands related to one another by hierarchies interested in competitivity, [individual] protagonism and selfishness'. (The words are Espaliú's own, cited in the exhibition notes.)

The litmus test of pluralist democracy today, whether in Spain or the rest of Europe, is in how the system treats its 'minorities', its new others, in all their forms. What is at stake, in the struggle for the civil and human rights of hundreds of thousands of people, is the very definition of Europe as the millennium approaches.

Conclusion

Spaniards' eager acceptance of their new 'European' identity is entirely comprehensible given their past sense of isolation and long-frustrated need to modernize social and economic structures. The feeling of having 'reached the goal' after a long process of economic, political, and social transformation explains something of 1992's celebratory nature. But while 'Europe' may seem a 'young idea', shiny and positive in its very intangibility, there is a more complex and problematic side. Spain's shift from Europe's margins to its mainstream means the assimilation of a certain Eurocentrism and participation in constructing its 'new others'; that is, new marginalized groups such as migrant workers and people living with HIV/ AIDS. In terms of prevailing political and social attitudes (the dominant ideology/ culture), then, Spain is now participating in the very structures once used to discriminate against it as a nation.

The result of Spain's fast-track transformation inevitably means that certain traditional values, such as solidarity and sense of community, have been eroded (though in some contexts these are being relearned in new ways) and others, associated with an individualistic, consumerist society, are more prominent. The greater marginalization of counter-culture—the result both of dictatorship and accelerated modernization—meant a crisis for the Spanish left which, after 1989, merged with the general crisis of the European left as a whole. Certainly, the culture of the market, above all in its 'post-history' phase, is at odds with the left's project for a 'social Europe'.

There is now, undoubtedly, a greater awareness of Spain's heterogeneity within the country. But one could argue that this is superficial: moreover, that it is not possible for Spain to sustain for long an identity based on the constant production of debased folkloric versions of its own culture. (See, for example, the descent from irony into pastiche in Bigas Luna's films *Jamón, jamón* (1993) and *Huevos de oro* (1994), and, arguably, also in Almodóvar's film *Kika* (1993).) But then again, it may be that the extinction of the European nation-state as we know it is written into the economic 'logic' of late capitalism; in other words, that the nation-state will suffer death by market fluctuation.

In the mean time, the present-centredness of the 1992 celebrations stands as a symbol of the most sterile aspect of the postmodern condition. Their form effectively precluded any real engagement with history (understood as the cultural mediation of the past). Yet without such an engagement we cannot read that past, cannot achieve the perspective that reveals to us the cultural process by which identity—national or otherwise—is actively constructed. Plurality and diversity are rightly celebrated, but they are not free-floating titbits in some sort of postmodern 'pick-'n'-mix'. They require context and structure, and that means history. Without history, cultural sense cannot be made.

Further reading
In addition to the titles specified below, the quality British press carried significant relevant coverage throughout 1992. *The Economist* is also a useful source, as is the digest *El País: Anuario de 1992* (Ediciones El País, Madrid, 1992).

Callinicos, A., *Against Postmodernism* (Cambridge, 1994).

Carr, M., 'Spain: Racism at the Frontier', *Race and Class*, 32 (1991).

Hall, S., 'European Cinema on the Edge of a Nervous Breakdown', in D. Petrie (ed.), *Image and Identity in Contemporary European Cinema* (BFI, London, 1992).

Harvey, D., *The Condition of Postmodernity* (Oxford, 1992).

Heywood, P., 'The Socialist Party in Power, 1982–92: The Price of Progress', *ACIS* (magazine of the Association for Contemporary Iberian Studies), 5/2 (1992).

Izquierdo Escribano, A., 'The EC and Spanish Immigration Policy', in A. Almarcha Barbado, *Spain and EC Membership Evaluated* (London, 1993).

Jameson, F., *Postmodernism; or, The Cultural Logic of Late Capitalism* (London, 1991).

Kirp, L., and **Bayer, R.**, *AIDS in the Industrialized Democracies* (Brunswick, NJ, 1992).

Morgan, R., and **Jordan, B.**, *'Jamón, jamón*: A Tale of Ham and Pastiche', *Donaire* (Consejería de Educación), 2 (1994).

Nederveen Pietersen, J., 'Fictions of Europe', *Race and Class*, 32 (1991).

Spencer, M., *1992 and All That: Civil Liberties in the Balance* (The Civil Liberties Trust, London, 1990).

Watney, S., *Practices of Freedom: Selected Writings on HIV/AIDS* (London, 1994).

Glossary

bachillerato formerly the secondary school leaving certificate. Replaced (under the terms of educational law of 1970 (LGE or *Ley Villar Palasí*)) by General Basic Education (EGB) from 6 to 14 which led on either to vocational training (FP) or to the new *bachillerato* (BUP)

cacique (caciquismo) deriving from the Carib term for an Indian chief, a *cacique* was the local political boss who 'delivered' the votes in the rigged elections which sustained the regular alternation in power (*turno pacífico**) of the two dynastic parties of the Restoration monarchy. In return for votes, the *cacique* would act as the representative/defender of local interests in Madrid, the remote political centre—although as social and economic change accelerated, the *caciques*' power came also to be based more crudely on bribery and intimidation (for example, through their control of the sole source of employment in a locality). The need for the *caciques* to act as brokers suggests the fragmentation of power and the weakness of the central state in Spain in the late nineteenth and early twentieth centuries. The term *caciquismo* denotes the institutionalization of this network of bosses as the basis of the *turno* system. It is usually employed critically, to sum up the impediments to Spain's political and economic development

Carlism (the Carlists) originally a rival monarchist cause in the early nineteenth century, Carlism was a brand of Catholic traditionalism attracting a substantial minority of mainly rural Spaniards to a crusade against the dominant developments of the modern age (i.e. urbanism/industrialization; religious tolerance/atheism; liberalism/socialism; administrative centralization). With its stronghold in the northern region of Navarre, Carlism called for the 'installation' of a traditional (but not absolute) monarchy, administrative devolution in the form of the historic *fueros*,* a corporative social and political system and infusing all this 'Catholic unity', implying uniformity of belief, expression, and behaviour. Militarily defeated three times by the Spanish state in the nineteenth century, Carlism underwent revival and reorganization in the 1930s becoming a major focus of violent opposition to the secularizing, modernizing Second Republic. Having backed the military rebellion in July 1936, the Carlists saw their militia—the *requetés*—absorbed along with the Falange's* into Franco's Nationalist forces and in April 1937 Carlism lost its organizational independence when Franco decreed its amalgamation with the Falange to form FET y de las JONS.* Francoism nevertheless sought to achieve one of the Carlists' most cherished aims—'Catholic unity'—and it also delivered a measure of administrative devolution for Navarre

casa del pueblo the socialist movement's (PSOE*/UGT*) workers' meeting houses, offering facilities for study (including a library), political activity, and relaxation/leisure. A source of great local pride to their members, they embodied the movement's strong sense of its own patrimony and its stress on worker self-improvement. The anarchist equivalents were known as *ateneos*

casticismo cultural nationalism (*casticista*: promoting cultural nationalism). The adjective *castizo* means 'typically Spanish'; derived from *casta* ('caste'), the term has strong racial overtones, and was much abused in Francoist ideology. It first became widely used in the late nineteenth century, at a time of growing nationalism, and was popularized by writers of the so-called 1898 Generation. Its association with belief in the need for a strongly centralized nation-state has meant that, in practice, what is meant by the 'typically Spanish' is the Castilian

castizo see **casticismo** above

Caudillo leader (often with military connotations)—as the title assumed by Franco, it is the equivalent of Führer or Duce (i.e. supreme political leader)

CEDA (Confederación Española de Derechas Autónomas) Spanish Confederation of Right-Wing Groups, a nation-wide mass Catholic 'umbrella' party formed in 1933. While hostile to the secularizing/modernizing thrust of the Second Republic, it professed social-Catholic principles. However, its defence of the Church's position and of social conservatism in general led both its leadership and the majority of its base to support the military rebellion in July 1936

CiU (Convergència i Unió) governing (conservative) Catalan nationalist formation led by Jordi Pujol. It was created in 1979 from a two-party merger and has been in power in Catalonia since the first Generalitat* elections of 1980. Its parliamentary support is currently crucial (1994) to the overall parliamentary majority of the ruling PSOE*

Civil Guard (Guardia Civil) national paramilitary police force created in 1844 to combat banditry. In the first third of the twentieth century it refracted the increasing social and political polarization of Spain. Seen by the élites and 'comfortable classes' as the Meritorious ['Benemérita'], for the poor and dispossessed it was a force of rural occupation brutally maintaining the status quo (i.e. the power of the large landowners), the guards' three-cornered patent leather hats symbolizing the authoritarian state and the social injustice and brutality it perpetuated

CNT (Confederación Nacional del Trabajo) anarcho-syndicalist labour union founded 1910–11; its traditional strongholds were some parts of Catalonia (especially Barcelona), Aragon, the Levante, and among the landless labourers of Andalusia. Its long-standing anti-parliamentarianism and strategy of direct action came to be questioned by some anarchists after the establishment of the Second Republic in 1931. Increasingly there were internal splits between the purists and those favouring political and parliamentary action. In November 1936 anarchist Ministers joined the wartime government. After Republican defeat in 1939, the CNT was more or less consigned to the margins of the anti-Franco opposition

Comisiones Obreras (CC. OO.) the Workers' Commissions—a clandestine labour organization which emerged in the late 1950s to operate inside the structure of the Francoist vertical trade unions.* Originally led by communists and Catholics (in a period of increasingly radicalized social Catholicism which would also give rise to worker priests), Comisiones' policy and leadership came increasingly to be formed by the Communist

Party (PCE*). The fact that by the 1970s the more dynamic sectors of Spanish capital (industry and business) were bypassing the vertical unions and negotiating directly with the (still illegal) CC.OO. came to be one prominent symbol of the Franco regime's final crisis. The CC.OO. were legalized in 1977

Consejo Superior de Investigaciones Científicas (CSIC) established after the civil war by the victorious Franco regime, the CSIC was the state body responsible for allocating grants for higher education and research. Its object was to undo the intellectual work of institutions such as the Republican Junta para Ampliación de Estudios whose 'successor' it was, and to disseminate the authoritarian-Catholic, irrationalist, and monolithic values of the new order. In the period up to 1951 the CSIC came to be dominated by the conservative lay Catholic organization the Opus Dei* which used the CSIC to further its aim of building up an élite leadership in Francoist Spain

costumbrismo (costumbrista) fostered by the Romantic cult of local colour, this Spanish form—which began as short articles, sketches and novellas in the 1830s, later developing into full length novels—depicts the distinctive features of regional life and customs. While *costumbrismo* was often a vehicle for a shallow, sentimental nostalgia for the rural, the form is significant because from it there developed first the regional and later the realist novel

desencanto the mood of political disenchantment/disappointment that prevailed in Spain in the later years of the transition period (1979–82), anticipated by the film *El desencanto* (Chávarri, 1976)

ETA (Euskadi ta Askatasuna) Basque Land and Liberty. Radical separatist Basque nationalist movement formed in 1959 by those critical of the mainstream Basque nationalist party, the PNV,* for its lack of active opposition to Franco. In the 1960s it committed itself increasingly to a strategy of violent direct action against the agents of the Spanish state (army/security forces) perceived as an occupying force. ETA's history is that of a succession of internal conflicts. There have been numerous splits over complex disputes, but in general the division has run between the partisans of a hard-line military approach and those favouring the incorporation of a more sophisticated political strategy to the tactics of direct action. The ongoing ETA campaign after 1975 enraged the military (the chief targets of its violence) thus complicating the consolidation of constitutional democracy. The post-Franco state's own direct action tactics against ETA (e.g. the counter-insurgency of the shadowy group GAL with links to the state security forces) and its treatment of ETA detainees has also revealed a significant democratic deficit which itself sustains a certain level of support/sympathy for ETA. The continuing appeal of radical Basque nationalism itself is now best understood as a protest against industrial restructuring (*reconversión industrial*) and the severe economic recession/unemployment and misery which have in consequence struck the Basque Country as an area traditionally dependent on shipbuilding and iron/steel production

FAI (Federación Anarquista Ibérica) purist wing of the anarchist movement, founded in 1927

Falange Española Spanish fascist party created in 1933 (from the amalgamation of smaller groups) under the supreme leadership of José Antonio Primo de Rivera, son of the dictator Miguel Primo de Rivera. A marginal party before the civil war, it grew rapidly during its early months. After José Antonio's execution in a Republican gaol in November 1936, the Falange descended into a period of warring factionalism which made it an easy political conquest for Franco. (See FET y de las JONS.*)

FET y de las JONS (Falange Española Tradicionalista y de las Juntas de Ofensiva Nacional Sindicalista) the basis of the single party of the 'New State', created in April 1937 when Franco forcibly amalgamated the two predominant political forces in the Nationalist camp: the Carlist* Communion (Traditionalists) and the Falange. (See also Movimiento Nacional*)

fueros the body of law, rights, and custom of a specific region—and more particularly the codes of traditional law embodying the political rights and social/economic privileges of the Basques *vis-à-vis* the Spanish crown/state. *Foralismo*: the political assertion/defence of these rights

Generalísimo literally General-in-chief/supremo of generals, title assumed during the civil war by Franco, as supreme military and political commander of the Nationalist forces

Generalitat Catalan autonomous government established by the statute of 1932. Abolished by Franco, it was re-established in September 1977 under the presidency of Josep Tarradellas

guerrilla an irregular form of warfare (literally 'a little war') whereby small groups of armed fighters (also known collectively as the *guerrilla*) are able to take on an army or much larger, better-equipped fighting force. It first appeared during the War of Independence (1808–14) when Spanish *guerrilleros* (guerrilla fighters) operated against the invading Napoleonic forces. The guerrilla strategy requires a supportive environment/ civilian population, hence the later emphasis on the battle for 'hearts and minds'. In the contemporary period there has usually been a connection between irregular forms of warfare and radical social/political goals—guerrilla struggles have had revolutionary aims

Institución Libre de Enseñanza Institute of Independent Education, founded in Madrid in 1876 by liberal educationalists and university teachers—most notably Francisco Giner de los Ríos—associated with the Krausist* movement. Its aim was to provide a non-official, secular education—freed of Catholic dogma—which would nurture the élite needed to modernize Spain

Izquierda Unida nation-wide coalition of the left whose nucleus is formed by the PCE.* It emerged from the PCE's own crisis and from the 'rainbow coalition' which mobilized in 1986 around the debate/referendum over Spain's NATO membership

Krausism (adj. **Krausist**) a strongly ethical school of philosophy dominant among Spanish liberal reformers in the 1870s and 1880s, based on the work of the post-Kantian German philosopher Krause, a contemporary of Hegel, and concerned particularly with the value of education in instilling a sense of responsible citizenship into individual Spaniards. The Krausists' lasting influence on the Spanish reform movement, particularly in education, was centred on the Institución Libre de Enseñanza*

latifundio deriving from the Roman occupation and consolidated during the Reconquista, and again in the nineteenth-century disentailments, *latifundios* are the large landed estates, entirely given over to one crop (monoculture)—usually olives or wheat—which traditionally dominated the economy, culture, and geography of southern (and parts of central) Spain. Until the 1950s, the owners of these estates (*latifundistas*) were the dominant economic interest group in Spain, forming the senior partner in the élite ruling coalition or oligarchy.* The term *latifundismo* refers to the predominance of this form of extremely antiquated agriculture but also—by implication—to the quasi-feudal social and political control exercised by *latifundistas* and their bailiffs and to the economic backwardness, parasitism, and social injustice perpetuated by the system

libertarian in this context, appertaining to anarchist beliefs/movement

LOAPA the Institutional Law for the Harmonization of the Devolution Process, commonly known by its initials (Ley Orgánica de Armonización del Proceso Autonómico). Born of an agreement between UCD* and the PSOE,* it was a notorious attempt to emasculate the concessions to the regions for fear of further military hostility in the wake of the attempted coup of 23 February 1981

movida (madrileña) the term applied to the explosion of creative activity, centred around youth culture, which dominated the Madrid cultural scene in the late 1970s through till the mid-1980s. Similar in many ways to British punk, it was nevertheless a response not to unemployment but to affluence and the new sexual permissiveness: in this sense it could be seen as a delayed form of 1960s culture, but of an aggressively apolitical nature. The term has by extension been applied to other subsequent explosions of youth culture, as in *movida galega* [Galician *movida*]

Movimiento Nacional known for short as el Movimiento, the Movement, it was an amalgam of all the different groups (or 'families') supporting Franco—Catholics, monarchists, soldiers, clerics, Falangists,* and Opus Dei* technocrats—as befitted the regime's totalizing intent

oligarchy state ruled by a small exclusive group, or, by derivation, this group itself. In Spain's case this élite was constituted by a senior partner—the large landowners (*latifundistas**)—and a junior one—the industrial bourgeoisie

Opus Dei founded by Escrivá de Balaguer in 1928, the Opus was a lay Catholic organization with an ultra-conservative, élitist philosophy. Secretive in nature, with lay and clerical members, its avowed goal was the conquest of the centres of state power for an authoritarian, integrist brand of Catholicism. It achieved prominence during the Franco regime (until 1973)—first via its control of the Consejo Superior de Investigaciones Científicas* and then through its major ministerial presence during the boom years of the 1960s (Franco's 'technocratic' ministers who oversaw the various economic plans were Opus members). The technocrats were wedded to neo-liberal ideas of 'pure' economic progress unmediated by social welfare policies. They embodied the regime's pivotal objective: to impel economic modernization while sustaining an authoritarian political structure and cultural project

PCE (Partido Comunista de España) orthodox (stalinist) Spanish Communist Party—founded in 1921 when a younger radical youth formation merged with members who had left the PSOE.* Until the civil war it existed on the margins of political life, unable to make any impact on either PSOE or CNT* memberships. During the war it acquired a large base—including a significant middle-class sector—and became a crucial part of the Republican wartime coalition. After the defeat of 1939, the PCE would reconstruct itself as the only enduring, organized clandestine opposition to the dictatorship in the interior. But its very strengths under the dictatorship (iron discipline, triumphalist ideology) would become its greatest weaknesses when the political circumstances changed. The PCE's mounting internal crisis and eventual collapse in the 1980s had much to do with membership discontent at the abiding lack of internal party democracy. Spanish voters (especially younger ones) also associated the PCE with the divisions and conflict of the past. The PCE lost out to its major rival the PSOE during the transition process and suffered a substantial reduction in electoral support in the October 1982 elections which brought the PSOE to power. (See also Izquierda Unida.*)

picaresque the European novel has its origins in the picaresque genre which developed in sixteenth-century Spain. This consisted of a loosely connected sequence of comic stories involving a low-life anti-hero or rogue (*pícaro*) who serves a series of masters, and whose misadventures and ability to get by on his wits provide an excuse for social satire

PNV (Partido Nacional Vasco) Catholic, conservative Basque nationalist Party founded by Sabino de Arana in 1894. It accepted the lay Second Republic and fought alongside it in the civil war because of the Republic's concession of autonomy to Vizcaya and Guipúzcoa in October 1936. After the demise of the Franco dictatorship, autonomy was restored by degrees to the Basque Country, although this was not a smooth process—see LOAPA*. The PNV is the dominant political force in the Basque Country today

poderes fácticos *de facto* powers—a term used to refer to those forces 'invigilating' Spain's democracy: predominantly the army, but also the financial establishment (the banks) and, to a lesser extent, the Church

PP (Partido Popular) Popular Party. Formed in 1976 as Alianza Popular (Popular Alliance), the PP has become since 1982 the major national conservative party and main parliamentary opposition to the ruling PSOE.* While the PSOE has stolen some of the PP's neo-liberal economic clothes, the latter remains significantly more conservative in matters of social values/policy

PSOE (Partido Socialista Obrero Español) Spanish Socialist Party (effectively social democratic in practice) founded in 1879 by Pablo Iglesias. Relatively marginal to the anti-Franco opposition, the PSOE underwent a crucial internal political renovation in the early 1970s which saw it emerge as a major contender—and the PCE's rival—during the transition process. Its low profile during the Franco years was an active advantage, adding to its appeal as a 'new' party for a 'new' Spain. The PSOE achieved an overwhelming victory at the polls in October 1982, since which time it has been in power continuously (although it no longer has an absolute majority). Always 'light' on ideology, this has facilitated the PSOE's pursuit, like several of its social democratic European counterparts, of deflationary economic policies that were once more usually associated with the political right. The PSOE's long period in office has led to a certain remoteness and a notorious arrogance in its dealings, which has led critics to refer to the problem of its institutionalized power. The PSOE is currently mired (1992–4) in a series of increasingly outrageous corruption scandals

PSUC (Partit Socialista Unificat de Catalunya) United Socialist Party of Catalonia. Formed in July 1936 when the Catalan branch of the PSOE merged with the PCE's Catalan section and two other organizations. By the end of the civil war the PSUC was effectively the Catalan Communist Party

Sección Femenina (SF) the Women's Section of the Falange* founded in 1934. In the post-civil war period it would become a state body and part of the Movimiento.* It was charged with the socialization and control of Spanish female youth and womanhood in accordance with the ideology of the new regime. In particular, it ran a form of labour service for unmarried women (compulsory for nearly all working women) through which the regime achieved rudimentary social services virtually gratis

topolino literally a small mouse, in the 1940s *topolino* was the name given to a very small car produced by SEAT. Its usage then extended to cover style-conscious teenagers—especially young women (the 'chicas/niñas topolino') who often wore 'zapatos topolino' (wedge-heeled shoes with raised soles and (sometimes) peep-toes)

turno pacífico (turno) the political system established with the monarchical Restoration of 1875 whereby the two, artificially created, dynastic parties (Conservatives and Liberals) alternated regularly (and 'peacefully') in power. The system depended on a national network of political bosses (*caciques**) who 'delivered' the vote in rigged elections. Intended to exclude the majority of Spaniards from political life (thus ensuring rule by a national élite or oligarchy*), the system began to break down under the pressures of imperial defeat and accelerating modernization, with the emergence of a powerful regional-industrial lobby in Catalonia and an organized urban labour movement. The *turno* system was killed off in the crisis of 1917 which saw the disintegration of the monolithic dynastic parties on which it depended

UCD (Unión de Centro Democrático), Union of the Democratic Centre: originally an electoral coalition formed in 1977 by a number of centre/centre-right tendencies (social democrats, Christian democrats, liberals, and prominent former-'career' Francoists concerned about their own political·futures) under the leadership of Prime Minister Adolfo Suárez (who had made his own career through the Francoist bureaucracy). After winning the June 1977 elections, UCD became the governing party of the transition period. Always fissiparous, and top-heavy, the stresses of power exacerbated a number of internal rifts and the party returned to its fragmented origins (the social democrats negotiated a transfer to the PSOE,* the conservative Christian democrats joined an electoral coalition and eventually merged with the right wing Popular Alliance (AP)). UCD's annihilation was confirmed by its disastrous showing in the October 1982 general elections, when it suffered the greatest electoral defeat of any governing party in Europe since the Second World War. These were the elections which brought the PSOE to power

UGT (Unión General de Trabajadores) socialist-led trade union founded in 1888, traditionally strongest in Madrid and the Asturian mining and Basque industrial zones

vertical trade unions (Sindicatos Verticales), also known as the **Organización Sindical (OS)** the Franco regime's official state unions set up (on the Italian fascist model) under the terms of the 1938 Labour Charter and staffed by the Falange.* By the 1960s the Sindicatos were increasingly influenced by the Comisiones Obreras*—which since the 1950s had been operating through the official union structures. A growing anachronism and a vast unwieldy bureaucracy, the Sindicatos were finally dismantled in 1977 (although their staff were transferred to other ministries/parts of the state administration)

zarzuela a Spanish variety of operetta, traditionally using lower class, mainly urban characters

Chronology

The editors have not listed major works in this chronology, except when indicative of cultural trends, since the aim of this volume is to encourage the study of cultural processes rather than products, and to break down the boundary traditionally separating 'high' and 'low' cultural forms.

Asterisked terms are explained in the glossary.

1890   Mallada's *Los males de la patria* [*The National Disease*] inaugurates a spate of publications on Spain's national identity and problematic relationship to modernity (by Isern, Unamuno, Ganivet, Picavea, Maeztu, Baroja, Azorín, Costa), tailing off after 1902

1891   Composer Pedrell's nationalist manifesto *Por nuestra música* [*For a Music of our Own*]

1893   First *Festa modernista* organized at Sitges by the painter and writer Rusiñol

1894   PNV* [Basque Nationalist Party] founded

1898   'The Disaster': Spanish navy defeated by USA with loss of remnants of colonial empire (Cuba, Puerto Rico, and Philippines)

1900   Ministry of Public Instruction created

1901   Lliga Regionalista founded: the party of Catalonia's industrial bourgeoisie.

1902   (February) First Spanish general strike in Barcelona

1903   Institute of Social Reform founded

1905   *Cu-cut* incident: army officers firebomb offices of satirical Catalanist magazine

1906   (February) Formation of Catalan Solidarity front: a coalition of independent republicans, Catalan republicans, Lliga, and Carlists
        (March) Law of Military Jurisdictions grants military courts power to try political protestors. Opposition to this attack on civil rights allows Catalanism to consolidate politically beyond the industrial bourgeoisie

1907   Junta para Ampliación de Estudios set up to encourage study abroad

1908   Education made compulsory till age of 12

1909   (July) 'Tragic Week' in Barcelona (anticlerical and anti-militarist popular protest)

1910–11	Anarcho-syndicalist trade union CNT* founded
1914	Limited administrative devolution ceded to Catalonia via the Mancomunitat Ortega y Gasset's first book *Meditaciones del Quijote* revives the debate on Spain's national identity Liga de Educación Política founded by liberal intellectuals
1914–18	European Great War.
1917	Three-pronged 'revolutionary crisis'—military juntas (junior officer revolt); Catalan (industrial bourgeoisie) and left-wing union-led protest movement—culminates in the Assembly Movement (August) general strike suppressed by army, signalling collapse of challenge to political establishment (though the *turno** system itself does not survive) Liberal national newspaper *El Sol* founded
1918	National Government formed. Catalan industrialists adhere, having deserted Assembly Movement
1918–20	'Bolshevik three years' (*trienio bolchevique*): labour/social conflict in rural south
1919	Intensification of labour conflict in Barcelona. CNT and employers involved in gang warfare (ongoing till Primo de Rivera's coup in 1923)
1921	PCE* [Spanish Communist Party] founded from merger of radical communist formation (created 1920) with section of the PSOE* (July) Disastrous military defeat at Anual in Morocco opens up the debate on 'political responsibilities' of old regime
1922	Falla, Lorca, and the painter Zuloaga organize *cante jondo* [flamenco] competition in Granada to revitalize 'primitive' Andalusian folk music (October) Italian fascists come to power (Mussolini becomes dictator from 1925)
1923	Ortega y Gasset founds *Revista de Occidente* (September) Military coup by General Miguel Primo de Rivera. All political organizations are effectively banned, though the regime initiates a collaboration with the UGT*
1925	End of war in Morocco
1926	Ortega y Gasset's *La deshumanización del arte* dissociates the avant-garde from mass culture Avant-garde magazine *L'Amic de les Arts* founded in Sitges by Gasch and Montanyà, with Dalí, Buñuel, and J. V. Foix as contributors (publ. till 1929)
1927	Celebration of tercentenary of the poet Góngora's death, giving its name to the '1927 Generation' of poets and musicians who sought to blend modernism with tradition *La Gaceta Literaria* founded by Giménez Caballero (swings to right in 1929, publ. till 1931) FAI* (purist anarchist organization) founded
1927–9	Failure of Primo dictatorship against background of cumulative economic problems
1928	Giménez Caballero founds Cineclub Español, embracing the mass media as an art-form with avant-garde potential

Catalan anti-art manifesto *Manifest groc* [*Yellow Manifesto*] published by Dalí, Gasch, and Montanyà

Opus Dei founded by Escrivá de Balaguer

1929 (January) Reform of Penal Code introduces penalties for persistent homosexual acts by both sexes (previously criminalized only for members of armed forces under martial law)

(March) Universities closed for opposing the regime

(October) Wall Street crash (USA) and onset of Great Depression

1930 (January) Fall of Primo dictatorship; military government instituted (under General Berenguer for most of period till April 1931)

(August) Pact of San Sebastián unites Republican and Catalan left against the monarchy. Leading monarchist politicians also alienated from King because of his desertion of them in 1923

1931 (April) Municipal elections. Monarchist candidates defeated in large towns (where vote was not rigged). Second Republic declared. King Alfonso XIII leaves Spain. Provisional government under conservative Catholic Alcalá Zamora. Left-wing Catalan nationalist party, Esquerra Republicana de Catalunya (ERC), founded. Generalitat* granted to Catalonia

(May) Cardinal Segura's pastoral letter (7th) reflects alienation of major part of ecclesiastical hierarchy from Republican regime. Burning of convents and churches in anticlerical protest (10–11th)

(June) Elections to constituent Cortes (parliament) gives a majority to left republicans and Socialist Party (PSOE)

(July) CNT telephone strike. Zaragoza military academy is closed

(August) Misiones Pedagógicas [Pedagogical Missions] set up by the Republic

(October) Resignation of Alcalá Zamora and Miguel Maura over religious provisions of the Constitution. Azaña ministry (coalition of left republicans and socialists). Law for the Defence of the Republic promulgated (20th)

Travelling student theatre company La Barraca set up with government funding, under Lorca's direction

Organization of liberal intellectuals, Agrupación al Servicio de la República, founded by Ortega y Gasset, Pérez de Ayala, and Gregorio Marañón

(December) Promulgation of Constitution, giving the vote to women* Civil Guards killed in incident at Castilblanco.

1932 (January) Workers clash with Civil Guards at Arnedo (Logroño), with fatalities. CNT revolts in Llobregat (Catalonia). Dissolution of the Jesuits. Cemeteries secularized

(February) Divorce Law enacted

(March) Debate on agrarian reform begins in the Cortes

(April) Catalan autonomy bill introduced

(July) In Germany, Nazis reach peak of their parliamentary strength in free elections, winning 230 seats in the Reichstag

(August) Attempted coup by General Sanjurjo

(September) Reaction against Sanjurjo unites progressive forces and Cortes passes Law of Agrarian Reform and Catalan Autonomy Statute. Elimination of death penalty

Reform of Penal Code decriminalizes homosexuality (except for members of armed forces)

1933 (January) State security forces responsible for fatal shootings at Casas Viejas (Andalusia); credibility of Azaña government eroded. Hitler appointed Chancellor in Germany

(February) Creation of clerical-conservative umbrella party CEDA,* which will bid for power on an anti-reformist platform

Parliamentary debate on proposals in 1931 Constitution to exclude the religious orders from teaching; culminates in Law of Congregations (May) establishing timetable for closure of all religious schools

Spanish Communist Party sets up Asociación de Mujeres Antifascistas (AMA)

(July) Repeal of Law for the Defence of the Republic

(October) Falange* Española founded

(November) General election in which centre-left defeated; victory of right. Government by Radical Party supported by CEDA strength in Cortes

(December) Anarchist risings in Catalonia and Aragon

1934 (February) Falange and other groups unite in a Spanish fascist movement led by José Antonio Primo de Rivera. Austrian dictator Dollfuss puts the left down in micro-civil war in Vienna

(June) Southern rural labourers' strike. Sección Femenina* de Falange (SF) created

(October) 3 CEDA ministers enter government. Uprisings in Catalonia and mining zone of Asturias; harsh military repression in latter (led by General Franco using Moroccan troops and Foreign Legion) lasts for months and presages Nationalists' strategy in civil war

1936 (February) Victory of Popular Front at polls, on a ticket of amnesty for political prisoners of October 1934. Left republicans form government under Azaña but without socialist participation

(March) Falange outlawed; José Antonio arrested. Germany occupies the Rhineland

(April) Communist-linked Alliance of Anti-Fascist Intellectuals for the Defence of Culture created. Library Section of Cultura Popular inaugurated (under Ministry of Public Instruction)

Anarchist organization Mujeres Libres created

(May) Azaña resigns as Prime Minister to become Republican President

(June) French Popular Front comes to power. Construction and other strikes in Madrid.

(July) Army uprising in Morocco on 17th; spreads to Spain 18th. Ministry of Public Instruction sets up Junta de Incautación y Protección del Tesoro Artístico to put valuable books, historical documents, and works of art in safe storage. PSUC* [United Socialist Party of Catalonia] founded (23rd). Hitler agrees to provide planes to fly Nationalists' Moroccan troops to mainland Spain (25–6th)

(July–August) Agrarian and industrial collectivization in parts of Republican zone. War of agrarian counter-reform as Nationalists (using the Army of Africa) sweep up through Andalusia

(August) French border closed (8th). Lorca shot by Nationalists in Granada

(19th). *El Mono Azul*, cultural magazine of the Alliance of Anti-Fascist Intellectuals, founded (publ. till end of civil war)

(August–September) Non-Intervention is mooted and a committee established in London with Britain and France as the initiating and leading powers

(September) Largo Caballero heads Republican cabinet of Socialists, republicans, and Communists (4th). Communist Jesús Hernández appointed Minister of Public Instruction; names Communist poster artist Josep Renau Director of Fine Arts. Nueva Escena theatre group created by Alliance of Anti-Fascist Intellectuals, under María Teresa León. Fall of Irún (5th) and San Sebastián (12th)

(October) Franco becomes Generalísimo* and Head of State (1st). Republic passes Basque Autonomy Statute (1st). Unamuno publicly castigates Nationalist general and Moroccan war hero Millán Astray for the inhumanity of the war and Nationalist philistinism (12th); he is dismissed as rector of Salamanca University (30th) and placed under house arrest. Republican agitprop cultural organization Altavoz del Frente created under 5th Regiment. Nationalist Culture and Education Committee set up under Catholic Monarchist Pemán, with responsibility for purging cultural and educational workers

(November) First Nationalist Press and Propaganda Office, with responsibility for censorship, set up at Salamanca under General Millán Astray. CNT joins Republican government which moves from a besieged Madrid to Valencia. Arrival of first International Brigaders. Despite all-out assault on Madrid, Franco fails to capture the city. Execution of Falange's leader, José Antonio Primo de Rivera, in a Republican gaol in Alicante

(December) Arrival of German Condor Legion and first Italian infantry units to aid Nationalists

1937   (January) Republican cultural magazine *Hora de España* founded under sponsorship of Ministry of Propaganda (publ. till January 1939)

Radio Nacional de España starts broadcasting from Nationalist headquarters at Salamanca

(February) Nationalists take Málaga

(March) Nationalists set up film censorship offices in Seville and Corunna (centralized at Salamanca in November). Nationalist offensive against the north begins with saturation bombing of Durango (31st), causing 127 civilian deaths. Nationalists broadcast threat to raze Basque industry to the ground if there is resistance

(April) Franco amalgamates Falange and Carlists* to form the FET y de las JONS.* Non-Intervention land and sea patrols inaugurated. Bombing of Guernica (26th)

(May) 'May Days' in Barcelona (failed popular/left revolt against reconstruction of the Republican state). Juan Negrín replaces Largo Caballero as Prime Minister (17th). Nationalist State Press and Propaganda Delegation set up in Burgos; institutes obligatory advance censorship

(June) Fall of Bilbao

(July) Second International Congress of Writers for the Defence of Culture held in Valencia, Madrid, Barcelona, and Paris. Spanish Republican pavilion at the Paris International Art and Technical Exhibition (till November). Spanish bishops endorse Nationalists in a collective letter.

(August) Private Catholic worship permitted once again in Republican zone
(September) María Teresa León sets up Teatro de Arte y Propaganda, evolving into Las Guerrillas del Teatro (formally constituted by Ministry of Public Instruction in December)
(October) Fall of the north. Republican government moves to Barcelona (31st). Republican Directorate of Fine Arts sets up Central Theatre Council, headed by Renau, María Teresa León, and Antonio Machado
Public use of Galician language formally banned in Nationalist zone

1938   (January) Nationalist government named in Burgos, with civilian members. The Falange is given control of culture via the Press and Propaganda Services (under Giménez Arnau and Ridruejo, responsible to Ministry of Interior), and the Church given control of education. Ridruejo creates Compañía del Teatro Nacional de FET y de las JONS
Public use of Basque language formally banned in Nationalist zone
(March) Nationalists promulgate Fuero del Trabajo (corporate Labour Charter modelled on that of fascist Italy): this makes strikes illegal and 'frees' married women from work. Italian planes bomb Barcelona. In response to Hitler's annexation of Austria (*Anschluss*), the French government under Blum temporarily reopens the frontier so aid may pass to the Republic (but Blum government resigns in June and border is closed again)
(April) Nationalists repeal Catalan autonomy statute, agrarian reform law, and divorce legislation. Nationalist troops reach Mediterranean coast between Barcelona and Valencia, dividing the Republican zone in two (15th). Nationalist Press Law formally institutes advance censorship of all printed, visual, or broadcast materials
(July) Battle of the Ebro begins; the longest of the war, it ends in November with the retreat of the Republican army
(September) Munich agreement effectively permits the dismemberment of Czechoslovakia by Hitler; this temporary triumph of appeasement also seals the Spanish Republic's fate. Soviet aid is wound down as Stalin seeks a defensive accommodation with Hitler
(November) International Brigades withdrawn (after Soviet Union agrees in June to Non-Intervention Committee's call for withdrawal of all foreign volunteers)
(December) Nationalist troops enter Catalonia

1939   (January) Fall of Catalonia. Nationalist troops enter Barcelona (26th). Refugees head for France
(February) Republican Cortes meets for last time in Figueras. Massive refugee exodus into France. Catalonia's border with France closed by Nationalists (10th). Nationalists promulgate the (retroactive) Law of Political Responsibilities: the blanket legislation which will facilitate Nationalist post-war repression. France and Britain recognize the Nationalist government of Burgos (27th). Azaña resigns as president of the Republic
(March) Casado coup in Madrid against PCE and against strategy of continued resistance. Casado attempts unsuccessfully to negotiate with Nationalists who demand and get unconditional surrender. German armies occupy Czechoslovakia.

Thousands of Republican refugees trapped in the centre-south zone try and fail to escape via the port of Alicante, where they are rounded up and interned
(April) Surrender of Republican armies (1st). USA recognizes Franco's government
(May–June) Repatriation of German and Italian troops
(June) Public use of Catalan language banned
(July) Advance censorship extended to theatre, song, and music

1939–43   Severe repression of Republicans (c.200,000 executions and over 400,000 imprisoned).

1939–45   European/World War; Spain remains a non-belligerent, although Franco provides logistic/intelligence support for Axis and 47,000-strong Blue Division (of Falangist volunteers) fights alongside German armies on Russian Front (1942–3)

1940   (October) Hitler and Franco meet at Hendaye
Cultural magazine *Escorial* founded by increasingly disaffected Falangist intellectuals

1941   Decree formally banning all public use of minority or foreign languages, and instituting obligatory dubbing into Spanish of all imported foreign films
Press and Propaganda Delegation renamed Vice-Secretariat for Popular Education and put under direct control of Falange
Official Journalists' School created
National Sports Delegation founded under General Moscardó
Satirical magazine *La Codorniz* founded by Miguel Mihura

1942   State-owned newsreel production company Noticiarios y Documentales Cinematográficos (NO-DO) created under Falangist control
(August) Tensions within the ruling élite surface in conflict between Carlists and Falangists

1943   (March) A Cortes of Francoist appointees is formed
Banditry and Terrorism decree promulgated
NO-DO given monopoly of newsreel production, and its newsreels made obligatory viewing in cinemas

1944   (October) Failed attempt by Spanish guerrilla* units to cross from France into Spain via Val d'Arán in order to form nucleus for popular uprising

1945   Censorship put under control of Ministry of Education
(May) Argentinian dictator Perón makes loan to Spain (a second loan negotiated April 1948)
(July) Promulgation of Francoist 'constitution', the Fuero de los españoles, as window-dressing for a regime made vulnerable by Axis defeat in the Second World War. With Axis defeat, the Falange becomes politically less prominent and the Church-linked authoritarian Catholic political 'family' increasingly so

1946   First books and plays in Catalan allowed since the civil war
(December) United Nations recommends diplomatic boycott of Spain (in reality a highly 'porous' boycott from the start)

1947   (March) Law of Succession names Franco as Caudillo* for life. Spain is defined as a Catholic state and a kingdom temporarily led by the Caudillo
First book in Galician published since the civil war

1948   Surrealist art group Dau al Set founded

1949   (February) Chase National Bank (US) makes private loan to Spain, though with
           state-department approval

1950   (November) Lifting of UN diplomatic boycott
           Spanish Communist Party begins withdrawal of its guerrilla units (process ends
           in spring 1951)
           First books in Basque authorized since the civil war
           Magazine *Laye* founded by young Barcelona intellectuals under aegis of Falang-
           ist student union

1951   (March) Barcelona tram strike, signifying a certain level of societal recovery
           from the depredations of post-war shortage and repression. USA make wheat
           loan
           Censorship put under newly created Ministry of Information and Tourism (MIT),
           under hard-liner Arias Salgado but with liberal García Escudero in charge of film
           Liberal Joaquín Ruiz Giménez appointed Minister of Education
           First Italian Film Week shows cycle of neo-realist films
           Falangist Nieves Conde's film *Surcos* marks the beginnings of opposition cinema

1952   García Escudero sacked for giving 'national interest' status to *Surcos* rather than
           to Orduña's *Alba de América*, and for authorizing Italian Film Week
           (May) End of rationing

1953   Second Italian Film Week; film magazine *Objetivo* founded by Communist
           activists Bardem and Muñoz Suay to promote neo-realism
           First San Sebastián Film Festival
           (August) Concordat with Vatican signed
           (September) Military base agreement between USA and Spain

1954   US military and economic aid starts to arrive in Spain
           First works by Juan Goytisolo, Jesús Fernández Santos, Carmen Martín Gaite,
           and Ignacio Aldecoa mark the consolidation of a new generation of social realist
           novelists
           Amendment to 1933 Anti-Vagrancy Law reintroduces penalties for homosexu-
           ality (previously had continued to be penalized under laws against dishonest
           abuse, corruption of minors, and public scandal)

1955   Bardem's *Muerte de un ciclista* consolidates neo-realism as the style of opposition
           cinema
           Salamanca Film Conversations organized by magazine *Objetivo*; *Objetivo*
           suspended
           Spain admitted to United Nations
           First agreements with OECD

1956   Young Writers University Congress organized with Communist backing.
           (February) Major student protest at Madrid University leads to sacking of Ruiz
           Giménez as Education Minister and declaration of 3-month state of emergency
           (April) Spain relinquishes Moroccan protectorate, but retains enclaves of Ceuta
           and Melilla.
           Spanish Television starts broadcasting

1957   (February) Opus Dei ministers join government

1958   (March) Strikes in Asturias spread to other industrial areas. Emergence of under-
            ground unions, the embryonic Comisiones Obreras*
            (April) Limited bargaining rights conceded to workers at plant level
            (May) 'Day of national reconciliation' sponsored by PCE (5th); it has little suc-
            cess, although this kind of inter-class social alliance will later provide the dy-
            namic of the transition. Principles of the National Movement (Movimiento
            Nacional*) presented to Cortes (17th). Spain joins IMF

1959   (June) Peaceful national general strike (*huelga nacional pacífica*) met with force
            (18th)
            (July) Stabilization Plan announced
            Inauguration of Valle de los Caídos
            (December) Visit of US President Eisenhower
            ETA* founded

1960   Banditry and Terrorism decree of 1943 implemented
            Intellectuals petition the MIT to relax censorship laws
            Basque priests sign letter protesting at human rights infringements in Basque
            Country

1961   Tourist boom starts
            Women's Political, Professional, and Employment Rights Law
            Buñuel's *Viridiana* wins Palme d'Or as Spain's entry to Cannes Film Festival; in
            the ensuing furore, Director-General of Film Muñoz Fontán is sacked, Spanish
            nationality is withdrawn from the film, and it is banned in Spain

1962   Martín-Santos's novel *Tiempo de silencio*, and the start of publication in Spain of
            the Latin American 'new novel', mark the beginning of a new phase of modern-
            ist fictional experiment
            (February) Spain requests negotiations with European Economic Community
            (April–June) Worker and student protest and consolidation of Comisiones Obreras
            (June) Opposition delegates meet in Munich (minus the PCE)
            State of emergency in Basque Country and Asturias
            Fraga Iribarne appointed head of MIT; contracts US advertising agents McCann
            Erickson to improve Spain's image abroad; puts García Escudero back in charge
            of film; the latter creates Official Film School to create a 'new Spanish cinema'
            Second Vatican Council convened by Pope John XXIII
            First bikini shown on Spanish cinema screens

1963   (April) Execution of Communist Party activist Julián Grimau for 'civil-war crimes'
            demonstrates the regime's continuing auto-legitimation on the basis of its highly
            exclusive version of the civil war
            Tribunal de Orden Público (civil court) set up to try crimes against law and
            order (previously subject to court martial)
            Literacy campaign introduced by Ministry of Education
            Conference on realism organized in Madrid by International Association for
            Cultural Freedom

Dissident magazine *Cuadernos para el Diálogo* founded by Ruiz Giménez (publ. till 1978)

1964 (March) Strikes in Asturias. Comisiones Obreras organize nationally as a permanent, though still illegal, labour organization. Repression of Asturian strike (September) Fraga organizes the regime's '25 Years of Peace' publicity campaign; writers, artists, and intellectuals lead protests, focusing on the repression in Asturias
400 Catalan priests sign letter protesting at suppression of Catalan culture
Primary education made compulsory to age of 14; technical education reorganized

1965 (February) Large student demonstrations in Madrid and elsewhere. Universities are closed, but the official student union SEU is abolished as result of student pressure

1966 (March) Fraga's Press Law abolishes obligatory advance censorship and press directives; although the new law allows some relaxation of censorship, it proves double-edged
(April) Universities closed in Madrid and Barcelona
(November) Ley Orgánica del Estado [Institutional Law of the State] proposes monarchy as the form of future government without specifying order of succession to throne
(December) ETA's fifth congress (continued in March 1967) moves from cultural nationalism to adopt national liberation theory and its direct action tactics; split between nationalist and socialist wings

1967 (March) Church hierarchy takes steps to control radical currents to the fore in the lay association Acción Católica [Catholic Action]

1968 Academy of the Basque Language draws up standardized version of Basque *euskara batua*
(March) Madrid University closed (28th, till 6 May)
(June) ETA's first assassination of policeman
(August) ETA assassinates Melitón Manzanas, a high-ranking member of police force in Basque Country. As a result, state of emergency declared (ended in summer 1969)

1969 Fraga sacked as head of MIT and replaced by hard-liner Sánchez Bella
(July) Franco presents Juan Carlos as his successor
(August) Eruption of MATESA corruption scandal, implicating Opus ministers

1970 General Education Law
Castellet's anthology *Nueve novísimos poetas españoles* marks rejection of earlier socially committed poetry
(December) Burgos trial of ETA members provokes widespread protests at home and abroad; further state of emergency declared

1971 Weekly news magazine *Cambio 16* founded
Amendment to 1970 Ley de Peligrosidad y Rehabilitación Social [Anti-Social Activities and Rehabilitation Law] sets up Homosexual Rehabilitation Centre at Huelva

1972	Barral starts to promote the New Spanish Novel
1973	(January) Spanish bishops vote for separation of Church and state. Opposition to regime mounts among staff and students in the universities

1972   Barral starts to promote the New Spanish Novel

1973   (January) Spanish bishops vote for separation of Church and state. Opposition to regime mounts among staff and students in the universities
(June) Admiral Carrero Blanco appointed Prime Minister of hard-line cabinet, signifying reversion of the regime under pressure
(December) ETA assassinates Carrero Blanco (20th). The same day Comisiones leaders receive prison terms of 12–20 years as their trial ends. Arias Navarro appointed Prime Minister

1974   (February) Arias government proclaims 'spirit of 12 February' and a series of liberalizing reforms, including an end to censorship (under Cabanillas as Head of Ministry of Information and Tourism) and the permitting of political associations. In practice these measures come to little in the attempt to avoid alienating hard-line Francoists (the 'bunker'). Increasing strains between central government and Church over cultural and national rights of Basque country and Catalonia; Bishop Añoveros of Bilbao is placed under house arrest (28th)
(March) Execution of Catalan anarchist Puig Antich
(April) Portuguese revolution
(July) Franco taken seriously ill, handing power to Juan Carlos (till September). Opposition forms Junta Democrática with institutional backing of PCE. Its programme demands a new provisional government, a political amnesty, full civil rights associated with a plural state and EEC entry
(September) Bomb attributed to ETA kills twelve in Madrid
Teatro-Museo Dalí opened in Figueras
(October) Cabanillas is sacked as head of MIT for having relaxed censorship
(December) New Law of Political Associations is less liberal than expected

1975   (April) State of Emergency in Basque Country
(June) Alliance of opposition groups—the Plataforma de Convergencia Democrática —formed by PSOE, social democratic, and liberal Christian democratic groups as a basis for negotiating a united opposition front with the PCE's Junta Democrática
Fundación Miró opened in Barcelona
(August) Prevention of Terrorism Act (27th). Under its remit, magazines *Destino*, *Cambio 16*, and *Posible* are confiscated
(September) In terminal crisis, the regime continues executing its left-wing opponents (five members of ETA and FRAP). Magazine *Triunfo* is banned
(October) Juan Carlos takes over as temporary Head of State (30th)
(November) Franco dies (20th); Juan Carlos crowned king (22nd)

1976   (January–February) Largest ever strike wave
(March) Five workers killed in clashes with police in Vitoria. Opposition Junta Democrática and Plataforma de Convergencia Democrática unite (the 'Platajunta')
(April) UGT holds its first legal congress in forty years
Congrés de Cultura Catalana
Catalan-language newspaper *Avui* founded
Royal Academy of the Basque Language officially recognized
Newspaper *El País* founded under editorship of Cebrián; magazine *Interviú* founded

(June) New Law of Associations approved by Cortes

(July) Adolfo Suárez appointed Prime Minister

(August) Political amnesty

(October) 'Platajunta' (left and centrist opposition coalition) merges with five regional political fronts (Valencia, Catalonia, Balearic and Canary Islands, Galicia) to form the Plataforma de Organismos Democráticos (POD) in bid to influence and accelerate Suárez's reforms. Right forms Popular Alliance (Alianza Popular) as a coalition party

(November) Cortes approves Law of Political Reform which re-establishes democracy (popular sovereignty, universal suffrage, and political pluralism) in Spain. Its provisions also abolish censorship (by amendment of January 1977)

(December) 27th Congress of PSOE, the first to be held in Spain for forty years. Referendum on political reform yields 94% yes vote

1977   (January) Atocha incident: four labour lawyers assassinated by rightists in their office in Atocha district of Madrid

(March) Poet Vicente Aleixandre awarded Nobel Prize for Literature

(April) The Movimiento Nacional is dismantled. Legalization of labour unions and Spanish Communist Party (PCE)

(June) The first democratic elections held since 1936 are won by UCD under Adolfo Suárez

(July) New parliament opens (22nd). MIT replaced by Ministry of Culture under Pío Cabanillas

(September) Agreement to re-establish the Generalitat reached between Suárez and Catalan leader Tarradellas

(October) Moncloa Pact signed by government and opposition (austerity/deflation in return for social and redistributive reform, but the latter scarcely materializes)

(December) Film censorship replaced by a rating system

1978   (January) Consejo General Vasco [Basque General Council] created to negotiate autonomy with central government on behalf of the Basque provinces excluding Navarre (i.e. Vizcaya, Alava, and Guipúzcoa). Adultery decriminalized

(February) First serious ministerial crisis of new democratic era when left challenges Suárez cabinet over its weak economic efforts; this will be a recurrent theme throughout UCD's period in office

First woman (Carmen Conde) elected to full membership of Spain's Royal Academy

(March) Catalan theatre group Els Joglars tried by court martial for offending the military with their play La toma

(April) PCE holds its first legal congress in Spain for forty years; leninism is dropped. Cortes legalizes contraception

(May) Debate on new constitution begins

(October–December) Heaviest ever ETA campaign. Large numbers of ETA members arrested and retaliatory escalation of violence

(October) Cortes approves new constitution. This recognizes constitutional monarchy as the basic form of government, and autonomy of the nationalities within the indissoluble unity of Spain. It disestablishes the Church

(November) Age of legal majority lowered to 18. 'Operation Galaxia' (plan for a military coup) is uncovered

National Theatre Centre created under Marsillach

(December) Constitution is approved by 87% in a national referendum, and endorsed by King. Amendment to Anti-Social Activities and Rehabilitation Law decriminalizes homosexuality

1979   (January) A series of agreements (dating back to 1976) are concluded between the Spanish state and the Vatican which together replace the Concordat of 1953. ETA assassinate Supreme Court judge Miguel Cruz Cuenca; thirty ETA cadres arrested in France

(February) Anti-terrorist legislation drafted by Cortes. Wage ceiling provokes labour protests

(March) National elections. UCD again forms government, winning 165 seats to PSOE's 121. Founding of Convergència i Unió (CiU*)

(July) Basque Autonomy Statute passed by Cortes (approved in referendum of 7 October)

(September) PSOE ceases formally to call itself a marxist party

(December) Controversy over an abortion trial leads to heated debate; campaign begins to liberalize the law

Negotiations to join European Economic Community open

Pilar Miró's film *El crimen de Cuenca* banned and threatened with court martial

Political *desencanto** sets in

Beginnings of the *movida* *madrileña* (till mid-1980s)

1980   (January) Basque and Catalan home rule begins

(March) Elections to Catalan parliament won by CiU. Jordi Pujol becomes Catalan president when Tarradellas steps down

(April) Basque parliament is opened

(May) Suárez continues to face criticism over economic conditions

(June) Radio and Television Statute regulates control of media. Spanish Television (TVE) signs collaboration agreement with Spanish film industry

(August) Hunger marches in Andalusia

(October) Autonomy bill for Andalusia approved by Cortes

(December) Similar autonomy bill approved for Galicia

1981   (January) Suárez resigns premiership after severe criticisms of his leadership style from inside UCD, which is split into rival power groups

(February) Attempted coup by Tejero and Milans del Bosch (the *Tejerazo*) fails (23rd–24th)

(March) New cabinet under Leopoldo Calvo Sotelo (UCD)

(April) Divorce Law approved

(July) Cortes passes LOAPA* in an attempt to curtail and slow up the autonomy process in view of military displeasure and its potential consequences

(September) Picasso's *Guernica* returns to Spain

(October) Popular Alliance (AP) defeats UCD in Galician elections

(December) UCD* government signs Spain's formal adhesion to NATO

1981–2   Licensing of 300 new FM radio stations

1982	(February) First ARCO [Arte Contemporáneo] fair, organized by Ministry of Culture, is major success
	(March) Defendants in abortion trial found guilty; campaign to liberalize the law stepped up
	(May) PSOE defeats UCD in Andalusian elections. Murcia votes for home rule, as do Valencia (June), Castile, Canary Islands, and Navarre (July). Basque government creates Basque Radio and Television (Euskal Irratia Telebista)
	(June) Plotters of *Tejerazo* (February 1981) found guilty
	(July) Suárez resigns from UCD to form a new party
	(September) ETA politico-military wing announces that it is abandoning armed struggle and folds
	(October) Army officers arrested when plans for another coup attempt (scheduled for day before national elections on 28th) are uncovered. PSOE wins overwhelming victory in national elections, with an unprecedented 47% of the vote (202 seats; Alianza Popular 107 seats; UCD 11; PCE 3)
	(November) Poor election showing precipitates PCE crisis; Santiago Carrillo resigns as general secretary; party split into pro-Soviets and renovators
	(December) Felipe González sworn in as Prime Minister
1983	(January) Wage controls are extended. Museum entrance made free for Spanish nationals
	(February) Spectacular collapse of RUMASA, a massive holding company controlling banks, insurance companies, and numerous industrial and agricultural concerns, whereupon it is found to be fraudulently insolvent. The state takes over control of RUMASA, injects it with public money, and later reprivatizes it (August 1985). Beginning of government's attempt to decriminalize abortion in certain circumstances. This will produce a draft bill by the end of 1983 which becomes law in 1985
	(March) Felipe González announces sweeping restructuring/rationalization of Spanish industry (*reconversión industrial*); bill approved by Cortes in July
	(August) University Reform Law (LRU). Supreme Court rules that LOAPA is neither 'organic' nor 'harmonizing' and enforces its modification in the direction of strengthening regional governments' control in matters of local policy. The ruling is a significant victory for the autonomies over the central PSOE administration
	(December) First appearance of GAL (Grupos Antiterroristas de Liberación) [Anti-Terrorist Liberation Squads], a shadowy, state-linked and financed 'counter-terror' unit, after ETA's assassination of army captain Martín Barrios in October. GAL's first communiqué declares intention to avenge ETA killings on one-to-one basis. (23 assassinations will be attributed to GAL between 1983 and 1986. In December 1994 revelations by the two policemen gaoled for their involvement in GAL make clear its close ties with the state and implicate leading PSOE figures.) Legislation authorizing autonomous governments to set up their own TV channels (Basque Television's first channel ETB1 had already started broadcasting in January). Generalitat de Catalunya creates the Corporació Catalana de Ràdio i Televisió (CCRTV). Miró Law introduces new system of advance subsidies to the film industry, related to takings

Instituto de la Mujer [Institute for Women's Affairs] set up under Ministry of Culture

1984   (January) Catalan Television's first TV channel TV3 starts broadcasting. PSOE government begins major offensive against ETA (September sees the start of bilateral approach with French government in this campaign)
(February) PNV emerges as premier party in elections to Basque parliament
(May) State-owned newspaper chain Medios de Comunicación del Estado privatized
(November) New state controls imposed on Church-run schools

1985   (March) First AIDS case in Spain diagnosed
LODE [Institutional Law on the Right to Education] passed
(June) PCE-led one-day strike against PSOE government's austerity measures: the first major national strike since 1977
(July) Abortion Law legalizes abortion in limited circumstances (rape, foetus defects, serious damage to health of mother). Televisión Galega starts broadcasting
(September) Europalia-85, dedicated to Spain, opens in Brussels
(December) TVE debate programme La Clave withdrawn as result of government pressure

1986   (March) National campaign and referendum on Spain's NATO membership sees a significant about-turn with a majority vote for continued membership
Ley de Extranjería [Aliens' Law] passed. This makes guest workers more vulnerable to expulsion, and non-white populations of Ceuta and Melilla lose *de facto* status of Spanish nationals
(June) PSOE wins 184 of 350 Cortes seats in national elections
(July) Nine Civil Guards killed in ETA attack in Madrid
(September) ETA assassinate one of their former leaders, María Dolores González Cataráin (Yoyes), in Guipúzcoa as a 'warning' to those who would avail themselves of the government's offer of a route back to mainstream society (*reinserción social*)
(October) Barcelona wins international competition to stage 1992 Olympic Games. First civilian head of Civil Guard appointed
(November) PSOE increases its seats in elections to Basque parliament (to second position after PNV). Significant government coup against ETA as a result of Franco-Spanish co-ordinated action. Seizure of documents and information gained via arrest of top leader of direct action commandos, Santiago Arróspide Sarasola, permits dismantling of major part of ETA's operational structure in Spain
Centro de Arte Reina Sofía opens as national modern art collection. Instituto Valenciano de Arte Moderno (IVAM) also opens

1987   (January) Students demonstrate for university reform and open admissions; largest protest in recent years
(February) PNV and PSOE form a coalition government in the Basque Country
(March) Trial opens of those accused of causing the 'síndrome tóxico' (first deaths had occurred in 1981), majority opinion attributing this to adulterated

cooking oil illegally sold for human consumption. Death in car accident of top ETA leader, Txomin, disrupts the negotiations between government and top ETA leadership in France, in which he was acting as go-between and broker
(June) PSOE loses control of twenty-one of twenty-seven large cities in local elections. ETA car bomb outside a Barcelona supermarket kills fifteen
(October) Police seal Spanish border to prevent ETA using French territory as base
(November) USA and Spain fail to agree provisions over US air base at Torrejón (Madrid)

1988   (February) Julio Anguita elected as PCE's general secretary
Regulation of Telecommunications Law opens up radio and TV to foreign investment
(November) Some of the participants in the *Tejerazo* are conditionally discharged from prison
(December) General strike to protest against impact of PSOE's economic policies (14th). Crystallization of division between PSOE and UGT: UGT secretary-general, veteran socialist Nicolás Redondo, resigns as a PSOE deputy; the PSOE rules that UGT membership is no longer a requirement of party membership
Parliament approves introduction of private television
Arrest of police officers implicated in GAL

1989   National Prize for Literature awarded for first time to a work in Basque (Atxaga's *Obabakoak*)
(October) PSOE wins 175 seats in national elections; PP* wins 107 seats, Izquierda Unida* (which includes the PCE) 17 seats. Nobel Prize for Literature awarded to the novelist Camilo José Cela

1990   Private TV franchises awarded to Telecinco, Antena 3, and Canal+
Institutional Law on Overall Structuring of the Education System (LOGSE)

1991   Creation of new private universities authorized
(September) Two police officers implicated in the organization of GAL death squads receive gaol sentences of more than 100 years each

1992   Celebration of Quincentenary of 1492 (Columbus's discovery of America, conquest of Granada from Arab rule, and expulsion of the Jews from Spain) with Expo '92 in Seville and other exhibitions throughout Spain: notably those on Hispano-Arabic culture in Granada, and on Judeo-Spanish culture in Toledo. Barcelona hosts the Olympic Games. (Funding for these events permits a major upgrading of Spain's communications infrastructure.) Madrid is Cultural Capital of Europe
Thyssen-Bornemisza Museum opens in Madrid
Economic recession punctures cultural boom

1993   TV franchises awarded for Spanish satellite system Hispasat; bids for cable TV franchises invited for 1994
(June) PSOE wins general elections but loses its absolute majority as the Partido Popular makes significant gains. (PSOE 159 seats, Partido Popular 141 seats,

Izquierda Unida 18 seats). A series of corruption scandals continuing throughout 1994 and into 1995, implicating major financial, police, administrative, and political figures, leads to a climate of generalized cynicism, aggravated by continuing economic recession

Proposed expansion of abortion law to include provision for economic hardship of mother/family. Draft legislation framed, but at the time of writing (January 1995) its progress is effectively frozen

Index

Readers should note that modernity and modernization are not indexed since these concepts underlie the whole volume.

army (*Cont.*):
war and postwar 152, 154, 174, 177, 179, 191, 204, 209, 213, 229, 233, 234, 237, 333, 429–32; political intervention of 31, 35, 38, 178, 316, 318, 427, 428, 429, 438, 439; reform and funding of 26, 100, 272; Republican 39, 110, 112–13, 155–8, 162–4, 229–30, 236, 431, 432; and state nationalism 29, 31, 36, 37, 333–4, 421, 426; see also *guerrilla*, Morocco
Arnold, Matthew 2, 7
Arp, Jean 75
Arribas, Alfredo 377–9
art, see visual arts
art galleries 71, 78, 300–1, 375, 377, 399; see also museums
Asturias 44, 85, 108, 232, 263, 321, 425, 429, 434, 435: language 34, 338
Atxaga, Bernardo 353, 354, 403, 441
Aub, Max 65, 66, 67, 288
Austria 100, 429, 431
Austria-Hungary 37
autarky: economic vii, 171, 173–82, 186, 188, 191, 192, 194, 237, 242, 243–4, 248, 259–60, 376; socio-cultural 16, 176, 237, 242, 243, 265
avant-garde 7, 13–14, 63–81, 100, 165, 223, 227, 299, 300–1, 348, 370, 374–5, 377, 398, 427; see also modernism
Azaña, Manuel 126, 127, 135, 141–2, 148, 287, 428, 429, 431
Azcárate, Gumersindo de 84, 125, 126
Azorín 65, 127, 426
Azúa, Félix de 297
Azúcar Moreno 394

Bacarisse, Salvador 226
Bajo Ulloa, Juanma 317, 329, 353
Bakunin, Mikhail 116
Balearic Islands 321
Balmaseda, Enrique 372
Banderas, Antonio 327
banking, banks 180, 262, 263, 264, 359–61, 373–4, 379, 403, 424, 439; see also economic development,

enterprise culture, foreign investment
Barce, Ramón 227
Barcelona: and Catalan nationalism 145–51, 206; and Church 44, 266, 280; and civil war 16, 110, 150–2, 431; as cultural centre 58–61, 64, 71, 72, 78, 91, 224, 225–6, 227, 299, 305, 339, 344, 376–9, 384, 433; as economic centre 83, 85, 107, 263, 265, 270, 273–4; gay culture 393–4, 399; social conflict 38, 43, 44, 87, 269, 426, 427; workers' movements 86, 88, 420, 430; see also 1992 celebrations
Bardem, Javier 327
Bardem, Juan Antonio 305–6, 433
Baroja, Pío 83, 85, 127, 354, 426
Barraca, La 7, 155, 163, 299, 428
Barradas, Rafael 72, 74
Barral, Carlos 210, 252–3, 254, 297, 298, 402, 436
Barro, Pepe 347
Barthes, Roland 217
Bartók, Béla 227
Basque Country (Euskadi) 27, 29, 85, 144, 273, 280, 332–6, 365, 412, 425, 434, 436: autonomous government, autonomy 39, 144, 155, 321, 347, 352–3, 371, 430, 437, 438, 439, 440; culture 155, 204, 280, 351–5, 365, 371, 372, 375, 403, 404, 439, 441; language 34, 37, 204, 208, 280, 337–41, 351–5, 371, 375, 403, 431, 433, 435, 436, 441; nationalism 15, 30, 35–9, 95, 105, 206, 236, 268, 269, 278, 279, 280, 327, 332–6, 404, 412, 421, 424, 435; see also ETA, Herri Batasuna, minority languages, nationalism (regional), PNV, regional autonomies, regional cultures
Bataille, Georges 78
Baudelaire, Charles 66
Bauhaus 13, 223–4
Bautista, Aurora 220–1, 308
Bautista, Julián 226
Beardsley, Aubrey 298
Beatles 265

Beckett, Samuel 210
Belén, Ana 328–9
Belgium 38, 361
Bella Dorita, La 91, 210
Bellmunt, Francesc 326
Bello, Pepín 74
Belmonte 86
Benet, Juan 297, 298
Benet, Rafael 72
Benidorm 270
Benjamin, Walter 3, 11, 13
Berenguer, Dámaso (General) 129, 428
Berenguer, Francesc 60
Bergamín, José 153, 287
Bergés, Augusta 91
Berlanga, Luis García 210, 304, 305–6
Berlusconi, Silvio 5, 359–60, 365, 383
Bernaola, Carmela 228
Best, Steven 398
Besteiro, Julián 131, 287
Bigas Luna, Juan José 327, 329, 417
Bilbao 58, 86, 88, 107, 145, 160, 206, 263, 269, 393, 430
Blake, William 75
Blancafort, Alberto 227
Blanco, Segundo 155
Blasco Ibáñez, Vicente 83, 88
Borau, José Luis 307–9, 328
Borges, Jorge Luis 211
Borges, Norah 64, 72
Bosé, Miguel 328, 394
Boulez, Pierre 227
Bourdieu, Pierre 6
Braque, Georges 71, 74
Brassens, Georges 292
Brecht, Bertolt 18 n. 1
Brenan, Gerald 318
Breton, André 71, 73, 75, 78
Brines, Francisco 395
Britain v, 48, 125, 232, 237, 327, 359, 374, 377, 382, 390, 430, 431; see also England
Brossa, Joan 300
Bulffi, Lluís 121
bullfighting 86, 238, 377
Buñuel, Luis 14, 64, 74–5, 78, 265, 427, 434
Burgos 86, 208, 431
Burgos, Carmen de 67, 87

Caballero, Fernán 83
Caballero, José 160
Caballero Bonald, José María 253
Cabanas, Juan 160